War and Peace in the Ancient World

The Ancient World: Comparative Histories

Series Editor: Kurt A. Raaflaub

Published

War and Peace in the Ancient World

Edited by Kurt A. Raaflaub

War and Peace
in the Ancient World

Edited by

Kurt A. Raaflaub

Blackwell
Publishing

© 2007 by Blackwell Publishing Ltd

BLACKWELL PUBLISHING
350 Main Street, Malden, MA 02148-5020, USA
9600 Garsington Road, Oxford OX4 2DQ, UK
550 Swanston Street, Carlton, Victoria 3053, Australia

The right of Kurt A. Raaflaub to be identified as the Author of the Editorial Material in this Work has been asserted in accordance with the UK Copyright, Designs, and Patents Act 1988.

First published 2007 by Blackwell Publishing Ltd

1   2007

Library of Congress Cataloging-in-Publication Data

War and peace in the ancient world/edited by Kurt A. Raaflaub.
    p. cm.—(The ancient world—comparative histories)
  Includes bibliographical references and index.
  ISBN-13: 978-1-4051-4525-1 (hardback: alk. paper)
  ISBN-10: 1-4051-4525-0 (hardback: alk. paper)
  ISBN-13: 978-1-4051-4526-8 (pbk.: alk. paper)
  ISBN-10: 1-4051-4526-9 (pbk.: alk. paper)
  1. Military history, Ancient.   I. Raaflaub, Kurt A. II. Series.
U29.W3475 2007
303.6'60901—dc22

                                        2006009425

A catalogue record for this title is available from the British Library.

Set in 10/13 pt Galliard
by Newgen Imaging Systems (P) Ltd., Chennai, India
Printed and bound in Singapore
by COS Printers Pte Ltd

The publisher's policy is to use permanent paper from mills that operate a sustainable forestry policy, and which has been manufactured from pulp processed using acid-free and elementary chlorine-free practices. Furthermore, the publisher ensures that the text paper and cover board used have met acceptable environmental accreditation standards.

For further information on
Blackwell Publishing, visit our website:
www.blackwellpublishing.com

Contents

Series Editor's Preface

The Ancient World: Comparative Histories

The application of the comparative approach to the ancient world at large has been rare. The new series inaugurated with the present volume intends to fill this gap. It will pursue important social, political, religious, economic, and intellectual issues through a wide range of ancient societies. "Ancient" will here be understood broadly, encompassing not only societies that are "ancient" within the traditional chronological framework of c. 3000 BCE to c. 600 CE in East, South, and West Asia, the Mediterranean, and Europe, but also later ones that are structurally "ancient" or "early," such as those in premodern Japan or in Meso- and South America before the Spanish conquest.

By engaging in comparative studies of the ancient world on a truly global scale, this series will throw light not only on common patterns and marked differences but also illustrate the remarkable variety of responses humankind developed to meet common challenges. Focusing, as it does, on periods that are far removed from our own time and in which modern identities are less immediately engaged, the series will contribute to enhancing our understanding and appreciation of differences among cultures of various traditions and backgrounds. Not least, it will thus illuminate the continuing relevance of the study of the ancient world in helping us to cope with problems of our own multicultural world.

Topics to be dealt with in future volumes include the role of private religion and family cults; geography, ethnography, and perspectives of the world; recording the past and writing history; and the preservation and transformation of the past in oral poetic traditions.

Kurt A. Raaflaub

Notes on Contributors

Victor Alonso is Professor of Ancient History at the University of La Coruña in Spain. He received his doctorate in 1984 with a dissertation published as *Neutralidad y neutralismo en la Guerra del Peloponeso* (1987). He has been *member libre* at the Casa de Velázquez and Spanish as well as Humboldt Fellow at the Universities of Heidelberg, Nancy, and Münster. In addition to numerous articles on Greek international law, he has published a book on archaic Greek commerce and is preparing the edition of the proceedings of a conference on succession in Hellenistic kingdoms.

Carlin A. Barton received her Ph.D. from the University of California at Berkeley. She is currently Professor of History at the University of Massachusetts at Amherst. Her research has been focusing on the psychological and emotional life of the ancient Romans. Her main publications include *The Sorrows of the Ancient Romans: The Gladiator and the Monster* (1993) and *Roman Honor: The Fire in the Bones* (2001). She is currently working on the emotions of Roman cultic life.

Richard H. Beal received his Ph.D. from the University of Chicago, where he is Senior Research Associate on the Hittite Dictionary Project of the Oriental Institute. His interests focus on Hittite and Mesopotamian political, military, religious, and social history. He has published numerous articles, including "Hittite Oracles" (2002) and "The Predecessors of Hattušili I" (2003), and *The Organisation of the Hittite Military* (1992).

Lanny Bell has a Ph.D. in Egyptology from the University of Pennsylvania. He served on the faculty of the University of Chicago and is now an independent scholar as well as an Adjunct Professor at Brown University. From 1977 to 1989 he was Field Director of the Epigraphic Survey of the Oriental Institute. He has edited a volume on *Ancient Egypt, the Aegean and the Near East: Studies in Honour of Martha Rhoads Bell* (1997) and published articles on "The Epigraphic Survey and the Rescue of the Monuments of Ancient Egypt" (1990) and "The New Kingdom 'Divine' Temple: The Example of Luxor" (1997), among others.

Neta C. Crawford is Professor of Political Science and African-American Studies at Boston University. She has a Ph.D. in Political Science from MIT and has written books and articles on war, peace, and the ethics of war, her main interests. Her most recent book, *Argument and Change in World Politics: Ethics, Decolonization and Humanitarian Intervention* (2002), received the American Political Science Association's Best Book Award in International History and Politics in 2003.

Jeri Blair DeBrohun received her Ph.D. in Classical Studies from the University of Michigan and is currently Associate Professor of Classics at Brown University. Her primary research interests are Roman Republican and Augustan poetry. Her main publication so far is *Roman Propertius and the Reinvention of Elegy* (2003). She is currently working on a book for the Duckworth series "Classical Interfaces," on Greco-Roman Dress as an Expressive Medium.

Fred M. Donner received his Ph.D. in Near Eastern Studies from Princeton University. He is currently on the faculty of the Oriental Institute and Department of Near Eastern Languages and Civilizations at the University of Chicago, where he teaches early Islamic history and some aspects of Islamic law. His research interests include the role of pastoral nomads in Near Eastern societies, the question of Islam's origins and the early expansion of the Islamic state, Islamic historiography, the early history of the Qur'an, and apocalypticism in the Near East. His publications include *The Early Islamic Conquests* (1982) and *Narratives of Islamic Origins: The Beginnings of Islamic Historical Writing* (1997).

Benjamin R. Foster (Ph.D. Yale University) is the Laffan Professor of Assyriology and Babylonian Literature and Curator of the Yale Babylonian Collection. His research interests focus on Mesopotamian, especially Akkadian, literature, and the social and economic history of Mesopotamia. His primary publications include *Before the Muses* (1993, several revised editions), an anthology of annotated translations from Akkadian literature of all periods; *Umma in the Sargonic Period* (1982), and a co-authored history of Iraq from earliest times to the present, *Iraq Beyond the Headlines: History, Archaeology, and War* (2005).

Ross Hassig has a Ph.D. from Stanford University. After teaching for many years at the University of Oklahoma, he is now an independent scholar. He specializes in Mesoamerican ethnohistory, with particular focus on political, economic, and military issues and the Aztec empire. His publications include *Aztec Warfare: Imperial Expansion and Political Control* (1988), *War and Society in Ancient Mesoamerica* (1992), and *Time, History, and Belief in Aztec and Colonial Mexico* (2001).

Catherine Julien's Ph.D. is in Anthropology from the University of California at Berkeley. She is Professor of History at Western Michigan University in Kalamazoo. She works on South America in the sixteenth century, before and after the arrival of Europeans in the hemisphere, including the transition from Inca to Spanish rule in the Andes and Inca genres used by Spaniards in the composition of their narratives of the Inca past. Her books include *Hatunqolla: A View of Inca Rule from the Lake Titicaca*

Region (1983); Condesuyo: *The Political Division of Territory under Inca and Spanish Rule* (1991), and the award-winning *Reading Inca History* (2000).

David Konstan took his Ph.D. in Greek and Latin at Columbia University. He is the John Rowe Workman Distinguished Professor of Classics and the Humanistic Tradition, and Professor of Comparative Literature, at Brown University. His major interests are in classical literature and culture. Among his most recent publications we find *Friendship in the Classical World* (1997), *Pity Transformed* (2001), and *The Emotions of the Ancient Greeks: Studies in Aristotle and Classical Literature* (2006). He is a past president of the American Philological Association.

Thomas Krüger (Dr. Theol., University of Munich) is Professor of Old Testament and Ancient Near Eastern Religions at the University of Zurich. He is author of *Geschichtskonzepte im Ezechielbuch* (1989); *Kritische Weisheit: Studien zur weisheitlichen Traditionskritik im Alten Testament* (1997); and *Qoheleth: A Commentary* (2004).

Susan Niditch received her Ph.D. from Harvard University. She is the Samuel Green Professor of Religion at Amherst College. Her publications include *War in the Hebrew Bible: A Study in the Ethics of Violence* (1993); *Oral World and Written Word: Ancient Israelite Literature* (1996), and *Ancient Israelite Religion* (1997). She is currently completing a commentary on *Judges* for the Old Testament Library and is working on a new monograph concerning hair and identity in the culture of ancient Israel.

Kurt A. Raaflaub has a Ph.D. from the University of Basel. He is David Herlihy University Professor and Professor of Classics & History at Brown University, where he is currently also Royce Family Professor in Teaching Excellence and Director of the Program in Ancient Studies. His interests focus on the social, political, and intellectual history of archaic and classical Greece and the Roman republic, and on the comparative history of the ancient world. His recent publications include a co-edited volume on *War and Society in the Ancient and Medieval Worlds* (1999), *The Discovery of Freedom in Ancient Greece* (2004), and a co-authored volume on *Origins of Democracy in Ancient Greece* (2006).

Nathan Rosenstein is Professor of History at Ohio State University. His Ph.D. is from the University of California, Berkeley. His principal research interests focus on the political culture, military history, and human ecology of Republican Rome. He was recently co-editor of *War and Society in the Ancient and Medieval Worlds* (1999), the author of *Rome at War: Farms, Families, and Death in the Middle Republic* (2004), and is co-editor of *A Companion to the Roman Republic* (forthcoming).

Richard Salomon received his Ph.D. from the University of Pennsylvania. He is Professor of Sanskrit and Buddhist Studies in the Department of Asian Languages and Literature, University of Washington. His main areas of interest are Sanskrit and Prakrit language and literature, Indian epigraphy and paleography, early Indian history, Indian Buddhist literature, and Gandhāran studies. His publications include *The Bridge* *to the Three Holy Cities* (1985); *Indian Epigraphy: A Guide to the Study of Inscriptions in the Sanskrit, Prakrit, and the other Indo-Aryan Languages* (1998), and *Ancient Buddhist Scrolls from Gandhāra: The British Library Kharostī Fragments* (1999).

Louis J. Swift received his Ph.D. at Johns Hopkins University. He is Professor Emeritus of Classics at the University of Kentucky, where he was Chair of Classics (1970–76), Dean of Undergraduate Studies (1990–99), and Distinguished Professor of Arts and Sciences in 1993. His principal research interests have been in the area of Latin patristics with a particular focus on social issues. He has written on Ambrose, Augustine, and ante-Nicene writers and is the author of *The Early Church Fathers on War and Military Service* (1983).

Lawrence A. Tritle has a Ph.D. from the University of Chicago. He is Professor of History at Loyola Marymount University in Los Angeles. He has published widely on Greek history and the social history of Greek warfare, including "Hectors's Body: Mutilation of the Dead in Ancient Greece and Vietnam" (1997); *From Melos to My Lai: War and Survival* (2000), and *The Peloponnesian War* (2004). His current projects include a social history of the Peloponnesian War and an edited volume on the ancient world at war for Oxford University Press.

Josef Wiesehöfer received his Ph.D. at the University of Münster. He is Professor of Ancient History, Director of the Institut für Klassische Altertumskunde, and a member of the Center for Asian and African Studies at the University of Kiel. His main interests lie in the history of the Ancient Near East, Greek and Roman social history, the history of the Jews in Antiquity, and the history of Scholarship. His publications include *Die 'dunklen Jahrhunderte' der Persis. Untersuchungen zu Geschichte und Kultur von Fars in frühhellenistischer Zeit* (1994); *Ancient Persia. From 550 BC to 650 AD* (2nd edn. 2001), and an edited volume, *The Arsacid Empire: Sources and Documentation* (1998).

Robin D. S. Yates is James McGill Professor of History and East Asian Studies at McGill University in Montréal and Chair of the Society for the Study of Early China. His Ph.D. is in Chinese Studies from Harvard University. His research focuses on early and traditional Chinese history, historical theory, archaeology of culture, traditional popular culture, Chinese poetry, and Chinese science and technology. He has published widely on the history of Chinese warfare and early China. Most notably, he is co-author of *Science and Civilisation in China*, vol. 5, part 6: "Military Technology: Missiles and Sieges" (1994), author of *Five Lost Classics: Tao, Huang-Lao and Yin-Yang in Han China* (1997), and co-editor of vol. 1 of the *Cambridge History of War*, covering the Ancient World (in preparation).

1

Introduction: Searching for Peace in the Ancient World

Kurt A. Raaflaub

This volume contains the revised proceedings of a lecture series and colloquium on "War, Peace, and Reconciliation in the Ancient World" that the Program in Ancient Studies organized at Brown University in 2002–3.[1] The papers presented at these events covered nine early civilizations from China via India and West Asia to the Mediterranean and Mesoamerica. They offered illuminating glimpses into a rarely treated topic. Other contributors joined our enterprise later on. I am most grateful to all of them and to many others whose help was indispensable in organizing the events and preparing the publication.[2] This introduction intends, on the one hand, to sketch the background of endemic war, violence, and brutality, against which we must assess thoughts about peace and efforts to preserve or re-establish peace in the ancient world, and, on the other hand, to survey some of the common traits that are visible in several ancient cultures.

"Ancient" is here understood in a broad sense, including some societies that are structurally "early" but transcend the commonly accepted chronological boundaries of antiquity (wherever one chooses to place those). "Peace" is an equally imprecise, or perhaps rather a polyvalent notion. It is here understood primarily in contrast to war (hence the volume's title), but it is clear that this contrast covers only part of the term's range of meanings. In some ancient cultures, indeed, other meanings were more important. Several contributors (Salomon, Konstan, and Barton, among others) discuss these issues as well as relevant terminology. To give just two examples, the ancient Egyptians were primarily interested in peace as a domestic issue, visible in the integrity of the country and the absence of internal strife; compared with this ideal, peace with the outside world was less significant. Accordingly, the condition of perpetual peace offered to pharaohs by the gods referred to the domestic sphere, and even in the treaty with the Hittites (Bell, this vol.), the result of peace was expressed in the statement that the two countries had become one (Helck 1977). By contrast, the concept of peace that became pervasive in ancient Indian culture was internal and referred to peace of mind and spirit (Salomon, this vol.).

Experts on war in the ancient world are numerous, those on peace hard to find; the bibliographies differ accordingly. Moreover, in books on peace in the ancient world, "ancient" is usually limited to the Greeks and Romans. This volume, to my knowledge, is one of only two that examine the issue of peace on a global scale.[3]

Prologue

The dramatic date of the Chinese film "Hero" (*Yingxiong*) is the end of the Warring State Period (403–221 BCE), in which the last seven kingdoms fought ruthlessly for supremacy, causing massive slaughter and suffering for the population. In the film, the king of Qin, determined to conquer all of known China, has defeated most of his enemies. Over the years, however, he has been the target of many assassins. Three of these are still alive, Broken Sword, Flying Snow, and Sky. To anyone who defeats these three, the king promises great rewards: power, riches, and a private audience with the king himself. For 10 years no one comes close to claiming the prize. Then an enigmatic person, Nameless, appears in the palace, bearing the legendary weapons of the slain assassins. His story is extraordinary: for 10 years he studied the arts of the sword, before defeating the mighty Sky in a furious fight and destroying the famed duo of Snow and Broken Sword, using a weapon far more devastating than his sword – their love for each other.

The king, however, replies with a different story: of a conspiracy between the four, in which Nameless' victories were faked to enable him to come close to the king and kill him. Nameless indeed has a chance to achieve his goal. The king, exposed to his sword, tells him of his true aspiration: to conquer the warring states in order to overcome war and violence once and for all, to create a unified empire, and to establish lasting peace. Overcome by this vision, Nameless draws back his sword and walks out of the great hall, to die willingly under the arrows of the king's bowmen.

This is a powerful and beautiful movie. Its message is exciting. It raises both hope and doubts: was there really an ancient ruler who pursued a true vision of peace – even if it could be realized only at the price of war and violence? Not unexpectedly, hopes prove illusionary. However we interpret the movie – a question that has raised intense debates – the first emperor – he who displayed his army in a now world-famous terracotta replica near his necropolis – was no visionary of peace. "Later Chinese historians did not celebrate the First Emperor as one of the greatest conquerors of all time …, but rather castigated him as a cruel, arbitrary, impetuous, suspicious, and superstitious megalomaniac."[4]

Peaceful Societies?

Still, it is worth asking whether the vision of a "peaceable kingdom" ever moved from utopia to historical reality. For a long time scholars thought that, unlike the Aztecs, the Maya in Central America had essentially created a peaceful civilization, untainted by incessant warfare and human sacrifice. As David Webster writes (*W&S* 336),

> To be sure, early Spanish expeditions were beset by large and effective Maya armies, and during the Contact period Maya fought incessantly among themselves. Such bellicosity was usually seen, however, as the unfortunate legacy of [outside intrusions]. Military imagery in Classic period art was ignored or explained away as portrayals of ritual conflict. Intellectual priest-bureaucrats rather than kings purportedly held sway over Classic Maya polities, exercising their theocratic benevolence from essentially vacant ceremonial centers. Huge temples, built by masses of devoted commoners, dominated a tranquil political landscape. Monuments portrayed gods, and associated dates and inscriptions conveyed religious and astronomical information.
>
> Beginning in the 1950s, developments rapidly undermined this charming if unconvincing set of conceptions. First, some temples were shown to be burial monuments for important individuals. Shortly thereafter, breakthroughs in decipherment of Maya texts demonstrated the existence of dynasties of kings who recorded their deeds, including military exploits, in public inscriptions. Third, the rapid maturation of Maya archaeology revealed much new data about the character and chronology of Maya centers, polities, and populations that were impossible to reconcile with the traditional theocratic view ... [Warfare], along with its attendant rituals and sacrifices, is now recognized as perhaps the single largest theme of Late Classic texts and art.

Along with the great contributions of archaeology, texts played a decisive role in changing modern perceptions of Maya culture. Once the number of available inscriptions reached a critical mass, decipherment progressed and increasing numbers of texts could be read and interpreted with sufficient confidence, and so the picture changed dramatically. For example, a set of inscriptions discovered recently in Dos Pilas in northern Guatemala reveals

> the largely unknown story of 60 years in the life of a Dos Pilas ruler ... It is at times a grisly account of flowing blood and piles of skulls after a battle was over and the vanquished were sacrificed ... Of particular importance ... the Dos Pilas glyphs support an emerging consensus that ... much of the Maya world in those years was apparently in an almost constant state of belligerence between Tikal and Calakmul and their respective blocs of allies.[5]

Such texts are confirmed by pictorial evidence. Images in reliefs and wall paintings display scenes of fighting, eminent warriors standing on the backs of naked defeated enemies or holding their cut-off heads in their hands, and eagles and pumas feasting on human hearts. The "Temple of the Skulls" in Chichen Itza, colorful paintings on ceramic vessels, and a long series of ceramic statuettes offer eloquent testimony.[6] The "peaceable Maya" landed on the large pile of discarded historical myths.

Another candidate for "peaceable kingdom honors" is the Indus Valley Civilization (ca. 3000–1600 BCE), contemporaneous with those emerging in Egypt, Mesopotamia, and China, highly developed, and interacting intensively with others. Jane McIntosh (2000: 177) defends the view that this culture was unusual in that it "seems to have been a land without conflict. There are no signs of violence and no depictions of soldiers or warfare in the Indus art." Sir Mortimer Wheeler, who excavated the two main sites (1966, 1968), thought he found

> evidence for Indus militarism. The massive walls that surrounded the citadels ... were clearly defensive in Wheeler's eyes. Many Indus artifacts could have been weapons – arrowheads, spearheads, daggers – though to Wheeler's credit he admitted that all of them could equally have been used for other purposes like hunting ... In the years since Wheeler's investigations, this evidence has all fallen away ... [A]ll the objects that could be weapons could equally be tools, such as knives for cutting food, carving wood, or projectiles for hunting. There are no swords, no maces, battle-axes, or catapults ..., no other pieces of military equipment ... Close consideration of the walls around Indus cities has shown that they cannot have been constructed for defense against people ... Nothing suggests that the walls ever sustained military attacks or sieges ... They were a defense against the constant threat of flooding, although they were also probably intended to impress. The gateways allowed some control over who passed in or out of the settlements and may have been used in collecting customs tolls or taxes (McIntosh 2000: 178–80).

McIntosh admits that "this picture of an idyllic Indus society – the first welfare state and the land without an enemy – seems too good to be true" (181). She justifies it by assuming that the agricultural resources in a very fertile region were abundant: there was no need to fight about them.

> This theory is borne out by the mutually beneficial and symbiotic relationship between settled communities and hunter-gatherers in the Indian subcontinent that existed in historical times and endured into the 20th century ... The distribution of resources within the bounds of the Indus Civilization was certainly uneven. But ... Indus society seems to have been organized to minimize these discrepancies and to spread the advantage enjoyed by each region to every other within the Indus realms. Trade and the internal distribution mechanisms of the civilization ensured that most households in the urban settlements at least had access to the full range of goods that were necessary for daily life, and to a more-than-adequate supply of food ... So when it comes down to it, whom would the Indus people have needed to fight? (183).

McIntosh certainly raises important questions, not least concerning the origins of warfare – a topic for anthropologists and military historians and beyond the scope of this volume.[7] Her interpretation of the Indus Valley Civilization, however, is controversial. While admitting that the "most striking difference" between this civilization and its Mesopotamian and Egyptian contemporaries is "the small amount of evidence for military conflict," Jonathan Kenoyer (1998: 15, cf. 42) remains cautious:

> The absence of images depicting human conflict ... cannot be taken to indicate a utopian society in which everyone worked together without warfare. We have to assume that there were periodic struggles for control and conflicts within a city as well as between cities. These battles and political confrontations may have been illustrated in other ways that are not preserved in the archaeological record. Painted cloth scrolls, carved wooden reliefs and narrative sculptures made from reeds and unfired clay are commonly produced in traditional India to represent important myths and legends that usually include battles (82).[8]

Future research will decide the issue. Meanwhile, the concept of "peaceful societies" itself seems fraught with problems. In searching for such societies, Matthew Melko and Richard Weigel (1981) define "peace," among other criteria, by the absence of physical conflict in a definable region for at least 100 years (1981: 2–7). This leads them to include among their "Cases of Peace," for example, "Ptolemaic Peace (332–216 BC)" or "Roman Republican Peace (203–90 BC)," because during these periods no wars were fought in Egypt or Italy. Moreover, they often call the societies involved "peaceful." Terms such as *"pax Romana"* (below) or *"pax Achaemenidica"* (Wiesehöfer, this vol.), however, commonly designate a condition of peace within a state that nevertheless was frequently involved in wars against outside enemies; such terms do not characterize the peoples who created and maintained such peaceful conditions. Although both Persians and Romans promoted an ideology of peace (below), they certainly were not "peaceful societies." Empire builders almost by definition cannot be peaceful. In particular, between 203 and 90 BCE, when no wars were fought in Italy, Romans and Italians were involved almost constantly in wars in the eastern and western Mediterranean. The same is true for Ptolemaic Egypt in the early Hellenistic period. To call these "peaceful societies" is therefore patently wrong. Melko and Weigel (and Melko in his even more comprehensive effort to identify 52 peaceful societies throughout history [1973]) choose not to differentiate between "areas of peace" and "peaceful societies," and they ignore crucial factors, such as mentalities, political cultures, and a society's long-term conditioning for war (below). Conversely, it would be naive to call Japan a peaceful society because for most of its history it was not involved in external wars, when, as is well known, it enjoyed few periods without domestic wars (A. Gonthier, in *LP* 179–88; Farris, in *W&S* 47–70).

By including the additional criterion that a society not be involved in any external wars, David Fabbro's quest for peaceful societies (1978) is more plausible but yields much less spectacular results: among the seven societies he identifies, none significant on the stage of world history, are the Kung Bushmen of the Kalahari desert, the Mbuti Pygmies of equatorial Africa, or the Copper Eskimos of Northern Canada. Similarly, discussion of peaceful societies at a 1986 conference on "The Anthropology of War" focused on the Buid, Semai, and Xinguano (Haas 1990: 13–16 and relevant chapters). Of course, even if the societies involved were historically insignificant (whatever that may mean) they may still yield important historical insights on our topic (Wiberg 1981).

Ideologies of Peace

All large religious movements of antiquity grappled with visions of peace. That of ancient Judaism, as reflected in the Hebrew Bible, broke through only in rare instances and remained mostly obscured by the need of a small people, embattled in an area much contested by great powers, to fight for survival and rely on an ideology that supported this fight (H. Graf Reventlow, in *K&F* 110–22: Ravitzky 1996; Walzer 1996; Niditch, Krüger, this vol.). Early Christianity focused on another world and was soon confused by dogmatic infighting and its rise to a state religion (see Swift's chapter). The Islamic "community of Believers" was initially tolerant of other monotheistic religions and ecumenical to a remarkable extent, but, preoccupied with empire building, civil wars, and dogmatic splits, it soon turned monopolistic and intolerant (Donner's chapter, see also Hashmi 1996; Tibi 1996).

As far as Buddhism is concerned, things seem to be more complex. According to some scholars, this religion was most explicit and uncompromising with regard to avoiding violence and causing pain to living creatures. For example, Richard Coudenhove-Kalergi writes (1959: 121–22),

> Among the greatest pacifists of all time was Gautama (or Buddha), the founder of the gentle religion of peace ... He forbade killing, not only of men, but also of beasts. He demanded the suppression of all bellicose instincts, lust for power, greed and ambition. A Buddhist ruler or statesman who adhered strictly to his faith must be a pacifist. If the world had then become Buddhist, and if the Buddhists had followed the teachings of the founder of their faith, the world would now have been at peace for two and a half thousand years.

This may be an idealizing view, however. Other scholars emphasize continuing disagreement not only about the details of Buddha's life but also about the contents of his teachings and the nature of the religious community he reportedly founded, and they hesitate to generalize, speaking of "Buddhisms" rather than Buddhism. Moreover, even if Buddhism at times was a powerful factor for peace, it tended to focus more on turning inward and achieving peace individually, omitted to address the problem of war explicitly, and was often unable to hold its ground against more aggressive and nationalist religions or interpretations of religion (see below and Salomon's chapter).

Rather, the "crown" for unwavering commitment to peace in the sense of nonviolence should perhaps be awarded to the Jains (Sanskrit Jainas), a small but significant religious community found mainly in western India and dating back to the fifth or sixth century BCE and perhaps even earlier. More than any other religious community, the Jains taught and exemplified the principle of *ahimsa* (non-harming), trying to avoid violence even against the smallest living beings. Gandhi grew up in an area with a large Jain population, and his early acquaintance with the ideal of *ahimsa* must have contributed greatly to his later pursuit of complete nonviolence even in the struggle for Indian independence.[9]

Some ancient empires, however, did embrace an ideology of peace. An impressive example comes from a rock inscription of King Asoka (ca. 250 BCE), perhaps the greatest ruler and empire builder in early Indian history (Thapar 2002: 174–208). Overwhelmed by the massive scale of suffering caused by his conquests, the king devoted himself "to the zealous study of morality." Hence he advised his descendants against new conquests; he urged them to be merciful if conquests could not be avoided, and to "regard the conquest by morality as the only true conquest." Unfortunately, this text is unique; Asoka's example was not followed by his successors (Salomon, this vol., and see below).

In China, before the creation of the first empire, warfare was endemic. Eventually efforts were made to control international relations, contain violence, and impose stability through a system of elaborate rituals and covenants (Yates, this vol.). Confucius and his successors played a significant role in promoting ways of maintaining peace and harmony (below).

According to Achaemenid Persian royal ideology, the king, placed in power and endowed with wisdom and special qualities by the supreme god Auramazda, is capable of telling right from wrong and promoting justice, order, and peace. While those who disobey imperial rule or revolt against it, following the path of "falsehood," are punished with the harshest measures, those who do obey and follow the path of "truth" are rewarded by the king's generosity and care and enjoy the blessings of imperial peace. "Order, not chaos, peace, not tension, good conduct of the subjects and royal generosity, not disloyalty and kingly misbehavior dominate the inscriptions and imagery of the royal residences." The *pax Achaemenidica* was thus based on an imperial ideology that "stressed the reciprocity of royal care and loyalty of the subjects"; within their far-flung empire, the kings pursued a deliberate "policy of reconciliation and peacekeeping" (Wiesehöfer, this vol.).

The Romans concluded peace only under their own terms and only from a position of victory and strength (Barton, this vol.). Usually, the resulting treaties of alliance (like those made by the Aztecs: Hassig, this vol.) were unequal and acknowledged Rome's superiority. The defeated handed themselves over (people, land, and property) into their trust (*fides*). During the republic, peace was essentially nothing but intermission between wars (Rosenstein, this vol.). The century of violence and civil war that destroyed the republic, however, also produced a change in thinking. Peace became a desirable goal. The emperor Augustus was the first to proclaim it as his policy, both in writing and through monuments, especially the elaborate "Altar of Peace" (*Ara pacis*),[10] and rituals, like the closing of the Gates of Janus, "when victories had secured peace by land and sea throughout the whole empire of the Roman people" (*Res Gestae* 13; DeBrohun, this vol.).

Augustus' major achievement, indeed, was to have ended the civil wars. The "Augustan peace" (*pax Augusta*) or "Roman peace" (*pax Romana*), permitting unprecedented prosperity and cultural unification, affected primarily the lands within the borders of the immense Roman empire (Momigliano 1940; Woolf 1993). External conquest continued – in fact, Augustus was the greatest conqueror and expander of imperial boundaries Rome ever had – but it was now officially called "pacification."

> I made the sea peaceful (*pacavi*) and freed it from pirates ... I extended the territory of all those provinces of the Roman people on whose borders lay peoples not subject to our government. I brought peace (*pacavi*) to the Gallic and Spanish provinces as well as to Germany ... I secured the pacification of the Alps (*pacificavi*) ..., yet without waging an unjust war on any people (*Res Gestae* 25–26).

The epic poet Virgil famously wrote: "Your skills, Romans, will lie in governing the peoples of the world in your empire, to impose civilization upon peace, to pardon the defeated, and to war down the proud" (*Aeneid* 6.850–53; see further R. Glei, in *K&F* 171–90).

Critics were not fooled. A century after Augustus, the historian Tacitus lets a Roman general remind Gallic tribal leaders, who were contemplating a revolt, of the simple Roman principles (that do not differ much from those adopted by earlier empires): they punish rebels with utmost severity but invite those who submit to share in the blessings of peace; although they will do so as subjects of the all-powerful emperor, even in this respect Gallic tribesmen will be equal to Roman citizens and the highest dignitaries (*Histories* 4.73). Tacitus also attributes to a Scottish leader, Calgacus, words that harshly indict Roman imperialism. Victory, he says, "will mean the dawn of liberty for the whole of Britain," but defeat will mean submission to the most arrogant and exploitative rulers. "To robbery, butchery, and rape, they give the lying name of government; they create a desert and call it peace" (*Agricola* 30; tr. H. Mattingly).

Despite such sentiments, the Roman subjects too profited from the *pax Romana* – so much so that, another 150 years later, during the crisis of the third century CE, most of them, thoroughly integrated and "Romanized" (see, e.g. Aelius Aristides' speech *To Rome*), defended the empire vigorously against persistent outside attacks.

Perhaps the most successful example of a vision of peace that was sustained over a long time comes from a different corner of the globe: the "Iroquois League" was forged around 1450 CE to foster peaceful relations among six North-American Indian nations, and lasted to 1777, more than 300 years (Crawford, this vol.). The League seems to have been created through negotiation among equal partners rather than compulsion from above or outside. Its foundation was codified in the "Great Law of Peace." The League's purpose, achieved to a remarkable degree, was to maintain general peace, unity, and order among its member nations. Nothing like this ever came about in the ancient world, despite numerous attempts.

The Nature of War in Antiquity

In most ancient societies war was pervasive. The "Warring States Period" in China well deserves its name (Yates, *W&S* 25–30; Loewe and Shaughnessy 1999: ch. 9). Peace "was a rare feature in India ... Indian society was used to war, and in many respects approved of war, and ... both the sacred and secular writings of India ... not merely treat war as a normal feature of life, but even extol it as an instrument of policy and a means of releasing heroic and praiseworthy human qualities" (Derrett 1961: 143–44). In Mesoamerica, city-states, grouped in dense clusters, were constantly fighting for control, territory, and prisoners of war; superpowers vied for supreme control, enveloping each other with alliances and subordinate states, or expanding their empires by war and alliance. War was a constant threat and reality (Hassig 1992; Webster, Hassig, *W&S* chs. 13–14). In South America (modern Peru) several warring societies extended their control over sizeable territories (Moseley 2001; Schreiber, in Alcock et al. 2001: ch. 3), long before the Inca built a huge empire within only a few generations (D'Altroy, ibid. ch. 8). Although it is difficult to reconstruct the reality of warfare from later evidence, what can be found out confirms that this did not happen without the application of massive threats and violence (Julien, this vol.). Warriors returning from battle with prisoners roped by their necks, depicted in murals, on pottery, and in ceramic figurines of the Moche culture, convey the same message.[11] In ancient West Asia, the Hittites, Assyrians, and Persians pursued large-scale conquests and remained frequently at war to defend their empires and suppress rebellions, despite intense diplomatic efforts to obviate the need for doing so.[12]

In Greece, war became endemic in the fifth century, culminating in a long war between two "superpowers" and their allies that was increasingly understood as a fight for domination over the entire Greek world.[13] Even after Athens' defeat, war remained virtually permanent until Philip II of Macedon subjected the Greek city-states and forced them to abandon their rivalries. Between the Persian and Peloponnesian Wars, Athens was involved in some kind of war for two out of every three years (Garlan 1975; Raaflaub, *W&S* ch. 6). The same was true during most of the Roman republic. Moreover, in the period when they conquered the Mediterranean, the Romans mobilized unprecedented percentages of their and their allies' adult male population: estimates based on ancient historical sources suggest, for example, that between 197 and 168 BCE on average 47,500 citizens (out of a total population of c. 250,000 adult male citizens) fought every year in long wars abroad (Brunt 1971: 422–26; see also Rosenstein, *W&S* ch. 8, 2004); if we applied the same ratio to the USA, many millions of Americans would be fighting for their country every year.

Grim though this picture looks, should we not beware of generalizing or exaggerating it? No doubt, there were many periods and areas in which war was indeed endemic. But in most of the ancient world, Melko and Weigel claim, "peace appears to have been normal, war an exceptional activity . . . Most of the time, even if war was occurring in some society, it was not in most other societies . . . At any particular time, if somewhere a boundary was being violated, tens or hundreds of others were being respected" (1981: 131).

No doubt, there is some truth in this. Why, then, do we tend to overlook it? In large part, I think, because war and its results tend to attract the attention, from antiquity to today, of historians and other observers. War prompts action, momentous events, and change; it deeply affects the lives of individuals, communities, and states; it is responsible, directly and indirectly, for the development of social and political structures and for advances in the sciences, technology, and virtually every aspect of culture (Carneiro 1994: 15); it offers opportunities for distinction and, as already the poet of the *Iliad* knew, eternal glory. By contrast, peace seems static, uneventful, devoid of opportunities, and boring (see also below). War, as the Greek philosopher Heraclitus observed, "is both king of all and father of all, and it has revealed some as gods, others as men; some it has made slaves, others free" (fr. 53 in Diels and Kranz 1961).

Still, it is likely that Melko and Weigel's view is too simple. Not only, as Robert Carneiro observes, has war "pervaded too much of human history to be merely an anomaly or a misadventure" (1994: 5), it really seems to have been ubiquitous in the history of humankind, at least from an identifiable and early stage of its development. Relying on anthropological research on war among early societies (see also n. 10) and using for historical times as an index "the number of wars fought per polity per decade," Ronald Cohen (1986) and Carneiro (1994: 16–20) leave no doubt about the elementary fact that war was pervasive and deeply ingrained in human thinking through most of world history.

Be that as it may, ancient war, when it occurred, was brutal. The Maya and Aztecs hunted for prisoners of war, whom they sacrificed to their gods: human blood was needed to oil the cosmic engine. The "Temple of the Skulls" in Chichen Itza symbolizes this attitude. One Aztec king, succeeding a weak predecessor and wishing to restore obedience among the subject cities, made a punitive expedition, supposedly returned with 80,400 prisoners and sacrificed all of them during a four-day festival at the Great Temple in Tenochtitlan (Hassig, *W&S* 369). Unless their opponents accepted submission, the Inca were likely to exterminate whole tribes, to leave the fallen enemies on the battlefield as food for scavengers and a grizzly victory memorial, and to expose prisoners of war to a fight for life with wild animals (Julien, this vol.). Wars among competing city-states and kingdoms in early China must have taken an enormous toll in human life and destruction (Yates, *W&S* ch. 2). Egyptian pharaohs and Mesopotamian kings displayed the bloody harvest of war in reliefs on their monuments – as a deterrent and a record of their achievement (Pritchard 1969: 92–132). Assyrians and Persians not only punished most cruelly those involved in rebellions, they also deported large segments of defeated peoples into the interior of their country and occasionally replaced them with their own settlers (Oded 1979; Briant 1996). About the fate of prisoners of war in ancient West Asia and Egypt, taken in huge numbers, we are unusually well informed through textual and pictorial descriptions (Helck 1979; Klengel 1981: 243–46; Hoffner 2002). For example, in Mesopotamia,

> in the tenth and ninth centuries the official inscriptions give an impression of unremitting cruelty: most were slaughtered or blinded, some hung on stakes or fortifications around city walls, as a warning to others. Heads, hands, or lower lips were cut off to facilitate counting. It is impossible to tell whether the texts exaggerate the violence in order to frighten waverers into submission (Dalley 1995: 419).

In ancient Israel, so the Hebrew Bible claims, Yahweh occasionally demanded "the ban," that is, the wholesale annihilation of defeated enemies, including animals and property (Niditch, this vol.).

In the Greco-Roman world, customs of war gave the victor the right to dispose of the defeated at will. The Romans accepted only the wholesale capitulation of defeated enemies (above). Anything better than physical or social death (through slavery) was a gift bestowed by the victor's generosity – hence the unusual success of Rome's alliance system that restored to the defeated their communal autonomy. Even so, the massive influx of enslaved war captives (*CAH* VII.2^2: 389), as well as the confiscation of parts of the former enemies' territories, enabled the Romans to abolish debt bondage and to provide their own citizens with land allotments, thereby multiplying their own territory and the size of their citizen body – and armies (Raaflaub 1996: 287–99). In Greece, in the long and bitter Peloponnesian War, prisoners of war, unless ransomed by their relatives, were likely to be sold into slavery or to die from neglect (Ducrey 1968; Panagopoulos 1989). Several communities that resisted integration into the Athenian empire, or defected from it, were annihilated (Karavites 1982). Thucydides commemorated through his "Melian dialogue" (one of the most famous passages in political literature) the fate of tiny Melos that, confronted with the might of the superpower Athens, refused "to give up, in a short moment, the liberty" it had enjoyed for 700 years. The Athenians "put to death all the men of military age whom they took, and sold the women and children as slaves. Melos itself they took over for themselves" (Thuc. 5.112, 116). At the end of the war, Athens, starved into submission, almost suffered the same fate (Xenophon, *Hellenica* 2.2.10–20). Yet Sparta's conduct was not much better (Rahe 2002). Nor was the Peloponnesian War unique. Carthage and Corinth, large and famous cities, were destroyed in 146, when Rome's patience with recalcitrant enemies wore out. After his victory over the Macedonian king at Pydna in 168, the Roman general Aemilius Paullus, authorized by the Roman senate, systematically organized the simultaneous sack of seventy communities in Epirus and sold 150,000 innocent civilians into slavery (Livy 45.33–34).[14]

Moreover, the prevailing political culture tended to encourage war rather than peace. With few exceptions, the voices we hear from antiquity are those of the powerful elites and rulers. They were concerned primarily with legitimizing, securing, and extending their status and power. According to Herodotus, who was familiar with Persian royal ideology, King Xerxes' decision in the late 480s BCE to conquer Greece was motivated by the desire to avenge previous defeat and especially to emulate his ancestors:

> We Persians have a way of living, which I have inherited from my predecessors and propose to follow. I have learned from my elders that . . . we have never yet remained inactive. This is God's guidance, and it is by following it that we have gained our great prosperity. Of our past history you need no reminder; for you know well enough the famous deeds of Cyrus, Cambyses, and my father Darius and their additions to our empire. Now I myself, ever since my accession, have been thinking how not to fall short of the kings who have sat upon this throne before me, and how to add as much power as they did to the Persian empire (Hdt. 7.8a).

In the Inca world, too, leadership qualities, even if expected to be inherited, needed to be demonstrated through martial success, thus prompting each ruler to prove his *capac* status by engaging in war and conquest (Julien, this vol.).

Victory on the battlefield, riches gained in war, and imperial might enabled kings and generals to erect monuments, palaces, temples, and inscriptions that eternalized their glory; poets in their service sang their praise. This is what we still see and hear today. In city-states too, such as mid-republican Rome (below), and even in democratic Athens, the monumental city-scape reminded the citizens constantly of their city's glory and power, achieved through victories in war, and conditioned them to emulate their ancestors (Hölscher 1998, 2001; Raaflaub 2001a). Leaders found that success in war and conquest provided them with glory, wealth, and continuing influence. Policies based on action and intervention paid dividends; policies of peace meant inactivity, lack of success, stagnation: nothing to fight and die for! So in 415 BCE Alcibiades, the ultimate demagogue, prevailed over the cautious Nicias in persuading the Athenians to send a magnificent armada to Sicily, aiming at conquest – and meeting disaster (Thuc. 6.1–8.1, with the debate in 6.8–26; Raaflaub 1994). In Thucydides, Athens' enemies observe that, in contrast to the cautious Spartans, the Athenians have been conditioned to be activists, and this is reflected in their collective character, their way of life, and their policies (1.70–71). In the Athenians' own view, this quality of *polypragmosyne* (activism, meddlesomeness), despised by others, has carried them to the peak of power and glory, made their city the "greatest and freest" (Raaflaub 2004: 181–93). An *apragmon* citizen, by contrast, is inactive, not involved, and essentially useless to the community (Thuc. 2.40).

In Rome, too, constant warfare over centuries had molded society (Raaflaub 1996; Rosenstein, this vol.): the commoners had been conditioned to accept war as inevitable and profitable; the community had learned to live with war and to use it to increase communal power and wealth, to impress allies and subjects with ever new victories and so to deter them from revolts, to satisfy communal needs (e.g. for dependent labor or land for poor citizens) at the expense of the defeated, and to deflect internal conflicts toward the outside. Most importantly, the aristocracy had developed a value system that focused entirely on service for the community, especially in war; hence *gloria* and *dignitas* (status based on one's own and one's ancestors' achievements), indispensable for rising to the highest ranks among the political elite, could only be gained through successful leadership in war. In the ceremonial "triumph" the victorious general, dressed in the star-studded purple coat of the former kings, rode in a chariot at the head of the victorious army displaying the spoils and prisoners of war to the Capitol, where he paid homage and thanks to Jupiter: in a fleeting moment of equality, the greatest mortal shook hands with the greatest god (Versnel 1970; Beard et al. 1998: 44–45). *That* was worth dying for.

Searching for Peace

All this is well known and has often been discussed. It seems important to look at the other side of the coin as well. Where in this world of constant war and violence do we find peace? What role did peace play in people's concerns, in the thoughts of the mighty and lowly? Was peace an ideal, promoted by propaganda and ideology, even if these intended to deceive and hide different realities? Was it reflected in religion? Did poets and philosophers think and write about peace? Was "peacefulness" ever a virtue, balancing manliness and bravery (Roman *virtus*, Greek *andreia*)?

In many parts of the ancient world we search in vain for traces of this elusive commodity. No doubt, peoples everywhere, oppressed by frequent war, conscription, destruction, and death, yearned for peace and security. But we rarely hear their voices – sometimes because this kind of evidence has simply not survived, in other cases because the extant evidence reflects only the perspective of the mighty elites. At any rate, what was written concerned war more often than peace, and our chances of success in our search for peace are limited. Yet there is evidence, and it is of considerable interest.[15]

Analyzing words and concepts

To begin with, we can look for words or concepts that formulate peace, explicitly or implicitly: for instance, *pax* in Rome, *eirene* in Greece. The examination of such terminology and of the forms in which it is expressed can yield important insights (C. Milani, in Sordi 1985: 17–29; M. Job, in *K&F* 27–44). Is there one term for "peace" or are there several, and how are they distinguished? And what spheres of life and relationships do they cover? The Greeks use *eirene* but also *hesychia* (quiet); *homonoia* (oneness of mind, concord) and *philia* (friendship) are closely related, both in domestic and foreign relations. The legal language designating peace accords is even more varied (Alonso, this vol.). In fact, friendship is a condition for treaties that establish peace, in Greece and ancient West Asia.[16] Roman *pax* is related to *paciscor* (making an agreement) and comes to reflect the pact between a superior and inferior power (Barton this vol.). Here the external aspects of the word dominate, while in India the internal ones (peace of mind) prevail (Salomon this vol.).

Do peoples conceptualize peace? It is surely significant that already Homer contrasts the condition of peace with that of war (*Iliad* 2.797–98; 9.403) and juxtaposes on the famous shield of Achilles a city in peace and a city in war (18.490–540; Zampaglione 1973: 18–23; Effe, in *K&F* 9–26). His slightly younger contemporary, Hesiod, distinguishes between a good and bad form of *eris* (competition and strife; *Works and Days* 11–26), makes all the negative traits associated with conflict the children of Night (*Theogony* 211–32), and compares a city of justice that enjoys peace and prosperity with a city of injustice that is haunted by infertility, drought, famine, and war (*Works and Days* 225–47; Zampaglione 23–26). In Homer, we also find reflection and laments about the misery caused by war and a desire for peace, voiced by the masses of warriors. Laments about the destructive impact of war are frequent in other cultures too, especially in Mesopotamia (Foster, this vol.). The Sumerian view of the Golden Age, found in the epic "Enmerkar and the Land of Aratta," "describes a once-upon-a-time state of peace and security, and ends with man's fall from this blissful state." At that time, man was not threatened by wild animals, "there was no fear, no terror, man had no rival." The lands had all that was necessary, rested in security, and, in unison, praised their god, Enlil (Kramer 1981: 255–58). "Peace," however, seems implied here; what the poem emphasizes is plentiful bliss, safety, and social harmony (see also Foster, this vol.).

Do peoples have deities of war and peace and what is their role in the pantheon? Is peace incorporated in monumental displays (statues, temples, inscriptions); does it serve as a title of honor? Of course, the question of cult applies only to polytheistic societies – although it is surely meaningful that Jahweh is a warrior god (Niditch, this vol.),[17] while both the god and the savior of the Christians lack martial attributes, however ambivalent Christian attitudes toward war and violence may have been (Swift, this vol.). The Hittites had a god of peace (Beal this vol.), the Mesopotamians and Egyptians apparently not.[18] In Greece, Peace was personified very early. Soon after 700 BCE, the poet Hesiod placed Peace high up in the divine hierarchy and made her, like Justice and Good Order, one of the Horai, goddesses of growth and prosperity, and the daughter of the supreme god, Zeus, and his wife Themis, Divine Law, thus emphasizing peace as one of the primary communal values (*Theogony* 901–02). Eirene was prominent on Athenian vases and in comedy and tragedy in the fifth century (Zampaglione 1973: 71–90; *LIMC* 3.1: 704), clearly reflecting a reaction to the time's intense experience of war (Tritle, Konstan, this vol.). Even so, Peace received an official cult in Athens only after the victory of Timotheus over the Spartans in 375 (*CAH* VI[2]: 174). As Robert Parker comments,

> Here then the association of the abstract cult with a specific event is explicitly attested. What is more, the character of that event sets the idea of "Peace" in a particular light which is not that of a nascent pacifism. Of course, the cult must also have been a celebration of "the blessings of peace": a famous statue by Cephisodotus, perhaps the cult statue itself, showed the cheerful goddess with the boy Wealth in her arms. But Isocrates, our earliest witness, explains that Timotheus' victory had forced the Spartans to make terms which destroyed their power, "in consequence of which from that day on we have sacrificed to Peace every year, in the belief that no other peace has brought such benefits to the city" ... The cult began and was for some time remembered as one of Glorious Peace, in a century in which Athens had to accept so many peaces that were bitter humiliations. It too was a kind of war-memorial.[19]

Because in the period of the Peloponnesian War external war often went together with internal strife or civil war (*stasis*), which was capable of producing unprecedented excesses of treachery and cruelty (Thuc. 3.81–84; Gehrke 1985; Price 2001), a contrasting concept, concord (*homonoia*), rose to political prominence in this period; the term was apparently invented in the late fifth century and mentioned in treatises and speeches of several thinkers (sophists). The concept was realized in a spectacular way in the Athenian "amnesty decree" of 403 BCE, that ended the civil war between the supporters of the "Thirty Tyrants" and those of democracy. A cult followed a few decades later; its earliest extant attestation concerns an altar in Olympia established in 363 (Pausanias 5.14.9). Anticipated by the famous teacher of rhetoric, Gorgias, in a speech probably given at Olympia in 408, the cult was expanded in the second half of the fourth century to include panhellenic unity against the Persians.[20]

In Rome, *pax* was conceptually important all along because every cult act had the purpose of securing "peace with the gods" (*pax deorum*; Sordi 1985: 146–54), but personification and cult followed much later. While "internal peace, concord" (*concordia*) was personified and received a temple already in the mid-republic (Hölscher 1990), this happened with Peace only in the aftermath of the disastrous civil wars that destroyed the republic, when peace was imposed by the victors and eventually became the *pax Augusta*. Caesar seems to have celebrated *Pax* on one of his late coins (Crawford 1974: 480/24); a celebratory coin (cistophor), minted in 28 by the city of Ephesus, praised Augustus as liberator of the Roman people and shows the word *Pax* on the reverse (Mattingly 1923: n. 691 p. 112 and pl. 17.4). Most importantly, Augustus emphasized his accomplishment of establishing peace not only in his *Res Gestae* (13, see above) and with the *Ara Pacis* (Weinstock 1960), but also by linking this monument symbolically and monumentally with the great sundial adjacent to it and with the sanctuary of Janus on the Forum, which served as "indicator of peace and war" (Livy 1.19.2). When the shadow of the obelisk fell through the door of the *Ara Pacis* on Augustus' birthday on the fall equinox, it was clear that the first emperor wanted to be seen as "born for peace" (Simon 1986a: 28–46, esp. 29–30; 1994). Finally, and only after another round of civil wars, the emperor Vespasian built a temple to *Pax* in 75 CE (Suetonius, *Vespasian* 9.1). Obviously then, even more than in Greece, in Rome the cultic and monumental elevation of Peace came late and was prompted primarily by political and ideological motives.

It is instructive to consider "war" in the same way. The Romans saw themselves as descendants of the war god Mars; his sacred animal, and the "totem animal" of the Romans, was the wolf, and statues of the wolf (with or without the twins, Romulus and Remus), were displayed prominently in the city (Wiseman 1995). A shrine of Mars (*sacrarium Martis*) in the center of the city housed an ancient weapon cult (Plut. *Rom.* 29.1). The cult image in his temple outside the Porta Capena, dedicated in 388 BCE, showed him surrounded by wolves (Livy 22.2.12). Bronze statuettes of the warrior god date back to the sixth century. He was connected with rituals of war already in the early republic (*DNP* 7: 946–51; Simon 1984). Julius Caesar planned a temple for Mars (Suet. *Div. Iul.* 44.1), Augustus built it, for Mars Ultor (the Avenger) in his new Forum (Simon 1986a: 46–51; Siebler 1988 on the cult statue). Moreover, Mars was not the only god connected with war: Jupiter and, to some extent, Juno, were as well. From the early third century, when the conquest of Italy reached its climax, Roman generals began to use spoils to erect monuments and shrines, celebrating their victories and honoring the gods who had supported their achievement. The list of gods honored in this way contains many variations of the war and victory theme: Salus, Bellona Victrix, Jupiter Victor, Venus Obsequens, Victoria, Jupiter Stator, Fors Fortuna (*CAH* VII.2^2: 408; Hölscher 1978). In subsequent centuries, the Capitol, Forum, Field of Mars, and adjacent areas became a vast "memorial space," shaping the Romans' identity and reminding ever new generations of the great deeds of their ancestors (Hölkeskamp 2001; Hölscher 2001).

By contrast, among the Greeks, the war god Ares enjoyed the worst possible reputation. Homer describes him as a "maniac who knows nothing of justice" (*Iliad* 5.761) and a "thing of fury, evil-wrought" (5.831). Even Zeus, his father, finds nothing good in him:

> To me you are the most hateful of all gods who hold Olympos.
> Forever quarrelling is dear to your heart, wars and battles (5.890–91; trans. R. Lattimore).

"Beginning with Homer, Ares embodies the most abhorrent aspects of war. Nothing noble, no dignity or decency is in him; hence he can be portrayed as a coward in battle, a cheater and adulterer" (my trans. of Schachter 1996: 1048; cf. Burkert 1985: 169–70). It is perhaps not surprising, therefore, that the city of Athens did not have a sanctuary of Ares in the Classical Period. But there was one in the deme (district) of Acharnai in Attica, famed for its feisty warriors, and its fifth century temple was moved to the Athenian Agora in the first century BCE (Travlos 1971: 104–11; Camp 1986: 184–85).

Conversely, monuments and inscriptions celebrating victories proliferated in Athens. The elegant little temple of Nike (Victory) near the entrance of the

Acropolis, decorated with friezes representing military victories and with Nike reliefs on the parapet, commemorated an important victory over Sparta in 425/4 (Travlos 1971: 148–57); statues of Nike stood as *akroteria* on each wing of the magnificent Stoa of Zeus the Liberator in the Agora, built around 430 (Travlos 1971: 527–33; Camp 1986: 105–07); even the gold accumulated in the treasury of Athena was cast in Nike statuettes. And the greatest temple of all, the Parthenon, served as a monument of Athens' Persian victories and imperial might (Smarczyk 1990: 31–57; Osborne 1994; Hurwitt 2004: 106–54). The virgin goddess worshipped there was a warrior (Herington 1955; Fehr 1979–81), and as such, fighting in the front rank and leading her people to victory (*promachos*), she stood in a famous bronze statue (Athena Promachos) on the Acropolis, the greatest among many dedications commemorating Athenian victories (Travlos 1971: 69 fig. 88; Hurwitt 2004: 79–84 and 63 fig. 56; *LIMC* 2: 969–74, esp. 972). Moreover, monuments celebrating Athenian martial exploits stood also in the Agora and elswhere, and the public tombs of the heroes fallen in Athens' wars formed a long "façade of honor" along the main road in the public cemetery outside the walls. By "monumentalizing and perpetuating with works of art the glory of her great citizens and their famous achievements, Athens gradually developed into a monument of her own historical identity" (Hölscher 1998 [quote: 182]; Raaflaub 2001a).

Did peoples create a spatial distinction between a sphere of peace and a sphere of war? Here Rome offers outstanding examples. The gate of Janus, the two-faced god of the threshold that separates inside and outside, was closed whenever peace prevailed in the Roman realm (DeBrohun, this vol.). In close analogy, the sacred boundary of Rome (and any Roman or Etruscan city), called *pomerium*, separated the inside, the sphere of homes (*domi*) and peace, from the outside, the sphere of violence and war (*militiae*).[21] Rome is also illuminating for distinctions in time: calendrical separations between seasons of war and seasons of peace (below).

Examining rituals

Another avenue to discovering the meaning of peace leads through a society's actions and rituals. This approach is useful also for societies that do not have an explicit terminology for peace or whose terminology we do not know. Such actions may aim in various directions: toward separating the spheres of war and peace, towards securing the justice of one's cause and thus the support of the gods if war proves necessary, towards avoiding war or achieving the same goal by different means (e.g. diplomacy), or explicitly toward preserving or restoring peace.

A certain amount of ritual separation of war and peace was provided by the sacrifices, attested in many societies (for instance, the Inca: Julien, this vol.), that were conducted when an army left for war and returned after war. In Athens, before leaving town, the army offered sacrifices at the shrine of heroicized maidens called *Hyakinthides*. Their cult was connected with the myth of the sacrifice of the daughters of Erechtheus, Athens' first king, whose death had brought Athens victory, and so the army's sacrifice, like the annual communal cattle-sacrifice celebrated with choruses of maidens, was intended to guarantee victory in battle (Euripides, *Erechtheus* fr. 65.65–89; Lonis 1979: 206–09; Burkert 1983: 64–66). All campaigning of the year ultimately ended with the elaborate and solemn rituals of the burial of the war dead, described by Thucydides for the fall of 431 and immortalized by Pericles' Funeral Oration (2.34–46; Clairmont 1983). Whether anything of this kind was fixed in Athens' ritual calendar (which otherwise was full of war-related events: Pritchett 1979: ch. 5) is uncertain, however.

In Rome, where every action related to war was preceded by sacrifices and consultation of the gods (Rüpke 1990; Beard et al. 1998: 43–45), a special priesthood (the *fetiales*) was responsible for making sure that the Romans always fought for a just cause (see below). The departing general visited the temple of Jupiter Optimus Maximus (the Best and Greatest) on the Capitol and made his vows; upon his victorious return, with the senate's approval, his triumphal procession ended at the same place with offerings to Jupiter (mentioned above). Rome's calendar, originating in the community's earliest period, lists numerous festivals connected with war (Scullard 1981: pt. 2 and appendices). In the spring and fall, the beginning and end of the campaign season were marked by war dances performed by the archaic priesthood of the Salii, by sacrifices and festivals honoring Mars, and by other specific rituals (Rüpke 1990: ch. 2; Rosenstein, this vol.).

Efforts to Avoid or End War and Preserve or Restore Peace

Avoiding war through intimidation or diplomacy

Efforts to avoid war were common in many ancient societies; after all, it usually seemed preferable to achieve one's goals without incurring the risks, expenses, and losses of war. Methods varied. To begin with intimidation, for example, the Persian king sent ambassadors to the enemy, demanding "earth and water" as symbols of submission; giving these tokens was identical with accepting the overlordship of the king and thus made a war of conquest unnecessary; refusing them meant war (Herodotus 7.32, 131; Kuhrt 1988; Briant 1996). Assyrian kings decorated the halls where they received foreign embassies with reliefs illustrating in horrendous detail the cruel fate of rulers and cities that revolted or failed to submit. Before the start of a campaign, ambassadors went to the intended targets, delivering an equally blunt warning (Dalley 1995: 420; Ferrill 1997: 68–70). Rather than risking outright wars of conquest, especially against formidable opponents, the Aztecs engaged them in so-called "Flower Wars." These displayed the skills of the Aztec warriors and were intended as a show of strength to intimidate the enemies, convince them of the futility of resistance, and force them into voluntary submission (Hassig, *W&S* 379). In the period of Inca expansion, too, opponents were usually offered a choice between peace resulting from voluntary submission, and war, conquest, and destruction (Julien, this vol.).

Efforts to avoid war by diplomatic means are attested especially well in ancient West Asia (e.g. Beckman 1999; Cohen and Westbrook 2000; Beal, Foster, this vol.)

and the Greco-Roman world (Adcock and Mosley 1975; Piccirilli 2002; Alonso, this vol.). Already the Homeric epics, alluding to the prelude of the Trojan War and other potential conflicts, mention diplomacy designed to settle conflicts before they erupted in war (Raaflaub 1997: 2–8).

Alliance and arbitration

In archaic Greece (750–480 BCE), among clusters of city-states that balanced each other, alliances and treaties (Baltrusch 1994; Alonso, this vol.) as well as arbitration were useful tools to avoid the violent resolution of conflicts. To focus here on the latter, communities frequently appointed arbitrators to help settle both domestic and interstate conflicts (Tod 1913; Piccirilli 1973; for a later period, Ager 1996). A group of men emerged, among them the "Seven Sages," who stood above the conflicting parties, thus assumed an independent "third position," enjoyed great prestige, and were acceptable as mediators to all involved (Meier 1990: 28–52; Martin 1993). For example, Solon the Athenian and Pittacus of Mytilene were endowed with a communal mandate to implement incisive reforms. Around 600 BCE, Athens and Mytilene, feuding over Sigeum, a town near Troy, appealed to Periander, the ruler of Corinth and one of the "Seven Sages," who determined that each side should keep what they held at the time. Henceforth, Sigeum belonged to Athens (Hdt. 5.94–95).

Several factors supported this general tendency. The highest religious authority in the Greek world, the oracle of Apollo in Delphi, promoted principles of moderation and humane conduct, even in warfare (Kiechle 1958). Sparta, by far the largest and most powerful city-state, was handicapped by the very condition upon which its power rested (a large population of collective slaves); hence, rather than further expanding its territory, it sought to maintain a large "security zone" through a hegemonial alliance (Cartledge 1979). Archaic Sparta was thus a "superpower" without imperial ambitions, enjoying great authority and able to serve as arbitrator. Moreover, periods of general peace before and during the quadrennial Olympic and other Games may have helped to cool down conflicts; representatives of many Greek cities, meeting at this and other panhellenic festivals, could use the occasion for negotiations on neutral ground.

By the mid-fifth century, however, the Greek world was polarized between two power blocs led by Athens and Sparta. At stake potentially was predominance over the entire Greek world – a confrontation often compared with that of the Cold War (Fliess 1966; Lebow and Strauss 1991). Those trying to remain neutral were viewed with suspicion by both sides (Thuc. 5.84–114; cf. 3.82.8; Alonso 1987; Bauslaugh 1991). This made arbitration and thus the peaceful resolution of conflicts very difficult. For how was arbitration between two states going to work if there was no superior agency that had enough authority to be recognized by both contestants, and if the prevailing political culture did not encourage peaceful rather than violent conflict resolution?[22] This is the main reason why the arbitration clause in the "Thirty Years' Treaty" of 446 between Athens and Sparta failed to be effective in the prelude to the Peloponnesian War in 432–31 (Kagan 1995: ch. 1; Tritle, this vol.). As Sheila Ager writes (1996: 3),

> it seems to be typical of international arbitration, in the ancient as in the modern world, that smaller states would often be the most likely to appeal to the process. For a powerful

state, submission to a binding judicial process could represent a restriction of goals that might otherwise easily be achieved by military action or economic pressures. A less significant power, incapable of pursuing its own interests through such means, would have nothing to lose and perhaps everything to gain by an appeal to arbitration.

Rejection of binding arbitration or binding international agreements by one or more major powers focusing on their own interests: sadly, this is a problem that haunts the world to this very day! Even so, arbitration remained an instrument that was used frequently, especially in the Hellenistic period and on levels below that of the "Superpowers" (Ager 1996).

Securing a just cause

Attempts to avoid war were often connected with efforts to ensure the justice of one's cause and thus to secure the support of the gods if war proved inevitable. In the first phase of the Peloponnesian War, the Athenians could maintain that they had justice and the gods on their side because they had offered arbitration, as provided by the existing treaty, and Sparta had rejected it (Thuc. 1.140–41, 144–45). After the interlude of the "Peace of Nicias," the situation was reversed:

> The Spartans considered that Athens had been the first to break the peace treaty. In the first war they thought that the fault had been more on their side, partly because [their allies had committed the first act of aggression] and partly because in spite of the provision in the previous treaty that there should be no recourse to arms if arbitration were offered, they themselves had not accepted the Athenian offer of arbitration. They therefore thought that there was some justice in the misfortunes they had suffered ... But now [the Athenians were the aggressors. Moreover,] whenever any dispute arose on doubtful points in the treaty, it was Sparta who had offered to submit to arbitration and Athens who had refused the offer. It was now Athens, the Spartans thought, who was in the wrong through having committed exactly the same faults as theirs had been before, and they went into the war with enthusiasm (7.18; trans. R. Warner).

In the late republic, the Romans were operating with an explicit doctrine of "just war" (*bellum iustum*). Their ideology even claimed that they had conquered their empire only by pursuing just causes, specifically by aiding their allies; modern scholars call this the doctrine of "defensive imperialism" (Harris 1979: sect. V; J. Linderski, in Harris 1984: 133–64; K.-W. Welwei, in *K&F* 85–109). The Roman historian Livy (1.32) describes the ritual that, so his contemporaries thought, lay at the origins of this doctrine. It involved a special priesthood (the *fetiales*), specific curses and prayers, including one to *fas* (righteousness), and offered the community that owed satisfaction an opportunity to comply with Rome's demands (Harris 1979: 166–75; Rüpke 1990: ch. 5).

Efforts to restore peace

No less solemn ceremonies were used in efforts to end war and restore peace (see, generally, de Libero 2002). Again, the *Iliad* offers a splendid illustration in a truce between Trojans and Greeks (3.67–323). Its purpose is to avoid costly communal involvement by permitting the primary parties in the conflict, Menelaus and Paris, to decide matters in a duel. The two leaders act in the presence of both armies; these witness and validate the procedures which consist of prayers, a solemn definition of the issue at hand, sacrifices, oaths, and curses. He who breaks the truce and the oaths will be responsible for the recurrence of the war; the other side will fight for a just cause and enjoy the support of the gods. The poet lays this out in great detail and with much drama: it was clearly a matter of concern for his audiences. Remarkably, he emphasizes several times how much both armies hope for an end of war and the restoration of friendship between the two peoples (e.g. *Il.* 3.73–75, 111–12, 297–301, 319–23). Friendship and peace thus go together (see above). Hence already in its formative period Greek society disposed of clearly formulated rituals and procedures to avoid war and to restore peace if war broke out. Such procedures, however, had long been practiced among West Asian societies, and it comes as no surprise that scholars have found close correspondences between these and those described in the *Iliad* (Karavites 1992; Knippschild 2002).

Efforts to stabilize peace

Naturally, here too, diplomacy and alliances played a major role. The Aztecs, it seems, lacked a peace god and rites for peace. Conquest was a primary goal and war was inevitable to achieve it; accordingly, they valued everything highly that was connected with war and battle. As Ross Hassig puts it (this vol.), long-term peaceful relations with other polities were not their goal; the main issue for them was "how to bring all other polities into a hierarchical relationship with themselves on top. There could be peace only with the subordinated, the dead, or with those too distant or too powerful to be conquered yet." Moreover, everybody in Aztec society profited from war and empire. Hence peace as such was not desirable. Once conquest was completed, however, two mechanisms were put in place to maintain continued subordination and make further war superfluous – in this sense to guarantee peace. One was alliance based on tribute, the other a dense system of intermarriage that made sure that Aztec princesses were married to subordinate allied kings and produced sons who had the best chances to succeed their fathers, thus soon establishing direct descendants of the Aztec king on most allied thrones. To the extent possible, this did guarantee stability of alliance and peace.

A similar tributary system operated in the Han empire of China (after 206 BCE). Foreign states wishing to enter into formal relations with China had to bring gifts and recognize the emperor's ritual superiority. According to Robin Yates (this vol.), "peace was maintained in this system by the ritual exchange of gifts, by the emperor conferring Chinese titles on the leaders of the subordinate peoples, and sometimes by marrying off a woman of the royal family to the leader of the tribe and conferring an imperial surname on him." Even earlier, during the "Spring and Autumn Period" (722–481 BCE), marriage served to cement good and peaceful relations. While in later China a man could have only one legitimate wife, in this earlier period frequently several women from one ruling family were sent as brides to the groom in another state. The purpose was to ensure at least one, and preferably several, offspring capable of continuing good relations between the ruling families.

A spectacular example of peace through alliance and intermarriage is the treaty concluded between the Hittite king and Egyptian pharaoh after 1274 BCE (Bell, Beal, this vol.). The two kingdoms had been allied before, but their spheres of influence overlapped, and military conflicts recurred frequently. When Tutankhamun died without a designated male heir, his widow tried to control the succession to the throne by asking for the hand of a Hittite prince. The young man fell victim to intrigues at the Egyptian court, and hostilities resumed, culminating in the battle of Kadesh. The battle ended in a draw; both sides claimed victory. A few years later they recognized their common interest and entered into a treaty of alliance. The purpose of the treaty was to provide "peace and brotherhood and to prohibit hostilities." It was reaffirmed twice by Ramses II's marriages to Hittite princesses.

In Greece, the Peloponnesian War was eventually decided largely by Persian money. As a result, the Persian king reclaimed sovereignty over the Greek cities on the west coast of Anatolia that had been liberated after the Persian Wars and soon become Athenian subjects. It was in the Persian king's interest to control affairs in Greece by playing the leading powers off against each other and keeping them from interfering in Asia Minor. In a treaty concluded in 387 under the king's sponsorship, the autonomy of all Greek states was guaranteed and general peace was declared in a system that was supposed to retain its stability under Spartan supervision. Several such treaties of "common peace" (*koine eirene*) followed; none succeeded for a long time until peace was imposed on Greece by the Macedonian kings (Larsen 1944; Ryder 1965; Jehne 1994; also Alonso, this vol.). Still, together with the Thirty-Years' Peace of 446 (Kagan 1995: 31–37), the concept of "common peace" is one of the ancient world's most impressive attempts to forge an instrument capable of stabilizing peace in a world plagued by constant war. It failed because the power entrusted with supervising it saw it mainly as a tool serving its own interests.[23]

Intellectual Concern with Peace

The modern world features an impressive array of leading intellectuals who thought and wrote extensively about peace (e.g. Chanteur 1992). What does the ancient world offer in this respect? India, as Richard Salomon observes (this vol.), did not develop a genre of narrative history of the type familiar to us from other cultures. The Indian or Sanskrit tradition "was much more interested in the presentation of theories, categories, and ideals than in recording their applications and results." Theoretical literature on "the application of statecraft and the uses and manipulations of power" exists in the *Arthasastra* or "Treatise on Worldly Gain," the so-called "Indian Machiavelli." This work discusses the arts of war and peace but, typically, does not provide historical examples of the application of these rules (Kautalya 1961; Boesche 2002).

Here and in the *Dharmasastra* (Derrett 1973, 1995) and other works of literature the prevailing ideology presents the king as destined for activism, progress, conquest, and rise to imperial rule. The inactive king attracts contempt and will fall victim to his more aggressive and ambitious neighbors. In a world full of petty kings and constant rivalry, peace was possible only in those short periods when a larger territorial empire was established. As in early China (below), therefore, it was generally recognized that the one condition for peace was forceful domination by one man:

> We must admit that the Hindus, and their great teachers, generation after generation, were not fools. There was a "method in their madness." The texts, and the ethos which they record, seek peace, and something rather wider than peace, that, in fact, which is the one absolute necessity for fruitful living – and they seek it constantly and relentlessly. There was only one means by which it could be achieved, namely by constant, unremitting, general, intimate, and painstaking preparation for war. Through the mutual emulation of the warrior caste, and not otherwise, an emperor could be expected to emerge (as he often did), and he alone could give the greatest gift a human can give, *abhaya* ..., "freedom from fear," greater even than peace ...: under his supervision [the conquered peoples and kings], will confine their energies to the pursuit of righteousness and the protection of the public (Derrett 1961: 174–75).

In China, centuries of increasingly widespread and ruthless warfare in the Spring and Autumn and Warring States Periods (722–221 BCE) prompted important social, economic, military, and technological advances as well as intense intellectual debates and the emergence of new ideas about the natural order, human society, war, and peace. As one would expect, the latter seems to have played an important role in many different contexts, from military and political practice to ethics, even if it did not acquire independent value. For example, in two short treatises written by unknown authors, the *Great Learning* and *Doctrine of the Mean*, moral self-improvement is the focus but peace in the realm is among the ultimate goals:

> Peace in the realm cannot be achieved without first transforming people: A ruler must perfect his own virtue before he can regulate his family; not until his family is in order can he hope to govern his state effectively; and only on the basis of a well-governed state can he bring peace to the entire realm. In other words, one must change oneself before one can change other people or improve the world (Ebrey 1996: 46).

So too, some of Confucius' successors argued that only a completely virtuous ruler could achieve permanent peace. The philosopher Xunzi (ca. 310 – ca. 215 BCE) offered the following definition of "perfect peace" (in book 12, "On the Way of a Lord": Knoblock 1990: 178):

> [W]hen taxes are assessed on the product of their fields, the people do not mind the cost; when they must perform public duties and responsibilities, they do not mind the toil; when difficulties arise with bandits, the people do not mind the threat of death; the city will be defensively secure without having to wait for its inner and outer walls to be raised; and the cutting edge of the army will be strong without having to wait for it to be tempered by dipping into water. Rival states submit without having first to be subjugated. All the People within the Four Seas are unified without waiting for a decree. This may indeed be described as Perfect Peace.

Among other ideas, some philosophers contemplated universal disarmament. At any rate, intense discussions about peace proliferated, and a comparison with such discussions in ancient Greece (below) might offer valuable insights. Ultimately, however, the possibility of establishing lasting peace remained elusive. Military treatises wasted no thought on peace and focused only on ways to gain victory and destroy the enemy, while virtually all thinkers agreed that lasting peace could only be established with the unification of all the contending states into a single empire, even though how that unification was to be achieved, what ideology would be adopted, and what form the imperial government would take as well as the scope and nature of its policies were the subject of intense disagreement (Yates, this vol.).[24]

In Rome, at various times the issue of peace elicited an intense discourse (Fuchs 1926; Zampaglione 1973: 131–84).[25] Especially in the age of the emperor Augustus, the greatest authors (including Virgil, Horace, and Livy) reflected in their works on the momentous change from war to peace their time witnessed, on Augustus' own programmatic statements and promises, and on each others' thoughts (DeBrohun, this vol.). Here I conclude with a few remarks on another culture, that of the Greeks, that reflected on war and peace around the same time as Confucius but more broadly, in the context of popular culture as well as philosophy (Arnould 1981; Spiegel 1990; Graeber 1992). It is a remarkable fact, though, that among the immense literary production of Greece and Rome not a single treatise "About Peace" (*Peri eirenes* or *De pace*) has survived and we know of only one that was written: *Pius de pace*, by the first century BCE Roman polymath M. Terentius Varro, may have left its imprint on Augustine's well-known chapters on peace in *De civitate dei* (19.11–13; Fuchs 1926; Zecchini, in Sordi 1985: 190–202).

As pointed out earlier, already Homer's *Iliad* expresses an intense concern for issues of peace and just war. It conceptualizes in images and words the contrast between the misery of war and the blessings of peace, and elaborates on rituals and procedures to prevent the escalation of conflicts into war and to restore peace. It mirrors a deep yearning among people for peace and friendship among communities: Paris who has brought war and misery over his compatriots is hated "as black death is hated!" (3.453–54). The farewell between Andromache, who has lost parents and brothers in war, and Hector, who knows that after his death in battle his wife will become the slave of one of the victors, belongs among the most moving scenes in world literature (6.390–496). Not much later, Hesiod presents peace as one of the greatest communal values. Like many other Golden Age utopias (Gatz 1967), the first of his declining ages characterized by metals (a concept clearly borrowed from West Asia: West 1997: 312–18; 1978: 172ff.; Most 1998) is characterized by abundance, lack of woes, and peace (*Works and Days* 109–26), while the Age of Bronze and especially that of Iron are plagued by incessant war, destruction, and many other woes (ibid. 143–55, 174–201). The ideal of peace thus plays a significant role already in the earliest manifestations of Greek thought.

In the fifth century, huge citizen crowds in the theater of Athens were confronted with plays, both tragic and comic (Zampaglione 1973: 71–90; Konstan, Tritle, this vol.), that openly criticized the brutality of war and emphasized the desirability of peace. We need think only of Euripides' *Suppliant Women, Trojan Women*, or *Hecuba* (Gregory 1991; Croally 1994), and Aristophanes' *Acharnians, Peace*, and *Lysistrata* (Newiger 1980). For example, in Thucydides' Funeral Oration, Pericles demands that the citizen be a "lover of his city," subordinating his own interests to those of his beloved, the community. He thus postulates the primacy of the citizens' political over their social identity (Thuc. 2.43; Connor 1971: ch. 3; Meier 1990: ch. 6). In *Lysistrata*, a hilarious utopia performed in 411, after the Sicilian disaster, Aristophanes pointedly subverts this civic ideology and dissects on stage the detrimental consequences of a division between political and social, public and private. The result of this division is revealed in stark tones: a war-crazy city destroying itself. It can only be healed and prosper, the poet claims, if community and family remain integrated and pursue the same goals, abandon a fratricidal war, and support a panhellenic effort to reestablish peace (Henderson 1980; Raaflaub 2001a: 329–34).

Soon the philosophers began to deal with the issue of war and peace (Zampaglione 1973: 44–64; Ostwald 1996). Historians talked more about the causes and results of war, but they also inserted into their narrative pointed reminders of the senselessness and cruelty of war and desirability of peace (Zampaglione 1973, 90–106; Cobet 1986; Luginbill 1999). Herodotus, for instance, lets a Persian general criticize the Greek ways of war (one of many instances of Greek self-reflection through the hostile "Other": Hartog 1988):

> The Greeks start fights on the spur of the moment without sense or judgement to justify them. When they declare war on each other, they go off together to the smoothest and levellest bit of ground they can find, and have their battle on it – with the result that even the victors never get off without heavy losses, and as for the losers – well, they're wiped out. Now surely, as they all talk the same language, they ought to be able to find a better way of settling their differences: by negotiation, for instance, or an interchange of views – indeed by anything rather than fighting (Hdt. 7.9b; trans. A. de Sélincourt and John Marincola).

The same Herodotus lets another speaker declare, "No one is fool enough to choose war instead of peace – in peace sons bury fathers, but in war fathers bury sons" (1.87; cf. 8.3). To Thucydides the problem of war and peace is of utmost importance. He analyzes this issue, like those of democracy and imperialism, through a series of case studies that reach a climax in the Sicilian debate. He consistently pursues questions like: why is war not avoided even if the instruments to do so (diplomacy, arbitration) exist? Why do efforts to preserve or restore peace fail so often? What are the factors that propel a community towards war, despite the hardships and losses it causes? What are the ideological dimensions of war and how can we unmask them? Are propensity for war and desire for domination typical of all types of community or mainly of democracy, and if the latter, why?[26] Much more could be said on this topic (see Tritle, this vol.).

One final question. Why is it that the Greeks, unlike most other ancient civilizations, developed such an intense discourse on questions of war and peace? I can think of two answers. First, in a world of city-states with a rich public culture and participation of large segments of the citizen population in public affairs, issues of communal concern were widely shared. Hence from early on they became part of political reflection and were embedded in the poetry performed at public festivals. One of the functions of the poets was to serve as a voice of communal conscience and concerns. This function was inherited by the dramatic poets and prose authors of the fifth and fourth centuries (Raaflaub 1987; 2000). Second, whatever the conditions in the period that Homer and Hesiod reflect, in the archaic period war was not endemic; it was a reality, of course, but intermittent, motivated by intercity rivalries and fought for booty and contested lands rather than imperial control or survival; losses were surprisingly limited, and the destruction of cities was extremely rare. All this changed radically when the Greeks were confronted with a very different form of imperialism in the Persian Wars and when, in their aftermath, forms of imperial control and rivalry emerged among the Greeks themselves. Especially in the second half of the fifth century and in the Peloponnesian War, the face of war changed radically: it became a permanent feature, ubiquitous, brutal and increasingly total (*W&S* ch. 6). This new reality transformed the way people, and especially intellectuals, were thinking about war, and it made them think in new ways about peace.[27]

Notes

1 Thanks for generous financial support are due to the Rhode Island Committee for the Humanities, the Kirk Foundation, and, at Brown University, the Charles K. Colver Lectureship Fund, the Department of Classics, and the Program in Ancient Studies. Thanks also to Faith and Fredrick Sandstrom for their enthusiastic endorsement of our activities over many years.

2 These include the administrator of the Program in Ancient Studies, Maria Sokolova, Classics graduate students Jennifer Thomas, Mark Thatcher, and David Yates, and, not least, my wife, Deborah Boedeker. I also acknowledge with gratitude generous contributions to the publication of this book by the Department of Classics, the Program in Ancient Studies, and the Royce Family Professorship in Teaching Excellence, all at Brown University.

3 The other, published more than forty years ago (Gilissen 1961–2), covers ancient, medieval, and modern history. John Gilissen's introductory essay, "Essai d'une histoire comparative de l'organisation de la paix" (5–75), therefore deals only marginally with the ancient world. For war in antiquity in a global sense, see *W&S* and the first volume of a new *Cambridge History of War* (in preparation). For peace in (Greco-Roman) antiquity, see Fuchs 1926; Nestle 1938; Momigliano 1940; Lana 1967; Zampaglione 1973; Sordi 1985. Melko and Weigel (1981) and *K&F* include other eastern Mediterranean societies as well. De Souza and France (2006) focus on the role of treaties in establishing peace. Studies of Christian views on peace are more frequent (see Swift, this vol.).

4 On the historical background, see M. Lewis, in Loewe and Shaughnessy 1999: 587–650; Ebrey 1996: 59–61 (with the quote on p. 61 and a picture of the terracotta army on p. 62); on the interpretation of "Hero," for example, Robert Eng in *AsiaMedia*, Sept. 7, 2004. I thank my colleagues, Hsin-Mei Agnes Hsu and Lingzhen Wang, for good advice.

5 *New York Times*, September 19, 2002; the inscription's translator is Federico Fahsen, whose final report can be read at www.famsi.org/reports/01098, accessed on April 7, 2006; his book is in preparation.

6 On Maya Warfare, see Hassig 1992; Webster, *W&S* 1999: 333–60; Martin 2000; for an attempt at historical reconstruction, Martin and Grube 2000.

7 See, for example, chs. by Jean Poirier and Annie Dorsinfang-Smets, in *LP* 77–98, 99–121; Keegan 1993; Carneiro 1994; Keeley 1996; Ferrill 1997: ch. 1; Guilaine and Zamit 2001; Lambert 2002.

8 Kenoyer 1989: 82 also mentions the possibility of extolling greatness of a ruler or community through dramatic enactments or puppet shows. Maisels 1999: 220–24 takes a position similar to that of McIntosh. For a general discussion of the Indus Valley Civilization, see recently Thapar 2002: 79–88.

9 On Buddhism, see, for example, Queen 1998; Strong 2002. On Jainism, see, for example, Basham 1981: 289–97; Caillat 1987; Laidlaw 1995; Chapple 1998; Cort 2001; specifically

on *ahimsa*, Shastri and Shastri 1998. I thank my colleague Donna Wulff for generous advice on this section.

10 On Augustus' monuments and rituals, see Simon 1986a; Zanker 1988; Galinsky 1996. His report on his achievements (*Res gestae*): Brunt and Moore 1967.

11 Warrior- and prisoner-shaped vessels: for example, Benson 1972: 45–48 with fig. 3-2; Donnan 2004: ch. 7; fighting on painted vases: Donnan and McClelland 1999. Painted murals: those recently discovered at the Huaca de la Luna are not yet published, but see those at the Huaca Cao Viejo, El Brujo complex, in Pillsbury 2001: 140, 149–51. On Moche warfare and human sacrifice, see chs. by Steve Bourget, John W. Verano, and Tom D. Dillehay, in Pillsbury 2001 (all with biblio.). Generally on the Moche civilization: Benson 1972; Bawden 1996. I thank Catherine Julien and Christopher Donnan for useful suggestions.

12 Hittites: Beal 1992, 1995, this vol.; Bryce 1998, 2002 (with a chapter on the soldier). Assyrians: von Soden 1963; Malbran-Labat 1982; Wiseman 1989. Persians: Cook 1983: ch. 10; Sekunda 1989; Briant 1996. On diplomacy, see below.

13 As Eric Robinson notes (2001, and see his discussion with Spencer Weart in the same volume), at least in antiquity the case of Athens does not support the "democratic peace" theory that postulates that democracies tend not to engage in war with each other – which, of course, says little about the theory's validity in modern history (ibid. 605). Duncan Derrett remarks, however (1961: 147 and n. 1), that at least in early India societies ruled by oligarchies were "nowhere nearly so liable to be involved in war as those which were monarchies." In *Mahabharata, Sabha-parva* 14, "we are given a debate on the bases of the two types of government: *samrajya* (kingdom) is founded on force (*bala*), whereas *paramestya* (oligarchy) is based on peace-and-quiet (*sama*).

14 The list of atrocities committed by Romans in this period is long. At the time, Rome had become the sole superpower in the world. Lack of outside checks nourished arrogance of power and abuses; see Harris 1979, 1984.

15 Given my own areas of expertise, I will take most examples from Greece and Rome. See also Van Wees 2001 and other chapters on antiquity in Hartmann and Heuser 2001; van Wees 2004: ch. 1. Expanding these lines of inquiry more systematically to other ancient cultures would offer a rich field of comparative research.

16 Baltrusch 1994: 7–8; Konstan 1997: 33–37 and this vol.; see also, for example, Nougayrol 1963; Karavites 1986.

17 See also, for example, the discussions triggered by von Rad 1958, summarized by Ben Ollenburger in a vol. containing an Engl. trans. (von Rad 1991) and an annotated bibliography on "War, Peace, and Justice in the Hebrew Bible," compiled by Judith Sanderson.

18 Neither the authoritative *Reallexikon der Assyriologie* nor Black and Green 1992 or Bottéro 2001 mention "peace." On the Egyptian side, peace is a domestic value (mentioned above) and subsumed in the blessings of good order.

19 Parker 1996: 229–30 with references in n. 45; also Simon 1986b; Stafford 2000: ch. 6. Plut. *Cim.* 13.5 (an altar dedicated by Cimon in the early 460s) is not authentic. On images of war and peace in Greece and Rome, see also G. Belloni, in Sordi 1985: 127-45; P. Kranz, in *K&F* 68–84.

20 Athens: Thuc. 8.93.3; Lys. 18.17; Arist. *Constitution of the Athenians* 39–40; Xen. *Hell.* 2.4.38–39; Loening 1987; Funke 1980; Munn 2000: 218–44. Panhellenic *homonoia*: Gorgias (below); Isoc. *Panath.* 13; Etienne and Piérart 1975. Sophists: Democritus no. 68 B255; Gorgias 82 B8a; Thrasymachus 85 B1; Antiphon 87 B45ff., in Diels and Kranz 1964; trans. in Freeman 1948. On the origins and cult of *homonoia*: de Romilly 1972; Shapiro 1990; Thériault 1996.

21 Rüpke 1990: ch. 3; Beard et al. 1998: 177–81; Rosenstein, this vol. Rüpke on the Roman and Lonis 1979; Pritchett 1979 on the Greek side offer comprehensive analyses of religious aspects of war.

22 This, of course, remains one of the greatest challenges even in our own time, despite thousands of years of recorded negative experiences and the existence of a world organization that was created not least for this very purpose. Limited to the domestic sphere, the quarrel between Achilles and Agamemnon in the first book of the *Iliad* illustrates the same problem (Raaflaub 2001b: 80–81).

23 For the complex topic of peace efforts in the Hellenistic period, see C. Préaux, in *LP*, 227–301; for arbitration, Ager 1996.

24 See also Lun 1998. I thank Robin Yates for good advice on this section.

25 This topic seems to me far from exhausted. A "Pacific Rim Roman Literature Seminar," held in Auckland in June 2005, focused on "War and Peace in Roman Literature."

26 On Thucydides' concern with democracy and imperialism, see Raaflaub 1994; 2006. The historian's concern with peace awaits further discussion; the politics of the Pylian campaign and its aftermath in bk. 4 are crucial here. For Herodotus' worry about the excesses of war and imperialism, see Raaflaub 2002.

27 I thank Thea Brennan-Krohn for useful insights on this topic, formulated in her 2003 Honors Thesis, "An End to the Glittering Steel: Greek Ideas of War and Peace from the Archaic Period through the Peloponnesian War."

Abbreviations

CAH	*Cambridge Ancient History*
DNP	*Der Neue Pauly. Enzyklopädie der Antike*
K&F	*Krieg und Frieden*: Binder and Effe 1989
LIMC	*Lexicon Icononographicum Mythologiae Classicae*
LP	*La Paix*: Gilissen 1961–2
W&S	*War and Society*: Raaflaub and Rosenstein 1999

References

Adcock, F., and D. Mosley. 1975. *Diplomacy in Ancient Greece*. London.

Ager, S. L. 1996. *Interstate Arbitration in the Greek World, 337–90 BC*. Berkeley.

Alcock, Susan E., Terence N. D'Altroy, Kathleen D. Morrison, and Carla M. Sinopoli (eds.). 2001. *Empires: Perspectives from Archaeology and History*. Cambridge.

Alonso Troncoso, Victor. 1987. *Neutralidad y neutralismo en la Guerra del Peloponeso (431–404 a.c.)*. Madrid.

Arnould, Dominique. 1981. *Guerre et paix dans la poésie grecque de Callinos à Pindare*. New York.

Baltrusch, Ernst. 1994. *Symmachie und Spondai: Untersuchungen zum griechischen Völkerrecht der archaischen und klassischen Zeit (8.-5. Jh. v. Chr.)*. Berlin.

Basham, A. L. 1981. *The Wonder that Was India: A Survey of the Culture of the Indian Subcontinent before the Coming of the Muslims*. Paperback edn. Calcutta. Originally New York, 1954 (many reprints).

Bauslaugh, Robert A. 1991. *The Concept of Neutrality in Ancient Greece*. Berkeley.

Bawden, Garth. 1996. *The Moche*. Cambridge (MA) and Oxford.

Beal, Richard H. 1992. *The Organisation of the Hittite Military*. Heidelberg.

——. 1995. "Hittite Military Organization." In Sasson 1995: 545–54.

Beard, Mary, John North, and Simon Price. 1998. *Religions of Rome*, I: *A History*. Cambridge.

Beckman, Gary M. 1999. *Hittite Diplomatic Texts*. Harry A. Hoffner, Jr. (ed.), 2nd edn. Atlanta.

Benson, Elizabeth P. 1972. *The Mochica: A Culture of Peru*. New York.

Binder, Gerhard, and Bernd Effe (eds.). 1989. *Krieg und Frieden im Altertum*. Trier.

Black, Jeremy, and Anthony Green. 1992. *Gods, Demons and Symbols of Ancient Mesopotamia: An Illustrated Dictionary*. London.

Boesche, Roger. 2002. *The First Great Political Realist: Kautilya and his Arthashastra*. Lanham, MD.

Bottéro, Jean. 2001. *Religion in Ancient Mesopotamia*. Trans. Teresa L. Fagan. Chicago.

Briant, Pierre. 1996. *Histoire de l'empire Perse de Cyrus à Alexandre*. Paris.

Brunt, P. A. 1971. *Italian Manpower 225 BC–AD 14*. Oxford.

——, and J. M. Moore (eds.). 1967. *Res Gestae Divi Augusti: The Achievements of the Divine Augustus*. Oxford.

Bryce, Trevor. 1998. *The Kingdom of the Hittites*. Oxford. New edn. 2005.

——. 2002. *Life and Society in the Hittite World*. Oxford.

Burkert, Walter. 1983. Homo necans: *The Anthropology of Ancient Greek Sacrificial Ritual and Myth*. Berkeley.

——. 1985. *Greek Religion*. Cambridge, MA.

Caillat, Colette. 1987. "Jainism." In Mircea Eliade (ed.), *The Encyclopedia of Religion*, vol. 7: 507–14. New York.

Camp, John M. 1986. *The Athenian Agora: Excavations in the Heart of Classical Athens*. London.

Carneiro, Robert L. 1994. "War and Peace: Alternating Realities in Human History." In S. P. Reyna and R. E. Downs (eds.), *Studying War: Anthropological Perspectives*, 3–27. Langhorne.

Cartledge, Paul. 1979. *Sparta and Lakonia: A Regional History, 1300–362 BC*. London. Rev. and updated edn. 2001.

Chanteur, Janine. 1992. *From War to Peace*. Trans. Shirley A. Weisz. Boulder. French edn. Paris 1989.

Chapple, Christopher K. 1998. "Jainism and Nonviolence". In Smith-Christopher 1998: 13–24.

Clairmont, Christopher. 1983. *Patrios Nomos: Public Burial in Athens during the Fifth and Fourth Centuries BC*. British Archaeological Reports, Intern. Ser. 161. 2 vols. Oxford.

Cobet, Justus. 1986. "Herodotus and Thucydides on War." In I. Moxon, J. D. Smart, and A. J. Woodman (eds.), *Past Perspectives: Studies in Greek and Roman Historical Writing*, 1–18. Cambridge.

Cohen, Raymond, and Raymond Westbrook (eds.). 2000. *Amarna Diplomacy: The Beginnings of International Relations*. Baltimore.

Cohen, Ronald. 1986. "War and Peace Proneness in Pre- and Postindustrial States." In M. L. Foster and R. A. Rubinstein (eds.), *Peace and War: Cross-Cultural Perspectives*, 253–67. New Brunswick.

Connor, W. Robert. 1971. *The New Politicians of Fifth-Century Athens*. Princeton. Repr. with new introduction, Indianapolis, 1992.

Cook, John M. 1983. *The Persian Empire*. New York.

Cort, John E. 2001. *Jains in the World: Religious Values and Ideology in India*. Oxford.

Coudenhove-Kalergi, Richard. 1959. *From War to Peace*. Trans. Constantine Fitzgibbon. London.

Crawford, Michael H. 1974. *Roman Republican Coinage*. 2 vols. Cambridge.

Croally, N. T. 1994. *Euripidean Polemic: The Trojan Women and the Function of Tragedy*. Cambridge.

Dalley, Stephanie. 1995. "Ancient Mesopotamian Military Organization." In Sasson 1995: 413–22.

Derrett, J. Duncan M. 1961. "The Maintenance of Peace in the Hindu World: Practice and Theory." In *LP* 143–77.

Derrett, J. Duncan M. 1973. *Dharmasastra and Juridical Literature*. Wiesbaden.

——. 1995. *Essays in Classical and Modern Hindu Law*, I: *Dharmasastra and Related Ideas*. New Delhi.

Diels, Hermann, and Walther Kranz (eds.). 1961, 1964. *Die Fragmente der Vorsokratiker*. I: 10th edn., II: 11th edn. Zurich and Berlin.

Donnan, Christopher B. 2004. *Moche Portraits from Ancient Peru*. Austin.

——, and Donna McClelland. 1999. *Moche Fineline Painting: Its Evolution and Its Artists*. Los Angeles.

Ducrey, Pierre. 1968. *Le traitement des prisonniers de guerre dans la Grèce antique des origines à la conquête romaine*. Paris.

Ebrey, Patricia B. 1996. *The Cambridge Illustrated History of China*. Cambridge.

Etienne, R., and M. Piérart. 1975. "Un décret du Koinon des Héllènes à Platée." *Bulletin de Correspondence Hellénique* 99: 51–75.

Fabbro, David. 1978. "Peaceful Societies: An Introduction." *Journal of Peace Research* 15.1: 67–83.

Fehr, Burkhard. 1979–81. "Zur religionspolitischen Funktion der Athena Parthenos im Rahmen des Delisch-Attischen Seebundes." *Hephaistos* 1: 71–91; 2: 113–25; 3: 55–93.

Ferrill, Arther. 1997. *The Origins of War from the Stone Age to Alexander the Great*. Boulder.

Fliess, Peter J. 1966. *Thucydides and the Politics of Bipolarity*. Baton Rouge.

Freeman, Kathleen. 1948. *Ancilla to the Pre-Socratic Philosophers*. Cambridge, MA.

Fuchs, Harald. 1926. *Augustin und der antike Friedensgedanke*. Berlin.

Funke, Peter. 1980. *Homónoia und Arché. Athen und die griechische Staatenwelt vom Ende des Peloponnesischen Krieges bis zum Königsfrieden (404/3–387/6 v. Chr.)*. Wiesbaden.

Galinsky, Karl. 1996. *Augustan Culture: An Interpretive Introduction*. Princeton.

Garlan, Yvon. 1975. *War in the Ancient World: A Social History*. Trans. Janet Lloyd. London.

Gatz, Bodo. 1967. *Weltalter, goldene Zeit und sinnverwandte Vorstellungen*. Hildesheim.

Gehrke, Hans-Joachim. 1985. *Stasis: Untersuchungen zu den inneren Kriegen in den griechischen Staaten des 5. und 4. Jh. v. Chr.* Munich.

Gilissen, John (ed.). 1961–62. *La Paix*. 2 vols. *Recueils de la Société J. Bodin*, vols. 14–15. Brussels.

Graeber, Andreas. 1992. "Friedensvorstellung und Friedensbegriff bei den Griechen bis zum Peloponnesischen Krieg." *Zeitschrift für Rechtsgeschichte. Romanistische Abteilung* 109: 116–62.

Gregory, Justina. 1991. *Euripides and the Instruction of the Athenians*. Ann Arbor.

Guilaine, Jean, and Jean Zammit. 2001. *The Origins of War: Violence in Prehistory*. Oxford.

Haas, Jonathan (ed.). 1990. *The Anthropology of War*. Cambridge.

Hackett, John (ed.). 1989. *Warfare in the Ancient World*. London.

Harris, W. V. 1979. *War and Imperialism in Republican Rome, 327–70 BC*. Oxford.

—— (ed.). 1984. *The Imperialism of Mid-Republican Rome*. Rome.

Hartmann, Anja V., and Beatrice Heuser (eds.). 2001. *War, Peace and World Orders in European History*. London.

Hartog, François. 1988. *The Mirror of Herodotus: The Representation of the Other in the Writing of History*. Trans. Janet Lloyd. Berkeley.

Hashmi, Sohail H. 1996. "Interpreting the Islamic Ethics of War and Peace." In Nardin 1996: 146–66; rep. in Hashmi 2002: 194–216.

—— (ed.). 2002. *Islamic Political Ethics: Civil Society, Pluralism, and Conflict*. Princeton.

Hassig, Ross. 1992. *War and Society in Ancient Mesoamerica*. Berkeley and Los Angeles.

Helck, Wolfgang. 1977. "Frieden." *Lexikon der Ägyptologie* 2: 331.

——. 1979. "Kriegsgefangene." *Lexikon der Ägyptologie* 3.5: 786–89.

Henderson, Jeffrey. 1980. "Lysistrata: The Play and Its Themes." *Yale Classical Studies* 26: 153–218.

Herington, C. J. 1955. *Athena Parthenos and Athena Polias: A Study in the Religion of Periclean Athens*. Manchester.

Hoffner, Harry A. Jr. 2002. "The Treatment and Long-Term Use of Persons Captured in Battle according to the Masat Texts." In K. Aslıhan Yener and Harry A. Hoffner Jr. (eds.), *Recent Developments in Hittite Archaeology and History: Papers in Memory of Hans G. Güterbock*, 61–72. Winona Lake.

Hölkeskamp, Karl-Joachim. 2001. "Capitol, Comitium und Forum. Öffentliche Räume, sakrale Topographie und Erinnerungslandschaften der römischen Republik." In Stefan Faller (ed.), *Studien zu antiken Identitäten*, 97–132. Würzburg.

Hölscher, Tonio. 1978. "Die Anfänge römischer Repräsentationskunst." *Mitteilungen des Deutschen Archäologischen Instituts (Rom)* 85: 315–57.

——. 1990. "Concordia." *LIMC* 5: 479–98.

——. 1998. "Images and Political Identity: The Case of Athens." In Deborah Boedeker and Kurt Raaflaub (eds.), *Democracy, Empire, and the Arts in Fifth-Century Athens*, 153–83, 384–87. Cambridge, MA.

——. 2001. "Die Alten vor Augen. Politische Denkmäler und öffentliches Gedächtnis im republikanischen Rom." In G. Melville (ed.), *Institutionalität und Symbolisierung. Verstetigungen kultureller Ordnungsmuster in Vergangenheit und Gegenwart*, 183–211. Weimar and Vienna.

Hurwitt, Jeffrey M. 2004. *The Acropolis in the Age of Pericles*. Cambridge.

Jehne, Martin. 1994. *Koine Eirene*. Stuttgart.

Kagan, Donald. 1995. *On the Origins of War and the Preservation of Peace*. New York.

Karavites, Panayotis. 1982. *Capitulations and Greek Interstate Relations: The Reflection of Humanistic Ideals in Political Events*. Göttingen.

——. 1986. "Philotes, Homer and the Near East." *Athenaeum* n.s. 64: 474–81.

——. 1992. *Promise-Giving and Treaty-Making: Homer and the Near East*. Leiden.

Kautalya. 1961. *Arthasastra*. Trans. R. Shamasastry. 7th edn. Mysore.

Keegan, John. 1993. *A History of Warfare*. New York.

Keeley, Lawrence H. 1996. *War before Civilization: The Myth of the Peaceful Savage*. Oxford.

Kenoyer, Mark J. 1998. *Ancient Cities of the Indus Valley Civilization*. Oxford.

Kiechle, Franz. 1958. "Zur Humanität in der Kriegführung der griechischen Staaten." *Historia* 7: 129–56.

Klengel, H. 1981. "Krieg, Kriegsgefangene." *Reallexikon der Assyriologie* 3: 241–46.

Knippschild, Silke. 2002. *"Drum bietet zum Bunde die Hände." Rechtssymbolische Akte in zwischenstaatlichen Beziehungen im orientalischen und griechisch-römischen Altertum*. Stuttgart.

Knoblock, John. 1990. *Xunzi: A Translation and Study of the Complete Works, II*. Stanford.

Konstan, David. 1997. *Friendship in the Classical World*. Cambridge.

Kramer, Samuel N. 1981. *History Begins at Sumer: Thirty-Nine Firsts in Recorded History*. Philadelphia.

Kuhrt, Amélie. 1988. "Earth and Water." In Amélie Kuhrt and Heleen Sancisi-Weerdenburg (eds.), *Achaemenid History, III: Method and Theory*, 87–99. Leiden.

Laidlaw, James. 1995. *Riches and Renunciation: Religion, Economy, and Society among the Jains*. Oxford.

Lambert, Patricia M. 2002. "The Archaeology of War: A North American Perspective." *Journal of Archaeological Research* 10: 207–41.

Lana, Italo. 1967. "La pace nel mondo antico." *Studia et documenta historiae et iuris* 33: 1–18.

Larsen, J. A. O. 1944. "Federation for Peace in Ancient Greece." *Classical Philology* 39: 145–62.

Lebow, Richard N., and Barry S. Strauss (eds.). 1991. *Hegemonic Rivalry: from Thucydides to the Nuclear Age*. Boulder.

Libero, Loretana de. 2002. "Vernichtung oder Vertag? Bemerkungen zum Kriegsende in der Antike," In Bernd Wegner (ed.), *Wie Kriege enden. Wege zum Frieden von der Antike bis zur Gegenwart*, 3–23. Paderborn.

Loening, Thomas C. 1987. *The Reconciliation Agreement of 404–403 BC in Athens: Its Content and Application*. Stuttgart.

Loewe, Michael, and Edward L. Shaughnessy (eds.). 1999. *The Cambridge History of Ancient China. From the Origins of Civilization to 221 BC*. Cambridge.

Lonis, Raoul. 1979. *Guerre et religion en Grèce à l'époque classique. Recherches sur les rites, les dieux, l'idéologie de la victoire*. Paris.

Luginbill, Robert D. 1999. *Thucydides on War and National Character*. Boulder.

Lun, Tam Wai. 1998. "Subverting Hatred: Peace and Nonviolence in Confucianism and Daoism." In Smith-Christopher 1998: 49–66.

McIntosh, Jane R. 2000. *A Peaceful Realm: The Rise and Fall of the Indus Civilization*. Boulder.

Maisels, Charles K. 1999. *Early Civilizations of the Old World: The Formative Histories of Egypt, the Levant, Mesopotamia, India, and China*. London.

Malbran-Labat, F. 1982. *L'armée et l'organisation militaire de l'Assyrie*. Geneva and Paris.

Martin, Richard. 1993. "The Seven Sages as Performers of Wisdom." In Lesley Kurke and Carol Dougherty (eds.), *Cultural Poetics in Archaic Greece: Cult, Performance, Politics*, 108–28. Cambridge.

Martin, Simon. 2000. "Under a Deadly Star – Warfare among the Classic Maya." In Nikolai Grube (ed.), *Maya: Divine Kings of the Rain Forest*, 175–91. Cologne.

——, and Nikolai Grube. 2000. *Chronicle of the Maya Kings and Queens: Deciphering the Dynasties of the Ancient Maya*. London.

Mattingly, H. 1923. *Coins of the Roman Empire in the British Museum, I*. London.

Meier, Christian. 1990. *The Greek Discovery of Politics*. Trans. David McLintock. Cambridge, MA.

Melko, Matthew. 1973. *52 Peaceful Societies*. Oakville (Ontario).

——, and Richard D. Weigel (eds.). 1981. *Peace in the Ancient World*. Jefferson.

Momigliano, Arnaldo. 1940. "Pace." In *Pace e libertà nel mondo antico. Lezioni a Cambridge: gennaio-marzo 1940*, 29–41. Ed. Riccardo Di Donato. Florence, 1996.

Moseley, Michael E. 2001. *The Incas and Their Ancestors: The Archaeology of Peru*. London.

Most, Glenn W. 1998. "Hesiod's Myth of the Five (or Three or Four) Races." *Proceedings of the Cambridge Philological Society* 43: 104–27.

Munn, Mark. 2000. *The School of History: Athens in the Age of Socrates*. Berkeley.

Nardin, Terry (ed.). 1996. *The Ethics of War and Peace: Religious and Secular Perspectives*. Princeton.

Nestle, W. 1938. *Der Friedensgedanke in der antiken Welt*. *Philologus* Supp. 31. Göttingen.

Newiger, H.-J. 1980. "War and Peace in the Comedy of Aristophanes." *Yale Classical Studies* 26: 219–37.

Nougayrol, J. 1963. "Guerre et paix à Ugarit." *Iraq* 25: 110–23.

Oded, Bustenay. 1979. *Mass Deportations and Deportees in the Neo-Assyrian Empire*. Wiesbaden.

Osborne, Robin. 1994. "Democracy and Imperialism in the Panathenaic Procession: The Parthenon Frieze in Its Context." In W. D. E. Coulson, O. Palagia, T. L. Shear, Jr., H. A. Shapiro, and F. J. Frost (eds.), *The Archaeology of Athens and Attica under the Democracy*, 143–50. Oxford.

Ostwald, Martin. 1996. "Peace and War in Plato and Aristotle." *Scripta Classica Israelica* 15: 102–18.

Panagopoulos, Andreas. 1989. *Captives and Hostages in the Peloponnesian War*. Amsterdam.

Parker, Robert. 1996. *Athenian Religion: A History*. Oxford.

Piccirilli, Luigi. 1973. *Gli arbitrati interstatali greci*. Florence.

——. 2002. *L'invenzione della diplomazia nella Grecia antica*. Rome.

Pillsbury, Joanne (ed.). 2001. *Moche Art and Archaeology in Ancient Peru.* Washington, DC.

Price, Jonathan. 2001. *Thucydides and Internal War.* Cambridge.

Pritchard, James B. (ed.). 1969. *The Ancient Near East in Pictures Relating to the Old Testament.* Princeton.

Pritchett, W. Kendrick. 1979. *The Greek State at War, III: Religion.* Berkeley.

Queen, Christopher S. 1998. "The Peace Wheel: Nonviolent Activism in the Buddhist Tradition." In Smith-Christopher 1998: 25–47.

Raaflaub, Kurt A. 1987. "Herodotus, Political Thought, and the Meaning of History." In Deborah Boedeker and John Peradotto (eds.), *Herodotus and the Invention of History. Arethusa* 20: 221–48.

——. 1994. "Democracy, Power, and Imperialism in Fifth-Century Athens." In J. Peter Euben, John R. Wallach, and Josiah Ober (eds.), *Athenian Political Thought and the Reconstruction of American Democracy,* 103–46. Ithaca.

——. 1996. "Born to Be Wolves? Origins of Roman Imperialism." In Robert W. Wallace, and Edward M. Harris (eds.), *Transitions to Empire: Essays in Greco-Roman History, 360–146 BC, in Honor of E. Badian,* 273–314. Norman.

——. 1997. "Politics and Interstate Relations in the World of Early Greek Poleis: Homer and Beyond." *Antichthon* 31: 1–27.

——. 2000. "Poets, Lawgivers, and the Beginnings of Greek Political Reflection." In Christopher Rowe and Malcolm Schofield (eds.), *The Cambridge History of Greek and Roman Political Thought,* 23–59. Cambridge.

——. 2001a. "Father of All, Destroyer of All: War in Late Fifth-Century Athenian Discourse and Ideology." In David R. McCann and Barry S. Strauss (eds.), *War and Democracy: A Comparative Study of the Korean War and the Peloponnesian War,* 307–56. Armonk, and London.

——. 2001b. "Political Thought, Civic Responsibility, and the Greek Polis." In J. P. Arnason and P. Murphy (eds.), *Agon, Logos, Polis: The Greek Achievement and Its Aftermath,* 72–117. Stuttgart.

——. 2002. "Herodot und Thukydides: Persischer Imperialismus im Lichte der athenischen Sizilienpolitik." In Norbert Ehrhardt and Linda-Marie Günther (eds.), *Widerstand – Anpassung – Integration. Die griechische Staatenwelt und Rom,* 11–40. Stuttgart.

——. 2004. *The Discovery of Freedom in Ancient Greece.* English edn., revised and updated from the German. Chicago.

——. 2006. "Thucydides on Democracy and Oligarchy." In A. Rengakos and A. Tsakmakis (eds.), *Brill's Companion to Thucydides,* 189–222. Leiden.

——, and Nathan Rosenstein (eds.). 1999. *War and Society in the Ancient and Medieval Worlds.* Washington, DC.

Rad, Gerhard von. 1958. *Der Heilige Krieg im alten Israel.* 3rd edn. Göttingen.

——. 1991. *Holy War in Ancient Israel.* Trans. Marva J. Dawn. Grand Rapids.

Rahe, Paul A. 2002. "Justice and Necessity: The Conduct of the Spartans and the Athenians in the Peloponnesian War." In Mark Grimsley and Clifford J. Rogers (eds.), *Civilians in the Path of War,* 1–32. Lincoln, NE.

Ravitzky, Aviezer. 1996. "Prohibited Wars in the Jewish Tradition." In Nardin 1996: 115–27.

Robinson, Eric. 2001. "Reading and Misreading the Ancient Evidence for Democratic Peace." *Journal of Peace Research* 38: 593–608.

Romilly, Jacqueline de. 1972. "Vocabulaire et propagande ou les premiers emplois du mot *omonoia.*" In Alfred Ernout (ed.), *Mélanges de linguistique et de philologie grecques offerts à Pierre Chantraine,* 199–209. Paris.

Rosenstein, Nathan. 2004. *Rome at War: Farms, Families, and Death in the Middle Republic.* Chapel Hill.

Rüpke, Jörg. 1990. *Domi militiae. Die religiöse Konstruktion des Krieges in Rom.* Stuttgart.

Ryder, T. T. B. 1965. *Koine Eirene: General Peace and Local Independence in Ancient Greece.* Oxford.

Sasson, Jack (ed.). 1995. *Civilizations of the Ancient Near East.* 4 vols. New York.

Schachter, Albert. 1996. "Ares." *DNP* I: 1047–50. Stuttgart.

Scullard, H. H. 1981. *Festivals and Ceremonies of the Roman Republic.* London.

Sekunda, Nick. 1989. "The Persians." In Hackett 1989: 82–103.

Shapiro, H. Alan. 1990. "Homonoia." *LIMC* 5: 476–79.

Shastri, Sunanda Y., and Yajneshwar S. Shastri. 1998. "*Ahimsa* and the Unity of All Things: A Hindu View of Nonviolence." In Smith-Christopher 1998: 67–84.

Siebler, M. 1988. *Studien zum augusteischen Mars Ultor.* Munich.

Simon, Erika. 1984. "Mars." *LIMC* 2: 505–59.

——. 1986a. *Augustus: Kunst und Leben in Rom um die Zeitenwende.* Munich.

——. 1986b. "Eirene." *LIMC* 3: 700–05.

——. 1994. "Pax." *LIMC* 7: 204–12.

Smarczyk, Bernhard. 1990. *Untersuchungen zur Religionspolitik und politischen Propaganda Athens im Delisch-Attischen Seebund.* Munich.

Smith-Christopher, Daniel L. (ed.). 1998. *Subverting Hatred: The Challenge of Nonviolence in Religious Traditions.* Maryknoll.

Soden, W. von. 1963. "Die Assyrer und der Krieg." *Iraq* 25: 131–44.

Sordi, Marta (ed.). 1985. *La pace nel mondo antico.* Milan.

Souza, Philip de, and John France (eds.). 2006. *War and Peace in Ancient and Medieval Europe.* Cambridge.

Spiegel, Nathan. 1990. *War and Peace in Classical Greek Literature.* Jerusalem.

Stafford, Emma. 2000. *Worshipping Virtues: Personification and the Divine in Ancient Greece.* London and Swansea.

Strong, John S. 2002. *The Experience of Buddhism: Sources and Interpretations.* Belmont.

Thapar, Romila. 2002. *Early India from the Origins to AD 1300.* Berkeley and Los Angeles.

Thériault, G. 1996. *Le culte d'Homonoia dans les cités grecques.* Lyon and Québec.

Tibi, Basam. 1996. "War and Peace in Islam." In Nardin 1996: 128–45, rep. in Hashmi 2002: 175–93.

Tod, M. N. 1913. *International Arbitration amongst the Greeks.* Oxford.

Travlos, John. 1971. *Pictorial Dictionary of Ancient Athens.* New York.

Versnel, H. S. 1970. *Triumphus: An Inquiry into the Origin, Development and Meaning of the Roman Triumph.* Leiden.

Walzer, Michael. 1996. "War and Peace in the Jewish Tradition." In Nardin 1996: 95–114.

Wees, Hans van. 2001. "War and Peace in Ancient Greece." In Hartmann and Heuser 2001: 33–47.

——. 2004. *Greek Warfare: Myths and Realities.* London.

Weinstock, Stefan. 1960. "Pax and the 'Ara Pacis'." *Journal of Roman Studies* 50: 44–58.

West, M. L. 1978. *Hesiod, Works and Days, Edited with Prolegomena and Commentary.* Oxford.

——. 1997. *The East Face of Helicon: West Asiatic Elements in Greek Poetry and Myth.* Oxford.

Wheeler, R. E. M. 1966. *Civilizations of the Indus Valley and Beyond.* London.

——. 1968. *The Indus Civilization.* 3rd edn. Cambridge.

Wiberg, H. 1981. "What Have We Learned about Peace?" *Journal of Peace Research* 15: 110–49.

Wiseman, D. J. 1989. "The Assyrians." In Hackett 1989: 36–53.

Wiseman, T. P. 1995. *Remus: A Roman Myth.* Cambridge.

Woolf, Greg. 1993. "Roman Peace." In John Rich and Graham Shipley (eds.), *War and Society in the Roman World*, 171–94. London.

Zampaglione, G. 1973. *The Idea of Peace in Antiquity.* Tr. R. Dunn. Notre Dame.

Zanker, Paul. 1988. *The Power of Images in the Age of Augustus.* Trans. Alan Shapiro. Ann Arbor.

2

Making War and Making Peace in Early China

Robin D. S. Yates

This chapter will concentrate on the problems of making war and making peace in early China during the Eastern Zhou dynasty of the late Bronze Age, during the Spring and Autumn and Warring States periods, roughly 722 to 221. Before that time, in the late second millennium during the Shang dynasty, the purpose of war was primarily to capture enemy victims. They were sacrificed to appease the spirits of the dead ancestors of the Shang king and their blood was used to feed the altars of the grain and soil, the symbols of the state, which required blood sacrifices for their continued existence and ability to provide aid for the Shang living. Campaigns were also necessary to protect the harvest from raiding enemy tribes and to seize territory from them. Sacrifice and war were essential, almost daily activities of the aristocratic elite and there is no indication of any concept of or efforts to establish peace (Yates 1999: 9–11).

After the First Emperor of China, who had united all the states and founded the Chinese empire in 221, his successors in the Han dynasty (206 BCE–220 CE) directed aggressive warfare primarily at external enemies, principally the nomadic Xiongnu people of the northern steppes. In this later period of unified empire, new forms of international relations and peace making came to be developed, known as the "tributary system" in which the Chinese emperor claimed to be the sole suzerain and foreign peoples who wished to have relations with the Chinese state had to bring offerings to him and recognize his ritual superiority (Fairbank 1968).[1] Peace was maintained in this system by the ritual exchange of gifts, by the emperor conferring Chinese titles on the leaders of the subordinate peoples, and sometimes by marrying off a woman of the royal family to the leader of the tribe and conferring the imperial surname on him. Often the value of the Chinese gifts was greater than those they received from the tribute bearers and the latter used the Chinese goods to distribute wealth among their followers. The titles, marks of social prestige, were valuable commodities in the competition with other tribal leaders for dominance in their local areas and sometimes the chiefs could call in Chinese arms to support their political ambitions. In addition, tribute missions were often occasions of extensive trade by other members of the foreign delegation, thus the economic benefits were diffused more widely in the societies of the trading partners. If the Chinese refused to trade, or limited trade by closing their markets, the foreigners would initiate war until tribute and trade delegations were once again permitted. Thus war, peace and trade were intimately connected.

In the first part of the period under study in this chapter (722 to roughly 450), international relations were initially dominated by a system of ritual, but, as numerous city-states and coalitions of city-states led by hegemons (*ba*) fought with each other for control of human and natural resources, for territory, for survival, and for a variety of other reasons, a system of covenants led by the Master of Covenants (*mengzhu*) tried to impose order and stability.

In the second part (450–221), after massive consolidation of the warring city states into a few large regional city-state systems (Yates 1997), warfare was conducted primarily among shifting alliances of coalition partners each trying to achieve hegemony over the others and each trying to prevent its rivals from achieving the same hegemony (Lewis 1999: 632–34). Peace was, therefore, "an interim condition between wars" (Caplow and Hicks 1995: 23), and lasting peace was only achieved when the warring parties were defeated and incorporated into larger political units, ultimately the unified empire of the Qin and Han dynasties.

Nevertheless, despite the chronic conflict during the Eastern Zhou period, statesmen and political and military theorists developed techniques and rituals to try to maintain peace and harmony between rival political entities, and elaborated theories of how rulers of states should act to ensure the survival of their states and how they should interact with their peers. These rituals and ideas had a profound impact upon the ways in which the later Chinese imperial state interacted with rivals and with peoples that were unwilling to be assimilated into the Chinese culture sphere. While the exercise of naked military force and the promotion of pure self-interest were encouraged by a series of peripatetic statesmen, called the Vertical and Horizontal Alliance Specialists (*Zongheng jia*) and by some military experts, another group advocated general disarmament, others that the ideal system of ritual of earlier times should be re-instituted, yet others that all behavior, military and otherwise, should be based on the patterns of the cosmos or in harmony with principles of virtue and righteousness and in accordance with the Dao, the origin of all things. It is these various systems of international relations and modes of grappling with conflict that will be the focus of this essay.

Three Systems of Making War and Making Peace

Basing himself primarily on the records preserved in the *Zuo Commentary* (*Zuo zhuan*) to the *Spring and Autumn Annals* (*Chunqiu*) of the State of Lu, said to have been edited by Confucius (died 479), and the *Discourses of the States* (*Guo yu*), Yuri Pines has recently suggested that there were three different systems for managing interstate rivalries in the Eastern Zhou that appeared successively on the international stage: ritual, covenants,[2] and military superiority (Pines 2002: 105–35). Ritual was the basis of the system in the Western Zhou and early Eastern Zhou, from roughly 1045 to 700. Covenants (*meng*) replaced ritual in the middle of the seventh century, when Duke Huan of the state of Qi (reigned 685–643), the modern Shandong province in east China, gathered his allies and forced them to accept his overlordship and recognize him as hegemon. Qi's hegemony did not outlive Duke Huan, as his five sons fought for the throne, leaving Duke Huan's corpse unburied until, it is recorded, worms crawled out from under the door of the room it was lying in, and Qi lost its authority to command the other states. After an abortive attempt by Duke Xiang of Song, a descendant of the Shang royal house, to gain hegemony, the rule soon passed to Duke Wen of the rising north-central state of Jin (reigned 636–628), modern Shanxi province, who had spent 19 years in exile wandering from state to state, pleading his cause to be established on the throne of his native land (Hsu 1999: 551–60). Thereafter Jin fought for a century and half with its southern rival, the state of Chu, based on the middle Yangzi River, until other non-Huaxia (Chinese) states rose to prominence and joined in the competition for dominance. This led to a free-for-all, where no state was able to command its rivals; rather, more and more of the petty smaller states were annexed by their aggressive neighbors and incorporated into their political, administrative and military systems. Towards the end of this period, wars came to last longer than before, and campaigns could extend over several years, in contrast to earlier times when a war was most often decided by a single battle. The final contest for total conquest was fought between seven major states in the Warring States, where military superiority alone counted, and the population of the states was put on an almost permanent war footing. Peace treaties were signed, but were broken without remorse or shame when short-term advantages seemed to offer better political opportunities.

In the following analysis, it should be remembered that practices developed in the earlier systems continued to be of importance in later times for managing violence and for attempting to create peace. Marriage alliances, the exchange of hostages, ritual visits where mutual presentations were made, and blood covenants were later supplemented by the exchange of ambassadors, the use of spies and merchants, the ceding of territory, cities and towns, and the acceptance of leading foreign officers as prime ministers of rival states.

The Ritual System

The system of ritual developed out of the form that political dominance had taken during the previous Western Zhou period, during which the Zhou kings, based on their capital in the Plains of Zhou in the Wei river valley, Shaanxi province (modern Xi'an), dominated the political scene after their conquest of the eastern Shang dynasty in about 1045. The Zhou kings were the heads of the principal clan, the Ji, and they parceled out the walled encampments and lands they had conquered to the heads of lineages closely related by blood, those that had been created by segmentation from the main clan line, or to those who assisted them in gaining supreme authority. The system was integrated by the heads of the lineages participating in the sacrificial and ritual system of the Zhou center and cemented by continuing marital ties and presentations of items of symbolic and ritual value in a cycle of gift-giving (Cook 1997). Relative rank was determined by the nature of the blood relationship between the head of the lineage and the Zhou king, and the members of the system referred to each other by their kin terms, such as "maternal uncle," "nephew," and so on. It was the ritual obligation of the participants to request permission of the Zhou king to engage in offensive warfare and to report the results of the campaign to him. Permission had to be asked for one state's armies to pass through the territory of another on the way to attack a third state. The system was therefore hierarchical and based on the structure and ranking of the extended patrilineal clan. Those peoples who lived either beyond the reach of the Zhou, or who lived as tribes in the interstices between the Zhou settlements, were assimilated to the system by fictive kin relations, although in time there were a number of examples of intermarriage between the Zhou aristocrats and the families of the chieftains of these non-Zhou tribes. Peace and order were maintained by this system of ritual exchange. Some indication of the extremely elaborate rules that had to be followed by ambassadors employed in interstate exchanges can be found in one of the three Confucian ritual texts, the *Yi li*, but since the record of the *Yi li* may represent a later idealization of these rites, it is beyond the scope of the present chapter to analyze them here (Steele 1966: 189–288). Those who refused to offer traditional gifts, who rejected the overlordship of the Zhou king, or were outside of the exchange cycle, like numerous native peoples in the southeast, could be attacked without excuse and without limit. Nevertheless, random killing within the system, without justification, could bring down retribution on the perpetrator. One story, recounting the circumstances of the death of King Xuan of Zhou, who died in 782, illustrates this point:

> King Xuan killed Dubo, but he was guiltless. Three years later King Xuan gathered the many lords to hunt in the royal game preserve. At mid-day, Dubo arose by the side of the road, and wearing a scarlet jacket and hat and wielding a scarlet bow and arrow, shot King Xuan, hitting him in the heart and splitting his sternum, so that he died (Shaughnessy 1999: 348).

No matter how King Xuan actually died, the Zhou people believed that a person who died of unnatural causes could become a ghost and threaten the living, and those with greater charisma, or *de*, in life had more power in death. The dead ancestors lived on in the Zhou world, or, rather, just below the surface, and could always cause difficulties to the living: they had to be appeased and supplicated by continual offerings of alcoholic drinks, grain, and cooked meats prepared in bronze vessels.[3] What we see here is the beginnings of the notion that the taking of life, if done at all, had to be done with justification. These were the beginnings of morality in war that culminated in the creation of the notion of "righteous warfare" (see below).

Zhou central political power began to wane in the last century or so of the Western Zhou period. This decline culminated in their defeat at the hands of a coalition of rebellious vassals and non-Zhou tribes in 771 and King Ping decided to move the capital to the east to Chengzhou, the modern Luoyang, Henan province. For a while this revived the fortunes of the dynasty, but soon the clan ties that bound the Zhou vassals to their king became looser and he was no longer able to command the respect of his distant kinsmen nor to field a sufficiently large and powerful army to force compliance with his demands. Furthermore, the system of ranking (there were five ranks of nobles) gradually weakened because changes in the relative political, economic, and military power of the various nobles no longer reflected the ideal order of the ranks. This led directly to the second system, that of covenants. Soon after the Zhou moved east, the rule that members of the same clan surname were not to attack each other was ignored. Duke Zhuang of the state of Zheng, located near the new Zhou capital, although defending the Zhou court, broke the previous rules of behavior by engaging in unprecedented attacks against members of the Zhou polity in addition to the Rong tribes. The king felt so threatened that he appointed another noble from another nearby state, that of Guo, to assist him as another high minister to balance Duke Zhuang's power. The duke was enraged and only mollified when the king sent him in 720 one of his own sons in exchange for the duke's heir apparent to act as hostages and guarantors of peaceful relations (Hsu 1999: 552).

The Exchange of Hostages and Marriage as Methods of Guaranteeing Peace

The exchange of hostages between the Zhou king and the Duke of Zheng was the beginning of a method of maintaining peace between essential equals or between unequal partners that continued down until the middle of the seventeenth century, when the Koreans sent hostages to the Manchus to assure their loyalty during the Manchus' ultimately successful attack on and conquest of the Chinese Ming dynasty. Lien-sheng Yang has analyzed this method of guaranteeing peace and has divided hostages into two types: "exchanged hostages" in which both sides sent hostages to the other to ensure continued amicable relations, and "unilateral hostages" (Yang 1961). In Yang's view, there were two varieties of this latter type. "External hostages" might be forced from the defeated party by the victor during peace negotiations to ensure continuing submission, or during a period of peace by a more powerful state from weaker dependent or vassal states, or by a lord from a group of individuals who were pledging allegiance to him. The second type of "unilateral hostage" was demanded by a ruler from civil officials or military officers, who were assigned to dangerous posts on the frontiers or who commanded expeditionary forces, to ensure their loyalty. In the late Warring States, in the military chapters of the book of *Mozi*, it is strongly recommended that spies who are to be sent out into enemy territory be also obliged to present family members as hostages, to ensure that they would report the truth, would not turn into double-agents, and would not betray the trust of their superiors. The family members were to be locked in a barracks and closely guarded, but were to be treated well, given good food, warm clothing, and other rewards.

Quite frequently, in both periods under consideration here, the heir apparent of a ruler was sent out as a hostage to another state, not only to guarantee friendly relations between the two states, but also to keep the son out of internal political infighting that could take his life, to enable him to gain experience in the wider world of interstate politics, to learn the customs of his hosts, and to grow up in the company of those who would ultimately hold power in the other state. Not infrequently, the hostage might be encouraged to take a wife from his host's ruling family, in the hopes that, on the hostage's return to his home state, she would work in the interests of her natal state and produce a son who might come to the throne eventually and be predisposed to continuing friendly relations with his mother's relatives. It was not uncommon, indeed, for states holding hostages to intervene in other states' succession struggles on behalf of the hostages they held. At the very end of the Warring States period, the father of the man who would unite China as the First Emperor, Prince Chu of Qin, was precisely in this situation. His father, the very long-lived King Zhaoxiang of Qin, had sent him as a hostage to the state of Zhao where he was practically forgotten. He was poorly treated by his hosts and neglected by his relatives back in Qin, so he lived an impoverished life in the Zhao capital of Handan. The rich merchant Lü Buwei saw the condition of the Qin royal prince as an ideal opportunity to advance his own interests. He gave the prince vast sums of money so that he could live as a prince should and also gave him one of his own concubines. This woman then gave birth to the future First Emperor and one story has it that she was already pregnant when she was given to the prince, implying that the First Emperor was the son of a merchant, and not of Qin royal blood. When the army of Qin besieged Handan and the plight of the Zhao population was extremely serious, they wanted to put Prince Chu to death, but Lü Buwei bribed them and Prince Chu was left unharmed. He then schemed to have the prince adopted as the son of the heir apparent of Qin who was himself childless. When old King Zhaoxiang died, the prince was recalled to Qin, and, when his adopted father, the new king, died one year later, the throne passed to Prince Chu. Shortly afterwards, he passed away in turn, and the young boy possibly fathered by Lü Buwei, inherited as King Zheng, choosing his benefactor, Lü Buwei as his prime minister. When King Zheng reached his majority, he forced his benefactor to commit suicide, imprisoned his mother, and wreaked vengeance on the state where he had been held hostage by destroying it utterly and incorporating it into his developing empire. Such then was the result of a policy that had been intended to ensure peace, but, of course, ultimately a greater peace resulted because the territory of Zhao forever afterwards was considered to be an integral and indivisible part of the Chinese heartland.

Melvin Thatcher has made a special study of marriage patterns in the Spring and Autumn period on the basis of evidence in the *Zuo zhuan* and states that "marriage and the maintenance of good relations with affines were of the first order of importance in the affairs of a new ruler. Rulers received brides from and gave daughters to other ruling houses to seal agreements, signal friendly intentions, extend recognition, and, most important, to secure the support and protection of affines in the interstate, and sometimes domestic, struggle for power and survival" (Thatcher 1991: 42). He observes that the principles of marriage in this period were quite different from later Chinese patterns. Frequently several women from one ruling family were sent as brides to the groom in another state. For example, a group of sisters would marry the same man, or, if the elder woman lacked sisters, her female cousins or nieces could accompany her as secondary wives. In later China, a man could only have one legitimate wife and it was not acceptable to have relations with women of the same family or of different generations: this was considered incest and was punishable by imperial law, as the state was the keeper of morality. The reason for the multiple-woman marriage was, however, to ensure that there would be at least one, and preferably several offspring from a marriage capable of continuing good relations between the marrying families. A drawback was, however, that, despite the generally recognized rule that succession would be by primogeniture, in fact there were usually several eligible sons to inherit the throne on the death of the ruler/father, and even more competition was created by the custom that a noble or ruler could take wives from a number of different states to encourage peaceful relations between his state and those of his wives.

Some of the ruling families of states intermarried over generations, while others, like the state of Jin as it was consolidating its hegemony, started by taking wives from weaker, nearby states, and then as its power increased, began to take wives from more distant polities. While this system perpetuated class endogamy among the ruling aristocratic elite, and while ideally war was not to be prosecuted with those with whom one had marriage relations, in the end such relations did not prevent one state from attacking another, and eventually wiping the other out.

Ritual in Warfare

Before discussing the system of covenants in the Spring and Autumn period, the second of Pines' systems of making peace, it is appropriate to review briefly how ritual functioned in the actual prosecution of wars. It would appear that the origins of military ritual and the adoption of ritual in war are probably to be found as early as the early Bronze Age, for there is ample evidence of the practice of military ritual in the oracle-bone inscriptions of the Shang dynasty (late second millennium) and the bronze inscriptions of the Western Zhou, as well as in the formulations of later texts such as the *Zhou li* (Rites or Institutions of Zhou), and in the *Zuo zhuan*. That the Shang divined about success and failure of even the most minor of military engagements indicates that war was ritualized in those times in some fashion. The *Shang shu* (Book of Documents) also records the oaths that the Zhou king Wu swore in a ritual at the beginning of his campaign to destroy the Shang.[4] This practice was transformed in later centuries into the ritual pronouncement of prayers during the course of a campaign and can also be seen as the beginning of the development of military law (see below). The ritual pronouncement was not actually a formal declaration of war issued to the adversary, though perhaps the latter's scouts or spies would have got wind of the impending attack, but it did bind the officers and men to a compact with the general in command to obey orders on pain of death, it formally announced the faults of the enemy, and it declared the justness of the cause for which the war was to be fought. As far as I have been able to determine so far, there was no formal declaration of war at any time in early China.

In Spring and Autumn times, it would appear that weapons, or at least the ones to be wielded by the generals, were stored in the ancestral temple and taken out only when war had been decided upon by the head of state in consultation with other heads of aristocratic lineages, a decision that was solemnly taken in the presence of the ancestral tablets in that very temple. This was another practice that continued through the centuries. The ruler also purified himself before issuing weapons to his troops (*Zuo Zhuan*, Duke Zhuang year 5; Legge 1970: 77). How we should interpret this rite of purification, however, remains in doubt. Was there a belief in those times that weapons were inauspicious instruments (*xiongqi*), as the *Laozi* stated in late Warring States times (Lau 1982: 89), and therefore they could not be touched without due religious preparation? And what did "inauspicious" (*xiong*) actually mean? Was it believed that war, because it involved killing, had necessarily to be separated from ordinary activity? In other words, was warfare a kind of rite of passage where warriors had to undergo a kind of expulsion from the community and were, in Victor Turner's terms (Turner 1977), deemed to be in a liminal state, only to be reincorporated into the community after the end of the conflict by sharing a communal feast when the left ears of enemy dead were offered in blood sacrifice to the altars of soil and grain of the state?[5] Or was warfare a type of exorcism that entailed getting rid of dangerous and polluting spirits, that is, the enemy who was a threat to order? Or was it because war would cause the death of numerous combatants who, if not buried, would become dangerous ghosts that could threaten the very lives of the living?[6] Or was the purification undertaken because all contact with the ancestors had to be prepared for in that manner?[7] All of these explanations are possible, not only because, generally speaking, the participants in any given rite or set of rites can interpret them in different ways (the ways women interpret rites often differ strongly from the ways men view them; Bloch 1982; Martin 1988), but also because a rite or set of rites can be characterized in different ways, for example, as a calendrical rite, a rite of affliction, a festival, or a rite of passage.[8]

Not only was the start and end of a war signaled by rituals in Spring and Autumn times,[9] so was the actual campaign and the fighting itself: historians were actually more interested in the rituals surrounding combat than in the details of the actual killing (Kierman 1974). Adversaries made a mutual decision as to when and where the battle was to be fought and rituals preceded and succeeded the engagement. Even in the combat itself, the warriors treated each other with elaborate ritual decorum, like the knights of medieval European chivalry, ensuring that they only engaged, for example, warriors of their own status. In one famous encounter, a noble met the chariot of the opposing ruler stuck in the mud. He dismounted and pushed the chariot out before continuing the fight, to ensure that the combat would be completely fair.

Honor and vengeance for slights received were important values for the warrior aristocracy in this period of ritual warfare (Lewis 1990: 36–43). Nobles would contest for the honor of driving the chariot of the commanding general, or for being his spearman. They would challenge enemy warriors to demonstrate their courage and skill, and would not hesitate to murder one of their own men who had slighted them even if their action imperiled the success of the enterprise for which their ruler had sent them on campaign. One noble even murdered his ruler and two of his leading ministers for shaming him. The embarrassment brought on by shame was one of the reasons that a state would go to war and why a warrior would fight in such a way that he would inevitably be killed, as long as it preserved the honor of his name. "We call into bright display the principle of shame in teaching men to fight, the object being that they should kill the enemy" (*Zuo zhuan*, Duke Xi year 22, quoted in Byrne 1974: 186–87). Once, in 537, the King of Chu was considering whether to humiliate two high-ranking emissaries from the rival state of Jin by cutting off the feet of the one and castrating the other. One of his ministers advised him:

> If you have sufficient military preparations, why shouldn't you? If you shame even a common man you must be prepared to fight, how much more if you shame a state? For this reason the sage kings devoted themselves to diplomatic ritual and never sought to shame anyone (*Zuo zhuan* Duke Zhao year 5; Legge 1970: 605; Lewis 1990: 37).

Ritual continued to play an important role in warfare in later times and came to be viewed as central to the maintenance of order in society and the means by which, in the teachings of Confucius and his followers in the Warring States period, a gentleman could achieve self-transformation and embody ideal morality. Perhaps the Confucians took this view because of the complete lack of trustworthiness of competing rulers in their times and the inability of the states to work out a replacement for the system of covenants that had given a modicum of stability to interstate relations in the earlier period. The Confucian philosopher Xunzi (third century) expressed the following opinion:

> Ritual is the ridgepole of order and discrimination, the basis of strengthening the state, the Way of awesome success, the sum of achievement and reputation. When kings and dukes follow it, that is how they obtain all under Heaven; when they do not follow it, that is how they ruin the altars of soil and grain. Thus strong armor and keen arms are not enough to be victorious; high walls and deep moats are not enough to be secure; strict commands and manifold punishments are not enough to inspire awe. Following the Way brings about success; not following it brings about downfall (Goldin 1999: 66–67).

He proceeded to argue that success in warfare was impossible without the people being unified. No matter how strong the weapons might be, without the rulers and the ruled having mutual trust and having close relations, repelling an invader or defeating an enemy would never be accomplished; such was the efficacy of correct ritual performance (cf. Knoblock 1990; Goldin 1999). In fact, in imperial times military ritual, together with rituals for foreign guests, came to be two of the five significant types of rituals recognized by the state, and there are numerous records of the changing nature of these rituals in the compendia devoted to dynastic institutions.

Reasons for Making War in Spring and Autumn Times

Rebecca Byrne has analyzed the reasons given by the participants themselves for making war in the first six books of the *Zuo Commentary*. Sixty-seven times no reason is given for wars, and on 212 occasions one or more reasons are cited, totaling 242 reasons (Byrne 1974: 214–15). She categorizes these reasons under seven broad headings: simple loss or gain, to pursue an advantage, rebellion, moral considerations, one state's influence over another, anger or retaliation, and part of a larger plan (Byrne 1974: 216–17, table 9).

More specifically, wars were started to obtain a particular valuable object, such as a rare piece of jade or a sword, to seize an individual enemy, or to obtain territory or seize lands that were in disputed border territory. In this latter instance, it is worth remembering that the city states essentially consisted of walled settlements and that their hold on the surrounding countryside was weak at best, since in many cases it was occupied either by non-Huaxia tribes or farmers who had not been incorporated into the state system. It was only after a centuries-long process in the Warring States period that states conceived of their territories as being fixed by specific boundaries and walls erected between their own territory and that of their neighbors. This process culminated in the construction of the Great Wall along the northern border to divide the territory exploited by nomads from that occupied by the sedentary Chinese (di Cosmo 2002). States in this later period guarded the roads and passes, building watchtowers and customs houses at strategic locations to monitor travelers and check their passports and to tax merchants carrying goods from one state to another. Penetration by an enemy force could be easily detected and would be considered a violation of territorial integrity and an *ipso facto* declaration of war. In the earlier period, a state was ritually obliged to request permission for safe passage over another's territory; yet borders were not guarded and the population in the countryside was relatively sparse so that a battle formation of chariots could proceed deep into another's territory, and even reach the walls of the target city-state, before being discovered. Other reasons for going to war within the category of "simple loss or gain" would be to remove a threat to a ruler or state or to launch a pre-emptive strike. The military theoreticians of the Warring States period speak frequently of such attacks, and they must have been more common in those times, especially when a new form of light chariot was developed and when cavalry was introduced from the northern nomads in the fourth century (Yates 2003).

In the category "pursuing an advantage" are included such reasons as taking advantage of another state's weakness, or attacking when the hegemon was weak and not able to defend his subordinates, and taking advantage of having troops already mobilized and, after a campaign against one state, on the return journey investing another state. In the category "rebellion" are the reasons of putting down a rebellion, or pursuing someone who had rebelled in one's own state. Quite frequently, as mentioned above, one state would intervene in a succession dispute and bring in forces to depose a ruler and set up another more well-disposed to the attacking power, for example, one who had lived as a hostage in the more powerful state.

Moral considerations included coming to the aid of a state in difficulty or punishing a state for not fulfilling its moral or ritual obligations, such as failing to provide the rush mats the Zhou King needed for his sacrifices. Moral considerations were an important part of the oaths of covenants, as described below. Another type of reason was to extend influence over another state, to prevent it from changing sides in the contest between the superpowers, or to punish it for failing to abide by signed treaty obligations, breaking a verbal promise, or refusing a request from a stronger power. The most common reasons for war within the category of "anger or retaliation" were revenge for a previous attack and the failure to treat the state or the ruler with proper ritual decorum. Alternatively, it was to satisfy an angry person or to redress a wrong done to a member of the state by the enemy. In this category, the ancient military theoreticians and statesmen of later times were in unanimous agreement that anger should not be a motivating factor leading to war. This emotion could quickly change and a ruler or general who succumbed to it could be easily duped and rapidly defeated. Since the survival of the state depended on success in warfare, every preparation had to be undertaken before a campaign or war was initiated, and careful assessment of both the enemy's and one's own resources had to be made. Sunzi's *Art of War* stated this view succinctly:

> If it is not advantageous, do not move. If objectives cannot be attained, do not employ the army. Unless endangered do not engage in warfare. The ruler cannot mobilize the army out of personal anger. The general cannot engage in battle because of personal frustration. When it is advantageous, move; when not advantageous, stop. Anger can revert to happiness, annoyance can revert to joy, but a vanquished state cannot be revived, the dead cannot be brought back to life (Sawyer 1993: 184).

This view was echoed by later theorists, such as the *Weiliaozi*: "The army cannot be mobilized out of personal anger. If victory can be foreseen, then the troops can be raised. If victory cannot be foreseen, then [the mobilization] should be stopped" (Sawyer 1993: 243).

Finally, the last two reasons for going to war, under the rubric "larger plans," included the initiation of a long-term strategy – the most effective of which came later, in the Qin's conquest of Sichuan at the end of the fourth century that more than doubled its territory and human and economic resources, and enabled it to outflank the southern state of Chu (Sage 1992) – or to engage in a campaign for domestic reasons, such as punishing a rival state for supporting a rival claimant to the throne.

System of Covenants

More than two hundred covenants (*meng*) were sworn in the Spring and Autumn period according to the historical records and they seem to have been one of the principal ways in which not only states managed interstate relations and tried to enforce agreements and alliances, but also lineages resolved differences of opinion over important issues, such as the leadership of the group, by vowing to abide by the oaths sworn (Walker 1953; Dobson 1968; Lewis 1990; Liu 1998; Pines 2002). There are even two cases in which a woman forced the man with whom she had sexual relations to recognize the offspring of the union. Dobson believes this latter practice is the earliest form of the covenant and possibly its origin, for the woman in one instance cut her arm and forced her partner, a Duke of Lu, to smear his lips with the blood and promise her that he would make her his wife (Dobson 1968: 278). In other words, Dobson believes that covenants originated in blood-oaths that created kinship ties. While this is possible, I believe it is more likely that the origin is to be sought much earlier, in the practice of allies gathering together to sacrifice enemies to the ancestral spirits and the gods of the Shang dynasty.

The covenant consisted of several steps. The agreement between the parties was drawn up in writing presumably by the person who was demanding the ritual pact (the Lord of the Covenant); an animal, usually a sheep or an ox, was slain, the left ear was cut off, and the blood that flowed from this wound was used to smear the lips of the participants in the rite. It was considered very important that a strict order of precedence was preserved, first in the right to hold the ear, and second in the order in which the blood was smeared: on several occasions competing claims of relative power among the participants led to serious disagreements. The document was then inscribed on jade tablets, apparently frequently in red ink (which, if not originally the blood of the sacrificed victim, was certainly symbolic of the blood shed), and the animals and jade tablets were buried in pits in the ground. The text consisted of several parts: a preamble that gave the precise day of the ritual and the names of the participants in order of precedence, a detailed description of the terms of the agreement, an oath or curse that called down disasters on those who might violate the oath, and a list of the ancestral spirits and other gods who bore witness to the oath and through whose spiritual power the violators would be punished. Copies of the covenants were given to each participant and stored in a special treasury of covenants. The records of these covenants were kept for many years, in one instance, at least 150 years, and states could use these records to call attention to violations of the oaths that had been sworn.

These covenants were supposed to be sworn willingly, and a forced oath was not considered legally or ritually binding: the participants were not supposed to bring armor and weapons with them. There are even cases in which belligerents forged covenants to try to trick an opponent into thinking that an agreement had been made when in fact none had. Covenants sworn by private parties in a state were often made right outside the walls of a city in a sacred field or in the ancestral temple in the presence of the ancestral tablets, but covenants between interstate partners (the joint covenant, *tongmeng*) were usually made in liminal spaces between states, for example, in the wilds near a river, especially after the practice of requiring covenants of subordinate allies by the dominant hegemon of the age began with Duke Huan of Qi in 678. These bilateral or multilateral treaties (one treaty was signed by twelve states) were subsequently known by the name of the location where the ritual had taken place. The ritual bonds of mutual obligations between the swearing parties essentially seem to have been of a personal nature, for when one of the principals died, the oath had to be "rewarmed" by his successor, although not all of the ritual steps were then considered obligatory. Thus in early times, it was the rulers of the states themselves who traveled to the ritual, but in late Spring and Autumn times it was powerful ministers who took over the right to swear on behalf of their states.

A typical example of the text of an interstate covenant is the one recorded for the year 562 between Jin, the dominant power and Zheng, who actually intended to betray it:

> Every participant of our alliance will neither accumulate grains nor monopolize profits [of mountains and rivers], neither shelter criminals nor keep traitors. [Everybody] should help others in the case of natural calamity, share likes and dislikes, and support the royal dynasty. If anybody violates this order, then let the Lord Inspector, the Lord of Alliances, [deities] of famous mountains and rivers, all the deities and all those who accept sacrifices, [spirits of] former kings, former lords, ancestors of the seven clans, and the twelve states [–let all these] numinous deities punish him; may he lose his people, may his life be cut short and his lineage destroyed, his state and family overthrown (Pines 2002: 123).

That alliance members sent each other grain supplies in time of famine is well attested in the historical records, as is the yielding by one state of criminals wanted by another, although it was equally common for exiles to find refuge in other states. Clearly the requirement to share allies and enemies was a very important element of the oath for it was what maintained peace between the parties. In other instances, the texts listed various types of moral behavior, such as filial piety, that had to be observed by the signatories. The curse at the end reveals just how embedded these treaties were in the contemporary religious beliefs and practices.

No physical evidence of multilateral treaties has yet been discovered by archaeologists, perhaps because they were sworn in out-of-the way places, but two examples of intra-lineage covenants have been discovered at Houma, the capital of the state of Jin, Shanxi province, probably dating from the early fifth century, and Wenxian, located near the bank of the Qin river. These texts were written on jade tablets in either red or black ink and are even more complex in structure and form than those recorded in the histories, comprising loyalty texts, pledge texts, restoration texts, curse texts, and divination texts (Weld 1997). It is quite possible that such texts were also prepared for the interstate meetings, but only the central texts recording the obligations of the parties have been handed down.

The system of covenants was able to keep the peace for several centuries, but in the late sixth century, more and more examples of cynical manipulation took place, especially by the southern state of Chu. The result was that interstate rivals no longer found the interstate meeting and the swearing of a covenant a practical means of resolving disputes and establishing and maintaining friendly relations. The legal force of oaths seems to have been ignored, a trend that led directly to the internecine warfare of the Warring States.[10]

War and Peace in the Warring States

Hsu (1965) has shown how the aristocratic elite lineages of the Spring and Autumn times destroyed themselves in the increasing warfare of the sixth century and, as a consequence, a new form of social order and a new type of state emerged in Warring

States times. Many of the smaller states were incorporated into larger regional polities and most of these few surviving states came to be ruled by a single dominant royal family with increasing central authority. Rulers administered their states using knights (*shi*) who, as their paid employees, owed their loyalty to them alone, and became less reliant on the few aristocratic lineages that had survived the slaughter. Commoners came to play an increasingly important role, because the system of corvée labor depended on their contribution, and able-bodied men were obliged to serve as infantrymen. Armies became much larger in size and the main fighting force shifted from the chariots to the infantry, supplemented from the fourth century by cavalry (Yates 1999).

As a consequence of these changes and the weakening of the legal and ritual force of covenants, the methods of making war and peace likewise changed. War became a free-for-all where yesterday's friend was tomorrow's enemy and there was no coherent method of ensuring peace between the warring parties. States were only interested in expanding their territory and holding on to what they had seized through force of arms or deception.[11] With fewer states in competition with each other, intermarriage between the royal families of different states played a much less prominent role in maintaining peaceful relations. The system of multiple-woman marriages seems to have given place to a new system where only a single principal wife was legally recognized. Therefore the opportunity for women to play an important role in interstate relations seems to have somewhat decreased. By contrast, the demand for or exchange of hostages maintained its significance as states attempted to bind each other to their interests, or at least to prevent them from interfering in their domestic and foreign policies.

As the states became larger and more centralized, and as the armies grew larger and were in the field for longer periods of time, specialized administrative expertise to manage the increased flow of business came to be developed. Most significantly, legal rules were elaborated in systems of statutes whereby the central authorities began to claim the right to punish those who committed crimes against the social order. No longer could an individual wreak vengeance for a slight he had received or to defend his honor. Even the smallest injury inflicted on someone not of the same family was to be punished by the state, not by the victim or the victim's family, and the precise punishment for each crime was specified in the laws depending on its severity (the value of the damage inflicted) or degree (how many participants had been involved).

Regulations for combat were proclaimed, and rules for reward for meritorious service elaborated, and these were enforced in the army and written into the statutes. The general gained the legal right to enforce these laws, once he had received the command in a religious ritual in the ancestral temple: his subsequent decisions could not be countermanded even by the ruler himself. Thus, while former methods of managing conflict between states broke down at the macro-level, a new system of laws for managing violence on the field of battle and in organizing the army emerged at the micro-level. In short, increasingly larger territorial units enforced peace among the communities that they incorporated. While violence *between* states increased, and larger and larger numbers of men were engaged and killed on the battlefield, violence *within* states diminished, and eventually the state that defeated all the others, Qin, succeeded in establishing a monopoly on the use of force that all later dynasties exercised.

Furthermore, a new system of selecting the top administrative leadership of the states emerged. A small group of highly intelligent and resourceful men moved from state to state selling their services to those rulers who rewarded them the most. Frequently they were given enormous sums of money or rare treasures, or they were enfeoffed as lords with towns or territory, whose population then remitted their taxes to the lord. War and peace were negotiated between these individuals, and the most famous of them were engaged in establishing alliances between the states either to oppose the rising power of Qin in the west (the vertical alliance), or to seek to unite with Qin (the horizontal alliance). Thus the states brought in foreign talent to help them manage their interstate affairs. Many of these peripatetic statesmen held the post of prime minister in different states, and one, Zhang Yi, even held five top posts concurrently. War and peace were decided by presenting persuasive arguments to the rulers, and the only thing that mattered was the self-interest of the state or of the individual orator.

Trust between states seemed to have been completely abandoned, much to the distress of philosophers, such as the Confucians Mencius and Xunzi, who lamented the passing of the age of ritual and sought to re-establish social order by re-instituting it on a social level and advocating that permanent peace could only be achieved by a ruler who was utterly virtuous. Other philosophers, such as the Mohist Song Xing, advocated complete disarmament by all parties, whereas his fellow Mohists chose to reduce offensive warfare by becoming experts in the defense of towns and cities, and hired themselves out to whichever ruler was under attack. Others, such as the Yin-Yang specialists, considered that a ruler could only survive by harmonizing all his actions with the changing rhythms of the cosmos. Not only did he have to perform all his actions in conformity with the changing seasons, all his vestments, all his food had to be in harmony, too, and his army could only be successful if it marched out on days that were auspicious for him and inauspicious for his enemy, and when certain powerful astral deities were in the right location of the sky to further his enterprise.

Yet, despite their differences of opinions, virtually all the various philosophers of the day came to the conclusion that the only way to re-establish a permanent peace and restore social order was for a single ruler to emerge who would unite the all-under-heaven in a single polity. A balance of power between equal states came to be simply inconceivable, a view also held by the numerous military theorists who flourished in this period of constant warfare, such as Sun Wu, his grandson Sun Bin, and many others. In the military treatises that have survived, there is not a single word about how to create a lasting peace between amicable neighbors. They are only concerned about the methods to be employed to utterly destroy an enemy without suffering significant damage to one's own army or state.

The "persuasions" of the "specialists in horizontal and vertical alliances," who were the most involved in manipulating war and peace between the rival states, are recorded in the text of the *Zhanguo ce* (Intrigues of the Warring States), although this is a work of literature, not an accurate rendition of actual speeches and historical reality. Nevertheless, the book allows us to observe and appreciate the flavor of these speeches of traveling persuaders and statesmen, and the methods whereby alliances were created only to be immediately broken when political circumstances changed (Crump 1970).

With the increasing violence of the late Warring States, when even the large states were subject to destruction or loss of large portions of territory resulting from defeat on the battlefield where hundreds of thousands of soldiers fought each other for months, even years on end, and where the survival of the state was often dependent on the competence of the rulers and the trustworthiness of their leading ministers, some philosophers began to develop a new doctrine on the justifications of war, "righteous warfare." This concept was elaborated on in the *Spring and Autumn Annals of Lü Buwei*, a work commissioned by Lü Buwei in the late 240s for King Zheng of Qin to enhance Qin's reputation as a viable contender for overlordship of all the states. The scholars employed by Lü created a manifesto justifying an offensive attack on other states, claiming superior morality for the punishment. A "righteous army" could seize the goods of those who acted immorally against the Way of Heaven and injured their own people, but preserved the lives and property of those who yielded, richly rewarding turncoats. Its actions and justifications were to be promulgated to the defeated in a formal, ritually correct, and public manifesto (Knoblock and Riegel 2000: 185–86). But, of course, in reality, what was being justified was the destruction of all those opposed to the Qin armies.

Conclusion

The state of Qin was ultimately successful in destroying all its rivals in a ten year blitzkrieg that culminated in the creation of the Chinese empire in 221. The historical records are silent on whether its heralds actually made the proclamations suggested by the *Lü Buwei* text. Certainly there was no mercy offered to those who resisted. The Qin imposed a peace by force of arms, a peace that was thought to be a renewal of the harmony that had existed at the beginning of cosmic time. It proceeded to dismantle all fortifications throughout the land and confiscated all the weapons that it then cast into a set of enormous bronze statues. One of these survived for close to 400 years before it was melted down for more weapons at the end of the Han dynasty. But Qin's methods of imposing peace, by extracting enormous amounts of forced labor from its population, by insisting that rank and social status could only be gained by success in battle, led to its rapid downfall. The Qin dynasty could not last for the ten thousand generations its architect, King Zheng, envisaged. But his draconian policies for integrating the population into a single empire, based on the rigid application of a fearsome set of laws, did survive, and for ever after the Chinese could only conceive of themselves as a single people living under a single cosmic ruler who linked the three realms, Heaven, Earth, and Man, into a harmonious whole.

Notes

1 The persistence and accuracy of the Fairbank model for imperial China's relations with foreign powers and peoples has been challenged in recent years (Hevia 1995). In the Song

dynasty, the Chinese emperor was obliged to negotiate for peace with the northern Liao, Jin, and Xixia emperors as an equal.

2 Pines calls them alliances because they were agreements between humans and not between humans and a supreme divinity.

3 Strictly speaking, the meats were offered on wooden platters, the grain and wine offerings in the bronze vessels (Chang 1977: 3–21, 25–52).

4 "Tai shi" and "Mu shi," in *Shangshu zhengyi, Shisan jing zhusu*, vol. 1, *juan* 11: 182–83.

5 Armies were, however, organized in a strictly hierarchical fashion, and the *Zuo zhuan* describes many examples of members of the elite competing with each other for the right to drive the leader, or command the forces into battle. There is no evidence of a sense of "communitas" and equality among the warriors that we would expect to see if Turner's hypothesis were applicable. For "rites of passage," see van Gennep (1960).

6 Cf. Kleeman 1994: 195: "Because these ghosts could not receive normal ancestral sacrifice, they wandered the world in search of food. Their liminal status, neither of the living nor among the safe, provided-for dead, gave them numinous power (*ling*)." According to the *Zhou li*, those who were killed in warfare were not permitted to be buried in the ancestral cemetery (Biot 1969: 2.21 "Zhongren").

7 In one of the three Han dynasty books of rites that were later incorporated into the Confucian canons, the *Li ji*, children were required to wash their hands and rinse their mouths, a form of purification, before speaking to their parents in the morning (Legge 1885, vol. 27, Book 10 "Nei Ze": 449).

8 Bell (1997: 93–137) categorizes the different types of ritual action into rites of passage, calendrical rites, rites of exchange and communion, rites of affliction, feasting, fasting, and festivals, and political rites.

9 The victorious warriors were re-integrated into society in a communal feast while the left ears of the defeated were offered to the altars of earth as a blood sacrifice.

10 Some covenants are recorded for the Warring States period, but they were not common.

11 "Warfare is the Way [*Tao*] of deception," in Sunzi's famous words (Sawyer 1993: 158).

References

Ames, Roger T. 1993. *Sun-tzu: The Art of Warfare: The First English Translation Incorporating the Recently Discovered Yin-ch'üeh-shan Texts*. New York.

Bell, Catherine. 1997. *Ritual: Perspectives and Dimensions*. New York and Oxford.

Biot, Edouard (trans.). 1969 (1851). *Le Tcheou-li ou Rites des Tcheou*. Taipei.

Bloch, Maurice. 1982. "Death, Women and Power." In Maurice Bloch and Jonathan Parry (eds.), *Death and the Regeneration of Life*, 211–30. Cambridge.

Byrne, Rebecca Zerby. 1974. *Harmony and Violence in Classical China: Study of the Battles of the "Tso Chuan."* Unpublished Ph.D. Dissertation. Chicago.

Caplow, Theodore, and Louis Hicks. 1995. *Systems of War and Peace*. Lanham.

Chang, K.C. (ed.). 1977. *Food in Chinese Culture*. New Haven.

Cook, Constance A. 1997. "Wealth and the Western Zhou." *Bulletin of the School of Oriental and African Studies* 60.2: 253–94.

Crump, J. I. (trans.). 1970. *Chan-kuo Ts'e*. Oxford.

di Cosmo, Nicola. 2002. *Ancient China and its Enemies: The Rise of Nomadic Power in East Asian History*. Cambridge.

Dobson, W. A. C. H. 1968. "Some Legal Instruments of Ancient China: The *Ming* and the *Meng*." In Chow Tse-tung (ed.), *Wen-lin: Studies in the Chinese Humanities*, I, 269–82. Madison.

Fairbank, John K. (ed.). 1968. *The Chinese World Order: Traditional China's Foreign Relations*. Cambridge, MA.

Goldin, Paul Rakita. 1999. *Rituals of the Way: The Philosophy of Xunzi*. Peru.

Hevia, James L. 1995. *Cherishing Men from Afar: Qing Guest Ritual and the Macartney Embassy of 1793*. Durham.

Hsu, Cho-yun. 1965. *Ancient China in Transition: An Analysis of Social Mobility, 722–222 BC*. Stanford.

——. 1999. "The Spring and Autumn Period." In Loewe and Shaughnessy 1999: 545–86.

Kierman, Frank A. Jr. 1974. "Phases and Modes of Combat in Early China." In Frank A. Kierman Jr. and John K. Fairbank (eds.), *Chinese Ways in Warfare*, 27–66. Cambridge, MA.

Kleeman, Terry. 1994. "Licentious Cults and Bloody Victuals: Sacrifice, Reciprocity, and Violence in Traditional China." *Asia Major* 3rd ser., 7.1: 185–211.

Knoblock, John. 1990. *Xunzi: A Translation and Study of the Complete Works*. Vol. II, Books 7–16. Stanford.

——, and Jeffrey Riegel. 2000. *The Annals of Lü Buwei*. Stanford.

Lau, D. C. (trans.). 1982. *Lao Tzu: Tao Te Ching*. Harmondsworth.

Legge, James. 1885. *The Sacred Books of China: The Texts of Confucianism*, part 3, *The Li Ki, I-X*, in F. Max Müller (ed.), *The Sacred Books of the East*. Oxford.

—— (trans.). 1970. *The Chinese Classics*, vol. 5, *The Ch'un Ts'ew with the Tso Chuen*. Hong Kong.

Lewis, Mark Edward. 1990. *Sanctioned Violence in Early China*. Albany.

——. 1999. "Warring States: Political History." In Loewe and Shaughnessy 1999: 587–650.

Liu, Yongping. 1998. *Origins of Chinese Law: Penal and Administrative Law in Its Early Development*. Hong Kong, Oxford, and New York.

Loewe, Michael, and Edward L. Shaughnessy (eds.). 1999. *The Cambridge History of Ancient China from the Origins to 221 BC*. Cambridge.

Martin, Emily. 1988. "Gender and Ideological Differences in Representations of Life and Death." In James L. Watson and Evelyn S. Rawski (eds.), *Death Ritual in Late Imperial and Modern China*, 164–79. Berkeley and Los Angeles.

Pines, Yuri. 2002. *Foundations of Confucian Thought: Intellectual Life in the Chunqiu Period, 722–453 BCE*. Honolulu.

Sage, Steven F. 1992. *Ancient Sichuan and the Unification of China*. Albany.

Sawyer, Ralph D. (trans.). 1993. *The Seven Military Classics of Ancient China*. Boulder.

Shangshu zhengyi, Shisan jing zhushu. 1980. Edited by Ruan Yuan. Beijing.

Shaughnessy, Edward L. 1999. "Western Zhou History." In Loewe and Shaughnessy 1999: 292–351.

Steele, John (trans.). 1966 (1917). *The I-li or Book of Etiquette and Ceremonial*. Taipei.

Thatcher, Melvin P. 1991. "Marriages of the Ruling Elite in the Spring and Autumn Period." In Rubie S. Watson and Patricia Buckley Ebrey (eds.), *Marriage and Inequality in Chinese Society*, 25–57. Berkeley and Los Angeles.

Turner, Victor. 1977. *The Ritual Process: Structure and Anti-Structure*. Ithaca.

van Gennep, Arnold. 1960. *The Rites of Passage*. Chicago.

Walker, Richard Louis. 1953. *The Multi-State System of Ancient China*. Hamden.

Weld, Susan R. 1997. "The Covenant Texts from Houma and Wenxian." In Edward L. Shaughnessy (ed.), *New Sources of Early Chinese History: An Introduction to the Reading of Inscriptions and Manuscripts*, 125–60. Berkeley.

Yang, Lien-sheng. 1961. "Hostages in Chinese History." In id., *Studies in Institutional History*, 43–57. Cambridge, MA.

Yates, Robin D. S. 1997. "The City State in Ancient China." In Deborah L. Nichols and Thomas H. Charlton (eds.), *The Archaeology of City States: Cross-Cultural Approaches*, 71–90. Washington, DC.

——. 1999. "Early China." In Kurt Raaflaub and Nathan Rosenstein (eds.), *War and Society in the Ancient and Medieval Worlds*, 7–45. Washington, DC.

——. 2003. "The Horse in Early Chinese Military History." In Huang Ko-wu (ed.), *Military Organization and War*, 1–78. Taipei.

3

Ancient India: Peace Within and War Without

Richard Salomon

Some Preliminary Remarks

Since the prevalent, if largely self-created image of traditional India is that of a realm of peace and nonviolence (*ahiṃsā*), I have chosen to emphasize peace, rather than war, in this chapter.[1] But in the process, I will try to offer some thoughts about how and why the image of a realm of peace has come to be attached to traditional India, what this image really means, and to what extent it corresponds to historical reality.

In introducing these subjects in connection with ancient and classical India, I find myself in the position, all too familiar to Indologists, of having to plead a special case. The priorities and foci of interest of the classical Indian tradition – by which I mean essentially the cultural tradition, or rather traditions, which are embodied in the Sanskrit language and its contemporary relatives, the Prakrit dialects – are in many regards very different from those, not only of the ancient western world, but also of the classical cultures of other parts of Asia. In broad terms, Indian civilization is far more concerned with the presentation and consideration of normative theories than in the recording of pragmatic realities.

The paradigmatic case of this pattern is what is sometimes called the "empty shelf" syndrome of the history of ancient India. From the very beginning of the modern study of Sanskrit and allied literatures, western scholars have been troubled and puzzled by the absence of a literary genre corresponding to what they knew as "history," which constituted such a fundamental body of knowledge not only in European classical culture but also, for example, in Chinese and Islamic civilizations. Many early scholars of what is nowadays known as the Orientalist school tended to see this "empty shelf" as a defect, whereas some nationalist-inclined Indian authors, in (over)reaction to the orientalist stance, denied the alleged absence of historical literature, citing among other exceptions to the rule relatively well-developed regional historical traditions in some parts of the Indian subcontinent, especially Kashmir (see n. 2).

Such debates, however, are ultimately unenlightening; depending on how one chooses to define and delimit "history," one can argue that the ancient Indians did or did not have a tradition and a literature of history. But what is beyond debate, and more important, is that history, however one might wish to define it, was conceived and presented in a very different way in classical Indian tradition than in most of the other traditions that are represented in this volume. The detailed chronicling and preservation of dates, events and personalities – the stuff of what for other civilizations was the very basis of history – was not a priority, and so we have precious little of this for early India. Here, as in most respects, the Indian/Sanskrit tradition was much more interested in the presentation of theories, categories, and ideals than in recording their applications and results. For example, if we can consider history in a traditional sense as concerning the doings of kings and nations, that is, the application of statecraft and the uses and manipulations of power, we do have in the Indian tradition a theoretical literature on these subjects, principally embodied in the *Arthaśāstra* or "Treatise on Worldly Gain" attributed to Kauṭilya or Cāṇakya, the so-called "Indian Machiavelli." This remarkable book (translated in Kangle 1960–65: vol. 2) presents, in the systematic and schematic pattern that is so characteristic of the Indian traditional sciences (*śāstras*), a detailed textbook of the art of statecraft, including, of course, the arts of war and peace (principally in books 7 and 10). But what it notably – though again, typically of the *śāstras* – does not provide are historical instances of the application of these rules. Everything is presented as theory and principle; of illustration or application there is virtually nothing.

For example, with regard to the issue of peace treaties, we do find in the *Arthaśāstra* a detailed presentation (in book 7) of the types, strategies and tactics of forming treaties and alliances (*sandhi*); but as usual, it gives us not a single instance of the actual historical application of such treaties. Searching through other branches of Indian literature, we once again find virtually nothing on the topic. In fact, I have been able to discover only a single instance of a direct citation of the text of a peace treaty anywhere in Sanskrit literature, including epigraphy, and that a rather minor case, which cites only the heading of the treaty.[2]

How, then, given the special nature of the sources available to us, are we to deal with issues of peace and war in such a way as to be meaningful and useful – and hopefully also interesting – in the comparative context of this volume? Fortunately, the foregoing caveats notwithstanding, there are some exceptions to the overall pattern which make it possible to address these questions meaningfully in the Indian context. Although peace, as usually conceived in modern usage, was not in and of itself a topic of discussion in classical Indian literature, there are nonetheless texts and sources which bear upon it in a very significant manner. Foremost among these sources are the great *Mahābhārata* epic and the *Bhagavad-gītā* which constitutes a central episode of it. The *Mahābhārata*, like the *Iliad* with which it has so much in common, is essentially about war and the ravages it afflicts on all it touches; in this sense, it is of necessity also about peace, if only secondarily.

Images of Peace and War in Indian Inscriptions

I will return to the *Mahābhārata* and *Bhagavad-gītā* in the next part of this chapter, but first I would like to present a pair of examples from what will be our other major source of information, namely the immense corpus of historical or quasi-historical inscriptions which have served, in the absence of a substantial body of historical literature, as the main body of information from which modern scholars have reconstructed, as far as possible, the history of ancient and classical India.[3] These two epigraphic specimens date from very different periods of Indian history, and reflect diametrically opposite attitudes toward war and peace. The first is an extract from the famous thirteenth rock edict of Aśoka, the great emperor (ca. 269–232 BCE) of the Mauryan dynasty who for the first time united nearly all of the Indian subcontinent under a single polity and who was, or presented himself, as the apostle of peace and righteousness. In this passage, Aśoka expresses his heart-felt remorse for the devastation caused by his conquest of the territory of Kaliṅga in southeastern India (modern Orissa):[4]

> When King Devānaṃpriya Priyadarśin [= Aśoka] had been anointed eight years, the country of the Kaliṅgas was conquered by him. One hundred and fifty thousand in number were the men who were deported thence, one hundred thousand in number were those who were slain there, and many times as many those who died.
>
> After that, now that the country of the Kaliṅgas has been taken, Devānaṃpriya is devoted to a zealous study of morality [*dhrama* = Sanskrit *dharma*], to the love of morality, and to the instruction of people in morality. This is the repentance of Devānaṃpriya on account of his conquest of the country of the Kaliṅgas. For this is considered very painful and deplorable by Devānaṃpriya, that, while one is conquering an unconquered country, slaughter, death, and deportation of people are taking place there...
>
> And this conquest is considered the principal one by Devānaṃpriya, viz. the conquest by morality. And this conquest has been won repeatedly by Devānaṃpriya both here and among all his borderers, even as far as six hundred leagues, where the Yona [Greek] king named Antiyoka [Antiochus] is ruling, and beyond this Antiyoka ... the king named Turamaya [Ptolemy], the king named Antikini [Antigones], the king named Maka [Magas], and the king named Alikasudara [Alexander]...
>
> And for the following purpose has this rescript on morality been written: in order that the sons and great-grandsons [*sic*] who may be born to me should not think that a fresh conquest ought to be made, that, if a conquest does please them, they should take pleasure in mercy and light punishments, and that they should regard the conquest by morality as the only true conquest.

The second example is a single verse from a long Sanskrit inscription, dated 953/4 CE, from the famous temple site of Khajuraho in the central Indian state of Madhya Pradesh. The inscription, recording the foundation of a temple of Viṣṇu-Vaikuṇṭha by King Yaśovarman[5] of the Candella dynasty, eulogizes in the verse in question the donor's grandfather Rāhila in the most bloodthirsty terms:[6]

> Skillfully, by means of his strategic counsels [which served as] the ritual prayers [*mantra*], he tirelessly sacrificed his enemies like cattle in the sacrificial rite of battle, in which his fearful whirling sword was the oblation ladle, the streaming blood [of his enemies] served as the clarified butter, the buzzing of his bowstring was the ritual cry "*vaṣat*," the soldiers marching in order were the priests, and his burning hatred was the fire, fanned by the winds of his unquenchable rage.

Aśoka's inscription is by far the more familiar of the two; in fact, it is probably the most-quoted passage from any Indian inscription, and the one with which anyone who has studied early Indian history at all is most likely to be familiar. And yet, it is actually most untypical and unrepresentative of Indian inscriptions. In fact, it is unique; after reading thousands of Indian inscriptions over some 35 years, I have yet to find a single comparable reference to the evils of war and the virtues of peace and gentle persuasion.

Contrast with this the eulogy of King Rāhila's bloody sacrifice of his enemies. In an extended or complex metaphor of the type which was a favorite device of classical Sanskrit poets, Rāhila's victory in battle is likened, point for point, to the sacred Vedic sacrifice: the slaughtered enemies are the sacrificial cattle, his fearful whirling sword is the oblation ladle, his victims' blood is the molten butter, and so on. Although this is admittedly a somewhat extreme example of the genre, it is not untypical of Sanskrit panegyric inscriptions (*praśasti*), in which the court poets sing in the most hyperbolic fashion the praises of their patrons' handsomeness, generosity, learning, and, especially, martial spirit. There are literally thousands of documents of this type, in contrast to the single example of the espousal of gentler values in Aśoka's inscription.

That Aśoka's famous invocation of peace and gentle government stands literally alone seems all the more surprising in that his were the first royal proclamations ever to be publicly inscribed in India. For although Aśoka apparently invented the practice of inscribing royal proclamations on pillars and stones, the generations of kings who followed him imitated only the physical practice; the contents and tone of his edicts were evidently ignored and forgotten. Whatever might have moved him to such sentiments – the calming influence of Buddhism, an innate nobility which led him to conceive such ideals long before their time, or a crafty strategy of hypocritical manipulation have all been suggested – his ideals did not, as he hoped, live on after him. For, despite his wish that his descendants should not aim at more conquests, apply "mercy and light punishments, and … regard the conquest by morality as the only true conquest," what little we know about the history of the Mauryan dynasty after Aśoka's death around 232 BCE indicates that it rapidly declined into disorder, fraternal strife, and war; in other words, into the pattern of violent dynastic rivalry and eventual decline that was typical of ancient India (as of other parts of the ancient world). And although Aśoka became the legendary model of the ideal emperor in the Buddhist tradition, the mainstream Brahmanical/Hindu tradition virtually ignored him and his lofty ideals, so that after Buddhism died out in its Indian homeland early in the second millennium CE, Aśoka was literally forgotten until his inscriptions were discovered and deciphered by European scholars in the first half of the nineteenth century.

Sanskrit Words for Peace

How, then, are we to reconcile the bloody reality of Indian history, as represented to us by the makers of that history themselves, with the prevalent image of classical India as a realm of peace and non-violence – an image which often takes as its emblem the words and monuments of Aśoka, despite the fact that, in the grand sweep of Indian history, they were actually so anomalous? And what, moreover, is this thing called "peace," of which we hear so much, and yet in another way so little, in the classical Indian tradition? The Sanskrit word (also commonly used in many other Indian languages) which is conventionally translated as "peace" is one which may already be familiar to many readers, even those without Indological background. It is *śānti*, nowadays frequently to be seen in the western world in the names of yoga schools and similar institutions, and also familiar in western literature from the closing line of T.S. Eliot's "The Wasteland": "Shantih shantih shantih."

But what does this word really mean? What kind of peace is "*śānti*?" To begin with a look at the dictionaries, M. Monier-Williams' standard *Sanskrit-English Dictionary* gives the following as its primary senses: "tranquility, peace, quiet, peace or calmness of mind, absence of passion, averting of pain, indifference to objects of pleasure and pain, alleviation, cessation, abatement, extinction." It should be noted that all of these definitions refer primarily, probably even exclusively, to inner states of the mind or spirit rather than to external political or social conditions. Only lower down in the lengthy entry under this word do we find references to later, secondary and generally less common meanings such as "peace, welfare, prosperity, good fortune, ease, comfort, happiness, bliss" which refer more to external circumstances; that is to say, meanings which correspond, if only approximately, to the sense of the English "peace" as it applies to the subject of this book.

Lest it be thought that these modern dictionary definitions reflect some cross-cultural misapprehension, I cite here the words which the *Amarakoṣa* (verse 2255), the definitive traditional Sanskrit lexicon, lists as the synonyms of *śānti: śamathas tu śamaḥ śāntir dāntis tu damatho damaḥ*. Instead of trying to translate this list of synonyms, I would rather point out that they all share the etymological sense of "calming" or "suppression." The list of six synonyms consists of two parallel sets of three nouns each, derived from the verbal roots *śam* "to calm" and *dam* "to suppress" respectively, and the primary sphere of reference of these terms is not the "calming" of the political sphere or the "suppression" of military enemies, but rather the "calming" of one's own mind and the "suppression" of one's own mental and spiritual deficiencies and negative inclinations.

The same point can be made by reference to any number of other Sanskrit sources; not to belabor the point, I will cite only one more. This is the *Subhāṣitaratnakoṣa* or "Treasury of Jewels of Eloquence," a medieval anthology of verses on diverse topics which was masterfully translated by Daniel Ingalls (1965) in his *Anthology of Sanskrit Court Poetry*. The forty-eighth of fifty chapters in this massive anthology is entitled *Śānti*, duly translated by Ingalls (418–27) as "Peace." A typical verse (no. 1617) from this chapter reads, in Ingalls' translation (424):[7]

> Of necessity the pleasures of the senses leave,
> though they have been with us for many a year.
> What difference is in the manner of the parting
> that men will not abandon them themselves?
> When pleasures leave without our will
> the heart is sorely grieved;

> but when we leave them on our own
> we gain the lasting joy of peace.

Here the word for "peace" at the end of the verse is *śama*, one of the synonyms for *śānti* given in the line from the *Amarakosa* lexicon cited above. This verse, chosen more or less at random, is typical of the anthology verses on "peace" in referring to the quest for inner peace through the suppression or rejection of worldly pleasures and cares. In fact, not a single verse from the 44 stanzas in this chapter on Śānti makes any reference whatsoever to peace in the sense of "absence or cessation of war"; without exception, "peace" always refers to inner, spiritual peace.

Having compared Sanskrit *śānti* and its synonyms to English *peace*, it seems prudent, by way of a control experiment, to compare *śānti* to words conventionally translated as "peace" in other ancient languages. For example, the entry in Cassell's *New Latin Dictionary* begins by defining *pax* as "a state of peace, *opp. to war*," (my italics), then goes on to give as secondary and transferred meanings, "calm, serenity, quiet." Thus the primary and secondary senses of Latin *pax* seem to be precisely the opposite of those of Sanskrit *śānti*, but, not surprisingly, more or less the same as those of English *peace*.

The same dictionary further informs us that *pax* is etymologically connected with the verb *paciscor*, "to make a bargain or agreement, covenant, contract" (whence English *pact*, etc.). This would seem to imply that in Latin peace is conceived as something resulting from an interaction and agreement between two individuals or groups (for discussion, see also Rosenstein's and Barton's chapters in this volume). Contrast with this the very different etymology of Sanskrit *śānti*, which is derived from the verbal root *śam* "to calm, control, quiet, suppress," referring not to external political or military activity, but rather, as noted above, to the suppression of one's own negative tendencies and emotions. Thus etymology confirms that Sanskrit *śānti* is an individual matter, something that is developed within oneself and applies to oneself, in contrast to Latin *pax* which, like English *peace*, refers to external interactions.

The question then arises, if *śānti* is not really a good correspondent to English *peace* or Latin *pax*, what would be a better Sanskrit equivalent for these words? Turning again to the dictionary, this time to Monier-Williams' *English and Sanskrit Dictionary*, we find at the very beginning of the entry for "peace" the specification "(Freedom from war)," followed by the correspondents *sandhi, sandhāna, ayuddha, yuddhābhāva, avigraha, asaṅgrāma*, and *nirdvandva*. These equivalents fall into two sets. The first set comprises the first two definitions, *sandhi* and *sandhāna*, which are etymologically cognate synonyms meaning literally "conjunction, combination, alliance, agreement," derived from the prefix *sam* "together" and the root *dhā* "to place."[8] As noted above (p. 54), *sandhi* is the technical term regularly used in the *Arthaśāstra* to refer to treaties and alliances. In this sense it is parallel to Latin *pax/paciscor* in the technical sense of "reaching an agreement" or "making a treaty." But *sandhi* in this sense connotes "peace" only in a limited and specific sense of "avoiding war by way of a tactical stratagem." It lacks any connotation of peace as a lasting and desirable state, and thus has none of the emotional overtones of *peace* or *pax*.

The second set of words given by Monier-Williams as the equivalents of English "peace," *ayuddha, yuddhābhāva, avigraha,* etc. are all essentially synonymous terms meaning "absence of war." For example, literal translations of the first three would be "non-war," "absence of war," and "non-strife," respectively. Thus they may seem to correspond to the primary sense of English *peace* (and Latin *pax*), but once again this is misleading, and in fact I suspect that they were plugged in by Monier-Williams for lack of any better equivalents. For I would think that anyone with a good knowledge of Sanskrit would have the reaction that, first of all, these are not very common words, and second, that even when they do occur, they too do not have the same connotations as *peace* or *pax*. For example, *ayuddha-*, literally "not war," actually refers in most cases to a strategic decision to avoid war in a particular situation, rather than to the absence of war as a lasting condition; thus, despite its different etymology, it is semantically similar to *sandhi*, "strategic peace/alliance," as used in the *Arthaśāstra*. For example, in his authoritative translation of the *Mahābhārata*, van Buitenen (1978: 524) correctly translates *ayuddha* (in the instrumental case form *ayuddhena*) as "without waging war," rather than "by means of peace."[9]

The sense of this and related key words is illustrated in a particularly interesting way in another passage from the *Mahābhārata*, which combines four of our key words, namely the nouns *ayuddha, yuddha,* and *śānti* and the verb *śam*. The context, as usual when the word *ayuddha* is used, is a discussion of strategy, in this case between Dhṛtarāṣṭra, the elder of Kauravas, and his kinsmen and allies:[10]

> tair **ayuddham** sādhu manye kuravas tan nibodhata /
> **yuddhe** vināśaḥ kṛtsnasya kulasya bhavitā dhruvam //
> eṣā me paramā **śāntir** yathā **śāmyati** me manaḥ /
> yadi tv **ayuddham** iṣṭaṃ vo vayaṃ **śāntyai** yatāmahe //
> Not to war [*ayuddham*] were best, I think – listen to
> me, Kurus! If there be **war** [*yuddhe*], the destruction of
> our entire lineage is assured. This is my last attempt at
> **peace** [*śāntir*], to **appease** [*śāmyati*] my mind. If you
> do **not want war** [*ayuddham*], let us then sue for **peace**
> [*śāntyai*].

Here again *ayuddha* has its usual sense of "not to war," as a tactical rather than an ethical strategy. Our key term *śānti*, however, appears twice, in two different but interlinked senses. In the second occurrence, "let us then sue for peace" (*śāntyai*, dative), it means "avoiding" or "ceasing war," and thus at least approximates the sense and connotation of English "peace." (I have not said, and do not mean to say, that Sanskrit *śānti* never has this meaning, but only that this is not its primary sense.) In this connection, it is striking that Dhṛtarāṣṭra juxtaposes this sense of *śānti*, which I consider to be the secondary one, with the other, primary one, when he prefaces this comment by saying, "This is my last attempt at peace (*śāntir*, nominative), to appease (*śāmyati*) my mind," in van Buitenen's translation; more literally, the phrase in question means, "This is my final peace, whereby my mind is put at peace." Here Dhṛtarāṣṭra seems to be making at once both an etymological and a psychological point; in juxtaposing the noun *śāntir* with the verb *śāmyati*, the present tense form of the aforementioned verbal root *śam* "to calm, control, quiet," he stresses the internal, personal dimension of *śānti*, that is, the sense which, as I am trying to argue, is the essential one. In other words, even when Dhṛtarāṣṭra talks about *śānti* in the political sense, he cannot or will not separate it from its primary sense of "personal" or "inner peace."[11]

War and Peace in Ancient India

This is not a trivial or accidental juxtaposition. Rather, it cuts to the very heart of the matter of the difference between the conceptions of peace that prevailed in ancient India and the modern world, as well as in at least some other ancient cultures. But why did the Indian concept of peace focus so strongly on internal states of the mind and spirit, rather than on political and social policies? The question can be addressed on two levels: the ideal on the one hand, and the pragmatic and historical on the other.

To dispose of the second one first: even a cursory study of the history of ancient India suffices to show that war was the rule and peace very much the exception. The number of times in premodern history that the entirety of the Indian subcontinent was brought under a single ruling authority is exactly – zero. There is one near-exception, namely the kingdom of Aśoka, one of whose inscriptions was quoted earlier in this chapter. During his reign, for a brief period of a few decades in the middle of the third century BCE, most, though not quite all of the Indian subcontinent was under a single ruler; so perhaps it is not a coincidence that it is precisely during this brief interlude that the ideal of peace as a lasting condition was voiced. But as we have seen, this moment of peace ended abruptly after Aśoka's death in about 232 BCE, whereupon the normal pattern of fragmentation into smaller states in more or less constant warfare reasserted itself. Other than this all-too-brief exception there was no lasting "Pax Indica" comparable to the "Pax Romana" or to the extended periods of peace and political unity that marked the history of Egypt, China, Iran, and other parts of the ancient world.[12] Rather, in the words of one author, speaking with reference to the attitudes expressed in the Sanskrit law books, "Peace is the interval between two wars... [W]ar is a permanent institution... Peace appears to be a compulsory adjustment to circumstances beyond the control of the king" (Tähtinen 1976: 91–2).

Why the history of India was so full of war and so empty of peace, why it was characterized by conflict and disunity rather than centralization and stability, is something that I have often pondered but never understood; so I will not try to explain it here. But of the fact itself there can be no doubt. If proof be needed, one need only refer to the thousands of inscriptions recounting and glorifying the bloody exploits of the kings of hundreds of dynasties, along the lines of the Khajuraho inscription cited above (p. 55). And while we need not and should not take literally the rhetorical bluster of these documents, the consistency of the overall picture, which is confirmed by the law books, epics, and other genres of classical literature from the Vedas on down, leaves us in no doubt of the matter: war was in ancient India the normal and more or less constant state of affairs, while peace was rare, abnormal, and apparently very fragile.

Turning now to the ideological, as opposed to the practical aspect of the question: whether it was because of this chronic state of war that the thinkers of ancient India turned inward and looked for some sort of peace within themselves, or whether it was rather because they turned inward that they did not pursue, and thus did not achieve peace in the public sphere, is a chicken-and-egg question which I would not venture to try to answer. But to delve a little deeper into the matter, I would like briefly to survey the attitudes toward war and peace expressed in the two dominant trends of thought in ancient India: first, Buddhism as represented in the texts which ostensibly record the original teachings of the Buddha, and second, the "orthodox" Brahmanical/Hindu tradition as represented in its best-known scripture, the *Bhagavad-gītā*.

In the Buddhist teachings, avoiding violence and the causing of pain to one's fellow creatures, human or otherwise, is emphatically and undeniably a cardinal value. And yet we find in the Buddhist scriptures very little indeed in the way of explicit and blanket condemnations of war as such. While violence and murder are criticized constantly, these criticisms are almost always expressed either with reference to individual relationships or ritual sacrificial slaughter, or in very broad and unspecific contexts. For example, a verse of the *Pāli Dhammapada*, a widely-read compendium of basic Buddhist ethics and principles, says simply:[13] "Everyone dreads violence; life is dear to everyone. Likening others to yourself, neither kill nor cause killing."

On occasion, we do find statements in Buddhist texts which at least approach condemnations of war and military violence. For instance, in one *sūtra*, the Buddha utters this verse in response to the news of the back-and-forth battle between Kings Ajātasattu of Māgadha and Pasenadi of Kosala:[14] "Victory produces hatred; the loser dwells in misery. [Only] the man of peace [*upasanto*] dwells in happiness, by rejecting both victory and defeat." But here, quite typically, the Buddha takes the latest news from the front as an occasion to give a lesson on individual human nature rather than to criticize war as such. To the Buddha, war is merely one of the many manifestations of the underlying cause of all suffering and unhappiness, namely the ignorance, delusion and self-centeredness of individuals. The solution is, as usual, for each of us to turn inward and cleanse ourselves of our internal defects; that is, to become *upasanto*, a man of peace.[15] Presumably the implication is that if people were to follow the Buddha's teaching and makes themselves "men of peace," war and other social problems would solve themselves. But significantly, this is, to my knowledge, never explicitly stated by the Buddha, who evidently did not see fit to address the abolition of war as a goal in itself.[16]

I turn now to the *Bhagavad-gītā*, representing the Brahmanical/Hindu tradition. The *Gītā* not only constitutes the authoritative Brahmanical voice on issues of war and peace, but also provides an interesting counterpoint to the Buddhist views on these issues. Although in origin the *Gītā* is a subsection of the *Bhīṣma-parvan* of the *Mahābhārata*, it has taken on a life of its own and in effect exists independently from its source text. It consists of a dialogue between Arjuna, one of the five Pāṇḍava brothers, and his charioteer, Kṛṣṇa, on the morning of the climactic battle with Arjuna's cousins and enemies, the Kauravas. At the critical moment before the battle, Arjuna is overwhelmed with doubts about the morality of fighting and killing his own kinsmen: "I cannot stand, my mind reels; I see evil omens; I find no good in killing my own people in battle" (1.30c–31). The remaining 18 chapters of the *Gītā* consist of Kṛṣṇa's explanations and revelations of the true nature of things, in the course of which he provides Arjuna with justifications for war in three respects:

1 Arjuna is by birth a *kṣatriya*, a member of the warrior class, and it is therefore by definition his inviolable personal duty (*dharma*) to fight and to kill: "Considering your own duty, you should have no doubt. For there is nothing better for a kṣatriya than a righteous battle. Happy are those kṣatriyas who are lucky enough to come upon a battle such as this, which is an open door to heaven" (2.31–2).
2 Everyone must do their duty without regard to its consequences: "Be concerned only with the act, and never with its results" (2.47ab).
3 On a metaphysical level, what seems to be killing is really not killing at all, since it is a delusion to identify the physical body with the immortal soul: "He who considers it [the soul] to be the killer and he who thinks that it is killed – neither of them understands it; it neither kills nor is killed" (2.19).

Kṛṣṇa therefore commands Arjuna, repeatedly and unambiguously, to fight and kill: "Therefore, Arjuna, fight!" (2.18d); "Therefore, arise and gain your glory! Conquer your enemies and enjoy a vast kingdom" (11.33ab).

What are we to make of this? How can we reconcile the bellicose counsel of Kṛṣṇa (who, later in the text, will reveal his true identity as lord of the universe) in this most influential and most quintessential of Hindu texts with the image of India as the land of peace and non-violence? For if we read the *Gītā* literally, assuming that it means exactly what it says, we have an explicit and emphatic justification of war and a legitimation and rationalization of all of its horrors. Needless to say, the matter is not quite so simple, and this literalist interpretation is one which is widely dismissed – a bit too quickly, perhaps – by commentators and translators both ancient and modern, Indian and western. Nearly all of them agree that Kṛṣṇa's goading Arjuna on to slaughter his uncles and cousins should, indeed must somehow or other be taken in a metaphorical sense. In fact, paradoxical as it may seem, the message of the *Gītā* has been taken by many, above all by Mahātmā Gandhi, as a justification for a philosophy of the strictest non-violence (*ahiṃsā*). For according to Gandhi, "[t]he poet has seized the occasion of the war between the Pandavas and the Kauravas on the field of Kurukṣetra for drawing attention to the war going on *in our bodies* [my italics] between the forces of good (Pandavas) and the forces of Evil (Kauravas)."[17]

Of course Gandhi realized that on a certain, perhaps superficial level there was a problem with his interpretation; but he disposed of this problem with the remarkable comment that "I believe that the teaching of the *Gita* does not justify war, even if the author of the *Gita* had intended otherwise."[18] Presumably, Gandhi did not mean that he thought he understood the *Gītā* better than its original author did. Rather, his comment indicates that (unlike many religious leaders) he recognized the differences between the historical situations and cultural values of the time of the composition of the *Gītā* and those of his own time, and understood that one can adapt ancient wisdom to the modern world without naively accepting the outdated or unacceptable cultural baggage that comes with it. In a word, Gandhi was no fundamentalist.

In this way the *Gītā* can be and generally is understood on an allegorical level, which paradoxically ends up making it mean quite the opposite of what it seems on the surface to mean: when Kṛṣṇa tells Arjuna to arise and fight and conquer his enemies, he means that he must arise and fight for what is good and against what is wrong. And this, in Gandhi's morality, means avoiding war and violence in any and every form. In short, we come, by a rather roundabout path, to the same conclusion as that of the Buddha: "avoiding causing suffering to all beings"[19] is the ultimate good.[20]

To return, finally, to our principal topic: one point of consistency throughout the vast and varied cultural sphere that we are lumping together as "Ancient India" is that peace – *śānti* – is conceived as essentially an internal matter, and it is to be sought within oneself, not in the outside world. For it was taken for granted that the world is by its very nature a place of strife and war, and it was apparently assumed that to try to change this would be a waste of time. There was (at least as far as the historical record tells us) no Indian Lysistrata mobilizing a women's peace movement; and although India never had any shortage of goddesses, there was never a goddess Śānti to whom the Indians could pray for peace, as did the Greeks to Eirene and the Romans to Pax. Peace, if it was to be found at all, was to be found within, and the great religious teachers saw it as their role to provide people with a means, a technology as it were, to find it and cultivate it there, and only there.

Whether it was assumed or implied that such individual efforts at self-improvement would inevitably lead to an end of war, we cannot judge, because such terms of discourse are entirely absent. But in any case, the historical record shows us all too clearly that this did not happen, except, perhaps, for the remarkable but isolated instance of Gandhi's non-violent independence movement. In the current social and political atmosphere in India, where an aggressive nationalism is in the ascendant, Gandhi and Gandhian ideals no longer hold any effective sway, and it is hard to avoid seeing his success in harnessing the power of non-violence and individual morality as a temporary exception.

Still, Gandhi's experiment, and the other great Indian experiment in peace, that of Aśoka some two millennia earlier, stand out as beacons in the long history of strife and warfare, so that, if the Indian approach to the cultivation of peace from within the individual soul has been less than entirely successful, it has at least had some shining moments. In any case, it can hardly be claimed that the western approach to the quest for lasting peace through the harnessing and manipulation of political power has been any more fruitful.

Notes

1 On war in Ancient India, see Chakravarti 1941; Dikshitar 1944; Singh 1965.
2 This appears in the curious story of the failed treaty (*sandhi*) between Kings Lalitāditya Muktāpiḍa of Kashmir (ca. 724–60 CE) and Yaśovarman of Kanauj related in Kalhaṇa's *Rājataraṅgiṇī* or "River of Kings," a history of Kashmir composed in the twelfth century CE. According to the account given there, the proposed treaty was rejected by Lalitāditya on a matter of protocol, namely the question of which king's name would be recorded first in the heading of the treaty (Salomon 1987).

3   On Indian inscriptions in general, see Salomon 1998; on their special importance and function as historical source materials, see ibid., 226–32.

4   The text is presented here according to the version of the Aśokan rock edicts from Shāhbāzgaṛhī in northern Pakistan. The translation is based on that in Hultzsch 1925: 68–70, with minor modifications.

5   This Yaśovarman is not to be confused with Yaśovarman of Kanauj referred to above in note 2. The duplication of the name is merely coincidental.

6   The translation is mine. The original text (from Kielhorn 1892: 126, verse 17) reads:

> *bhīmabhrāmyadasisruci sravadasṛkdsampāditājyakriye*
> *jyāniṛgghoṣavaṣaṭpade kramacaratsamrabdhayodhartviji /*
> *aśrāntaḥ samarādhvare 'pratihatakrodhāniloddīpite*
> *vairoddarccisi yaḥ paśūn iva kṛtī mantrair juhāva dviṣaḥ //*

7   The original text reads:

> *avaśyaṃ yātāraś cirataram uṣitvāpi viṣayā*
> *viyoge ko bhedas tyajati na jano yat svayam imān /*
> *vrajantaḥ svātantryāt paramaparitāpāya manasaḥ*
> *svayaṃ tyaktvā hy ete śamasukham anantaṃ vidadhati //*

The verse is cited by the anthologist Vidyākara from an earlier anthology, Bhartṛhari's *Śatakatrayam* (verse 157).

8   Some readers may recognize the word *sandhi* from its usage in English as a technical linguistic term for sound changes conditioned by the juxtaposition ("placing-together") of phonemes.

9   *Mahābhārata* 5.192.13a, *ayuddhena nivṛttiṃ ca manasā cintayābhibho,* "Think with your mind, my lord, on how to make him desist without waging war" (van Buitenen, ibid.).

10   Here I have given the original Sanskrit text (5.52.14–15) in the body of the chapter with the key words in bold face, so that non-Sanskrit readers will be able to get a sense of their distribution in the passage in question. The translation is van Buitenen's (316).

11   Readers who are familiar with the *Mahābhārata* may recall at this point that the word *śānti* has another very important function in that epic, namely as the title of the twelfth of its eighteen books (*parvan*), the Śānti-parvan, or, as it is conventionally translated, "The Book of Peace." Since this book follows shortly after the end of the cataclysmic war that forms the central theme of the epic, one could easily jump to the conclusion that the *śānti* of its title refers to the permanent peace that, one might hope, would follow a destructive and disastrous war; but in fact this conclusion would be wrong. Actually, *śānti* in this context is used in another of its technical senses, referring to various apotropaic rituals; the "*śānti*" of the Śānti-parvan refers to a kind of ritual "cooling off" of King Yudhiṣṭhira. In the words of Fitzgerald in his translation of the Śānti-parvan (2004: 95), the main subject of the book is "a grand *śānti* of the newly inaugurated king, one intended to bring his disabling inner heat to rest and allow him to rule." So once again, and in yet another way, the semantic field of Sanskrit *śānti* turns out to be not at all congruent with that of English *peace*.

12   See, for instance, the various examples cited in Melko and Weigel 1981.

13   Dhammapada 130:

> *sabbe tasanti daṇḍassa sabbesaṃ jīvitaṃ piyaṃ /*
> *attānaṃ upamaṃ katvā na haneyya na ghātaye //*

14   Saṃyutta-nikāya 1.83.31–2:

> *jayaṃ veraṃ pasavati dukkhaṃ seti parājito /*
> *upasanto sukhaṃ seti hitvā jayaṃ parājayaṃ //*

15 Note that the Buddha uses a term (*upa-santo*) derived from the Pāli equivalent, √*sam*, of the previously discussed Sanskrit root √*śam*, the source of *śānti*.

16 On attitudes towards kings and war in a later Buddhist text of the Mahāyāna school, see Lang 2003: 103–6, 199–201.

17 As cited by J.T.F. Jordens in Minor 1986: 98.

18 Ibid 97.

19 *Ahiṃsā sabbapānānaṃ*, Dhammapada 270c.

20 The question of whether scriptural references to war are to be taken as literal or figurative – that is, whether war is a metaphor for the struggle between good and evil, or rather is the actual means to effect the conquest of good over evil – can hardly fail to bring to mind the ongoing controversy over the Islamic concept of *jihād*. The etymological meaning of the word is "effort" or "struggle," and a common application of the word in the *Qur'an* and Islamic law books is "armed struggle against the unbelievers." There are those, as we know all too well, who maintain that this sense of the term remains in full effect in the modern world. On the other hand, many others prefer to understand the primary referent of *jihād* as a metaphorical *internal* struggle against one's own evil inclinations. Thus the paradoxical problem of the interpretation of *jihād* is precisely analogous to that of the *Gītā*: the external struggle may be a metaphor for the internal struggle, or vice versa, and the text, as Gandhi wisely realized, can mean whatever you want it to mean.

References

Buitenen, J. A. B. van. 1978. *The Mahābhārata. 4: The Book of Virāṭa. 5: The Book of the Effort.* Chicago.

Chakravarti, Prithwis Chandra. 1941. *The Art of War in Ancient India.* Dacca.

Dikshitar, V.R. Ramachandra. 1944. *War in Ancient India.* Madras.

Fitzgerald, James. 2004. *The Mahābhārata. 11: The Book of the Women. 12: The Book of Peace,* Part 1. Chicago.

Hultzsch, Eugen. 1925. *Inscriptions of Aśoka.* Corpus Inscriptionum Indicarum 1. 2nd edn. Calcutta.

Ingalls, Daniel H.H. 1965. *An Anthology of Sanskrit Court Poetry: Vidyākara's "Subhāṣitaratnakoṣa."* Harvard Oriental Series 44. Cambridge, MA.

Kangle, R.P. 1960–65. *The Kauṭilīya Arthaśāstra.* 3 vols. University of Bombay Studies: Sanskrit, Prakrit, and Pāli 1–3. Bombay.

Kielhorn, F. 1892. "Inscriptions from Khajuraho." *Epigraphia Indica* 1: 121–53.

Lang, Karen. 2003. *Four Illusions: Candrakīrti's Advice for Travelers on the Bodhisattva Path.* Oxford.

Melko, Matthew, and Richard D. Weigel. 1981. *Peace in the Ancient World.* Jefferson.

Minor, Robert N. (ed.). 1986. *Modern Indian Interpreters of the* Bhagavadgītā. SUNY Series in Religious Studies. Albany.

Salomon, Richard. 1987. "An Ancient Indian Diplomatic Dispute." *Brahmavidyā: The Adyar Library Bulletin* 51: 71–9.

——. 1998. *Indian Epigraphy: A Guide to the Study of Inscriptions in Sanskrit, Prakrit, and the Other Indo-Aryan Languages.* South Asia Research. New York.

Singh, Sarva Daman. 1965. *Ancient Indian Warfare with Special Reference to the Vedic Period.* Leiden.

Tähtinen, Unto. 1976. *Ahiṃsā: Non-Violence in Indian Tradition.* London.

4

Water under the Straw: Peace in Mesopotamia[1]

Benjamin R. Foster

Situation, conflict, and resolution are key elements in the narrative self-presentation of many human beings, past and present, perhaps under the assumption that their audiences generally find conflict more interesting, both narratively and expressively, than peace and harmony. Thus in ancient Mesopotamia, some of the earliest representational art showed warlike activity, such as bashing bound prisoners over the head, and some of the earliest narratives focused on conflict and its outcome. The usual iconography of peace was not universal happy conditions, but submission of the enemy, and the narrative equivalent was triumph and victory. Their stories turned on conflict, as do ours, and their lions did not lie down with lambs but ate them. Does this mean, based on a quick survey of written and cultural remains, that the Mesopotamians, or certain of them, such as the Assyrians, were an especially warlike people? Shall we assume that they saw conflict as the normal state of being in human society, history, and the world around them? If we excavated a New England town center, we would find monuments to wars – should we foreground these and say that New Englanders were a warlike people? Most residents of that New England town would probably have said, "Not so, we were attacked, responded, defeated our enemies, and this is to remember our fallen soldiers. If you want to understand us, go down the street to the town hall, the school, the churches, the public library, or out to the mall; these are places where our cultural values might better be apprehended." So I will start by bewaring war memorials, important as they may be.

My second caveat is the extraordinary richness of the tradition we can explore from ancient Mesopotamia. Our New England town might approach 300 years of age, and modern residents might consider the Civil War era quite foreign in its values to those of their own times. As much time, on the other hand, separates the earliest Mesopotamian references to peace from the latest as separates George Patton from Alexander the Great. King Hammurabi of Babylon was remoter in time from King Assurbanipal of

Assyria than William the Conqueror from Eisenhower. Thus my examples are drawn from a much wider range of space and time than might seem suitable to a European historian, who would not speak of King Alfred and Napoleon in the same informative sentence. I set forth my choices, however, in a kind of orderly progress, from the most straightforward to the most difficult.

This chapter considers peace in ancient Mesopotamia from four perspectives: first, peace as a formal agreed-upon state between individuals and social groups; second, peace within a single social group as a consequence of good leadership; third, peace within the realm of a person's own private life and actions, and finally, intellectual speculations about peace as an element in the world order.

As for peace as a formally agreed-upon state among individuals and social groups, obvious evidence for this is peace treaties, for which over 40 examples exist, from the later third millennium to the seventh century. We have treaties between small city states, for example, in the early second millennium, and between great national states of the outgoing second and first millennia. In the early second millennium, for example, Mesopotamia was part of a larger cultural continuum that bore some resemblance to the Arab countries of western Asia today. From Syria to the Gulf along the Euphrates, and up the Tigris to the foothills of Iran and Anatolia we find peoples who shared a common language, religion, and cultural background, as well as a common myth of origins and an agreed-upon set of diplomatic principles (Lafont 2001). We call them the Amorites and see them historically as newcomers to Mesopotamia, absorbing and transforming the 1000-year-old pre-existing culture there. The states the Amorites built up tended to be in tiers of first to third-rate powers, the essence of strategy being to line up as many of these on your side as possible, through alliance, conquest, marriage, whatever was required. One king tells us he defeated 26 kings in less than six months, so there were many intrigues afoot, and the archives of Mari know of 160 different kings within their horizon over a period of 30 years (Lafont 2001: 214). Treaties from this period give us specifics of peace. One, what we would call a "trade agreement," deals with customs dues, ransom and release of people, and protection of personal property of merchants, all this, no doubt, with a view to profit for both sides, although the motivation was not expressed (Eidem 1991). Orderly conduct of business is a kind of peace and worth a treaty. Another treaty defines peace in terms of a subservient relationship of one ruler to another, what we would call a vassal treaty, from an example of which I quote a few lines:

> By the sun in heaven, Atamrum son of Warad-Sin, king of the land of Andariq, has sworn, "From this day forth, so long as I live, I will commit no misdeed against Zimri-Lim, son of Yahdun-Lim, king of Mari and the land of the Hanaeans, nor against his city, his army, nor his land... I swear that I have written herewith no lie nor falsehood and that what I have written I have done so without reserve. I swear that I will follow closely and act wholeheartedly in the best interests of Zimri-Lim, son of Yahdun-Lim, king of Mari and the land of the Hanaeans" (Joannès 1991).

Here peace is defined as cooperation with one's overlord.

The title of my chapter, water under the straw, was drawn from an oracle, or speech of a god, pronounced by someone in an ecstatic state to this same Zimri-Lim, warning him that his prospective peace partner, Ibalpiel II of Eshnunna, was not to be trusted. A flurry of letters and a fair draft of the proposed treaty between these two have come down to us, so we can, in effect, watch the peace process at work (Charpin 1991; see further Charpin 2003: 159–97). What strikes the reader is the detailed and vivid suspicions that underlie the exchange. I quote from the draft of the treaty sent from Eshnunna:

> I swear that if the king of Eshnunna my father and his great vassals should come to discuss before me the wording of any document concerning their military preparedness, I will communicate nothing about it or the discussion they held, for better or worse, to any king or dignitary whatsoever in this entire region, be he enemy or ally of Ibal-pi-El son of Dadusha, king of Eshnunna, nor let the same be told of it, nor shall I tell any of those who serve me of its secret content.

Zimri-Lim goes on to swear that he will not reveal any intelligence about the Eshnunnan army, "be it in the open country, on road or route, in a defile, wadi, or streambed, in quarters, at night, or on stand-down."

In the tangled political and military affairs of this period, "peace" was mutual assistance, support and intelligence, honesty and forthrightness, all qualities desirable in national leaders. Yet people did not always honor these commitments, despite the ghastly oaths summoned upon the heads of violators, backed up by solemn gestures, rituals, and resounding prose. A disgruntled sovereign describes one unreliable ally as follows:

> He makes peace with one king and swears an oath, then he makes peace with (another) king and swears an oath, then he repudiates the previous king he made peace with, and the (new) king he made peace with, his peace-making and repudiation [will change] in a few [months]! (Eidem 2001: no. 1).

One of the most famous treaties of the late second millennium (see in general Liverani 1990: 115–202) was drawn up between Ramesses, king of Egypt, and Hattushili, king of the Hittites, about 1280 (Edel 1997; see also Bell's chapter in this vol.). This was drafted in Akkadian, the international language of the time, then translated into Hittite and Egyptian, the wording altered somewhat for the benefit of the local audience. Thus the Egyptian preamble tells us that the Hittites begged for peace, whereas the Hittite version has the Egyptians making the first move. This preamble states the purpose and terms of the treaty:

> In order to establish great peace and great brotherhood between them forever... Behold, the will of the great king of the land of Egypt and the great king of the land of the Hittites: from eternity no god permits the waging of war between them, because of a treaty valid for eternity... Ramesses, the great king, king of the land of Egypt, has entered into a treaty, written on a silver tablet, with Hattushili, the great king, king of the land of the Hittites, his brother, for all time, to establish good peace and brotherhood between us forever, for he is brother to me and I am brother to him and at peace with him forever. Behold, we make herewith our brotherhood and our peace, and this will be better than the brotherhood and peace which existed formerly of the land of Egypt with the land of the Hittites.

This last sentence refers diplomatically to a major war between Egypt and the Hittites. As for "brotherhood," this term referred to kings of equal status; lesser kings were called "sons" (Liverani 1990: 197–202). Although the gods of both sides sanction the peace, they do so as witnesses to a contract, not explicitly because peace was a good thing in and of itself. The rhetoric to the effect that peace was the normal state between these two great powers referred only to a prior treaty between them, but was standard in Late Bronze Age diplomacy (see in general Cohen and Westbrook 2000).

An ideology of righteous war as a consequence of broken peace developed particularly in Assyria at the end of the second millennium and was proclaimed thereafter in the commemorative inscriptions of the Assyrian kings. An Assyrian royal epic of the thirteenth century portrays in fulsome language the Assyrian king's righteous indignation that his Babylonian counterpart would break a sworn treaty (Foster 2005: 298–317). In a prayer to Shamash, the sun-god, the patron deity of treaties, he says:

> O Shamash, great lord, I respected your oath, I feared your greatness,
> He who does not do so has transgressed before you, but I observed your ordinance.
> When our fathers made a pact before your divinity,
> They swore an oath between them and invoked your greatness.
> You are the hero, the valiant one, who from of old was incorruptible judge of our fathers,
> And you are the god who rights wrongs, who sees now our loyalty.
> Why has the king of the Kassites from of old invalidated your plan and your ordinance?
> He had no fear of your oath, he transgressed your command, he schemed an act of malice.
> He made his crimes enormous before you, judge me, O Shamash!
> By your great command bestow victory on the observer of oaths,
> He who does not acknowledge your command, obliterate his people in the rout of battle!

The Babylonian king is understandably consumed by guilt:

> He was appalled on account of the appeal to Shamash and became fearful and anxious about what was laid before the gods,
> The mighty king's utterance constricted his body like a demonic presence.
> So Kashtiliash deliberated with himself, "I did not listen to what the Assyrian said, I did not take the messenger seriously.
> I did not conciliate him, I did not accept his favorable intention before.
> Now I understand how grievous the crimes of my land are become, how numerous its sins.
> Mortal punishments have smitten me down, death has me in its grip!
> The oath of Shamash hounds me, it catches me by the fringe of my garment.
> You have entered in evidence against me an unalterable tablet with the seal impression of my forefathers,
> They too have introduced evidence before me, a treaty whose wording cannot be changed.

In this instance, battle became a trial in which the condemned liar, Kashtiliash, was defeated by the plaintiff, the Assyrian king. The last preserved episode deals with looting of cultural property: the Assyrians collected Babylonian manuscripts and archives and brought them back to Assyria. Theft of the statues of gods, for example, and

Appropriation of Visigothic church, later transfusion of Muslim culture to crusading christians (El Cid)

Like the Cordoban Caliphate (10th century) Iberia

reorganization of the pantheon to account for it, was known in Assyrian military practice; so in effect peace could be a matter of appropriating your opponent's identity so
that he and his land simply ceased to be (example in Mayer 1983: 103; Foster 2005:
808–09; see in general Cogan 1974: 22–41; Mayer 1995: 478–82). Defeated people
were incorporated into the Assyrian administrative and ideological network. Peace
meant only inclusion within Assyria, rather than Assyrian tolerance of some other
state. The Mesopotamians expressed this as "causing to hear as one" or "speaking
with one mouth."

This leads to the second category of peace, peace as an internal state within a unified group, as opposed to a formally agreed-upon state between two groups. The
Assyrian version of peace which I just mentioned was rather like this, as it meant that
one formerly independent party to a contract was then included within Assyria. The
opposite state to peace would therefore be described as rebellion, unrest, insubordin-
ation, terms for which the Mesopotamians had a rich vocabulary. Hammurabi, for
example, gives a vision of such a peace, using an age-old comparison of his human
subjects browsing contentedly like sheep and cattle near the city: "I caused the people
of this land to lie down in safe pastures nor did I allow anyone to affright them" (Roth
1997: 133). The inner logic of the comparison is intriguing: the subjects were happy
and safe, but outside the walls of his palace. Hammurabi referred to himself in his
own inscriptions as a shepherd. This means that he was entrusted with his subjects by
their owners, the gods, to protect, nurture, and guide them, and at the same time to
make a legitimate profit from them – this is how shepherds made their living (Kraus
1974; Charpin 1996). Peace and prosperity were signs that the gods approved of how
the king was carrying out his contract. Hence, peace in the land was the sign of a
responsible and effective king.

Han dynasty "mandate of Heaven" similar to this

The Mesopotamians did not expect freedom or democracy from their rulers, but
they did expect justice (Charpin 1996). Justice was not only morally correct, it was a
paternal duty. Furthermore, like any good householder, the king should rule under
conditions of prosperity. Some kings went to the trouble of proclaiming the ideal market conditions of their reigns, both in general terms and even with lists of commodity
prices, wonderfully, even fantastically low (Foster 1995). One king proclaims:

> As if for sheep, I sought out forage and fed the people in green pastures. I lifted the
> heavy yoke from their necks. I settled them in secure abodes. . . I made the land content.
> I reduced to one tenth the grain tax that formerly was one fifth. I made the ordinary
> citizen perform labor service only four days a month. The cattle of the palace which used
> to graze in certain fields, and which were a source of complaint, I removed those cattle
> from the plowed land. I made anomalous the person with a complaint.

Another king of the eighteenth century, Sin-kashid of Uruk, boasted that three large
measures of barley cost only one shekel of silver in his reign.

A thousand years later, the Assyrian king Assurbanipal wished at his coronation that
30 large measures of grain would be bought during the rest of his reign for one shekel of
silver. The coronation prayer concluded, "May the great listen when the lesser speak,
may the lesser listen when the great speak, may harmony and peace be established

in Assur" (Foster 2005: 815–16). We may accept this as a rare Assyrian definition of domestic peace.

There is nothing unusual in the correlation of prosperity with peace. The old Puritan hymn sums it up pungently, "Peace, prosperity, and health; private bliss and public wealth." The Mesopotamians, like the hymnist, would probably see some superior agency behind prosperity; at least, rulers took credit for such conditions. The Sumerians, however, the people who lived in southern Babylonia before the Babylonians, during the third millennium, saw things differently. As I will argue below, they thought that peace and harmony were a natural and original condition of the human race, rather than the result of human management. The gods did not give peace as a reward for good behavior but had provided it to human society when the divinely ordered world was set up. Peace, in this view, was a reversion to the way society was supposed to be, rather than a remarkable individual human achievement. One may illustrate this in practice with a passage from an inscription by a Sumerian ruler, Gudea of Lagash, who tells us that when he was going to build a new house for the city god, he sought to do so in conditions of perfect social harmony:

> The ruler issued orders to his city as if to a single person, making the land of Lagash of one accord as the children of one mother. They took tools in hand, pulled up thorn bushes, raked the thorn bushes into piles. Gudea barred argument and sent crime packing. He untied the lash of whip and goad and put wool in the overseers' hands. No mother would scold her child and no child would disobey its mother. No master would hit his servant on the head when he bungled, and no mistress would slap a serving girl's face who had done the wrong thing (Edzard 1997: 76–77).

Perfect harmony achieved, Gudea was then ready to proceed.

Our third consideration, peace and reconciliation between individuals, is attested in a late second and first millennium corpus of magic rituals and spells intended for peace and harmony (Foster 2005: 1005). Some were general in purpose, so that when you met people in positions of responsibility they would be pleased to see you and would feel satisfied with you. One of these spells, for example, was to be said when you put on your shoes in the morning, so that everyone you met that day would be favorably disposed to you. Another group of spells was aimed specifically at reconciling a person who was angry with you. These were to be said as part of a rather complicated and somewhat distasteful procedure. The magic words go as follows: "I have escaped the spittle of your mouth, I have given the word of your father, the word of your mother, the word of your sister, as if it were the word of a traveling mountebank, or of a city whore, to the covering earth, which makes no effort to speak, which does not wag its tongue." This means that anything the angry man or his close relations may want to say against you will have no effect. The ritual was as follows (Ebeling 1931: 16):

> You take spittle of the man who is angry with you, you say this spell over it three times, then you bury it in earth. Next, on the same day, you take juniper, sulphur, and alkali and pound them and drop them into water. You recite the spell 'O alkali, O alkali' over it, then you pour water over the spittle, you take up oil in a wooden container and you put the paste (you have just made) in it. You say the spell and rub yourself over your whole

body with the paste. The man who was angry with you will be reconciled with you and your words will please him.

Spells of this type were gathered into a collection called "When you enter a public building." One of these guaranteed that "king, dignitary, prince, palace staff, courtier, or anyone among the palace personnel will be reconciled with the subject." This sort of magic activity would require a specialist, who presumably had to be paid, as most people did not know the words of the spell beginning "O alkali" or how to make the magic paste.

The notion of individual reconciliation had an important place in religious discourse as well. Misfortune was a sign that some god was angry with you, so it was important to find out who and why, and to do something about it. Hymns and prayers were therefore full of the language of reconciliation and appeals to restore a sufferer to the god's good graces (Foster 2005: 722):

> O my god, clear, forego, dispel your ire,
> Disregard my iniquities, accept my entreaties,
> Transmute my sins into good deeds.
> Your hand is harsh, I have seen your punishment,
> Let anyone who does not revere his god and goddess learn from my example.
> O my god, be reconciled, O my goddess, relent!
> Turn hither your faces to the entreaty of my prayer,
> May your angry hearts be calmed,
> May your feelings be soothed, permit me reconciliation.

I believe an interesting letter from the early second millennium makes oblique reference to wooing an estranged deity with choice foods (Kraus 1964: 80). A man writes to an associate as follows:

> You know very well that last year I divided everything equally with you, but this year so far you haven't sent me a thing. Apil-ilishu the comptroller has laid an obligation on me, so send me garlic, onions, fresh water fish, and doves, so I can reconcile the one who is angry. Pack up and send me what is needed for my obligation. This year may you feel the desire to do the right thing!

I assume that this refers to materials needed for some religious ritual to assuage the anger of a god.

To begin the fourth consideration, peace as an element in the cosmos, one may begin with anti-war sentiment, and first with an argument from silence. Assyrian kings routinely made military exploits part of their commemorative discourse, whereas the later Babylonian kings, just as routinely, did not. Nebuchadnezzar II, for example, was well known as a warrior king, but his formal inscriptions confined themselves to pious utterances. No one has explained this Babylonian reluctance to mention what Assyrian kings boasted of, but I should add that we have Babylonian chronicles (Glassner 1993) and heroic poetry (Grayson 1975) that make abundant mention of warfare, so this reticence seems to be restricted to commemorative prose.

Although oracles and prophecies frequently urge Mesopotamian kings to take care of themselves and not to embark on foolish adventures, overt anti-war sentiment is rare. Perhaps the best known example comes from a first-millennium text that was composed as if it had been written by an ancient king of long ago and inscribed on a stone monument. This king, named Naram-Sin, explains that previous kings had not left such monuments; so he is going to do so, in the hope that future kings will not have to experience the terrible defeats and blood-lettings he had to go through (Westenholz 1997: 300–31; Foster 2005: 344–56). He addresses future rulers with good advice:

> Behold this stela: You should not be confounded, you should not be bewildered,
> You should not be afraid, you should not tremble,
> Your stance should be firm.
> You should do your task in your wife's embrace.
> Make your walls trustworthy,
> Fill your moats with water.
> Bring into your well-fortified city your treasure boxes, your grain, your silver, your
>   goods and chattels.
> Gird on your weapons but stay out of sight,
> Restrain your valor, take care of your person.
> Though he raids your land, go not out against him,
> Though he drives off your livestock, go not nigh him,
> Though he eats the flesh of your soldiery, though he murder your citizens,
> Be moderate, control yourself, answer them "Yes, my lord!"
> To their wickedness, repay kindness,
> To kindness add gifts and gratification,
> You should not trespass against them.

Although this sounds a little like the 1960s chant "make love, not war," it really speaks for a strong defensive posture, and the king's task in his wife's embrace was to produce an heir to the throne, for the stability of the realm.

The most spectacular Mesopotamian denunciation of violence and warfare is found in a long and dramatic poem, dating perhaps early in the first millennium, called the *Epic* (or *Poem*) *of Erra* (Foster 2005: 880–911). The author of this poem had undoubtedly experienced civil strife and its aftermath. He was deeply troubled about how such disasters could occur in a world supposedly directed by the gods in their own self-interest. Now their temples and cities had been destroyed, their subjects, good and evil alike, killed, maimed, and dispersed. His narrative suggests that violence was latent in the universe and that there was indeed a god, Erra, whose dominion was random violence and destruction. This god could become bored and restless if no constructive outlet was found for his energies. Once he broke out of his confines, nothing was safe – whatever the original objective may have been, it fell lost in a welter of destruction and killing. I quote from the bragadocio of Erra, god of indiscriminate violence:

> Why sit at home like a helpless child?
> Shall we eat woman food, like non-combatants?
> Have we turned timorous and trembling, as if we can't fight?
> Going to the field for the young and vigorous is like to a very feast,
>   but even the nobleman who stays in the city can never eat enough.
> His people will hold him in low esteem, he will command no respect,
> How could he threaten a campaigner?

However well developed is the strength of the city dweller,
How could he possibly best a campaigner?
However toothsome city bread, it holds nothing to the campfire loaf.
However sweet fine beer, it holds nothing to water from a skin,
The terraced palace holds nothing to the wayside sleeping spot!
Let the great gods hear and extol your name,
Let the lesser gods hear and flinch at the mention of you,
Let all the gods hear and bend for your yoke,
Let sovereigns hear and fall prostrate before you,
Let countries hear and bring you their tribute,
Let the lowly hear and perish of their own accord,
Let the mighty hear and his strength diminish,
Let lofty mountains hear and their peaks crumble,
Let the surging sea hear and convulse, wiping out her creatures,
Let the stalk be yanked from the tough thicket,
Let the reeds of the impenetrable morass be shorn off,
Let men turn cowards and their clamor subside,
Let beasts tremble and return to clay!

He goes on and on for hundreds of lines:

I am the smiter of wild beasts, battering ram against the mountain,
I am the conflagration in the reed thicket, the broad blade against the rushes,
I am the banner for the march, I blast like the wind, I thunder like the storm,
Like the sun, I scan the circumference of the world.
I am the wild ram striding forth in the steppe,
I invade the range and take up my dwelling in the fold.
All the gods are afraid of a fight!

He describes with relish the destruction of war:

He who did not die in the battle will die in the epidemic,
He who did not die in the epidemic, the enemy will plunder him,
He whom the enemy has not plundered, the bandit will murder him, the king's weapon
    will vanquish him.
He whom the king's weapon did not vanquish, the prince will slay him,
He whom the prince did not slay, a thunderstorm will wash him away,
He whom the thunderstorm did not wash away, the sun will parch him...
   * * *
The man in charge of the city says to his mother: "If only I had stuck in the womb
    the day you bore me,
If only our lives had come to an end,
If only we had died together"...
He who begot a son, saying, "This is my son,
When I have reared him he will requite my pains,"
I will put that son to death, his father must bury him,
Afterwards I will put that father to death, but he will have none to bury him.
He who built a house saying, "This is my home, I built it for myself, I shall spend my
    leisure time in it,
On the day fate claims me, I shall fall asleep in it,"
I will put him to death and wreck his home, afterwards, though it be wreckage, I will
    give it to another.

Finally, in his madness, the god of random violence goes on to scream:

> I will make hell shake and heaven tremble,
> I will make the planets shed their splendor,
> I will wrench out the stars from the sky,
> I will hack the tree's roots so its branches cannot burgeon,
> I will wreck the wall's foundation so its top crumbles.

Then, of course, the mourner is left to mourn. The chief of the gods, Marduk, mourns the ruin of his own city:

> Alas for Babylon, whose crown I fashioned luxuriant as a palm's, but which the wind has scorched!
> Alas for Babylon, that I had laden with seed, like an evergreen, but of whose delights I could not have what I had hoped for!
> Alas for Babylon, that I tended like a thriving orchard, but whose fruit I could not taste!
> Alas for Babylon, that I suspended like a gemstone seal on the neck of the sky.

This poem is perhaps the most powerful denunciation of war to come down to us from the ancient world.

Another Babylonian poem, about a 1000 years older than the above, dwells at length on the stupidity of fighting. In this narrative, Enki, the god of intelligence, became so annoyed with Ishtar, the goddess of battle, that he created a hideous monster named "Discord" to challenge her and so leave the other gods in peace (Foster 2005: 96–106). The middle of the poem is lost, but towards the end, Ishtar asks Enki what he meant by creating such a monster and demands that he get rid of it. He replies that as soon as she, Ishtar, stops acting the way she has been, the monster will of course disappear, he merely created it to show her what she looked like. To create a remembrance, he ordains a festival every year that involves a mock battle or war dance, so people will keep in mind what battle looks like. This too is a remarkable tractate against the gory glory of battle.

A second Babylonian poem of that same period suggests that the gods created the human race with a divine element of rebelliousness or conflict in its nature (Foster 2005: 227–80). Once upon a time, it says, the lesser gods were enslaved by the greater gods but rebelled, worn out by the hard work. The gods decided to create the human race to do their work for them. To do so, they killed the ringleader of the revolt and mixed his blood with clay to make the first human being. The throb of the human pulse reminds us of this dead god, who had the inspiration for the revolt that led to the creation of the human race. By this teaching, opposition to injustice and oppression was the god-like element in human nature.

We may conclude by going further back in time and considering some Sumerian views of war and peace. These wrestled with the same question that the later *Epic of Erra* did: what place does violence have in the cosmos? Do the gods plan it and why, since it tends to set back all the civilized accomplishments of the human race? Three short examples may be cited here that touch on this question.

The first is a witty and elegant Sumerian epic called *Enmerkar and the Lord of Aratta* (Jacobsen 1987: 275–319; Vanstiphout 2003: 49–96). Enmerkar was a king of Uruk who needed foreign goods to build a temple for his goddess, Inanna, the Sumerian counterpart to Ishtar, goddess of war. He could think of no way to get these goods save by demanding them as tribute from the far-off city of Aratta. When this was refused, he sent out an army to take them by force. Just at the point the armies of Uruk were about to triumph over Aratta, which was starving for lack of rain, the same goddess Inanna, who was goddess of both Uruk and Aratta, arranged for rain to fall there so the city was revived and did not have to submit to Uruk. At this point in the story, an unnamed woman speaks up. She suggests that, after all, war is a stupid way to go about getting things you need, why not exchange goods on a mutually profitable basis? And so, the poet tells us, international trade was born.

The delicate satire of this poem strongly suggests that war is a consequence of male ego, as the two kings jousted for the favors of the same goddess in trials of strength and cunning. It takes a clever woman to resolve the dilemma of the plot. But this is not all there is to this poem, by any means. Embedded within it is a further reflection on the origins of conflict, which in fact it blames on the god of intelligence, Enki. The poet portrays an idyllic stage of history when there was no conflict:

> In those days, there were no snakes, no scorpions,
> No hyenas, no lions, no dogs, no wolves,
> Neither fear nor terror: Humanity had no enemy!

What then, did the god of intelligence do but make man his own worst enemy: he broke the human race up into different peoples, speaking different languages, to dilute the authority of the god who had executive control of human beings, purely out of jealousy for his power over so many servants (Klein 2000).

This fascinating doctrine can explain conflicts between peoples, as I illustrated above, in connection with peace treaties. But in a world created by intelligence, how can we explain conflict within a single people, a single family, a single couple? Here too a large body of Mesopotamian tradition offers answers. I choose first another Sumerian poem. This one, which we call *Enki and the World Order* (Bottéro and Kramer 1989: 165–88), suggests that Enki, the god of intelligence, arranged and ordered the whole world so it operated perfectly. Everything was beautiful, lush, and running smoothly, so peace and harmony were the natural state of a well-ordered universe, as suggested above. All the gods had their roles and all was proceeding well. But there was one who did not have prerogatives, Ishtar, or, as the Sumerians called her, Inanna, goddess of love, sex, and war. She went to Enki and harangued him bitterly, complaining that her sisters had been given pretty things, but she had been given nothing. She says:

> My sister, the birth goddess, was given the birth stool and the midwife's tools, and is midwife even to kings,
> My sister, the goddess of healing, is grandfather's favorite;
> My sister, the goddess of crafts, has been given gold and silver implements,
> My sister, the goddess of the literate arts, has been given a beautiful surveyor's measure,
> My sister, the goddess of fishing, has been given wonderful seafood,

But what about me, what did you do for me?

Enki's answer to Ishtar is oblique and difficult, but he says:

> I gave you the coat of mail,
> I gave you the young warrior's boast,
> I gave you the encouraging word in battle,
> Although you are no raven, I gave you the croak of doom.
> You are to twist the straight thread, you are to straighten the twisted thread.
> You pile up boasts like burial mounds, you sow words that grow up rank.
> You destroy what cannot be destroyed, you set up what cannot be set up.
> You take the cover off the drum for laments, you put the cover on the drum for happy
>   songs.
> Your eye never wearies of your admirers.

Ishtar, as we may call her, is the beautiful face with the hard cruel eyes, exhausting seven and seven young men at once in what Casanova called "the sweet combat" (see Foster 2005: 678). Her dominion was opposites and contrasts, to bring misery where there was happiness, to suborn the rational order with temptation and irresistible allure that brought catastrophe. Otherwise, perhaps, human beings would be smiling and efficient automatons, just as Enki first created them and Gudea brought about when his temple was ready for building.

[margin handwriting: Contrast in Norse goddess "Hel"]

A Babylonian poem (Groneberg 1997: 1–54; Foster 2005: 281–85) tries in its own way to explain Ishtar's role as provoker of violence and conflict. It starts by praising Ishtar as goddess of the bedroom, and says of the neophyte lover:

> He's on the way, that one who had no experience of your power,
> Your footsteps will guide (him) to the end of time.
> The inexpert man will learn from this,
> He will seek out your door ere you have laid your hand on him,
> Your doings are strange, your ways unfathomable,
> Your handiwork is spectacular, what god would not be like you?

In other words, our poet says, when men feel the need of Ishtar, and once they have fallen under her spell, they are transformed and, as the poem later explains, will never know contentment again.

> Leveling a home and plundering its bricks are yours, O Ishtar,
> Overturning the broad seat of emotion and contentment,
> Fickleness and rejection at night are yours, O Ishtar.
> Discord, disturbance, uncertainty, estrangement,
> Torch of strife and extinguishing conflict are yours, O Ishtar.
> Anger, fighting, smoulder then cooling,
> Cursing, holding the tongue are yours, O Ishtar.
> Falsification of truth (?), ... in the land, parlaying fair words,
> Doubling tasks and dispersing stores are yours, O Ishtar.
> Vigor, entreaty, good fortune, and divine protection,
> Wealth, abundance, and a bed on the ground are yours, O Ishtar.
> Blood relative, kinless, foreigner, underling,
> Stranger, to make them brethren, is yours, O Ishtar.

[Bestowing?] success on a house and the woman who dwells there,
Causing an angry breach wherever you will are yours, O Ishtar...
Raising loud battle cries, teeth chattering in fear,
Coiffing, toying with hair, are yours, O Ishtar.
Misogyny, taking goddess and harlot for lover,
Making engagements, providing gifts are yours, O Ishtar.
Opening the loins to the lover's urge,
Twin babies, founding a family, then watching (it grow) are yours, O Ishtar.

In a later passage, this composition goes on to describe role reversal in a slap-stick festival, where men act like women and the women burlesque the behavior of men, apparently by acting out all the things they hate most about them: sexual aggressiveness, rudeness, obsession with weaponry:

Role reversed, he looks quite different!
Yes to your mockery, shiver at that "Yes!" O Ishtar.
You make men observant to clothes and locks, O Ishtar.
The women are feeling over a splendid young man, they are bold with their hair.
A man carries a salad leaf in his hand,
A woman carries a quiver like a man, she's holding a bow,
A man carries a hairpin, a cosmetic shell, kindling wood, and a girl's harp,
Women carry throw sticks, slingshots, and slingstones.
A man holds their gear for them, he looks quite different!

So the Mesopotamians had no simple explanation for peace in the heart or in the world. They developed mechanisms for making peace, they prayed for peace and spoke well of it, but they spoke of conflict as inherent in an intelligent and complete creation. They could blame the origins of conflict in creation on the vanity of rulers or on the selfishness and caprice of a jealous male or female deity; they could ascribe the resolution of conflict to the superior intelligence of a woman or to male valor and leadership. They had a goddess of discord but none of harmony. Harmony and love were the more intensely experienced because their mistress presided over hatred and alienation as well. Mesopotamian literature described and denounced the effects of conflict using the vivid language of bitter experience, and with no promise of peace at the last. There was, in fact, no thought of future paradise or state of bliss in another life, so peace, if it was to be enjoyed, had to be sought in the here and now.

Note

1   This essay is adapted from a public lecture given at Brown University. All translations from Mesopotamian sources are my own and may in some cases show a different understanding from that in the source indicated – there is no comprehensive study of Mesopotamian treaties. For the third millennium, see for example Fronzaroli 2003: 43–76; for the second Hess in Durand 1986; Charpin 1991; Eidem 1991; Joannès 1991; Hallo and Younger 2000: 329–52; for the first Watanabe and Parpola 1988. The standard survey by McCarthy 1963 is now antiquated – all dates are BCE.

References

Bottéro, J., and S. Kramer. 1989. *Lorsque les dieux faisaient l'homme. Mythologie mésopotamienne.* Paris.

Charpin, D. 1991. "Un traité entre Zimri-Lim de Mari et Ibal-pi-El II d'Ešnunna." In Charpin and Joannès 1991: 139–66.

———. 1996. "'Le bon pasteur': idéologie et pratique de la justice royale à l'époque paléo-babylonienne." *Les Moyens d'expression du pouvoir dans les sociétés anciennes. Lettres Orientales* 5: 101–14.

———. 2003. *Hammu-rabi de Babylone.* Paris.

———, and F. Joannès (eds.). 1991. *Marchands, diplomates et empereurs. Études sur la civilisation mésopotamienne offertes à Paul Garelli.* Paris.

Cogan, M. 1974. *Imperialism and Religion: Assyria, Judah and Israel in the Eighth and Seventh Centuries BCE.* SBL Monographs 19. Missoula.

Cohen, R., and R. Westbrook. 2000. *Amarna Diplomacy: The Beginnings of International Relations.* Baltimore.

Durand, J. 1986. "Fragments rejoints pour une histoire élamite." In L. de Meyer (ed.), *Fragmenta Historiae Aelamicae. Mélanges offerts à M.-J. Stève,* 111–28. Paris.

Ebeling, E. 1931. *Aus dem Tagewerk eines assyrischen Zauberpriesters. Mitteilungen der Deutschen Orient-Gesellschaft* 5/3. Berlin.

Edel, E. 1997. *Der Vertrag zwischen Ramses II. von Ägypten und Hattušili III. von Hatti.* Wissenschaftliche Veröffentlichungen der Deutschen Orient-Gesellschaft 95. Mainz.

Edzard, D. 1997. *Gudea and His Dynasty. The Royal Inscriptions of Mesopotamia, Early Periods* 3/1. Toronto.

Eidem, J. 1991. "An Old Assyrian Treaty from Tell Leilan." In D. Charpin and F. Joannès (eds.), *Marchands, diplomates et empereurs. Études sur la civilisation mésopotamienne offertes à Paul Garelli,* 185–208. Paris.

———. 2001. *The Shemsharra Archives, The Letters.* Det Kongelige Danske Videnskabernes Selskab 23. Copenhagen.

Foster, B. 1995. "Social Reform in Ancient Mesopotamia." In K. Irani and M. Silver (eds.), *Social Justice in the Ancient World,* 165–77. Westport.

———. 2005. *Before the Muses, An Anthology of Akkadian Literature,* 227–80. 3rd edn. Bethesda.

Fronzaroli, P. 2003. *Testi di cancelleria: I rapporti con le città (Archivio L. 2769).* Archivi Reali di Ebla, Testi XIII. Rome.

Glassner, J.-J. 1993. *Chroniques mésopotamiennes.* Paris.

Grayson, A. 1975. *Babylonian Historical-Literary Texts.* Toronto.

Groneberg, B. 1997. *Lob der Ištar. Gebet und Ritual an die altbabylonische Venusgöttin.* Groningen.

Hallo, W., and K. Younger (eds.). 2000. *The Context of Scripture, Monumental Inscriptions from the Biblical World.* 3 vols. Leiden.

Jacobsen, T. 1987. *The Harps that Once . . . Sumerian Poetry in Translation.* New Haven, CT.

Joannès, F. 1991. "Le Traité de vassalité d'Atamrum d'Andarig envers Zimri-lim de Mari." In Charpin and Joannès 1991: 167–77.

Klein, J. 2000. "The so-called 'Spell of Nudimmud' (ELA 135–135): A Re-Examination." In Simonetta Graziani (ed.), *Studi sul Vicino Oriente Antico dedicati alla memoria di Luigi Cagni,* 563–84. Istituto Universitario Orientale, Dipartimento di Studi Asiatici, Series Minor 61. Naples.

Kraus, F. 1964. *Briefe aus dem Britischen Museum. Altbabylonische Briefe* 1. Leiden.

———. 1974. "Das altbabylonische Königtum." In P. Garelli (ed.), *Le palais et la royauté (archéologie et civilisation), xix* rencontre assyriologique internationale, 235–61. Paris.

Lafont, B. 2001. "Relations internationales, alliances et diplomatie au temps des rois de Mari." *Amurru* 2: 213–328.

Liverani, M. 1990. *Prestige and Interest: International Relations in the Near East ca. 1600–1100 BC.* Padua.

Mayer, W. 1983. "Sargons Feldzug gegen Urartu – 714 v. Chr. Text und Übersetzung." *Mitteilungen der Deutschen Orient-Gesellschaft* 115: 65–132. Berlin.

——. 1995. *Politik und Kriegskunst der Assyrer.* Münster.

McCarthy, D. 1963. *Treaty and Covenant: A Study in Form in the Ancient Oriental Documents and in the Old Testament.* 2nd edn. Analecta Biblica 21. Rome.

Parpola, S., and K. Watanabe. 1988. *Neo-Assyrian Treaties and Loyalty Oaths.* State Archives of Assyria 2. Helsinki.

Roth, M. 1997. *Law Collections from Mesopotamia and Asia Minor.* 2nd edn. Atlanta.

Vanstiphout, H. 2003. *Epics of Sumerian Kings: The Matter of Aratta.* Writings from the Ancient World 20. Atlanta.

Westenholz, J. 1997. *Legends of the Kings of Akkade.* Winona Lake.

5

Making, Preserving, and Breaking the Peace with the Hittite State

Richard H. Beal

For the Indo-European Hittites of second millennium BCE Anatolia (modern Turkey), peace could be considered literally a benefaction grantable by the gods. There was a Storm God of Peace who received offerings in the Festival of the Month (van Gessel 1998: 659, 778). A prayer of Great King Muwattalli II[1] asks, "[may] wealth, peace, well-being, growth, plenty and *tarawiya* come about in the land." In the same prayer he says, "May the gods look upon the land with peaceful eyes, and may they make wealth, *tarawiyan*, well-being and growth." Similar lists occur in two other places in this prayer (Singer 2002: 83–84). Other Hittite prayers with similar lists of requests to the gods do not include "peace." Interestingly the major event of this king's reign was his costly victory in perhaps the Hittites' greatest battle, that at Qids (wrongly known today as "Qadesh or Kadesh") against the Egyptian pharaoh Ramses II (see Bell's chapter in this volume). We do not know when in Muwattalli's reign the prayer was composed. Did he ask the gods for "peace" in the hopes (eventually to be dashed) of settling his dispute with Ramses by diplomacy or was he sick of the bloodshed he saw at Qids and so added "peace" to his list of requested divine benefactions?

The Hittite word for "peace" *takšul* is derived from the verb *takš-/takkešš* – "fit together, devise." Its opposite *kurur* "enmity" may be related (correctly or incorrectly) to the verb *kuer* – "to cut apart" (Puhvel 1997: 285f.). Perhaps that means that the original meaning of *takšul* was not the absence of war, but "togetherness" or "something put together." Alternatively, perhaps *takšul* was something one devised, or worked at.

Peace making was the king's business. "His Majesty, the Great King Zidanza (II), King of the Land of Hatti and [Pilliya] King of the Land of Kizzuwatna made peace and devised [a treaty between themselves]" (Otten 1951: 129 obv. 1–3). In foreign areas where there was little beyond the most local forms of government groups of individuals could come and make peace with the Hittite king. A letter from the king to General Kaššu, resident in the city of Tapigga in the march facing the land of the barbarian Kaška, reads: "This is what you wrote to me: 'At this very moment large numbers of Kaškaeans are coming for peacemaking. How will you, Your Majesty, write to me?' Keep sending before My Majesty the Kaškaeans who are coming for peace" (Hoffner 2003b: 48.17–22). Perhaps not all peacemaking was done at such a high level since the same royal letter to Kaššu records, "I got your message that you wrote me concerning the matter of Pihapzuppi and Kaškanu: 'They have already made peace (with us)' " (ibid. 14–16). A treaty with the elders of several border localities stipulates, "[If] the population of some city [of] the enemy comes for peace, do [not slander] Hatti before them" (Beckman 1999: 165).

Sometimes it was fear of Hittite armies that inspired the making of peace. "My father (Šuppiluliuma I) sent Hannutti, the Chief of the Chariot Fighters, to the Lower Land and gave him [troops] and chariotry. When Hannutti arrived [in the Lower Land] and when the people of Lalanda [saw] him, they became afraid and made peace, [and they again became a possession of the Land of Hatti]" (Houwink ten Cate 1966: 28). King Muršili II reminds Manapa-Tarhunta, king of Šeha River Land: "Because you [sided with Uhha-ziti (of Arzawa),] whom the oath gods seized [and I destroyed], I [would] have destroyed you too. [But your mother] fell [down] at [my feet] and [you dispatched] old men [and old women] to me. And your messengers [fell] down at [my] feet. You sent [to me] as follows: 'Spare me, my lord. [May my lord not] destroy [me]. Take me as your subject and [save] my person ...' Then I, My Majesty, had compassion for you and made peace with you ... I will take you as my servant" (Beckman 1999: 83).

However, peace gave opportunities for commerce: "Because all of the Kaškaean land was at peace, some of the Hittites had inns behind Kaškaean towns and some had again gone into towns" (Hoffner 2003a: 189). However, the Kaškaeans, even those who had made peace, were not trusted. "Furthermore, if a friendly comes in to Hatti, let him trade in whatever city the Governor of the Rural Province assigns him, let him not trade in another city on his own authority" (von Schuler 1965: 122.87). Hittite merchants from the port of Ura (mod. Gilindere?) were making so much money trading with the subordinate state of Ugarit and investing it in real estate in Ugarit that the protectionist instincts (for real estate) of the king of Ugarit were powerfully aroused. In response to his complaints his overlord Hattušili III banned the Urans from buying land in Ugarit or from staying there during the winter hiatus in sea-trade (Beckman 1999: 177). The decision was pretty much a win-win situation for Hattušili. The king of Ugarit was happy – lower real estate prices and no more danger (real or imagined) of being king of a city that was owned mostly by foreigners; the Urans' lucrative trade was unaffected; and their money would presumably now be invested at home in Hatti.

War brought the opposite: the cutting of trade. The subordinate king of the Syrian coastal state of Amurru is told by his Hittite overlord: "As the King of Assyria is (now) at war with My Majesty, let him also be at war with you. Your merchants shall not go into the land of Assyria. Do not let his merchants into your land. Don't let them pass through your land. If one comes into your land, seize him and send him to My Majesty" (Beckman 1999: 106).

Hittite kings made no claims to being gods or even universal kings. They saw them-selves simply as appointed by the gods of Hatti to rule Hatti. Thus they had no problem recognizing other important friendly kings as their "brothers" or friendly minor kings as "sons." When hostile Great Kings decided to make peace, it was necessary to draw up a formal treaty of "brotherhood." To this purpose one king would send an embassy with a message to the other. If the response was positive, the other would send back the first king's embassy accompanied by his own messenger. Eventually after more exchanges the text of a treaty would be hammered out. The Hittite gods were asked whether, if the treaty were to be concluded, this would end Hittite worries. If the answer was positive each side would send an official, sealed copy to the other (Klengel 2002). The word for treaty is *išhiul*, which is derived from the verb "to bind." Thus a "treaty" is a binding/sworn set of obligations concerning a foreign power. The same word, *išhiul* is used for what we would call "instructions" that is, a binding/sworn set of obligations concerning individual Hittites.[2]

In treaties between great powers complete equality of partners would be expected. The one preserved, between the Hittite king Hattušili III and the Egyptian pharaoh Ramses II,[3] was designed to establish

> good brotherhood and good peace between us and in order to establish good peace and good brotherhood in [the relations] of Egypt with Hatti forever ... The sons of Ramses, Beloved of Amon, <Great King>, King of Egypt, will be at peace and brothers with the sons of Hattušili, Great King, King of Hatti, forever. And they will remain as in our relationship of brotherhood [and of] peace, so that Egypt will be at peace with Hatti and they will be brothers like us forever. And Ramses, Beloved of Amon, Great King, King of Egypt, for all time shall not open hostilities against Hatti in order to take anything from it. And Hattušili, Great King, King of Hatti, for all time shall not open hostilities against Egypt in order to take [anything] from it.

If an enemy attacks Hatti or there is a revolt in Hatti, if Hattušili asks for help, Ramses is obliged to send his infantry and chariotry. In exact parity, if an enemy attacks Egypt or there is a revolt in Egypt, if Ramses asks for help, Hattušili is obliged to send his infantry and chariotry. If anyone flees from Hatti to Egypt they are to be returned but not punished, and similarly if anyone flees from Egypt to Hatti, or to Hatti's subordinate state of Amurru, they are to be returned but not pun-ished. Interestingly the only clause that is not reciprocal is one stipulating that should Hattušili's son be ousted from the kingship Ramses is obliged to send his army to aid or avenge him. No such clause involves Ramses' son. Hattušili, a usurping uncle, cer-tainly had legitimate grounds to worry about this possibility, but apparently Ramses, himself the legitimate heir, had no such worries (Klengel 2002: 88–89). Alternatively, perhaps Egyptian insularity could not contemplate large numbers of foreigners on Egyptian soil.

When a small state sought the embrace of the Hittite Great King, either semi-voluntarily (to escape a worse fate either at Hittite hands or at the hands of a nastier neighbor) or as a result of Hittite conquest, the smaller state was in no position to negotiate and the terms were dictated by the Great King. To avoid any misunderstand-ings between the subordinate state and Hatti, or between the subordinate state and

its neighboring subordinate states, the borders of the subordinate state were set out.
Some clauses were one-sided: if anyone fled from Hatti to the subordinate, he had to
be returned, but if a gentleman fled from the subordinate to Hatti, "I (My Majesty)
will not give him back to you. It is not permitted to give back a fugitive from Hatti"
(Beckman 1999: 91 §15). The subordinate king is further required to report/check
out any rumors he hears about the Great King, but the Great King is under no obligation to report rumors he hears to the subordinate. Furthermore subordinate kings
were required to visit the Great King once a year. There are many clauses basically
saying that the subordinate is to send his army to help his overlord against all external
or internal enemies, even if no messenger has made it to him to ask for help. There are
no reciprocal clauses for each of these many variations on the theme. But mutuality
is not entirely lacking. The western Anatolian subordinate kings are all ordered to
get along with one another, and should any of them attack his neighboring subordinate land, the king of Hatti promises to come to the aid of the attacked. Anyone
who revolts against the subordinate king and flees to Hatti is to be considered an
enemy of the Great King. The subordinate king may summon military help from his
overlord, and while the subordinate must provision these troops while they are in
his territory, they may not do harm against or seek territory from the subordinate
king: "They shall walk like brothers before him" (Beckman 1999: 38–39, 56, 61,
66, 72, 88, 91, etc.). The treaties also require the subordinate king and his descendants to support not just their current overlord, but also the overlord's designated
heir, and his heir's heir. In return, the Hittite king and his descendants undertake
to support the subordinate king, his designated heir and his heir's heir (assuming of
course that the subordinate kings keep the other provisions of the treaty). The treaties
are often further fortified with examples from the history of the subordinate king's
loyal predecessors to whom the Hittite king had been loyal in return and/or disloyal
ancestors who had met a bad end at the hands of their overlord. Although the treaties are supposed to be binding for all the future, in practice it seems that it was felt
prudent to renew them with each change of ruler (for many examples, see Beckman
1999).

Subordinate kings were expected to follow the Great King's lead in matters of peace
and war:

> If the King of Egypt is at peace with My Majesty (Tudhaliya IV), he shall also be at peace
> with you (Šaušgamuwa of Amurru). If he is at war with My Majesty, he shall also be at
> war with you. If the King of Babylonia is at peace with My Majesty, he shall also be at
> peace with you. If he is hostile to My Majesty, he shall also be hostile to you. As the King
> of Assyria is (now) at war with My Majesty, let him also be at war with you (Beckman
> 1999: 106).

Curiously, few of the treaties mention a requirement that the subordinate state pay
tribute. Requirements to pay tribute are preserved in treaties with the Syrian states of
Nuhašše, Amurru, Ugarit and in a letter concerning Niya (van den Hout 1998: 223;
Beckman 1999: 37, 55, 60). The treaty Šuppiluliuma made with Niqmad II of Ugarit
at about the same time has a separate treaty detailing Ugarit's yearly tribute, payable

to the Great King, Queen, crown prince and five other enumerated officials but no one else (Beckman 1999: 166–68). The renewal of the treaty by these rulers' sons, Muršili II and Niqmepa, preserves the details but reduces the amount, reflecting the detachment of the kingdom of Siyannu from Ugarit's control (Beckman 1999: 175–77). The treaty with Amurru mentions that they had previously paid tribute to Egypt (Beckman 1999: 60, cf. 37). None of the treaties with Anatolian states mentions tribute. It is possible that tribute clauses have managed to be broken away in every treaty with an Anatolian state or that separate treaties concerning tribute have not come down to us. That this is indeed a possibility may be seen in the following texts: from the earlier Middle Hittite period the indictment of the freebooter Madduwatta states, "he did not allow the tribute which [had been imposed] on anyone to be brought before My Majesty, but he always took it for himself" (Beckman 1999: 158). A prayer from the reign of Muršili II, containing many recycled requests, complains: "Moreover, the lands which belong to Hatti, the Kaška land … Kalašma, Lukka and Pitašša have declared themselves free from the Sun Goddess of Arinna. They discontinued [the payment of] their tributes and began to attack Hatti" (Singer 2002: 52–53). Muršili's youngest son, Hattušili, King of Hakpiš, states: "The lands which were around Nerik – Nera and Haštira I made the border – I subjected them all and made them tributary" (van den Hout 2003: 202 iii 48–51).

Nonetheless, in the best-preserved and most detailed history of a reign, the Annals of Muršili, there is no hint that cessation of tribute caused a war, and only one mention of imposition of tribute at the end of a war: "I made Kappēri, Kāraššuwa and Hurna 'of' tribute. They present wine to Hattuša" (Götze 1933: 176f. iii 48–51). The usual requirement to give troops is not mentioned for these three places; so this would appear to be a special case. Similarly *ṢĀRIPU* – men (dyers?) under attack by the freebooter Piyamaradu on Lazpa (Lesbos) plead that some of them are tributaries (*argamanalliuš*) of the Hittite king and some of the gods, and should be allowed to render their tribute (*argaman*) and go home (Houwink ten Cate 1984: 39–40). Perhaps significantly they do not use the usual term "subjects." Since the Akkadian verb *ṣarāpu* means "to burn, refine metals, and dye red," its deverbal profession noun may mean "dyers" perhaps specifically of that color ("Tyrian purple") whose name (*argaman*) also means "tribute" in Hittite. That the word *ṢĀRIPU* is attested only of people of Mediterranean seaports (Lesbos or Miletus and Ugarit) raises the possibility that these "tributaries" were suppliers of a rare commodity to the Hittites, which would make them another special case. Several documents refer to Anatolian places, usually smaller ones, but including the appanage kingdoms, as being tributary to one or more gods: "[If] I (Great King Hattušili III) give the Upper Land, Palā and Tum[manna to so]me boy, if to [my son], if to some other boy, I will make them tributary to Šaušga of Šamuha, my lady. Whatever tribute I claim(?) from them [i.e. from the sons to whom he gave conquered lands], they shall present it to Šaušga of Šamuha, my lady" (Götze 1930: 48–49). Indeed this is the primary usage of the term "tributary" outside of the Syrian treaties, and it may well represent an obligation imposed on all Hittite subjects. There is no evidence that being tributary to Hittite gods was an obligation incurred by subordinate states (other than appanage kingdoms); even in the case of the appanage state of Tarhuntašša the king was responsible only for the gods of his own state (Beckman 1999: 111 §6; 120f. §§22–24). When military assistance was needed less urgently than other forms of material support, one could be converted into the other (Beckman 1999: 182–183).

The clauses of treaties with subordinate states, like instructions to the Hittite king's direct underlings, tend to end with stipulations such as, "if you do not act in accordance with this clause, the oath gods will pursue you unrelentingly."

In an effort to bind both sides to their agreement, a long list of the gods of both parties are invoked as witnesses and thus guarantors. This list is followed by a list of curses on those who break the treaty, and blessings for those who keep it. In a treaty between equals these are strictly mutual. In a treaty with a subordinate king, all of the blessings and curses apply only to the subordinate ruler and his country:

> If you, Alaksandu, transgress these words of the tablet, which stand on this tablet, then these Thousand Gods shall eradicate you, together with your person, your wife, your sons, your lands, your cities, your vineyard, your threshing floor, your field, your cattle, your sheep, and including your possessions. They shall eradicate your progeny from the dark earth. But if you do observe these words, then these Thousand Gods whom I, My Majesty, the Labarna, Muwattalli, Great King, have summoned to assembly – the deities of Hatti, the deities of Wiluša, and the personal Storm-god of Lightning of My Majesty – shall benevolently protect you together with your wife, your sons, your grandsons, your cities, your threshing floor, your vineyard, your field, your cattle, your sheep, and including all your possessions. You shall thrive in the hand of My Majesty, and you shall live to an old age in the hand of My Majesty (Beckman 1999: 92f.).

Although the treaties with subordinate kings do not contain any explicit curses and blessings on the Hittite Great King – unless the subordinate king was a member of the Hittite royal family (see, e.g. Beckman 1999: 120–22) – the gods of both parties are still witnesses to promises the Great King has made to the tributary; it would therefore be clear to any Great King that he was also bound by what he had promised, and that the gods would punish him and his land for breaking the treaty. A well-justified retaliatory attack on Egypt by Šuppiluliuma I was nevertheless found by his son Muršili II to have broken the long forgotten Kuruštama treaty and so to be one of the causes of divine anger that had prompted a plague ravaging Hatti and killing Šuppiluliuma himself and his successor Arnuwanda II (Singer 2002: 56–69; Beal 2003: 83 with n. 2; Hoffner 2003a: 190–91).

In a further effort to keep peace, Hittite garrisons were stationed in the capitals of some of the less trustworthy or less stable subordinate states (Beckman 1999: 70 §4, 79 §19, attested only for the three states that had been under Arzawa until Muršili destroyed that kingdom). These ostensibly served to aid the subordinate ruler against enemies foreign and domestic, but obviously also to remind the subordinate ruler of his obligations to the Hittite state.

In addition to the treaty binding each individual state within the Hittite system to the Great King, there were bilateral treaties which bound subordinates to one another. Still preserved is a parity treaty which regulates the extradition of those who murder each other's merchants; it was concluded between the kingdom of Ugarit and its immediate overlord, the Hittite viceregal kingdom of Kargamiš (Nougayrol 1956: 152–60).

In yet another effort to preserve peace, the Hittite Great King served as mediator in disputes between two subordinate states or between the citizens of two states. As we saw above, King Hattušili III settled a dispute between the king of Ugarit and merchants of the Hittite port of Ura. He also agreed to return fugitives who had fled from Ugarit and joined bands of displaced persons (*hapiru*) in Hatti. In a case between a Ugaritan boat owner and his allegedly negligent Hittite (?) captain, Queen Puduhepa decided in favor of the former. Disputes among Syrian subordinate states were settled by the King of Kargamiš, a member of a cadet line of the Hittite royal family. Ini-Teššub, King of Kargamiš, arbitrated in a case, among others, that involved the banishment to Alašiya (Cyprus) of two brothers of Ammištamru II of Ugarit; this was an interstate dispute because their mother was a princess of Amurru (Beckman 1999: 177–80). Several times the same king assessed blood-money against Ugarit for foreign merchants killed in the city (Nougayrol 1956: 169–74). He also imposed a three-fold compensation on a Hittite merchant, who stole a bronze kettle and a bronze cauldron from a Ugaritan (ibid. 179), and adjudicated a number of cases of cross-border problems between the states of Ugarit and Siyannu (ibid. 161–63). An edict tells the king of the southern Syrian kingdom of Amurru to go to "the Priest," that is, the Hittite king of Aleppo, for arbitration, but if the problem is too difficult, it should be referred to the Great King himself (Beckman 1999: 172). Sometimes trusted aides were sent to render judgement (e.g. Nougayrol 1956: 231–32, 234–39).

When two countries were at peace, a vigorous correspondence between the two courts helped to maintain the positive relationship created by the treaty. Complaints could be aired and responded to before they festered. In a letter to the Kassite Babylonian king Kadašman-Enlil II, Hattušili III responds to a number of complaints by the Babylonians. Since the Babylonians are not happy with a judgement by the king of Kargamiš concerning merchants, he offers to hear an appeal of the judgement himself or to send all parties to Babylonia so that the Babylonian king himself can make the judgement. Upon a complaint that "My merchants are being killed in the subordinate states of Amurru and Ugarit," Hattušili gives Kadašman-Enlil a lecture on Hittite law: the Hittite government will investigate a murder, apprehend the murderer, purify the place of murder, but will not execute the murderer. Instead he is turned over to the next of kin who may accept blood money or make him a slave. "Would those who do not kill a malefactor kill a merchant?" He then suggests that the relatives of the murder victims be sent to Hattuša to present their case to him. Kadašman-Enlil is also unhappy that Bentešina, king of Amurru, is casting spells on Babylonia. Hattušili has investigated and discovered that Bentešina claims the Babylonians owe him the tremendous sum of three talents of silver. Hattušili reports that he has sent a representative of Bentešina to Babylon so that the Babylonian king can judge the dispute over the debt. Meanwhile, Bentešina has been made to swear an oath in the presence of the Babylonian ambassador that he has not been cursing Babylonia. "If my brother does not believe this, let his servant who heard Bentešina when he continually cursed the land of my brother come here and oppose him in court. I will put pressure on Bentešina. Bentešina is my subject. If he has cursed my brother, has he not cursed me too?" (Beckman 1999: 141 §§9–11).

Not only did the Great Kings write their greetings, good wishes and concerns to their "brothers," but Great Queens wrote greetings to their "sisters" or to their "brothers(-in-law)," and princes received letters from their "fathers." Such letters were usually accompanied by expensive gifts, carefully detailed in the letter (Edel 1994; Beckman 1999: 127–52). "Brothers" had no compunction about asking for specific gifts or complaining about the quality of those they had received (Beckman 1999: 143 §§17–18). Specific aid could also be requested. Ramses informed Hattušili that even Egyptian doctors could not help Hattušili's 50 or 60-year-old sister get pregnant, but that he would send the doctor that Hattušili had requested anyway (Beckman 1999: 137–38, cf. 142–43 §§12–13). Later in a time of famine in Hatti, Ramses' son and successor Merneptah sent shiploads of grain to help (Klengel 1974: 167–68). On a lighter note, Hattušili III asks Kadašman-Enlil II to lend him a Babylonian sculptor (Beckman 1999: 143 §16). On the death of one great king, his "brother" king was expected to mourn, to send a letter of congratulations to his heir, and, in accord with the treaty, to ask if he needed any help (Beckman 1999: 138–46).

In a further effort to bind the parties together in peace and friendship, marriage alliances were arranged. Šuppiluliuma I made a Kassite Babylonian princess his queen (Bryce 1998: 173), and later Tudhaliya IV, when still crown prince, was married to another Kassite Babylonian princess (Beckman 1999: 134). Unlike the Egyptians, the Hittites had no problem reciprocating by sending their daughters out to be married to foreign princes. Hattušili III sent a daughter to Egypt. Apparently, he was so interested in keeping peace with Ramses II (who was holding Hattušili's nephew Muršili III, the rightful Hittite king) that he did not insist that his daughter become Ramses' queen, as would have been expected between equally great powers. Even in this case, negotiations were long and drawn out, with much long-distance haggling (Bryce 1998: 310–12; Klengel 2002: 127–43).

Marriage alliances were not just made between the great powers. Šuppiluliuma I married off one of his daughters to Šattiwaza, a refugee claimant to the throne of the once great kingdom of Mittanni, before sending his new son-in-law with a Hittite army to claim his kingdom (Beckman 1999: 180–82). He married another of his daughters, Muwatti, to another princely refugee, Mašhuiluwa of Mira and Kuwaliya. Mašhuiluwa had to wait for his father's throne until his brother-in-law finally placed him there as a subordinate king (Beckman 1999: 74). Šuppiluliuma I even gave a sister to Huqqana of Azzi-Hayaša, a state with sexual mores that were (or were reputed to be) so far beyond the pale that Šuppiluliuma felt it necessary to include in the treaty with Huqqana clauses (amounting to five full paragraphs) that say, in effect, we know you are a bunch of perverted barbarians, but now that you are marrying my sister, you yourself must conform to our (spelled out) code of sexual conduct (Beckman 1999: 26–34, esp. 31–32). Hattušili III sealed an alliance with the large Syrian subordinate state of Amurru by sending a daughter to Amurru and marrying his son Nerikkaili to a princess from that state (Beckman 1999: 101–2, 134). As naval warfare increased in importance, Hammurapi III, king of the subordinate state of Ugarit, after much begging, was rewarded with a Hittite princess, whom he later had the ill grace to divorce, forcing the king of Kargamiš to act as divorce court judge (Beckman 1999: 183–84).

Subordinate states were bound to each other by such marriage alliances as well. A previous king of Ugarit, Ammištamru II, married a princess of Amurru; the marriage ended in disaster when the king of Ugarit not only divorced her but then demanded the right to kill her. Needless to say, the Hittites went to great pains to prevent the very hostilities between subordinate kings that this marriage had intended to forestall. Hittite justice, which frowned on death sentences, was eventually sacrificed to political expediency. The King of Kargamiš and eventually the Great King as well, after unsuccessfully trying other solutions, eventually signed off on a peace-preserving but reeking agreement between the king of Ugarit and his former wife's brother, the king of Amurru, in which the husband was allowed to buy her extradition and murder by a large cash payment to her brother (Nougayrol 1956: 125–48; Bryce 1998: 344–47; Beckman 1999: 180–82).

Peace could be fragile. Cities were walled, gates locked and a seal affixed at night, and guards posted on the walls. In times of trouble people and animals were herded into the city at night (Beal 1992: 246–76). The barbarian Kaška in particular were not trusted. According to the decree of Hattušili III for the border city of Tiliura, a Kaškaean man was not to spend the night in the city, even if he was married to a woman from the place and Kaškaean soldiers serving the Hittites were not to enter the city at all, even if they were chariot-drivers for some high Hittite officer (von Schuler 1965: 146–47).

Any sign of weakness in the Hittite state could cause an outbreak of war. When the warrior king Šuppiluliuma I got sick and died, quickly followed by his crown prince and second-in-command Arnuwanda II, leaving the empire in the hands of an untried youth, Muršili II, all the enemy lands began hostilities (Beal 2003: 83–84). We saw above how during times of peace Hittites had gone into Kaškaean towns and had set up inns near them. However, "When the Kaškaean men saw that there was a plague in the (Hittite) army, they seized the people who had again gone into their towns. They killed some and seized others. Then the enemy came by night, split up, and attacked all the forts" (Hoffner 2003a: 189).

Aside from an attack on Hatti, a frequent reason for the breakdown of peace was the failure by the other side to observe a treaty it had sworn with the Hittites. Sometimes the Hittites were very patient, willing to overlook treason, oath-breaking, and even overt military action against Hatti in return for future peace and good behavior. At a time when probably the bulk of the Hittite armies were tied up elsewhere, the "Indictment of Madduwatta," detailing Madduwatta's perfidy and attempts both diplomatic and military by the Hittite kings Tudhaliya II and Arnuwanda I to get him to behave, reads either like a last chance for diplomacy or a justification for war, depending on what one thinks was said on the missing second tablet of the composition (Beckman 1999: 153–60). About five generations later a freebooter named Piyamaradu aggrandized himself in Hatti's western borderlands by playing the two great powers, Hittites and

Ahhiyawans, off against one another. A letter to Tawagalawa, the prince of Ahhiyawa concerned with eastern affairs, details Hittite offers to Piyamaradu of friendship and districts to rule, if he will just obediently settle down and not disturb the peace (Sommer 1932: 1–18).

In the following case, failure to deal with a district that had sworn to supply troops to the Hittites, prompted that district to turn the tables and raid Hittite lands. "The district of Tipiya had become hostile and ceased giving me troops" (Beal 2003: 84b). "While my father was in Mitanni, Pihhuniya, man of Tipiya, marched and repeatedly attacked the (Hittite) Upper Land. He advanced as far as Zazziša and he looted the Upper Land and carried (the loot) down into the land of the Kaška. He took all the land of Ištitina and turned it into his pasture" (Beal 2003: 87a). A successful counter raid in Muršili's second year failed to solve the problem (Beal 2003: 84b). By his seventh year Tipiya had grown even more dangerous. Muršili first tried diplomacy. Remarkably, the primary Hittite demand was not the return to the original situation (a subordinate status, primarily with the obligation of supplying troops) or even the return of the booty, but rather the return of the Hittite king's most important economic and military asset, his subjects, whom Pihhuniya had carried off.

> I, My Majesty, went toward him and sent him a messenger saying "Send out to me my subjects whom you took and led down into Kaška." Pihhuniya wrote back to me as follows: "I will not give anything back to you. And if you come to fight me, I will not take a stand to fight you in my own field and meadow, I will come to your land and I will take a stand to fight you in the midst of your land." When Pihhuniya had written this back to me and did not give my subjects back to me, I went to fight him (Beal 2003: 87).

The desire for the return of fugitives, who by right of conquest of their lands belonged to the Hittite king, could also be a *casus belli* with the land harboring them.

> When my brother [Arnuwanda conquered …], the troops [of Attārimma, Huwaršanašša and Šuruda fled before him and went] to [Arzawa. I sent a messenger] to Uhha-ziti. [I] wrote to him [as follows:] "People [who belong to me – the troops of Attārimma,] Huwaršanašša [and Šuruda] – came [to you. Give them back to me.]" But Uhha-ziti [wrote back] to me [as follows]: "I will not [give anyone back] to you." … He mustered his troops … I set my infantry and horse-troops in motion and in that same year I went against Arzawa. I sent a message to Uhha-ziti (as follows): "Because I asked you to return my subjects who came to you and you did not give them back – you kept calling me a child and you kept belittling me – now, come, we will fight. Let the Stormgod, my lord, decide our lawsuit" (Beal 2003: 85, restoration based on parallel sections; see Götze 1933: 38–41 ii 25–35, 44–46 ii 7–14).

The final phrase in the preceding quotation shows another typical Hittite belief about warfare: it was a trial in which the gods would give victory to the just. King Hattušili of Hakpiš justified his rebellion and attempted usurpation from his nephew, the Great King Muršili III, by listing the latter's ingratitude and successive attempts to strip him of his various lands and offices. He ends by saying:

> When I became hostile to him, I did not commit a moral offense by revolting against him on the chariot or revolting against him within his house. (No!) In a manly way I declared

to him: "You opposed me. You are Great King, whereas I am king of the single fortress that you left me. So come! Šaušga of Šamuha and the Stormgod of Nerik will judge us."

After the success of his rebellion, Hattušili III writes, "If he had in no way oppressed me, would the gods really have made a Great King succumb to a petty king? Because he has now opposed me, the gods have made him succumb to me by their judgement" (van den Hout 2003: 203).

When war seemed necessary, the gods were consulted through oracles. They were presented with a series of proposals. For each they were asked to write their approval or disapproval in a particular divine language on the entrails of a particular sheep, in the flight of birds, or in the pattern of moving symbols on a game board. The answers received in one "oracular language" would be checked by asking that the same question be answered in another language. Questions typically asked aimed at finding out which enemies would cause trouble, who among a list of generals would be successful on a particular campaign, and what very specific route a particular campaign should take. Importantly, the oracles did not give just one answer; rather, they eliminated certain possibilities while leaving it to the king to choose one of the remaining possibilities (Beal 2002: 11–37).

Soldiers had to be prepared for combat. By a series of rituals the soldiers signaled the dire fate that would befall them should they be disloyal. For example:

> [The officiant] places wax and mutton-fat into their hands. Then he throws them into the fire and says, "As this wax melts and mutton-fat fries, so may he who breaks the oath and deceives the Hittite king melt like wax and fry like mutton-fat." (The soldiers) reply: "So be it!" ... They bring in women's clothing and a distaff and a spindle (symbols of womanhood); and they break an arrow (symbol of manhood). You speak to them (the troops) as follows: "What are these? Are these not the dresses of a woman, which we have here for (your) oath? Whoever breaks these oaths and does evil to the king and the queen and the royal princes, let these oath-gods change him from a man into a woman. Let them change his soldiers into women. Let them dress them like women and cover their heads with kerchiefs. Let them break their bow, arrows and (other) weapons in their hands and put in their hands distaff and spindle" (Beal 1995b: 63–64; Collins 2003).

Before departing, the ritual, "When the soldiers go away from the land to campaign and [they go] to the enemy land to fight," was performed over them. Chariot horses also went through a purificatory ritual to remove, burn away, and wash off evils from them. Another ritual written by Azzari, the Hurrian female pharmacist, anointed with magical oil the general, his horses, his chariot and his implements of war. A third made a figurine of cedar labeled with the name of the enemy leader and a figurine of clay labeled with the name of the Hittite leader. When these were thrown into the fire, the enemy was destroyed and the Hittite strengthened. When the Hittite army reached the enemy's border, another ritual was performed in which legal justification for the war was laid out and the gods were asked for victory.

> The gods of the Hatti land have done nothing against you, the gods of the Kaškaean country. They have not put you under constraint. But you, the gods of the Kaškaean country, began war. You drove the gods of the Hatti land out of their realm and took

over their realm for yourselves. The Kaškaean people also began war. From the Hittites you took away their cities and you drove them out of their field (and) fallow and out of their vineyards. The gods of the Hatti land and the (Hittite) people call for bloody vengeance. The vengeance of the Hatti gods and the vengeance of the (Hittite) people will be wrought on you, the gods of the Kaškaean country and the Kaškaean people (translation adapted from Goetze, in Pritchard 1969: 354–55).

Hittite gods were expected to run at the head of the army. Other rituals sought to convince, coax, or lure the enemy's gods away from the enemy's land. Since more soldiers probably died of disease on a campaign than in battle, there were rituals to rid the army of disease and afflict the enemy with it. In case none of this worked and the Hittite army was defeated, yet other rituals offered magic to repurify the army and restore its morale (Beal 1995b).

In the conflict with Tippiya described above, the magic worked. Muršili records: "I captured Pihhuniya and brought him back to Hattuša ... Since Pihhuniya had taken Ištitina, I rebuilt it and made it a Hittite land again" (Beal 2003: 87b).

In one case we have a rather full description of relations between the Hittites and a foreign state, leading to war and eventually back to peace. The country of Azzi(-Hayaša) had become a subordinate state and had signed a treaty relatively early in the days of Šuppiluliuma I. While this king was busy defeating the long-time enemy Mittanni and annexing their Syrian territories, he ignored small problems in the north, as we saw above with Tippiya. It was left to his son Muršili II to solve these problems which were caused by Hittite subjects who had either voluntarily gone over or been carried off to Azzi-Hayaša. First Muršili tried diplomacy:

> I sent a messenger to Anniya, king of Azzi(-Hayaša) saying: "[Return to me] my subjects who came to you while my father was in Mittanni ... You came, marched to Dankuwa, attacked it, plundered it of transportees (on whom see below), cattle, and sheep and carried them down into Hayaša." Aniya, the king of Azzi, wrote back to me as follows: "[Why] do you keep writing to me? If some [transportees] came and (if) there are some who are (still) coming in to me, [we do not give them up]." I wrote back to him: "I came and encamped at the border of your land. I did not attack your land and I did not plunder it of transportees, cattle and sheep. You started hostilities [with My Majesty]."

Interestingly, Muršili nowhere invokes the treaty between his father and a previous king of Azzi-(Hayaša). Obviously, despite language invoking permanence, new kings needed to renew existing treaties. Since this had not been done here, Aniya was not accused of oath-breaking.

In the following year, Muršili determined that diplomacy had failed and force was inevitable:

> [I] would [have led] my troops and horse troops [against Azzi-Hayaša], but when the [men] of Hayaša [heard]: "His Majesty is coming," they sent [a messenger] to [me] saying, "O lord, ... we will bring back the Hittite transportees who are coming in to us and hand them over." When the men of Hayaša replied to me in this way (I decided to celebrate the festival of Invocation of Hebat of Kummanni).

Despite the promise, made under threat of an invasion, nothing happened. A year later, Muršili again wrote to Azzi:

> I said, "Hand over the Hittite transportees who are coming to you … and I will not then go against the men of Hayaša." However the men of Hayaša did not hand over the Hittite transportees. So I wrote again to Anniya saying: "[You have not] yet [begun] to give anything back to me." … He sent word to Hattuša: "The Hittite transportees have not been compensated for [by?] Azzian [transplantees] either. If some Hittite transportees are coming over to us, we will not give them over."

The situation changed dramatically when Muršili's brother, Piyašili/Šarri-Kušuh, the King of Kargamiš and Viceroy of Syria suddenly died. Nuhašše revolted and Assyria threatened Kargamiš. "When the men of Hayaša heard that enemies were arising against My Majesty, they did not return any Hittite transportees. They mustered their troops and attacked the Land of Ištitina … and destroyed it." Muršili sent General Nuwanza who successfully drove the Azzi-Hayašans out of Hittite territory, but no attack on Azzi-Hayaša could be contemplated until the following year (Götze 1933: 96–131; Beal 2003: 87–90).

Finally, in the fourth year running that Azzi-Hayaša had failed to return the fugitives, Muršili invaded their country. The Azzi-Hayašans' plan to destroy Muršili's army by a night attack on his camp failed when Muršili got wind of it and took precautions. Thereupon, the Azzi-Hayašans changed their strategy, refused battle and retreated into mountain fortresses. After Muršili had besieged and taken one of these (Aripša) by storm and allowed his troops to plunder it, the next fortress (Dukkama) capitulated.

> When the Azzians saw that I was beginning to take down their fortified cities by storm, the Azzians holding fortified cities, mountain fastnesses, and difficult places became afraid. The elders of the land came to me and fell at my feet saying to me: "O lord! Don't destroy us. Take us as your subjects. We will begin to give you infantry and horse troops. We will give over the transportees of Hatti who are in our (land)." So I, My Majesty, then did not destroy them and took them as my subjects. But since the campaign season was over, I did not then reorganize Azzi, but I made the Azziyans swear an oath and I then came back to Hattuša. When it became spring, I would have gone back to Azzi to reorganize it, but when the Azziyans heard, they sent Mutti of Halimanā with orders to say: "Our lord, since you have already defeated us, don't come again. Take us as your subjects and we will begin to give infantry and horse-troops." They handed over to me the one thousand Hittite transportees who were in their (land). Because they handed over to me the Hittite transportees, I did not again go to Azzi and I took them as my subjects" (Götze 1933: 130–37: KBo 4.4 iii 57-iv 52; cf. the summary in Beal 2003: 90).

Failure to make peace often resulted in conquest. Sometimes, whether for reasons of law or realpolitik, only the leaders were judged guilty; they were replaced by more cooperative members of the dynasty, and life went on (e.g. in Kinza: Beal 2003: 88–90; for Nuhašše see below). When the military or political situation called for it, cities were looted, the booty being divided between the gods, the king and the soldiery. When an example needed to be made or a city was not intended to be held, it was burned (e.g. Aripša, Götze 1933: 134–35).

An interesting text lays out some possible consequences of rebellion. When Tette of Nuhašše and EN-urta of Barga revolted against Muršili II, a member of the royal family of Barga, "Abiradda, went over to My Majesty's side. He chased EN-urta out … And I, My Majesty, utterly destroyed EN-urta, together with his household and his land. But his kingship, throne, household and land which I spared I gave to Abiradda and made him king in the land of Barga." Abiradda then asked Muršili for the town of Iyaruwatta which had been taken from Abiradda's grandfather and given to Tette's grandfather by the Mittannian king, who at the time was his overlord. In reply Muršili writes:

> I, My Majesty, made a commitment to him as follows: "If I, My Majesty, conquer Iyaruwatta by the sword with infantry and horsetroops of Hatti, I will take up its civilians to be resettled, and property, and carry them off to Hatti. However, I will give the empty city of Iyaruwatta with its bare walls, gods and ancestral spirits to you Abiratta. But if not, and if before I, My Majesty, have conquered Iyaruwatta, a son or brother of Tette should anticipate and kill Tette, or capture him and [turn] him over to me, saying 'I am the subject of Your Majesty in (this) place', then I, My Majesty, will not take Iyaruwatta away from him" (Beckman 1999: 170–71).

Sometimes the temple district was spared out of respect for the local deity. After a long siege and eight days of attack, the great city of Kargamiš fell to Šuppiluliuma I. "When my father conquered the city, because my father feared the gods, in the citadel he let no one into the presence of the god/goddess […] or the Tutelary Deity. He even worshiped them and gave […]." From the lower city, however, people, gold, silver, and bronze were plundered (Hoffner 2003a: 190). "I went further into the Land of Hurna. I destroyed the Land of Hurna, and the city of Hurna. But because there was a temple of the Storm God of Hurna behind the city of Hurna, I spared it and they did not plunder it. The servants of the god who were behind, I left alone, and they are still there" (Götze 1933: 176–77 iii 41–46). At other times the deities found themselves with a new home in Hattuša.

The animals of a newly conquered territory were usually carried off. In cases of conquest, the civilian population became the property of the Hittite king. Known as "transportees," they could be left "in place" (Beckman 1999: 172 §10) which probably did not cause any difference in their lives. Perhaps more frequently, they were divided between the king and the soldiers. The latters' prisoners were enslaved. Of the king's share, some became slaves of the victory-giving gods, working in the temples or as dependent peasants on land belonging to the gods. Others were settled on land in Hatti, given the seed and materials to start a new life, exempted from taxes for three years, and expected to turn into contented subjects of the Hittite state (von Schuler 1965: 146; Hoffner 1997: 107–08 §112; McMahon 2003: 224 §§39, 44–45). In newly conquered or reconquered territory, the king would "reorganize the land," constructing forts for defense, rebuilding the towns, returning Hittite refugees from the area, and bringing in transplantees (e.g. von Schuler 1965: 146; Beal 2003: 89–90; van den Hout 2003: 201 §8, 202–03). More distant areas would be given to a subordinate king, either a member of the old dynasty or, if no kingdom had existed there, a junior member or in-law of the Hittite dynasty (Beal 1992: 320–27, esp. 326 with n. 1249).

Soldiers of conquered enemy lands were incorporated into the Hittite army. Tudhaliya II writes:

> When I destroyed Aššuwa, I returned to Hattuša, and I brought to Hattuša *alšantan* ten thousand troops, six hundred horses, chariots and chariot drivers and I settled them in Hatti. I (also) brought back to Hattuša Piyama-Kurunta, Kukkulli and Piyama-Kurunta's in-law [Mala]ziti and their children and grandchildren. When I had returned to Hattuša, I gave Piyama-Kurunta and Malaziti to the Stormgod of the Gatehouse at the Gatehouse. But I took Kukkuli into my service and released him (Carruba 1977: 158–61).

Yet such a large body of men, settled as a still cohesive unit, proved a major problem, for Kukkuli soon stirred them to revolt. Subsequently, when larger states were defeated, Hittite policy was to install a subordinate king, tied by treaty and oaths to the Hittite king (see above), who was responsible for maintaining his own army both to defend himself and to aid the Hittites when called upon.

With smaller decentralized places, however, this proved more difficult. From the reign of Tudhaliya III, when Hatti was fighting for survival against neighboring small states and barbarians, a list of Kaškaean men by name, village, and ransom price, and an indication of whether he is "seeing" or "blind," survives from the northern frontier fortress of Tapigga. The differentiation and the great number of blind men suggests that this does not reflect debilitating war wounds but, at least in the reign of Tudhaliya III, a policy of blinding some prisoners of war; as other texts from the same period tell us, they were put to work grinding grain. Some, whether blinded or not, were eventually ransomed back by their compatriots (del Monte 1995: 103–11; Hoffner 2002: 67–68). Such a policy is not mentioned in other reigns. Since the oath sworn by soldiers joining the Hittites mentions that the oath gods would (among many other things) blind disloyal soldiers and turn them into women, it seems likely that these blinded Kaškaean men who ended up doing women's work were the leaders of Kaškaean soldiers who had joined the Hittite army and broken their oath of loyalty (Siegelová 2002).

In conclusion, although the Hittites considered peace a beneficial gift of the gods, they understood that they needed to work for it. To that end they drew up elaborate treaties, expecting the gods to do their part by blessing those who kept the treaties and cursing those who broke them, while humans tried to maintain peace through political marriages and intensive correspondence and diplomatic exchanges. Although the treaty partners were often unequal, justice, overseen by the gods and their appointee, the king, was the glue holding the system together. Where these techniques did not work, vigilance and strength were keys to peace. Success in war was perceived as the just gods' decision in a legal case in favor of the Hittite plaintiff. At least in the Late Bronze Age New Kingdom what mattered was not just victory over the enemy army but the number of the most valuable of resources, namely taxpaying farmers, craftsmen, slaves and especially soldiers that were added to the empire. Depopulated lands could thus be resettled and reorganized. Lands further afield signed treaties to keep the peace and provide soldiers. This completed the cycle from peace to war and back again to peace.

Notes

1 For easier orientation, I list here the Hittite kings:

Pithana (king of Kuššara)	Zidanta II (nephew)
Anitta (son, fl. ca. 1790)	Huzziya II (?)
(succession unclear)	Muwattalli I (usurper)
Huzziya 0 (?)	Kantuzzili (son of Huzziya II)
(succession unclear)	Tudhaliya II (son)
Tudhaliya I (?)	Arnuwanda I (son-in-law)
Pu-Šarruma (son)	Hattušili II (brother)
Labarna (son-in-law)	Tudhaliya III (son of Arnuwanda)
Hattušili I (nephew)	Šuppiluliuma I (son, ca. 1350–1323)
Muršili I (grandson, ca. 1610–1594)	Arnuwanda II (son, ca. 1323–1322)
Hantili I (brother-in-law)	Muršili II (brother, ca. 1322–1290)
Zidanta I (son-in-law)	Muwattalli II (son, ca. 1290–1269)
Ammuna (son)	Muršili III (a.k.a. Urhi-Teššub, son,
Huzziya I (son)	ca. 1269–1262)
Telipinu (half-brother-in-law)	Hattušili III (uncle, ca. 1262–1240)
Tahurwaili (grandson of Ammuna)	Tudhaliya IV (son, ca. 1240–1205)
Alluwamna (son-in-law of Telipinu)	Arnuwanda III (son, ca. 1205–1204)
Hantili II (son)	Šuppiluliuma II (brother, ca. 1204–1178)

2 Cf. the use of the derived verb *išhiulahh-*: "When I heard that the Azziyans planned to attack my army camp at night, I gave sworn instructions (*išhiulahh-*) to my troops – just as they marched battle-ready during the day, so at night they should be ready for an ambush" KBo 4.4 iii 65–70 (annals of Muršili II), ed. Götze 1933: 132–33.

3 Edel 1997. The Egyptian version is preserved in Hittite (Beckman 1999: 96–100), the Hittite version in Egyptian (with a bit of Egyptian political ideology incongruently added): Wilson: 1969: 199–201. For a more detailed discussion of this treaty, see Bell, this vol.

Abbreviation

KBo　　　　　*Keilschrifttexte aus Boghazköi*. Multiple vols. Leipzig and Berlin.

References

Beal, Richard H. 1992. *The Organisation of the Hittite Military*. Texte der Hethiter 20. Heidelberg.

——. 1995a. "Hittite Military Organization." In Sasson 1995: 545–54.

——. 1995b. "Hittite Military Rituals." In Marvin Meyer and Paul Mirecki (eds.), *Ancient Magic and Ritual Power*, 63–76. Leiden.

——. 2002. "Gleanings from Hittite Oracle Questions on Religion, Society, Psychology and Decision Making." In Piotr Taracha (ed.), *Silvia Anatolica: Anatolian Studies Presented to Maciej Popko*, 11–37. Warsaw.

——. 2003. "The Ten Year Annals of Great King Muršili II of Hatti." In Hallo 2003: 2.82–90.

Beckman, Gary M. 1999. *Hittite Diplomatic Texts*. 2nd edn. Atlanta.

Bryce, Trevor. 1998. *The Kingdom of the Hittites*. Oxford.

——. 2002. *Life and Society in the Hittite World.* Oxford.

Carruba, Onofrio. 1977. "Beiträge zur mittelhethitischen Geschichte I. Die Tuthalijas und die Arnuwandas." *Studi Micenei ed Egeo-Anatolici* 18: 137–74.

Collins, Billie Jean. 2003. "The First Soldiers' Oath"; "The Second Soldiers' Oath." In Hallo 2003: 1.165–68.

del Monte, Giuseppe. 1995. "I testi amministrativi da Maşat Höyük/Tapika." *Orientis Antiqui Miscellanea* 2: 89–138.

Edel, Elmar. 1994. *Die ägyptisch-hethitische Korrespondenz.* Rheinisch-Westfälische Akademie der Wissenschaften, Abhandlung 77. Opladen.

——. 1997. Der Vertrag zwischen Ramses II. von Ägypten und Hattušili III. von Hatti. Wissenschaftliche Veröffentlichungen der Deutschen Orient-Gesellschaft 95. Berlin.

Gessel, B. H. L. van. 1998. *Onomasticon of the Hittite Pantheon.* Handbuch der Orientalistik 1.33. Leiden.

Götze, Albrecht. 1930. *Neue Bruchstücke zum großen Text des Hattušiliš und den Paralleltexten.* Mitteilungen der vorderasiatisch-aegyptischen Gesellschaft 34.2. Leipzig.

——. 1933. *Die Annalen des Muršiliš.* Mitteilungen der vorderasiatisch-aegyptischen Gesellschaft 38. Leipzig.

Hallo, William W. (ed.). 2003. *Context of Scripture.* 3 vols. Leiden.

Hoffner, Harry A. 1997. *The Laws of the Hittites.* Leiden.

——. 2002. "The Treatment and Long Term Use of Persons Captured in Battle." In K. Aslıhan Yener and Harry A. Hoffner, Jr. (eds.), *Recent Developments in Hittite Archaeology and History,* 61–71. Winona Lake.

——. 2003a. "Deeds of Šuppiluliuma." In Hallo 2003: 1.185–92.

——. 2003b. "Letters: Middle Hittite Period." In Hallo 2003: 3.43–51.

van den Hout, Theo. 1998. *The Purity of Kingship.* Documenta et Monumenta Orientis Antiqui 25. Leiden.

——. 2003. "Apology of Hattušili III." In Hallo 2003: 1.199–204.

Houwink ten Cate, Philo H. J. 1966. "A New Fragment of the 'Deeds of Suppiluliuma as Told by His Son, Mursili II'." *Journal of Near Eastern Studies* 25: 27–31.

——. 1984. "Sidelights on the Ahhiyawa Question from Hittite Vassal and Royal Correspondence." *Jaarbericht Ex Oriente Lux* 28: 33–79.

Klengel, Horst. 1974. "'Hungerjahre' in Hatti." *Altorientalische Forschungen* 1: 165–74.

——. 2002. *Hattuschili und Ramses: Hethiter und Ägypter – ihr langer Weg zum Frieden.* Kulturgeschichte der antiken Welt 95. Mainz.

McMahon, J. Gregory. 2003. "Instructions to Commanders of Border Garrisons (*BEL MADGALTI*)." In Hallo 2003: 1.221–25.

Nougayrol, Jean. 1956. "Textes accadiens des archives sud." In *Le Palais Royal d'Ugarit* 4. Mission de Ras Shamra 9. Paris.

Otten, Heinrich. 1951. "Ein althethitischer Vertrag mit Kizzuvatna." *Journal of Cuneiform Studies* 5: 129–32.

Puhvel, Jaan. 1997. *Hittite Etymological Dictionary,* K. Berlin.

Pritchard, James B. (ed.). 1969. *Ancient Near Eastern Texts Relating to the Old Testament.* 3rd edn. Princeton.

Sasson, Jack M. (ed.). 1995. *Civilizations of the Ancient Near East.* 4 vols. New York.

Schuler, Einar von. 1965. *Die Kaškäer.* Berlin.

Siegelová, Jana. 2002. "Blendung als Strafe für den Eidbruch." In *Anatolia Antica: Studi in memoria di Fiorella Imparati,* 735–37. Eothen 11. Florence.

Singer, Itamar. 2002. *Hittite Prayers.* Writings from the Ancient World 11. Atlanta.

Sommer, Ferdinand. 1932. *Die Ahhijavā-Urkunden.* Abhandlungen der Bayerischen Akad. der Wiss.: Phil.-hist. Abt. NF 6. Munich.

Wilson, John A. 1969. "Treaty Between the Hittites and Egypt." In Pritchard 1969: 199–201.

6

Conflict and Reconciliation in the Ancient Middle East: The Clash of Egyptian and Hittite Chariots in Syria, and the World's First Peace Treaty between "Superpowers"

Lanny Bell

Late Bronze Age Egypt and Anatolian Hatti, separated only by the petty kingdoms of Syro-Palestine, had become bitter rivals for control of the resources, ports, and overland trade routes of Syria. These powerful states, once seemingly committed to mutual destruction, were nevertheless destined to sign a historic peace treaty.[1]

Relative Chronology

I append here, for the sake of clarity, a brief chronological chart. I list only select pharaohs, and the dates are approximate. Since much of ancient Mediterranean history is still calibrated in terms of synchronisms with Egypt, I indicate only the relative chronology of individual Hittite rulers.

Archaic Period = Dynasties 0–2	ca. 3250–2675	
Old Kingdom = Dynasties 3–8	ca. 2675–2155	
First Intermediate Period = Dynasties 9–11 (1st half)	ca. 2155–2020	
Middle Kingdom = Dynasties 11 (2nd half)–13 (1st half)	ca. 2020–1710	
Second Intermediate Period = Dynasties 13 (2nd half)–17	ca. 1710–1550	
		Hattusili I
		Mursili I
New Kingdom = Dynasties 18–20 Thutmose III (ca. 1479–1425)	ca. 1550–1070	

Amenhotep II (ca. 1428–1400)	
Thutmose IV (ca. 1400–1390)	
Amenhotep III (ca. 1390–1353)	Suppiluliuma I
Amenhotep IV/Akhenaten (ca. 1352–1336)	
Tutankhamun (ca. 1334–1325)	
Aye (ca. 1324–1321)	
Horemheb (ca. 1321–1293)	
Ramesses I (ca. 1293–1291)	
Sety I (ca. 1291–1279)	Muwattalli II
Ramesses II (ca. 1279–1212)	Urhi-Teshshup/ Mursili III
	Hattusili III
	Tudhaliya IV
Merenptah (ca. 1212–1202)	
Ramesses III (ca. 1182–1151)	Suppiluliuma II

Egyptian Background

In order to understand the relationship between the two states, it is necessary to look briefly at Egyptian foreign relations prior to the New Kingdom. Ancient Egyptian attitudes toward foreigners reflect several fundamental cultural assumptions, the most important of which are summarized here in Egyptian terms.[2] The king of Egypt was a living god; son of a mortal woman, he ruled the earth as the heir of his divine father. Because of his hybrid nature, he was the proper intermediary between humankind and the gods; the gods expressed their will through his words and deeds. Egypt was the center of the universe, and the Egyptians were the gods' chosen people – the only true humans.[3] It was traditional Egyptian culture, embodied in the abstract concept of *ma'at*, "truth, justice, righteousness, correct behavior, and divinely ordained cosmic order" – in short, the status quo of the Egyptian way of life – that distinguished the Egyptians from their barbaric neighbors. One of the primary duties of the king was to secure the frontiers and prevent aggressors from penetrating them. Glorified as a mighty hunter and heroic warrior, he perpetuated the warlike deeds of the god who had harnessed or repelled the formless and all-encompassing waters of chaos to create the island oasis of Egypt at the beginning of time.

The tribal peoples living just beyond Egypt's borders consisted of small semi-nomadic groups; like the untamed herds and other wild animals occupying the fringes of the deserts and the marshlands, they symbolized vestiges of the chaotic preexistent, whose potential return always constituted a threat to Egypt's security. Isolated by deserts, cataracts, and seas, for the first 1500 years of its recorded history the Egyptian Nile Valley was effectively protected against major foreign incursions. On the other hand, Egyptian expeditions, with superior manpower, weaponry, and organization, felt free to exploit the greater world at will in the quest for needed raw materials and luxury trade goods. Their activities were concentrated in Lower Nubia, the Eastern Desert, and the Sinai, where the pacification of hostile natives could be achieved through coercion or intimidation. Peace, for the Egyptians, meant simply that foreigners submitted to them. Meanwhile, more distant contacts, probably on more equal terms, were maintained with African Punt and the Egyptianized port city of Byblos in Syria (Kemp 1983: 136–37; O'Connor 1983: 270–71). Because there was no standing army, troops were conscripted throughout the country for each such occasion, relying on the long-established corvée system. Foreign warriors and their dependants were frequently brought back from these campaigns. Settled into detention camps until they were Egyptianized (i.e. domesticated or civilized), they were then integrated into Egyptian society without prejudice, serving, for example, as soldiers or household servants.

The Egyptian Empire in Western Asia

Small-scale Canaanite infiltration into the Eastern Delta is attested during the troubled times of the decentralized First Intermediate Period (the transition between the Old and Middle Kingdoms). The Middle Kingdom response was to fortify the northeastern frontier, and a few punitive raids were launched into Canaan and possibly Syria (Cohen 2002: 33–50). However, the crisis of the Second Intermediate Period (the transition between the Middle and New Kingdoms) – when rulers of foreign descent controlled most of Egypt – had a dramatic impact on the Egyptian mentality, resulting in a major shift in foreign policy. After forcing the Hyksos kings and their Kushite allies to withdraw from the land at the beginning of Dynasty 18, the Egyptians set about trying to convert Syro-Palestine into a defensive barrier, modeled after the buffer zone which had long existed in Lower Nubia, thus in fact establishing an empire in Western Asia. The kings' obligations were no longer limited to defending the frontiers, but were now redefined to emphasize their expansion. The Egyptians rapidly extended their control toward the north and east, taking possession of numerous prosperous city-states and encountering previously unknown territorial states. Very different from Egypt, but equally powerful, these claimed prior rights in the areas where Egypt was now operating. Confronted with such new conditions and challenges, the Egyptians were forced to develop a professional army that is amply attested to in the proliferation of military ranks and titles borne by many individuals during the New Kingdom (Schulman 1964, 1995; Yoyotte and López 1969). The same circumstances, however, also prompted the emergence of Egyptian diplomacy.

Western Asiatic Powers

The Second Intermediate Period had also seen the emergence of two newcomers to the realm of international politics:[4] the Hurrian kingdom of Mitanni[5] in northern Mesopotamia and the Hittite Old Kingdom, based at the capital city of Hattusa (modern Boghazköy) in north central Anatolia. The first two Hittite kings, Hattusili I and his grandson Mursili I, were energetic opponents of Mitanni, in both its Anatolian and Syrian operations; in search of trade routes and natural resources, they extended Hittite dominion into northern Syria. Conquering Aleppo and crossing the Euphrates into Mitannian territory, they even raided Babylon. Their efforts in this direction, however, were short-lived, as they were beset by interference from competitors in Western Anatolia, and dynastic rivalries soon resulted in the temporary eclipse of Hatti from the international arena.[6] Mitanni immediately moved back into northern Syria to fill the vacuum.

International Relations: Egypt and Western Asia

The first Egyptian references to Hatti occur during the reign of the Dynasty 18 pharaoh Thutmose III, who was busily extending the northern frontiers of Egypt and consolidating its newly acquired Asiatic empire. In the course of 17 campaigns during 21 years, his armies must have interfered in, or operated very close to, the Hittite sphere of influence. However, the Hittites were not yet prepared to address this aggression.[7] A scene in a private tomb represents a man, identified as the chieftain of Hatti, kneeling before the Egyptian king in the act of extolling, along with other foreign leaders, "the might of his Majesty, their 'tribute' (i.e. diplomatic gifts)[8] being upon their backs – consisting of all the [valuable materials][9] from the East, namely silver, gold, lapis lazuli, turquoise, and every (other) semi-precious stone – in exchange for their being granted the breath of life" (cf. Wilson 1969: 248–49). This man is not depicted as an actual Hittite, but rather a Syrian vassal in Hittite service (Darnell 1991: 113 and n. 1). So the Egyptians were well aware of the existence of the Hittites at this time, but had only an indirect relationship with them (Oosthoek 1992: 343).

The rulers of the Syrian states of Tunip and Qadesh are also represented in the scene mentioned above. In the year 22/23, during his first victorious Asiatic campaign against Megiddo, Thutmose III had faced a coalition of independent local forces led by the king of Qadesh. Always a regional center of agitation against Egypt, Qadesh had to be dealt with again subsequently. Its fortifications were breached in the great campaign of the year 33, when the Euphrates was crossed and Tunip was also captured. Following Egypt's military successes against Mitanni, even on its own turf, neighboring Hatti quickly joined in dispatching diplomatic gifts to the Egyptian court.[10] Meanwhile, Mitanni, always in competition with Hatti – which was now enjoying a resurgence of power and influence – did not hesitate long to offer itself as an ally of Egypt;[11] diplomatic marriages were arranged since at least the time of Thutmose IV (Moran 1992: 93). As Egypt enjoyed an era of unprecedented power and wealth, the "Hittite problem" faded into the background.

In the reign of Amenhotep III Hatti appears in several geographical lists, as letters written in the Hittite language were exchanged with the Anatolian kingdom of Arzawa. Although the circumstances are unknown, it seems to have been a Hittite scribe who taught the Egyptians how to write cuneiform Babylonian, the language of diplomacy

(Moran 1992: xviii–xxii; Gianto 1997: 426–27, 433). New regional troubles late in Amenhotep's reign were connected with the rise of the "rogue state" of Amurru, whose ambitious rulers took advantage of the ambiguity of their frontline location along the Egypto-Mitannian border to foment trouble with their neighbors, perhaps relying on the reluctance of either Egypt or Mitanni, now ruled by Tushratta, to intervene militarily so close to the other's domain. Although both Mitanni and Hatti continued to challenge one another over control of north Syria, as well as southeastern Anatolia, that situation was temporarily stabilized in a sort of gridlock, with only limited movement possible on either side. But soon they would become embroiled in another major power struggle.

Egypt's Withdrawal from the International Scene

Upon the accession of Akhenaten, the founder of the Hittite empire, Suppiluliuma I, dictated a congratulatory letter to the new ruler. He expressed the wish that Hatti and Egypt would continue in the friendly and mutually beneficial relationship they had enjoyed under Akhenaten's father (Moran 1992: 114). The Egyptian hieroglyphic translation of the Hittite version of the later treaty between Ramesses II and Hattusili III in fact refers to this prior treaty:[12] "As for the treaty which was in place in the time of Suppiluliuma, the king of Hatti, likewise the treaty which existed in the time of Muwattalli, the king of Hatti, my predecessor, I hold to/embrace it" (cf. Wilson 1969: 200; Davies 1997: 102–03). This is undoubtedly the same treaty mentioned in the annals of Suppiluliuma (composed by his son Mursili II), the violation of which, according to the interpretation of the plague prayers of Mursili, led to the punishment of Suppiluliuma (his death in a plague) at the hands of the Hittite Storm God: "Then my father asked for the tablet of the treaty again, (in which there was told) . . . how the Storm God concluded a treaty between the countries of Egypt and Hatti, and how they were continuously friendly with each other" (Güterbock 1956: 98);

> although the Hattians as well as the Egyptians were under oath to the Hattian Storm-god, the Hattians ignored their obligations; the Hattians promptly broke the oath of the gods. My father sent foot soldiers and charioteers who attacked the country of Amqa, Egyptian territory . . . "Those arrangements which were made by the Hattian Storm-god – namely that the Egyptians and the Hattians as well were put under oath by the Hattian Storm-god . . . and that the Hattians promptly broke their word – has this perhaps become the cause of the anger of the Hattian Storm-god, my lord?" (translation adapted from Goetze 1969: 395).

Akhenaten was surely highly flattered by Suppiluliuma's offer, but the implementation of such an alliance was hardly one of the priorities of his reign. He was preoccupied with internal affairs, including the realization of his new vision of a universal god, the Aton cult. As Egypt's military control over its share of the border states of northern Syria loosened, the vassal princelings resumed their ceaseless squabbling. Egyptian detachments stationed in Syro-Palestine could be moved around in response to appeals for aid from Egypt's dependents, but Egypt was unwilling or unable to commit additional troops to the area. The management of provincial affairs was left in the hands of Egyptian administrators and local coalition partners. On the whole, Egypt reacted passively to these new developments. Only one particularly duplicitous ruler, Aziru of Amurru, was actually summoned to appear at the Egyptian court to explain his behavior; he was detained for some time before being sent home again. He is next found firmly in the Hittite camp (Moran 1992: xxxiii; Beckman 1999: 36–41, 59–60, 101, 104).

Collapse of Mitanni

The previous balance of power in northern Syria was now upset. The audacity of Mitanni's king Tushratta, who seems to have intervened in nominally Egyptian-controlled territory more than once, apparently alarmed Suppiluliuma. A festering dispute over control of the inland border state of Isuwa, located to the north of Mitanni and east of Hatti, provided him with an excuse to respond; Egypt refused to take sides in the conflict, probably conveniently citing the treaty obligations it had with both combatants. At first Suppiluliuma was careful to avoid attacking rulers who at least formally owed their allegiance, and their tribute, to the pharaoh. Instead, he focused directly on Mitanni, which found itself facing Hatti alone. After a lightning fast raid into its heartland, Mitanni collapsed suddenly; Tushratta fled and was subsequently murdered by one of his sons (Beckman 1999: 41–44). The Hittites had unexpectedly achieved supremacy in the whole region! On his homeward march, Suppiluliuma was rashly attacked by Egypt's ally, the king of Qadesh, who was defeated, his state incorporated into the Hittite empire. Henceforth Qadesh (Babylonian Qinsa/Hittite Kinza) found itself located precariously close to the front now separating Egypt and Hatti; it became the prize sought after in the ensuing tug of war between the two remaining world powers.

Egypto-Hittite Confrontation

The neutralization of Mitanni and the fall of Qadesh lifted some of the restraints which heretofore had moderated Hittite ambitions. Flushed with success, Suppiluliuma pushed further into the fringes of formerly Egyptian-dominated territory, while still avoiding a direct confrontation with Egyptian forces. His favorite target seems to have been the fertile agricultural lands of the Amqa district, lying in the Litani River basin of the Beqa'a Valley of Lebanon, south of the headwaters of the Orontes River, not far from the fortified town of Qadesh. Some of the Syrian city-states rushed to welcome Hatti, while others once more appealed desperately to Egypt for help as the tides of war and the currents of local politics fluctuated endlessly. Several loyal vassals sent identical reports to their Egyptian overlord: "Look, we are in Amqa, in cities of the king, my lord; and Etakkama, the ruler of Qadesh, assisted the troops of Hatti, and set the cities of the king, my lord, on fire. May the king, my lord, take cognizance, and may the king, my lord, give archers that we may (re)gain the cities of the king, my lord, and dwell in the cities of the king, my god, my Sun" (translation collated and adapted from Moran 1992: 260–61, 361–62). This situation is verified by a remark in another letter: "Moreover, troops of Hatti under Lupakku have captured cities of Amqa" (adapted from Moran 1992: 257). Even if, belatedly, Akhenaten did send an expedition to the area, it must have served little or no practical purpose (Moran 1992: xxxiii).

Finally, under Tutankhamun, the general Horemheb launched a counterattack in Syria,[13] for the first time bringing Egyptians and Hittites face to face across the field of battle, as they struggled for control of Qadesh and Amqa (Darnell 1991: 120–21). The pattern seems to have been this: the Egyptians headed straight for their erstwhile possession Qadesh, intent on recovering it; Hatti repulsed them and retaliated by attacking Amqa. The historical questions concerning who had actually started the current cycle of violence, and whether the inevitable retaliation was justified, seem to have become largely matters of indifference, as the partisans of each side rushed to avenge the latest outrage committed by the other.

Missed Opportunity

Shortly afterwards, Tutankhamun died without a designated male heir. Suppiluliuma's shock and disbelief can only be imagined, when Ankhesenamun, the young widow of Tutankhamun, in a daring bid to control the succession to the throne, sent two letters requesting the dispatch of one of his sons to marry her and take over the kingship of Egypt:

> He who was my husband died and I have no son(s). Shall I perhaps take one of my servants and make him my husband? [variant: Never shall I take a servant of mine and make him my husband!]. I have not written to any other country, I have written (only) to you. People say that you have many sons. Give me one of your sons and he is my husband and king in the land of Egypt (collated from texts translated by Goetze 1969: 319; Güterbock 1956: 94–97).[14]

Following an understandable period of hesitation and investigation, after he had finally received all the proper assurances, Suppiluliuma accepted the remarkable offer, and the boy was duly escorted across the mountains. However, he was doomed. "But when my father gave them one of his sons, they killed him as they led him there" (Goetze 1969: 395). "The people of Egypt killed Zannanza[15] and brought word: 'Zannanza died!' And when my father heard of the slaying of Zannanza, he began to lament for Zannanza" (Güterbock 1956: 108). His assassination at the hands of treacherous Egyptian agents (we may infer that they acted on the orders of Aye and/or Horemheb) led to his outraged father's renunciation of the standing treaty with Egypt and sparked a fresh round of attacks on Egyptian interests in Syria,[16] as Suppiluliuma reasserted his control over any territory he had just surrendered to Horemheb. But an epidemic broke out and spread with captives taken from Syria back to the Hittite capital, ravaging the whole land for more than 20 years. In its wake, both Suppiluliuma and his eldest son lay dead (Goetze 1969: 394–96).

Renewed Hostility

Skirmishes may have persisted throughout Horemheb's reign as king; it is also possible that a treaty regarded as still in effect during the reign of Muwattalli II (mentioned above) was arranged at this time. In Dynasty 19 an uprising in Egyptian Canaan once more escalated the level of tension in the area. Having dealt successfully with this problem at the beginning of his reign, Sety I later turned his attention to Amurru and the lost Qadesh. This time there would be no doubt that Egypt was responsible for disturbing the fragile peace. Sety's family had originated in the Eastern Delta near the old Hyksos capital of Avaris (now Tell el-Dab'a) at the site which would come to be known as Pi-Ramesse (modern Khata'na-Qantir). His father, the general Pa-Ramessu (later Ramesses I), served as commander of the nearby frontier fortress of Sile (modern el-Qantara), before his promotion to vizier and heir apparent under Horemheb; Sety had succeeded his father in these positions, before becoming king himself. Under Sety the capital of Egypt was moved to Pi-Ramesse, giving his armies easier access to Western Asia; with an extensive harbor located on the Pelusiac branch of the Nile, this site also had easy access to the sea. Royal rhetoric styled the reign of Sety as a Renaissance; one aspect of this conceit was his plan to reconstitute the empire of the glory days of Thutmose III. Amurru's return to the Egyptian fold under Sety is apparently referred to in the historical introduction to a later treaty between Tudhaliya IV and a Hittite prince, his nephew and brother-in-law, ruler of Amurru: "But when Muwattalli, uncle of My Majesty, became King, the men of Amurru committed an offense against him, informing him as follows: 'We were voluntary subjects. Now we are no longer your subjects.' And they went over to the King of Egypt" (Beckman 1999: 104–05). Sety's campaign is designated "The ascent which Pharaoh . . . made in order to take apart/dismantle the land of Qadesh and the land of Amurru," and the surrender of the fortress of Qadesh is depicted in the accompanying scene at Karnak (Epigraphic Survey 1986: pl. 23).

Sety would soon boldly move north to challenge the Hittite army directly. Charging into the amassed Hittite forces, and claiming to have scattered them in disarray and to have annihilated them, he is represented returning their leaders to Egypt to be dedicated to the service of the imperial god Amun-Re (Epigraphic Survey 1986: pls. 33–36). Hatti is described as "the wretched land of the Hittites, of whom his Majesty . . . made a great heap of corpses." The many images used to portray Sety include

> a ferocious [var.: mighty] lion, who (freely) roams over [var.: treads] the (most) impenetrable pathways of every mountainous land, a mighty [var.: young] bull, sharp-horned and implacable [var.: resolute], who tramps/stamps all over the Asiatics [var.: utterly devastates the mountainous lands] and tramples down the Hittites [var.: the land of Hatti], one who slays their chieftains – thrown to the ground in (pools of) their (own) blood – who forces his way through them like a hot flame and annihilates them (composite text collated from Epigraphic Survey 1986: pls. 34–35).

Nevertheless, not long after Sety's withdrawal, Qadesh defected again to the Hittites, thus prompting the next assaults mounted under Ramesses II, who unsuccessfully pressed his father's claim to it.

Battle of Qadesh

In the 4th year of his 67-year reign, Ramesses II set out from the frontier fortress of Sile and marched northward through Canaan to the Lebanese coast, turning inland through the mountains via the Eleutheros River Valley (the modern Nahr el-Kebir along Lebanon's northern border with Syria) to capture Amurru, which would serve as a base for his planned attack on Qadesh. Sure enough, in his fifth year, massed Egyptian and Hittite forces headed straight toward each other for a final showdown in Syria; not surprisingly, they met at Qadesh.[17] This was undoubtedly the first time an Egyptian king and a Hittite king had ever personally faced off against one another. The ensuing battle – the subject of an epic poem, and clearly regarded by Ramesses as the highpoint of his career – is documented, with the usual Egyptian spin,[18] in large-scale relief renderings (the *Pictorial Record*) and the complementary texts known as the *Bulletin* (or Record) and the *Poem*.[19] All details about the battle come from the Egyptian side, except as noted.

The regular Egyptian forces were organized into four divisions. Ramesses' chariot was prominent at the head of his army; and the Hittites were led by their king, Muwattalli II (grandson of Suppiluliuma). Ramesses crossed the Orontes just south of Qadesh. Although this detail is suppressed in the famous artistic renderings of the onslaught (most notably in the Great Temple of Abu Simbel),[20] the literary compositions depict Ramesses as arrogant and overconfident, easily deceived by Muwattalli's clever and successful ruse in sending out two of his bedouin agents to be apprehended and mislead the Egyptian king with false intelligence: "the villain of Hatti is (still) in the land of Aleppo, north of Tunip; he is (too) frightened of Pharaoh ... to come (further) south, since he has heard that Pharaoh ... has already come north" (*Bulletin* §§15–16). In his impetuousness, Ramesses rushed ahead to position himself at an advantageous site overlooking the town, where he began setting up camp before all his forces were in place. It was a foolish mistake, one which almost cost him his life. Imagine his horror when two genuine Hittite spies were captured and interrogated with a sound beating, leading to their confession of the truth just as the battle was getting underway – the Hittite army had actually been concealed all the time on the opposite side of Qadesh!

The Hittites launched a sneak attack, ambushing stragglers on the road; these fled headlong toward the camp, hotly pursued by enemy chariots. Confident of victory and distracted by the great wealth of the camp, the Hittites temporarily broke off the chase to begin looting, postponing mopping up operations for later (Beal 1995: 549).[21] Meanwhile, Ramesses found himself surrounded and nearly alone. In desperation he cries out to Amun-Re, asking why he has forsaken him; the invisible god replies, comforting the king: "Forward (into battle), (for) I am with you! I am your father; my hand is joined to yours – and I am more effective than hundreds of thousands of persons. I am the lord of might, who loves valor" (*Poem* §§125–27). So assured by the god, and enwrapped in his protection,[22] Ramesses suddenly charged like a suicidal berserker, pure adrenaline driving his frenzy, as he tried to take out as many

Hittites as possible: "He had a savage look in his eyes the moment he saw them, his numinous/mystical power[23] glowing like fire against them" (*Bulletin* §92). Ramesses' shield bearer despaired, disheartened at the seemingly hopeless odds; and he advised the king: "We're standing (all) alone in the thick of battle, while the infantry and chariotry have abandoned us. For what (possible) reason should you make a stand to (try to) save them? Let's clear out; (at least) you can rescue (the two of) us!" (*Poem* §§210–13). However, caught off guard, the Hittites were so terrified at the sight that they fell back in disarray just as Egyptian special forces, coming up from Amurru, reached the scene. Muwattalli, depicted fleeing in his chariot, is labeled "The wretched chieftain of Hatti standing, (his face) twisted around (i.e. looking over his shoulder), frightened of his Majesty"; he is further described as "apprehensive and distressed" (*Pictorial Record* §§41, 42).[24] When the battle is finally over for the day, Ramesses' wayward troops come creeping into camp under cover of darkness; and Ramesses harangues them for their cowardice in deserting him.

After further missteps and generally much confusion, the great battle turned out to be a stalemate, with each side later claiming victory. Egyptian accounts describe Muwattalli suing for a truce after some fighting on the second day: "Do not make your terms (too) harsh, (O) mighty king! Accord is more advantageous than fighting, so grant us (the) breath (of life)." When Ramesses reports this to his officers, they respond in one voice: "Accord is good – exceedingly (so) – (O) sovereign our lord; there's no reproach for peace(making) when you do it" (*Poem* §§319–20, 328–29). Keenly aware of the overextension of his own supply lines, and the precariousness of his tactical position, Ramesses was eager to assent. Muwattalli shadowed his withdrawal until he entered the mountainous ranges of the Lebanon. The Hittite king then occupied the Egyptian province of Damascus and left his brother Hattusili (the later Hattusili III) in charge while he returned to Hattusa, stopping off along the way to depose Benteshina, the wayward king of Amurru;[25] Damascus was relinquished a year later (Beal 1995: 549). In the wake of this retreat, practically all of Canaan rose up in rebellion, seeing the contest as a defeat for Ramesses and a clear indication of Egyptian weakness. Having dealt with this insurrection and reorganized his forces, in his eighth year Ramesses returned to northern Syria, raiding deeply into Hittite territory along the Orontes, north of Qadesh; and some degree of hostility between Egypt and Hatti persisted for more than a decade.

Aftermath of Battle

All the while, Ramesses' "greatest victory" was portrayed in temples throughout his realm and described on monuments set up at Pi-Ramesse, where the cult of the divine Ramesses flourished. Texts inscribed on obelisks originally raised in the capital city loudly proclaim that he "brought back the chieftains of Syria as prisoners of war and trampled the land of Hatti into the ground," and "smashed this land of Hatti, plundering them by (his own) valor, and making a great heap of corpses (out of them)"

(Montet 1935–37b: pls. 26, 18).[26] Ramesses also presents a brief account of the battle in a letter to Hattusili III; once again he emphasizes his own heroism. Nevertheless, the matter-of-fact tone he uses here indicates that the events he relates were already well known to the Hittite king (Edel 1994: vol. 1, 58–61, vol. 2, 100–01; Archi 1997: 11). Hittite allusions to the wars culminating in the Battle of Qadesh speak simply of Egypt's defeat by Muwattalli: "At the time that Muwattalli took the field against the king of the land of Egypt and the country of Amurru, and when he then had defeated the king of the land of Egypt and the country of Amurru" (translation adapted from Goetze 1969: 319),[27] "then My Majesty's uncle Muwattalli and the King of Egypt fought over the men of Amurru. Muwattalli defeated him, destroyed the land of Amurru by force of arms, and subjugated it" (Beckman 1999: 104–05). The hieroglyphic text of the subsequent treaty negotiated between Ramesses and Hattusili speaks only of Ramesses and Muwattalli having fought one another (Wilson 1969: 199; Davies 1997: 100–01).

The Egyptians, of course, took Ramesses' miraculous escape from the jaws of death as proof of his incomparable bravery and a sign of his great favor among the gods, even his own divinity.[28] The human failings so colorfully recounted in the literary account were interpreted positively: it was not merely Ramesses the man, but Ramesses *the god* who had achieved such unexpected success under seemingly impossible circumstances; Ramesses' godhood was actually enhanced!

> One of them cried out to his companion, saying: "He is not a human being, this one who is in our midst, but (rather) supremely powerful Seth, Ba'al in the flesh! Beyond what a(ny) human can do is that which he does!" ... (Another) one of them cried out to his companion: "Stay back! Watch out that you don't get (too) close to him! No question about it, Sakhmet the Great is the one who is with him; she is (joined) with him on his horses, (working) hand in hand with him. Anybody who goes (too) close to him, a hot blast of fire will come and roast his flesh!" (*Poem* §§157–59, 285–89).

Egypto-Hittite Treaty

In time, the subjugation of Mitanni by Suppiluliuma had left Hatti increasingly vulnerable on its eastern flank, without an adequate buffer against the growing territorial ambitions of Assyria. Just to cite an example, in the account of a raid he made to the west in his accession year (around year 35 of Ramesses II), the Assyrian king Tukulti-Ninurta I (ca. 1244–1208) claims: "I uprooted 28,800 Hittite people from Syria (lit. 'Beyond the Euphrates') and led (them) into my land" (Grayson 1972: 118, 121). At the same time, Egypt's western frontier was coming under increased pressure from Libyan encroachment; in an attempt to curb intruders from that direction, Ramesses built a chain of fortresses extending from the western approaches to the Delta almost to the border of modern Libya (Habachi 1980; O'Connor 1983: 272–75).

In an extraordinary turn of events, in the year 21 Ramesses II and Hattusili III (the brother of Muwattalli II and grandson of Suppiluliuma – his reign corresponds approximately to Ramesses' years 16–46), finally recognizing their common interests, entered into an alliance of peace. This great treaty has survived in copies recovered from both lands.[29] It was sealed through the exchange of large silver tablets written in Babylonian and carried by envoys between the two courts; needless to say, these have not survived.[30] However, even the great seals of the Hittite ruler and his queen Puduhepa (one on each side of the tablet sent from Hatti) are described in full detail in the hieroglyphic version of the text.[31] Three clay archival tablets containing substantial parts of the Babylonian text of the Egyptian silver tablet have been discovered during excavations conducted at ancient Hattusa.[32] A nearly intact Egyptian translation of the Hittite silver tablet into hieroglyphics is preserved on a wall just outside the south entrance to the Great Hypostyle Hall at Karnak Temple.[33] The format of this parity treaty[34] (an agreement between acknowledged equals) is similar to that employed in Hittite vassal treaties, which generally consist of preamble, historical introduction, specific provisions or stipulations, details of deposition of copies, list of divine witnesses, curses and blessings (Beckman 1999: 2–4). The particular obligations incumbent upon the signatories in this case are "the reaffirmation of former treaties, the mutual renunciation of aggression, a mutual defense pact, the guarantee of succession to the throne for the designated heir of the Hittite ruler, and the extradition of fugitives" (Beckman 1999: 4). The agreement recognized the territorial status quo, leaving Qadesh and Amurru in Hittite hands; in other words, the existence of the natural boundary between Egypt and Hatti was confirmed precisely where it had been ever since the days of Suppiluliuma, when the great struggle began! (Archi 1997: 4, 6).

The treaty is spoken of as "an arrangement for instituting the conditions/relationship which (the gods) Re and Seth set for the land of Egypt with the land of Hatti, in order to prevent hostiliti(es) from occurring between them forever" (cf. Wilson 1969: 199; Davies 1997: 100–01); "the eternal regulation which the Sun-god and the Storm-god made for Egypt with Hatti ... (to provide) peace and brotherhood and to prohibit hostilities between them" (Beckman 1999: 98). Egyptian and Hittite gods, summarized as "a thousand gods [variant: gods and goddesses] of the land of Hatti, together with a thousand gods [variant: gods and goddesses] of the land of Egypt," act as witnesses and guarantors of its provisions.[35] The official versions of the treaty were deposited "at the feet of the [Hittite] Storm-god ... [and] the Sun-god of Heliopolis and before the Great Gods" (translation adapted from Beckman 1999: 131). The purpose of the treaty is said to be the establishment of "good peace and good brotherhood" between the parties. The participants are spoken of as brothers, and they profess eternal peace and friendship. The hieroglyphic text reads: "he is in brotherhood with me and he is at peace with me, and I am in brotherhood with him and I am at peace with him forever." Nefertari, Ramesses' queen, writes similarly to Puduhepa: "And I am likewise in a condition of peace and brotherhood with you, my sister" (Beckman 1999: 129).[36] In the later court correspondence, Hattusili writes: "Have not you and I established (a relationship of) brotherhood, and are we (not) as of (only) *one* father, and are we (not) as of (only) *one* mother, and do we (not) live as in *a single* country?" (Edel 1994: vol. 1, 86–87; Archi 1997: 14).

The rulers swear an oath binding their descendants and heirs likewise down through the ages, forswearing any further hostilities between them and pledging to intercede on each other's behalf in the event of attack by rebels or foreign enemies. They also vow to extradite political opponents or other fugitives seeking exile in their lands. The humane treatment of returning fugitives is described as follows: "and let his house not be torn down, nor his women and children (dispersed); let him not be executed; let no injury be inflicted on his ears, eyes, mouth, or feet; and let no criminal charge(s) be raised against him" (translation collated from parallel hieroglyphic texts); the Babylonian version specifies: "They shall not tear out their tongues or their eyes. And they shall not mutilate(?) their ears or their feet. And they shall not destroy(?) their households, together with their wives and their sons" (Beckman 1999: 99). The issue of forced repatriation, as well as the question of royal succession, were especially important to Hatti, since Hattusili had deposed his nephew Urhi-Teshshup, who had reigned for seven years as Mursili III (approximately Ramesses' years 9–16). Urhi-Teshshup had been sent into exile, where attempts were made by his supporters in Anatolia and Hittite-controlled Syria to set him free; he apparently escaped to Egyptian territory (ca. year 18), and was eventually taken to the Egyptian court at Hattusili's request (in lieu of his forced repatriation).[37] Hattusili worried that he might mount a challenge to his uncle's legitimacy in a bid to regain the throne for himself – perhaps even with Egyptian help (Archi 1997: 6, 10–11; Beckman 1999: 105, 114, 130–32, 141). Finally, a curse is laid upon any ruler who might violate the terms of the treaty, and a blessing upon those who perpetuate them. The Egyptians could not resist inserting at the beginning of the hieroglyphic version, before the preamble, the claim that Hattusili had sued for peace (Wilson 1969: 199; Davies 1997: 98–101).

Royal Marriages

The pact with Hattusili was reaffirmed in the year 34 and again around years 40–42 by Ramesses' marriages to Hittite princesses.[38] The Hittite king was now Ramesses' father-in-law; and the former was represented along with his eldest daughter, a Chief Queen of Egypt, on marriage stelae set up in several Egyptian temples,[39] and in the decoration of a colossal statue of the Egyptian king at Pi-Ramesse itself! (Montet 1935–37a: pl. 7; Bittel 1986; Goyon 1987: 48; Desroches Noblecourt 1991: 162, fig. 19; Klengel 2002: 132–36). We are not certain of her Hittite name,[40] but she was given the Egyptian name Maat-Hor-Neferure.[41] With characteristic hyperbole and bombast, Ramesses uses the event to memorialize his "great victory" over the Hittites, portraying this marriage as a logical outcome. The princess was accompanied in her train by a sumptuous dowry, and the clear evidence of the strength of the Egypto-Hittite coalition would let their Syrian vassals know that any opposition against either in the future would be fruitless. The description of preparations made for her reception at the border between Hatti and Egypt, in the mountains of Syria, contains the first Egyptian reference to snow,[42] because it was winter and Ramesses was worried they might have a hard journey on the difficult roads. But Ramesses appealed to Seth, the god of (bad) weather, not to make rain, cold wind, or snow; Seth obliged him: the skies remained clear, and the days were like those of summer. So the Syrian chieftains said of Ramesses: "Even the sky is sealed/controlled by him; it behaves in whatever way he has commanded!" (cf. Wilson 1969: 257–58; Davies 1997: 136–41).

The joyous occasion of the meeting of the Hittite and Egyptian parties to escort the girl to Egypt is depicted as follows: "the infantry, chariotry, and officials of his Majesty ... mingling with the infantry and chariotry of Hatti, ... all the people of the land of Hatti mingling with those of Egypt. They ate and drank together, being of one mind, like brothers, no one disdainful of his partner, (rather) peace and brotherhood being between them in accordance with the plan/design of God himself." From the Hittite side, we know that Queen Puduhepa played an especially important role in the negotiations preceding the signing of the marriage contract (Archi 1997: 8). Despite his impatience at the delay in her arrival – due to difficulties in raising an appropriate dowry – when the beautiful young girl, whom her mother describes as "the daughter of heaven and earth," is finally about to set out for Pi-Ramesse, Ramesses is delighted (Beckman 1999: 131–36). One of the main issues at stake was the assurance that the princess would become a ruling queen in Egypt (Archi 1997: 13–14).[43] When he hears the glad news that his daughter is pregnant, Hattusili writes that, if the child is a boy, he would have a chance to succeed to the Hittite throne. Here we envision the proposed reciprocal arrangement of the ill-fated Zannanza affair! Later we learn that a daughter has been born; and the gods have proclaimed that she will become queen of a foreign land, which will thereby be united with Egypt (Edel 1994: vol. 1, 166–67, 226–31, vol. 2, 251, 254, 256, 349, 352–53). The letter to Ramesses expressing the Hittite grandparents' elation reads, in part: "I have rejoiced at (hearing the news of) your daughter; likewise the (whole) land of Hatti. Heaven, earth, the mountains, and the rivers were (also) joyful that the gods have granted you (such) good fortune!" (Edel 1994: vol. 1, 228–29, vol. 2, 352). Indeed, one of Ramesses' daughters bears the name Neferure, undoubtedly derived from her mother's name (Desroches Noblecourt 1991: 136; Edel 1994: vol. 2, 257; Archi 1997: 14, n. 51; Leblanc 1999: 270, fig. 73).

A Hittite Queen at Pi-Ramesse

Ramesses' new queen took up residence in a palace at the Egyptian capital. Hittite ladies-in-waiting served her, and a detachment of Hittite charioteers formed an honor guard for her. It was also here that she received the emissaries of her father (Edel 1994: vol. 1, 214–15, vol. 2, 321–22).[44] Excavations undertaken in the palace area since 1980 by the Pelizaeus Museum of Hildesheim have revealed a large installation associated with a chariotry garrison at Pi-Ramesse, including an armory, stables, workshops for repairing chariots and shields, and a training and exercise yard for horses. The most significant finds for our immediate purpose are several large limestone molds employed in forming the bronze fittings to be attached to Hittite figure-eight shields and Anatolian trapezoidal shields (Pusch 1989, 1991, 1996; Gore 1991: 16–17). "And if one finds not only the weapons of the fiercest enemy of Egypt, but also the tools of their production …, then their presence can only be understood as proof that the Egyptians and the Hittites were working side by side in a spirit of friendship. This leads inevitably to the conclusion that Hittites were producing or repairing Hittite shields to be used by Hittite contingents within Pi-Ramesses" (Pusch 1996: 143).

Letters continued to be exchanged between the courts, mostly cordial, while a few are a bit testy in tone. The international renown of Egyptian medical skills is referred to more than once. In replying to a request from Hattusili that a gynecologist might be sent to prepare potions for enhancing the fertility of his sister, Ramesses – obviously taken aback somewhat at the thought – responds: "She is said to be fifty or sixty years old. It is not possible to prepare medicines for a woman who has completed fifty or sixty years so that she might still be caused to give birth" (Beckman 1999: 137–38). He believes that only a miracle could accomplish what Hattusili wants! Nevertheless, he graciously consents to send her a physician – accompanied by a priest.

Fall of Hatti

The treaty remained in effect, and peaceful relations persisted, until the fall of the Hittite empire under pressures from both the Assyrians and the migrating Sea Peoples (who ushered in the Iron Age), just about the beginning of the reign of Ramesses III of Dynasty 20. The Hittite empire would be succeeded – in name only – by the biblical Hittites, the Neo-Hittites of North Syria; and Egypt would be left as the only remaining one of the three original superpowers. In an inscription dated to his fifth regnal year, Merenptah, the successor of Ramesses II, mentions that he had supplied shiploads of grain to Hatti after a disastrous crop failure (Kitchen 1982: 215; Davies 1997: 156–57).[45] In the historical inscription of his year 8 at Medinet Habu, Ramesses III describes the destruction of Hatti by the Sea Peoples (presumably under its last known king, Suppiluliuma II, the younger son of Tudhaliya IV):[46] "No land could stand before their arms" (Edgerton and Wilson 1936: 53; Peden 1994: 29). The lands of Qode/Kizzuwatna, Carchemish, Arzawa, and Alasiya/Cyprus also fell in the same series of assaults, as did Ugarit and Troy. Egypt, itself in turmoil at the time, was in no position to come to Hatti's aid.

Nevertheless, the Egyptian propaganda machine, always operating at a fever pitch, continued to portray the Hittites in typically xenophobic fashion. In a series of undated battle scenes, set pieces from his great temple at Medinet Habu, Ramesses III – eager to emulate his illustrious predecessor, Ramesses II – anachronistically records fictitious victories over three Hittite-controlled towns! (Edgerton and Wilson 1936: 94–96).[47] At Karnak he also borrows freely from Sety I in describing himself as "one who has trampled down the Hittites and slain their chief – (all) thrown to the ground in (pools of) their (own) blood" (Epigraphic Survey 1936: pl. 82A).[48] The symbolic value of

Hatti as an enemy overcome was maintained down into the Roman period (Gauthier 1927: 188). However, it was not a time for celebration. There would be no "peace dividend," as Egypt was already suffering the beginnings of internal instability – the economic, social, and civil disorders which characterize the end of the New Kingdom. Shortly after the death of Ramesses III, Egypt would lose all claim to superpower status for the better part of two centuries – just as the Israelite and Philistine/Palestinian kingdoms were organizing themselves in Canaan. But that is another story.

Concluding Remarks

The New Kingdom Egyptian empire in Western Asia was associated with the rise of a new line of kings who originated at the provincial center of Thebes in Upper Egypt, the home of the god Amun-Re. The creation of the empire had the effect of promoting this god to the status of national, imperial, and eventually universal deity. Henceforth, the fortunes of Amun-Re (and later also Seth of Avaris/Pi-Ramesse)[49] were based on the deeds of the warrior kings of Dynasties 18–20, and vice versa: the extent of the wealth of the god's estate was determined by victories in war, which, in turn, depended on the god's goodwill. This interdependence resulted in removing military actions from the realm of mere human political ambition to the realm of the divine. War was justified by invoking divine sanction: one was simply carrying out God's will. In this way, every war became a holy war.

At Karnak the treaty with Hatti is the centerpiece of a highly visible tableau occupying a prominent position on a wall regularly accessible to pilgrims entering or leaving the Hypostyle Hall during festival processions. Surrounded by battle scenes, here the conclusion of the peace treaty is interpreted as the achievement of victory (i.e. the submission of the foreign enemy) through war: peace results from war. Nevertheless, the success of the treaty was a milestone marking Egyptian recognition of peace as an acceptable alternative to war as a means of resolving conflict while achieving desired political objectives. This quantum leap became possible only after the Egyptians had been forced by circumstances to broaden their definition of "human" by conceding that at least some foreigners were basically human – even though they continued to villainize foreigners and blame them for their problems: primitive habits of thought die hard!

As is usually the case in history, the more things change, the more they remain the same. In the human condition, making war seems to be too easy; peacemaking is much more difficult. It took a long time for Egypt and Hatti to learn to cooperate peacefully. A simple lesson for today's world may be drawn from this remarkable human drama of more than 3,200 years ago – a lesson which is directly relevant to many of the long wars and other conflicts which currently beset the Middle East: Even the worst enemies of yesterday can become the best friends of today. For the sake of peace and the avoidance of further bloodshed, it is incumbent upon the participants in such hostilities, and their various supporters around the world, to recognize this fact sooner rather than any later!

Notes

1　I first lectured on this topic in 2001, in Emory University's "Year of Reconciliation" program, together with Hittitologist Billie Jean Collins. While we were both teaching at the University of Chicago, we enjoyed portraying the competing Egyptian and Hittite sides of this story. I thank Billie Jean for teaching me how to think about this subject, and for references and other help. However, any errors in this chapter are entirely my own. I thank Leonard Lesko for suggesting this topic for the Ancient Studies lecture series. Originally, I spoke of "the World's First Peace Treaty," but Assyriologist Alice Slotsky reminded me of Mesopotamia's long history of international treaties, citing the twenty-fourth century treaty between Ebla and Abarsal (Archi 1997: 6). Finally, I thank the editor for his valuable suggestions and encouragement in developing my lecture for publication.

2　For an introduction to these concepts, see Morenz 1973: 42–54; Assmann 1990; Hornung 1992: especially chapters 2–3, 7–9; Quirke 1994; Bell 1997: 127–32, 137–44.

3　The word for "human being" was applied originally only to Egyptians.

4　Due to the incomplete and biased nature of the extant written evidence on events marking relationships among Egypt, Mitanni, and Hatti – and the fact that its authors assume much prior knowledge – scholars disagree particularly on matters of relative chronology. (For some of the complications involved, see Murnane 1990: 115–37.) I restrict my background narrative to the most relevant data, set into a simplified framework, hoping to facilitate appreciation of the complex developments that eventually resulted in the treaty concluded between Ramesses II and Hattusili III.

5　First mentioned by name in an Egyptian text from the beginning of Dynasty 18 (Helck 1975: 110).

6　Even as late as the reign of Amenhotep III, a letter to the king of Anatolian Arzawa refers to the Hittites as completely out of the picture (Moran 1992: 101).

7　On Hittite foreign relations and attitudes toward war and peace, see, for example, Gurney 1961: 113–16; Goetze 1969: 201–06, 354–55; Beal 1995, and Beal's chapter in this volume; Beckman 1999, and relevant sections in Hallo and Younger 2003.

8　See Bleiberg 1996.

9　Text damaged; some such restoration is called for.

10　The annals refer to gifts sent by Great Hatti itself, in conjunction with the campaigns of years 33 and 41 (Sethe and Helck 1905–58: 701, 727).

11　The receipt of diplomatic gifts from Mitanni is referred to under Amenhotep II (Sethe and Helck 1905–58: 1326; cf. 1309 [mentioned in the same context with Hatti and Babylon – Mitanni is here designated as Naharin, "River Land": for a discussion of this term and its usage by the Egyptians, see Hoch 1994: 187–91]).

12　Fragmentary tablets preserve scraps of the Hittite version of the actual treaty between unidentified Hittite and Egyptian kings (Murnane 1990: 31–35; Beckman 1999: 7, 8, n. 2).

13　In Horemheb's tomb at Saqqara (dating to the reign of Tutankhamun) it is said of him: "His name was renowned in the land of the Hittites(?) when he travelled northwards" (Martin 1989: 80 and pl. 91; the captives taken during this campaign are represented in pls. 99–105). The earliest Egyptian depictions of classic or standard Hittites come from this tomb (Darnell 1991: 120–21). For the recently identified fragmentary Theban narrative battle reliefs of Asiatic campaigns during the reigns of Tutankhamun and Horemheb, see Johnson 1992. No classic Hittites are portrayed, nor does the small amount of extant text mention Hatti or Hittites.

14　An original fragment of the Queen's second letter has survived (Edel 1994: vol. 1, 14–15, vol. 2, 22–26; Archi 1997: 2).

15　Apparently Zannanza is not the prince's name; it represents a Hittite rendering of the Egyptian for "king's son" (Liverani 1971; Archi 1997: 3 and n. 6).

16 The badly damaged draft of an accusatory letter to be sent by the Hittite king to the Egyptian king (probably Aye), written in the aftermath of these events, has survived (Murnane 1990: 25–28; van den Hout 1994; Archi 1997: 3–4). It appears that the Egyptian king had professed his innocence in the boy's death.

17 For a diagram of the setting at the time of the battle, see Kitchen 1982: 52, fig. 17.

18 In large measure, of course, determined by the intended audience, whether mortal or divine – especially bearing in mind that no more than 5 percent of the Egyptians were literate, and very few of those were trained to read monumental hieroglyphs. But many more people could recognize and "read" the essential elements of the relief decoration.

19 For the narrative of the reliefs, see Kantor 1957: 50–51, and pls. 13–14 (Luxor), 15 (Abu Simbel); Gaballa 1976: 113–19, and fig. 9 (Abu Simbel); for representations of the battle at Luxor Temple, see Kitchen 1982: 55, 57, figs. 18–19. Easily accessible English translations of the *Bulletin* and *Poem* are available in Lichtheim 1976–80: vol. 2, 57–72; Davies 1997: 55–96. For translations of the texts associated with the reliefs, see Gardiner 1960: 35–45, who also offers a synthesis of the Egyptian documentation and a summary of the course of the battle (48–52, 54–56).

20 The battle is also represented at the Ramesseum, Luxor Temple, Karnak Temple, and the Ramesses II Temple at Abydos.

21 Beal presents a good summary account of the battle from the Hittitologist's point of view.

22 For the representation of the Theban war god Montu shielding Thutmose IV in a charging chariot and acting through him, see Bell 1985: 33–35 and pl. 2.

23 Associated with divine intervention in human affairs (Borghouts 1982).

24 The *Poem* (§146) also describes him as "standing up and turning around, apprehensive and afraid."

25 His submission to Ramesses in year 4 was considered treasonous. He was reinstated on his throne by Hattusili III, as a reward for his support of Hattusili against Urhi-Teshshup (Beckman 1999: 100).

26 For obelisks as abstract representations of the powers of divine kings, see Bell 2002.

27 Text known as the Apology of Hattusili III.

28 Cf. the discussion of the Qadesh reliefs in Broadhurst 1992.

29 Easily accessible English translations of the hieroglyphic text are available in Wilson 1969: 199–201; Davies 1997: 97–116. For a collation of the overlapping cores of the Hittite and Egyptian texts, see Langdon and Gardiner 1920: 187–91.

30 The preparation and exchange of the silver tablets is the subject of a series of letters written by Ramesses to Hattusili (Edel 1994: vol. 1, 16–29, vol. 2, 27–29; Archi 1997: 1, n. 1, and 6). A well-preserved bronze treaty tablet was discovered at Boghazköy in 1986 (Hoffner 1992: 47–48; Klengel 2002: 79, figs. 40–41). For a photograph and drawing of an impression of the great seal of Hattusili III, see Kitchen 1982: 81, fig. 26B; Klengel 2002: 71, fig. 38. In fig. 26A, Kitchen presents a drawing of a sealing of Muwattalli with a design similar to that described in the treaty.

31 Puduhepa had a particularly prominent position at court, and seems to have "officially shared power with her consort" (Archi 1997: 7–8). For the corresponding extraordinary position of Nefertari in Ramesses' court, see Kitchen 1982: 98–100; Hornung 1990: 186–87; Leblanc 1999: 23–140. Ramesses' mother, Queen (Mut-)Tuy – another imposing figure at Pi-Ramesse – also wrote two letters to the Hittite court in year 22 (she died in year 22/23), one to Hattusili and the other to Puduhepa (Edel 1974; Kitchen 1982: 97; Desroches Noblecourt 1982: 232–43; 1991: 129–30; Archi 1997: 8).

32 For a photograph of one of the clay tablets and a drawing of its text, see Kitchen 1982: 77, fig. 25; Klengel 2002: 81, fig. 42. For the most complete translation of the Babylonian text, with §§12–19 reconstructed on the basis of the corresponding sections of the Egyptian text, see Beckman 1999: 96–100; for §§1–11, see also Goetze 1969: 201–03.

33 A very fragmentary copy has also been identified at the Ramesseum.

34 Hittite treaties are attested at least as early as the last years of the Old Kingdom, at the end
    of the sixteenth century (Beckman 1999: 1). Whether written in Babylonian or Hittite,
    cuneiform treaties are designated as "a binding and an oath," with reference to the stipula-
    tions and the divine curses and blessings (Beckman 1999: 2). The corresponding Egyptian
    term may be translated as "an agreed arrangement" (Murnane 1990: 73–74).

35 For the gods in the Hittite pantheon who so serve, and the order in which they are named,
    see Gurney 1977: 4–6. For the equivalence of Hittite and Egyptian gods in the Ramesses-
    Hattusili treaty, cf. Langdon and Gardiner 1920: 185, 194–97.

36 For the "kind of family relationship ... established between the two courts," see Archi
    1997: 8; cf. Beckman 1999: 127.

37 Most, if not all, of the letters dealing with Urhi-Teshshup date from after the conclusion
    of the treaty; one clearly shows him still residing at Pi-Ramesse in year 34 (Edel 1994: vol.
    2, 74–76; Beckman 1999: 131–32). For a global attempt to grapple with the complex set
    of issues surrounding the whole Urhi-Teshshup affair, see Houwink ten Cate 1974.

38 Ramesses' first two Chief Queens, Nefertari and Isetnofret, had both died by year 34. The
    much less known second Hittite marriage was recorded in temples at Coptos and Abydos;
    it is also referred to in the Hittite correspondence. No name is attested for this queen (Edel
    1994: vol. 2, 264–67; Archi 1997: 14; Davies 1997: 144–49). The first Hittite marriage is
    memorialized in a Dynasty 30 legend intended to promote the cult of a healing form of the
    god Khonsu in Thebes. It revolves around the demonic possession and successful exorcism
    of (Maat-Hor-)neferure's younger sister, Bentresh (Wilson 1969: 29–31; Lichtheim 1976–
    80: vol. 3, 90–94; Ritner 2003: 361–66). For this latter name, apparently attested in the
    27th Dynasty Aramaic papyri associated with the Jewish garrison stationed at Elephantine,
    see Wilson 1969: 30, n. 8. See further Grelot 1972: 467; Porten and Lund 2002: 334.

39 Abu Simbel, Karnak, Amara West, Elephantine (4 blocks), Aksha/Serra West (1 block),
    and the Mut Temple complex (abbreviated version). Complete English translation available
    in Davies 1997: 117–43; cf. Wilson 1969: 256–58.

40 Edel suggests Šauškanu (Edel 1994: vol. 1, 226–27, vol. 2, 349, 351).

41 It is possible that her personal name was really just Neferure, and that maat-hor indicated
    her particular role as queen. She appears in the Bentresh Stele as a Chief Queen named
    Neferure. The queenly title "She who sees Horus" is attested in Dynasties 1 and 3, and
    occurs at least once in the Ptolemaic Period; the form "She who sees Horus and Seth"
    occurs in Dynasties 4–6, 11, 12, 18, and 19: see Troy 1986, pp. 64, 81, 84, 152–58, 163,
    165, 168, 179, 189; Kuchman 1977; 1993. Perhaps the title "She who sees Horus" was
    revived to satisfy in some way the Hittite insistence that she should actually be a ruling
    queen. The only Dynasty 19 queen who seems to have borne the title "She who sees Horus
    and Seth" was (Mut-)Tuy – the distinction may have been intended to specify the different
    court functions and ranks of Ramesses' mother and his foreign wife.

42 Employing a word borrowed from Semitic – ultimately related to English "snow" (cf.
    Hoch 1994: 264–65).

43 Her parents insisted on having the princess so anointed at a betrothal ceremony conducted
    by Egyptians at Hattusa before she was sent off to Egypt (Edel 1994: vol. 1, 130–31,
    134–39, 218–19, 224–25, vol. 2, 204, 207–08, 215, 337, 347).

44 Later in the reign, she is found (in retirement?) at a harim palace near Ghurab/Gurob at
    the entrance to the Fayoum (Gardiner 1948: 23–23a; Kitchen 1982: 110). She probably
    died before Ramesses' second Hittite marriage was undertaken (cf. Edel 1994: vol. 2, 266).

45 An earlier grain shipment from Egypt is mentioned in the correspondence between
    Ramesses II and the Hittite court, in conjunction with which the Hittite prince Heshmi-
    Sharrumma – formerly identified as the later Tudhaliya IV – visited Pi-Ramesse (Güterbock
    1956: 121; Hoffner 1992: 49; Edel 1994: vol. 1, 182–85, vol. 2, 275, 279–82).

46 For the serious chronological problems associated with the end of the Hittite Empire, see Güterbock 1992; Hoffner 1992.

47 The specific implications of these representations probably rest on Hatti's recent fall: it should be no surprise to the (ancient) viewer that Egypt survived the attacks of the Sea Peoples, and gloriously defeated them, whereas Hatti did not – after all, Egypt has always been stronger than the Hittites, as witnessed by its great victories over them.

48 A hymn addressing Ramesses VII as "one who has charged into the land of the Hittites, so that you might overturn its mountains" (Condon 1978: 13) was certainly derived from an original composition for Sety I or Ramesses II (Condon discusses the dating on pp. 4–5).

49 On Seth's later fall from grace and demonization resulting from his identification with the Syro-Palestinian storm god Ba'al, see te Velde 1977: 138–51.

References

Archi, Alfonso. 1997. "Egyptians and Hittites in Contact." In *L'impero ramesside: Convegno internazionale in onore di Sergio Donadoni*, 1–15. Rome.

Assmann, Jan. 1990. *Ma'at: Gerechtigkeit und Unsterblichkeit im Alten Ägypten*. Munich.

Beal, Richard H. 1995. "Hittite Military Organization." In Sasson 1995: 545–54.

Beckman, Gary. 1999. *Hittite Diplomatic Texts*. Atlanta.

Bell, Lanny. 1985. "Aspects of the Cult of the Deified Tutankhamun." In *Mélanges Gamal Eddin Mokhtar*, 31–59. Bibliothèque d'Etude 97.1. Cairo.

——. 1997. "The New Kingdom 'Divine' Temple: The Example of Luxor." In Byron E. Shafer (ed.), *Temples of Ancient Egypt*, 127–84. Ithaca.

——. 2002. "Divine Kingship and the Theology of the Obelisk Cult in the Temples of Thebes." In Horst Beinlich et al. (eds.), *Ägypten und Altes Testament* 33.3:5. *Ägyptologische Tempeltagung . . . 1999*, 17–46. Wiesbaden.

Bittel, Kurt. 1986. "Bildliche Darstellungen Hattušili's III. in Ägypten." In Harry A. Hoffner, Jr., and Gary M. Beckman (eds.), *Kanissuwar: A Tribute to Hans G. Güterbock on His Seventy-Fifth Birthday . . .*, 39–48. Chicago.

Bleiberg, Edward. 1996. *The Official Gift in Ancient Egypt*. Norman, OK, London.

——, and Rita Freed (eds.). 1991. *Fragments of a Shattered Visage: The Proceedings of the International Symposium of Ramesses the Great*. Memphis.

Borghouts, J. F. 1982. "Divine Intervention in Ancient Egypt and its Manifestation (*b3w*)." In R. J. Demarée and Jac. J. Janssen (eds.), *Gleanings from Deir el-Medîna*, 1–70. Leiden.

Broadhurst, Clive. 1992. "Religious Considerations at Qadesh, and the Consequences for the Artistic Depiction of the Battle." In Alan B. Lloyd (ed.), *Studies in Pharaonic Religion and Society in Honour of J. Gwyn Griffiths*, 77–81. London.

Cohen, Susan L. 2002. *Canaanites, Chronologies, and Connections: The Relationship of Middle Bronze Age IIA Canaan to Middle Kingdom Egypt*. Winona Lake.

Condon, Virginia. 1978. *Seven Royal Hymns of the Ramesside Period: Papyrus Turin CG 54031*. Munich and Berlin.

Darnell, John Coleman. 1991. "Supposed Depictions of Hittites in the Amarna Period." *Studien zur altägyptischen Kultur* 18: 113–40.

Davies, Benedict G. 1997. *Egyptian Historical Inscriptions of the Nineteenth Dynasty*. Jonsered.

Desroches Noblecourt, Christiane. 1982. "Touy, mère de Ramsès II, la reine Tanedjmy et les reliques de l'expérience amarnienne." *L'Egyptologie en 1979: Axes prioritaires de recherches*, vol. 2, 227–43. Paris.

——. 1991. "Abou Simbel, Ramsès, et les dames de la couronne." In Bleiberg and Freed 1991: 127–66.

Edel, Elmar. 1974. "Zwei Originalbriefe der Königsmutter *Tūja* in Keilschrift." *Studien zur altägyptischen Kultur* 1: 105–46, 295.

——. 1994. *Die ägyptisch-hethitische Korrespondenz aus Boghazköi in babylonischer und hethitischer Sprache*. 2 vols. Opladen.

Edgerton, William F., and John A. Wilson. 1936. *Historical Records of Ramses III: The Texts in Medinet Habu vols. I–II*. Chicago.

Epigraphic Survey. 1936. *Ramses III's Temple within the Great Inclosure of Amon*, Part II, *and Ramses III's Temple in the Precinct of Mut*. Chicago.

——. 1986. *The Battle Reliefs of King Sety I*. Chicago.

Gaballa, G. A. 1976. *Narrative in Egyptian Art*. Mainz am Rhein.

Gardiner, Alan. 1948. *Ramesside Administrative Documents*. Oxford.

——. 1960. *The Kadesh Inscriptions of Ramesses II*. Oxford.

Gauthier, Henri. 1927. *Dictionnaire des noms géographiques contenus dans les textes hiéroglyphiques*, vol. 4. Cairo.

Gianto, Augustinus. 1997. "Script and Word Order in *EA 162*: A Case Study of Egyptian Akkadian." *Orientalia* 66: 426–33.

Goetze, Albrecht. 1969. "Hittite Treaties," "Hittite Historical Texts," "Hittite Rituals, Incantations, and Description of Festival," "Hittite Prayers." In Pritchard 1969: 201–6; 318–19; 346–61; 393–401.

Gore, Rick. 1991. "Ramses the Great." *National Geographic* 179, no. 4: 2–31.

Goyon, Georges. 1987. *La découverte des trésors de Tanis: Aventures archéologiques en Egypte*. Paris.

Grayson, Albert Kirk. 1972. *Assyrian Royal Inscriptions*, vol. 1. Wiesbaden.

Grelot, Pierre. 1972. *Documents araméens d'Egypte*. Paris.

Gurney, O. R. 1961. *The Hittites*. Baltimore.

——. 1977. *Some Aspects of Hittite Religion*. Oxford.

Güterbock, Hans Gustav. 1956. "The Deeds of Suppiluliuma as Told by His Son, Mursili II." *Journal of Cuneiform Studies* 10: 41–68, 75–98, 107–30.

——. 1992. "Survival of the Hittite Dynasty." In Ward and Joukowsky 1992: 53–55.

Habachi, Labib. 1980. "The Military Posts of Ramesses II on the Coastal Road and the Western Part of the Delta." *Bulletin de l'Institut Français d'Archéologie Orientale* 80: 13–30.

Hallo, William W., and K. Lawson Younger, Jr. (eds.). 2003. *The Context of Scripture*. 3 vols. Leiden.

Helck, Wolfgang. 1975. *Historisch-biographische Texte der 2. Zwischenzeit und neue Texte der 18. Dynastie*. Wiesbaden.

Hoch, James E. 1994. *Semitic Words in Egyptian Texts of the New Kingdom and Third Intermediate Period*. Princeton.

Hoffner, H. A., Jr. 1992. "The Last Days of Khattusha." In Ward and Joukowsky 1992: 46–52.

Hornung, Erik. 1990. *The Valley of the Kings: Horizon of Eternity*. New York.

——. 1992. *Idea into Image: Essays on Ancient Egyptian Thought*. New York.

Houwink ten Cate, Philo H. J. 1974. "The Early and Late Phases of Urhi-Teshub's Career." In K. Bittel et al. (eds.), *Anatolian Studies Presented to Hans Gustav Güterbock on the Occasion of his 65th Birthday*, 123–50. Istanbul.

Johnson, W. Raymond. 1992. *An Asiatic Battle Scene of Tutankhamun from Thebes: A Late Amarna Antecedent of the Ramesside Battle-Narrative Tradition*. Unpublished Ph.D. dissertation, University of Chicago.

Kantor, Helene J. 1957. "Narration in Egyptian Art." *American Journal of Archaeology* 61: 44–54.

Kemp, Barry J. 1983. "Old Kingdom, Middle Kingdom, and Second Intermediate Period *c.* 2686–1552 BC." In Trigger et al. 1983: 71–182.

Kitchen, K. A. 1982. *Pharaoh Triumphant: The Life and Times of Ramesses II*. Warminster.

Klengel, Horst. 2002. *Hattuschili und Ramses: Hethiter und Ägypter – ihr langer Weg zum Frieden*. Mainz.

Kuchman Sabbahy, Lisa. 1977. "The Titles of Queenship: Part I. The Evidence from the Old Kingdom." *Newsletter/Journal of the Society for the Study of Egyptian Antiquities* 7.3: 9–12.

——. 1993. "Evidence for the Titulary of the Queen from Dynasty One." *Göttinger Miszellen* 135: 81–87.

Langdon, S., and Alan H. Gardiner. 1920. "The Treaty of Alliance between Hattušili, King of the Hittites, and the Pharaoh Ramesses II of Egypt." *Journal of Egyptian Archaeology* 6: 179–205.

Leblanc, Christian. 1999. *Nefertari, "L'aimée-de-Mout."* Monaco.

Lichtheim, Miriam. 1976–80. *Ancient Egyptian Literature: A Book of Readings*, vols. 2–3. Berkeley.

Liverani, Mario. 1971. "Zannanza." *Studi Micenei ed Egeo-Anatolici* 14: 161–62.

Martin, Geoffrey Thorndike. 1989. *The Memphite Tomb of Horemheb, Commander-in-Chief of Tut'ankhamūn*. London.

Montet, Pierre. 1935–37a. "Les fouilles de Tanis en 1933 et 1934." *Kêmi* 5: 1–18.

——. 1935–37b. "Les obélisques de Ramsès II." *Kêmi* 5: 104–14.

Moran, William L. 1992. *The Amarna Letters*. Baltimore.

Morenz, Siegfried. 1973. *Egyptian Religion*. Ithaca.

Murnane, William J. 1990. *The Road to Kadesh: A Historical Interpretation of the Battle Reliefs of King Sety I at Karnak*. Chicago.

O'Connor, David. 1983. "New Kingdom and Third Intermediate Period, 1552–664 BC." In Trigger et al. 1983: 183–278.

Oosthoek, Ann-Laure. 1992. "Hittite ou pas Hittite? Trois représentations à charactère hybride." In Claude Obsomer and Ann-Laure Oosthoek (eds.), *Amosiadès: Mélanges offerts au Professeur Claude Vandersleyen par ses anciens étudiants*, 335–46. Louvain-la-Neuve.

Peden, A. J. 1994. *Egyptian Historical Inscriptions of the Twentieth Dynasty*. Jonsered.

Porten, Bezalel, and Jerome A. Lund. 2002. *Aramaic Documents from Egypt: A Key-Word-in-Context Concordance*. Winona Lake.

Pritchard, James B. (ed.). 1969. *Ancient Near Eastern Texts Relating to the Old Testament*. Princeton.

Pusch, Edgar B. 1989. "Ausländisches Kulturgut in Qantir-Piramesse." In Sylvia Schoske (ed.), *Akten des vierten Internationalen Ägyptologen-Kongresses München 1985*, vol. 2, 249–56. Hamburg.

——. 1991. "Recent Work at Northern Piramesse: Results of Excavations by the Pelizaeus-Museum, Hildesheim, at Qantir." In Bleiberg and Freed 1991: 199–220.

——. 1996. "'Pi-Ramesses-Beloved-of-Amun, Headquarters of thy Chariotry': Egyptians and Hittites in the Delta Residence of the Ramessides." In Arne Eggebrecht (ed.), *Pelizaeus Museum Hildesheim: The Egyptian Collection*, 126–44. Mainz.

Quirke, Stephen. 1994. "Translating Ma'at." *Journal of Egyptian Archaeology* 80: 219–31.

Ritner, Robert K. 2003. "The Bentresh Stela (Louvre C 284)." In William Kelly Simpson (ed.), *The Literature of Ancient Egypt: An Anthology of Stories, Instructions, Stelae, Autobiographies, and Poetry*, 361–66. New Haven.

Sasson, Jack M. (ed.). 1995. *Civilizations of the Ancient Near East*, vol. 1. New York.

Schulman, Alan Richard. 1964. *Military Rank, Title and Organization in the Egyptian New Kingdom*. Berlin.

——. 1995. "Military Organization in Pharaonic Egypt." In Sasson 1995: 289–301.

Sethe, Kurt, and Wolfgang Helck. 1905–58. *Urkunden der 18. Dynastie: Historisch-biographische Urkunden*. 22 fascicles. Leipzig and Berlin.

te Velde, H. 1977. *Seth, God of Confusion: A Study of his Role in Egyptian Mythology and Religion*. Leiden.

Trigger, B. G., B. J. Kemp, D. O'Connor, and A. B. Lloyd 1983. *Ancient Egypt: A Social History.*
    Cambridge.
Troy, Lana. 1986. *Patterns of Queenship in Ancient Egyptian Myth and History.* Uppsala.
van den Hout, Theo P. J. 1994. "Der Falke und das Kücken: der neue Pharao und der hethitische
    Prinz?" *Zeitschrift für Assyriologie und Vorderasiatische Archäologie* 84: 60–88.
Ward, William A., and Martha Sharp Joukowsky (eds.). 1992. *The Crisis Years: The 12th Century
    B.C. from Beyond the Danube to the Tigris.* Dubuque.
Wilson, John A. 1969. "Egyptian Myths, Tales, and Mortuary Texts," "Egyptian Treaty,"
    "Egyptian Historical Texts." In Pritchard 1969: 3–36; 199–201; 227–64.
Yoyotte, Jean, and Jesús López. 1969. "L'organisation de l'armée et les titulatures de soldats
    au nouvel empire Egyptien." *Bibliotheca Orientalis* 26: 3–19.

7

From Achaemenid Imperial Order to Sasanian Diplomacy: War, Peace, and Reconciliation in Pre-Islamic Iran

Josef Wiesehöfer

To Rüdiger Schmitt on the occasion of his 65th birthday with gratitude

Introduction

The history of the Near East was crucially shaped by the rule of the three great Iranian dynasties of the Achaemenids (ca. 550–330 BC), Parthians (ca. 250 BC–AD 224), and Sasanians (AD 224–651). The realm of Cyrus the Great and his successors is rightfully called the first world empire of antiquity, since, by incorporating the former empires, it temporarily covered the entire area between Thrace and Egypt in the west and Sogdia and the Indus valley in the east. By contrast, the Parthians and Sasanians shared their rule over the Near East with the Romans. For a long time, ancient historians have looked upon the history of these realms almost exclusively from a Greco-Roman point of view; this applies to the selection of the sources, to the determination of topics relevant to research (Wiesehöfer 2005b), and to the treatment of Iranian foreign policy that is usually considered only in the context of Greco-Roman eastern policy. Although, at first sight, a western perspective appears inevitable because of the abundance of Greek and Roman sources, it fails to do justice to the extant tradition as a whole and to take the priority of the indigenous sources into consideration; methodologically, both are indispensable if we want to achieve a fair understanding of foreign cultures. We should also remember that the relegation of Iran to the "outer fringes" or its designation as a "marginal civilization" ("Randkultur") was due less to reasons of evidence than to the assignment of unequal cultural potential to the Greeks and Romans on the one side and the Iranians on the other, and to the distorting influence of ancient and modern stereotypes of the "Barbarian" or the "Oriental." Although this chapter, due to the available evidence, will also primarily deal with the relations between Iran and its neighbors in the west, it will nevertheless try to adopt an Iranian perspective on the problem of peace and war in pre-Islamic times. I will begin, however, with some general remarks on the relationship between Iran and the Greco-Roman world (see ibid.).

With regard to foreign policy and cultural contacts, educated western readers still seem convinced today that the relations between Greeks, Romans, Byzantines, and Iranians were of a primarily bellicose and unfriendly nature. Historically powerful key words like "Marathon," "Issus," "Carrhae," "barbarians," or "oriental despotism" have helped shape the perception that the ancient Iranians and their western neighbors were hardly ever able to engage in real communication and peaceful exchange. Yet a closer look at the history of their relations will teach us otherwise. That we owe Greek views of the "barbarian" (Achaemenid) neighbors to Greek authors is understandable; that relations, whether belligerent or peaceful, between Persians and Greeks are a central theme almost exclusively in Greek literary sources is informative; the fact, however, that, in addition, almost all Persian views of the Greeks are due to Greek versions of Persian views of the Greeks ("Persians on Greeks are really Greeks on Persians and therefore Greeks on Greeks": Sancisi-Weerdenburg 2001: 340), is disturbing. Therefore, Greco-Persian relations in Achaemenid times disclose themselves to us only (1) through an exact analysis of the Greek testimonies, embedded in a history of ideas and mentalities and in a synchronic and a diachronic comparison, (2) through non-literary (especially epigraphic and archaeological) material found in the Persian Empire itself,[1] and (3) through the critical interpretation of historical myths and of literary *topoi* that, though influential, are only partly historical.[2]

For a long time, the military conflicts between Greek *poleis* ("city-states") and the Persian Great King and, in their wake, an evolving contempt for barbarians in Athenian literature, rhetoric, and art that soon became a *topos* itself, were seen as predominant in relations between Athens, or even Greece, and Iran in classical times. However, as is well known, not all Greeks were enemies of the Great King at all times; on the contrary, many of them were his subjects, mercenaries, and servants. The Persians even became highly valued allies in Greek interstate conflicts and guarantors of Greek Common Peace settlements (Alonso, this vol.). Greek literature and art typically reflect multifaceted views of the Persians, not a uniform outlook. Furthermore, new excavations in Gordium and Dascylium in Asia Minor prove unreduced continuation of imports of fine Attic pottery after 480 BC (de Vries 1997; Tuna-Nörling 1998), and recent historical research has demonstrated that the border regions between the Delian League and the Persian Empire in Western Anatolia were zones of intensive cultural interaction (Balcer 1985; Miller 1997; Whitby 1998). All these findings warn us not to equate political and military antagonism with the absence of cultural exchange. Besides, in Achaemenid times cultural transfer took place not only in an easterly, but also in a westerly direction. The fact that military enemies might be "archetypal opponents" for the political identity of a community, but "models in some regard" for its cultural identity, can be exemplified by Athens in the third generation after Marathon (Hölscher 2000: 308, 313). At this time, when to rich Athenian youths the orient no longer appeared as a cultural opposite, but as an ideal and fascinating "other world," we can observe a change of social ideals and patterns of behavior that used Persian models but, at the same time, adapted them to the Athenians' own needs. Moreover, in myth (we need think only of Orpheus) and reality representatives of Greek culture, such as diplomats and artists, met "ready Oriental listeners" (Hölscher 2000: 310). Changes in life-style and world-view were connected with the import of eastern products and the local imitation of Oriental luxury goods (Miller 1997). As far as Iranian contacts with the west are concerned, Iranian visits to Greek cult places (for instance Delos) are well attested, and they continued after the end of Achaemenid rule (Baslez 1986). Besides, in regions like Anatolia, due to the proximity of Iranians, Greeks, Lydians, Phrygians, and others, we notice simultaneous Iranian, Greek, and indigenous influences on culture, and there emerged new cultural phenomena in which we cannot always easily distinguish and attribute individual components. The favorable conditions created by Achaemenid rule for the spreading of scientific and philosophical ideas have once more been emphasized recently with regard to the history of astronomy and cosmology (Panaino 2001: 92–95). It was also in this period that Zoroaster and Iranian religious concepts entered the cultural horizon of Europe for the first time.[3]

Contempt and imitation of the barbarians, fear and admiration of a dangerous and decadent but also fascinating opposite and "other" world, military confrontation and transcultural exchange, acculturation and new creations – all these were almost contemporaneous forms of Greek mental as well as practical preoccupation with their powerful neighbors in the east. In contrast, in Persian royal ideology the Greeks (the "Ionians," *Yaunā*, of the royal inscriptions) were worth mentioning only as subjects of the Great King. In practice, however, he welcomed the contributions of Greeks from outside his realm, from whose cultural stimulation as well as advice in political affairs he hoped to profit.

Heirs to the Achaemenids and Seleucids in Iran and Mesopotamia were the Parni, an originally semi-nomadic people who invaded the Iranian province of Parthia around 250 BC and conquered all of western Iran and Mesopotamia after the Seleucids' defeat by Rome in 190 BC. Eventually, the Parni, calling themselves Parthians soon after their first successes, and their kings of the Arsacid clan became familiar with Greek culture and with various forms and processes of transculturation, first in Parthia and later in other parts of Iran and Mesopotamia. For centuries, they shared borders with the Seleucid and then the Roman empires in the west and for more than 100 years with the Greco-Bactrian empire in the east, and they ruled over a large number of Greek subjects or subjects affected by Greek culture. It is no wonder, therefore, that the Arsacid era was particularly marked by cultural exchange in various forms and by phenomena of syncretism. It might have been bad experiences with their Roman neighbors and their destabilizing effect on Arsacid rule,[4] domestic necessities, and/or a new concept of safeguarding their power which, in the first century AD, induced Vologeses I and his successors to stress the Iranian foundations of Arsacid kingship and imperial rule. Compared with such "Iranianism," which anticipates later Sasanian times, the Greco-Hellenistic foundations of royal self-legitimation, self-perception, and views of their realm faded in importance, although Greek cultural traditions in Mesopotamia and Iran did not disappear. It was, after all, the role of the Parthians as transmitters of goods and ideas between the Roman Empire and India, Central Asia, and China that opened up the east to Greek culture and the west to eastern cultures (Wiesehöfer 2001b).

On April 28, 224 AD the Parthian king Artabanus IV lost his life in a battle against his challenger Ardashir, the vassal king of Fars. This marked the end of the almost

500-year-old Arsacid reign over Iran. The new masters from the "house" of Sasan had begun their ascent as local dynasts of Istakhr near Persepolis and from 205/6 extended their domain at the expense of other "petty kings" of the south. In the following years they came into possession of all Parthian territories as well as north-eastern Arabia. So far, scholars have paid little attention to the history of relations between the Sasanian Empire and the Mediterranean world.[5] Normally, they have limited themselves to an account of the military encounters between Iran and Rome or Byzantium and of the Romano-Byzantine views of Iran. Many of the older studies that deal with peaceful contacts between Romans/Byzantines and Sasanians subscribe to the conventional west-east perspective, overlook the variety of cultures and traditions on both sides of the Euphrates and the multifaceted processes of cultural interaction, and think of the reception and transformation of western cultural elements in Iran chiefly as "barbarization" (Hauser 2001). Only recently, regional studies (such as Fowden 1999 on the monastery of Saint Sergius) have begun to underline the multicultural character of the border regions, the extent of cross-border transcultural contacts, and the inadequacy of holistic cultural concepts based on ideas of ethnic isolation and purity. Other studies have demonstrated the importance and variety of official as well as unofficial friendly exchange between Romans and Sasanians in the fields of philosophy, medicine, religion, mythology, and magic as well as art and technical knowledge.[6] And only recently has the role of Rome and Byzantium in the Iranian view of world history been uncovered (Wiesehöfer 2005a).

In view of the state of our sources, and because there is no Iranian historiographical tradition comparable to the Greco-Roman, it is impossible to deal with the topic of this volume in the context of a history of events. It makes more sense to illustrate its importance by way of three case studies, focusing, for the Achaemenids, on the royal ideology of a *pax Achaemenidica* ("Achaemenid Peace") and Persian strategies of reconciliation in a regional or local context; for the Parthians on the Arsacids' liking of Greek culture and their dealings with the "Greek" cities of their realm in times of peace and war; and for the Sasanians on the procedures of peace negotiations and the motif of the chivalrous single combat.

Pax Achaemenidica: Royal Ideology of Peace and Achaemenid Strategies of Reconciliation

> Proclaims Darius, the king: May Auramazda bring me aid together with all the gods; and may Auramazda protect this country from the (enemy) army (*hainā*), from crop failure (*dušiyāra*) (and) from Falsehood (*drauga*)! Upon this country may not come an (enemy) army, nor crop failure nor Falsehood! This I pray as a favour of Auramazda together with all the gods; this favour may Auramazda grant me together with all the gods (*DPd* 12–24; trans. R. Schmitt).

The ideological traits of Achaemenid kingship, heralded empire-wide in images and inscriptions, can be summarized as follows: first, kingship is firmly rooted in Persia or, more precisely, in the region of Persis and the Aryan ethnic and cultural community, and it requires descent from the family of Achaemenes.[7] The Persians, at the same time, stand out among all peoples on account of their abilities and their special relationship to the ruler. Persian kingship differs from that of any neighbors and predecessors in that it exceeds them in power ("king of kings"), not least because an unprecedented number of "lands" or "peoples" acknowledges its rule. Second, Persian kingship is characterized by a special relationship between ruler and gods, although neither divine descent nor godlike qualities are attributed to the king. Auramazda "and the other gods that are" have bestowed the kingdom on Darius (or Xerxes); "by the favor of Auramazda" he has been elected and installed, and – successfully – rules the empire. As the god's "representative" on earth, he is vested with a kind of royal charisma (*farnah). Third, as he owes his kingship to the favor of Auramazda, the king is obliged to protect the god's good creation. He is capable of doing so because the god has given him the ability to tell right from wrong and because he has special qualities which are conducive to the promotion of justice and the protection of order. Although an absolute monarch, he is capable of being impartial and self-controlled; he judges, rewards, and punishes not at his own discretion, but always on the basis of fairness; as a good horseman, warrior, and farmer he is able to ward off the dangers threatening his empire. This is why the violent death of a king (by murder or on the battlefield) endangers god-given imperial order no less than the disloyalty of the king's subjects (bandakā) does. Order, not chaos, peace, not tension, good conduct of the subjects and royal generosity, not disloyalty and kingly misbehavior dominate the inscriptions and the imagery of the royal residences.

The Persian kings had no problems in adapting their behavior to the royal ideologies of foreign cultures. They were, on the contrary, eager to gain advantage from them (thus in his cylinder inscription from Babylon Cyrus shows himself to be the tool of Marduk, and Darius calls himself "king by the favor of Bel" in a copy of his record of deeds in the same place). In the context of his official and social functions both in the palace and as a traveling king, the ruler on the one hand emphasizes the *master-servant* relationship between himself and all his subjects (e.g. when distributing gifts or arranging banquets). On the other hand, and at the same time, he gives the impression of being accessible and concerned with the worries of his subjects.

The inscriptions of the Achaemenid kings take the loyalty of the subjects for granted, presenting it as the necessary consequence of divine instruction and royal efforts to guarantee justice, "truth," and the well-being of all inhabitants of their realm. These efforts are desired by the gods, and it is Auramazda in particular who enables the king to fulfill his tasks.[8] By contrast, the inscriptions threaten with sanctions the man who is not inclined to follow divine and royal law.[9] Greek tradition and royal proclamations (cf. DB) know of merciless revenge and cruel punishment of rebels and insurgents, even if kings Cambyses and Xerxes, presented as particularly cruel by Greek sources, must be acquitted of some of the crimes they purportedly committed and their acts hardly differed from those of their more popular fathers, Cyrus and Darius. Carrot and stick, guarantee of well-being (although within traditional relationships that were economically and socially unbalanced) and graveyard peace after the quelling of rebellions were the two sides of the pax Achaemenidica at all times.

Provincial elites imitated the royal life-style and adopted royal images and proclamations. The significance of this phenomenon might become clearer if we reconsidered it, for example, in the light of recent research on Augustan culture. Did this "semantic" and "pragmatic" system "of large scope" not also prevent the hatching of counter or alternative plans? Is it enough to explain its spreading to the private sphere only by joyful agreement of the recipients or could it partially be an expression of "noncommittal political applause" or a rather opportunistic mentality? Could the ancient spectators and listeners not have grown weary of the constant repetition and ubiquity of royal imagery and epigraphic set phrases, even if we today might like their emphasis on peace and order and their renouncement of images of war and strife?[10] Moreover, political reality was not as peaceful as proclaimed.

Up to now, the positive image the Persian kings created of themselves and their policy has remained quite powerful – if we leave aside the equally imaginative Greco-occidental representation of the Persian Wars with the Greeks. Emphasis is often placed on the "tolerance" of the Achaemenids which, especially in comparison with their Assyrian forerunners, appears as the exact opposite of the strictness, severity, or even brutality of Sargon, Sanherib or Assurbanipal. Such statements are based particularly on the great difference in tenor between the Assyrian and Achaemenid royal proclamations in both their epigraphic and pictorial forms. But three points are easily overlooked. First, when the Achaemenids established, extended, and secured their rule, they must have had in mind the Assyrian example of the foundation, maintenance, and downfall of an empire. Second, Cyrus and his successors emulated their Assyrian forerunners in words (e.g. in Cyrus's famous cylinder inscription from Babylon in which Assurbanipal is mentioned), in pictures (for instance, in the sculptural art of the palaces, which shows Assyrian influence),[11] and in deeds (deportations, quelling of rebellions; van der Spek 1983; Bedford in press); they also left no doubt about the fact that their empire had been established by means of war (Briant 1999). Third, Achaemenid minor (e.g. glyptic) art knows martial subjects very well, and the Achaemenid images of imperial peace are affixed to the external façades of the palaces, whereas the Assyrian images of conquest and submission are found inside the palace rooms (Kuhrt 2001: 168). In addition, much else suggests that the Persians had learned their lesson from Assyrian ideology and practice and were probably also imitating the Neo-Babylonians.[12] The result was an imperial ideology that particularly stressed the reciprocity of royal care and loyalty of the subjects. The Persians also showed greater flexibility in the administration of their empire (omitting universal provincialization and promoting local autonomy); they did not impose hierarchization on the divine sphere (the local divinities were not subordinated to Auramazda), and they did not engage in mass deportations on an Assyrian or Roman scale as a means of pacification.[13]

The well-considered and successful Achaemenid policy of reconciliation and peace-keeping can be illustrated with two historical case studies; these, however, are not meant to give the impression that there were no irrational elements in Persian governmental practice.[14] A Milesian inscription indicates that around 390 BC the cities of the Ionian Federation settled a border dispute between two members, Miletus and Myus, under the supervision of the satrap Struses (Struthas). The Federation's Court of Justice (perhaps called up by the satrap after an appeal of the cities to the king) carried out an investigation which, however, did not lead to a verdict because the Myusians gave up beforehand. The satrap was informed about the fact and confirmed that the land was to belong to the Milesians. In other words, a local instance usually made a decision after independent proceedings, and the satrap ratified, that is, recognized it and made a note of it and its political and fiscal effects in the provincial archives. We know of such decisions and regulations of local or regional administrative bodies in the fourth century BC that were sanctioned by the Persian governor because of their political and fiscal relevance for the satrapy.

The second example comes from a completely different cultural area within the empire. At the end of the fifth century BC, a conflict erupted at Elephantine, on the southern border of Egypt, between the Jewish worshippers of Yahweh and the Egyptian priests of Khnum, in the course of which the Jewish sanctuary was destroyed. The official Persian decision, which was made after repeated requests of the Jewish military settlers, is characteristic of Persian religious policy: the administration agreed to the reconstruction of the temple or altar house because the Jews could refer to privileges dating to the time of Cambyses. The Persians did not interfere with the religious and ritual issues; instead, these were decided by the authorities in Jerusalem who made arrangements for a further offering of food and incense, but no longer for burnt offerings which before had probably included rams, the sacred animals of Khnum. Even in the religious and ritual sphere, therefore, we observe the interaction of local autonomy and central control. The latter could even authorize the destruction of a sacred place like the temple of Apollo at Didyma that had been involved in the Ionian Rebellion and was therefore regarded by the Persian king as a place of demons.

Even if the extent of the subjects' acceptance or refusal of the royal Persian "order of peace" cannot really be determined, the Achaemenid Empire came to an end mostly because of the tactical skills of a military opponent, not because of a lack of internal cohesion or administrative or economic crises. Such cohesion had been the result of consistent royal actions for the well-being of the subjects and the successful combination of an amazing degree of autonomy granted to the subjects (structural "tolerance") and strict and, when necessary, severe supervision by the central authorities. Its conqueror, Alexander, regarded many of the institutions of the Persian empire as exemplary, and thereby earned the title of the "last of the Achaemenids" (Briant 2002: 876); this, too, explains the Achaemenid traits of later Near Eastern empires.

Political Calculation or Genuine Philhellenism? The Parthian Relationship with Greek Culture and Greek Subjects in Times of Peace and War

Roman views of the barbarian and devious, exotic, and soft, and also beautiful Parthian enemy, who, belonging to an *orbis alter* ("counter world"), is not able to behave like a Roman, stand in the literary and iconographic tradition of Greek images of barbarians, especially Persians.[15] Not surprisingly, therefore, in Augustus' time (after 20 BC) the Greek victories of 490 (Marathon) and 480–479 BC (Salamis and Plataea) were systematically "updated," and the identification of the Parthians with the Persians became a central topic of Roman imperial ideology. All this aimed at stressing the superiority of the occident over the orient as a singular achievement of occidental history (Schneider 1998: 110–11). Like Alexander, who had passed off his Persian campaign to the Greeks as a war of revenge for Xerxes' invasion of Hellas, so too the first Roman Emperor represented Roman preparations against Parthia since Caesar's time as retaliatory measures. When the Augustan poets call the Parthians Medes, Persians or Achaemenids (cf. Wissemann 1982), this is equivalent to the Parthians' Achaemenid-Persian dress in Roman pictorial art or the imitation of the naval battle of Salamis during the inaugural ceremonies of the temple of Mars Ultor in 2 BC.[16]

While the Greek conquerors of the Persians served the Romans of Augustan times as models which they had not only imitated but even surpassed, the Achaemenid Persians were useful to the Parthians not only as royal predecessors, but also as legitimizing "forefathers": they not only adopted Achaemenid institutions and titulature, most probably through the agency of the Seleucids, but also discovered the newly conquered Parthia as their "home country" and the Achaemenid Artaxerxes II as their royal ancestor. When, according to Tacitus (*Ann.* 6.31), the Parthian king Artabanus II in a letter to Tiberius reclaimed the public treasury bequeathed to the Romans by the Parthian prince Vonones, referred to the old Persian and Macedonian borders, and threatened to invade the areas formerly ruled by Cyrus and Alexander, this may be regarded as an exaggerated use of ideology in diplomacy. Yet it should also be seen as an attempt to confront the Roman imitation of the Greeks with their own adoration of Cyrus, who was also highly renowned in the west, and the Roman imitation of Alexander with the Parthian emulation of the Macedonian (Wiesehöfer 1986: 177–85, 1994).

The references to Alexander and his successors lead us to the question of the Parthian relationship to the culture of their numerous Greek subjects and of the Arsacid strategies of peacekeeping and reconciliation in a Greek environment.[17] Surely, the Arsacids were not eager to embrace the Greek winners of Salamis and Plataea, but does this mean that they were not able or willing to relate to the Greeks of their realm, that they had only a superficial interest in their cultural achievements, and that their philhellenism was only governed by reasons of political utility? Is Augustus right when he shunts the Parthians off to the eastern barbarian counter world, where Greek education and culture is hardly even conceivable? Many Romans of Augustan times would have answered these questions positively, and even today such verdicts are still common. It is frequently assumed that the Arsacids lacked familiarity with Greek culture and that their policy was determined by a hostile attitude towards their unreliable pro-Seleucid or pro-Roman subjects. A closer look at some sources proves both assumptions wrong.

In his biography of Crassus, Plutarch introduces the Parthian king Orodes (II) as follows (33.2):

> Whilst these things were doing [Surena's triumph over Crassus, 53 BC], Orodes had already struck up a peace with the Armenian Artabazes [Artavasdes], and made a match between his son Pacorus and the king of Armenia's sister. Their alternating feastings and

entertainments in consequence were very sumptuous, and various Greek compositions, suitable to the occasion, were recited before them. For Orodes was not ignorant of the Greek language and literature, and Artavasdes was so expert in it that he wrote tragedies and orations and histories, some of which are still extant (trans. John Dryden).

Plutarch then describes the famous scene, when, during a performance of Euripides's *Bacchae*, Crassus's head is brought into the throne hall and the actor Jason of Tralles connects the stories of Pentheus and the Roman general. Plutarch explicitly stresses that *both* kings liked Greek plays, which they used to stage in the course of their *mutual* invitations; and it was only the contrast between the Greek education of the Arsacid king and his barbaric treatment of Crassus's corpse that induced the biographer to describe this scene in full detail or, at least, to provide it with a special meaning: "Plutarch's Parthians are dangerously violent readers of Euripides" (Zadorojniy 1997: 182). The Arsacid kings' personal preference for Greek culture is also proven by the art of the Parthian royal residences in an Iranian, non-Greek environment: the excavators of the first Arsacid residence at Nisa in Turkmenistan detected both Greek workshops and Greek cultural imagery (Invernizzi 1998; Wiesehöfer 2000, with bibliography). Everything points to an intensive preoccupation of the Parthian kings of the second and first centuries BC with Greek art and Greek ideas for the purpose of royal self-representation.

But what about Arsacid policies towards the Greeks of Mesopotamia and Parthian methods of preserving the peace in Seleucia on the Tigris or Susa in the politically turbulent days of Roman interference with Parthian affairs? This question leads us back to real political life and the time of Augustus and his successors. Whenever in their days a pretender to the Arsacid throne looked for Roman support or was even sent from Roman Syria into Parthian territory, it became crucial, for strategic, economic, and political reasons, on which side the "Greek" cities of Mesopotamia stood. For example, the Parthian king Artabanus II (AD 10/11–38) not only abstained, in a specific situation, from using the normal epithet *philhellēn* ("Friend of the Greeks") on his coins (Sellwood 1980: 200–02), he also intervened in the autonomy of the Greek cities and took up a clear position in their internal conflicts.[18] The example of Seleucia proves that this policy was clearly connected with fights about the throne and Roman interference in Parthian internal affairs by supporting pretenders to the throne. Artabanus sought the support of the *primores* (the political "elite"), a group which, because of its small size, could be influenced more easily (Tac. *Ann.* 6.42.2) and, for its part, hoped to profit from its bond of trust to the king. Not surprisingly, the *populus* (the people) supported Artabanus's opponent Tiridates who, after his initial success, provided for a "democracy" in Seleucia (ibid. 6.42.3) and probably promised to respect the city's autonomy. Seleucia's later rebellion against Artabanus and his son Vardanes was probably intended to defend this constitution and autonomy, as is proven by the winner's first measure (ibid. 11.9), the transfer of power to the *boulē*, the council dominated by the "elite."[19] The kings' support for the undoubtedly Greek "aristocracy" of the city and consequent opposition to the majority of the population, and Artabanus's abstention from bearing the epithet *philhellēn*, clearly suggest that the *populus*, to a large extent, must have been made up of Greeks or at least hellenized non-Greeks (cf. Dabrowa 1983: 84ff.; 1994: 195ff.). It is therefore unnecessary to interpret the hostilities in the city and its rebellion as an ethnic conflict and to insinuate that Artabanus acted for reasons of fundamental enmity with the Greeks. All that can be said is that this king, in a certain situation, hoped to profit from a curtailment of the autonomy of the "Greek" city,[20] a policy that was obviously also in the interest of the Greek "elite" of Seleucia.[21]

There can be no doubt that the Arsacids and their court were more than superficially hellenized. Surrounded by hellenized neighbors, emulating the Seleucid kings and satraps, and contacted frequently by Greek cities and individuals, they had opportunities and good reasons for being acquainted with Greek traditions. In doing so, however, they did not forget their Iranian roots. Like all rulers of the Hellenistic world, they did not firmly decide on one way or the other in cultural and political affairs. Yet the Arsacid kings of the second and first centuries BC not only showed great personal interest in the achievements of Greek civilization but were eager to emulate their predecessors and contemporaries politically and ideologically and to find acceptance in their circles. Political marriages and contacts served this goal no less than the imitation of Greek institutions and ideas, and both measures also provided for the strengthening of their rule inwards and outwards. Placing Hellenistic royal epithets, symbols, and guarding divinities on their coins, the Parthians aimed at impressing their Greek subjects and royal neighbors. It signaled that the Arsacids, like other kings, considered themselves successors of Alexander the Great and promoted Greek culture. Here, personal and public philhellenism in foreign and domestic affairs came together for their mutual benefit. Good Parthian relations with the Greeks of the empire guaranteed peace and order and facilitated an intensive experience of their cultural achievements. A disturbance of this mutually profitable relationship between rulers and Greek subjects did not necessarily cause the royal renunciation of their personal interests. To assume this would be equal to regarding philhellenism exclusively a phenomenon of royal Arsacid ideology and considering political measures against Greek cities proof of a merely superficial attachment of the Parthian kings to Greek traditions. Anybody confronted with Roman punitive measures against Greek states in the second century BC would not interpret these as proof of Roman lack of interest in Greek culture but would try to describe the reasons for such measures. Just so, Artabanus's dealings with Seleucia (and Susa) should be explained against the background of the specific political situations, and without connecting them with the issue of the king's personal philhellenism.

Chivalrous Jousting and Rules of Protocol: Images of War and Peace in Sasanian Iran

In that year Blasses [Wahram V], king of the Persians, came, making war on the Romans. When the emperor of the Romans learnt of this, he made the patrician Procopius *magister militum per Orientem*, and sent him with an army to do battle. When he was about to engage in battle, the Persian king sent him a message, "If your whole army has a man able to fight in single combat and to defeat a Persian put forward by me, I shall immediately make a peace-treaty for fifty years and provide the customary gifts." When these terms had been agreed, the king of the Persians chose a Persian named Ardazanes from the division known as the Immortals, while the Romans selected a certain Goth, Areobindus, (who was) *comes foederatorum*. The two came out on horseback fully armed. Areobindus also carried a lasso according to Gothic custom. The Persian charged at him first with his lance, but Areobindus, bending down to his right, lassoed him, brought him down off his horse and slew him. Thereupon the Persian king made a peace treaty (Ioh. Mal. 14.23; trans. E. Jeffrys and R. Scott).

This episode in Malalas' description of the battle of AD 421, which led to a stop in the fighting between Romans and Sasanians and to a peace treaty between Theodosius II and Wahram V one year later, is probably not historical. Nevertheless, it was chosen by the historian with good reason, as he seems to have been familiar with the motif of the single combat in an Iranian context. From its very beginning, the Sasanian art of rock sculptures had known jousting scenes (probably derived from Hellenistic-Parthian models) that referred symbolically to important historical decisions and turning points.[22] More complex historical processes were depicted through additional jousting scenes both juxtaposed to and underneath each other. Most probably, those big-sized scenes of combat were originally designed for the mosaics and paintings of Sasanian palaces and then found their way into other genres of art. The fact that the Iranian heroic tradition also presents important historical and military decisions in the form of duels (such as jousting or wrestling matches) speaks for a common root of the literary and iconographic versions of such ordeal-like situations.

It has long been known that both Romans and Sasanians, in the context of their triumphal art, tended to use the visual imagery and ideological vocabulary of their enemies. Thus the famous triumphal reliefs of Shabuhr I show the exact reversal of the visual ideology used by the Roman emperors (Schneider 2006). On the other hand, Galerius celebrated his triumph over Narseh on the triumphal arch in Thessalonica not only through the motif of a tribute procession of barbarians offering gifts to the Roman emperor but also by depicting a jousting scene involving the victorious Roman Emperor and the defeated Sasanian "King of Kings" (ibid.). Iran's superiority over Rome is stressed both in the Sasanian royal inscriptions and Iranian mythological tradition. When Eranshahr ("Land/Empire of the Aryans": Gnoli 1989, 1993) became the official and prescribed point of reference for all Sasanian subjects, the idea of a dangerous, hostile outer world developed accordingly. The importance of Rome for the identity of the Sasanian Iranians is particularly obvious in the *Res Gestae Divi Saporis*, Shabuhr's report on his personal deeds and his court. There, the neighbor in the west – despite the special danger he poses, which lifts him far above the other enemies and justifies a personal royal account at a memorial place such as Naqsh-i Rustam – is portrayed not as a second world power but as a tributary to Iran (Rubin 1998: 181). In §91 of his *Res Gestae* at the tower of Paikuli, Shabuhr's son Narseh explicitly stresses the fact that, at the beginning of his rule, there were peaceful and friendly relations between himself and the Roman Emperor, and that these were the result of Roman efforts to attain peace and friendship from him. This idea imitates the style of Roman panegyric with its emphasis on Persian supplication (Rubin 1998: 181–82; Wiesehöfer in press). On the other hand, the Romans are the only foes to whom the principle of *bellum iustum* ("just war") is applied (Rubin 1998: 182). Apart from inscriptions, the Sasanians also used other media to give expression to their striving for superiority over Rome. Particularly famous are the scenes of triumph on Sasanian rock reliefs (Schneider 2006) and the "Shabuhr-Cameo" of the Bibliothèque National in Paris which has been interpreted correctly as a Roman piece of art made upon Sasanian instructions (von Gall 1990: 56–59). However, the ways the Iranians tried to cope with Roman ideas of world domination and with the Roman language of visual art have not yet been properly analyzed.

In Sasanian royal ideology, the Romans and later the Byzantines were never dismissed from their subordinate position, even if in diplomatic contacts the Sasanians had to be content with acknowledging the equal rank of both realms and dynasties (see below). In an episode of Ibn al-Balkhi's *Farsnama*, probably mirroring late Sasanian propaganda, the throne of the Byzantine emperor is given a preferred place among all the neighbors' thrones, a place, however, from which he is forced to look up to Husraw I (Le Strange and Nicholson 1921: 97). There is much to suggest also that the Iranian rulers of the fifth and sixth centuries, similar to Shabuhr's pecuniary demands on Philip the Arab, propagandistically passed off Byzantine payments as tribute, although they were part of well-balanced diplomatic agreements and intended to support Sasanian efforts to protect the borders against nomads or mountain tribes (Yarshater 1983: 410; Rubin 1998: 178–79).

Even if both Sasanian and Roman triumphal art leaves no doubt about the outcome of the respective duel portrayed (very often the enemy is unseated or taken by his hand), and even if the two great powers ideologically stressed their own superiority,[23] the peace treaty at the end of the Malalas anecdote quoted earlier suggests that, in practice, both sides had to recognize their equal rank and get along with each other for better or worse. It is no surprise, therefore, that the peace treaties of the Romans or Byzantines and Sasanians were not only regarded as historically most relevant events but also arranged in a special ceremonial way.[24] This becomes particularly clear in Menander Protector's report on the peace treaty of 562 AD between Justinian and Husraw I (fr. 6.1 Blockley). The author, a man with a profound rhetorical and legal education and, as a member of the emperor Maurice's court, familiar with Byzantine diplomatic customs, offers insight into all substantial aspects of international law at his time. He talks about the special position of the envoys, the choice of a suitable place for diplomatic negotiations, the ceremonial protocol, the linguistic problems of communication, and, last but not least, the dealings of the two rulers with each other. First, Petrus, *magister militum praesentalis*, and Jesdegusnaph, Husraw's chamberlain, both high-ranking functionaries and experienced diplomats with imperial authorization to negotiate and decide matters, meet at a neutral place in the frontier region near Dara and convene a meeting of the commanders of the surrounding territories. The two negotiators speak in their native tongue, describing their own starting position in as favorable, just, and benevolent terms as possible; interpreters translate these inaugural speeches. Menander summarizes the following discussion by briefly defining the demands of the two parties and the main final agreements. Documents (*sacrae litterae*) are then executed and sent to both rulers for ratification;[25] of the rulers' letters, Menander quotes the Persian (in Greek translation) quite literally. Afterwards, in further meetings and negotiations between the envoys of both empires all details are clarified. Finally, the official contract is issued both in Greek and Middle Persian and compared word for word. Menander concludes his report on the negotiations with the following words:

> When matters had progressed to this stage of orderly development, those whose task it was took the texts of the two documents and polished their contents, using language of equivalent force. Then they made facsimiles of both. The originals were rolled up and secured by seals both of wax and of the other substance used by the Persians, and were impressed by the signets of the envoys and of twelve interpreters, six Roman and six Persian. Then the two sides exchanged the treaty documents, the Zikh [Jesdegusnaph] handing the one in Persian to Peter, and Peter the one in Greek to the Zikh. Then the Zikh was given an unsealed Persian translation of the Greek original to be kept as a reference for him, and Peter likewise was given a Greek translation of the Persian. After this the conference ended (Men. Prot. fr. 6.1; trans. R.C. Blockley).

In the preamble to the Sasanian document of ratification (in Menander's version) "the divine, good, father of peace, ancient Chosroes [Husraw], king of kings, fortunate, pious and beneficent, to whom the gods have given great fortune and a great kingdom, giant of giants, formed in the image of the gods,"[26] calls his Roman opponent "Justinian Caesar, our brother."[27] Even if the titulature given to Justinian is plainly shorter than his own, the form of address ("brother") nevertheless shows clearly that the "king who reigns over kings" and the "victor of wars" grants the "lord of all things and of the world"[28] equal rank in a diplomatic context. This is stressed eloquently and colorfully in the words Byzantine authors like Petrus Patricius and John Malalas put into the mouth of Sasanian kings and diplomats. There is mention of the two empires as two lights, which, "like eyes, are adorned by each other's light" (Petr. Patr. fr. 13 Müller), or as two divinely planned centers of civilization, which are called "the moon of the west" and "the sun of the east" (Ioh. Mal. 18.44, p. 449 Thurn). Rome and Byzantium equally grant the same rank, dignity, and autonomy to the eastern opponent, although, ideologically, the eastern *natio molestissima* ("most annoying nation") would actually deserve to be destroyed (Amm. Marc. 23.5.19), and although, or precisely because, Rome's claim to universal rule was in reality substantially limited by the existence of the Sasanian empire.

It was also usual for the two great powers to announce accessions to the throne by a special message and to answer this report by a special greeting.[29] And it was also custom and practice to ask the foreign envoys during a solemn audience about the well-being of the royal "brother" and to exchange gifts. The fulfillment of requests also served to keep good terms with the neighbors.[30]

We are particularly well informed about one special form of communication between the Emperor and the Great King: embassies (Güterbock 1906; Sako 1986). The Byzantine sources make a difference between the so-called "great" and "small" embassies and envoys, designations which refer both to the respective importance of the legation and the rank of the envoys. Each legation had to be formally announced to the ruler with whom it was going to be authenticated, by state couriers or an announcement to the border authorities; however, neither ruler was obliged to receive it. We also know numerous cases of legations and counter-embassies that struggled to find agreement during difficult and lengthy negotiations; and we hear about the intentional delay of negotiations to improve one's own position, as well as about suspicions of espionage (Lee 1993: 166–70). Both rulers selected particularly distinguished envoys for the more important negotiations; if they proved successful, the kings repeatedly entrusted them with missions. We know about limited and unrestricted authorization for the envoys as well as secret instructions. The envoys, among whom the highest-ranking dignitary normally acted as a spokesman, were accompanied by attendants, assistants and interpreters (cf. above). They enjoyed certain privileges both in times of peace and war: they were sacrosanct, traveled in the neighboring country at public expense, were accommodated and entertained in accordance with their rank, and were not subject to the usual customs regulations and trade restrictions. While most sources inform us only about diplomatic procedures and ceremonies at the court in Constantinople, Menander uniquely describes Byzantine negotiations with Husraw I and his successor Ohrmezd IV in detail; not surprisingly, the diplomatic failures of the Byzantines are attributed to the improper behavior (pride and slyness) of the Sasanian kings:

> When Hormisdas [Ohrmezd] had made this arrogant reply, Zacharias and Theodorus were finally dismissed, having spent almost three months there and having suffered all manner of discomforts. For the guard assigned to the envoys did not allow them to breathe fresh air or even put their heads out of the building where they were lodged. Their lodging itself was dark and poorly ventilated and particularly unsuitable for the summer, so that it actually seemed like a prison. When they had been worn out by these bad conditions, the Persians dismissed them and harassed them far worse on their return trip. For they supplied them with provisions insufficient for their needs, forced them to delay and made their journey very long. They led them forward for one day's journey and on the next led them back by another path, until they had so distressed them that they both fell seriously ill. Then they sent them out of Persia (Men. Prot. fr. 23.9; trans. R. C. Blockley).

Outlook

Both the Achaemenid ideology of a divinely requested order of peace, maintained by just rulers and loyal subjects alike, and the Sasanian symbol of the duel have shaped the view of Ancient Iran for centuries. The *pax Achaemenidica* has been influential in Europe (despite the usual European preference for the Greek way of civilization and the survival of ancient stereotypes of barbarians and of myths of the Persian Wars), not least because it was viewed much more favorably than the alleged deathly quiet of the *pax Assyriaca*. In Iran, such views were based on the myth of a history of 2500 years of human rights and religious tolerance.[31] On the other hand, the Sasanian motif of chivalrous jousting lives on in the entire Iranian-speaking Near East, because it was excessively used by Iranian poets. Tradition and research have not been fair to the Parthians. The Sasanians drove them out from tradition and the Romans relegated them to an "outer" or even to a "counter world," and this has been their place until now. In reality, their success in founding an empire and keeping peace in it, was rather impressive.[32]

Notes

1 Successful attempts to describe Persian (i.e. the Great Kings') views of the Greeks on the basis of royal inscriptions and reliefs were made by Sancisi-Weerdenburg 2001; Kuhrt 2002: 19–22, who show that, ideologically, the kings were interested only in their Greek subjects, not in the Greeks outside their realm.

2 Briant 2002; Wiesehöfer 2001a: 79–88; 2002a; Funke 2002 (all with bibliography).

3 Stausberg 2002: 159. Cf. also de Jong 1997 (who compiled and analyzed the accounts of Greco-Roman authors); Panaino 2001: 100–08.

4 Wiesehöfer 2002b. For the Roman imagery of "Orientals" and Parthians respectively, see Schneider 1998, for the role of the Parthians in Roman literature, Lerouge, in press.

5 A first attempt is made in Wiesehöfer and Huyse 2006.

6 Gignoux (2006); Gyselen 1999, 2002; Huyse 2002; Panaino 2001; Rubin 2002; Schneider (2006).

7 Huyse (in press) shows how Darius I and his successors used Avestan (Zoroastrian) and secular (oral) Iranian folk traditions (about legendary Iranian kings) to make their rule part of an Iranian "historical" continuum.

8 Cf. *DPd* 12–24 (quoted above); cf. 56–60: "O man, the commandment of Auramazda – let not that seem evil to you! Do not leave the right path! Do not be disobedient!" and *XPh* 1-6.46-56: "A great god (is) Auramazda, who created this earth, who created yonder heaven, who created man, who created blissful happiness for man, who made Xerxes king, the one king of many, the one master of many ... You, whosoever (shall be) hereafter, if you shall think: 'Blissful may I be (while) living and (when) dead may I be blessed,' obey the law, which Auramazda has established! Worship Auramazda at the proper time and in the proper ceremonial style!" (trans. R. Schmitt).

9 Cf. *DB* IV 61–67: "Proclaims Darius, the king: For that reason Auramazda brought me aid and the other gods who are, because I was not disloyal, I was no follower of Falsehood, I was no evil-doer, neither I nor my family, (but) I acted according to righteousness, neither to the powerless nor to the powerful did I do wrong, (and) the man who strove for my (royal) house, him I treated well, who did harm, him I punished severely" (trans. R. Schmitt).

10 I have profited greatly from Hölscher 1999.

11 Matthiae 1999: 209–63; Roaf 2004. In comparison with Assyrian sculpture, which had come to depict flexible, complex, and overlapping plots, its Achaemenid counterpart appears to be noticeably timid, immobile, and lacking major stylistic development. On the other hand, this type of representation correlates with the indeterminacy of time and place in the royal inscriptions.

12 Jursa 2004; Schaudig 2001 reveal the dependence of Achaemenid royal inscriptions on Assyrian and Babylonian models.

13 For example, in Miletus in 494 or Eretria in 490 BC parts of the population were deported to the East, but the cities' history did not come to an end (Ehrhardt 2003).

14 Cf. Wiesehöfer 1995; for the allocation of responsibilities, see Jacobs 2003 (although based on a highly disputed model of administration).

15 For Greek views of the Persians, see Raeck 1981; Schmal 1995; Hutzfeldt 1999. For the variety of actual contacts between Greeks and Persians, see the excellent study of Miller 1997.

16 *Res Gestae divi Aug.* 23; Vell. Pat. 2.100; Plin. *HN* 16.190, 210; Stat. *Silv.* 4.4.7; Tac. *Ann.* 14.15; Suet. *August.* 43.3; *Tib.* 7.3; Cass. Dio 55.10.7.

17 I have discussed these problems extensively elsewhere and cited many examples (Wiesehöfer 2000); here, I confine myself to three particularly disputed case studies.

18 The discussion centers on the famous letter of Artabanus II to the magistrates of Susa (*RC* 75) and Tacitus's report on this king's policy towards Seleucia (*Ann.* 6.42ff.). See Le Rider 1965: 408–33; Dabrowa 1983: 79ff.; 1994: 185ff. (with earlier literature).

19 This follows from Vardanes's coins, which show the image and the legend of the *boulē*; cf. Sellwood 1980: 211–12. According to Philostr., *Vita Apollonii* 1.32, Vardanes was Apollonius's interlocutor, that is, a monarch open to Greek culture.

20 On the other hand, we would misunderstand Tiridates and his political aims, if we regarded him as an unreserved Grecophile. In his efforts to gain political backing, he turned to the *populus* of Seleucia, which had been disappointed by Artabanus; however, at the same time, he wooed the favor of the Parthian aristocracy.

21 Because of this assessment, but also in the light of the archaeological and epigraphic testimonies, we would be mistaken in regarding the year AD 42 as the starting-point of an unstoppable "decline" or even a kind of "orientalization" of the "Greek" city of Seleucia.

22 See von Gall 1990: 97 for the temporary adoption of Roman imagery.

23 The Sasanians did not programmatically invent and systematically cultivate a similar preoccupation with the Occident as the Romans did with the Orient, although Rum appears as one of the two deadly foes of Iran in the "Iranian National History" (Wiesehöfer 2005).

24 For the Romano-Sasanian diplomatic encounters and peace treaties, see Güterbock 1906; Winter 1988, 1989; Winter and Dignas 2001: 141–81.

25 The Roman or Byzantine emperors and Sasanian kings did not meet personally. At that time, official visits and meetings of monarchs were unusual.

26 Justinian normally uses for himself a titulature which was still in use in the tenth century AD: "the pious, the lucky, the renowned, the victorious, the triumphant, always the illustrious emperor": *pius (eusebēs), felix (eutychēs), inclutus (endoxos), victor (nikētēs), triumphator (tropaiouchos), semper augustus (aeisebastos augoustos)*.

27 Totally different is the protocol of Husraw II's letter, when he asks the emperor Maurice for help: "Chosroes king of the Persians greets the most prudent king of the Romans, the beneficent, peaceful, masterful, lover of nobility and hater of tyranny, equitable, righteous, savior of the injured, bountiful, forgiving" (Th. Sim. 4.11, trans. M. and M. Whitby).

28 These are the words in Amm. Marc. 19.2.12 (*rex regibus imperans et bellorum victor – dominus rerum et mundi*). Cf. 17.5.3: "I, Sapor, king of kings, partner of the stars, brother of the sun and the moon, send my best regards to the Caesar Constantius, my brother" (*Rex regum Sapor, particeps siderum, frater Solis et Lunae, Constantio Caesari fratri meo salutem plurimam dico*), a formula which Constantius answers in the following way: "I, Constantius, the victor on land and on the sea, always the illustrious Emperor, send my best regards to king Sapor, my brother" (*Victor terra marique Constantius semper Augustus fratri meo Sapori regi salutem plurimam dico*).

29 Ioh. Mal. 18.34, 36 (pp. 445, 448) Thurn; Men. Prot. fr. 9.1 Blockley; Th. Sim. 3.12; Theophan. Chron. 250 de Boor; Chr. Pasch. 735 Dindorf. Such an announcement is omitted by Ohrmezd IV (Th. Sim. 3.17), whereas Husraw II does not accept the letter of the murderer of his patron Maurice, Phocas (id. 8.15).

30 Inquiry: Petr. Patr. *apud* Constantin. Porphyrogen. *De caeremoniis* 1.89 Bonn; gifts: ibid. 1.89, 90; Procop. *Pers.* 1.24 et al.; gifts of the Augusta to the Persian queen: Ioh. Mal. 18.61 (p. 467) Thurn. Requests: for example, Justinian granted Husraw I his wish and allowed the neo-Platonic philosophers, who had come to the Sasanian court at Ctesiphon,

to return (Hartmann 2002); he also sent the physician Tribunus, whom Husraw had asked for, to Persia for one year to cure the Sasanian king (Procop. *Goth.* 4.10).

31 Wiesehöfer 1999. That this idea is still common in Iran, even under intellectuals, is shown by the Nobel Lecture of the admirable Shirin Ebadi (www.nobel.se/peace/laureates/ 2003/ebadi-lecture-e.html): "I am an Iranian. A descendent of Cyrus the Great. The very emperor who proclaimed at the pinnacle of power 2500 years ago that ... 'he would not reign over the people if they did not wish it.' And [he] promised not to force any person to change his religion and faith and guaranteed freedom for all. The Charter of Cyrus The Great is one of the most important documents that should be studied in the history of human rights."

32 I would like to thank Kurt Raaflaub for inviting me to contribute to this publication and for improving the English version of my text.

Abbreviations

CII	*Corpus Inscriptionum Iranicarum.* London
DB	Inscription of Darius I from Bisutun
DPd	Inscription d of Darius I from Persepolis
MMAI	Mémoires de la Mission Archéologique Française en Iran
OrOcc	Oriens et Occidens. Stuttgart
RC	Welles 1934
SOR	Serie Orientale Roma dell'Istituto Italiano per il Medio ed Estremo
XPh	Inscription h of Xerxes I from Persepolis

References

Balcer, J. M. 1985. "Fifth Century Ionia: A Frontier Redefined." *Revue des études anciennes* 87: 31–42.

Baslez, M.-F. 1986. "Présence et traditions iraniennes dans les cités de l'Egée." *Revue des études anciennes* 87: 137–55.

Bedford, P. In press. "The Assyrian Empire."

Briant, P. 1999. "The Achaemenid Empire." In K. Raaflaub and N. Rosenstein (eds.), *War and Society in the Ancient and Medieval Worlds*, 102–28. Cambridge, MA.

——. 2002. *From Cyrus to Alexander. A History of the Persian Empire.* Winona Lake.

Dabrowa, E. 1983. *La politique de l'état parthe à l'égard de Rome – d'Artaban II à Vologèse I (ca. 11 – ca. 79 de n.è.) et les facteurs qui la conditionnaient.* Kraków.

——. 1994. "Dall' autonomia alla dipendenza: Le città greche e gli Arsacidi nella prima metà del I secolo d.C." *Mesopotamia* 29: 85–98.

—— (ed.). 1998. *Ancient Iran and the Mediterranean World.* Electrum 2. Kraków.

Ehrhardt, N. 2003. "Milet nach den Perserkriegen: ein Neubeginn?" In E. Schwertheim and E. Winter (eds.), *Stadt und Stadtentwicklung in Kleinasien*, 1–19. Bonn.

Fowden, E. 1999. *The Barbarian Plain: Saint Sergius between Rome and Iran.* The Transformation of the Classical Heritage 28. Berkeley.

Funke, P. 2002. "Europäische *lieux de mémoire* oder *lieux de mémoire* für Europa im antiken Griechenland?" *Jahrbuch für Europäische Geschichte* 3: 3–16.

Gall, H. von. 1990. *Das Reiterkampfbild in der iranischen und iranisch beeinflußten Kunst parthischer und sasanidischer Zeit.* Teheraner Forschungen 6. Berlin.

Gignoux, P. 2006. "Prolégomènes pour une histoire des idées de l'Iran Sassanide: Converg-
ences et divergences." In Wiesehöfer and Huyse 2006: 71–81.

Gnoli, G. 1989. *The Idea of Iran: An Essay of Its Origin.* SOR 62. Rome.

——. 1993. *Iran als religiöser Begriff im Mazdaismus.* Rheinisch-Westfälische Akademie der
Wissenschaften, Vorträge G 320. Opladen.

Güterbock, K. 1906. *Byzanz und Persien in ihren diplomatisch-völkerrechtlichen Beziehungen im
Zeitalter Justinians.* Berlin.

Gyselen, R. (ed.). 1999. *La science des cieux: Sages, mages, astrologues.* Res Orientales 12.
Bures-sur-Yvette.

—— (ed.). 2002. *Charmes et sortilèges: Magie et magiciens.* Res Orientales 14. Bures-sur-Yvette.

Hartmann, U. 2002. "Geist im Exil: Römische Philosophen am Hof der Sasaniden." In Schuol,
Hartmann, and Luther 2002: 123–60.

Hauser, S. R. 2001. "'Greek in Subject and Style, but a Little Distorted': Zum Verhältnis
von Orient und Okzident in der Altertumswissenschaft." In S. Altekamp et al. (eds.),
*Posthumanistische Klassische Archäologie. Historizität und Wissenschaftlichkeit von Interessen
und Methoden, Kolloquium Berlin 1999,* 83–104. München.

Hölscher, T. 1999. "Augustus und die Macht der Archäologie." In Adalberto Giovannini (ed.),
La révolution romaine après Ronald Syme: Bilans et perspectives, 237-73. Entretiens sur
l'Antiquité Classique 46. Vandoeuvres and Geneva.

——. 2000. "Feindwelten-Glückswelten: Perser, Kentauren und Amazonen." In T. Hölscher
(ed.), *Gegenwelten zu den Kulturen Griechenlands und Roms,* 287–320. Munich and
Leipzig.

Hutzfeld, B. 1999. *Das Bild der Perser in der griechischen Dichtung des 5. vorchristlichen
Jahrhunderts.* Serta Graeca 8. Wiesbaden.

Huyse, P. 1999. *Die dreisprachige Inschrift Šābuhrs I. an der Kaba-i Zardušt (ŠKZ) (CII, pt.
III, vol. 1, texts I).* 2 vols. London.

——. 2002. "Sprachkontakte und Entlehnungen zwischen dem Griechisch/Lateinischen und
dem Mitteliranischen." In Schuol, Hartmann, and Luther 2002: 197–234.

——. In press. "Histoire orale et écrite en Iran ancien entre mémoire et oubli."

Invernizzi, A. 1998. "Parthian Nisa: New Lines of Research." In Wiesehöfer 1998: 45–59.

Jacobs, B. 2003. "Mechanismen der Konfliktbewältigung in der Verwaltungsorganisation
Kleinasiens zur Achämenidenzeit." In W. Henkelman and A. Kuhrt (eds.), *Achaemenid
History 13: A Persian Perspective. Essays in Memory of H. Sancisi-Weerdenburg,* 239–63.
Leiden.

de Jong, A. 1997. *Traditions of the Magi: Zoroastrianism in Greek and Latin Literature.* Leiden.

Jursa, M. 2004. "Observations on the Problem of the Median 'Empire' on the Basis of
Babylonian Sources." In Lanfranchi, Roaf, and Rollinger 2004: 169–80.

Kuhrt, A. 2001. "The Persian Kings and Their Subjects: A Unique Relationship?" *Orienta-
listische Literaturzeitung* 96: 165–73.

——. 2002. *"Greeks" and "Greece" in Mesopotamian and Persian Perspectives.* Oxford.

Lanfranchi, G., M. Roaf, and R. Rollinger (eds.). 2004. *Continuity of Empire (?): Assyria, Media,
Persia. Proceedings of the International Meeting in Padua, 26th–28th April 2001.* Padova.

Lee, A. D. 1993. *Information and Frontiers. Roman Foreign Relations in Late Antiquity.*
Cambridge.

Le Rider, G. 1965. *Suse sous les Séleucides et les Parthes.* MMAI 38. Paris.

Lerouge, C. In press. L'image des Parthes dans le monde gréco-romain du début du
premier siècle av. n.-è. jusqu'à la fin du Haut-Empire romain. Diss. University of Paris
X-Nanterre.

Le Strange, G., and G. A. Nicholson (eds.). 1921. *Ibn al-Balkhi: The Farsnama.* London.

Matthiae, P. 1999. *Geschichte der Kunst im Alten Orient (1000–330 v.Chr.): Die Großreiche der
Assyrer, Neubabylonier und Achämeniden.* Darmstadt.

Miller, M. C. 1997. *Athens and Persia in the Fifth Century: A Study in Cultural Receptivity.* Cambridge.

Panaino, A. 2001. "Greci e Iranici: confronto e conflitti." In S. Settis. (ed.), *I Greci*, vol. 3: *I Greci oltre la Grecia*, 79–136. Torino.

Raeck, W. 1981. *Zum Barbarenbild in der Kunst Athens im 6. und 5. Jahrhundert v.Chr.* Bonn.

Roaf, M. 2004. "The Median Dark Age." In Lanfranchi, Roaf, and Rollinger 2004: 13–22.

Rubin, Z. 1998. "The Roman Empire in the *Res Gestae Divi Saporis* – the Mediterranean World in Sāsānian Propaganda." In Dabrowa 1998: 177–85.

——. 2002. "*Res Gestae Divi Saporis*: Greek and Middle Iranian in a Document of Sasanian Anti-Roman Propaganda." In J. N. Adams, M. Janse, and S. Swain (eds.), *Bilingualism in Ancient Society: Language Contact and the Written Text*, 267–97. Oxford.

Sako, L. 1986. *Le rôle de la hiérarchie syriaque orientale dans les rapports diplomatiques entre la Perse et Byzance aux Ve–VIIe siècles.* Paris.

Sancisi-Weerdenburg, H. 2001. "Yaunā by the Sea and across the Sea." In I. Malkin (ed.), *Ancient Perceptions of Greek Ethnicity*, 322–46. Cambridge, MA.

Schaudig, H. 2001. *Die Inschriften Nabonids von Babylon und Kyros' des Großen.* Alter Orient und Altes Testament 256. Münster.

Schmal, S. 1995. *Feindbilder bei den frühen Griechen.* Frankfurt.

Schneider, R. M. 1998. "Die Faszination des Feindes: Bilder der Parther und des Orients in Rom." In Wiesehöfer 1998: 95–146.

——. 2006. "Orientalism in Late Antiquity: The Oriental in Imperial and Christian Imagery." In Wiesehöfer and Huyse 2006: 241–78.

Schuol, M., U. Hartmann, and A. Luther (eds.). 2002. *Grenzüberschreitungen: Formen des Kontakts zwischen Orient und Okzident im Altertum.* OrOcc 3. Stuttgart.

Sellwood, D. 1980. *An Introduction to the Coinage of Parthia.* 2nd edn. London.

Stausberg, M. 2002. *Die Religion Zarathushtras*, I. Stuttgart.

Tuna-Nörling, Y. 1998. *Attische Keramik aus Daskyleion.* Izmir.

Van der Spek, R. 1983. "Cyrus de Pers in Assyrisch perspectief." *Tijdschrift voor Geschiedenis* 96: 1–27.

de Vries, K. 1997. "The Attic Pottery from Gordion." In J. H. Oakley (ed.), *Athenian Potters and Painters*, 447–55. Oxford.

Welles, C. Bradford. 1934. *Royal Correspondence in the Hellenistic Period: A Study in Greek Epigraphy.* New Haven.

Whitby, M. 1998. "An International Symposium? Ion of Chios fr. 27 and the Margins of the Delian League." In Dabrowa 1998: 207–24.

Wiesehöfer, J. 1986. "Iranische Ansprüche an Rom auf ehemals achaimenidische Territorien." *Archäologische Mitteilungen aus Iran N. F.* 19: 177–85.

——. 1994. "Zum Nachleben von Achaimeniden und Alexander in Iran." In H. Sancisi-Weerdenburg, A. Kuhrt, and M. C. Root. (eds.), *Achaemenid History* VIII: *Continuity and Change*, 389–97. Leiden.

——. 1995. "'Reichsgesetz' oder 'Einzelfallgerechtigkeit'? Bemerkungen zu P. Freis These von der achaimenidischen 'Reichsautorisation'." *Zeitschrift für Altorientalische und Biblische Rechtsgeschichte* 1: 36–46.

—— (ed.). 1998. *Das Partherreich und seine Zeugnisse – The Arsacid Empire: Sources and Documentation. Historia* Einzelschriften 122. Stuttgart.

——. 1999. "Kyros, der Schah und 2500 Jahre Menschenrechte: Historische Mythenbildung zur Zeit der Pahlavi-Dynastie." In S. Conermann (ed.), *Mythen, Geschichte(n), Identitäten: Der Kampf um die Vergangenheit*, 55–68. Asien und Afrika 2. Hamburg.

——. 2000. "'Denn Orodes war der griechischen Sprache und Literatur nicht unkundig ...' Parther, Griechen und griechische Kultur." In R. Dittmann et al. (eds.),

Variatio delectat: Iran und der Westen. Gedenkschrift für P. Calmeyer, 703–21. Alter Orient und Altes Testament 272. Altenberge.

Wiesehöfer, J. 2001a. *Ancient Persia*. 2nd edn. London and New York.

——. 2001b. "Griechen, Iraner und Chinesen an der Seidenstraße." In U. Hübner, J. Kamlah, and L. Reinfandt (eds.), *Die Seidenstraße*, 17–33. Hamburg.

——. 2002a. "'Griechenland wäre unter persische Herrschaft geraten ...': Die Perserkriege als Zeitenwende?" In H. Brinkhaus and S. Sellmer (eds.), *Zeitenwenden*, 209–32. Hamburg.

——. 2002b. "Die 'Sklaven des Kaisers' und der Kopf des Crassus: Römische Bilder des Ostens und parthische Bilder des Westens in augusteischer Zeit." In P. Freeman et al. (eds.), *Limes XVIII: Proceedings of the XVIIIth International Congress of Roman Frontier Studies Held in Amman, Jordan (September 2000)*, I: 293–300. Oxford.

——. 2005a. "Rum as Enemy of Iran." In E. S. Gruen (ed.), *Cultural Borrowings and Ethnic Appropriations in Antiquity*, 105–20. OrOcc 8. Stuttgart.

——. 2005b. *Iraniens, Grecs et Romains*. Paris.

——. In press. "Narseh, Diokletian, Manichäer und Christen." In J. Tubach (ed.), *Christen im Sasanidenreich*. Halle.

——, and P. Huyse (eds.). 2006. *Eran and Aneran. Beiträge zu den Beziehungen zwischen Ost und West in sasanidischer Zeit*. OrOcc 13. Stuttgart.

Winter, E. 1988. *Die sāsānidisch-römischen Friedensverträge des 3. Jahrhunderts n. Chr. – ein Beitrag zum Verständnis der außenpolitischen Beziehungen zwischen den beiden Großmächten*. Frankfurt am Main.

——. 1989. "Legitimität als Herrschaftsprinzip: Kaiser und 'König der Könige' im wechselseitigen Verkehr." In H.-J. Drexhage and J. Sünskes (eds.), *Migratio et Commutatio: Studien zur Alten Geschichte und deren Nachleben. Th. Pekáry zum 60. Geburtstag ... dargebracht*, 72–92. St. Katharinen.

——, and B. Dignas (eds.). 2001. *Rom und das Perserreich: Zwei Weltmächte zwischen Konfrontation und Koexistenz*. Berlin.

Wissemann, M. 1982. *Die Parther in der augusteischen Dichtung*. Frankfurt and Bern.

Yarshater, E. 1983. "Iranian National History." *Cambridge History of Iran*, III/1: 359–477. Cambridge.

Zadorojniy, A. V. 1997. "Tragedy and Epic in Plutarch's 'Crassus'." *Hermes* 125: 169–82.

8

War and Reconciliation in the Traditions of Ancient Israel: Historical, Literary, and Ideological Considerations

Susan Niditch

Methodological Considerations

The lore preserved by ancient Israelites is rich in images and tales of war. As in the wider ancient Near East, creation is often perceived in terms of a battle against chaos, while the deity, Yahweh, is frequently depicted as "a man of war," powerful and victorious in battle. Israelites' accounts of their own history describe both military successes and failures and include sophisticated intellectual engagement with issues pertaining to the causes and conduct of war. Exploring attitudes to war in ancient Israel, however, involves a number of methodological challenges. Questions arise about date, Israelite identity, and the relationship between the literature preserved in the Hebrew Bible and actual Israelites set in place and time. When one writes of attitudes to war in "biblical times," in the earliest period of Jewish history, precisely whose attitudes is one uncovering?

The first eight books of the Bible trace a chronology from a period before the rule of kings in Israel (pre-tenth century), to the time of the monarchies (tenth century – 586), to a period after the monarchies when foreign superpowers take control (586 on).[1] It would be wonderfully convenient for the study of ancient Israelite history and culture if sources describing the various periods were historically accurate and if views of war expressed in biblical sources paralleled actual political developments. As is the case with the great epic literature of any culture, however, the relationship between the Bible and actual historical events is often difficult to ascertain, while trajectories of intellectual and social history and threads of ideology are difficult to unravel.

Biblical narratives, often expressed in the formulaic language and conventionalized patterns of traditional discourse, have a long history, written and oral. Layers of voices and contributors are reflected in any one account along with the point of view of the composer who "got the last word." Variations persist in the rich array of manuscript traditions that lie behind the edited Bible that one now reads. In addition, extra-biblical literary sources and archaeological evidence must also enter any analysis of aspects of ancient Israelite history and culture. We begin, in fact, with a brief overview of the history of ancient Israel as revealed by archaeological evidence that richly, if sometimes enigmatically, informs our knowledge of the course of Israel's social and political history, both of these being intimately interwoven with attitudes to war, its causes and conduct.

Israelite History and the Material Culture of War

Before the monarchy

The earliest known extra-biblical source in which Israel is mentioned is the Egyptian Merneptah Stele of the thirteenth century, and it is with this date that most contemporary scholars feel confident in beginning the history of Israel. Archaeological evidence reveals settlement activity in the central frontier highlands of Israel including sites such as Ai, Bethel, and Shiloh. Hilltop villages were small in size and arranged in clusters of small pillared, multi-room houses, probably reflecting kinship ties (Stager 1985: 11–23). Water was stored in bell-shaped cisterns carved into the bedrock and the villagers engaged in subsistence agriculture, growing grapes, figs, cereals, legumes and other foodstuffs on terraced plots, with some variation depending upon the climate in each eco-niche (Meyers 1997: 10–11). They were also engaged in pastoral activities, raising sheep, cows, and goats. Archaeologists picture an essentially pre-state, non-urban culture having much in common with the lifestyles of other Northwest Semitic peoples of the area. Many scholars suggest, in fact, that it is difficult to identify houses, communities, or villages that are specifically Israelite. We can assume the existence of a lively oral culture, the political role of certain local chieftains, and the presence of traders. Additional archaeological finds that are intriguing but difficult to interpret include religious artifacts such as an eighteen centimeter bronze bull or a perhaps sacred circle of stones (see Mazar 1992: 350–51). We can also imagine the likelihood of the need for defense and the possible disputes that may have arisen between groups vying for control of land or water rights.

Certain features of war in ancient Israel pertain to this early period and all subsequent times. In Israel as in any traditional, pre-modern culture, wars, as T. R. Hobbs notes (1989: 18), were "close order affairs" in which warriors "smelled their opponents as they fought." The fighting took place largely "on foot," while "weapons were simple, thrown or pulled by the human arm." "The quality of materials was poor" and "firepower notoriously inaccurate." Such physical realities inevitably are going to affect not only images of war but also attitudes to fighting, one's views of the enemy. Many cameo scenes in the Hebrew Bible such as the confrontation between David and Goliath (1 Samuel 17), the deadly wrestling match between young men of opposing sides in the civil war between forces of David and Saul (2 Sam 2:12–17), and the confrontation between Asael and Abner (2 Sam 2:18–23) invoke the flavor of such war-making up-close, while some of the ideologies of war, which I will argue evidence guilt and inner-conflict about killing in war, may be rooted in the realities of face-to-face combat in which one's enemy dies before one's eyes and at one's hand.

Another ongoing feature of war throughout the ancient Near East involves the role of the deity. Not only is the deity himself a warrior who fights with or without human supporters, but he decides the outcome of battles and may use defeat in war as a means of punishing an unfaithful people. The deity is usually consulted before battle via oracle or another method to help leaders decide whether or how to engage in battle (see Kang 1989: 56–72, 98–107, 215–22; Niditch 1993: 125). The integral, physical presence of the deity in battles fought by humans as well as the bigger-than-life cosmogonic pattern in which worlds are created, lead to a particularly macho divine portrait. God marches to battle, he confronts the enemy, and his sword devours unmercifully. This personification of the deity poses an ethical dilemma to many within the latter traditions for whom the Hebrew Bible is sacred literature. What sort of model is here offered? Should we imitate God in dealing with those we perceive to be the ungodly, the forces of evil, or should we wait for that all powerful warrior to finish them off himself? While the former can lead to extremely agonistic behavior by human beings, the latter can actually encourage a kind of *de facto* pacifism. Before exploring these varying ideologies of war, we complete our historical overview.

The monarchy

While essential aspects of pre-monarchic culture continue for all biblical times, the late tenth century evidenced the existence of a new urban culture as well, characterized by monumental architecture with fortifications, casement wall systems, six chambered gateways, streets, drainage canals, and water projects (Mazar 1992: 382, 406, 416–17, 424, 470–71, 484; for a summary, Niditch 1997: 14–22). Archaeological evidence includes the remains of buildings used to support the military and bureaucratic infrastructure (Meyers 1998: 250) and increased use of the technology of writing. Finds also include hints of popular religious practices that differ in some respects from "proper" modes of religious behavior enjoined in the Bible. Actual references to wars in which Israelite kingdoms engaged are found, for example, in the ninth century Mesha Stele and Tel Dan Stele inscriptions (King and Stager 2001: 223). Weapons such as "clubs, maces, spears, lances, daggers, and swords" would have been common in the ancient Near East throughout biblical times (ibid. 224). In addition to the continued use of bronze, this period saw manufacture of weapons from the stronger metal iron, imported to Israel and hardened via a carbonizing "quenching" system (ibid. 167, 169, 225). As Israel made the transition from decentralized, pre-state society to a more centralized state that controlled the lowlands as well as the hill towns, state-supported armies found use for chariots with iron axles (ibid. 189, 244). As Hobbs notes, the monarchies led to more fully equipped armies and somewhat "more effective weaponry" (1989: 111).

Post-monarchy

The northern kingdom was conquered by Assyria in 721, the southern kingdom by Babylonia in 587/6. The elites were sent into exile by these superpowers in order to lessen the possibility of organized revolt. Major population centers were disrupted, and a new frontier, in a sense, opened with the Persian conquest of the area in the late sixth century; for Persia allowed Jews from the exiled aristocracy to return to Judea to live and lead under Persian rule. The temple in Jerusalem, which had been destroyed by the Babylonians, was rebuilt with Persian assistance. Some would suggest that these literate returnees, from the upper and priestly classes, were those who collected many of the Biblical traditions and wrote them down, putting their own ideologies and stamp on the material. They played an important role in preserving images of war in ancient Israel although the activity of actual, independent armies was over for the time being.

Certain threads in the archaeological record thus provide information about the evolution of weaponry and modes of warfare in ancient Israel, and these aspects of Israel's material culture do have a bearing on the way Israelites may have viewed participation in battle or their relationship to the enemy. On the other hand, artifacts lead only so far, and so we must turn to the Hebrew Scriptures to explore attitudes expressed by Israelites themselves about war, albeit keeping in mind the methodological challenges and complexities discussed above.

Ideologies of War

The integrated anthology of ancient Israelite writings, the Hebrew Bible, preserves a number of views of war, some of which overlap, while some seem at odds with one another. Again, assigning these various ideologies of war to specific periods in Israelite history or to specific groups in Israelite society is no easy task, but one can, at least, provide an overview of some of the major threads in Israelite thinking about war and speculate about whose views they reflect and how such views may have operated in the complex process of asserting and understanding cultural identity.

The ban

Perhaps the most troubling war ideology in the Hebrew Bible is that of the ban or *herem*, a term rooted in the sacrificial meaning, "devote to destruction," and sometimes associated with non-warring contexts (see Lev 27:21, 28). The ban in war is imagined to be commanded by God and requires that all human enemies and sometimes also their animals be slaughtered and often burned in entirety, "a whole burnt offering to God" as Deut 13:16 states overtly. Spoil is often destroyed or set aside for God's use, unless exception is granted.

There are, in fact, two banning ideologies, the ban which treats the enemy as a sacrifice vowed to God, explicitly or implicitly (see Num 21:2–3; Deut 2:34–35; Josh 6:17–21; 8:2, 24–28; 11:11, 14, and I Kgs 20:35–43), and the ban which regards the killing as an execution of God's justice. In the latter version, the enemy is described as unclean, contaminating, and sinful. He must be rooted out (see Deut 7:2–5, 23–26 concerning foreign enemies, and 13:12–18 on the idolatrous enemy within Israel). Both versions of the ban may reflect an attempt to rationalize killing in war. God exacts the dead from the Israelites.

This notion that God is pictured to desire the dead as spoils of war is a shocking one to modern readers, to be sure. We have to remember, however, that Israelite religion was a sacrificial religion in which animals were offered up on the altar, part going to the deity, sometimes the whole as in the "whole burnt offering," to which indeed the ban is compared in Deut 13:16. Blood is a multi-vocalic symbol in the Hebrew Bible, the stuff of the soul, the life-force, splashed upon the altar for purification, daubed upon the right earlobe, right big toe, and right thumb of priestly initiates (Lev 8:22–24). A frequent refrain in the Hebrew Bible declares that all that first emerges from the womb belongs to Yahweh. Most such references quickly make clear that human young are to be redeemed (e.g. Num 3:12; 18:15; Ex 13:2, 13–14), but Ex 22:28 (Hebrew; 22:29 in English Bibles) declares more starkly, "The firstborn of your sons shall be given to me." Perhaps redemption is assumed or cultic service of some kind, but the story of the binding of Isaac suggests that life is God's to demand or exact even though in this case Yahweh relents. Jephthah's daughter is not so lucky and is an exchange item in a war vow made by her father to God, victory in exchange for whomever or whatever he sees first upon his return from successful battle, and she becomes the offering (Judg 11:29–40). This myth, probably an etiology for a young woman's ritual of maturation (for the young virgins go off yearly to the mountains to mourn her "sacrifice," her becoming a gift to a demanding God) parallels the ban as described clearly in Num 21:2–3, in which the Israelites promise to devote their enemies to destruction if the deity grants them victory:

> And Israel vowed a vow to Yahweh, saying,
> "If you will give this people into my hand,
> I will devote to destruction their towns."

Relevant in this context is the episode in Joshua 7 in which a man named Achan takes some of the material "devoted to destruction" for himself, and he and his immediate family, believed to be contaminated by (his essentially) having stolen from God, are rounded up, encircled physically and separated socially, and killed. Prophetic interactions with kings, Saul in Samuel 15 and Ahab in 1 Kings 20, also point to this theme of God's due in battle. In each case, the Israelite political leader sensibly and pragmatically takes animal spoil or spares the captured enemy leader who is worth much more to his captors alive rather than dead, in political status and economic value. Certain prophets, however, regard the enemy, especially the most important enemy, the leader of his people, as God's booty. He is to be slaughtered under the demands of the ban. Thus in one important thread in the Hebrew Bible, the treatment of enemies in battle is seen in the context of a god who appreciates or demands sacrifice in human terms.

The ban as sacrifice is described in a Moabite Inscription of the ninth century and appears to have been a concept shared by Israel's neighbors. "Now Kemosh (the Moabite deity) said to me, 'Go seize Nebo from Israel' (here we see war from the point of view of one of Israel's traditional enemies). So I went and fought against it from the break of dawn until noon. I seized it and killed everyone of [it], seven thousand native men, foreign men, native women, foreign women, concubines – for I devoted it (that same *hrm* root is used here) to 'Ashtar Kemosh'" (lines 14–17, trans. Jackson 1989: 98; see also Albright's trans. in Pritchard 1969: 321). In the narrative traditions of the Hebrew Bible as well, Moabites are pictured as believing in the efficacy of human sacrifice in the context of war. In 2 Kings 3 the battle goes poorly for his people until the Moabite king slays his own son, "his firstborn son who was to succeed him and offered him as a burnt offering on the wall. And great wrath came upon Israel, so they withdrew from him and returned to their own land" (2 Kgs 3:27). Whose great wrath? Yahweh's, that of the Moabite god Kemosh, Wrath itself somehow personified? In any event, the devotion of a human being, especially one of high political status and personal value, the king's nearest kin, turns the tide. Deities appreciate the blood of sacrifice.

We have no way of knowing for certain when or if the ban was ever carried out by Israelites in actual war settings. The ban, treated as God's justice, may well be a response by Deuteronomic writers of the seventh century to ancient traditions about devoting enemies for destruction, for such writers regarded Israel as a pristine entity that had become soiled by foreign influences and sin. The ban is thus treated not as a means of providing human offerings to a demanding deity, a notion which in unadorned form would have been anathema to these writers who purposely condemn human sacrifice under any circumstances, but as a way of cleansing Israel from a contamination that separates them from God. According to this line of thought, the enemy left alive could serve as a temptation and a snare, given the temptations posed by their idolatrous practices. Again, we have no way of knowing if the ban was ever enacted or publicly proclaimed as a call to specific battles. The biblical descriptions of the seventh century reforms of Josiah, influenced by Deuteronomic thought, in fact, make no overt reference to the ban. It is rather interesting that in one of the instances in biblical historiography when one would most expect the ban to be mentioned, it is absent. Religious reforms forced upon people often require just such inducements and cleansings if other means of persuasion fail. Perhaps Josiah's reform was an unusually peaceful transition or perhaps the biblical writers wished to portray it as such implying some writers' discomfort with the notion of extirpating the internal "Other." This ideology is perhaps implicit in the coup of Jehu described in 2 Kings 9–10 as a violent change of power in the ninth century northern kingdom. Because the ban is regarded as imposed or expected by God, it appears to come under the heading of just cause and just conduct in Israelite thought, which distances these traditions from modern concepts of just war. The war is not a matter of self-defense and no degree of proportionality applies. It can be argued, however, that these troubling traditions do reveal the Israelites' discomfort with the violence of war in that the writers attempt to place responsibility for the killing outside Israel's own hands. God is propitiated by or demands the enemy's death and/or the enemy deserves to die in a grand plan of divine justice.

The bardic tradition

The bardic tradition, which is preserved in traditional narrative style, glorifies the courage, daring, and skill of warriors. Enemies sometimes engage in stylized duels and taunting behavior, while war is described as men's sport (e.g. 2 Sam 2:14) in which a code of fair-play operates. Men should fight their equals in skill, for example. In several passages, offense is taken or concern expressed when the combatants are not equally matched in status and experience of war. It is for this reason that Goliath resents the Israelites' sending forth the young David to engage in single combat with him. Rightfully he shouts, "Am I a dog that you come to me with sticks?" (1 Sam 17:43). Similarly, Abner does not want to fight Asael, younger brother of the rival general Joab, when the lad insists upon engaging him. Abner says, "Turn to your right or left, and seize one of the young men, and take his spoil." And again, "Turn away from following me; why should I strike you to the ground? How then could I face your brother Joab?" (2 Sam 2:21–22). Thus elements of just conduct emerge, and it could be argued that the bardic tradition preserves a warrior's code of some kind, however idealized, romanticized or conventionalized in the style of traditional literatures. Spoil is desired and acquired in the bardic tradition, and sometimes leads to conflict among allies. This view of war, so similar to war as described in the epic traditions of other cultures, may have originated in the royal courts of Judah or Israel during the period of the monarchies from the tenth century on, but could also have been prominent in pre-monarchic oral literature, extolling the heroes of old. Like the American war movies of John Wayne, such tales may have encouraged young men to want to fight, helping to define a particular view of manhood.

Tricksterism

Akin to guerrilla warfare, tricksterism is a war ethic of the oppressed who must use deception to improve their lot. Such war tales are a subset of the large fund of trickster tales in narrative portions of the Hebrew Bible, describing the victory of the marginal over the establishment. No guilt is implicit concerning the enemy's death and no code governs fighting, although the cause is always just from the perspective of those out of power. As currently framed in the Book of Judges, a rich repository of such war tales, the success of Israel and her charismatic leaders depends upon God's mercy to a sinful, backsliding nation. The ideology of tricksterism may be as old as Israel itself and was no doubt available as a justification and explanation for war throughout its difficult history of subjugation. Tales of Samson (Judges 14–15), Ehud (Jud 3:12–30), and Jael (Judges 4–5) exemplify this ideology. One particularly interesting thread in stories of Samson, Ehud, and Jael is the powerfully affective juxtaposition of eroticism and death which Emily Vermeule (1979: 102, 157) has noted also in connection with Homeric battle literature. The conquered or slain warrior is the "woman" raped, subdued, controlled. The Jael tale includes a powerful ironic twist in which the oppressed, now victorious, identify with the feminine who is the one who conquers the male warrior Sisera by means of her womanly wiles. Jael exemplifies what folklorists call the

"the iron fist in the velvet glove," while the description of the death throes of Sisera in Jud 5:27 richly employs double entendres of battle defeat and sexual seduction (Niditch 1989).

> Between her legs he knelt, he fell, he lay
> Between her legs he knelt, he fell,
> Where he knelt, there he fell despoiled.

The language has a rhythmic, intoning, repetitive quality, capturing, as Robert Alter has noted, Sisera's death in slow motion, falling, lower, lower, dying (1985: 45). Each image equates the act of dying with sex (Zakovitch 1981; Alter 1985: 43–49; Niditch 1989). To be sure, the terms "to kneel" and "to fall" are used in contexts of defeat and death in the Hebrew Bible (see, for example, Ps 20:8; v. 9 in Hebrew). "To lie with one's ancestors" is simply to die, but these terms are also associated with overt sexual contexts. Job defends himself to those who accuse him of sin and impropriety by saying,

> If my heart has been enticed by a woman,
> And at my neighbor's door I have lain in wait,
> Let my wife "grind" for another (note the sexual euphemism here),
> Upon her may others kneel.

"To lie" is also used in sexual contexts, frequently in those dealing with incest, rape, and a variety of unsanctioned sorts of relationship. The term I translate "despoiled" is usually associated with the destruction of enemies and in such contexts might be translated more generally as "deal violently with" (e.g. Isa 15:1; 23:1; Jer 47:4), but in Jer 4:30 the root is used in an erotic metaphor as Jeremiah compares the unfaithful Israel to a sleazy harlot, beautifying herself for her lovers. Finally the opening phrase "between her legs," erotic enough if simply translated without explanation, becomes more erotic once one realizes that the legs or feet are used in ancient Israel as a euphemism for genitals (Deut 28:57; Ezek 16:25; Isa 7:20; Judg 3:24; 1 Sam 24:3). War is thus eroticized. In the ideology of tricksterism, war is about liberation from oppression, but as always it is also about power, and the sexual language serves this theme exquisitely.

Expediency

This ideology suggests that any degree of cruelty is acceptable in order to achieve victory in battle. War is hell. War is business as usual; naked aggression and brutal conquest are the activities of kings, including the great hero David (2 Sam 5:7–8; 8:2).

> He defeated the Moabites and, making them lie down on the ground, he measured them with a cord; he measured two lengths of a cord for those who would be put to death, and one length for those who were to be spared.

Coldly and arbitrarily, David claims for himself the power of life and death, striking down survivors with the potent weapon of inducing fear.

> At this time Menachem struck Tiphsah and all that was in it . . .; because it did not open (to him) he ripped open all its pregnant women (2 Kgs 15:16).

The Danite founding myth of Judges can be read to suggest that it was good that the Laishians, targets of Danite conquest, were a quiet, peaceful, and unsuspecting people, the better to conquer their land and eliminate them (Jud 18:7, 10, 27). Victory results in spoil, enslavement of enemies, and the paying of tribute by the losing state. Others' lands are there to be conquered. This pragmatic ideology of war was common in the ancient Near East and possibly best relates to the ways in which actual wars were fought throughout Israel's history.

Non-participation

Rooted in biblical traditions that describe God's capacity to save Israel through miracles, the ideology of non-participation suggests that Israel need not fight wars itself, for God who redeemed the helpless Israelite slaves in Egypt will rescue his people again. This ideology, reflected, for example, in 2 Chronicles 20, is the closest concept to pacifism found in the Israelite tradition because human beings need not fight, but of course Yahweh himself is often expected or pictured to kill the enemy with the utmost violence and bloodshed. In 2 Chronicles 20, a huge contingent of enemy soldiers is arrayed against a vulnerable Judah. The king Jehoshaphat responds not with the bravado of the bardic ideology, nor with the pragmatic preparations of the ideology of expediency, nor does he plan a clever strategy of tricksterism. Instead, as the text reports, "He was scared and gave himself over to seek the Lord" (2 Chron 20:3). God loves the weak. He appreciates their obeisance and their prayer, and revels in their admitted inadequacies. The people join Jehoshaphat in humble prayer and confession of sin, and in return God sends a prophecy: "It is not for you to fight. Station yourselves and stand still and see the victory of the Lord for you" (2 Chron 20:17). To be sure, victory is always ultimately in divine hands, and Israelites are frequently enjoined to reduce the number of human soldiers in order to enhance God's victory in holy war (e.g. the case of Gideon's "lappers" in Judges 7; the dismissal of certain categories of able bodied fighters in Deuteronomy 20), but in 2 Chronicles 20 and comparable material the divine role is so absolute as to totally exclude humans from fighting. Such an ideology thus offers the powerless an alternative to ethics of war that involve overt human aggression and seems to have been popular with the post-monarchic, fifth century writers of 1 and 2 Chronicles.

Codes of War

In addition to those texts which fall under the headings of one or more of the ideologies discussed above, in which attitudes to war are often implicit, there are a number of interesting passages which overtly grapple with the justness of war and whether or not an occasion calls for one sort or other of martial response.

One such text frequently cited by scholars as a biblical code of war is Deuteronomy 20. Within the Bible's own chronology, the passage is presented as advice given by Moses before his death concerning the execution of the coming wars of conquest.

This passage is interesting on many levels, for example, the way in which battle duties reflect a particular priestly social hierarchy typical of Deuteronomic priestly ideals and the exemption from battle provided for those who have left certain aspects of their civilian lives unfinished as well as for those who are overcome by fear. What interests us here are rules governing the engagement of the enemy (Deut 20:10–20). The Israelites are to offer the enemy terms of peace and, if they accept, to spare their lives, although they will become "forced laborers" to the conquering Israelites – which does not exactly correspond to the Geneva Convention. If they resist, the victorious Israelites (victory is of course assumed) may kill all males, taking women and children as spoil.

V. 15, however, draws a distinction between towns that are "far away" and those that are nearby. In the latter the ban obtains with wholesale killing of men, women, and children and no opportunity for surrender. As Norman Gottwald (1964) and others have shown, in fact, the traditions of the conquest in Joshua-Judges are not so neat and do not seem to follow this near-far distinction that is based on the Deuteronomic notion that neighboring towns cannot be allowed to survive lest their inhabitants tempt the Israelites into foreign worship and apostasy. Rather, Deuteronomy 20 may reflect two war views, the ban and a somewhat more lenient view that looks like some sort of code. Within this code are rules for the treatment of trees in conquered territory (20:19–20) and captive women (21:10–14), a passage to which we will return. The writers admittedly seem more sympathetic to botanic than to human life (see 20:19, in which Israelites are enjoined to spare fruit-bearing trees) and envision cruelly wrenching enemy women from family and home. Nevertheless some small protections are imagined for the ecosystem and for the captive woman taken as wife.

Equally interesting in the context of passages that verge on codes of war is Judges 11:4–28, in which the Israelite hero Jephthah insists upon the justness of his people's cause. In a lengthy peroration composed of historiographic traditions preserved also elsewhere in the Hebrew Bible, concerning the route from Egypt and claims to certain territories, Jephthah seeks to show that the Ammonites have no right to wage war against Israel. He argues most diplomatically that Israel is in the right in defending itself against unjust Ammonite aggression. Texts such as Deuteronomy 20 and Jud 11:4–28, which suggest concern with proportionality in the fighting or matters of just cause, intertwine with Israelite notions about the power of the divine warrior, the ritualization of battle, and divine promises concerning the land and Israel's special status.

Emotions of War and the Passage to Peace

Having examined in some detail the material culture behind biblical images of war, matters of historical background, and some of the ideologies at play in the tradition, we shift focus and turn to themes of peace, exploring implicit and explicit critiques of warring behavior in the biblical tradition, and contrasts that were drawn between enmity and reconciliation.

How do biblical writers describe and explain the emotions of war (hatred, anger, fury, vengeance) and, once an individual or group has been consumed and propelled by the emotions of war, how do they return to normalcy, regaining equanimity? How do they reconcile, if at all, with the hated enemy and, once the battle is over, how do they resume the quotidian and constructive activities of life? What, moreover, is the relationship in Israelite literature between personal enmity and public or political opposition? And how does the suffering of combat and the trauma of losing one's comrades personalize the seemingly impersonal or political aspect of war, making reconciliation all the more difficult? This is precisely the question posed by classicist David Konstan in an examination of ancient Greek literature of war (see Konstan, this vol.).

Konstan pays close attention to the terminology of enmity, noting that the Greeks distinguished lexically between varieties of enemies. The "personally detested enemy" is called *ekhthros* from the verb meaning "to hate." The "military enemy" is the *polemios* from the root designating "war." Konstan notes how in the events of battle the *polemios* may well come to be regarded as a hated, personal enemy, an *ekhthros*, thereby making the end of hostilities less likely, the aftermath of war more bitter. Does ancient Israelite literature provide a similar terminology for the more and less personally hated enemy?

The Hebrew Bible does of course use many different terms for combatants and they range from neutral and unemotional designations to more emotional ones. In the former category, for example, are the many terms for warrior or hero: *'îš milḥāmāh*, lit. "man of war," *'îš ḥayil*, "man of strength," that is, "a valiant hero," *gibbôr*, "mighty man" or "hero" from the root meaning "strong" and *gibbôr ḥayil*, lit. "mighty man of valor," "valiant hero." These terms are used not only for Yahweh, the divine warrior, as in the ancient poem of Exodus 15, but also for Israelite heroes and enemy heroes alike. Thus Josh 10:2 refers to "all the men of Gibeon, mighty men/heroes" (*gibbôrîm*). Similar is Josh 6:2 in which God declares that he has "handed Jericho over to you along with its king and valiant heroes" (*gibbôrê ḥayil*). Enemies who are treated as the hated "Other" to be extirpated and exterminated in certain threads of the Deuteronomic corpus and its conquest account are here implicitly, through the very terminology used, paid the respect due one's heroic counterparts in battle. At 2 Kgs 5:1 Naaman, commander of the King of Aram, is also given the designation *gibbôr ḥayil*, while in Judges 3:29, the defeated Moabite enemy is *'îš ḥayil*, "man of strength." Throughout Judges 20, in the powerful account of a civil war between Benjamin and Israel, each side is described with one or more of these neutral or respectful terms for warrior as well (20:15, 17, 25, 34, 35, 46). This sort of language for enemies tallies well with aspects of the bardic ideology in which a certain code of reciprocity applies between warriors and one seeks, in fairness, to face one's respected equal in combat. Other terms for those one faces in war are more emotional, overtly negative, and implicitly personal.

Two roots in particular come to mind *śn'*, "to hate," which lends itself to one of the common words for an enemy, *śônē'*, and *'yb*, "to be hostile towards," "to treat as an enemy," as in the synonym for *śônē'*, *'ôyēb*. One might be tempted to see the word rooted in "hate" to be the more negative and the more associated with negative emotions, but, in fact, the literature of ancient Israel does not reveal a distinction between the use of these two terms, each of which can refer to personal and to public or political enemies. The terms are often used in synonymous parallelism in the traditional style of ancient Israelite rhetoric as in Ex 23:4–5. "When you come upon your enemy's (*'yb* root) ... ox or donkey ... When you see the donkey of your enemy (*śn'* root)." The enemy seems to be personal in each case and the message is that when your hated neighbor has a problem with his livestock, you are to come to the assistance of the animal and by doing so, serve the enemy neighbor's economic well-being, an important message in ethics.

It is illustrative, in fact, to look at some cases in Joshua and 2 Kings for the use of these two roots, as we did for the more neutral language of warriors; one begins to see that in many biblical threads, war is often overtly personal, accompanied by the emotions and terminology for hatred and hostility. Some of these references to the personal aspect of warring behavior are grounded in the framework of kinship which envelops much of biblical heroic narrative. As Lawrence Stager (1985), Carol Meyers (1997), and others have pointed out, kinship undergirds the very social structure of ancient Israel and, more importantly, shapes Israelite representations of essential foundation myths concerning that social structure. No strife is more bitter than internecine strife. The term "enemy" (*'ōyēb*) is put in the mouths of the Philistines as an epithet for the temporarily subdued Samson, "ravager of (their) land," an obvious political competitor, but the "personal" is also part of Samson's relationship with the Philistines; for he has unsuccessfully intermarried with them in the case of the Timnite woman, and the vengeance and counter-vengeance following from that unhappy event has, as David Konstan observed about other traditions, made the war personal.

This nexus between the personal and the political is even more obvious in the use of the term *'ōyēb*, "enemy," in tales of Saul and David. Saul is referred to as "David's *'ōyēb*" from the time that the younger man succeeds in gaining the love of Saul's daughter Michal (1 Sam 18:28). The biblical writer of these tales of intrigue, in fact, always sensitive to human emotions and the psychology behind them, couples the enemy or hostile relationship to David in Saul's mind with Saul's fear of being supplanted and his jealousy. David's very success in Saul's service is read by Saul as an indication of divine favor, a favor which he himself has lost. Michal's love for the young warrior is implicitly viewed by Saul as a sign of her transfer of loyalty from her father to David. Saul sees in David not a faithful servant and son-in-law but probably correctly a would-be usurper of his power. The reluctance of the father to give away his daughter, perhaps a universal feature of the human family, is thus intertwined with warring emotions and political notions about taking sides. Saul's hostility is political but is thoroughly imbued with the personal even before any real combat breaks out between the military forces of each side. Later when David has escaped with the help of Michal, Saul asks her, "Why have you deceived me like this and let my enemy (*'ōyēb*) go ...?" (1 Sam 19:17).

It is interesting that biblical characters themselves are sometimes portrayed as insensitive to the intensely complicated and ambivalent nature of Saul's being an enemy of David. When the sons of Rimmon proudly come to a now victorious David with the head of Ishbaal, "son of Saul, your enemy," David reacts in anger and has the assassins brutally executed (2 Sam 4:5–12). Saul, the hated enemy, on some level was loved; at least his death is cause for guilt or shame on David's part. Some of the same complication between the personal and the political attaches to other biblical uses of the term enemy. Ahab, husband of Jezebel, northern king of the ninth century, detested by the biblical preservers of tales about him and his zealous Baal-worshiping wife, calls Elijah the prophet of the Lord, "my *'ōyēb*/enemy" (1 Kgs 21:20). On the one hand Elijah is politically opposed to him and his tolerance or support of the pro-Baal clique in the palace, on the other their relationship is complicated like that between parent and child. The biblical narrator insists that Ahab has been "urged on" by his evil wife (21:25) and shows Ahab capable of repentance (21:27–29) and responsive to Elijah's admonition. At 1 Kgs 18:41–42, Elijah and Ahab have another interesting interaction implying a personal dimension to their complicated relationship.

Another mixture between the personal and the political that is difficult to untangle is implied in the term for enemy derived from the verb "to hate" and in uses of the verb itself in relation to adversaries. While many references to "enemies" appear to be impersonal and political – for example, Gen 24:60 ("may your offspring gain possession of the gates of their foes," *NRSV*) and Ex 1:10 (Pharaoh about the Israelites in Egypt: "Come let us deal shrewdly ... or they will join our enemies and fight against us," *NRSV*) – the verb itself is often used in personal feuds or clashes, such as Absalom's hatred for his half-brother Amnon who had raped Absalom's full sister Tamar (2 Sam 13:15). The hatred spills over into assassination but it is difficult to see where the personal ends and the political begins for the hated Amnon is also a rival for the kingdom of an increasingly ineffectual King David, their father. As William Moran (1963) showed in relation to the formulas of ancient Near Eastern treaties, to "love" and "to hate" are political terms connoting the vassal's loyalties to his suzerain and the latter's reciprocal responsibilities to him. Thus when Yahweh loves those who love him and hates those who hate him, on one level, the biblical writers are referring to political, in the sense of covenantal, enemies or allies. In this vein, Joab accuses David of loving those who hate him and of hating those who love him, for David mourns, in his view, too much for his defeated and killed rebel son Absalom who had waged war against his own father to usurp the throne (2 Sam 19:7).

Indeed one begins to wonder if the "enemy" derived from the word "hate" is a less loaded term than *'ōyēb* (explored above) or, alternatively, if some of the intense emotion of hatred – with all its implicit resentment, increased heart-rate, and heat – is always implied even in the seemingly political or covenantal usages. When God as divine warrior is jealous, is he jealous only in the technical sense one reserves for disloyal vassals or, as the furious emotions of the passages seem to imply, is it much more personal? At Num 11:1–3, the Israelites again complain (lit. "murmuring bad in God's ears"). He hears and "his anger burned and he burnt against them the fire of Yahweh and it consumed the outskirts of the encampment." There are two words for "burn," one for "fire," another for "hot anger" just in this one little scene – emotions are displayed!

Biblical writers recognize the over-the-top, out-of-control quality of the emotions of war, hatred, anger, vengeance, and in several instances criticize and condemn the destructive behavior to which they lead. They urge reigning in these emotions. War may be necessary in certain situations but it need not be excessive. For example, Genesis

49 curses the "anger" of the brothers Simeon and Levi, two of the sons of Jacob, who decimate the Shechemites in the foundation myth preserved in Genesis 34. In this tale of war motivated by vengeance, the prince Shechem has raped Dinah and the brothers use trickery to weaken their foes. They convince them to become circumcised so that the two peoples may intermarry and the relationship between Dinah and Shechem be socially regularized and sanctioned. The demand for circumcision and attendant promises of political and economic alliance are of course a clever ruse to incapacitate the enemy. The particular trickery involved symbolically points to matters of manly status and self-definition and to the fact that the war is less about Dinah than about men's honor and shame. Shechem had helped himself to Dinah's sexuality without the permission of the men around her. They are portrayed as feeling fully justified in employing what I have called "the ideology of tricksterism" and in the extensive nature of the vengeance taken, as they kill every man and take the women and children as captives (34:25). Jacob the father is not so sure that what they did was wise and, in fact, the tale reveals a kind of generation gap between the hot-blooded young men on both sides and their elders who seem to prefer deal-making and treaties to conflict. While the sons speak of "defilement" and treating "our sister as a whore" (34:27, 31), Jacob says that war will only lead to more war and greater instability. "You have stirred up trouble for me, making me (lit.) stink among the dwellers (natives) of the land, the Canaanites and the Perizzites, and I am few in number and they will gather against me and destroy me and my household" (34:30). It is not that Jacob believes the vengeance to be unjustified or unethical but rather that he considers it not practical.

Genesis 34 is a fascinating tale for students of ancient war. Pragmatic self-preservation is not a bad deterrent. The composer of Genesis 49 goes even further: the young men's actions indicate an anger that is too strong, a fury or arrogance, an overflow of anger ('evrāh, lit. from the root 'ābar meaning "cross/pass over") which is too severe, difficult (Gen 49:7). They have gone overboard and in this catalog of the ancestor heroes of the tribes they are characterized as hotheads, not to be admired or imitated. In a similar vein, the eighth century prophet Amos condemns Edom. Edom, a southeastern neighbor of Israel who is linked to the Israelites in biblical foundation myth as Jacob/Israel's twin brother, is condemned for pursuing his brother or kin with the sword.

> He brought to ruin his compassion (or brotherly love)
> And ravage forever did his anger
> And his fury lasted (kept) to eternity (Am 1:11).

The terms for "anger" and "fury" are the same as those in Gen 49:7. Amos pictures anger as literally tearing at its enemy like a wild beast. Here the additional dimension of directing this destructive behavior towards kin intensifies the condemnation.

Finally, at 2 Chronicles 28 another prophet named Oded comes forward to condemn Northern Israelites who as military allies of Aram have captured some southerners or Judahites in battle. He says, "You have killed them with a storming rage that unto the heavens reaches." He insists that the captives be returned. It was only Judah's sin that has allowed the Northerners' victory over fellow Israelites. And so, guiltily

(2 Chron 28:13), strongly urged by their fellows from Ephraim in the North, they release their enemies and the spoil, "clothed them, shod them in sandals, fed them, and gave them drink, and they anointed them and led on donkeys all those unsteady on their feet, and they brought them to Jericho, city of Palms, to their kin, and they returned to Samaria" (2 Chron 28:15). This scene is the polar opposite of biblical ban texts in which all captured foes are "devoted to destruction," and lest it be thought that such reconciliatory treatment be reserved only for kin, we have another interesting passage from 2 Kings 6. In this case, invading Aramaeans are prevented from conquering Samaria when God blinds them in one of his miraculous battle displays. The King of Israel asks Elisha the prophet whether he should kill the captives whose eyes have now been opened and who find themselves prisoners of the Israelites. The prophet declares that indeed he should not kill these enemy troops, for they are God's not his. He asks, "Did you capture with your sword and your bow whom you want to kill?" (2 Kgs 6:22). In the view of the prophet – and the word of the prophet is oracular advice, telling what the deity wants – the Israelites are to "set food before them that they may eat and drink, and let them go to their master." This scene thus ends very much like the one about prisoners who are fellow Israelites in 2 Chronicles 28. The author adds, "And the Aramaeans no longer came raiding into the land of Israel." Their aggression is stayed, to be sure, by the certainty of divine intervention, but is there also an implication that peace is easier to maintain without total war, massive retaliation, or extermination of enemy soldiers whose friends and family in Aram will not forget?

The Passage to Peace

A final issue to be explored here is the way in which Israelite writers describe the passage from war, a way out of what David Little (1995) has called "the pathology of violence." How might conquered peoples be integrated into the society of the conquerors? How might warriors who have experienced the sensations of battle with its death, bloodshed, and mayhem make the passage back to the workaday world of peace? If war is participation in sacral activity, which in some cases it is in Israelite conception, how does one return successfully to the realm of the mundane?

First on dealing with captives. As noted above, one option is to return survivors on the other side to their own people. Such behavior generously undertaken can make reconciliation possible. Another, terrifying, option seen in the Hebrew Bible and mentioned earlier is to kill all captives imagining one's own group as responding to divine orders to place the "idolatrous Other" under the ban or as fulfilling a promise, a war vow. Defeated humans will be "devoted to destruction" as a kind of offering to the deity in thanks for his allowing one's own side to be victorious in battle. Anthropologists of an "ecological materialist" bent might suggest that both of these options, to let them go or to kill them, betoken a society which is unable to absorb more members even as slaves or second class citizens. The availability of protein resources prevents, or the amount of labor necessary in that society precludes, the desirability of adding to the conquerors' population. Perhaps such a pragmatic approach gives some hint as to the date or provenance of these varying Israelite war views. But there is a third option that does involve the absorption of the enemy or some of the enemy, and here we find recognition of the need for transition, rite of passage, transformation of identity that follows battle. Deuteronomy 21 describes the treatment of women taken as spoils of war. It is an extremely troubling passage, written from a male and Israelite victors' point of view. As in the rape of Dinah (Genesis 34), women have no voice. The passage is interesting nevertheless in what it says about its writers' sense of the group and of the conquered Other. Here the enemy is neither personally hated nor expressly described as deserving of mistreatment because of wrongs done by their people who have been defeated with the help of God. The women captives are the unfortunate victims of circumstance. The Israelite writer suggests that they must in some way be integrated into the world of the victors.

The text from Deuteronomy sets the scene. "If you go to war against your enemies (*'ôyēb* term discussed earlier) and Yahweh gives them into your hand, and you take captives of his (group) . . ." The war is thus not one in which the total ban has been imposed, and implicit is the assumption that the people will go warring from time to time, which is an interesting and disturbing feature of the writer's worldview in and of itself. In any event, should an Israelite see a beautiful woman from among them (notice that all is addressed to the males) and wish to take her as his wife, he may do so, and the woman may be brought into his household, but she is to be ritually purified and transformed: she is to shave her head, pare her nails, and remove her captive's garments (21:12, 13). She is to remain in his house for a full month's days, literally "crying," that is mourning over her father and her mother. After that time the man can "go into her" (that is, consummate the marriage) and become husband to her, and she for him a wife (21:13). The writer adds that if the woman displeases her husband, he must set her free. He cannot sell her as a slave woman since he has had his way with her. The Hebrew uses the term *'ānāh/'innāh*, which literally means "oppress," "humiliate" and is sometimes used for rape (Gen 34:2: Dinah; Judges 19:24; 20:5: the Levite's concubine; 2 Sam 13:12, 14: the rape of David's daughter Tamar; Deut 22:24, 29). This root is also used to describe what the Egyptians do to the Israelites in slavery (Ex 1:11) and how Sarah treats Hagar (Gen 16:6).

On the one hand Deuteronomy 21 evokes modern comparisons with "ethnic cleansing" whereby rape is one vicious weapon used to subdue, humiliate, and dehumanize the enemy. The least we can say is that women are regarded as chattel and are subjected to forcible abduction as spoils of war. One might counter that such was the way of war in the ancient world, thinking of parallels in classical Greek tradition, but this acknowledgement does not let the tradition off the ethical hook. Similarly, one might aver that in ancient Israelite society, all women marginals were subject to brutish methods of "neatening up" the social structure defined in terms of male lineages: rape victims who could be married off to their rapists; young widows to be married off to their brothers-in-law; adulteresses to be stoned. This passage takes its place along the others and is on one level a priestly passage about absorbing the spoils of war, making unclean booty clean and usable.

On the other hand, it is possible to see in Deuteronomy 21 an acknowledgement, albeit patronizing of women and prejudiced against the Other, that the enemy is a human being. Given the realities of war in the ancient world that were taken for granted, the woman is imagined as undergoing a passage that allows her integration into the people of Israel. Having her head shaved must have been a humiliating experience. Her body, her fertility, like that of the matriarchs' slave women is treated as a commodity to be plucked and utilized. For the framers of this material as for the conquered, the body is a powerful symbol, a template that signifies status and change of status. By shedding old hair, old nails, and old clothing, the woman is transformed, made anew. Again, she would not want to be remade by her enemies, nor would she probably experience reconciliation. For the victors whose voice dominates the passage, her transformation marks an end to military hostilities, a possibility for some degree of reconciliation, although of course the terms are dictated by the winners. The humanity of those she left behind is acknowledged. Their loss is to be mourned by their child. It is not certain, by the way, whether she cries because they died in the war or because she has been permanently separated from them and her former way of life. The association with the parents as guardians left behind implies the youth of the woman. Finally, she is not treated as a slave that can be sold for money. Sex with the Israelite has made her a part of the group; she has been branded in a sense – again the paternalistic and androcentric bent of the material is clear. At the same time, however, the use of the verb 'innāh implies an admission that all is not proper in this method of obtaining a wife, further enforcing the sense that the Israelite writer on some level recognizes the humanity of his enemies. The end of war and the transfer of conquered peoples requires a process of passage and transformation.

Another descriptive text that concerns itself with such transition and transfer is the priestly account in Numbers 31 of a military encounter with the Midianites. Within a thread of the biblical founding myth, alluded to in Num 31:16 (cf. Num 25:6–18; 23:28: Josh 13:21–22), the Midianites, their women in particular, have tempted the Israelites into the worship of Baal Peor. This temptation is given as justification for a war of vengeance. The victorious Israelites take women and children as spoils, but Moses, whose point of view dominates the scene, insists that male children and adult women who have known a man (sexually) be slaughtered. Only the young virgin girls are blank slates who can be integrated into the group. As I have argued elsewhere and is perhaps implicit in Deuteronomy 21 where the captive women weep for their mother and father (but not for husband or children left behind), the young women are as yet unmarked by the contagious Other – they have not become "one flesh" with them – and unlike young boys who will grow into the "Other" can be transformed by possession into members of Israel, fresh gardens into which Israelite seed may be sown. Again, we are dealing with an alien worldview in which women are objects, men determine identity. Women are presented here and in Deuteronomy 21 as receptacles; ethnicity is rooted in paternity.

Significantly, both the warriors who have killed or touched a corpse and the captives who are to be integrated into the community must undergo a process of purification, as must any inanimate spoil that is to be brought into the camp. Implicit in this particular priestly passage is the notion that death defiles (cf. Num 5:1–4; 19, and compare rules applying to priests alone in Lev 21:1, 2, 11; also 11:39 on the defiling characteristics of animal carcasses). For this reason, virtually all war defiles some of the combatants. To emerge from the uncleanness, time must be passed outside the encampment (Num 31:19); seven days as in other purification rituals, with purification on the third and seventh days. Material booty is to be cleansed with fire if it can survive fire, or with water if not. Clothes are to be washed on the seventh day and then they are permitted to enter the encampment.

The passage is interesting in various ways. First is the reason given for the attack on Midian, an implication that the events of collective memory have long-lasting influence and staying power. In the case of Midian and Numbers 31, at least according to the biblical chronology, we are still dealing with the pre-conquest period, but other misdeeds of the various populations encountered after the emergence from Egypt, e.g. not allowing Israel to pass through their land in spite of peaceful requests to do so, will generations later be cited as cause for war (see, e.g. 1 Sam 15:2–3 regarding Saul's war with the Amalekites). Stories of past hostilities are recognized to have lots of staying power within the tradition itself. In our own time, we have observed the ways in which ancient tales of hostility serve as justification for war in the present, for example, when the Serbs in former Yugoslavia justified their attacks on Muslims in the 1990s by the aggression of their enemies in 1389. These stories of past indignities take on a life of their own; they assume importance as fixtures of a foundation myth thoroughly interwoven with a group's sense of its own identity. This process too is surely part of the "pathology of violence."

Numbers 31 is also interesting from the perspective of gender, the body, and identity; sexual contact transforms and demarcates, altering ethnic status and branding identity. The priestly source of this tale is acutely aware of the way in which the body serves as a cultural code. While the world is filled with the uncontrollables of chaos, especially in the form of death, one can impose some degree of order on the body, having it serve as symbol of renewal and transformation. One can mark upon the body the emergence from unclean to clean and thereby the passage from death to everyday life, from crisis to the quotidian. Death defiles, and war is intimately associated with the chaos of death, but through rituals of purification one may emerge from the status of the unclean, death-stained warrior. In a similar vein, the Chronicler suggests that David was not allowed by God to build the temple because he had been a warrior, his hands stained with blood. His peacetime son "Shlomo" will build the sacred space.

In contemporary war situations we have learned about the danger of returning the warrior to his old life too quickly after combat, and before allowing him or her some sort of passage. We deal in terms of human psychology and state of mind, and as has sometimes been the case, we fear that the fury of war might spill over to the peace-time setting with wife and children, resulting in violence, aggression, and even death (see, for an impressive analogy in early Greece, Shay 1994). Perhaps the ancient writers of Numbers 31, albeit in their own priestly terms of "purity and danger," as Mary Douglas (1966) calls it, recognized a similar need to demarcate clearly between war status and peace status, to give the warrior some means by which he could effect the return to his former life. He requires transformation in order to rejoin the community much as the foreign wife needs to be transformed from an Israelite perspective to become a part of the people.

Our analysis moves the study of Israelite war in some interesting directions. The emotions and experiences of war are acknowledged by several biblical voices who not only implicitly explore the boundary shared by personal and political enmity but also critique the violent excesses resulting from the furious emotions of war. Biblical writers do examine possibilities for reconciliation between enemies after war and ritually mark not only the entrance into battle but also the emergence from war. And thus in a wide range of biblical texts pertaining to war we not only see the need ideologically to justify the killing, but also a desire to find a way back to the sentiments and the state of peace.

Note

1 All dates are BCE.

Abbreviation

NRSV   *The Holy Bible New Revised Standard Version*

References

Alter, Robert. 1985. *The Art of Biblical Poetry.* New York.

Douglas, Mary. 1966. *Purity and Danger. An Analysis of Concepts of Pollution and Taboo.* New York.

Gottwald, Norman. 1964. "'Holy War' in Deuteronomy: Analysis and Critique." *Review and Expositor* 61: 297–310.

Hobbs, T. R. 1989. *A Time for War. A Study of Warfare in the Old Testament.* Wilmington, DE.

Jackson, Kent P. 1989. "The Language of the Mesha Inscription." In Andrew Dearman (ed.), *Studies in the Mesha Inscription and Moab,* 96–130. Atlanta.

Kang, Sa-Moon. 1989. *Divine War in the Old Testament and in the Ancient Near East.* Berlin and New York.

King, Philip J., and Lawrence E. Stager. 2001. *Life in Biblical Israel.* Louisville.

Little, David. 1995. "Introduction." In David R. Smock (ed.), *Perspectives on Pacifism. Christian, Jewish, and Muslim Views on Nonviolence in International Conflict,* 3–9. Washington, DC.

Mazar, Amihai. 1992. *Archaeology of the Land of Israel.* New York.

Meyers, Carol. 1997. "The Family in Early Israel." In Leo G. Purdue et al. (eds.), *Families in Ancient Israel,* 1–47. Louisville.

——. 1998. "Kinship and Kingship. The Early Monarchy." In Michael D. Coogan (ed.), *The Oxford History of the Biblical World,* 221–71. New York and Oxford.

Moran, William L. 1963. "The Ancient Near Eastern Background of the Love of God in Deuteronomy." *Catholic Biblical Quarterly* 25: 77–87.

Niditch, Susan. 1989. "Eroticism and Death in the Tale of Jael." In Peggy L. Day (ed.), *Gender and Difference in Ancient Israel*, 43–57. Minneapolis.

——. 1993. *War in the Hebrew Bible. A Study in the Ethics of Violence.* New York and Oxford.

——. 1997. *Ancient Israelite Religion.* New York and Oxford.

Pritchard, James A. (ed.). 1969. *Ancient Near Eastern Texts.* Princeton.

Shay, Jonathan. 1994. *Achilles in Vietnam. Combat Trauma and the Undoing of Character.* New York.

Stager, Lawrence E. 1985. "The Archaeology of the Family in Ancient Israel." *Bulletin of the American Schools of Oriental Research* 260: 1–35.

Vermeule, Emily. 1979. *Aspects of Death in Early Greek Art and Poetry.* Berkeley.

Zakovitch, Yair. 1981. "Siseras Tod." *Zeitschrift für die Alttestamentliche Wissenschaft* 93: 364–74.

9

"They Shall Beat Their Swords into Plowshares": A Vision of Peace Through Justice and Its Background in the Hebrew Bible

Thomas Krüger

In the year 1959 the government of the USSR presented to the United Nations a bronze sculpture created by Soviet artist Evgeny Buchetich. The sculpture which is now located in the North Garden of UN Headquarters in New York is called "Let Us Beat Our Swords into Plowshares." It depicts the figure of a man holding a hammer aloft in one hand, and a sword in the other, which he is making into a plowshare.[1] There is a bit of irony in this present, since the USSR at that time was ruled by the explicitly atheist Communist Party, whereas the sculpture obviously alludes to a prophetic vision recorded in the Hebrew Bible in the books of the prophets Isaiah (2:2–5) and Micah (4:1–5). Two decades later, Ingeborg Geissler, a German designer living in Dresden, used a drawing of the sculpture, surrounded by the circular inscription "Schwerter zu Pflugscharen" ("swords into plowshares"), as an emblem of the Christian peace movement in the GDR, circulating first on bookmarkers, later on sew-on labels. Especially young people openly wearing this appeal for peace and disarmament were faced with harsh reprisals taken by the communist government of East Germany. A little later the Christian peace movement in West Germany took over the slogan "swords into plowshares," protesting against the deployment of new NATO missiles aimed mainly at East Germany.

Beating swords into plowshares seems to be a powerful image that is able to focus a whole lot of claims and convictions in one attractive and convincing scene. It depicts disarmament as a transformation of dangerous weapons into harmless farm implements. Blacksmiths with their special know-how will not loose their work but get new tasks. Instead of preparing tools for hurting and killing one another, people will devote themselves to the production of food. Contrasting swords = war = death with plowshares = food production = life, the image of beating swords into plowshares reduces the complexity of reality to one simple and clear opposite. That swords are used not only for war but also for defending law and justice in one's own country, and that rivalry can turn food production into a struggle for survival (cf. Isaiah 5:8–10; Micah 2:1–5), is kept out of view. Finally, the image of beating swords into plowshares can be understood as an appeal for action. Directed at one particular nation or government – as in the peace movements of East and West Germany – this appeal would demand unilateral steps toward disarmament; directed at the community of nations – as with the gift of the USSR to the UN – it would ask all governments to act together.

In its original biblical context the image of beating swords into plowshares is part of a more detailed and complex prophetic prediction (cf. Otto 1999: 144–51). Its slightly more elaborated version in the Book of Micah (4:1–5) reads as follows:[2]

> (1) In days to come the mountain of the LORD's house shall be established as the highest of the mountains, and shall be raised up above the hills. Peoples shall stream to it, (2) and many nations shall come and say: "Come, let us go up to the mountain of the LORD, to the house of the God of Jacob; that he may teach us his ways and that we may walk in his paths." For out of Zion shall go forth instruction, and the word of the LORD from Jerusalem. (3) He shall judge between many peoples, and shall arbitrate between strong nations far away; they shall beat their swords into plowshares, and their spears into pruning hooks; nation shall not lift up sword against nation, neither shall they learn war any more; (4) but they shall all sit under their own vines and under their own fig trees, and no one shall make them afraid; for the mouth of the LORD of hosts has spoken. (5) For all the peoples walk, each in the name of its god, but we will walk in the name of the LORD our God forever and ever.

In the center of this text is the expectation that one day the conflicts between peoples and "nations" (a somewhat anachronistic translation for Hebrew *goyim*) will be settled not by means of force and violence, but on the basis of jurisdiction and moral sense. As a consequence, the people will give up war, weapons, and military training. That all shall sit under their own vines and under their own fig trees, illustrates not only a state of security and prosperity but also the absence of economic struggle thanks to an equal distribution of property, especially of the means of (agricultural) production. A prerequisite of this pacification of all peoples is the acceptance of Israel's god Yahweh ("the LORD") as the central authority of moral instruction and the administration of justice. In this respect the prophetic oracle of universal peace remains attached to the perspective of a particular culture. However, this Israelite culture enjoyed at best a marginal international status at the time of this oracle. And it is not clear whether it is expected that all peoples will become Israelites or only that some aspects of Israel's culture and civilization will be accepted by the other peoples. Perhaps the last verse of the oracle makes exactly this point: if the peoples listen to Yahweh's teaching and accept his judgments, this does not imply that they give up their particular gods – that is, their cultural identity (cf. Rendtorff 1999: 274). But it is also possible, that v. 5 gives expression to the experience that the hope articulated in v. 1–4 has not yet become reality: instead of learning the ways of Yahweh the peoples continue to walk in the ways of their gods (cf. Wolff 1982: 94). In this case the oracle would have to be understood as an expectation of universal acceptance of Israelite culture and civilization.

Even if one takes into account the obvious limits of this vision of universal pacification, the hope that war could finally be overcome by justice sounds amazingly modern. As clear and definite as this expectation is formulated here, it is unique in the Hebrew Bible as well as in the Ancient Near East (cf. Otto 1999: 11). How could such a perspective of a peaceful coexistence of peoples be developed in an environment in which war was a constant experience and widely held as an inevitable ingredient of reality? What were the prerequisites that made it possible to imagine a world in which conflicts between peoples can be settled without violence?

One factor which pointed in this direction was probably the experience that within society violence had already successfully been tamed by justice. The Hebrew Bible depicts the danger of an escalation of violence, caused by the practice of vengeance, in the figure of Lamech who boasts in front of his wives:

> I have killed a man for wounding me,
> a young man for striking me.
> If Cain is avenged sevenfold,
> truly Lamech seventy-sevenfold (Genesis 4:23).

That "the earth was filled with violence" was, according to Genesis 6:11, the reason for the great flood which Yahweh had brought over the earth in the days of Noah. After the flood, God commanded humankind to protect human life by the threat and application of capital punishment:

> For your own lifeblood I will surely require a reckoning: from every animal I will require it and from human beings, each one for the blood of another, I will require a reckoning for human life. Whoever sheds the blood of a human, by a human shall that person's blood be shed; for in his own image God made humankind (Genesis 9:5–6).

Finally, the laws given to Israel at Mount Sinai limit the right to exact vengeance for bodily injuries. In such cases,

> you shall give life for life, eye for eye, tooth for tooth, hand for hand, foot for foot, burn for burn, wound for wound, stripe for stripe (Exodus 21:22–24)

– not a life for a wound or a stripe, as Lamech did (cf. also the limitation of blood revenge by law in Numbers 35). Thus, in the perspective of the Hebrew Bible, history showed that violent ways of settling conflicts between humans could be overcome by justice and moral sense – taught to Israel by Yahweh! Why should it not be possible to transfer this model of pacification through justice from internal quarrels to international conflicts?

Considerations of this kind probably could have been supported by experiences with current political powers. There is a relatively broad consensus in present research that the nearly identical oracles of Isaiah 2:2–5 and Micah 4:1–5 did not originate in the times of the prophets Isaiah and Micah, that is, roughly, the second half of the seventh century, but in the period of Persian dominion over Jerusalem and Judah, between 539 and 332 – more probably in the first half of this period than in the second (cf. Otto 1999: 145–46 n. 259). It seems that the rule of the Persians was perceived as largely positive in Jerusalem and the province of Jehud. Unlike the Assyrians, the Babylonians, and later the Greeks, in the Hebrew Bible the Persians are never the subject of a prophetic oracle of doom. Zechariah 1:11 characterizes the state of the world under the rule of Darius I: "The whole earth remains at peace." In fact, the Persian kings were nearly constantly engaged in wars with their neighbors and in the suppression of rebellions within their empire. But in their textual and visual artifacts they presented themselves as fighting for truth, law and justice, peace and well-being of their subjects (cf. the inscription of Darius I in Behistun/Bisotun: *TUAT* 1: 419–50). In his famous "Cyrus Cylinder" Cyrus calls himself a "shepherd with justice and righteousness" and depicts the capture of the city of Babylon (539) as a peaceful act of liberation:

> When I entered Babylon in a peaceful manner, I took up my lordly reign in the royal palace amidst rejoicing and happiness ... My vast army moved about Babylon in peace; I did not permit anyone to frighten (the people of) [Sumer] and Akkad. I sought the welfare of the city of Babylon and all its sacred centers. As for the citizens of Babylon, upon whom he [i.e. Nabonidus, the last king of Babylon] imposed corvée which was not the god's will and not befitting them, I relieved their weariness and freed them from their service (?). [The Babylonian god] Marduk, the great lord, rejoiced over my [good] deeds. He sent gracious blessings upon me, Cyrus, the king who worships him, and upon Cambyses, the son who is [my] offspring, [and upo]n all my army, and in peace, before him, we move [about] ... (*COS* 2: 315).

To mention just one other example, the architecture and the decoration of Persepolis, one of the Achaemenid royal capitals built under Darius I and his successors, intended

> to present to the world the concept of a *Pax Persica* – a harmonious, peaceful empire ruled by a king who contained within his person and his office the welfare of the empire (T. Cuyler Young, Jr., in *ABD* 5: 236, cf. Ahn 1992; Koch 1996).

The positive experience of Persian rule and the concept of a "Persian Peace" (*pax Persica*) propagated by the Achaemenid rulers (Wiesehöfer, this vol.) probably supported the hope for a peaceful co-existence of peoples on the basis of a common ethos and a judicial settlement of conflicts, as it is articulated in Isaiah 2 and in Micah 4. However, the biblical visions go beyond the Persian concept of a peaceful world order in two respects. First, they do not mention any human king as guarantor of peace; the peoples are judged and instructed by God himself. Second, they see no need for an army to maintain and protect the peaceful order of the world, contrary to the decoration program of Persepolis which included numerous depictions of troops of the Persian army. These differences between the concept of a *pax Persica* and the biblical visions of world peace point to the fact that the latter were influenced not only by the experience of Persian rule but also by specific historical experiences and cultural traditions of Ancient Israel.

One important factor was that Israel viewed world affairs from a perspective at the margin of the Persian empire. Living at the border of Egypt, a constant trouble spot for the Persian rulers, people in the province of Yehud were thoroughly familiar with the atrocities of war (cf. Winn Leith 1998; Stern 2001: 576–82). And after the breakdown of the state of Judah, in consequence of its conquest by the Babylonians in the first decades of the sixth century, the Israelites had learned to live without a king on the basis of their moral and legal traditions.

Paradoxically, one strand in Israelite traditions that was a crucial condition for the development of a concept of peace without war was the idea that success in warfare depended on divine support. In Psalm 2 Yahweh hands over the enemies to the king who is the representative of divine rule on earth:

> I have set my king on Zion, my holy hill.
> … You are my son;
> today I have begotten you.
> Ask of me, and I will make the nations your heritage,
> and the ends of the earth your possession.
> You shall break them with a rod of iron,
> and dash them in pieces like a potter's vessel (Psalm 2:6–9).

That Yahweh fights for his people is emphasized in the narratives about wars in the pre-monarchic period of the history of Israel (Niditch, this vol.). It is much debated whether these narratives refer to real historical experiences. In any case, they got their present literary form only in the monarchic period or even later, and were influenced by ancient near eastern, particularly Neo-Assyrian, war accounts, to which they partly try to formulate a critical alternative (cf. Kang 1989; Otto 1999: 13–75).

In a famous battle of the Israelites against a Canaanite army commanded by Sisera, reported in the book of Judges (chapters 4 and 5), Yahweh supports his people by striking the enemies with panic:

> The LORD threw Sisera and all his chariots and all his army into a panic before Barak [the leader of the Israelites]; Sisera got down from his chariot and fled away on foot (Judges 4:15).

Fleeing, Sisera is finally killed by a woman in whose tent he tries to hide. In the equally famous narrative about the capture of the city of Jericho under Joshua, Yahweh miraculously causes the walls of the city to collapse so that the Israelites can take the city (Joshua 6). In a battle near Gibeon (Joshua 10), Yahweh not only throws Israel's enemies into a panic (v. 10) but also "threw down huge stones from heaven on them" so that "there were more who died because of the hailstones than the Israelites killed with the sword" (v. 11). In the end, at Joshua's request, Yahweh causes the sun and the moon to stand still for nearly a day so that the Israelites can take vengeance on their enemies (v. 12–13).

These examples illustrate how Yahweh supports his people in battle in often miraculous ways. After their departure from Egypt, the Israelites do not have to fight at all against the Egyptian army pursuing them. "The LORD will fight for you, and you have only to keep still," Moses exhorts his people in the face of the enemy (Exodus 14:14). And, indeed, the Israelites watch in amazement as their enemies drown in the sea. "Thus the Lord saved Israel that day from the Egyptians; and Israel saw the Egyptians dead on the seashore" (Exodus 14:30). If one takes narratives like this seriously, it is easy to be convinced that Israel does not need any sort of armament or preparation for war. On this premise the prophet Isaiah criticizes his contemporaries' lack of trust in God:

> Thus said the Lord GOD, the Holy One of Israel:
> In returning and rest you shall be saved;
> in quietness and in trust shall be your strength.
> But you refused and said,
> "No! We will flee upon horses" –
> therefore you shall flee!
> and, "We will ride upon swift steeds" –
> therefore your pursuers shall be swift!
> A thousand shall flee at the threat of one,
> at the threat of five you shall flee,
> until you are left like a flagstaff on the top of a mountain,
> like a signal on a hill (Isaiah 30:15–17; cf. Isaiah 7).

The conviction that Yahweh fights for Israel can thus have different consequences. It can warrant the preparation for and the waging of wars by the Israelite kings, but it can also criticize and question such actions. As a result, expectations concerning the conduct of a king can differ quite substantially, as two war narratives from the book of Kings may illustrate.

In 1 Kings 20 King Ahab of Israel, according to the demand of Yahweh transmitted to him by a prophet, wages war against King Ben-hadad of Aram. Having defeated his army, Ahab makes a peace treaty with Ben-hadad and releases him. For that he is criticized in strong terms by a prophet: "Thus says the LORD, 'Because you have let the man go whom I had devoted to destruction, therefore your life shall be for his life, and your people for his people'" (1 Kings 20:42). Since the king must not wage war on his own authority and owes his success to Yahweh, he must also not make peace on his own authority. Rather, he has to exterminate the defeated enemy completely, according to the tradition of the "ban" (or "dedication to destruction," cf. Niditch 1993: 28–77 and this vol.).

In contrast to this story, 2 Kings 6 narrates how, once upon a time, an Aramean army was miraculously blinded by Yahweh and led right into the center of the city of Samaria by the prophet Elisha.

> When the king of Israel saw them he said to Elisha, "Father, shall I kill them? Shall I kill them?" He answered, "No! Did you capture with your sword and your bow those whom you want to kill? Set food and water before them so that they may eat and drink; and let them go to their master." So he prepared for them a great feast; after they ate and drank, he sent them on their way, and they went to their master. And the Arameans no longer came raiding into the land of Israel (2 Kings 6:21–23).

Here, Yahweh's deliverance from the enemies does not lead to their destruction but to a peaceful coexistence, according to the tradition of hospitality.

Another tradition of Israelite thought underlying Isaiah 2 and Micah 4 is the hope for divine intervention that will bring war to an end. In the face of the atrocity of wars, it is quite understandable if people hope that the end of a present war or of a war expected in the near future will bring the end of all wars. "Never again war!," many people in Germany said, when the Second World War had come to an end about 60 years ago. In the Hebrew Bible the hope for an end of all wars is linked with the idea that Yahweh supports Israel's wars or that he fights for his people. One may hope, therefore, that Yahweh will win such a decisive and lasting victory over the enemies that they will never again want or have the means to wage war against Israel. So, for example, Psalm 46 says:

> Come, behold the works of the LORD;
> see what desolations he has brought on the earth.
> He makes wars cease to the end of the earth;
> he breaks the bow, and shatters the spear;
> he burns the shields with fire (Psalm 46:8–9).

What follows is obviously spoken by Yahweh to the enemies:

> Be still, and know that I am God!
> I am exalted among the nations,
> I am exalted on the earth (v. 10).

As in Isaiah 2 and Micah 4, here too Yahweh instructs the peoples in his "ways" and thereby prevents them from waging war. A decisive difference between these texts and Psalm 46 is that there Yahweh settles the conflicts between the peoples by jurisdiction, whereas here he threatens them with brute force. The latter is also the case in later prophetic texts which express the eschatological expectation of a final and universal war against the peoples who are hostile to Yahweh and Israel, which will lead to a universal and lasting world peace (cf., e.g. Isaiah 60, 65; Joel 4; Micah 5; Zephaniah 3; Zechariah 9). The horizon of expectations is thus expanded from limited wars of liberation to an extensive disarmament and pacification, as we see it in Isaiah 2 and Micah 4.

A model for a way of driving away enemies without fighting a war is the liberation of Jerusalem from the Assyrian siege under Sennacherib in the year 701 (cf. 2 Kings 18–19; Isaiah 36–37). According to 2 Kings 19:35, "the angel of the LORD set out and struck down one hundred eighty-five thousand in the camp of the Assyrians." Thereupon Sennacherib left and went home to Nineveh (v. 36). A historically more credible version of these events seems to be preserved in 2 Kings 18:14–16: King Hezekiah of Judah paid a heavy tribute of silver and gold to Sennacherib (cf. Sennacherib's own account of the events: COS 2: 302–03). In the legend of 2 Kings 6:24–7:20, God caused an Aramean army which laid siege to Samaria "to hear the sound of chariots, and of horses, the sound of a great army" (7:6), so that they were frightened and fled away for their lives. Isaiah 9 seems to look back to the withdrawal of the Assyrian occupying forces from the Assyrian provinces in northern Israel in 620 which had been conquered by the Assyrian king Tiglath-pileser III in 732 (cf. Otto 1999: 121–24) – an event that had been caused not by military actions of Judah but by the decline of the Assyrian empire in the context of larger changes in the Ancient Near East:

> In the former time he brought into contempt the land of Zebulun and the land of Naphtali, but in the latter time he will make glorious the way of the sea, the land beyond the Jordan, Galilee of the nations.
> The people who walked in darkness
> have seen a great light;
> those who lived in a land of deep darkness –

on them light has shined.
You have multiplied the nation,
you have increased its joy;
they rejoice before you as with joy at the harvest,
as people exult when dividing plunder.
For the yoke of their burden,
and the bar across their shoulders,
the rod of their oppressor,
you have broken as on the day of Midian.
For all the boots of the tramping warriors
and all the garments rolled in blood
shall be burned as fuel for the fire (Isaiah 9:1–5).

This passage emphasizes the possibility of a state of peace that is not brought about by warfare. Isaiah 2 and Micah 4, however, go one step further, envisioning a state of peace that is based on a judicial settling of conflicts. In this development two other strands of Israelite tradition seem to play a part: the idea of connecting war with justice, and the expectation that law will spread so widely as to become universal.

The conviction that success and failure in warfare depend not only on arms and military know-how, but also on right or wrong, justice or injustice, is not foreign to the Ancient Near East (see for Assyria, Oded 1992). In the Hebrew Bible it is articulated particularly in the prophetic books (e.g. Amos 3:9–11) from which it found its way into the historical sections. Thus the books of Kings explain the destruction of the states of Israel and Judah by attacking Assyrian and Babylonian armies as a consequence of the constant offenses of these two states against the laws that Yahweh had given them. At the end of the Mosaic laws, Deuteronomy 28 promises the Israelites in blessings and curses success or failure in warfare, depending on whether they comply with these laws or violate them. If Israel obeys the laws, "the LORD will cause your enemies who rise against you to be defeated before you; they shall come out against you one way, and flee before you seven ways" (v. 7). But if Israel flouts the laws,

the LORD will cause you to be defeated before your enemies; you shall go out against them one way and flee before them seven ways. You shall become an object of horror to all the kingdoms of the earth. Your corpses shall be food for every bird of the air and animal of the earth, and there shall be no one to frighten them away (v. 25–26).

Genesis 15:16 promises Abraham that his descendents will take over the promised land of Canaan – but only in the fourth generation, because the injustice of the Amorites first has to be "completed," so that Yahweh may justly drive them out of their land. Deuteronomy 9:4–5 also emphasizes that Yahweh thrusts out the inhabitants of the promised land before the Israelites because of their "wickedness." The prophet Nahum interprets the destruction of Nineveh as a just punishment for the injustices committed by the Assyrians. Accordingly, the prophet Habakkuk predicts the end of the Babylonians because they committed injustice when they occupied Judah.

It is only a small, but distinctive, step from the conviction that in history, in the end, not power but justice will prevail, to the vision that justice might prevail not only through war and force but also without violence. This step is taken in the prophetic predictions recorded in Isaiah 32 – not yet concerning the whole world but focusing only on Israel. They promise a better future after the expected military defeat of Israel, when a new ruler will care for peace by promoting law and justice:

> For the palace will be forsaken,
> the populous city deserted;
> the hill and the watchtower will become dens forever,
> the joy of wild asses, a pasture for flocks;
> until a spirit from on high is poured out on us,
> and the wilderness becomes a fruitful field,
> and the fruitful field is deemed a forest.
> Then justice will dwell in the wilderness,
> and righteousness abide in the fruitful field.
> The effect of righteousness will be peace,
> and the result of righteousness, quietness and trust forever.
> My people will abide in a peaceful habitation,
> in secure dwellings, and in quiet resting places (Isaiah 32:14–18).

In expanding this expectation of a peace based on law and justice from Israel to the whole world, Isaiah 2 and Micah 4 pick up another traditional line of thought in the Hebrew Bible: that law and justice will radiate and spread out from Israel to all peoples of the world. This expectation is articulated in a rather similar way in chapters 40–55 of the book of Isaiah which Old Testament scholars are used to call "Second Isaiah" or "Deutero-Isaiah," and which originated in the time of the Babylonian exile or perhaps more probably in the Persian period (cf. Baltzer 2001). Here Cyrus, covering the world in a campaign of conquest, in which he "trampled on rulers as on mortar, as the potter treads clay" (Isaiah 41:25), is represented as the precursor of a new world order. This new world order, however, shall not be based on military power, as in Cyrus' case, but on the laws and ethos contained in the "instruction" (*torah*) of Yahweh. Thus Yahweh says in Isaiah 51:4–5:

> … a teaching will go out from me,
> and my justice for a light to the peoples.
> I will bring near my deliverance swiftly,
> my salvation has gone out
> and my arms will rule the peoples;
> the coastlands wait for me,
> and for my arm they hope.

In Isaiah 42:1–4 Yahweh appoints his "servant" or "minister" to spread his law and his instruction to all peoples:

> Here is my servant, whom I uphold,
> my chosen, in whom my soul delights;
> I have put my spirit upon him;
> he will bring forth justice to the nations.
> He will not cry or lift up his voice,
> or make it heard in the street;
> a bruised reed he will not break,
> and a dimly burning wick he will not quench;
> he will faithfully bring forth justice.
> He will not grow faint or be crushed

until he has established justice in the earth;
and the coastlands wait for his teaching.

In the present literary context this anonymous "servant" of Yahweh is identified with Israel.

As another example of this line of tradition we could mention Deuteronomy 4:6–8 where the conviction is expressed that the Mosaic laws are sensible and fair, and that this fact will be acknowledged by the peoples as soon as they will become acquainted with it. We could also point to numerous statements in the book of Psalms according to which Yahweh as the judge of the whole world will dispense justice for all peoples and all humans (e.g. Psalm 82; 96:10, 13; 98:9 as well as Genesis 18:25).

Isaiah 2 and Micah 4 devise a "program for a state of peace ... that leaves behind any expectation of peace that the Ancient Near East could ever formulate" (Otto 1999: 11). Even in the Hebrew Bible it is rather unique (Yoder and Swartley 1992). The observations outlined above tried to point to some lines of tradition in the Hebrew Bible (and in the Ancient Near East) that help us understand, at least in broad outlines, the way that led to this conception of peace without war. They also show that this vision of peace based on justice and moral sense did not simply arise from pious wishful thinking but is founded on the historical experiences of Ancient Israel – experiences of failure in the age of monarchy, protection during the exile, and a new beginning in the early Persian period. However, the most important condition, based on experience, for a vision of overcoming violence in the international realm through justice and peaceful settlement of conflicts, seems to have been the fact that analogous developments had already taken place successfully within individual peoples and communities – in simplified terms: the overcoming of revenge through law. This achievement did not eliminate violence from human society but, restricted by law, violence was more and more reduced in the course of history.

Corresponding efforts in our time to regulate the co-existence of peoples and nations in a non-violent way by law and justice seem promising – even if they have suffered some set-backs in the recent past. In any case, the vision of completely overcoming war and violence between peoples, as it is formulated in Isaiah 2 and Micah 4, remains a challenge even today – not least because it expects peace without war to be realized by God and thus points out that this goal is beyond human control. However, the God about whom Isaiah 2 and Micah 4 speak, does not work through force but tries to convince people through word, law, and moral instruction. Therefore, he cannot achieve his goal without the cooperation of humans.

Notes

1 See www.un.org/av/photo/subjects/art.htm. April 7, 2006. The following is a revised and expanded version of a lecture given in May 2003 at a conference on the subject of "War – Society – Institutions" in Wittenberg (Germany). All dates are BCE.
2 Quotes from the Hebrew Bible here and below follow the *NRSV*.

Abbreviations

ABD	Freedman 1992
COS	Hallo and Younger 2003
NRSV	*The Holy Bible: New Revised Standard Version*. New York, 1989
TUAT	Kaiser 1982–97

References

Ahn, Gregor. 1992. *Religiöse Herrscherlegitimation im achämenidischen Iran*. Leiden.

Baltzer, Klaus. 2001. *Deutero-Isaiah*. Minneapolis.

Freedman, David (ed.). 1992. *The Anchor Bible Dictionary*. 6 vols. New York.

Hallo, William, and K. Lawson Younger Jr. (eds.). 2003. *The Context of Scripture*. 3 vols. Leiden.

Kaiser, Otto (ed.). 1982–97. *Texte aus der Umwelt des Alten Testaments*. 3 vols. Gütersloh.

Kang, Sa-Moon. 1989. *Divine War in the Old Testament and in the Ancient Near East*. Berlin.

Koch, Klaus. 1996. "Weltordnung und Reichsidee im alten Iran und ihre Auswirkungen auf die Provinz Jehud." In Klaus Koch and Peter Frei (eds.), *Reichsidee und Reichsorganisation im Perserreich*. 2nd edn, 45–119. Fribourg and Göttingen.

Niditch, Susan. 1993. *War in the Hebrew Bible: A Study in the Ethics of Violence*. New York.

Oded, Bustenay. 1992. *War, Peace, and Empire: Justifications for War in Assyrian Royal Inscriptions*. Wiesbaden.

Otto, Eckart. 1999. *Krieg und Frieden in der Hebräischen Bibel und im Alten Orient: Aspekte für eine Friedensordnung in der Moderne*. Stuttgart.

Rendtorff, Rolf. 1999. *Theologie des Alten Testaments: Ein kanonischer Entwurf*, 1: *Kanonische Grundlegung*. Neukirchen-Vluyn.

Stern, Ephraim. 2001. *Archaeology of the Land of the Bible: The Assyrian, Babylonian, and Persian Periods, 732–332 BCE*. New York.

Winn Leith, Mary Joan. 1998. "Israel among the Nations: The Persian Period." In Michael D. Coogan (ed.), *The Oxford History of the Biblical World*, 367–419. Oxford.

Wolff, Hans Walter. 1982. *Dodekapropheton* 4: *Micha*. Neukirchen-Vluyn.

Yoder, Perry B., and Willard M. Swartley (eds.). 1992. *The Meaning of Peace: Biblical Studies*. Louisville.

10

"Laughing for Joy": War and Peace among the Greeks

Lawrence A. Tritle

In 421 and after 10 years of war, plague, and destruction, Athens and Sparta managed to find a way to stop fighting and find peace for themselves and their allies in what today is known as the Peace of Nicias. It ended the first phase of the Peloponnesian War of 431–404 and was an event that even the comic playwright Aristophanes took seriously. In a drama called simply *Peace*, he tells how "the reconciled cities greet and blend in peaceful intercourse, and laugh for joy" (ll. 538–40). Clearly the Greeks believed that peace was preferable to war, but finding it and keeping it was as elusive for them as it is for us today.

War is as old as man and even some of its most horrific practices, mutilation of the dead for example, have survived into the twentieth century (Keeley 1996; Tritle 1997: 123–36). Time will tell about the twenty-first. War's impact on society and culture should not be ignored, though many modern scholars seem to think that its study is somehow ignoble and beneath them. Yet it remains as true for us as for Heraclitus, an Ionian Greek philosopher around 500, that "war is the father of all things" (22 B53 Diels-Kranz 1961).

The first Greeks, the Mycenaeans, were accomplished practitioners of war. In the video program *Greek Fire*, a forensic scientist reconstructing the faces of warriors buried at Mycenae calls them a "group of thugs." In other words, their very portraits depict them as violent men who fight hard, ask for no quarter and give none. It is tempting to think that they are the heroes we know from Homer's *Iliad* and *Odyssey*. These rightly famous poems provide not only our earliest accounts of the nature of Greek culture and society, but also of the practice of war and the dream of peace.

The *Iliad* is perhaps the greatest story of war yet written. Two works that explore its themes of war, violence, and their consequences, Simone Weil's famous essay "The *Iliad*, or the Poem of Force" (originally published 1940–41, most recently in Holoka 2003: 45–69) and Jonathan Shay's *Achilles in Vietnam* (1994), are as compelling as they are moving. Yet the *Iliad* also tells of the quest for peace. In Book 18 Homer describes the blessings of peace emblazoned on the new shield of Achilles, made for him after Hector took his first from Patroclus who had carried it into battle (Taplin 1998: 96–115). The scenes that the smith-god Hephaestus depicted revolve around two cities, one peaceful and the other violent, that call to mind Renaissance Italy's "Allegory on Good Government" by A. Lorenzetti in the Sienese town hall (Hartt and Wilkins 2003: 145–49). Scenes of pastoral serenity and justice evoke visions of peace that contrast sharply with war's brutalities. Homer surely does this deliberately – he shows what the warriors have left behind and will likely never see again – wives, children, parents, and the good things in life that most people aspire to have and enjoy. Achilles' shield reveals that the early Greeks knew war all too well and saw peace as an elusive good (see also the introduction to this volume).

At about the same time that the stories of the *Iliad* were first circulating, an unknown potter on the island of Mykonos made a *pithos* (a large storage jar) that depicted the great tale of Troy (Osborne 1998: 53–7). On the neck of the *pithos* stands the Trojan horse in which the heads of warriors are visible in square portholes, surrounded by yet more warriors, all about to sack Troy. Below are several horizontal bands that depict the fate of a sacked city, not just Troy but any fallen town. Here warriors, having already killed the men, freely assault women and may be even seen grabbing children by their heels, dashing their heads into the ground. Like Homer, the artist of the Mykonos *pithos* knew what really happened when a town fell to its enemies.

The earliest Greeks grimly understood war's realities and valued the blessings of peace. In the historical era of the fifth and fourth centuries, however, we find clearer evidence of how the Greeks attempted to avoid war; we also learn of the traumas and stresses they experienced, how they suffered and in the end were changed. In fact, there can be no mistaking the consequences of war – how it transforms those who experience it and how those experiences change the society and culture of which they are part.

The Greek classical era is dominated by war as told to us by the founding fathers of history, Herodotus and Thucydides, each writing in response to the first great teller of war, Homer (Havelock 1972: 19–78). Herodotus thought war was so much foolishness that it was best avoided. He makes this point in several ways. Early in his *Histories*, he attributes to the Lydian king Croesus a telling statement: "No one is stupid enough to prefer war to peace; in peace sons bury their fathers and in war fathers bury their sons" (1.87). He follows this sentiment up with an analysis of the Greek "art" of war that he ascribes to the Persian commander Mardonius, a cousin of King Xerxes. Trying to convince Xerxes that a conquest of Greece would pose few problems, Mardonius says:

> From all I hear, the Greeks usually wage war in an extremely stupid fashion, because they're ignorant and incompetent. When they declare war on one another they seek out the best, most level piece of land and that's where they go and fight. The upshot is that the victors leave the battlefield with massive losses, not to mention the losers, who are completely wiped out. What they should do, since they all speak the same language, is

make use of heralds and messengers to settle their differences, since anything would be preferable to fighting (7.9; tr. Waterfield 1998).[1]

Herodotus' opinion reveals an understanding of war and violence that comes from firsthand experience as well as contemporary reflection on the fighting in Greece which he observed.

Herodotus remains our basic guide to the Persian Wars. In explaining how the Greeks and Persians came to blows, he resorts to myth in connecting the war of his generation to the great Trojan War and to divine intervention. The human contribution to war is hidden by this, though it does occasionally peek through his account. It would be the achievement of his younger contemporary, Thucydides of Athens, to provide a rational analysis of the outbreak of his generation's great war between Athens and Sparta. On no other conflict in the ancient world do we have as much information as on this one, thanks to Thucydides' rich and intense report. Modern readers will find themselves at home here as he relates factors that have a curiously modern ring – power politics, ambition, and the drive to acquire greater wealth. It is necessary, therefore, to spend some time examining this account, not least since Thucydides also describes how the Greeks tried to avoid war.

The Outbreak of the Peloponnesian War

Shortly after 435 the cities of Corcyra and Corinth began squabbling and then fighting over Epidamnus, a city in the Adriatic in which both had interests. Their feud entangled Athens and Sparta, each leading a powerful group of allies. As the dispute worsened and expanded to include Potidaea (a city in the northern Aegean founded by Corinth but dominated by Athens), the likelihood of a greater conflict gradually increased (Thuc. 1.24–55).[2] Historian E. Badian (1993: 125) is surely right that after the war ended there was much discussion over responsibility (who started the war?) – an ancient version of the 1919 Paris Peace Conference's "war-guilt issue" – and what Thucydides wrote must be placed within this context. It is also clear that Thucydides gives us his own account of how things unfolded and in doing so downplays those events where Athens' responsibility was greater (Rhodes 1987: 161–63; Badian 1993: 125–63). Yet wars are complex; given the practical limitations of his time and the limits imposed by his own perspective, Thucydides deserves credit for relating as ably as he does what drove the Greeks to war in 431.

In discussing the conflicts over Epidamnus and Potidaea, Thucydides identifies what historians today would refer to as "short-term causes." He recognizes, however, that there were "long-term causes" as well, particularly the growth of Athenian power that so worried the Spartans that in their view there was no alternative but war (1.23.6; for discussion, see Hornblower 1991–6: 1.62–66). Thucydides identifies also what could be defined as the "necessary" cause, that is, the type of cause without which a conflict could not begin, in the Theban "sneak" attack on Plataea (2.1–6). Like the events following the assassination of the Austrian Arch-Duke Franz Ferdinand in 1914, these factors led to the mobilization of the armies after which war could not be stopped (2.7). Moreover, after the failed Theban attack on Plataea, the Plataeans executed 180 Theban prisoners and this surely hardened attitudes. Thucydides makes clear that this sparked the mobilization of the armies of Greece and the war that so many feared became a reality.

Yet Thucydides states that in going to war both Athens and Sparta broke the 30 Years Peace that had been in place since 446/5 when the Greeks negotiated a settlement ending an eight-year period of undeclared war.[3] When Thucydides' account of the outbreak of war in 431 is probed, several factors emerge that shed light on the origins of this great war. First, and perhaps most critical, is the issue of arbitration.[4] The historian advances this issue first in the Athenian speech at Sparta at the beginning of the dispute between Corcyra and Corinth. He returns to it in Pericles' first speech to the Athenians urging them to vote for war with Sparta in the late fall of 432. Pericles states plainly that the Spartans have refused, or at very least have failed to accept, Athenian offers to arbitrate their differences as called for by the 30 Years Peace.[5]

Arbitration and the Greeks

How could such a dispute be arbitrated? Modern political scientists observe that among the features of the international system that prompts states to fear each other is the absence of a central authority that can protect them from the aggressions and ambitions of other states.[6] There can be little doubt that as early as Homer the Greeks recognized the same problem. The dispute between Agamemnon and Achilles over Briseis in the first book of the *Iliad* is analogous insofar as it involves the two greatest leaders and thus can only be resolved by the gods.[7] But even divine intervention does not always work. The Aristophanic hero Trygaeus, upon arriving in heaven in his search for Peace (discussed below), finds that the gods have left in disgust, unable to resolve the disputes that have led the Greeks to war. The reported Spartan refusal to arbitrate, their presumed responsibility for plunging Greece into war, is not then an argument that should be accepted at face value. If the Spartans indeed provoked war, they followed a most unusual diplomatic strategy. For on at least four occasions Spartan ambassadors approached the Athenians attempting to find some way to stop the escalation to violence.[8] What did the Spartans hope to accomplish with these negotiations? Why did the Athenians refuse to deliberate?

In late fall 432 the Athenians took up the issue of war with Sparta, which had been brewing for a year. A Spartan embassy (the third?) now arrived and announced, "Sparta wants peace. Peace is still possible if you give the Hellenes their autonomy" (Thuc. 1.139.3). Pericles, architect of Athenian power, responded with a speech intended to incite not only rejection of the Spartan overture but a vote for war with Sparta. It was in this speech that Pericles claimed the Spartans were plotting against Athens and had refused offers of arbitration. He referred specifically to a treaty clause stipulating the grant of arbitration upon the offer of one party in a dispute and that, until a decision was reached, "each side should keep what it has" (Thuc. 1.140.2, 144.2). This statement would appear to put the Spartans in the wrong in causing a war that the Athenians scrupulously tried to avoid. Yet the Spartans, as Thucydides makes clear, knew of the obligation to accept arbitration. In an earlier speech at Sparta, King Archidamus refers to it, as he tells the Spartans that it would be wrong to initiate war while arbitration was pending (Thuc. 1.85.2).

Many scholars would argue, following Thucydides, that the Spartan embassies were only buying time to prepare for war and to gain the moral advantage in the dispute. After all, Thucydides asserts, some Spartans later admitted Spartan responsibility in failing to rein in the Thebans (before their attack on Plataea) or to take up the Athenian offer to submit to arbitration.[9] But this admission, placed in the context of the Sicilian expedition, comes some 15 years after the war's outbreak. How well did these *anonymous* Spartans know their city's efforts – undertaken by Archidamus, Polyalces and others, most of whom by then must have been dead – to stop the march to war? If the statement is genuine and not simply Thucydidean editorializing, it might just as easily reflect the limited knowledge and understanding of younger men of events of which they had no direct knowledge.[10]

A greater problem seems to be a flaw in the process: the difficulty of identifying an arbitrator that would satisfy each aggrieved party. The Greek city-states by this time had fallen into two armed camps now preparing for war. The only major non-aligned state in Greece proper was Argos, a community involved in a long-standing relationship with Sparta of mutual hatred and hostility and thus unacceptable to Sparta as a mediator.[11] In western Greece, Corcyra had been the major non-aligned state, but Corcyra was now party to the dispute and could not possibly act as an arbiter. There were several other non-aligned communities in western Greece, but these – Aetolia and Achaea – lacked the necessary political organization, sophistication, and authority to arbitrate the complex issues involving the two Greek superpowers.[12] Furthermore, even in the relatively sophisticated Athenian democracy of the fourth century, domestic arbitration was hardly foolproof. Judgments of arbitrators (*diaitetai*) were only final if both parties accepted them, and either party could appeal.[13] These pitfalls of domestic arbitration suggest that inter-state arbitration (particularly in the fifth century) would have been even more problematic and likelier to fail.

The difficulties of implementing arbitration played into the hands of the Athenians. In the speeches Thucydides creates for the Athenians, as well as in the words of the Corinthians and Spartans, the Athenians come across as intellectually quick, able to solve any problem.[14] The Athenians seem to have seized upon a diplomatic technicality that they used to confuse the less sophisticated Peloponnesians. They realized the difficulty in finding and then agreeing on an arbiter and this suited them just fine. It allowed them to assume the role of the injured party in the negotiations, as they could always claim that they were prepared to submit their quarrel to a third party, when in fact they knew it would be difficult if not impossible to settle on one. With such delaying tactics they could put off negotiations and at the same time continue their provocative policies, which were at the root of Spartan fears and anxieties all along. It seemed perhaps a perfect strategy, yet in the end it backfired and brought about a war that Pericles and many Athenians believed they could win.

The Spartan embassies to Athens

Before arrival of the "autonomy" embassy mentioned above (n. 8), the Spartans had already approached the Athenians on several occasions attempting to find some way to head off war.[15] The first embassy is a strange affair of demands and counter-demands to acknowledge religious-political misdeeds of the past. Thucydides' intent is not clear. It appears that he creates an occasion to recount old instances of Athenian–Spartan conflict while also revealing the realities of religious pollution in political affairs.

The second embassy, however, was much more of a diplomatic effort. The Spartans told the Athenians that war could be avoided if they abandoned the siege of Potidaea and restored autonomy to Aegina, an island community the Athenians had subjected 20 years earlier (Thuc. 139.1).[16] From this point on, freedom took on a new and greater meaning as a political slogan that Sparta would use in order to win influence with the other Greeks.[17]

The Athenians, however, remained inflexible. They refused to lift the siege of Potidaea. The Spartan envoys then told the Athenians there would be no war if they revoked the Megarian Decree (Thuc. 1.139.1), enacted several years earlier, that had barred Megarian goods from markets controlled by Athens. This punitive measure had created an economic slump that, if we believe Aristophanes (*Acharnians* 535–40), had reduced many Megarians to near starvation. The Athenian response was again unyielding. Pericles justified the ban by accusing the Megarians of cultivating sacred land and providing shelter to fugitive slaves (Thuc. 1.139.2). He added that in any case the decree could not be repealed, to which Polyalces, one of the Spartan envoys, said, "Well, turn it to the wall. There's no law against that, is there?"[18] The simplicity of Polyalces' statement argues for its authenticity – who else but a Spartan could say something so plain and direct? It also reveals Athenian intellectual arrogance, their unwillingness to enter into meaningful discussions that might defuse the crisis they all faced.[19] What can be learned, then, about this embassy from other sources suggests that Sparta undertook serious diplomatic efforts and that the Athenians consistently rebuffed them.

The final Spartan attempt to avert war came shortly after the Theban sneak attack on Plataea. Archidamus, moderate in his views and not eager for war, sent Melesippus to Athens in a last ditch measure to avert war.[20] Archidamus hoped that the Athenians might now talk as they could see that the Peloponnesian allies had not only mobilized for war but were moving. The Athenians would still not budge. This was largely the work of Pericles, who had persuaded the Athenians to enact a decree that upon Peloponnesian mobilization further negotiations would be barred. Refused entry to Athens and escorted to the borders of Attica, Melesippus went home. As he departed, he said to those present, "This day will be the beginning of great misfortunes for Greece."[21] He was right.

The "inevitability" of war (Thuc. 1.23.6)

Was this war preventable? Or was it, as Thucydides seems to suggest, inevitable?[22] I would argue that Thucydides understands the reasons behind the actions of individuals and states too well to be satisfied with arguments of inevitability in explaining what happened in Greece between 433 and 431. His reference to inevitability may be no more than a reflection of popular opinion.[23] This finds support in his explanation of the War's short- and long-term causes, the "necessary" cause in the Theban attack on Plataea, and his own interpretation that the growth of Athenian power led Sparta to conclude that there was no recourse but to fight when diplomatic overtures failed.[24]

As noted by a number of scholars (e.g. Kagan 1969: 205), Thucydides' sophisticated account of the war's outbreak bears an eerie resemblance to Europe in August 1914 and the outbreak of World War I. In both instances we observe complex causes that combined to bring war about, the apparent enthusiasm of young men who were inexperienced in war and thereby drawn to it, the willingness of many to imagine that a war would follow a predictable course (an idea that even modern politicians and statesmen adhere to) or the hard "no negotiations" line assumed by one of the parties in the conflict. All this suggests that Thucydides had thought long and hard on what happened in 433–31 and saw war not as inevitable but rather as the result of decisions made by those caught up in the events. The factors just mentioned require further examination.

In discussing the aftermath of the Theban attack on Plataea, Thucydides observes that there was widespread enthusiasm for war. Not unlike the youth of Europe in 1914, many Peloponnesian and Athenian young men, who had never been to war, were thrilled at the prospect.[25] They feared that unless they became personally involved the whole effort itself would be handicapped (Thuc. 2.8.1). Thucydides notes further that support for the Spartans was widespread in Greece. The Athenians' suppression of Naxos, Samos, and other allies had created such bitterness that other communities feared they might be next (2.8.4). "Enthusiasm" for war, then, was nourished by youthful exuberance for the unknown, and a wider belief that Athens was indeed the "tyrant city," as the Corinthians said, and that those upholding the "freedom" of the Greeks were the Spartans, as they increasingly proclaimed.[26]

Enthusiasm for war was matched by the popular belief that it was predictable. Yet early in his *History*, Thucydides stresses the unpredictability of war.[27] In his speech after the Theban attack on Plataea, Archidamus reminds the allies that war is uncertainty and that too often attacks are made on a sudden impulse. This reference to what we know today as the Clausewitzian "fog of war" underlines the idea of popular enthusiasm for war – that people think they can anticipate the sequence of events once war begins – just like so many did on the eve of World War I and often since.

Enthusiasm for war among the Greeks may in part be explained by cultural attitudes that saw war as a way of life (Havelock 1972: 19–52). They were related to concepts familiar from heroic epics that saw success in war as the clearest expression of manly excellence; in other words, war brought out the best in man. Herodotus' work on the Persian Wars enhanced this ethos by extending it to the larger community, the *polis*, as demonstrated in Athens' heroic leadership in the Greeks' victory over the Persians. Moreover, war was not only glorious and noble, it also brought power and wealth.

After the Persian Wars, Athens and Sparta had taken divergent paths. Sparta remained a somewhat old-fashioned community whose goal was still that of preserving the status quo – maintaining control over the Peloponnesians to ensure control over the helots. Athens, however, was increasingly becoming a "modern" state where, as Pericles emphasizes in Thucydides, democracy had reshaped its citizens into lovers of the *polis* (2.43.1; Raaflaub 1994: 130). Democratic institutions established at the end of the sixth century continued to be expanded and refined throughout the fifth – magistrates with defined tenures of office, a functioning assembly that wielded real authority, law courts and juries that expressed the will of the people. To maintain this development – and the wealth of empire that came with it – Athens had to stay the course, to exercise power and authority wherever possible.[28] But this argument may be taken a bit further. Political scientist John Mearsheimer (2001: 367–68, 406; cf. Doyle 1997: 76–80) has argued that democratic states are as driven by power politics as their authoritarian counterparts and will practice the same sort of policies that lead to aggression and expansion. This also fits democratic Athens on the eve of the Peloponnesian War. In stark contrast to slow and "conservative" Sparta, as the Corinthians emphasize in an illuminating comparison (Thuc. 1.70), Athens was constantly looking for opportunity wherever it could be found. The dispute that erupted between these two states was not only between a "land" power and a "sea" power, but between two communities that for more than two generations had developed in diametrically opposed directions.

Diplomatic maneuvers, particularly of Corinth, were closely related to these conditions. In explaining how states pressure and influence each other in attempting to balance power, Mearsheimer (2001: 156–59) identifies one method which he calls "buck-passing," whereby a state that chooses not to act itself pressures another to act in its place. In this instance, Corinth – unwilling and unable to challenge Athens' greater power – maneuvered its leader and protector Sparta to do exactly what it could not. Buck-passing remains a tried and tested diplomatic technique today and its practice among the Greeks supports the suggestion presented above that the Peloponnesian and Athenian conflict "feels modern."

Influenced by the new and "enlightened" thinking of the sophists (Woodhead 1970: 3–6; Solmsen 1975: 116–22; de Romilly 1992: 135–37), Thucydides recognized that this quest for power drove the "modern" state that Athens had become. Power brought security, power brought the good things in life that the Athenians had fought so hard to win since defeating the Persians. Thucydides saw that states flourish or decay as they are militarily effective and that success in wielding power allows them to rule others as an empire – an experience altogether preferable to being ruled – and to achieve that greatest of political values – freedom (Havelock 1972: 75). Homer and Herodotus composed their works to keep the deeds of brave men from being forgotten. Thucydides had this in mind too, but he went further in showing how men's exploits in war enabled states to become strong and successful. For the same reason he relates the fate of those states like Melos that, lacking power, were overcome by their more powerful opponents and had no choice but to accept whatever the strong imposed upon them (Thuc. 5.84–116).

What happened, then, in 433–431? Athens, Corinth, and Sparta, and the lesser states of Greece, had become locked into a way of looking at life that saw conflict as natural, even manly, the solving of disputes by recourse to war as lying in the nature of both men and states. Kurt Raaflaub (2001) speaks eloquently of the powerful images and associations that conditioned the Athenians to think of war and violence, in the words of Wilfred Owen in *Dulce et decorum est* (Owen 1973: 79), as "glorious and proper."

In some ways the Athenians imagined that war would bring out the best in them – it would protect their power and predominance and they would prevail in their adversities as their history demonstrated. One Athenian who suffered no illusions about what was at stake was Pericles. He realized that war brought with it the opportunity to increase Athenian power and wealth and so took advantage of a legalistic interpretation of the arbitration clause of the 30 Years Peace to disguise an Athenian bid for domination.[29]

To carry this argument a step further, for the Athenians to negotiate would be to show weakness, to retreat from the prospects of winning even greater power. Athens had to stand up to Sparta (and Corinth) because not to do so would be to deny the opportunity for greater gain and to surrender the power it possessed. Such an admission of weakness might well lead to further conflicts that could deprive the Athenians of their empire. In the debate over Mytilene in 427 Thucydides attributes this very idea to the Athenian politician Cleon as justification for imposing a reign of terror over the subjects of the empire (3.37.2, 40.4). In his Melian Dialogue, Thucydides ascribes to the Athenians the same motive: they must control or conquer Melos in order to avoid appearing weak or indecisive to the subjects of their empire (5.91–96). Driven by such perceptions, Athens, then, in a sense had no choice but to frustrate and deny Spartan overtures and go to war in 431.

Koine Eirene and the Search for Peace

After 27 years of war, Sparta finally defeated Athens, but the peace that Sparta imposed on Athens and her unhappy allies did not last long. By 395 another major conflict among the Greek states erupted, the Corinthian War, which ranged Sparta against her former allies Corinth and Thebes with a recovered Athens joining those who had once argued for Athens' destruction (Hamilton 1979). This conflict dragged on for some eight years, finally ending with an agreement sometimes called the "Peace of Antalcidas" or the "King's Peace," as the Persians were now involved in Greek affairs. Contemporary authors such as Isocrates and Xenophon began using the term *koine eirene*, "common peace," to describe the settlement that all parties could accept so as to end conflict and bring about peace (Ryder 1965: xi–xvii, 1–2; Jehne 1994; see also Alonso, this vol.). Intended among other things to guarantee local autonomy, these agreements were repeated a number of times during the fourth century (e.g. in 375, 371, 368, 366/5, 362/1, 346, 338/7, and 311; Ryder, xi–xiii).

Such emphasis on "common peace" suggests that fifth century experiences, in particular the Peloponnesian War, had encouraged the Greeks to find a way not only to end conflict but preempt it, that is, to protect communities and establish a process by which conflicts might be resolved without recourse to war. The "common peace" was an effort to solve the very problem that had proved detrimental in 432 when there was no means to enact arbitration in the conflict between Athens and Sparta over Corinth and Corcyra. Now representatives of states would gather and discuss the points of conflict that separated them, hoping that such a "congress" would find a generally acceptable solution.[30] Such an effort failed in 371, with dire consequences for Sparta. Sparta attempted to break the looming power of Thebes over central Greece by refusing Theban demands to sign a treaty for all Boeotians. Rebuffed, the Thebans defiantly resorted to war which resulted in the great Spartan defeat at Leuctra, the end of Spartan power in Greek affairs forever, and the meteoric but short-lived rise of Thebes to domination in Greece (Buckler 1979: 50–69; Cartledge 1987). In 337/6, following his defeat of the major Greek states at Chaeronea, Philip of Macedon created the League of Corinth and imposed a "common peace" upon the Greeks (Ellis 1994). While the former powers – Athens, Sparta, and Thebes – were far from pleased, the smaller states of Greece found an organization that would both protect their rights and provide a place to resolve their differences.

The process of the "common peace" shows that like the fifth century peace efforts that preceded it, the Greeks attempted to find a process by which they might avoid the horrors of war that Homer described so powerfully in the *Iliad*. Try as they might, their efforts met with only modest success as ambitions for power and domination drove communities to give priority to their own needs and goals. Such conflicting ambitions resulted in war, and war's effects rippled through society like a stone tossed into a still pond.

War's Impact on Society and Culture

There can be no doubt that Greek soldiers witnessed horrific scenes amid the battles they fought. Herodotus tells of an Athenian soldier, Epizelus, at Marathon, who was struck blind as he witnessed the man next to him cut down (6.117). A similar account of hysterical blindness is preserved in the Epidaurian miracle lists, which also record wounded men waiting years for arrowheads to work their way out of their chests, spearheads to be dislodged from jaws.[31] Additional contemporary evidence is to be found in the *Encomium of Helen* by the sophist Gorgias. In this rhetorical treatise Gorgias refers to the traumatic experiences of men confronted with the violence of battle; even if they survive they "have fallen victim to useless labor and dread diseases and hardly curable madnesses."[32] The traumatic impact of these men's sufferings on their personal lives and their families can only be imagined. Such information is valuable not only because it is contemporaneous but also because literary historians are primarily concerned to tell the "big picture" of war. By contrast, the Epidaurian miracle lists and Gorgias reveal the trauma of war and how those caught up in its grip attempted to return to "normal" everyday life.

The militaristic society of Sparta offers other intriguing glimpses into this process. In the heroic stand at Thermopylae in 480, all but two of the three hundred Spartans and their king Leonidas died fighting the Persians. The two survivors, Pantites and Aristodamus, returned home to a decidedly unfriendly welcome: Pantites soon hanged himself in disgrace while Aristodamus remained scorned and dishonored and was known as Aristodamus the "coward" (Hdt. 7.229–232; Ehrenberg 1937: 2292–97; Lewis 1977: 30–31). At the battle of Plataea in the following year, Aristodamus fought to his death to erase the stain on his honor. After the battle the Spartans discussed who should receive prizes for valor: Aristodamus' name came up but was dismissed as the Spartans felt he had fought to die while others had fought to live.[33]

This incident has been discussed often, but its significance has not been fully appreciated. While Aristodamus bore the label "coward," it remains clear that he was not so shunned that he was banished from the ranks, but in fact took his place alongside his fellow Spartans.[34] What happened to Aristodamus at Thermopylae is uncertain, but what drove him to go "berserk" at Plataea was not a desire to die but rather to restore his name and reputation, his status in the community.[35] Herodotus heard from his Spartan sources a combination of gossip and backbiting which, to his credit, did not deceive him, for in his view Aristodamus showed the greatest courage in the battle (Hdt. 9.71.2). This story is not dissimilar from a modern one that has inspired at least three film versions, *The Four Feathers* (see, e.g. Pym 2003: 418).

In the years following the Persian Wars, the elite population of *homoioi* or Spartiates continually declined (Hodkinson 2000: 399–445). Such losses clearly affected attitudes toward behavior in battle. In 425, a force of over four hundred Spartans, sent to garrison the island of Sphacteria near Pylos, was surrounded; during an Athenian attack the survivors did the unthinkable – they surrendered. Of the 292 survivors, 120 were Spartiates. When they were later released and returned home, the Spartans feared that they might become revolutionary and stir up trouble and so revoked their citizen rights. There were so many, however – and a number appear to have come from influential families as well – that later their lost rights were restored.[36]

It will be clear from this incident that Aristodamus' problem was that Pantites took his own life. While one man can be easily dismissed as a coward, multiple cases, let alone those of more than a hundred, rather confuse things and make condemnation more difficult. This is confirmed by the aftermath of the Spartan defeat at Leuctra in 371. Here a king, Cleombrotus, was killed along with nearly a thousand Spartans of whom some four hundred were Spartiates (Xen. *Hell.* 6.4.6). The survivors had no stomach for further fighting and, surrendering the battlefield to the Thebans, returned home. Again the charge of cowardice came up. This time, however, Agesilaus, the surviving king, said that the laws should be allowed to "sleep for a day"; in other words, the punishments normally meted out to cowards should be suspended.[37] Spartan behavior perhaps only lies at the extreme range of Greek reaction to war's disasters, and in the treatment of those who failed in battle or proved cowards similar reactions, regulations, and customs appear elsewhere. Numerous references in Attic comedy and oratory about throwing away one's shield indicate that this brought not only shame but also criminal charges. A Macedonian could not tie his clothes with a belt until he had killed his first enemy in battle; until then, he basically wore the clothes of a girl.[38]

From Homer's time on the Greeks knew that the experience of war was as horrifying as it was exhilarating – that war brought out the best and the worst in men, just as it does today. The Greeks also realized, I think without knowing exactly why, that something needed to be done to return warriors to the routine of peacetime existence and to enable them to live peacefully with their families and neighbors. This was accomplished, for example, through ritualistic dance and, in Athens, the theater.

Rituals, as E.R. Dodds notes, are "usually older than the myth by which people explain [them] and [have] deeper psychological roots" (1960: xiv; see also McNeil 1995: 13). In such rituals, dance plays a key part; this appears to be a phenomenon shared by numerous if not all cultures, from Kazantzakis' Zorba the Greek to the Lakota Sun Dancers. William McNeil has discussed the physiology of dance and how it induces calming and joyful emotions in both dancers and audiences (1995: 7–8). Many reports of dance competitions and related athletic contests after battle, from Homer's *Iliad* (23. 257–897) to Xenophon's *Anabasis* (6.1.5–13; cf. Arr. 3.6.1; 6.28.3), argue that the Greeks practiced these for their therapeutic value, just as American Indian Vietnam veterans (and non-Indian veterans as well) did in order to cleanse themselves of the trauma of battle and so leave the violence behind.

In Athens, dance and shared experience with violence came together in the theater. While reading Attic tragedy remains a rich and rewarding experience even today, at the time it was also "the occasion for elaborate symbolic play on themes of proper and improper civic behavior, in which the principal component of proper male citizenship was military" (Winkler 1990: 23). Both tragedy and comedy possessed a "civic-military aura" and took place before an audience not simply of male citizens, but of men who had been exposed to war's violence and paradoxes.[39] It has been said that drama was the "instruction of the Athenians" and this apt description applies here (Gregory 1991: 2; see also Konstan, this vol.). The dramatists were (in part) reaching out to their fellow citizens who had returned home and were faced with the difficult task of living in a world where war's paradoxes – killing, raping, looting – were not acceptable modes of conduct. In an effort to sensitize their fellow citizen-soldiers to the world of civilian life, the poets challenged them to contemplate what was right and wrong, so that they might be restored to a semblance of normality. Educating the Athenians, then, with dance and theater allowed society and culture to flourish, not entirely untouched by war, but able to overcome it. We might learn something from them even today.

Aristophanes and the Comedy of Peace

The title for this chapter drew upon the war-time comedy of Aristophanes, perhaps the greatest writer of that literary form. Most of his extant comedies (of forty-four known by title, eleven survive) were written during the Peloponnesian War, and all of them reflect at least to some degree the war's impact on Athenian and Greek culture and society. Four plays, however, *Acharnians* (425), *Peace* (421), *Birds* (414), and *Lysistrata* (411), focus on issues of war, peace and reconciliation, and so merit some attention here.

In three plays, *Acharnians*, *Peace*, and *Lysistrata*, the main issue Aristophanes addresses is the return of peace to war-torn Greece. Readers of these dramas might wonder at just how serious Aristophanes is here – after all, he is writing comedy. He wants the audience to laugh and be entertained, he wants to win the prize of victory in the competition and so win acclaim for himself. That war was regarded by the Greeks as a natural part of the life cycle is a scholarly commonplace. Yet it remains, as we have seen, that the Greeks saw war as a horrifying spectacle that left many men devastated for life (Tritle 2000: 167–68, and nn. 36–37 below). This suggests that while the Greeks recognized war as a "fact" of life, they also, as Aristophanes suggests, considered it something to be avoided if possible.[40]

That this is the case seems clear from the three plays just mentioned. In *Acharnians*, Dicaeopolis (whose name means "Just city," which is perhaps not insignificant) makes a separate peace with the Spartans, in spite of the objections of his own countrymen, the Acharnians of the play's title. These remain intent on war as the Spartans have devastated their lands and they will have their revenge. Dicaeopolis must literally fight them in order to achieve his goal of peace (205–390). Four years later, Aristophanes took up the same theme of the quest for peace in *Peace*. Here the comic hero Trygaeus abandons war-weary (and crazed) Athens and flies on a giant dung-beetle up to Olympus to have a face-off with the gods (81–108). When he arrives he finds that the gods have abandoned Olympus, disgusted with the conduct of the humans – the Greeks – below, and have left War and his henchman Riot in charge of things (195–220). Trygaeus perseveres, however, and with the help of a group of common Greek citizens, rescues the goddess Peace whom War has imprisoned, and brings her back to the Greeks (221–25, 288–526).

Common to both plays is the quest for peace, and while Dicaeopolis acts for himself and Trygaeus for all Greeks, the unifying theme is the superiority of peace to war and how dearly it is coveted. This same idea Aristophanes expressed in what is surely his best-known play, *Lysistrata*. Written 10 years after *Peace*, it too concerns all Greeks, not the Athenians alone. Here, Lysistrata ("She who dissolves armies") of Athens creates pan-hellenic solidarity among women who join in a sex-strike to achieve peace in Greece (65–180). There are scenes of great comedy – for example, when Cinesias, son of Paion, whose two names are slang for sexual intercourse, attempts unsuccessfully to bed his wife Myrrhine (845–979) – which mask the more serious issue of Greeks killing each other, while the Persian enemy stands off-stage waiting to profit (1133–34). The play ends with the women's triumph, and in a subtle touch that reveals again its pan-hellenic message, Aristophanes ends the play with allusions and references to Spartan song and places (Henderson 1987: 218–22).

These dramas, in spite of their apparent comic nature, should be seen as serious statements on the desirability of peace over war. As author and veteran Paul Fussell has noted in examining the World War I experience, farce and comedy are more appropriate literary forms to express the tragedy of war (Fussell 1975: 203–04). This is visible in other issues Aristophanes touches upon. He describes several prominent figures of the Peloponnesian War as war-lovers. In *Peace*, he caricatures Brasidas of Sparta and Cleon of Athens, calling them the "pestles" used by War to keep stirring up the Greeks (230–85). In *Acharnians*, the Athenian general Lamachus is described in the same manner (566–70, 620–23; *Peace* 1175–76), as are essentially all the Greeks in *Lysistrata*. Similarly, in *Peace* Aristophanes lists those "ruined" by the return of peace, namely weapons makers who remind us of arms manufacturers (i.e. the "military-industrial complex") of the modern era (1198–1264). It might even be possible to compare Hierocles, the well-known oracular authority, and all the others who preyed on peoples' anxieties in war-time, with modern popular media broadcasting news of mayhem and destruction without analysis or meaningful comment (*Peace* 1046–1125).

Aristophanes, then, takes aim at virtually all segments of Greek society (not just Athenians) for their unwillingness to perceive their situation realistically and to resolve their problems by talking rather than fighting each other (see also Hdt. 7.9b.2). Thus in *Acharnians* he relates the sufferings of the Megarians, who are oppressed by the Athenian-imposed Megarian Decree (discussed above) that has destroyed their economy (515–35). He also criticizes Pericles for refusing a peaceful settlement, when the Spartans kept asking for terms to resolve their widening dispute (535–40). The hard stance taken by Pericles in the negotiations that preceded the Peloponnesian War was assumed again by Cleon in 425/4: the Athenians threatened to kill the Spartan prisoners of war captured at Sphacteria in order to influence Spartan policies and so to broker a settlement – which they then declined, hoping to gain even more by continuing the war (Thuc. 4.21–22, 41.). While critical of his own countrymen, Aristophanes does not spare the sensibilities of other Greeks who also choose war over peace. In *Peace* of 421, for example, he notes the reluctance of the Argives, Boeotians, and Corinthians to support the settlement that the two "great" powers were negotiating at the time (465–508).[41]

Conclusion

The Greeks, no less than we moderns, knew war as a frightening and constant threat. They, like ourselves, experienced moments when cooler heads prevailed and ways were found to end the suffering. As in the modern era too, there were intellectuals like Aristophanes, who saw that war was not the only or right solution; while he may have been able to find answers to the prevailing problems only in comedy, he realized that efforts to find peace were crucial. Filmmaker Oliver Stone once remarked, "I've been to war and it's not easy to kill. It's bloody and messy and totally horrifying, and the consequences are serious."[42] I share his experience and sentiment, and would argue that so too did the people and writers of ancient Greece.[43]

Notes

1　Herodotus' commentators, How and Wells 1912: 2.129, suggest (rightly) that Herodotus puts his own ideas into the mouth of Mardonius.

2　The standard accounts of the outbreak of the war are Kagan 1969 (see now also Kagan 2003) and de Ste. Croix 1972. Cawkwell 1997 is also useful. De Ste. Croix takes a strong anti-Spartan position, arguing that Sparta aimed to destroy Athenian power, a position which Badian 1993 has challenged. Kagan 1969: 345–56 argues for blame all around.

3　Thuc. 1.115.1, 2.2.1 refer to the 30 Years Truce, 1.23.4 to both Athens and Sparta breaking it (passed over without comment by Hornblower 1991–6: 1.64).

4　Kagan 1969: 353–54 and Badian 1993: 142–44 refer to the issue, but do not discuss the problems confronting the Greeks to make it work.

5　Thuc. 1.78.4, 1.104.2. Note also 1.28.2 referring to a Corcyraean offer to arbitrate its dispute with Corinth by bringing in a third party from the Peloponnese acceptable to both. But, again, no mechanism appears to be in place to make this work.

6　For discussion see Mearsheimer 2001: 3, 32, who notes the problems posed by the lack of mediation and arbitration in the international political arena. While he focuses on the modern day political scene, there can be little doubt that the same factors influenced great powers in antiquity, such as Athens and Sparta, as well as the less great such as Corinth.

7　My thanks to Kurt Raaflaub for reminding me of this.

8　Thucydides reports these embassies as: (1) the "curse" embassy (1.139.1); (2) the "Potidean and Megarian" embassy of Polyalces (1.139.1); (3) the "autonomy" embassy of Ramphias, Melesippus, and Agesandrus (1.139.3); and (4) the "last ditch" embassy of Melesippus (2.12.1–3). The chronology of the embassies is uncertain, but the Theban attack on Plataea at the beginning of spring, probably about February/March 431 helps. The third embassy dates to late fall or early winter 432, with the first two falling between spring 432 and early fall 432, that is, after the Spartans voted that the Athenians had broken the 30 Years Peace in its 14th year. Melesippus' last ditch effort came after the attack on Plataea, perhaps in March 431.

9　Gomme, Andrewes, and Dover 1970–81: 4.394, commenting on Thuc. 7.18.2, argue that the Spartan embassies were designed to provoke refusal. This seems overly cynical. See the discussion below, and Badian 1993: 125–62 (esp. 143–44) who argues that Thucydides misrepresents Spartan "plotting and deviousness."

10　The Peloponnesian War would not be the last conflict to be started by one generation and ended by another; we might compare it with the medieval 100 Years' War and the 30 Years' War of the seventeenth century.

11　Peloponnesian neighbors Argos and Sparta were enemies from the sixth century when Sparta's Peloponnesian League began expanding at Argos' expense. In c. 494 the Spartan king Cleomenes I destroyed an Argive army at Sepeia (Hdt. 6.76–80); Argos was so weakened that it played no part in the Persian Wars and into the later years of the fifth century.

12　Syracuse, the dominant state in Greek Sicily might be considered as an alternative. Yet Syracuse had been founded by Corinth, and the two states maintained the ties appropriate to mother-city and colony, which would have made Syracusan mediation unacceptable to Athens.

13　[Arist.] *Ath Pol.* 53.2, with Rhodes 1981: 589–90. Busolt-Swoboda 1920–26: 1.485–86 refer to other domestic arbitrators from the Hellenistic period. Note also Solon's arbitration of the Athenian land crisis ([Arist.] *Ath. Pol.* 5, 11–12) and his ensuing 10 year absence from Athens to exclude the possibility of overturning his decisions!

14　Archidamus (Thuc. 1.84.3) says that the Spartans are wise because they are not educated to despise the law, a clear jibe at the Athenians. In his famous Funeral Oration, Pericles (2.40.2) refers to Athenian daring in taking on bold, though calculated ventures and danger. See also Thuc. 1.70–71 and Raaflaub 1994: 105–06.

15 As Badian 1993: 154 notes, after Thuc. 1.139.1, there were "many" such embassies, though Thucydides only comments on those discussed here.

16 The issues of both freedom and autonomy had emerged during and after the Persian Wars and became influential ideas in Herodotus' and Thucydides' *Histories*, for discussion, see Raaflaub 2004.

17 Thuc. 1.124.3; 2.8.4, 12.1; 3.32.2, 63.3; 4.85.1, 86.1; see also Lewis 1977: 65; Raaflaub 2004: 193–202.

18 Plut. *Per.* 30.1, confirmed by Ar. *Ach.* 537 (*pace* Stadter 1989: 274); see Lewis 1977: 49 n. 157 with bibliog.

19 According to Thuc. 1.144.2, Pericles replied that the Megarians and their goods would be admitted to Athenian ports, but only when the Spartans agreed not to expel Athenians and their allies from Sparta. This seems to be a reference to an old custom whereby "foreigners" were periodically expelled from Sparta. Thucydides does not explain how this might be connected to the Megarians. If he reported accurately, the argument might be nothing more than an issue raised by the Athenians to confuse things further.

20 Thuc. 2.12.1. Lewis 1977: 48 questions Archidamus' authority in Sparta, but here Thucydides says that it was Archidamus who sent Melesippus on this mission which argues not only for his views on the imminent war but also for his ability to influence politics.

21 Thuc. 2.12.1–3, and Hornblower 1991–6: 1.250, who considers this quote genuine. One final embassy deserves mention here though it is not Spartan. In the months preceding the outbreak of war, the oligarchic rulers of Mytilene – the strongest *polis* in Lesbos and an old Athenian ally – sent an embassy to Sparta, attempting to win Spartan support for a takeover of the island and a defection from Athens. The Spartans refused even to hear this delegation's offer, which argues additionally that the Spartans were not eager for war; otherwise the Mytilenian embassy would surely have been heard; see Thuc. 3.2, with Hornblower 1991–6: 1.382–83.

22 The key word here is *anagke*, or "necessity"; Thucydides (1.23.6) uses the verb *anagkasai*, or "to force" (so Hornblower 1991–6: 1.66). The standard translations (Crawley, Lattimore, Warner) render this as "inevitable," which is close enough but not quite the same: readers need to beware of several nuances that "inevitable" does not quite convey.

23 Cf. Rhodes 1987: 154–60, who notes that Thucydides took "pleasure in showing that he knows better than popular opinion."

24 Kagan 1969: 365–66 discusses the idea of inevitability and the positions taken by scholars on this issue. F. E. Adcock (in *CAH* 5: 182) seems alone in rejecting Thucydidean inevitability.

25 See also Thuc. 6.24 on the enthusiasm in Athens for the Sicilian expedition – which ended in disaster.

26 Thuc. 1.122.3, 124.3 (Corinth on Athens, echoed by Pericles in 2.63.2, Cleon in 3.37.2). For arguments that the Spartan drive to "free" the Greeks was only propaganda, see de Ste. Croix 1972: 154–58, a position challenged by Lewis 1977: 108–09; see also Raaflaub 2004: 197–202.

27 Thuc. 2.11.4 (Archidamus' speech); 1.78.1 (unnamed Athenians at Sparta), and other passages cited in Gomme 1945–56: 2.2, 13. The argument that war is unpredictable would seem to undercut the idea that war is inevitable – how can that which is changeable be predicted? Cf. n. 24 above.

28 See Raaflaub 1994: 113–18, 130–31, also Raaflaub 1998 for discussion of Athens' rise to "world power" and its development of political institutions and active participation of its citizens in political and military activities. This is essentially state-building of a modern type.

29 Cf. Kagan 1969: 334, who argues that Pericles proposed a "defensive" war but with Athenian incursions into the Peloponnese to hurt Sparta and her allies. Not only were such operations offensive in nature, they also served as counterstrokes to the Spartan-led invasions of Attica. Cf. Raaflaub 1994: 130–46 on power and the citizens' and leaders' motives.

30 It should be noted, however, that "peace" negotiations were dominated by the leading states of Greece, and that military power and considerations were never far removed from diplomatic activities. The Peace of 375 may be considered an example of a "peace" (briefly) ending a period of war. See Buckler 1979: 46.

31 See LiDonnici 1995: 109, 95 (text and translation); Salazar 2000: 212–15; Plut. *Mor.* 217C, 241F for other examples of battle injured men.

32 Gorg. no. 82 B11, 16–17 Diels Kranz 1961 (trans. G. Kennedy, in Sprague 1972: 53–54).

33 Hdt. 9.71. That even 40 or 50 years after Plataea Herodotus heard the story of Aristodamus can only mean that the Spartans, his informants, were still trying to sort it all out. Also of interest is Herodotus' analysis of the story and his ability to reach an independent judgment.

34 Noted by Lazenby 1985: 56; Shipley 1997: 332, but without explanation. Flower and Marincola 2002: 233 note the practice of shunning practiced still by the Amish in Ohio and Pennsylvania.

35 See discussion below on the Spartans who surrendered at Sphacteria.

36 Thuc. 4.26–40, 5.34.2. See also Gomme, Andrewes, and Dover 1970–81: 4.36, with additional references to Xen. *Lac. Pol.* 9.4–5, and Plut. *Ages.* 30.

37 Plut. *Ages.* 30.6; Shipley 1997: 331–34. Additional examples: Xen. *Hell.* 1.2.10; Plut. *Alc.* 29.1–5; Thuc. 1.105.3–106; Paus. 1.29.9.

38 See Pritchett 1971–91: 2.233–36 for discussion of legal charges of cowardice at Athens and Sparta; also Winkler 1990: 29 who discusses the oath of the Athenian ephebes who pledged not to throw away their weapons or abandon their post (see Dem. 19.303; Ar. *Nub.* 1220; *Horai* F579 Kassel-Austin 1984); Hammond-Griffith 1979: 23 on Macedonia.

39 See Shay 1995, who refers to the "paradoxical logic of war," after a phrase coined by Luttwak 1987/2001: 3–15.

40 See discussion in Sommerstein 1980: 5; McDowell 1995: 248, who argue that Aristophanes' comedy is actually serious, that is, that it cloaks a genuine effort to "educate" the Athenians on the need for peace; I share this position; *contra:* Dover 1972: 158–59. For other views, see Rutherford 2005: 63.

41 The perception that peace was beneficial only to the "great" powers may well have been the reason for the lesser powers' negative response.

42 Cited in *Newsweek*, "Quotes of the Week," October 13, 1997.

43 My thanks to Kurt Raaflaub for organizing the 2003 conference at Brown University and for his helpful comments on this chapter.

Abbreviations

CAH	*Cambridge Ancient History*
RE	*Realencyclopädie der classischen Altertumswissenschaft*

References

Badian, Ernst. 1993. *From Plataea to Potidaea. Studies in the History and Historiography of the Pentecontaetia.* Baltimore.

Buckler, John. 1979. *The Theban Hegemony, 371–362 BC.* Cambridge, MA.

Busolt, Georg, and Heinrich Swoboda. 1920–26. *Griechische Staatskunde*. 2 vols. Munich.

Cartledge, Paul. 1987. *Agesilaus and the Crisis of Sparta*. London.

Cawkwell, George. 1997. *Thucydides and the Peloponnesian War*. London.

Diels, Hermann, and Walther Kranz (eds.). 1961. *Die Fragmente der Vorsokratiker* I. 10th edn. Berlin.

Dodds, Eric R. 1960. *The Greeks and the Irrational*. Berkeley.

Dover, Kenneth J. 1972. *Aristophanic Comedy*. Berkeley.

Doyle, Michael W. 1997. *Ways of War and Peace. Realism, Liberalism, and Socialism*. New York.

Ehrenberg, Victor. 1937. "*Tresantes.*" *RE* VIA: 2292–97.

Ellis, J. R. 1994. "Macedonian Hegemony Created." *CAH* VI: 782–85. 2nd edn. Cambridge.

Flower, Michael A., and John Marincola (eds.). 2002. *Herodotus, The Histories. Book IX*. Cambridge.

Fussell, Paul. 1975. *The Great War and Modern Memory*. New York.

Gomme, Arnold W. 1945–56. *A Historical Commentary on Thucydides*. Vols. 1–3. Oxford.

——, Anthony Andrewes, and Kenneth J. Dover. 1970–81. *A Historical Commentary on Thucydides*. Vols. 4–5. Oxford.

Gregory, Justina. 1991. *Euripides and the Instruction of the Athenians*. Ann Arbor.

Hamilton, Charles D. 1979. *Sparta's Bitter Victories: Politics and Diplomacy in the Corinthian War*. Ithaca.

Hammond, Nicholas G. L., and Guy T. Griffith. 1979. *A History of Macedonia*. II. *550–336 BC*. Oxford.

Hartt, Frederick, and David G. Wilkins. 2003. *A History of Italian Renaissance Art*. 5th edn. London.

Havelock, Eric A. 1972. "War as a Way of Life in Classical Culture." In E. Gareau (ed.), *Classical Values and the Modern World*, 19–78. Ottawa.

Henderson, Jeffrey. 1987. *Aristophanes, Lysistrata. Ed. with Intro. and Comm.* Oxford.

Hodkinson, Stephen. 2000. *Property and Wealth in Classical Sparta*. London.

Holoka, John P. (ed.). 2003. *Simone Weil's the Iliad, or the Poem of Force: a Critical Edition*. New York.

Hornblower, Simon. 1991–6. *A Commentary on Thucydides*. 2 vols. Oxford.

How, Walter W., and Joseph Wells. 1912. *A Commentary on Herodotus*. 2 vols. Oxford.

Jehne, Martin. 1994. *Koine Eirene. Untersuchungen zu den Befriedungs- und Stabilisierungsbemühungen in der griechischen Poliswelt des 4. Jahrhunderts v. Chr.* Stuttgart.

Kagan, Donald. 1969. *The Outbreak of the Peloponnesian War*. Ithaca.

——. 1987. *The Fall of the Athenian Empire*. Ithaca.

——. 2003. *The Peloponnesian War*. New York.

Kassel, R., and Austin, C. 1984. *Poetae Comici Graeci*, III.2: *Aristophanes, Testimonia et Fragmenta*. Berlin.

Keeley, Lawrence H. 1996. *War Before Civilization*. New York.

Lazenby, John F. 1985. *The Spartan Army*. Warminster.

Lewis, David M. 1977. *Sparta and Persia*. Leiden.

LiDonnici, Lynn R. 1995. *The Epidaurian Miracle Inscriptions*. Atlanta.

Luttwak, E. N. 1987/2001. *Strategy: The Logic of War and Peace*. Rev. and enlarged edn. Cambridge, MA.

McDowell, Douglas M. 1995. *Aristophanes and Athens: An Introduction to the Plays*. Oxford.

McNeil, William. 1995. *Keeping Together in Time. Dance and Drill in Human History*. Cambridge, MA.

Mearsheimer, John. 2001. *The Tragedy of Great Power Politics*. New York.

Osborne, Robin. 1998. *Archaic and Classical Greek Art*. Oxford.

Owen, Wilfred. 1973. *War Poems and Others*. Ed. with Introduction and Notes by D. Hibberd. London.

Pritchett, W. K. 1971–91. *The Greek State at War*. 5 vols. Berkeley.

Pym, John (ed.). 2003. *Time Out Film Guide*. London.

Raaflaub, Kurt A. 1994. "Democracy, Power, and Imperialism in Fifth-Century Athens." In J. P. Euben, J. R. Wallach, and J. Ober (eds.), *Athenian Political Thought and the Reconstruction of American Democracy*, 103–46. Ithaca.

Raaflaub, Kurt A. 1998. "The Transformation of Athens in the Fifth Century." In D. Boedeker and K. A. Raaflaub (eds.), *Democracy, Empire, and the Arts in Fifth-Century Athens*, 15–41. Cambridge, MA.

——. 1998. "Father of All, Destroyer of All: War in Late Fifth-Century Athenian Discourse and Ideology." In D. McCann and B. S. Strauss (eds.), *War and Democracy: A Comparative Study of the Korean War and the Peloponnesian War*, 307–56. Armonk, NY and London.

——. 2004. *The Discovery of Freedom in Ancient Greece*. Chicago.

Rhodes, Peter J. 1972. *The Athenian Boule*. Oxford.

——. 1981. *A Commentary on the Aristotelian* Athenaion Politeia. Oxford.

——. 1987. "Thucydides on the Causes of the Peloponnesian War." *Hermes* 115: 154–65.

Romilly, Jacqueline de. 1992. *The Great Sophists in Periclean Athens*. Oxford.

Rutherford, Richard B. 2005. *Classical Literature. A Concise History*. Oxford.

Ryder, Timothy T. B. 1965. *Koine Eirene. General Peace and Local Independence in Ancient Greece*. London.

Ste. Croix, Geoffrey E. M. de. 1972. *The Origins of the Peloponnesian War*. Ithaca.

Salazar, Christine F. 2000. *The Treatment of War Wounds in Graeco-Roman Antiquity*. Leiden.

Shay, Jonathan. 1994. *Achilles in Vietnam. Combat Trauma and the Undoing of Character*. New York.

——. 1995. "The Birth of Tragedy – Out of the Needs of Democracy." *Didaskalia: Ancient Theater Today* [on-line journal] 2: 2.

Shipley, D. R. 1997. *Plutarch's Life of Agesilaos. Response to Sources in the Presentation of Character*. Oxford.

Solmsen, Friedrich. 1975. *Intellectual Experiments of the Greek Enlightenment*. Princeton.

Sommerstein, Alan H. 1980. *Aristophanes, Acharnians*. Ed. with Translation and Notes. Warminster.

Sprague, Rosemary K. (ed.). 1972. *The Older Sophists. A Complete Translation*. Indianapolis.

Stadter, Philip. 1989. *A Commentary on Plutarch's Pericles*. Chapel Hill.

Taplin, Oliver. 1998. "The Shield of Achilles Within the *Iliad*." In I. McAusland and P. Walcot (eds.), *Homer*, 96–115. Oxford.

Tritle, Lawrence A. 1997. "Hector's Body: Mutilation of the Dead in Ancient Greece and Vietnam." *Ancient History Bulletin* 11, 4: 123–36.

——. 2000. *From Melos to My Lai. War and Survival*. London.

Waterfield, Robin (trans.). 1998. *Herodotus, The Histories*, with Introduction and Notes by Carolyn Dewald. Oxford and New York.

Winkler, John J. 1990. "The Ephebes' Song: Tragoidia and Polis." In id. and F. I. Zeitlin (eds.), *Nothing to Do with Dionysos? Athenian Drama in Its Social Context*, 20–62. Princeton.

Woodhead, A. Geoffrey. 1970. *Thucydides on the Nature of Power*. Cambridge, MA.

11

War and Reconciliation in Greek Literature

David Konstan

> Revenge is pleasant . . . , and victory is pleasant too, not only for those who are competitive but for everyone; for there arises a sense [*phantasia*] of superiority, for which everyone has a passion, whether less or more (Aristotle *Rhetoric* 1.11.13–14).

> Attic tragedy remembers vengeance as an honorable imperative essential to the preservation of order (Burnett 1998: 6).

By tracing the course of the Peloponnesian War and its aftermath, Lawrence Tritle exhibits brilliantly the kinds of problems that war leaves in its wake, as combatants return to peacetime activities and deep wounds between former enemies remain to be healed. In my chapter, which originally took the form of a response to Tritle's discussion, I propose to complement his account with some additional illustrations, drawn from classical Greek literature, of how these rifts in the ideological fabric manifested themselves – sometimes in subtle ways and implicitly, as an undercurrent or subtext to the surface narrative. For tragedy, with which I shall be principally concerned, indeed reflected contemporary social reality, but indirectly. I begin with the problem of the warrior's homecoming, and then turn to the difficulty of reconciling enemies once hostilities were ended.

At the beginning of Euripides' *Heracles*, Amphitryon, Heracles' father, explains to the audience that he, his daughter-in-law Megara, and the children she has had with Heracles are being forced to leave the sanctuary where they have taken refuge and submit to being killed by Lycus, the tyrant who has taken possession of the throne of Thebes.[1] Lycus' motive is to eliminate all the relatives of the former king, Creon, so as to get rid of potential rivals for the throne and secure the sovereign power for his own line. Heracles is in no position to help his family, since he has gone to Hades on a mission to capture Cerberus, the hound of hell. Just when Amphitryon and Megara have given up all hope and are ready to accept death with dignity, Heracles appears, and when Lycus returns to kill his family, he slays Lycus instead.

At this juncture, just over half-way through the play, Iris, the messenger of the gods, and Lyssa, that is, "Madness" personified, arrive and announce, without the least preparation in what has happened so far, that at Hera's instructions they are going to drive Heracles mad, with the result that he will murder his own wife and children. Lyssa protests against her assignment on the grounds that Heracles has been a good man.

To this, Iris replies coldly: "The wife of Zeus did not send you here to be reasonable" (857), and Lyssa reluctantly performs her task.

The results are instantaneous. Heracles begins foaming at the mouth, and imagines that he has driven in a chariot to Argos, where he will take vengeance on Eurystheus, the king who was responsible for sending him on his labors. His father asks in alarm: "My son, what is happening to you . . . ? Is the slaughter of the corpses whom you just now killed making you frenzied?" (965–67). Under the impression, however, that he is in Eurystheus' palace and that his father and children are those of Eurystheus, he slays his three sons and Megara as well, collapsing just before he manages to add his father Amphitryon to the carnage. When Heracles awakens and becomes aware of what he has done, he contemplates committing suicide, but at this point Theseus, whom Heracles had rescued from Hades, arrives with troops from Athens, with the intention of driving out the tyrant Lycus. Heracles accepts Theseus' offer of refuge, and departs for Athens with him.

Heracles unintentionally slays the very people whom Lycus had sought to destroy. True, he believed, in his deluded condition, that they were rather the family of Eurystheus. But a question arises: was the vengeance Heracles proposed to take against Eurystheus – slaying his entire family – also a symptom of his madness, or did his madness reside simply in his confusion over the identity of his victims? If his madness consists solely in his mistake or delusion concerning whom he was killing – his own sons rather than those of Eurystheus – then his behavior in attacking the presumably innocent children and wife of his enemy is not different, in principle, from that of Lycus in regard to Heracles' own family, and the moral distinction between the two men is blurred if not altogether eradicated.

The tragedy itself passes over in silence the analogy between Heracles' intention to kill Eurystheus' children and Lycus' plan, focusing instead on the moral and psychological disaster of slaughtering one's own family. But what the audience sees is a berserk warrior who acts out of character only in that he misdirects his martial savagery. The tragedy presents us with a man who is renowned for aggressive valor in confronting every kind of antagonist, human or monstrous, and who suddenly turns his fierce strength against those dearest to him. This behavior is explained within the play itself as an episode of insanity inflicted upon the hero by a jealous deity, and having nothing whatever to do with Heracles' own nature or activities – as though domestic violence were quite foreign to such a man, however ferocious he might be toward outsiders when the occasion required it. Brutality in the home and at war are neatly quarantined, with no possibility that the latter might seep into and contaminate the former. What the play conceals but simultaneously intimates is that killing other people's children and killing your own are closer than the story itself makes you think.[2]

The Greeks were well aware of this problem. Plato, for example, stresses how difficult it is to train the guardians of his ideal state in the *Republic* to be at once violent toward strangers and tender toward their own people. "How, then, Glaucon," Socrates asks, "will those who have such a nature" – that is, a fierce one (*thumoeidēs*) – "not be savage toward each other and their fellow citizens?" "It won't be easy," Glaucon replies. "And yet," Socrates says, "they must be gentle toward their own, but rough toward their enemies. Otherwise, they won't wait for others to destroy them but will do it first themselves" (*Republic* 2, 375B5–C6). In Menander's comedy, *The Shorn Girl*, a soldier, in a fit of jealous rage, cuts off the hair of the woman he has been living with. In the end, the woman is reunited with her father, who reconciles her with the soldier and gives her to him in wedlock. But he warns the soldier: "In the future, be careful not to do anything rash, given that you're a soldier" (1016–17). Men conditioned to violence are potentially dangerous.

One more point. Lyssa, the name of the goddess who drives Heracles mad, in Homeric epic always signifies battle lust. Later, it comes to represent madness of all sorts, including erotic passion and, for that matter, rabies in animals (we may recall that the name of his antagonist, Lycus, means "wolf"; the word "lycus" may actually be cognate with "lyssa"). When Amphitryon asks his deranged son, "Is the slaughter of the corpses whom you just now killed making you frenzied?," he may be alluding not just to the vengeful spirits of the dead but to the persisting wildness of Heracles in his battle mood. Having tasted blood, it is difficult for him to calm down and be rational again.

So much for the warrior's homecoming. As for reconciling enemy states, the problem was no doubt rendered particularly difficult by the extreme measures a conquering power might take against a defeated enemy. Tritle mentions in passing Thucydides' account of the attempt by Mytilene, an ally of Athens, to shake off Athenian hegemony in the early years of the Peloponnesian War (428 BC). As punishment, the Athenians voted in the Assembly to kill all the adult males of Mytilene and sell the women and children into slavery.[3] On the subsequent day, the Athenians met again to deliberate over whether to rescind that decision and settle instead for the execution of the leading conspirators, numbering about a thousand. One wonders whether this act of generosity would have mollified the surviving Mytilenaeans, as Diodotus, who spoke in favor of leniency, hoped and expected, or would instead have increased the danger that they posed to Athens, since they might be expected to seek revenge. If those slain were mostly aristocrats, perhaps the partisans of a broader democracy would have felt more grateful than resentful; such are the passions of war, as Thucydides explains in his famous analysis of civil conflict in Corcyra (3.83).

The plot of Euripides' *Suppliant Women* is unusual in that it involves actors representing three different cities – Athens, Argos, and Thebes. The suppliant women who make up the principal chorus in the play are Argives; they have come to Eleusis, a village in Attica, together with their king Adrastus and their grandsons, to enlist Athens' aid in reclaiming their dead, who lie unburied outside Thebes. After the death of Oedipus, his sons agreed to share the throne of Thebes, but Eteocles refused to vacate it when his turn was up, and Polyneices, who had married the daughter of Adrastus, sought the aid of Argos to replace Eteocles. The Argive forces were defeated, Polyneices and Eteocles having slain each other in combat, and the new Theban king refused to surrender the corpses of the besiegers for proper burial. The women of Argos beg Aethra, the mother of the Athenian king Theseus, to pity them and affirm the justice of their cause. At first, Theseus is reluctant to intervene, in part because he believes that Adrastus was foolish to have approved the expedition against Thebes; finally, however, he yields to his mother's argument that it is in Athens' interest to uphold the common laws or customs of the Greeks, among which the right to lay one's dead to rest is fundamental (304–13; see Konstan 2005 for discussion).

Theseus first tries diplomacy, but when a Theban herald haughtily rejects his appeal, Theseus reaffirms his decision to safeguard the laws of all Greeks (522–63), and leads his troops to the attack. He duly trounces the Thebans, but refrains from following up his advantage and sacking the city, limiting himself to bringing back the Argive bodies, as he promised, for cremation by their kin (723–25). Back in Athens, Adrastus urges the chorus – mothers of the fallen heroes – to approach the corpses, but Theseus cautions him against augmenting the women's grief (941–47). The women conclude the scene with a choral lament.

At this point, the play takes one of those surprise turns that are characteristic of Euripides' art – we have already seen one such sudden twist in the *Heracles*, when Iris and Lyssa descend from Mount Olympus, on instructions from Hera, to drive Heracles mad. In all liklihood those two goddesses entered by means of the so-called "machine," a crane-like apparatus that was employed to carry deities and other air-borne characters (e.g. ghosts and griffins) onto the stage and which is the source of the Latin expression, *deus ex machina*. In *Suppliant Women*, too, a female character unexpectedly arrives more than three quarters into the play (in line 990; Iris and Lyssa enter at line 822) and takes up a position above the action, probably on the rear wall that served as the backdrop of the stage or else, conceivably, on the "machine" itself. This time it is not a goddess who appears overhead, however, but a mortal woman, Evadne, the wife of the fallen Argive hero, Capaneus. Because Capaneus was struck by a lightning bolt outside Thebes, rather than by an enemy sword or spear, Theseus has granted him his own pyre, separate from the rest, and Evadne declares her intention to cast herself upon it and so to die together with her husband. On her heels comes Iphis, her father and father too of another of the slain Argive leaders, Eteoclos. Iphis tries to dissuade Evadne from her self-immolation, but in vain: she is driven by a desire to make manifest her virtue and, by her deed, achieve fame as the noblest woman under the sun (1059–63).[4] She leaps to her death, and leaves her father to lament his childless old age.

In the meantime, a second chorus – not unparalleled, but rare in Greek tragedy – begins its song; this chorus is composed of the young children of the fallen heroes, who sing antiphonally with their grandmothers, that is, the women who make up the main chorus. The boys announce their intention to avenge the deaths of their fathers (*antiteisomai*, 1143–46), and are unmoved by the elder women's forebodings of fresh slaughter and grief. In the finale, Athena arrives on the "machine," enjoins Adrastus to swear an oath that Argos will never invade Athens, and prophesies the successful capture and destruction of Thebes by the sons of the slain Argives (1213–26).

The complex movement of the play has puzzled commentators, since the conclusion seems to fly in the face of the moderation and restraint in international relations that Theseus so impressively defends both by word and by example.[5] Whereas Theseus acts out of respect for panhellenic custom, which, at least according to the ideals enunciated in this drama, did not permit the abuse of the dead, the Argive children are prepared to renew hostilities and destroy Thebes utterly – something Theseus deliberately refrained from doing – just because their fathers were killed outside that city, without regard for the rights and wrongs of the case: the bodies of the dead have, after all, already been recovered, so that is not their motive. The ritual lamentation appears to have ignited a desire for revenge, and no sooner will the boys reach manhood – at the moment, that is, when their beards first sprout – than they will exact it, as Athena herself predicts (1219). Even more difficult to integrate into the plot of the play is the self-sacrifice of Evadne, who intrudes abruptly upon the action with a gesture that seems wholly out of tune with the solemn style of mourning that Theseus has, until now, managed to impose upon the last rites, in part by keeping the mothers at a distance to avoid hysterical displays of grief.[6] Clearly, the finale of the tragedy is marked by a drastic change of mood.

This, surely, is Euripides' intention: Theseus' sober and restrained approach to the recovery of the Argives' bodies, inspired by respect for holy custom and aloof to motives of revenge and personal enmity, is displaced by what seems like a fanatical attachment to the dead and an act of passionate martyrdom. So too, the scions of the heroes will only be satisfied in their thirst for vengeance by the utter annihilation of Thebes. It is tempting to suppose that Euripides is deliberately contrasting Athenian moderation with the reckless passion of the Argives, celebrating the virtue and piety of his own city while exposing the excesses of Athens' off-and-on rival. On a more immediate political level, the Argives are being reminded of their debt to Athens as a way of encouraging their loyalty, which was at times ambivalent over the course of the Peloponnesian War. Hence the emphasis, in the epilogue to the play, on the Argive oath never to invade Athens.[7]

Nevertheless, it is Athena herself, the patron deity of Athens, who to all appearances endorses, even as she prophesies, the destruction of Thebes, Athens' enemy during most of the fifth century BC (cf. Grethlein 2003: 190–93). In the tragedy, Athens has no motive of its own for attacking Thebes; it does so only at the behest of Argos, as we have seen, and the defense of panhellenic norms is its only excuse. It is not entirely clear that such a reason for launching a war was universally regarded as legitimate, or that Athens had any title to acting as the ritual policeman of Greece. Be that as it may, the Athenians' interest in the war – so far as the action of the play is concerned – is at best indirect. The Argives, however, have a personal grievance against Thebes: their men died in battle, and the impious treatment of the corpses is an affront to the whole city. If the reaction of the Argive boys and of Evadne is more extreme than that of Theseus, it may be explained not just as a sign of a more violent disposition or a flaw in their political system but also as a consequence of their different circumstances. What would the Athenians' response have been had their dead been left unburied on the battlefield? Could it be that the intensity of the Argives' reaction, and their desire for vengeance, would have been seen by the Athenians as entirely plausible and even reasonable, given the provocation? One might even speculate that the destruction of Thebes was the realization of a wish, perhaps not entirely unconscious, on the part of the Athenians themselves – not those within the play, but in the audience.[8]

Self-sacrifice and revenge: today, the two seem not unrelated. Both are popularly associated with extremism, at least in the United States. But it may be that our own attitudes constitute an obstacle to our appreciation of their role in Euripides' *Suppliant Women*. What is at stake, for example, in labeling Evadne's gesture fanatical? In a brilliant investigation of Western attitudes toward the practice of the self-immolation of widows in India, which was never, in fact, so common or so enduring as to constitute the "tradition" it has often been taken to represent, Uma Narayan speculates on why "sati" (sometimes transliterated as "suttee") has so mesmerized observers and been "singled out for such extensive debate" both inside and outside India, as compared to "more routine forms of mistreatment of women" and other manifestations of human suffering. "I suspect," she writes, "that *sati*'s fascination for the British had something to do with *sati* being simultaneously deeply familiar in its invocation of wifely devotion and womanly self-sacrifice, and deeply alien in endorsing actual self-immolation on the husband's funeral pyre. The reactions of British officials to actual incidents of *sati* reveal horror mixed with admiration for the 'courage and devotion' of the women involved, reactions in which their admiration for the women's 'nobility' mixes uneasily with distaste for the 'savagery' of immolation."[9]

Might it be that modern readers (more particularly, perhaps, male readers) experience a comparable ambivalence in respect to Evadne's audacity and commitment? The patriotic reading of the play, which understands Euripides to be extolling Athenian moderation in contrast to Argive fanaticism, may represent an effort to distance ourselves from Evadne's zeal and the militancy of the Argive boys. Theseus, as a polar contrast within the play to the violent passion of the widows and orphans from Argos, provides us with a locus of identification. But the possibility remains that this reading imports into the play our own desire to construct a qualitative difference between such vengeful fervor and our own ostensible rationality and restraint. To quote Narayan once more (66): "I suspect that what was arguably a 'difference in degree' between British and Indian scripts about women's cultural place had to be converted to a substantive 'difference in kind' to support the sense of vast difference between colonizers and 'natives' that the colonial project required as moral justification." Extremes of vengeance were a fact of life in classical Greece, and perhaps the unexpected finale of *Suppliant Women* was not simply Euripides' way of pointing a moral by means of the negative example of Argive fury. War and defeat ineluctably arouse bitter passions. Might it be that Argos is in fact Athens' twin?[10]

As we have seen, Euripides concluded *Suppliant Women* with a prediction, by the patron goddess of Athens, of the future destruction of Thebes at the hands of the Argives. To be sure, this event had the authority of myth behind it: according to legend, the heirs or "epigoni" of the defeated Thebans attacked and defeated Thebes a generation later. But the tragedy dramatizes the longevity of such animosities, and how war inaugurates a cycle of reprisal, ending only – if at all – with the extermination of one of the contending parties. It may appear shocking that the image of Thebes' obliteration should have provided a satisfactory ending to a tragedy in the theater of Dionysus. It is impossible to know how Athens would have treated Thebes in the event that Athens had emerged victorious in the Peloponnesian War. We do know that at the end of the war, when Athens itself lay open to vengeance on the part of its enemies, the Thebans, along with the Corinthians, pressed Sparta to destroy the city, and that Athens was spared thanks only to the opposition of the Spartans (see Xenophon, *Hellenica* 2.2.19–20). The young Argives' ire at Thebes, like the shadow of madness under which Heracles slays the wife and children, as he imagines it, of his arch enemy Eurystheus, reveals at the same time as it masks or displaces the murderous passions that war let loose, in Athens just as much as in Argos or Thebes. *Suppliant Women* implicitly confirms that no city – not Athens itself – is immune to them.[11]

Euripides' *Children of Heracles* has often been paired with *Suppliant Women* as a eulogy of Athens, and the two are remarkably similar in structure. Like *Suppliant Women, Children of Heracles* too centers on an appeal to Athens on the part of foreign suppliants: Heracles' sons and daughters, together with Heracles' mother Alcmene and Iolaus, Heracles' now aged comrade in arms, have taken refuge in the temple of Zeus in Marathon – located, like Eleusis, in the outskirts of Attica – to escape persecution by Eurystheus, the king of Argos (also called by the ancient name Mycenae in the play). It was Eurystheus who had obliged Heracles to undertake his famous labors; now, after Heracles' death, he is intent upon killing his surviving kin, and especially his children, so as to eliminate the potential threat they pose to his throne (cf. 465–70). Like the ruler of Thebes in *Suppliant Women*, Eurystheus sends a herald to dissuade the Athenians and their king Demophon (the son of Theseus) from acceding to the suppliants' plea. The herald argues that Argos has a right to punish its own (139–43), and warns against provoking war with a mighty foe for the sake of a few helpless strangers. Iolaus protests that, having been expelled, they are no longer under Eurystheus' jurisdiction (184–89), and Demophon decides to protect the suppliants, since they are related to him and because his own honor – like that of Theseus in *Suppliant Women* – is at stake.

At this point, there occurs another of those abrupt and shocking twists in the plot that one expects of Euripides. It is suddenly announced that, according to the consensus of a series of prophecies, the Athenians can only emerge victorious from battle with the Argives if the virgin daughter of a noble family is sacrificed (408). Demophon refuses to immolate a daughter of his own or compel another Athenian family to do so (411–13), but Heracles' eldest daughter (named Macaria in other sources) offers herself in behalf of her relatives and the city that has given them refuge (501–02).[12] Here again, as in *Suppliant Women*, a foreign woman gives her life in a splendid gesture of self-sacrifice. Of course, Macaria is not moved simply by a desire for glory, as Evadne seems to have been; that the survival of her family depends on her act endows it with an element of compulsion. In this, Macaria resembles other youngsters in Euripidean tragedy who immolate themselves in behalf of their city – above all Menoeceus, the son of Creon king of Thebes, in *Phoenician Women*, and to a lesser degree Iphigenia in *Iphigenia in Aulis*; in his *Erechtheus*, which survives only in fragments, Euripides treated a similar episode in the mythology of Athens itself, in which the daughters of Erechtheus consent to die so that the city may not fall to a Thracian invasion. The scenes of Evadne and Macaria have in common the motifs of proud self-sacrifice and intense devotion to kin.

As Macaria is led off to die, news arrives that Hyllus, the eldest of Heracles' sons, has returned to Athens with a company of soldiers, and old Iolaus girds himself for battle. As in *Suppliant Women*, the Athenians are victorious (784–87), and Iolaus, who has been magically rejuvenated (796, 857–58), succeeds in capturing Eurystheus alive (859–63).

Here the action once again takes a surprising turn, apparently without precedent in the myth.[13] Alcmene protests that Iolaus should have killed Eurystheus (879–82) on the battlefield rather than spare his life, but the messenger who has brought her the news of the victory explains that Iolaus wished precisely to put Eurystheus in her power (883–84). Iolaus' squire leads Eurystheus in, bound and humbled, and Alcmene vents her rage upon him, declaring that he must be killed: indeed he ought, she says, to die many times over for what he has done (958–60). The squire objects that it is not permitted to slay him, but Alcmene is adamant: "In vain, then, have we taken him captive" (962). If Athenian tradition (*nomos*) prohibits killing a prisoner of war (963–72), then she will execute him herself, for however much she loves the city of Athens, Eurystheus must not live, now that he has fallen into her hands (973–80).[14]

Here again, as in *Suppliant Women*, the Athenians' defense of suppliants in a just cause and their triumph over an arrogant enemy give way to a mood of bitter vengeance, in which the former victims turn against their enemies with a violence and hatred that seem no less extreme than what they had previously suffered. In both plays, a woman's self-immolation appears to set the stage for passionate revenge, as though selflessness and retribution were naturally paired.[15] Once more the question arises as to how one is to understand the venomous anger of the foreign (i.e. non-Athenian) characters in the finale of the play, which appears to contrast so sharply with the moderation and respect for law and custom that characterize Athens' intervention in their behalf.[16]

Here too, we may begin by noting the difference between Alcmene's relation to Eurystheus and that of Demophon and the Athenians generally. Athens undertakes to wage war in defense of a principle, whether the right to burial or the respect due to suppliants (though self-interest and other motives are not entirely lacking); the enemy has done no prior harm to Athens, nor does it intend any. Strictly speaking, Athens is the aggressor against Thebes. In the case of Argos, it is Eurystheus who begins hostilities, but his goal is limited to reclaiming the Argive refugees. Alcmene, on the contrary, is moved by a fierce personal antagonism toward Eurystheus, going back to the time when he imposed the twelve labors on Heracles. Thus two kinds of enmity are active in the play. The difference between the two is clearer in ancient Greek than in English, moreover, since they are distinguished lexically.

Classical Greek, like Latin, had two words for "enemy." The term *polemios* (corresponding to the Latin *hostis*) signified a military enemy; it derives from the noun *polemos*, meaning "war." The word *ekhthros* (analogous to the Latin *inimicus*) denoted rather a personal enemy. The word is connected with the verb *ekhthairō*, "to hate." The abstract noun *ekhthra* carried the senses both of "enmity" and "hatred"; Aristotle, for instance, in his analysis of *misos* ("hatred") in the *Rhetoric* (2.4, 1381b30–1382a20) uses the word interchangeably with *ekhthra* as the opposite of *philia* or affection.

In English, "enemy" does service for both types, although the term "foe," which is now obsolete in the United States except in certain formulas such as "friend or foe," is used principally in reference to military antagonists.

In *Children of Heracles*, Iolaus may refer to the Argives as *polemioi* insofar as he thinks of them as a hostile army (315–16); this is the term he employs, for example, in connection with news from the battlefield (382, 655), or again in reference to the enemy ranks (676; cf. 738). The squire speaks of his desire to return to battle and engage with the *polemioi* (678–79). But when Iolaus declares that his only concern about dying is the possibility that his death may bring joy to his enemies (443–44), the term is *ekhthroi* (cf. 449–50 on the shame of death at the hands of an *ekhthros*, that is, Eurystheus; also 458, 468). In battle, he prays to be rejuvenated so that he can take vengeance on his *ekhthroi* (849–53), here clearly thinking of the Argives as his personal enemies. Macaria, having volunteered to die, tells Iolaus that he need no longer fear the enemy's spear (*ekhthrōn doru*, 500; cf. 512, 530).[17] But it is Alcmene who is most conscious of the deep hatred that exists between herself and Eurystheus. She insists that it is unwise not to avenge oneself when one has one's *ekhthroi* in one's power (881–82). The squire, as he leads Eurystheus in, tells Alcmene that "it is most pleasant to see an *ekhthros* suffer misfortune after he has prospered" (939–40). Face to face with Eurystheus, Alcmene calls him "a hateful thing" (*misos*, 941), and berates him for daring to look his enemies (*ekhthroi*) in the face (943). So too, she justifies her intention to kill Eurystheus with the words, "Don't the Athenians think it a fine thing to slay their *ekhthroi*?" (965), to which the squire replies, "Not one who has been taken alive in battle," pointing to the contrast between personal antagonisms and the protocols of war.[18]

If Alcmene's vengeful assault on Eurystheus comes as a surprise, no less so is Eurystheus' own response in the face of her hostility.[19] After refusing to confront Hyllus, the son of Heracles, on the battlefield in what, at least according to the report of the messenger, seemed to be an open display of cowardice, Eurystheus suddenly acquires an unanticipated dignity as he confesses his earlier crimes and accepts his death with calm assurance. He explains that he had previously lived in fear of his *ekhthroi*; nor will he deny that Heracles, though an *ekhthros*, was a noble man. After Heracles' death, he knew that he was hated (*misoumenos*) by his children thanks to their inherited hostility toward him (*ekhthra patrōia*), and he tried to eliminate them as well; Alcmene would have done the same, he says, concerning the cubs of a hostile (*ekhthros*) lion. He concludes by reminding Alcmene that Athens has spared him, respecting the laws of the Greeks and honoring the god above enmity (*ekhthra*) toward him (994–1013).

Alcmene is unappeased, and Eurystheus, prepared to die, announces – in yet another unexpected twist of the plot – that, in accord with an ancient prophecy of Apollo, if he is buried in Attica he will prove a savior of the city, although he will remain forever at war (*polemiōtatos*) with the descendants of Heracles (1032–34). The tragedy concludes as Alcmene orders her servants to kill Eurystheus, since he is an *ekhthros* and on top of that his death will aid Athens, and to throw his body to the dogs (1045–51). In their final comment, even the chorus of Athenians agrees that it is best for Eurystheus to die (1053–55), which would seem to put in question all that Athens stood for earlier.

I have dwelled on the distinction in terminology between *polemios* and *ekhthros* because it points the way to an interpretation of the action of *Children of Heracles* that does not simply contrast the ostensible savagery of Alcmene with the civilized restraint of Athens and its king. Revenge is a fierce motive, and it demands satisfaction. Euripides is not, I think, out to put its claims in doubt, or to pretend that it is an eliminable motive in times of war. Athens, it is true, is aloof to the passions that drive the primary antagonists. It is thus in the lucky position of being able to receive the Heraclids as suppliants and simultaneously to benefit from the presence on its soil of the defeated and slain king of Argos. This is all very well, but the difference between Athens and Alcmene is due to their situation, not to a fundamental disparity of character.[20] That Alcmene's defiant decision to have Eurystheus killed is approved by the Athenians and redounds to their advantage confirms the sense that their motives and hers are not so much at odds as responsive to different relationships with the defeated king. The vengeance motif is not undermined but incorporated into the larger plot of the play and rendered crucial to Athens' destiny. As Justina Gregory observes in connection with Euripides' *Hecuba* (1991: 107): "For the Greeks, retribution, whether publicly or privately obtained, was an essential component of justice." As in *Suppliant Women*, so too in *Children of Heracles* Euripides portrays war in all its aspects, both as an engagement based on principle and as a function of personal hatreds and revenge.[21]

The desire for revenge makes reconciliation difficult or impossible. The startling conversion of Eurystheus into a talismanic savior of Athens is something of a sleight of hand, or perhaps a manifestation of wishful thinking. Deep-seated hatreds give rise to wars, which in turn augment hostile sentiments. To the extent that such fierce and enduring resentment was typical of Greek warfare, it is difficult to imagine how reconciliation might be achieved. At one point in Homer's *Iliad*, which was the paradigm text of the Greek warrior culture, the Greek general Agamemnon admonishes his brother Menelaus against taking prisoners alive:

> . . . let not one of them go free of sudden
> death and our hands; not the young man child that the mother carries
> still in her body, not even he, but let all of Ilion's
> people perish, utterly blotted out and unmourned for
> (6.57–60; trans. Lattimore).

The reader knows, of course, that the war will in fact end with the utter obliteration of Troy.[22]

Two centuries after Euripides, the historian Polybius described how Antigonus Doson of Macedon, allied with the Achaeans, besieged the city of Mantinea, which subsequently surrendered (2.54.11–13; see Konstan 2001: 85–88; 2007). In the aftermath, the adult males were slain and the rest of the population sold into slavery. Polybius, a partisan of Antigonus, explains that when Aratus had conquered Mantinea four years previously, he had treated the inhabitants with exemplary humanity: no people had ever encountered kindlier enemies. But when the Mantineans went over to the Spartans, they slit the throats of the Achaeans in their midst, in violation, Polybius says, of the laws common to mankind. They thus deserved an angry response, and no penalty would have been sufficient; mere enslavement, he affirms, is simply the recognized outcome of defeat (2.58.9–12). The Spartan king Cleomenes III, taking the part of Mantinea, struck back and attacked the Achaean Megalopolis, penetrating the city by night although the inhabitants put up a heroic resistance. Cleomenes so ravaged it that no one believed it could ever be resettled (2.55.7–8). Such is the image and the reality of ancient warfare.

There were, of course, some inhibitions on the pursuit of vengeance. Self-interest, for example, might put brakes on the most extreme measures. We have already mentioned the instance of the fate of Mytilene, as recorded by Thucydides. Although self-interest may not seem the most enlightened or humane basis for the conduct of international affairs, in a context in which war was often justified by anger at past offenses and the need to avenge them, a pragmatic approach might help to calm hostile feelings and promote prudence. In Euripides' *Suppliant Women*, Theseus is guided by practical considerations, and he reproaches Adrastus for going to war with Thebes because of the pressure exerted by the young men of Argos, who are eager for battle irrespective of justice; Theseus compares their influence to that of the mob or *plēthos* in a democratic city (232–37). It was doubtless self-interest, along with respect for Athens' role in repelling the Persian invasion, that induced Sparta to refrain from extirpating Athens at the end of the Peloponnesian War, as the Thebans had urged. And, as Tritle points out, Athens was soon prepared to enter into an alliance with Thebes itself.

There were, in addition, some norms of war, although they did not approach modern ideals concerning the rights of captives and non-combatants, and the proper treatment of soldiers who have surrendered. Polybius believed that mass execution and enslavement were in accord with prevailing custom, after all.[23] Limits on cruelties inflicted on a defeated enemy make possible an end to the cycle of rage and revenge that threatens to result in a permanent state of feud, save in the case of the complete extermination of the foe. One might also respect a foe who was a *polemios*, a military opponent, as opposed to a detested personal enemy or *ekhthros*. In Homer's *Iliad*, the Trojan hero Hector invites Ajax, after a duel that has come to a draw, to be reconciled in a spirit of noble courtesy:

> Come then, let us give each other glorious presents,
> so that any of the Achaians or Trojans may say of us:
> "These two fought each other in heart-consuming strife, then
> joined with each other in close friendship, before they were parted"
> (7.299–302; trans. Lattimore, modified).

But the pain of war bred a desire for harsh retribution, as the Greeks clearly and coldly recognized. In the *Iliad*, Achilles expresses the wish that he could eat Hector's flesh raw for the harm that he has done to him, and Hector's mother, Hecuba, feels similarly toward Achilles for the murder of her son (22.346–47, 24.212–13). Polybius blithely suggests that an enemy general ought not only to have been tortured but also led round the cities of the Peloponnese as an example before being permitted to die (2.60.7).

In Euripides' war tragedies, the motive of revenge is part and parcel of the larger action. The surprising twists and turns of the plots trace the complex pattern of motivations of the characters. We may wish to separate out the noble purposes of Theseus and Demophon from the violent passions of Alcmene or of the young Argives in *Suppliant Women*, but the plays weave them together to produce a single outcome, favorable to Athens. Patriotic they may be, but they are not preachy or naive. Vengeance was a fact of war, and achieving a lasting peace between former enemies was as difficult as it was desirable.

Notes

1 The discussion of Euripides' *Heracles* is based in part on Konstan 1999.
2 Riley 2004: 115 remarks of recent revivals of Euripides' *Heracles*: "The concept of the warrior, the trained killer who misdirects his aggression against his own household, has found very powerful resonances in our own society, where marital violence and the male child-killer are pressing social concerns."
3 This was not an uncommon form of retribution; cf. Pritchett 1991: 312: "Cities were regularly destroyed and the inhabitants killed or sold into slavery. It is only on rare occasions that the victor concerned himself with coming to terms with the vanquished."
4 It is notable that Evadne herself makes no mention of grief among the motives for her self-immolation.
5 For a review of earlier judgments on the "chauvinistic" or "propagandistic" import of *Suppliant Women* and *The Children of Heracles*, as well as of the ostensible incoherence of their story lines, see Mendelsohn 2002: 3–4, 6–9.
6 Mendelsohn 2002: 197 cites some earlier views to this effect.
7 Mendelsohn 2002: 1–5 reviews the patriotic interpretations of this play and *The Children of Heracles*. For a nuanced view of the praise of Athens, with extensive bibliography, cf. Grethlein 2003: 123–89.
8 The Athenians had reasons to feel hostile toward Thebes during the Peloponnesian War, and more particularly shortly after 424, to which years the *Suppliant Women* is most commonly assigned on metrical grounds (cf. Grethlein 2003: 189 for literature). For one thing, the Thebans were regarded as having precipitated the war by launching an unprovoked attack on Plataea in 431; after the attackers were overcome by the Plataeans, the Thebans were instrumental in persuading the Spartans to destroy Plataea and execute the defenders (Thuc. 3.53–59). It is worth noting that, in the peroration to their speech before the Spartans, the Plataeans represent themselves as suppliants (3.59.2), appeal to the common laws of the Greeks (*ta koina tōn Hellēnōn nomima*, 3.59.1), and entreat the Spartans to be moved by reasonable pity (*oiktōi sōphroni*, 3.59.1). Still more relevant in the context of the *Suppliant Women* is the fact that, after the Athenians were defeated in a battle with the Thebans in 424, the Thebans balked for two or three weeks at returning the Athenian dead for burial (Thuc. 4.96–101).
9 Narayan 1997: 65–66; on the construction of difference between modern, progressive institutions and the ostensibly traditional culture in which honor crimes are framed in Turkey, see Kogacioglu 2004.

10 That it is a woman who, by her gesture, stimulates the desire for revenge raises the question of gender in the play. But women are not simply identified with violent passion; Aethra is moved principally by pity, and it is she who convinces Theseus to intervene against Thebes in behalf of the Argives. For a full discussion of gender roles in *Suppliant Women* and *Children of Heracles*, see Mendelsohn 2002. It may be worth noting that, according to the late mythographer Hyginus (*Fables* 243), Aethra herself committed suicide when she learned of the death of Theseus.

11 Kurt Raaflaub suggested to me that the hatred and desire for revenge fostered by war might account, in part, for the Athenians' unwillingness to accept Sparta's peace offers after the surrender of the Spartan force in Pylos in 425–24 (Thuc. 4.41). The demagogue Cleon was thus able to play upon a pre-existing disposition in the Athenian population to "pay the bastards back."

12 Mendelsohn 2002: 88 argues that Demophon's refusal to allow the sacrifice of an Athenian maiden shows that for him, "the affairs of the *polis* are a private, even family affair." But this is not Athens' war; gestures of sacrifice are appropriate when one's own group is at risk. In general, Mendelsohn seems to me to place excessive emphasis on the contrast between loyalty to the values of the city and a more narrow commitment to the clan, represented above all by Iolaus (79; cf. 91, 97 on Macaria's role).

13 Mendelsohn 2002: 17–18; on the surprising, even shocking character of the scene, cf. Seidensticker 1982: 99–100.

14 Mendelsohn 2002: 120 observes: "Not surprisingly, this scene has been the object of especially harsh critical puzzlement and outrage"; like other critics, Mendelsohn notes that "in pursuing her terrible revenge Alcmene becomes the double of her arch-enemy" (126). I am not convinced, however, by Mendelsohn's claim that Alcmene's "mad scene" (120) "is motivated by an extreme version of the *genos*-creed" (121; cf. 124–25), that is, loyalty to clan values as opposed to those of the city. A desire for vengeance is equally characteristic of civic hostilities.

15 It is tempting to see a contrast in *Children of Heracles* between two models of femininity, submissive (Macaria) and vindictive (Alcmene); cf. Rabinowitz 1993: 14, with Mendelsohn 2002: 22–26; cf. 120 on the "structural parallels" between the scenes involving Macaria and Alcmene. In *Suppliant Women*, however, it is the Argive youths who assume the role of agents of vengeance, and while it is usually women who are sacrificed in Euripidean tragedy (e.g. *Hecuba, Iphigenia in Aulis*), in *Phoenician Women* Menoeceus, the son of the Theban king Creon, plays a role analogous to that of Macaria; see Wilkins 1990. I am inclined to agree with Mendelsohn that "In tragedy's critique of political ideology, the definition of proper behavior for both the city and the citizen is never exclusively aligned with either the wholly masculine or the wholly feminine ..., but is instead arrived at as the result of complex negotiations between the two poles" (2002: 35; cf. 48). In regard to *Suppliant Women* and *Children of Heracles*, Mendelsohn contrasts the roles of Macaria and Aethra, who help to save the city, with the "more harrowing instances of feminine transgression" represented by Alcmene's revenge and "Evadne's erotic Mad Scene" (47).

16 For the positive representation of Athens in the play, with bibliography of earlier views, see Grethlein 2003: 396–424.

17 The expression *ekhthrōn doru* is also used in 312–15, where Iolaus says that the Heraclids must forever regard the Athenians as *philoi*, that is, friends, and never raise a hostile spear against them. *Philos*, which may mean "ally" as well as "friend," is usually paired with *ekhthros* as its opposite; cf. 19–20, 690–91 (on the order of the lines, see Wilkins 1993: 138).

18 When the messenger reports to Alcmene the Athenian victory, he says (786–87): "We are victorious over our *ekhthroi* and a trophy has been set up bearing all the arms of your *polemioi*"; I presume that the trophy elicits the idea of a defeated army. At 410, however, Demophon announces that it is necessary to sacrifice a girl to be a trophy over their *ekhthroi*.

Cf. Eur. *Electra* 832–33 (Aegisthus speaking): "the son of Agamemnon is the most hated [*ekhthistos*] of mortals and a foe [*polemios*] to my house."

19 I do not see that Eurystheus has "become a double" of Macaria, however, as Mendelsohn 2002: 128 suggests, nor that there is an implicit feminization of his character.

20 Mendelsohn 2002: 86–87 observes that "if the point of the play were merely to demonstrate Demophon's admirable qualities, it would surely end at line 380."

21 Cf. Burnett 1998: 145: "Only the final revenge section has attracted much notice, and that negative, as indignant critics discover there a crazed old lady who performs an action both repulsive and illegal and thereby betrays the noble masculine city that has befriended her. I would argue, on the contrary, that Alcmena is proposed as a justice-bearing avenger after the pattern of her hero son." I disagree, however, with Burnett's view that "civilized Attic legalism [offers] a paradoxical protection to the tyrant" Eurystheus, thereby demonstrating that "even in a righteous contest, the man of scruples may be crippled by the very order that he wants to defend" (148; cf. 153, 156: "The rule of law, like the right to asylum, survives, but only because a fierce old woman was not afraid to do the Heraclean work of brute revenge."). The Athenians do not have a motive for revenge, but Alcmene does; this, I believe, is the reason for their different responses to the crisis.

22 Other, more conciliatory, sentiments are also expressed in the *Iliad*; cf. the aspirations for peace on both sides in 3.111–12, or the mutual respect between the Greek Ajax and Trojan Hector at the conclusion of their duel in 7.287–305 (partly quoted below).

23 Contrast the modern view that slavery is a form of "social death," in Orlando Patterson's phrase (Patterson 1982), and that to be a slave is to be "radically deprived of all rights that are supposed to be accorded to any and all living human beings" (Butler 2000: 73).

References

Burnett, Anne Pippin. 1998. *Revenge in Attic and Later Tragedy*. Berkeley.

Butler, Judith. 2000. *Antigone's Claim: Kinship between Life and Death*. New York.

Gregory, Justina. 1991. *Euripides and the Instruction of the Athenians*. Ann Arbor.

Grethlein, Jonas. 2003. *Asyl und Athen: Die Konstruktion kollektiver Identität in der griechischen Tragödie*. Drama: Beiträge zum antiken Drama und seiner Rezeption, Beiheft 21. Stuttgart.

Kogacioglu, Dicle. 2004. "The Tradition Effect: Framing Honor Crimes in Turkey." *Differences* 15: 118–51.

Konstan, David. 1999. "What We Must Believe in Greek Tragedy." *Ramus* 28: 75–88.

——. 2001. *Pity Transformed*. London.

——. 2005. "Pity and Power." In Rachel Sternberg (ed.), *Pity in Ancient Athenian Life and Letters*, 48–66. Cambridge, MA.

——. 2007. "Anger, Hatred, and Genocide." Forthcoming in *Common Knowledge* 13.1.

Mendelsohn, Daniel. 2002. *Gender and the City in Euripides' Political Plays*. Oxford.

Narayan, Uma. 1997. *Dislocating Cultures: Identities, Traditions, and Third-World Feminism*. New York.

Patterson, Orlando. 1982. *Slavery and Social Death: A Comparative Study*. Cambridge, MA.

Pritchett, W. Kendrick. 1991. *The Greek State at War*. Vol. 5. Berkeley.

Rabinowitz, Nancy. 1993. *Anxiety Veiled: Euripides and the Traffic in Women*. Ithaca.

Riley, Kathleen. 2004. "Heracles as Dr Strangelove and GI Joe." In Edith Hall, Fiona Macintosh, and Amanda Wrigley (eds.), *Dionysus Since 69: Greek Tragedy at the Dawn of the Third Millennium*, 113–41. Oxford.

Seidensticker, B. 1982. *Palintonos Harmonia: Studien zu komischen Elementen in der griechischen Tragödie*. Hypomnemata 72. Göttingen.

Wilkins, John. 1990. "The State and the Individual: Euripides' Plays of Voluntary Self-Sacrifice." In Anton Powell (ed.), *Euripides, Women, and Sexuality*, 177–94. London.

——. 1993. *Euripides: Heraclidae. Edited with Introduction and Commentary*. Oxford.

12

War, Peace, and International Law in Ancient Greece

Victor Alonso

Greek Civilization begins with a great poem celebrating war, the *Iliad*. This work's strength and beauty emanate largely from the fact that Homer does not hide the terrible face of the conflict between Achaeans and Trojans. Heroes fight and die on the battlefront before the walls of Ilium, the city which will one day be taken amidst a bath of blood. But all is not tragedy and pain in this hermeneutically inexhaustible story. The bard reserves the poem's final song to relate an act of reconciliation that belongs among the most moving and inspiring in world literature. Under the cover of night, King Priam, a desolate and unarmed old man, approaches Achilles' tent as a suppliant, with the consent of the gods, to reclaim, for appropriate burial and funerary rites, the body of his son Hector, whom Achilles still keeps as testimony of his victory and vengeance. Overcoming his legendary wrath, Achilles concedes to Priam's supplication with a display of recognition and pity. The work thus concludes with a funeral celebrating the fallen hero, the greatest of the Trojans, and according him a measure of poetic justice that cannot but bring us a sense of relief.

George Steiner (1984: 242–43) says that

> The more one experiences ancient Greek literature and civilization, the more insistent the suggestion that Hellas is rooted in the twenty-fourth Book of the *Iliad*. There are not many primary aspects of Greek moral, political, rhetorical practice which are not incipient in and, indeed, given unsurpassed imaginative formulation by, the night encounter of Priam and Achilles and the restoration of Hector's body. Much of what Greek sensibility knew and felt about life and death, about acceptance of tragic fate and the claims of mercy, about the equivocations of intent and of mutual recognition which inhabit all speech between mortals, is set out in this climactic, most perfect part of the epic.

There is, of course, an essential harmony between this song and Sophocles' *Antigone*, that pinnacle of Hellenic tragedy in the Classical Period. But three centuries before Sophocles, the singers of tales already understood that all military confrontations must obey a set of limits and rules, for as Antigone puts it, men are obliged to respect the unwritten and unfailing statutes of divine law (*Ant.* 454–55). And they are also compelled to search for reconciliation, provisional or definitive, beyond the imperatives of war.

Interestingly, the *Iliad*'s conclusion contains, along with Achilles' return to civilized order (to *humanitas*, as a reader of Cicero would have said), a complete retraction of his earlier position, when, at the culminating moment of his duel with Hector, he had rejected any accord with his opponent. The proposal the Trojan leader had offered conformed to a fundamental principle of the Greek code of war:

> But come here, let us call the gods to witness, for they will be the best witnesses and guardians of our covenants: I will do you no violent maltreatment if Zeus grants me strength to endure and I take your life; but when I have stripped from you your glorious armor, Achilles, I will give your dead body back to the Achaeans; and so too do you (*Il.* 22.254–59).

Achilles' immediate response had been a vow to fight to the bitter end:

> Hector, talk not to me, curse you, of covenants. As between lions and men there are no oaths of faith, nor do wolves and lambs have hearts of concord but plan evils continually one against the other, so is it not possible for you and me to be friends, nor will there be oaths between us till one or the other has fallen, and glutted with his blood Ares (22.261–67).

In other words, Achilles had announced that his personal conflict with this enemy, the killer of Patroclus, was situated at the margins of culture, in a natural state of brute force and simplicity, unmediated by cultural norms, and dominated by blind formlessness and moral chaos. The emblem of this chaos within the *Iliad*, as James Redfield has indicated (1975: 183), is the anti-funeral: the dead are stripped and left to the scavengers, "a prey to dogs and a feast for birds" (*Il.* 1.4–5).

Both the *Iliad* and the *Odyssey* conclude with scenes of reconciliation fostered by the gods who for their part have had to make an effort to overcome their own differences about the fates of the mortals. In the first poem, the private compromise between the two leaders has no political or military consequences, as it is limited to the retrieval of Hector's body, and does not end the hostilities (although it does serve symbolically to reaffirm the civilized condition of Achilles – that almost superhuman, ambiguous son of a god and a mortal). In the case of Odysseus, as we shall see shortly, the avenger's pact with the dead suitors' relatives will once again bring peace (*eirene*) and prosperity to Ithaca or, if we prefer, the end of civil discord (*stasis*) and the deactivation of the logic of *vendetta* (which is further complicated in this case by its international ramifications). Both episodes might be read as metaphors of Greek political history in its totality. In effect, the dynamics of war – with its multiple ways of suspending and overcoming conflict – along with the precariousness of peace, in the framework of intra-communal and inter-Hellenic dissensions, constituted the great argument of this history, from the Homeric epic to the Hellenistic period.[1]

The Institutionalization of International Relations: Friendship, War, and Reconciliation

War represented a structural component of the Greco-Roman world, as much or more than slavery or agriculture; from Herodotus to Xenophon and from Thucydides to Polybius, Greek historiography is above all political-military history. Any college graduate with a degree in Classical Studies understands this fact, and there are even surveys that elucidate for us the chain of conflicts to the end of the Hellenistic Period.[2] It is important, however, not to oversimplify the complexity of international relations by generalizing on the basis of its most dynamic actors, that is, precisely those the extant historical sources inform us about. Hellenic communities found themselves involved in armed conflicts in a variety of ways, a crucial fact which unfortunately remains insufficiently emphasized in the most recent studies on Greek political history. There were many *poleis* and federal states (*koina*) that found a way to keep themselves out of the great confrontations, pursuing a policy of neutrality (Alonso 1987, 2001), or concluding compromises with Greek superpowers (as did the Aegean cities of the Delian League, who freed themselves from military service in exchange for a monetary contribution), or even waging an indirect war. Argos and Corcyra offer well-known examples of abstinence from war during most of the fifth century, as do Megara in the fourth or Rhodes and Athens in some periods of the Hellenistic era (Habicht 1997: 173ff.). Prior to the prominent role it would play in the second half of the third century, the Achaean Confederacy presented an enviable case of splendid isolation. There were entire regions, like Aetolia, Epirus, or Crete, that refused to participate in the great conflagrations of the classical age, anchored as they were in policies of neutrality and non-alignment which do not lack certain present-day analogues. The same could be said for the colonial world occupied by Greek cities – Libya, the Black Sea region, Magna Graecia. Certainly, many of these areas experienced periods of hostilities of a more or less local character, but the fact is that these cannot have been important enough for our historical sources to pay them much attention.

We should therefore remain critical toward generalizations and occasional phrases on the phenomenon of war that we read in the works of some Greek philosophers (Phillipson 1911: 167–68, 173). They thought that war should be considered a natural and inevitable state inherent in both human and animal life on earth. Heraclitus called war the father of all things, in the sense that it is the fundamental principle causing all change and development (22 B53 in Diels and Kranz 1961). And so Cleinias, at the beginning of Plato's *Laws* (626a), addressing the Athenians on the subject of Cretan institutions and assuming that strife is inevitable for attaining political exclusiveness and national self-realization, says: "In reality every city is in a natural state of war with every other, not indeed proclaimed by heralds, but perpetual." In the "Melian Dialogue," the Athenian ambassadors, not without sophistry, say that the rule of the strongest, operative in nature, always prevails over law in governing relations between peoples. That well-known discussion between Melians and Athenians (Thucydides 5.84–116) might induce us to conclude that the Law of the Jungle defined interstate relations in Hellas. Yet not even those most convinced of the prevalence of a naturalist ideology of war among the Greeks (like Momigliano 1960) would be willing to subscribe to this conclusion. The problem with such sharp and doctrinary pronouncements, typical of Greek theoretical thinking (although less of historiography), is that they have contributed to confusing modern authors.[3]

Here it is necessary to mention Bruno Keil (1916: 5ff.). In a celebrated study, he defended the idea that during the first centuries of Greek history peace was nothing but a contractual interruption of the normal state of war between the *poleis*, little more than a respite, and that after the expiration of an international treaty the parties returned automatically to their natural situation of "war of all against all" (*bellum omnium contra omnes*). A decisive point for Keil was the fact that the word *eirene* did not emerge as a legal term in diplomatic language until the fourth century, with the "common peace" of 386, the first *koine eirene*. In effect, to label the legal instrument designated to stop an armed conflict between cities, international law still employed in the fifth century the noun *spondai*, "libations," in combination with the terms *synthekai* and *horkoi*, "stipulations" and "oaths."[4] The lack of a concept of "peace treaty" corresponded precisely with the establishment of a period of time for the *spondai* negotiated at the close of a conflict (50, 30, 10, 5 years of guaranteed non-aggression). This model of negotiation definitively reveals a negative conception of *eirene* as "not-war" or, if we prefer, as the provisional suspension of general belligerency between states.

Recent research has thus confirmed the validity of Keil's philological analysis in its essential points, but it has at the same time convincingly refuted the historical and legal premises he deduced from his analysis.[5] Our current understanding suggests that, far from being rooted in a naive belligerent state of everyone-against-everyone, early Greek communities maintained at least three types of external relationships: none at all, war, or friendship.[6]

1. A lack of relationship between parties (*ameixia*) is typically the starting point in the history of international law. This state of non-relationship corresponds with the absence of ties and contacts that Thucydides (1.2.2, 3.4) postulates for many early Greek communities that were closed off from each other in their autarky and too distant to maintain external relations, given the conditions of navigation and the difficulties of land travel. As Achilles recalls, he and his Myrmidons found themselves before the walls of Troy solely because of their commitment to Agamemnon:

> I did not come here to fight because of the spearmen of Troy, since they are in no way at fault toward me. Never did they drive off my cattle or my horses, nor ever in deep-soiled Phthia ... did they lay waste the grain, for many things lie between us – shadowy mountains and sounding sea (*Il.* 1.152–57).

Legal uncertainty – rather than lawlessness (*anomia*) – essentially characterizes any contacts with the exterior (*epimeixia*). These contacts usually assume the form of peaceful commerce (the Hesiodic *ergon*, the plebeian *emporie*), of piracy or banditry (*lesteia*), or of both simultaneously (the elite *prexis*).[7] It is in this context that we should interpret the first mythological frictions between Asia and Europe, in the form of the abduction of women, as narrated by Herodotus (1.1–5). Corresponding to the doubts that invariably beset the sailor upon arriving in a strange land, "whether its people are cruel, and wild, and unjust, or whether they are kind to strangers and fear the gods in their thoughts" (*Od.* 9.175–76), there appears the typical formula of salutation to the unknown visitor: "Whence do you sail over the watery ways? Is it on some business, or do you wander at random over the sea, as pirates do, who wander hazarding their lives and bringing evil to men of other lands?" (*Od.* 3.72–74).

The mute exchange practiced by the Carthaginians in some regions of Africa, as described by Herodotus (4.196), might be considered one degree above this state of incommunication. This minimal, but conventional (in the strict sense of the word) form of *epimeixia* illustrates the difficulties that divergent referential systems, beginning with language and religion, pose for human groups. The source of the Cyclopses' savage conduct is precisely their lack of understanding of the *themis* common to civilized societies (*Od.* 9.106), where *themis* refers to a customary rule of divine origin consecrating norms of behavior, such as hospitality, under the protection of Zeus Xenios (*Od.* 9.270). Hence the confrontation between man-eating Polyphemus and his unsuspecting guests in Book 9 of the *Odyssey*, or the impossibility of the Cyclopses' cohabitation with the Phaeacians, who are forced to emigrate to Scheria, a sort of promised land (ibid. 6.2–8). It is not by chance that in the Homeric world the utopian image *par excellence* is this Scheria, an island that barely "mixes" with the exterior (*Od.* 6.205, 279), although Nausicaa, perhaps overcome by *ennui*, will fall in love with a foreign shipwreck. Naturally, as is the case with Rokovoko, the isle of Queequeg, Phaeacia did not appear on maps.

2. For a negative relationship marked by a state of war (*polemos*) between communities, the struggle of the Achaeans against the Trojans might serve as a paradigm. In the Homeric poems, war already constitutes a well-defined legal situation, in which the fury of Ares appears counterbalanced by the rational calculation of Athena. Given that any confrontation potentially endangers the entire population and implies the mobilization of all or most of the military force, the decision to initiate hostilities is made public before the corresponding governing bodies (kings, counselors, and the assembly of the people). Before it comes to war, the offended party can request or receive a conciliatory proposal on the basis of satisfaction (*poine*). If armed conflict proves inevitable, the combatants have at their disposal a series of institutions and customary rules to limit and avoid its devastating effects: the proclamation of the conflict, the inviolability of heralds (*kerykes*), the possibility of diplomatic negotiations through ambassadors (*angeloi*), the recourse to single combat (*monomachia*) with the intention of sparing widespread bloodshed, the use of truces for the recovery of bodies, the condition of suppliant (*hiketes*), the inviolability of sanctuaries and sacred persons (*asylia* of priests like Chryses in *Iliad* 1), the contractual status of ally (*epikouros*), the regulated distribution of booty, including the honorary share of the leader (*geras*), and, of course, the figure of the primary combatant or head of the coalition (Agamemnon, Priam).[8]

Precisely because armed conflicts have causes and a beginning, and because they do not represent the natural state of relations between peoples, it is also recognized that they can be ended by means of a binding treaty. This is *philotes*, a pact of reconciliation and friendship which originates in the sphere of penal law and early on comes to be applied at the international level.[9]

Paris hopes that differences will cease altogether after his single combat with Menelaus:

> And whoever wins, and proves himself the better man, let him duly take all the wealth and the woman, and take them home. But you others, swearing friendship and solemn oaths (*philoteta kai horkia pista*), may you all live in deep-soiled Troyland, … , and let the others return to Argos, … and Achaea (*Il.* 3.71–75).

Philoteta kai horkia pista: this formulaic expression is repeated by both sides as many as three times (*Il.* 3.94, 256, 323), announcing the solemn accord that establishes first the celebration of a decisive duel (*monomachia*) and afterwards a new bond of friendship (*philotes*) between the contracting parties.[10] Agamemnon and Priam, the supreme leaders, grant their consent to the proposal and execute the oaths, the sacrifices, the pouring of libations (*spondai*), and the shaking of hands that sanction the pact, taking the gods as their witnesses and guarantors.[11] The process, however, will be suspended by the intervention of Aphrodite, who carries Paris away from the battlefield in the very moment of his defeat. It seems important to underline that, at this point, because none of the contracting parties is involved in the goddess' ploy,[12] the agreement has not yet been invalidated irreversibly. Zeus knows this and therefore continues to seek the possibility of a solution: "But surely victory rests with Menelaus, dear to Ares" – a thoroughly just ruling.

> Let us therefore take thought how these things are to be; whether we shall again rouse evil war (*polemon*) and the dread din of battle, or place friendship (*philoteta*) between armies. If this should in any way be welcome and sweet to all, then might the city of king Priam still be inhabited, and Menelaus might take back Argive Helen.[13]

A wise judge, the father of the gods makes a legally impeccable analysis of the situation: either leave things as they were, continuing with the hostilities, or conclude the accord in favor of the Achaeans (but with the unforeseen survival of the loser in the duel). The latter is Zeus' preferred option, because it leaves Troy safe, while at the same time preventing either of the two provokers of this absurd war from getting away completely with their own designs: Menelaus recovers Helen, but fails to avenge himself by killing Paris (a perfect *kadi* justice, as Max Weber would say). Nevertheless, the agreed-upon *philotes* will not be realized because Hera resists adamantly, sways her husband, and sends Athena to convince Pandarus to shoot his arrow at Menelaus, thus making the Trojans "the first in defiance of their oaths."[14]

The *Odyssey* concludes with a successful negotiation of a pact of reconciliation and friendship (*philotes*) to bring definitive resolution to an armed conflict. Odysseus returns to Ithaca and butchers without mercy all of Penelope's suitors who have defiled his house and squandered his possessions. In exacting vengeance, the hero has been assisted by Athena, who is nevertheless the first in attempting to restore peace to the community of Ithaca and to root out the insurrection of the dead suitors' relatives against the king and his house. The danger for Odysseus is all the more serious as the conflict exceeds the borders of his homeland and, since some of the fallen hail from "other *poleis*" (24.418), acquires an international character. Athena now proposes to Zeus the alternative that he himself had considered at Troy: "Will you still further bring to pass evil war and the dread din of battle, or will you establish friendship (*philoteta*) between the two sides?" (*Od.* 24.475–6). Zeus' answer confirms the judicial wisdom of the king of the gods:

> Do as you will, but I will tell you what is fitting. Now that noble Odysseus has taken vengeance on the suitors, let them swear a solemn oath, and let him be king all his days, and let us on our part bring about a forgetting of the killing of their sons and brothers; and let them love one another as before, and let wealth and peace (*eirene*) abound (24.481–86).

Athena judiciously follows Zeus' counsel: after a mock attack that causes the death of Eupeithes – the inconsolable father of one of the leaders of the suitors and head of the uprising – the goddess imposes on both sides the exchange of oaths validating the accord of reconciliation.

The vocabulary employed in this episode speaks eloquently to one of the fundamental principles of Greek international law in the archaic and classical periods. For the agreement as such, Zeus uses the technical term *horkia pista*,[15] while the resulting legal relationship is defined as *philotes*, friendship in a positive and institutional sense. The immediate and basic consequence of this solemn covenant is the return of *eirene* to Ithaca, but technically this word neither designates the new relationship between the parties nor the legal instrument itself. Typologically, the pact reached is not an agreement of peace, but rather of friendship, from which the reality of *eirene* derives logically, with all its benefits (beginning with *ploutos*, wealth, its inseparable companion).[16] The idea of peace, therefore, does not figure in the legal culture of early Greece as an institutional category *per se*, as an independent legal concept, but rather as a state produced by a conventional relationship of *philotes* (or, later, *philia*). Not only is Greek thought incapable of conceiving of peace as a natural and universal right of all peoples (barbarians and Hellenes); as yet it cannot even conceive of peace as a legal relationship in and of itself. Peace must be enveloped and supported by a stronger bond with a bilateral character: friendship (which in this period can entail mutual assistance in warfare).[17]

3. A completely positive and conventional relationship with a foreign community can in principle be reached by means of two institutions: exogamic matrimony (*gamos*) and guest friendship (*xenia*). Both of these ties create friendship and eventually military alliance between two kings or Homeric nobles from different communities (Finley 1977: 98ff.). If the wife who is handed over may be considered in a certain sense a token of the *philotes* between father-in-law and son-in-law, the figure of the guest friend (*xenos*) is intimately associated in Homeric language with the notion of *philos* and the emotional and legal values of friendship (Benveniste 1969: I, 341, 345). For this reason,

the verb *philein* expresses the conduct required of an individual who welcomes the *xenos* into his home and treats him according to ancestral customs (perfectly expressed in *Il.* 3.207). Moreover, it is not uncommon to seal a *xenia* (or a *philotes*) with matrimony, reinforcing the friendship between sides (*FGrHist* 26 F1; *Il.* 9.285–90). The classic scene illustrating the early *xenia*'s great potential is found in the *Iliad*, when Glaucus of Lycia and Diomedes of Argos shake hands upon recognizing one another as *xenoi* before the walls of Troy. Although one is an ally of Priam and the other of Agamemnon, they refuse to fight as enemies and instead exchange gifts in the middle of battle with the aim of renewing the guest friendship they inherited from their parents (*Il.* 6.119–231). It was precisely Paris' violation of the law of hospitality, with his abduction of Helen, that unleashed the Trojan War (Hdt. 2.115). Myth and legend offer other instances of similar transgressions, while also illuminating the great capacity of *xenia* for diplomatic mediation. For example, Antenor, the Trojan noble hosting Menelaus and Odysseus in his home when they arrive as ambassadors to negotiate a deal and avoid the war (*Il.* 3.207), will later be the first to argue before Priam and the assembly for the return of Helen and for reconciliation (7.347–53). His actions cannot but remind us of the functions of the *proxenos*, a sort of "consul," representing in one Greek city the interests of another, who later on the public level will replace the old *xenos* (Gschnitzer 1973: 632).

The institutions of international law that develop in the seventh and sixth centuries are directly derived from these experiments and achievements of early Greece that are reflected in the epics. In the Homeric world, the contracting subjects are always individuals, the kings, whose words bind the community as a whole: it is not the Cretans who conclude the alliance with the Argives, but rather Idomeneus who joins the king of Mycenae to fight against Troy; nor is it the Trojans or the Achaeans who ratify Paris' proposal, but Priam and Agamemnon. Which is not to say that their peers – those nobles who are also called *basileis* – and the people (*demos*) are marginalized in decisions concerning war and peace (Carlier 1991). In matters that are vital to them all, the members of the council are consulted by the king (Gschnitzer 2001: 199–211), and the men in the assembly make their voices heard through their shouts of consent or disagreement (Raaflaub 1997). These are the origins of war as an institution, that is, organized interstate violence, subjected to legal and political norms and differentiated from banditry and piracy (Ilari 1980: 41; Nowag 1983: 94ff.).

That the actors in inter-state relations were individuals and not the entire citizen body remained typical until the Hellenistic period of states and cities that were less developed politically or ruled by monarchs. Thus the tyrants in the archaic epoch were recognized as contracting parties by the other states: Thrasybulus of Miletus, for example, reached an agreement of reconciliation (*diallage*) with his enemy, the Lydian king Alyattes, in which "they agreed to be guest friends (*xeinous*) and allies (*symmachous*) of one another" (*StV* 105); Polycrates of Samos formed bonds of *xenia* with pharaoh Amasis of Egypt (*StV* 117); Peisistratus of Athens made an alliance with the Thessalians (*StV* 108). However, with the triumph of the idea of the *polis* and the transfer of sovereignty to the citizen body – both in oligarchies and democracies – a general change took place. As international relations were in this way "politicized," treaties were fixed in writing and publicly exhibited on monuments of stone and other materials; moreover, such displays were not confined to the cities involved but, for enhanced effect and publicity, also extended to the large panhellenic sanctuaries. Along with oral and customary traditions – that are historically the first source of international law – an ever more flexible and technical written law began developing as an expression of an ever more diversified and autonomous will to conclude contractual agreements.[18] Corresponding phenomena within the *polis* obviously were the codification of internal law and the appearance of great legislators (van Effenterre and Ruzé 1994; Hölkeskamp 1999), and in this sense every diplomatic instrument could also be considered a legal instrument. The sixth century represented a turning point in this process, as demonstrated in extant documents.

Toward the middle of that century King Croesus of Lydia entered into diplomatic relations with Sparta, the leading power in Greece, negotiating a pact of *xenia* and *symmachía* that was in line with the traditional uses of guest friendship. Nonetheless there were two differences: this pact incorporated a diplomatically more modern concept of military alliance, and it designated as the contracting party no longer the two Spartan kings, but rather the Lacedaemonians in their function as a sovereign political entity (*StV* 113). The old terminology is maintained on a bronze plate that the Sybarites and the Serdaioi deposited at Olympia prior to 510, establishing *philotes* "forever" (*StV* 120), that is to say, a pact of friendship that, I believe, put an end to hostilities between the Achaean colony and its Italic neighbors. This was surely the case with Cyrene and Amasis, who concluded a treaty of *philotes* and *symmachía* around 565, following upon the previous pharaoh's invasion of the territory of the Greek city.[19] We know from another bronze plate that the priests of Olympia intervened actively to facilitate a settlement of *philia* of 50 years' duration between two Elean communities, the Anaitoi and the Metapioi (*StV* 111); the covenant surely signaled the end of a period of confrontation between the contracting parties and established an arbitration procedure to resolve future differences between them (Gschnitzer 1973: 636–37). Significantly, interpersonal *xenia* became an increasingly antiquated way of designating and articulating relations between two civic collectivities; it was replaced by the more abstract and neutral terms *philotes* or *philia*.[20]

In all these interstate treaties we find a confirmation of the general principles governing the laws of peace and war in Greece since the Dark Age: from a non-existent relationship groups could arrive at a state of friendship (with the rather attractive possibility of an alliance) or they could go to war, after which they could also achieve definitive reconciliation, again by means of a friendship treaty. This fundamental distinction was maintained to the end of the Hellenistic age. In the most critical moment of diplomatic contacts between Antiochus III of Syria and Rome, which began at the no-relationship level, the Seleucid king's ambassadors proposed to the Roman senate a treaty of alliance and friendship (*philia kai symmachia*).[21] The agreement failed and war broke out, but the peace treaty concluded after the decisive victory of the Romans at Apamea (188) consecrated a new relationship precisely of *philia* "forever" between the two parties.[22]

Steps on the Way to Open War (*phaneros polemos*)

War, then, did not represent the primary and normal state of affairs between Greeks, but was just one of several normal and legitimate ways of relating to one another.[23] War represented an institutionalized procedure for settling differences and imposing decisions and sanctions at the international level; from the Homeric period, it coexisted with diplomacy and was increasingly subject to a series of rules and limitations. In general, the outbreak of hostilities was preceded by diplomacy in order to avoid, if possible, a military confrontation (which almost always proved very costly in human and economic terms). The essential functions of such diplomacy were prevention, dissuasion, and arbitration; the diplomatic agents working towards these ends often continued to operate once an armed conflict had begun. They included primarily the consul (*proxenos*), the arbiter (*diallaktes*), and the ambassador (*presbys*). At least in theory, Greek international law sought to limit the use of force in two respects: concerning the right to resort to war (*ius ad bellum*), and the laws of war (*ius in bello*). The institutionalization of war required that lines were drawn separating it from the state of peace and from other forms of violence (legitimate or not), and, in particular, that the condition of open war (*phaneros polemos*) was clearly defined.

A characteristic feature of Greek international law, at least until the third century, resided precisely in its definition of the state of open war, distinct from that of indirect war. *Phaneros polemos* between cities or federal states was considered an irreversible fact when one side had invaded another's territory (*chora*). The crossing of borders, that is to say, direct aggression against a community, constituted the reason for war and alliance (*casus belli* and *casus foederis*) par *excellence* among the Greeks. We have already heard Achilles express this idea very clearly: between his people and Troy there existed no cause for enmity, no Trojans had invaded his land to destroy crops or steal livestock. Conversely, King Cleomenes III of Sparta became the open enemy of the Achaeans when he used military force to occupy a place in the territory of Megalopolis (Pol. 2.46.6–7), thus causing the Cleomenic War (229/8-222). Such direct aggression is the only sort prohibited by post-war non-aggression treaties (long-term *spondai*) and treaties of friendship and alliance. For example, the *symmachia* of 367 between Athens and Dionysius I of Syracuse reads, "It shall not be permitted for an attack to be made by Dionysius or his descendants against the territory of the Athenians with hostile intent, either by land or by sea."[24] These legal instruments also regulated the conditions of alliance (*casus foederis*), which in any case were met by an outside attack against the allied territory: "If anyone comes against the land of the Athenians for the purpose of making war either by land or by sea, assistance shall be given by Dionysius and his descendants."[25] Shortly before the so-called "War of the Allies" (220–217) broke out, the *casus foederis* alleged by the Achaeans before the Hellenic coalition presided over by Philip V (*StV* 507) was that the Aetolians had invaded the confederation's territory (Pol. 4.15.1–2). Furthermore, nothing prevented two allied cities from fighting one another in the territory of a third party, in fulfillment of another contractual obligation: after the victory at Leuctra (371), the Athenians concluded a *symmachia* with the Spartans in 369 (*StV* 274) to put an end to Thebes' dominance, but in 366 they negotiated another alliance treaty with the Arcadians (*StV* 284), who for their part were in open war with Sparta because of their participation in the invasion of Laconia by Epaminondas. The Athenian assembly approved this second treaty because of the diplomatic benefit it brought (Xen. *Hell.* 7.4.2), and Sparta did not cancel its pact with the Athenians.[26]

Relations between Athens and Sparta during the (so-called) Peace of Nicias (*StV* 188), concluded in 421 after the first phase of the Peloponnesian War, are even more illuminating. The fact that the two cities had also forged an alliance between themselves (*StV* 189) proved no obstacle when, three years later in the battle of Mantinea, the Athenians and Lacedaemonians fought one another alongside their respective *symmachoi* (Thuc. 5.66ff.); nor was this an impediment for the Athenian deployment of Messenians and helots at Pylos with orders to ravage Spartan territory (5.56.3) – not to mention repeated violations of the stipulated terms of their agreement that were mutually tolerated (5.48.1; 56.3). For this reason Thucydides says:

> For six years and ten months the two powers abstained from invading each other's territory; in other regions, however, there was only an unstable cessation of arms and they kept on doing each other the greatest possible damage. But at last they were forced to break the treaty which had been concluded after the first ten years, and again engaged in open war (*polemon phaneron*, 5.25.3).

The breaking of *spondai* and the eruption of the Decelean War were results of an offensive action which was relatively unimportant from a military point of view but decisive from a legal standpoint: a raid against some Laconian communities perpetrated by the Athenian fleet in the summer of 414 (6.105.1). It was these thirty ships that "in the most clear way" (*phanerotata*) broke the state of peace: "For before this," comments Thucydides (6.105.2),

> the Athenians waged the war in cooperation with the Argives and Mantineans by predatory excursions from Pylos and by making landings round the rest of the Peloponnesus rather than in Laconia; and although the Argives frequently urged them only to make a landing with arms on Laconian territory, devastate in concert with them even the least part, and then go away, they refused.[27]

Things were simpler when military aid was lent to an ally fighting against a third state with whom peaceful relations were maintained by means of a post-war non-aggression treaty (long-term *spondai*), or against a state with whom there was no relationship at all. Let us take the well-known example of the events leading to the Peloponnesian War (431–404). Athens was able to ally itself with Corcyra (*StV* 161) in 433 and defend Corcyra against Corinth's attacks in the battle of Sybota despite the fact that the 30 Years' Peace of 446 between the Delian and Peloponnesian Leagues was still in force (*StV* 156). In order to avoid breaking this treaty, which included Corinth as an ally of Sparta, a specific type of alliance (called *epimachia*) was concluded between Athenians and Coryraeans, in which the contracting parties committed themselves to the defense of their respective territories and allies (Thuc. 1.44.1), while excluding their participation in offensive military campaigns (1.45.3). Accordingly, during the naval clash at Sybota the Athenian triremes limited themselves to repelling attacks against the Corcyraean fleet, but did not threaten the territory of Corinth or its allies (1.48–54). Hence the state of peace between Athens and the Peloponnesians was formally preserved (1.55.2, 66), even though henceforth Athens' relations with Corinth were strained and as a result also those with Sparta. When in the spring of 431 the Thebans decided on their own to attack Plataea, *eirene* was still intact on the Athenian side between the Peloponnesian and Delian Leagues (2.2.3).

The Corinthian War (395–386) offers an equally, or perhaps even more, eloquent testimony of this sort of situation. To my knowledge, scholars have generally supposed that Athens (and Argos) entered into war with Sparta and its allies in 395, without ever pausing first to consider in what type of conflict they were getting involved (Alonso 1999). The Athenians (as well as the Argives) entered a treaty of *symmachia* with the Boeotians in 395 (*StV* 223) and, not long thereafter, with the Corinthians (*StV* 224, l. 2), and they did, in effect, come to blows with the Peloponnesians at Coronea (in 394) in defense of Boeotia, and at Nemea (in 394) in defense of Corinth (*casus foederis par excellence*). But the direct war against Attica began only after 389, as a consequence of the failure of negotiations in 392–391, and, above all, of the Athenians' initiation of *phaneros polemos* at sea, as specified by Xenophon (*Hell.* 5.1.1), who reaches here Thucydidean quality. The Spartans were true masters in the art of economizing their forces, exposing themselves to a minimum of risk while achieving a maximum of results; indirect war afforded them a certain amount of relations (*epimeixia*) with third parties and, most importantly, allowed them to avoid the terrible danger of enemy counter-attacks in Laconian or Messenian territory (which Athens could very well have done from the sea, and why it did not do so is indeed a crucial question).[28]

What, then, were the established procedures for initiating *phaneros polemos*? In modern international law a simple diplomatic act is sufficient to establish a new legal relationship between two states: "A declaration of war is made by means of a unilateral notification to the other (...). The notification takes effect upon receipt. Thereupon a state of war comes into existence, without the need for subsequent military action."[29] Hence, the commencement of war in the legal sense does not need to coincide with the actual commencement of hostilities. However, things were neither so simple nor so profane in the ancient world, where wars were frequently initiated by ritual ceremonies. The Romans, for example, had an elaborate mechanism for maintaining a just cause in commencing war (the traditional rites of the *ius fetiale*, Livy 1.32). The Greeks could have agreed with us that war in the legal sense begins at the time when a legally recognized state of war comes into existence, that is to say, when the laws of war – the *nomoi tou polemou* of Polybius 5.11.3 – replace the law of peace in relations between the parties. But this definition certainly would have seemed insufficient to them, because it ultimately corresponds to the current state of our culture that conceives of law, like economy and the market, as an autonomous sphere, while antiquity did not produce anything approximating a "pure theory of law" or "principles of economics." Rather, representative thinkers like Herodotus, Xenophon, or Plutarch would have added that the transition from *eirene* to *polemos* also constituted a religious act, as it implicated certain changes in the war parties' relations with the gods – beginning with the divinities protecting the places that were to be attacked or crossed by the army. Hence the declaration of a war, a practice considered mandatory among the Greeks,[30] assumed a character *sui generis* or, to put it differently, was inserted in and conditioned by a group of rites of passage (or crossing) that could be more or less strict according to the religious customs of each *polis*.

Fourth century Sparta still mounted a veritable sacred and political spectacle when hostilities were to begin – in this sense King Agesilaus best embodied the ideal Spartan citizen (Spartiate). Following the failure of diplomatic negotiations with the other party and the assembly's approval of the armed conflict (which was not equivalent to a declaration of war nor did it necessarily imply breaking *epimeixia*), came the order, forwarded by the ephors to one of the king-priests, to mobilize the army. Mobilization was possible as long as the Spartans had not accepted a sacred truce for the Olympian, Isthmian, Pythian, or Nemean games and there was no conflict with the Karneia and Hyakinthia, two religious festivals of the Dorian-Spartan calendar which imposed an interruption of hostilities.[31] The king, who commanded the army, performed border-crossing sacrifices (*diabateria*) upon leaving Laconia; he also paid close attention to signs and portents (e.g. an earthquake) that might necessitate the campaign's interruption. During the campaign he received all embassies arriving from the adversary and transmitted ultimatums through such embassies, hoping (sometimes successfully) that the other side would yield at the last moment. Before entering enemy territory and thereby making the *phaneros polemos* manifest, the king appealed to the gods and heroes of the other country (*epitheiasmos*).[32]

In Greece, as in Rome, the passage of time and the expansion and increasing complexity of the international stage in the Hellenistic period led to the simplification of the formalities that preceded the start of hostilities and determined how a campaign was conducted. Polybius (13.3) laments the disappearance of the old customs of honest and noble war, above all censuring the Aetolians and their "politics of plunder" (Scholten 2000). This complaint echoes the nostalgia of Demosthenes (9.47–51), who was infuriated by the new methods employed by Philip II. Of course, there is a certain irony to the fact that the Athenians, of all people, reproached the Macedonian monarch for dehumanizing war, when it had been Athenian imperialism in the fifth century that had completely revolutionized traditional warfare (Meier 1990: 583; Hanson 2001). In reality, as we know all too well, criticism against violations of international law, whether in the form of undeclared war (*anepangeltos polemos*) or mistreatment of the conquered (Ducrey 1968) or any other sort, continue to the present day. Nostalgia for gentlemanly forms of battle has a long history, from at least as early as Xenophon to Katsumoto, most quixotic of all. Still in the first century AD, Onasander in a treatise about the good general insisted "that he should call heaven to witness that he is entering upon a war without offence" (*Strat.* 4.3).

All of this definitely contradicts the supposition that it was simple and easy for the Greeks to unleash *phaneros polemos*. The concept of open war served concrete purposes and had a teleological explanation. As already noted by Bickerman (1950: 125ff.), within an extremely fragmented political map, comprised mostly of dwarf states beset by endemic contentiousness and engaged in multiple sets of alliances, the limiting of *casus belli* and *casus foederis* helped preserve the state of peace between cities whose territories had not been attacked by armies.[33] The "philosophy" behind all this might be summarized as follows: if war is indeed frequently inevitable, let us limit it in space, delay its outbreak for as long as possible, leave a wide margin for diplomacy, and, once it begins, establish generally accepted formal procedures (such as truces, capitulations, and the protection of heralds) that will allow us to maintain relations between belligerent parties. In fact, *phaneros polemos* represented an extreme in a wide spectrum of legitimate uses of force in international relations. Excepting piracy, considered by most an illegal activity, the scale of tensions might be summarized as follows:

1   Diverse forms of private extralegal violence (self-help) were tolerated by Greek international custom in cases in which there were no agreements of legal assistance between two cities (*symbola*), that is to say, conventions offering non-violent, judicial means of settling claims between their respective citizens. Self-help meant in some cases the right to engage in reprisals (*sylan, rhysiazein*) against every fellow citizen of the debtor.[34] These were actions between individuals, and as such clearly distinguished from war, as specified by Polybius (22.4.15).

2   The right to raiding on land and sea conceded by public authority to private individuals under its jurisdiction against the citizens and territory of another state (*to laphyron epikeryttein*) was a kind of paramilitary action that was normally proclaimed either as a preliminary measure just before a war (Pol. 4.26.7, 4.53.2) or at the start of one (Pol. 4.36.6; Xen. *Hell.* 5.1.1). This proclamation did not necessarily produce open war between the parties (Thuc. 5.115.2), did not involve the mobilization of the citizen army, and cannot be considered an official declaration of war.[35]

3   Indirect war in the territory of a third party, as we have seen, did not cause a state of war between all parties engaged in such fighting. Obviously, indirect war did not require that war be declared or justified through diplomatic channels to the ally's enemy.

4   For open war (*phaneros polemos*) an announcement or declaration of war was required.

Long-term *spondai* and Peace Treaties (*koine eirene*)

Pataikos, a character in Menander's early Hellenistic comedy *Perikeiromene* ("Rape of the Locks"), says at the end of the work: "I greatly like your 'I'll make it up'. Accepting a fair settlement when you've been lucky – that's a mark of Greek behavior!" This does not differ much from Phoenix's advice to Achilles to make peace with Agamemnon in exchange for compensation for the offenses committed against his honor (*Il.* 9.496–605). Achilles' problem, in terms of modern sociology, is that he was completely unadapted, an absolutely heroic character who in some sense lived in conflict with the very idea of social contract. Hence his accord with Priam took place at the margins of the coalition, as a strictly private act, almost an act of natural law. Now,

Achilles obviously was an exceptional case. The distance between him and Pataikos is greater than that separating Roland from any bourgeois in the comedies of Molière. Ultimately, internal tensions within each *polis* needed to be controlled by some sort of arrangement; the same is true of corresponding tensions on the international level in the wide spectrum of conflicts just enumerated.

What is characteristic of the Hellenic experience, as already suggested, is that in order to discover the idea of peace as an autonomous legal category, international law had to take a roundabout route. Agreements in the form of *spondai*, which guaranteed *eirene* only for a specified period, were probably the diplomatic procedure adopted by Sparta in its relations with some cities that joined the Peloponnesian League after a military confrontation. In the fifth century, as demonstrated above all by the period of the so-called Peace of Nicias (421–414), the formula *spondai* or *spondai + symmachia* became the standard diplomatic model.

Before the Persian Wars in the early fifth century, Greece presented a panorama of local, seasonal, and quantitatively limited warfare. Scholars have often stressed the ritual, agonistic, and symbolic (although no less bloody) character of archaic land warfare.[36] Changes occurred, however, as a consequence of the challenges of the confrontation with Persia in 480–79, which represents the first globalization of the phenomenon of war in Greek history. Xerxes' invasion had a positive effect insofar as a great diplomatic effort was required to reconcile rivaling cities and unite forces in a great coalition under the hegemony of Sparta: the "Hellenic League" (*StV* 130; Brunt 1993: 47–83). In response to the globalization of war by the Achaemenid empire, the Greeks made a first attempt at globalizing the state of peace among themselves (Hdt. 7.145.1; Plut. *Them.* 6.3). Athens and Aegina, for example, had to settle their long-standing differences under Sparta's mediation, while the coalition's ambassadors opened negotiations to induce Argos to join the alliance, although the Argives preferred neutrality (Alonso 2001). We know that Argos then proposed to Sparta to agree on *spondai* for 30 years to terminate the old confrontation over Cynuria (Hdt. 7.148.4–149.2). I suggest that the Argive proposal copied an accord reached toward the middle of the sixth century between Tegea and Sparta (*StV* 112), the starting point of the "Peloponnesian League." Just as this league became the nucleus of the Hellenic League (Baltrusch 1994: 34–35), so must the Argives have been inspired by the Tegean model of relations with Sparta: post-war *spondai* as the basis of their *symmachia*, with both *spondai* and *symmachia* forming a single diplomatic instrument.

With the victory over Persia and the birth of the "Delian League" in 478–77 under the hegemony of Athens (*StV* 132), a dynamic interplay of power blocs emerged in Greek history. Sparta and the Peloponnesians observed a prudent moderation in their dealings with Athens until 461, when a regional conflict erupted in the Saronic Gulf that dragged the two superpowers into open war (beginning in 457). In a first attempt to resolve this conflict, in 451 the two sides agreed upon *spondai* for just five years (*StV* 143), essentially keeping swords drawn and ready. Taking advantage of this diplomatic opportunity, Pericles announced the convocation of a great Panhellenic Congress to ensure free navigation and peace among all parties (Plut. *Per.* 17, with comments by Stadter 1989: 201ff.). Perhaps this ambitious idea, which was crushed by the Peloponnesians' mistrust, was the first attempt to achieve something akin to a "general peace" (*koine eirene*) between the Hellenes. In any case, the Spartans and their allies invaded Attica when the pact of 451 expired, which left the dispute unresolved and eventually necessitated the negotiation of a balanced and realistic accord. The treaty of the "Thirty Years' Peace" of 446/5 recognized the Athenian empire, while at the same time confirming the Spartan coalition's dominance on the Greek mainland (*StV* 156). This excellent diplomatic instrument acknowledged the right to neutrality and prescribed arbitration for the resolution of differences between the contracting parties, but still failed to stabilize the Greek political map. Only 15 years later, in 431, the Peloponnesian War (431–404) broke out. It is worthwhile to read Thucydides' first book and draw our own conclusions about whether or not this "Great War" was inescapable (see also Tritle, this vol.). The so-called Peace of Nicias (421) was technically based on *spondai* for 50 years and a subsequent *symmachia* between Athens and Sparta. Rather than resolving conflicts, it only succeeded in further muddling international relations, until Sparta finally achieved victory.

It was only after the Corinthian War that Greek diplomacy managed to create a new institution of international law that overcame the provisional nature of treaties in the form of *spondai*. This was the *koine eirene*. In 386 the "King's Peace" (*StV* 242) inaugurated a series of common peace treaties, ranging over 50 years, leading to the "League of Corinth" in 337 (*StV* 403), and even inspiring the foundation of the Hellenic League under Antigonus and Demetrius in 303/2 (*StV* 446). Successively adapted and refined, these general peace treaties contain fundamental changes: the diplomatic instrument is designated as *eirene* and is now formally and properly a peace treaty; as in the modern law of nations, the peace treaty is concluded for an unlimited duration and therefore politically and legally terminates war. It is therefore not restricted to simply containing the conflict while leaving open the possibility of an eventual renewal of hostilities after the accord's expiration (as usually occurred with long-term *spondai*);[37] the pact ceases to be bilateral, restricted to two parties, and becomes genuinely multilateral, extending to all Greek states (whether adherent to the pact or not); it consecrates as universal the principle of *polis* autonomy; and beginning with the common peace concluded at Athens in 371, the contracting parties also swear to a guarantee-clause which obliges all parties to ward off with arms any assault against these agreements of peace and independence.[38] Politically and legally, this was, without doubt, the first great diplomatic movement in the history of Greece to organize peace on a general level.[39]

Notes

1 Martin 1940: 7ff. offers a good introduction to the general conditions of Greek international life. For *stasis*, see Gehrke 1985. Translations of Greek authors are taken from the Loeb Classical Library (A. T. Murray for Homer, C. F. Smith for Thucydides).

2 See, for example, Adcock and Mosley 1975: 14ff.; Ilari 1980: 373ff., and, masterfully, Will 1979–82.

3 "Trop souvent on commet l'erreur qui consiste à identifier l'histoire du droit international
   et l'histoire des idées sur ce droit" (Schwarzenberger), cited by Bierzanek 1960: 121;
   cf. Martin 1940: 493, 585ff.

4 The pouring of libations (to the gods) served to seal an agreement between belligerents;
   by extension it referred to the diplomatic instrument solemnized by the libation: Baltrusch
   1994: 92ff.

5 See Santi 1985 for the vocabulary. For an accurate account, see Heuss 1946: 56 n.18;
   Fernández 1975: I, 94 n.3; Bravo 1980: 977ff. Ilari 1980: 38ff. Baltrusch 1994: 94 n.2.

6 Schmitt 1983: 33; Baltrusch 1994: 94. See also Paradisi 1974: 312 (with a quotation of
   Rousseau); Nowag 1983: 99–100.

7 Mele's masterful book (1979) is indispensable on this subject.

8 On these customs and institutions, see Bierzanek 1960; Wéry 1967; Ducrey 1968;
   Fernández 1975: II, nos. 1–7, 14–16; Nowag 1983: 98–99, 107ff.; Baltrusch 1994:
   97 n.30, 104ff.; and, especially, Karavites 1992.

9 Glotz 1904: 135ff., 151–52; Trümpy 1950: 183–84. See also Benveniste 1969: I, 342–44,
   and Karavites 1992: 18ff.

10 As noted, correctly, by Baltrusch 1994: 105, 112.

11 *Il.* 4.245ff., 267ff.; 4.158–59. In the Achaean assembly Agamemnon had already
   mentioned the possibility of agreeing to *horkia pista* with the Trojans: *Il.* 2.123–4.

12 After all, the gods cannot violate a pact of which they themselves are named guarantors.
   Cf. also Karavites 1992: 69 n.45.

13 *Il.* 4.14–19. Meanwhile, the combatants have realized that Paris' disappearance is Zeus'
   doing and that his fate will determine whether the war is to go on or peace to be restored
   (4.82–84).

14 *Il.* 4.67, 72; 7.351–2: cf. Fernández 1975: II, 14; Karavites 1992: 78, 176.

15 "The religious ritual of the *horkia* ceremony prepared the contracting parties to enter into
   the type of binding political friendship which imposed reciprocal obligations and duties
   upon the parties ... *Horkia*, on the other hand, could denote pledges accompanied by
   oaths, pledges accompanied by sacrifice in confirmation of the pledges, the sacred items
   employed in confirmation of the newly established relationship, and, by extension, the
   agreement consecrated by the ceremonial procedure" (Karavites 1992: 65, 76).

16 As in Aristophanes' *Peace* and in the statue of Eirene carrying Ploutos by Kephisodotos:
   Keil 1916: 48; Pritchett 1979: 161.

17 See also Baltrusch 1994: 95 n.13, 124 n.188, 148, 204; Grewe 1997 for the concept of a
   peace treaty.

18 For the normative structure and sources of Greek international law, see Alonso 2003a.

19 Hdt. 2.181.1 (and Hdt. 2.161.4; 4.159.5), not included in Bengtson 1975. As in the case
   of Achaeans and Trojans, the *philotes* agreement closes a period of direct war.

20 This last institution, in reality, socialized the values of guest-friendship: the correspondence
   between *philos* and *xenos* (Benveniste) can be seen, for example, in Hdt. 1.69–70.1 and
   2.182.2; 3.39.2 (Diod. Sic. 1.95.3).

21 Diod. Sic. 28.15.2; App., *Syr.* 6: see Will 1982: II, 197–98.

22 Pol. 21.43.1; App., *Syr.* 38: see Will 1982: II, 221ff.

23 The stance adopted by Polybius (4.31.3) is probably representative of the prevailing
   enlightened circles: "That war is a terrible thing I agree, but it is not so terrible that
   we should submit to anything in order to avoid it."

24 *StV* 280, l. 23–26 (tr. Harding 1985). See also ibid. nos. 188, 193, 201–02, among others.

25 *StV* 280, l. 12–15 (tr. Harding 1985).

26 See Mosley 1974: 49, and the comment by Bengtson 1975: 242. If we take this practice
   of Greek diplomacy into account, Polybius' criticism (4.15.8–11) of the resolution of the
   Aetolian *koinon* is more understandable.

27 See also Thuc. 7.18.2–3, and Busolt 1904: III 2, 1355; Alonso 1987: 38ff.

28 The same question should be asked, conversely, about the reasons for Sparta's inactivity (against Attika) after its victory over Athens at Tanagra in Boeotia in 457.

29 Meng 2000: 1339. The latter was the case in the war between the Latin American states and the German Reich in World War II.

30 See Alonso 1995, and Klose 1972: 148ff.

31 For Spartan delays in the Persian Wars because of the Hyakinthia and other religious scruples, see Hdt. 7.107, 120; 9.7–11.

32 See Popp 1957; Pritchett 1971: 113ff., 116ff.; 1979: 296ff., 322f.; Lonis 1979: 95ff.; Hanson 1991: 202f.; Alonso 1995: 218ff.

33 Even if a direct attack on a state's territory automatically resulted in an immediate state of war between the parties, this would not necessarily preclude the existence of other reasons for going to war. But in such cases the *casus belli* was a subjective determination.

34 See Gauthier 1972: 209ff.; Bravo 1980, and Gauthier's reply 1982.

35 See Ducrey 1968: 4 n.2; Klose 1972: 152 n.659 (against Bengtson 1963: 102); Bravo 1980: 844ff., 858ff. (and Gauthier's comments, 1982: 558ff.); Pritchett 1991: 86ff., 137f. No consensus has been achieved.

36 See Lonis 1979: 25ff.; Connor 1988; Hanson 1989: 27ff., 222f. For a comparative perspective, see Raaflaub and Rosenstein 1999.

37 Unlike Baltrusch 1994: 92ff., 123–24, 187, 192, I do not believe that the expiration of the *spondai* automatically signaled a return to war between the parties; cf. Hampl 1938: 2. The fact that the reasons for the conflict had not disappeared (although they may have become less important with the passage of time), did not negate the obligation to resuscitate the war in accordance with established procedures (discussed earlier). The resulting situation, I think, was a mixture of legal uncertainty and a *de facto* persistence of *epimeixia*. This explains the behavior of Argos in 420, already *aspondos* but sending ambassadors, and not heralds, to Sparta (Thuc. 5.40–1), and treating war as a possible outcome, not an existing state (5.44.1). On the other hand, the Athenian *spondai* (5.47.1: *StV* 193) with the Argives and the Mantineans were not post-war treaties, though those with the Eleans were (Alonso 1987: 154ff., 175ff., 479), and there was by no means any suggestion that hostilities would be renewed between the parties once the 100 years had elapsed.

38 Ryder 1965: xvi; Jehne 1994: 26 n.91, 28; Alonso 2003b.

39 I would like to thank Kurt Raaflaub for his corrections and suggestions on the final draft of this chapter.

Abbreviations

FGrHist	Jacoby 1923-
RE	*Realencyclopädie der classischen Altertumswissenschaft*
StV	Bengtson 1975; Schmitt 1969

References

Adcock, F., and D. J. Mosley. 1975. *Diplomacy in Ancient Greece*. London.

Alonso, V. 1987. *Neutralidad y neutralismo en la guerra del Peloponeso (431–404 a.C.)*. Madrid.

——. 1995. "Ultimatum et déclaration de guerre dans la Grèce classique." In E. Frézouls and A. Jacquemin (eds.), *Les relations internationales*, 211–95. Strasbourg.

——. 1999. "395–390/89 a.C., Atenas contra Esparta: ¿ de qué guerra hablamos?" *Athenaeum* 87: 57–77.

Alonso, V. 2001. "Die neutralen Staaten in den Perserkriegen und das griechische Völkerrecht." In D. Papenfuss and V. M. Strocka (eds.), *Gab es das griechische Wunder?* 365–77. Mainz.

——. 2003a. "L'Institution de l'hégémonie: Entre la coutume et le droit écrit." In G. Thür and F. J. Fernández Nieto (eds.), *Symposion 1999*, 339–54. Cologne.

——. 2003b. "La KOINH EIPHNH del 371 y el sistema griego de alianzas." *Les Etudes Classiques* 71: 353–77.

Baltrusch, E. 1994. *Symmachie und Spondai*. Berlin.

Bengtson, H. 1963. "Bemerkungen zu einer Ehreninschrift der Stadt Apollonia am Pontos." *Historia* 12: 96–104.

—— (ed.). 1975. *Die Staatsverträge des Altertums*, II: *Die Verträge der griechisch-römischen Welt von 700–338 v. Chr.* 2nd ed. Munich.

Benveniste, E. 1969. *Le Vocabulaire des institutions Indo-Européennes*. Paris.

Bickerman, E. 1950. "Remarques sur le droit des gens dans la Grèce classique." *Revue historique de droit français et étranger* 4: 99–127.

Bierzanek, P. 1960. "Sur les Origines du Droit de la Guerre et la Paix." Revue historique de droit français et étranger 38: 83–123.

Bravo, B. 1980. "Sylân." *Annali della Scuola Normale Superiore di Pisa* 10: 675–987.

Brunt, P. A. 1993. *Studies in Greek History and Thought*. Oxford.

Buraselis, K. 1982. *Das hellenistische Makedonien und die Ägäis*. Munich.

Busolt, G. 1904. *Griechische Geschichte bis zur Schlacht bei Chaeroneia*, III. 2. Gotha.

Carlier, P. 1991. "La procédure de décision politique du monde mycénien à l'époque archaïque." In D. Musti (ed.), *La transizione dal miceneo all'alto arcaismo*, 85–95. Rome.

Connor, W. R. 1988. "Early Greek Land Warfare as Symbolic Expression." *Past & Present* 119: 3–29.

Diels, H., and Kranz, W. 1961. *Die Fragmente der Vorsokratiker*, I. 10th ed. Berlin.

Ducrey, P. 1968. *Le Traitement des prisonniers de guerre dans la Grèce antique*. Paris.

Effenterre, H. van, and Ruzé, F. 1994. *Nomima: Recueil d'inscriptions politiques et juridiques de l'archaïsme grec*. 2 vols. Rome.

Fernández Nieto, F. J. 1975. *Los acuerdos bélicos en la antigua Grecia*. Santiago de Compostela.

Finley, M. I. 1977. *The World of Odysseus*. 2nd edn. London.

Gauthier, P. 1972. *Symbola*. Nancy.

——. 1982. "Les saisies licites aux dépens des étrangers dans les cités grecques." *Revue historique de droit français et étranger* 60: 553–75.

Gehrke, Hans-Joachim. 1985. *Stasis. Untersuchungen zu den inneren Kriegen in den griechischen Staaten des 5. und 4. Jh. v. Chr.* Munich.

Glotz, G. 1904. *La solidarité de la famille dans le droit criminel en Grèce*. Paris.

Grewe, W. G. 1997. "Peace Treaties." In Macalister-Smith 2000: 938–46.

Gschnitzer, F. 1973. "Proxenos." *RE* Suppl. XIII: 629–730.

——. 2001. *Kleine Schriften zum griechischen und römischen Altertum*, I. Stuttgart.

Habicht, C. 1997. *Athens from Alexander to Antony*. Cambridge, MA.

Hampl, F. 1938. *Die griechischen Staatsverträge des 4. Jahrhunderts v. Chr.* Leipzig.

Hanson, V. D. 1989. *The Western Way of War: Infantry Battle in Classical Greece*. New York.

——. 1991. *Hoplites: The Classical Greek Battle Experience*. London and New York.

——. 2001. "Democratic Warfare, Ancient and Modern." In D. R. McCann and B. S. Strauss (eds.), *War and Democracy: A Comparative Study of the Korean War and the Peloponnesian War*, 3–33. Armonk.

Harding, P. 1985. *From the End of the Peloponnesian War to the Battle of Ipsus*. Translated Documents of Greece and Rome 2. Cambridge.

Heuss, A. 1946. "Die archaische Zeit Griechenlands als geschichtliche Epoche." *Antike & Abendland* 2: 26–62.

Hölkeskamp, K.-J. 1999. *Schiedsrichter, Gesetzgeber und Gesetzgebung im archaischen Griechenland*. Stuttgart.

Ilari, V. 1980. *Guerra e diritto nel mondo antico.* Milano.

Jacoby, F. 1923–. *Die Fragmente der griechischen Historiker.* Multiple vols. Berlin, then Leiden.

Jehne, M. 1994. *Koine Eirene.* Stuttgart.

Karavites, P. 1982. *Capitulations and Greek Interstate Relations: The Reflection of Humanistic Ideals in Political Events.* Göttingen.

———. 1992. *Promise-Giving and Treaty-Making: Homer and the Near East.* Leiden.

Keil, B. 1916. *EIPHNH: Eine philologisch-antiquarische Untersuchung.* Leipzig.

Klose, P. 1972. *Die völkerrechtliche Ordnung der hellenistischen Staatenwelt in der Zeit von 280–168 v. Chr.* Munich.

Loenen, D. 1953. *Polemos: Een Studie over Oorlog in de Griekse Óudheid.* Amsterdam.

Lonis, R. 1979. *Guerre et religion en Grèce à l'époque classique.* Paris.

Macalister-Smith, P. (ed.). 2000. *Encyclopedia of Public International Law*, III. Amsterdam.

Martin, V. 1940. *La vie internationale dans la Grèce des cités (VIᵉ–IVᵉ s. av. J.-C.).* Paris.

Meier, C. 1990. "Die Rolle des Krieges im klassischen Athen." *Historische Zeitschrift* 251: 555–605.

Mele, A. 1979. *Il commercio greco arcaico: prexis ed emporie.* Naples.

Meng, W. 2000. "War." In Macalister-Smith 2000: 1334–42.

Momigliano, A. 1960. "Some Observations on the Causes of War in Ancient Historiography." In A. Momigliano, *Secondo Contributo alla Storia degli Studi Classici*, 13–27. Rome.

Mosley, D. J. 1974. "On Greek Enemies Becoming Allies." *Ancient Society* 5: 43–50.

Nowag, W. 1983. *Raub und Beute in der archaischen Zeit der Griechen.* Frankfurt.

Paradisi, B. 1974. *Civitas Maxima: Studi di storia del diritto internazionale.* Florence.

Phillipson, C. 1911. *The International Law and Custom of Ancient Greece and Rome.* London.

Popp, H. 1957. *Die Einwirkung von Vorzeichen, Opfern und Festen auf die Kriegführung der Griechen im 5. und 4. Jahrhundert v. Chr.* Erlangen.

Pritchett, K. 1971, 1979, 1991. *The Greek State at War*, I, III, V. Berkeley.

Raaflaub, K. 1997. "Politics and Interstate Relations in the World of Early Greek *Poleis*: Homer and Beyond." *Antichthon* 31: 1–27.

Raaflaub, K., and Rosenstein, N. (eds.). 1999. *War and Society in the Ancient and Medieval Worlds. Asia, the Mediterranean, Europe, and Mesoamerica.* Cambridge, MA.

Redfield, J. M. 1975. *Nature and Culture in the Iliad: The Tragedy of Hector.* Chicago.

Ryder, T. T. B. 1965. *Koine Eirene.* Oxford.

Santi Amantini, L. 1985. "Semántica storica dei termini Greci relativi alla pace nelle epigrafi anteriori al 387/6 a.C." In M. Sordi (ed.), *La pace nel mondo antico*, 45–68. Milano.

Schmitt, H. H. 1969. *Die Staatsverträge des Altertums*, III: *Die Verträge der griechisch-römischen Welt von 338 bis 200 v. Chr.* Munich.

———. 1983. "Friedenssicherung im griechischen Völkerrecht." In H. Kreutzer (ed.), *Wendepunkte, Acta Ising 1982*, 31–44. Munich.

Scholten, J. B. 2000. *The Politics of Plunder: Aitolians and their Koinon in the Early Hellenistic Era, 279–217 BC.* Berkeley.

Stadter, Philip A. 1989. *A Commentary on Plutarch's Pericles.* Chapel Hill.

Steiner, G. 1984. *Antigones.* New York.

Trümpy, H. 1950. *Kriegerische Fachausdrücke im griechischen Epos.* Basel.

Wéry, M. 1967. "Le Fonctionnement de la diplomatie à l'époque homérique." *Revue internationale du droit de l'antiquité* 14: 169–215.

Will, E. 1979–1982. *Histoire politique du monde hellénistique (323–30 av. J.-C.).* 2 vols. Nancy.

13

War and Peace, Fear and Reconciliation at Rome

Nathan Rosenstein

The *pax Romana* – the long era of peace that prevailed throughout the ancient Mediterranean under the aegis of Rome's imperial rule during the first and second centuries CE – might seem to make Rome a natural fit for any colloquium on peace and reconciliation. Those who examine the evidence carefully, however, quickly discover that the facts belie the Empire's pacific image. Rome fought plenty of wars between 31 BCE and the early third century CE. Most were defensive in nature, but major conquests were not lacking – Britain under the Emperor Claudius and Dacia under Trajan, who also undertook to overcome the mighty Parthian empire, an endeavor that only his untimely death cut short. Serious conflicts also were waged in Spain, Germany, Armenia, and North Africa. The image of peace in the first three centuries of our era masks an ongoing bellicosity not all that different from the period of Rome's greatest conquests, between the fourth and first centuries BCE, when Romans saw the doors of the temple of Janus, which were closed whenever Rome was at peace, shut precisely twice. It was among the proudest boasts of Rome's first Emperor, Augustus, that during his 45-year reign the temple's doors were closed three times (*Res Gestae* 13). And indeed, the inauguration of Augustus' rule in 31 brought peace, but one that it had taken nearly 20 years of periodic, bloody civil war to achieve. Yet even under Augustus, *pax* is not much in evidence, at least for those beyond Rome's frontiers. For if that emperor thrice closed Janus' temple doors, they did not stay fastened very long. At the end of his long life he recorded a litany of conquests on the inscription he set up in front of his mausoleum to underscore his claim to be Rome's greatest conqueror:

> I extended the boundaries of all the provinces of the Roman people bordering those not subject to our rule … I pacified the Gallic and Spanish provinces and Germany … I subdued the Alps … I sent two armies simultaneously into Ethiopia and Arabia Felix; great numbers of both enemies were killed and many towns fell … I recovered military standards from the Spanish, Gauls, and Dalmatians after defeating them. I forced the

Parthians to return to me the spoils and standards of three Roman armies … I subjected
the Pannonians to the rule of the Roman people and extended the boundaries of Illyricum
to the Danube (*Res Gestae* 26–30; Galinski 1996: 106–07).

If the Romans throughout their history made a lot of war, however, they also made
a lot of peace when those wars concluded. As Virgil famously wrote, "Remember,
Roman, these will be your arts: / to teach the ways of peace to those you conquer, /
to spare defeated people, to tame the proud" (*Aeneid* 6.851-3, tr. Mandelbaum). But
as these lines suggest, and as Carlin Barton argues in her contribution to this volume,
peace to the Romans meant something quite different from modern conceptions. It
was the product of victorious war, something imposed on the vanquished, the product
of surrender, humiliation, and a breaking of the enemy's spirit. *Deditio* ("capitulation")
was its symbol, a ritual act of utter and complete surrender of the vanquisheds' lives
and property into the *fides* – the good faith – of a victorious Roman general. It was a
precarious state. Although accepting an enemy's surrender might imply a moral obligation not to take extreme measures, there were no guarantees. The fate of the *dediticii*
(those who had surrendered) depended totally on the whim of a single man or, at times,
on the collective whim of the Roman senate, who could set them free, sell them into
slavery, or even butcher them as he or they saw fit (Polybius 20.9.10–10.9, 36.4.1–4).

The notion of ending a war on any other terms was anathema to the Romans. During
the Republic's very difficult wars against the Spanish city of Numantia in the 130s BCE,
one Roman commander reached a negotiated settlement with the enemy, but insisted
the Numantines go through a sham surrender because the treaty they were making
would not stand a chance of ratification at Rome without one. Even so, the peace was
rejected when the circumstances of its making came out, and the war went on (Appian,
Iberica 79). Later these same Numantines defeated another Roman general and forced
him to conclude a treaty to save his army. The senate repudiated that agreement, too,
and ceremoniously handed its author, bound and naked, back to the Numantines to
do with as they wished. Interestingly, the general in question, C. Hostilius Mancinus,
spoke in the senate in favor of the bill to turn him over to the enemy and, when the
latter refused to take him, returned to Rome, resumed an honored place in the senate,
and even had a statue made depicting himself being delivered to the enemy. It was a
point of pride to the Romans that they never surrendered, never made peace on any
terms other than the defeat of their enemy, and when Mancinus failed to live up to that
high ideal, he took the only course that honor allowed and willingly sacrificed himself
to nullify the disgrace and religious obligations he had imposed upon the city (Appian,
Iberica 80, 83; Plutarch, *Tiberius Gracchus* 5.1–7.4; Rosenstein 1986). This attitude
persisted long after the Republic's fall and the establishment of a monarchy in its place.
When the emperor Domitian negotiated a settlement with the Dacians that spared the
Romans the cost of a major war in return for modest subsidies to the Dacian king, he
came in for heavy censure: this was not at all in keeping with the Romans' conceptions
of their dignity. Domitian's successor, Trajan, represents the ideal: he renewed the
Dacian wars, and his conquests wiped away what a panegyrist considered the stain of
Domitian's peace (Pliny, *Panegyricus* 11.4–12.4).

t all this really tells us is that the Romans measured war and peace against ...y different yardstick of values than do contemporary Americans or Europeans. The principles involved were articulated and explained long ago by antiquity's greatest student of conflict, Thucydides, who placed in the mouths of the Athenian spokesmen in the Melian Dialogue the chilling sentiment that "right ... is in question only between equals in power, while the strong do what they can and the weak suffer what they must" (5.89, trans. Wick). By that logic, if the Athenians did not conquer the tiny island of Melos, their subjects would take it as a sign of weakness and be led to revolt, endangering not only Athens' empire but the very existence of the city itself, for the Athenians could expect no better treatment at the hands of their subjects than they had meted out to the latter. And so, in 416 BCE the Athenians destroyed Melos, put the men to death, and sold the women and children into slavery (5.116). Not much changed in the ensuing 500 years. By the time Domitian and Trajan reigned, Rome had controlled for nearly three centuries an empire stretching the length and breadth of the Mediterranean. Peace not only beyond its boundaries but also within the empire's confines depended ultimately on the perception of Rome's military might. Rome's British subjects revolted in 61 CE and the Jews of Judea followed suit in 66, 115, and one last time in 131. These and other risings were brutally repressed, but they demonstrate that the rulers of Rome could not take their subjects' contentment with the blessings of the *pax Romana* for granted. As the Roman historian Tacitus has the British war-leader Calgacus famously say during the Empire's conquest of the island, "Theft, slaughter, and plunder they falsely term empire; where they create a wasteland, they call it peace" (*Agricola* 30.6). Likewise, it was largely the certainty of swift and terrible retribution that deterred Rome's neighbors from attacks on the cities and settlements within Rome's borders.

The Romans were imperialists and unapologetic about it, but one should not necessarily condemn them for that. They lived in a very different world from ours, one where violence against individuals as well as between states was much more prevalent than today, something accepted as normal and unavoidable. In the ancient world, no police forces protected the weak against the depredations of the powerful, only the force of moral censure, which might afford very little protection indeed. Nor was there any international organization like the United Nations to guarantee the sanctity of international borders and to step in with peace keeping forces whenever war threatened to break out between (or even within) nations. In a world where the strong did what they could and the weak suffered what they had to, Rome faced a simple choice between being strong and being a victim (Eckstein 2006). Yet there were real limits to Rome's strength. War was expensive to wage, and standing armies costly to maintain. The empire's 400,000–450,000 man military establishment was the finest the ancient world ever knew, incomparably superior to any of its opponents. But even though this force represented only a tiny fraction of the empire's total population, it probably accounted for about half of the government's annual expenditures (Mattern 1999: 82–3, 123–49). That set firm limits on the size of the armies Rome could field and consequently shaped its military posture decisively. For a strategy founded on deterrence to succeed, Rome had to do everything in its power to enhance the perception of its military strength, to prevent challenges from arising that might, if they were numerous enough and came all at once, overwhelm its limited capacity to respond effectively. In that sense, Rome's army was like a modern, urban police force: highly effective against individual criminals or small gangs, but when anarchy threatens, even the best trained and equipped police force can find itself outnumbered and impotent.

It is this fundamental economic constraint on Rome's military capacity that accounts for the stress on vengeance and retribution in Roman thinking about relations with other nations. No slight could be allowed to pass unavenged for fear that the perception of weakness would spawn other challenges that could escalate into a serious threat. Hence, too, the Romans' emphasis on their own prestige and, correspondingly, on the abasement of their opponents. Potential enemies had constantly to be kept mindful of the might and majesty of Rome and of their own weakness and humility in the face of it. The men who ruled the Roman Empire, whether under the Republic or the monarchy, exalted Roman honor and could react with what might seem to us extreme violence to real or perceived affronts. Keeping the peace required teaching other nations to know their place, demonstrating to them in the most unmistakable terms that they would not stand a ghost of a chance against the Roman colossus and that horrible things would happen to them if they were so foolish as to try. As the Roman orator Pliny put it, in lauding the effect of the emperor Trajan (98–117 CE) on the barbarians across the frontiers, "The enemy had lifted up their spirits, they had thrown off the yoke … But now terror is back among them all. They are in fear and beg to be allowed to obey orders" (*Panegyricus* 11.5–12.1). Peace for the Romans, in other words, was founded on the potential violence that kept those weaker than Rome cringing (Mattern 1999: 162–94).

However, long before Rome became this colossus astride the Mediterranean and Europe, things were otherwise. In the earliest period of Rome's history, war wore a different aspect. Rituals constrained violence and marked it off from the ordinary state of peace. When the city or its citizens were wronged by others, priests known as *fetiales* presented formal claims for redress in the offenders' marketplace, a ceremony known as a *rerum repetitio* ("demand for things to be handed back"). If satisfaction was not forthcoming after a specific period of time, the *fetiales* returned to the borders of the enemy and proclaimed that fact. After a vote for war at Rome, they returned a third and final time and ritually declared war by casting a spear into the enemy's territory (Livy 1.32.5–14; Rich 1976: 56–60). The point was to ensure that the war the community of the Romans was about to embark on was a *iustum bellum*, a just war, one that was defensive in nature and in response to wrongs suffered, and so enjoying the support of the gods.

To some scholars these rituals indicate that war in this period was an anomalous interruption in an otherwise general state of peace and that in the *fetiales* Rome and its neighbors possessed an institution for resolving disputes without recourse to violence. Other rituals similarly worked to reinforce the notion of a firm separation between war and peace in early Rome. A physical barrier existed in the ritual boundary that surrounded the city itself, the *pomerium*, within which the carrying of weapons, and so all military activity, was enjoined. The city's leaders in civilian life, the king and, after the establishment of the Republic ca. 509 BCE, elected magistrates known as consuls and praetors, likewise symbolized their separation from the civilian sphere and their assumption of the role of military leader by donning a special military costume, the *paludamentum* or military cloak, and carrying out specific rituals and vows as they left for war (Livy 21.63.9). At a later date, after citizens obtained the right of appeal from a death sentence imposed by a magistrate, the axes in the bundles of rods, the *fasces*, borne by a consul's or praetor's attendants (*lictores*), with which executions were carried out, were removed while the magistrate was in Rome. When he took up a military command, however, the return of the axes to the *fasces* symbolized the power of life and death that a war leader wielded over all those under his command, excepting only Roman citizens (Marshall 1984). And upon assembling his army, a general performed a *lustratio*, a ceremony of purification, before he began his campaign.

The religious calendar reinforced this spatial separation between war and peace. A complex of ceremonies in March – the month of Mars, the god of war among other things – opened the season of warfare: priests danced in archaic military garb, cavalry horses were raced, and the war trumpets were purified. Other rites in October – the sacrifice of a war-horse and the cleansing of the army's weapons – marked its close (Scullard 1981: 82–95, 193–95). The celebration of a triumph, a procession of the army and its general to the temple of Jupiter on the Capitoline hill, the citadel of the city, to offer thanks for victory, likewise signified the termination of a war and a return to peace. Possibly, too, forms of violence short of full-scale war were available to resolve the conflicts of this era, as is suggested by the legend of the Horatii, three brothers who fought as champions for Rome against three brothers from a neighboring city (Livy 1.24.1–25.14). And, it has recently been suggested, conflicts with neighboring groups carried on by clans or bands of condottieri need to be distinguished from full-scale warfare involving the community as a whole (Rawlings 1998).

However, to the extent that this state of generalized peace and delimited space for war existed (and this picture, like nearly everything else touching upon early Rome, is highly conjectural; other scholars on the contrary would argue that war was endemic and islands of peace highly circumscribed), it depended upon the prevalence of a particular kind of warfare that was largely the product of cross-border raiding between neighbors for cattle and other movable booty (Rich 1976: 58). When the nature of Rome's wars changed, the institutions described in the preceding paragraph became far less effective in controlling it. The changes arose, in part, because under its last three kings (ca. 570?–ca. 509; Cornell 1995: 122–27) Rome grew to be a powerful hegemon in west central Italy, leading a coalition of its neighbors, the so-called Latin League, forged through war. Conflict came about less over rivalry, prestige, and booty, and far more to increase power and establish dominance. But even more crucial was the crisis that engulfed the whole region beginning around 475.[1] Overpopulation and famine elsewhere in Italy led to large-scale migrations and displacements throughout the peninsula. Although serious problems with the reliability of our sources make information about events in this period quite unreliable in its particulars, the general outlines of military developments during the fifth and fourth centuries BCE are tolerably clear. Rome along with the other Latin cities began to come under increasingly severe pressure that led to a long series of wars, not only between newcomers and local populations but also even amidst the latter, including Rome, as each city was tempted to make good what it lost to the immigrants at the expense of its neighbors. Institutions such as the *fetiales* that might have worked to prevent war in disputes over cattle rustling or conflicts over border territory were simply inadequate to deal with endemic warfare over something so basic to survival as control of farmland.

Severe social conflicts among the Romans themselves exacerbated this complex inter- and intra-regional crisis. As individual Roman farmers lost land in these wars, they seem to have been forced to turn to their wealthier fellow citizens for assistance. These found themselves able to impose increasingly harsh terms upon the landless as the price of access to the cropland they needed to support themselves and their families, thereby reducing them to a condition of near-servitude. The resentment that this deterioration in social relations engendered found its outlet in a series of general strikes, called *secessiones*, in which ordinary Romans, the plebs, protested the conditions many of them were being forced into by withdrawing from the community and, in particular, refusing to serve in the army (Raaflaub 2005: 196–97). These strikes naturally exacerbated the external threats confronting the city, and Rome faced a crisis that threatened its very existence.

The severity of the situation forced Rome to grapple with the problems of both internal and external peace and reconciliation in new and quite unprecedented ways (Cornell 1995: 265–71, 327–44; Raaflaub 2005). Internally, a series of compromises gradually softened the harshest features of the dependence that landless Romans were being subjected to until this practice was formally abolished in 326. Other compromises slowly opened the doors to the exercise of leadership to wealthier plebeians whom the dominant social group, the patricians, had long excluded from political, military, and religious office-holding. These leading plebeians, having realized that the Republic's troubles beyond its borders made additional manpower and commanders necessary and thus represented their opportunity to gain access to high offices, had put themselves at the head of a movement to organize ordinary plebeians and to use their collective power to ameliorate their lot by withholding military service to enforce their demands. As a result, the patricians were gradually forced to yield on this front, too, and slowly the Roman upper class lost its caste-like character. Wealthy plebeians and patricians not only began to exercise a joint leadership of the community both in the senate and in public offices but also started to intermarry until, by around 300 BCE, the city was ruled by a new aristocracy, the *nobilitas*, that defined itself by birth as well as by service to the community, meaning in large part exemplary service in war (Hölkeskamp 1993).

Fear, therefore, impelled the Romans to find an accommodation with one another in order to achieve social and political peace. They acted out of the simple realization that if they did not make peace among themselves something far worse than the consequences of compromise would befall them all: civil strife, military weakness, and possibly the destruction of Rome itself. This kind of internal peace was something quite different from the peace that ended Roman wars. It was not a mark of triumph, something imposed by the victors to humiliate and degrade the vanquished; instead it represented a yielding on the part of both sides. Significantly, although we recognize this process as one of making civil peace, the Romans did not use the term *pax* for this sort of reconciliation but rather *concordia* or harmony. According to legend, the Romans built a temple in 367 for the goddess *Concordia* to commemorate the end of a particularly important phase of this struggle between patricians and plebeians (Plutarch, *Camillus* 42.1–5).

Similarly, fear seems to have been the fundamental force shaping Rome's dealings with its neighbors in this same period. The city faced the same choice in its diplomacy that it did in its social and political arrangements: the Romans and the other Latin cities could either come to some sort of workable arrangement for cooperation on the basis of a community of interests or be destroyed piecemeal. For Rome, the urgency of forging such an accord was only underscored by the trauma that befell the Republic in 390, when a Gallic raiding party from northern Italy destroyed a Roman army at the Allia River and sacked the city. Rome was forced to buy its freedom, and the episode served ever after as a vivid object lesson of the consequences of military weakness (Livy 5.37.1–48.9; Cornell 1995: 313–18). Over the two centuries between about 500 and 300, Rome constructed a network of alliances with other cities in Latium as well as peoples farther afield, and this coalition not only succeeded in resisting incursions that threatened them all but laid the foundations for the Romans' ultimate success against such formidable opponents as Pyrrhus and Hannibal. Rome's successful coalition-building was exemplary and stands in striking contrast to the fate of Campania, the rich agricultural region to the south of Latium, where the Greeks and Etruscans who peopled the region in the early fifth century were by the close of the fourth all but completely displaced by Oscan-speaking immigrants from the highlands to the east.

Perhaps the most striking example of Rome's ability to make peace and find a basis for reconciliation following conflict lies in its willingness to extend its citizenship to some of those it defeated in war. The first case occurred in 381 at Tusculum, but the most important instance came in the aftermath of the great Latin revolt. The Republic's military might had long depended to a considerable extent on manpower supplied by neighboring Latin towns on the basis of a long-standing treaty of mutual assistance. But the victories this coalition won mainly benefited Rome, and by 341 the Latins had had enough. They rose in revolt but quickly met defeat, and in the after-math, the Roman leadership faced the task of imposing a settlement on its rebellious allies. In a strikingly far-sighted decision they elected to take drastic measures against only a few Latin cities. Rome enrolled many of the others among its own citizens, either with full rights or as half-citizens without vote (Livy 8.14.1–12; Cornell 1995: 347–52; for another alternative, continuous existence as an autonomous ally with specific obligations, see below).

This decision had both long- and short-term implications that need to be under-scored. Although Roman writers of a later age, looking back on this settlement, tended to view it as a remarkable act of generosity on the part of their forebears, they wrote at a time when Roman citizenship bestowed the highly-prized rights and privileges of members of the most powerful state in the Mediterranean (Cicero, *De officiis* 1.35).

In the latter fourth century few Latins would have seen it that way. Instead, their independence was being ended and their individual civic identities terminated. In their place came new and potentially more onerous obligations: military service and the payment of taxes to support Rome's wars. With citizenship also came the opportunity for political participation, it is true, either immediately for those awarded full citizenship, or in prospect for those whose citizen rights did not include the vote. But in practical terms such participation would not translate into substantial power and influence in the Republic for a long while. Election to public office, which brought access to political authority, was very much a matter of alliances and coalition building. New citizens, particularly members of the elite of the former Latin cities – those most interested in influencing the conduct of public affairs – were entering an electoral arena where powerful families already had well-oiled organizations that kept their members, if not on top of the political heap, then consistently in contention for that position. There was very little room for newcomers except in the role of junior partners. But junior partners had their value. Political competition was constant and intense among the Republic's aristocracy. Because the nobility defined itself in large part by public service, and because the paramount service that anyone could render the Republic was leadership, particularly in war, election to the public offices that entailed this responsibility became the *sine qua non* both for entry into the highest circles of the elite and, equally important, for maintaining that status. Every generation of young *nobiles* was expected to equal or if possible better the achievements of its forebears. But there were always more aspirants than offices. The resulting competitiveness among the aristocracy made coalition building imperative, and in return for help to a powerful figure in the form of their and their followers' votes and other forms of political support, newly enfranchised members of the Latin elite could expect to see their own ambitions gradually advanced.

In the short run, therefore, enrollment among the Roman citizenry would not have seemed a terribly desirable outcome to the Latins or any of the other peoples in central Italy who over the course of the fourth and third centuries suffered this fate when they, too, met defeat. But citizenship laid the foundations over the long run for reconciliation between Rome and the limited number of its vanquished enemies upon whom it chose to impose this status. To local aristocrats it offered gradual integration into the ruling circles of a much larger and more powerful state. It gave back to ordinary Latins all of the civil rights they had long enjoyed vis-à-vis Roman citizens (the rights to intermarry, to trade and make binding contracts, and to take up residence in Roman territory) that they lost when their Latin identity was ended. And it replaced that identity with that of Rome, a powerful, increasingly successful regional hegemon. As will be explained below, it further allowed ordinary new citizens as well as their leaders to share in the spoils of the Republic's successful wars. And it also left them a considerable degree of not only political but spiritual autonomy: local cults continued to function at the same time that new citizens were included in those of Rome (Sherwin White 1973: 38–73). Not an ideal solution from the Latins' point of view, perhaps, but certainly better than what could be the fate of a defeated community in the ancient world: butchery of the men and the sale of the women and children

into slavery, and the confiscation of the ancestral land by the victors, as happened at
Melos. Or a highly unfavorable treaty that imposed heavy burdens, particularly the
payment of a money tribute, a demand very difficult to meet for agrarian populations
with limited if any circulation of specie and little participation in a market economy.

The incorporation of new citizens was also smoothed by the Romans' own self-
image. Rome's founders, according to legend, were Romulus and Remus, migrants
from the Latin city of Alba Longa, who gathered a collection of shepherds, outcasts
and vagrants to populate their new city on the site of the seven hills (Livy 1.6.3,
8.4–7). A shortage of women was remedied by what is today called the "Rape of the
Sabine Women," a tale in which the kidnapping of spouses by the first Roman men led
ultimately to the integration of a substantial Sabine contingent into the city and a con-
dominium in rule between Romulus and the Sabine king, Titus Tatius (Livy 1.9.1–16,
11.5–13.8). In other words, the Romans of later generations thought of themselves
as a mixed people from the very beginning, drawn from a variety of sources, and imagining their origins in this way undoubtedly helped them accept newcomers into the
citizen community on equal terms. This foundation myth stands in sharp contrast to
examples from Greece that emphasize either the conquest of an indigenous population
by invaders that served to justify the rule of one group over another in archaic *poleis*
(city-states) or claims of autochthonous origins, such as that of the Thebans, who supposed that their ancestors were created when Cadmus sowed the dragon's teeth and
saw the Thebans literally spring up out of the soil behind him. Self-images like these
certainly helped underwrite the high degree of exclusivity that Greek *poleis* cherished.
In a parallel development, Rome also in these years began to conceptualize citizenship
as a collection of specific rights and responsibilities that could be conferred entirely or
in part on others. Again, the contrast with classical Greece is striking, where citizenship
in a *poleis* stemmed from ethnic identity and membership in an age-cohort that had
gone through a ritualized process of initiation, a status that was nearly impossible to
confer on anyone outside the restricted circle of its members.

But what also paved the way to forms of peace that sought reconciliation was certainly a keen sense of the military realities that Rome faced in Italy, realities that the
Latin revolt had brought vividly home to Rome's ruling class. The Latins represented
a considerable portion of the manpower that Rome depended on in the wars it fought.
Imposing a settlement that permanently subjugated and alienated the Latins would
have made them undependable allies and ultimately only weakened Rome. Finding
a way to retain and enhance their loyalty on the contrary increased the Republic's
might. For a city that had been brutally sacked only half a century before, the choice
was clear. Fear of the consequences of military weakness led to peace, reconciliation,
and ultimately integration between Rome and its former Latin allies as well as other
strategically important peoples in central Italy that Rome conquered over the next
century.

The same overriding concern with security shaped the nature of the Romans' peacemaking in other conflicts as well. The Romans could be quite brutal towards those
they defeated: they were not above the kinds of atrocities that the Athenians visited upon the Melians, and we have some truly horrific descriptions of the atrocities

Roman soldiers inflicted in such cases: "one may often see in towns captured by the Romans not only human beings who have been put to the sword, but even dogs cloven down the middle, and the limbs of other animals hewn off," as Polybius, an eye-witness, observed (10.15.4–16.9, trans. Shuckburgh; Ziolkowski 1993). But the Romans were also capable of stopping well short of extreme measures; traditionally, at least as the Romans claimed, they were inclined to be merciful to those opponents who surrendered to them before the assault on their city walls had begun (Cicero, *De officiis* 1.35). After that point, Roman commanders gave their soldiers free rein to pillage and kill indiscriminately when a city fell. Survivors were enslaved, a fate that befell tens of thousands of the Republic's opponents (Harris 1979: 59, 81). Brutality could be an extremely effective diplomatic tool, as distasteful to modern sensibilities as such a view is, and the usefulness of a reputation for ferocity ought to be self-evident: soldiers died in battles, particularly in desperate fighting against an enemy making its last stand. Consequently, Rome's leaders, concerned above all else to husband and if possible increase their military manpower, saw an advantage in not letting matters reach the stage where combat of this sort was required. The Romans held out the carrot of generous treatment with one hand and the stick of savagery with the other, and from the point of view of those to whom these alternatives were offered, the choice was simple. Or at least the Romans could hope so, and the atrocities that they from time to time inflicted upon their victims only served as an object lesson to others to avoid the same fate.

For the alternative, surrender to the Romans before it came to that point, could be far more attractive. Many of those Rome conquered in the fourth and third centuries BCE were forced to become the Republic's allies. They might be mulcted of a portion of their land, but otherwise the main burden alliance imposed on them was the obligation of furnishing fixed contingents of soldiers for Rome's army under a stipulation known as the *formula togatorum*. Allies were also obliged to surrender control of their foreign policy to the senate. Beyond that, however, they were left largely alone. They continued to elect their own magistrates and manage their own domestic affairs without interference from Rome. Once again, in other words, the Romans sought terms of peace that, while far from constituting an equitable agreement between its participants, still might represent a basis for future cooperation instead of hostility and lead to the reconciliation of the vanquished to their new lot. In a memorable analogy, the situation was not unlike that of a robber gang that obliged its victims to join it in future depredations in exchange for a share in any loot that might result – a cynical but not inaccurate depiction of the situation (Cornell 1995: 364–68). But it points up once again the Roman senate's overriding concern in making peace to increase its military potential.

This policy created a great reservoir of Italian manpower on which the senate could draw for Rome's armies; in turn, it could direct such military power anywhere it saw fit. The extent of its success is evident in a passage of Polybius, drawn from the earliest Roman historian, Fabius Pictor, that gives the Republic's total military strength in 225, shortly before the outbreak of the Second Punic War. The interpretation of the figures is difficult and, recently, controversial, but conventionally they are said to report that

:ould call on 271,000 infantry and cavalry drawn from its own citizens and 361,000 from among its Italian allies.[2] For comparison's sake, Macedon at its height, under Philip and Alexander the Great, probably could mobilize no more than 30,000 infantry and cavalry. In light of these figures, it is obvious how Rome could defeat the greatest battlefield commander of antiquity apart from those two men, Hannibal. It simply wore him down until it was able to deliver the final blow at Zama in 202.

Yet Hannibal reminds us that the Roman senate's efforts to bring about reconciliation through the peace treaties it made with defeated enemies could never be completely successful because these were fundamentally unequal arrangements. The strong did what they could and the weak suffered what they had to; Rome simply chose to do less than fully what it could, but few states preferred to live on Roman sufferance rather than in freedom when there was a choice. Throughout most of the third and second centuries, the allies opted for the former because no realistic alternative existed. Hannibal's early successes for a brief time changed all that, and a number of Rome's Italian allies responded by going over to his side in hopes of regaining their liberty, and in some cases, their former dominance over their neighbors. With the tide running strongly in Hannibal's favor after his victory at Cannae in 216, where nearly 50,000 Romans and allies may have died, the Carthaginian offered to open talks with Rome, but the senate firmly rejected the overture.[3] Peace on any terms other than victory was not only repugnant to the majesty of Rome in the senators' view but a threat to its very existence. Agreeing to accept defeat signaled weakness, and in light of such an acknowledgment Rome could foresee the rest of its allies rallying round the victor rather than remain loyal. The senators knew the score: the Italian allies outnumbered the Romans, and were they to side massively with Hannibal, the Republic would face a potentially crushing combination. Like Athens, Rome could expect little in the way of mercy from its subjects once they gained the upper hand. Fear, in other words, again is the key to understanding Roman peacemaking, but here it precluded any sort of compromise with Hannibal and the Republic's rebellious allies and so led to many more years of grinding struggle and, in the end, victory.

The Republic's success in making peace both internally and with those it conquered created a dynamic that, paradoxically, continuously required more war. The social and economic conflicts among the Romans themselves during the fifth and fourth centuries had in large part grown out of a lack of access to land, and while military necessity had ultimately led wealthy landowners to agree to limit the abuses they could inflict on the poor, they had not given in to demands for a redistribution of the land itself. So while this stance had made an accommodation between the two sides possible, it left the basic problem unresolved. Consequently, the only solution to a rising population and a shortage of land was to acquire more of the latter, and that meant war. And as the poor gained new land and escaped their status as dependant laborers on the estates of the rich, the owners of large estates required a new supply of workers to replace them. The slaves the Romans captured in their wars would fit the bill nicely.[4] Finally, the willingness of defeated enemies to reconcile themselves to their new status as Roman allies was predicated in large measure on being cut in for a share of future spoils. This was particularly true for those from whom Rome had recently confiscated land to satisfy the needy among its own citizens and prior allies. That, too, necessitated further conquests to replace the land of which they had been deprived as well as to accommodate the natural population increase among the rest.

The political peace established among patrician and plebeian members of the Republic's upper class by the close of the fourth century likewise created a propensity to war. The long crisis of the fifth century coupled with the trauma of the Gallic sack of Rome in 390 had brought about the development of a strong military ethos within Roman society, both among ordinary male citizens and especially within the nobility, the new upper class amalgamated from the patrician and plebeian elite (Raaflaub 1996). War was where an individual won the prominence necessary to gain election to the public offices that validated a man's title to membership in the ruling class and gave him charge of the community's weightiest affairs (Harris 1979: 10–41). And because those affairs often entailed leading the Republic's armies to war, they brought opportunities to acquire further glory and even greater prestige. When the Roman senate deliberated over war and peace, therefore, many of its members could see their interests served by opting for war. This is not to say that in any particular case the Roman senate was looking to pick a fight – although this may have happened on more than one occasion, since many considerations influenced any particular decision (Rich 1993) – but only that when a choice between a peaceful and a bellicose resolution of a foreign conflict presented itself, many members of the senate could see much to incline them to choose the latter path and little incentive to take the former.

The senators were further confirmed in this inclination by the realities of ancient interstate relations. As the Republic gradually conquered Italy between the mid-fourth and the mid-third centuries BCE and then expanded its hegemony overseas between the mid-third and the late second centuries, it found itself at the center of a complex hegemonic web that one might call an empire. These relationships, some based on treaties, others informal in nature, constituted much of its military power, since these alliances, mainly in Italy but also to some extent overseas, furnished Rome with half or more of its armed forces. But they also obligated the frequent deployment of that same military power, for with hegemony came the responsibility for protection. Any sign of irresolution on Rome's part, any failure to respond to provocation, any refusal to avenge the injuries done to itself or its friends would be perceived as weakness not only by those beyond Rome's control but by those under it, raising the prospect both of further aggression as well as possible revolt. The logic of empire, in other words, made it incumbent on Rome to project an image of strength, and the best way to do that was to keep the conquests coming. Not that the men who made the decisions in this period would have put the matter in the cold terms of realpolitik. Matters would have been couched in the language of morality and honor – upholding the majesty and dignity of Rome, punishing arrogance, humbling the proud, protecting the weak, defending the Republic's friends.[5] But ultimately the effect of this sensitivity to claims of honor was to create a propensity to mete out terrible retribution for slights real or imagined and thereby to perpetuate an image of the Romans as people not to cross. In that respect, little changed between the period of the Republic's great conquests and the high Empire four centuries later.

In such circumstances, it is hardly surprising that the nature of war during this era was anything but ritualistic. Conflicts were long and hard, and combatants could visit great brutality on enemy soldiers and civilians alike. No mechanisms at this stage existed for arbitration, for bringing Rome's conflicts to quick and relatively bloodless conclusions, or for limiting the exploitation of a victory.[6] If "battles of champions" had once attempted to settle wars without engaging the whole of the two sides' forces, the practice had become otiose by the middle Republic. A few single combats are on record, but they settled nothing save individual disputes over personal honor and martial prowess (Livy, *Epitome* 48; Appian, *Iberica* 53). The complex rituals of the *fetiales* had, probably by the early third century, been altered due to the increasing remoteness of the enemies against whom the city fought. A plot of ground near the temple of Bellona (a war goddess) was designated as "enemy territory" into which the priests could cast their spear and thereby invoke the support of the gods (Rich 1976: 56–118). But more importantly, even before that date the claims for redress that the *fetiales* (and the ambassadors who later replaced them) conveyed had become in essence non-negotiable demands and so excessive that acceding to them was tantamount to surrender (Harris 1979: 166–75).

To wage its wars Rome mobilized Italy's population on a vast scale – as many as seventy-five percent of Roman citizens aged 17 to 30 (some 75,000–80,000 men) were conscripted during the crisis of the Hannibalic War, a rate equaled only by the Confederate States during the American Civil War (Rosenstein 2004: 98, cf. 251 n. 1). During the last two centuries of the Republic the proportion of citizens under arms rarely dipped below 20 percent of men aged 17 to 46, but even that figure represented a far greater percentage than any other western nation would conscript before the modern era (Lo Cascio 2001: 135–37). And Italian allies served in equal or even greater numbers. Many of the practices that in early Rome had ritually separated war from peace for soldiers had long since fallen by the wayside. Although the religious celebrations that once marked the opening and closing of the season of war were still carried out, they no longer corresponded to the actual beginnings and terminations of fighting. Campaigning often lasted well into the fall and winter months, and men remained under arms for years at a time. Instead of experiencing an annual alternation between their roles as soldiers and civilians, most young men saw their lives shaped by a much longer cycle of war and peace. At 17, they began a lengthy period of military service that often lasted as long as 12 or 14 years. This was punctuated by occasional temporary demobilizations, often following victory and the celebration of a triumph, which still served to mark the end of a war. But conscription for a new conflict usually followed soon thereafter until a soldier was around thirty. By this point, he was nearing the maximum term of service and also getting ready to wed. The end of a man's time at war and his reintegration into civilian life was marked by taking a wife, obtaining a farm, and beginning a family. Thereafter, he would rarely if ever be called to war (Rosenstein 2004: 26–106).

What is unexpected however, given all the factors predisposing Rome to go to war, is that the senators' practice of viewing diplomacy in moral and ethical terms constituted one of the few consistent brakes on the Republic's warmaking. The lack of a justifiable *casus belli* more than once gave the senators pause in their deliberations upon war and peace. As the second century Greek historian Polybius noted, "The Romans took special care not to give the impression of beginning an unjust war or in undertaking wars to be laying hands upon their neighbors, but always to seem to be defending themselves and compelled to go to war" (fr. 99). So as early as 264, the senators wrestled with the question of whether or not to provide military aid to the Mamertines, a contingent of mercenaries who had seized the city of Messina on Sicily (particularly repugnant suppliants owing to the crimes they had committed to gain control of the city and to Rome's having not long before punished others for similar transgressions inspired by the Mamertines). In the end, they could reach no consensus and so left the decision to the assembly, where the general's desire for glory and the citizens' eagerness for loot tipped the scales in favor of war (Polybius 1.7.1–11.3). More than a century later, in 151, the *patres* once again found themselves for some time frustrated in their desire to declare war on the Carthaginians because the latter refused to afford them a suitable pretext. However, once one came to hand, the senators voted for war with alacrity (Polybius 36.2.1–3.9).

Yet it was rare that the Republic found itself in such a quandary. There was nearly always a way to see justice and Roman honor as needing to be requited by war, although it could sometimes take the senators a while to work this out. Otherwise, the main constraints inhibiting Roman warmaking were practical and short-term: the number of other conflicts being waged or in prospect at the same time, manpower limits, and occasionally political jealousy. Such contingent factors, along with ethical concerns, could and often did cause the senate to hesitate and resort to diplomacy before committing the Republic's armies to war to resolve its disputes. But in the end, despite such delays, the wars that won Rome its empire broke out anyway, in part because of the structural factors discussed above, and in part because in the absence of internationally accepted institutions for the resolution of inter-state conflicts, the Romans were prepared to fight when what they perceived to be their vital interests were at stake.

The hallmark of the Republic's peacemaking – its readiness in many cases to end conflicts on terms that would reconcile the defeated to their new status as partners (and sometimes fellow citizens) rather than subjects and thus increase Rome's military might – emerges strikingly once again in the early first century. By 91, for reasons that are complex and controversial, the relationship between Rome and its allies in Italy had deteriorated. The latter now reckoned that the disadvantages of the partnership far outweighed its benefits, and they rose in revolt.[7] The conflict (known as the Social War, from the Latin term for ally, *socius*), although relatively brief, was hard-fought and very bloody. Rome only prevailed when the senate offered what at least a substantial part of the Italians at that point wanted (or were willing to accept), namely full citizenship (Appian, *Civil Wars* 1.49). From that date on Rome's citizen community encompassed the whole of Italy south of the Po River. Once again, the senate realized that it had to find a way to achieve reconciliation with its enemies in order to remain strong. The Italian allies constituted at least 50 percent of the peninsula's manpower and contributed at least 50 percent of the forces that Rome led to war. The Romans were prepared, in the interests of preserving their power and empire, to take the long view and offer terms that their Italian allies could live with. One would like to imagine the senators as wise statesmen who understood the necessity of offering peace with honor to their opponents. And perhaps they were. The settlement of the Latin Revolt and the grants of citizenship that accompanied it surely offered an attractive and salutary precedent. But pragmatic concerns also must have played their part. Little more than a decade earlier the Republic had faced a desperate crisis when migrating tribes of Germanic peoples, the Cimbri and Teutones, having inflicted a series of massive defeats on Roman armies in southern France, threatened to invade Italy and sweep all before them with their overwhelming numbers. The Romans turned back this threat in 102 and 101 only with great difficulty, surely bringing home to them the vital importance of being able to call upon the full military resources of Italy. Once again, the fear arising from a grave threat served to temper the peace that Rome made with its defeated Italian allies.

Ironically, however, this willingness to reconcile with the defeated and seek in peace a basis for future cooperation that is so evident during the Social War is almost wholly absent in the Republic's domestic conflicts in this period. A case in point followed almost immediately upon the end of that struggle. The issue of how exactly to integrate the enormous number of new citizens into Rome's political structures spawned a contentious political dispute that, along with a number of other causes, led to the outbreak of civil war beginning in 88 and ending, after a lull of several years, in 82. The terms that the victor, L. Cornelius Sulla, imposed were harsh: highly-placed opponents were hunted down and summarily executed; their property was confiscated as was the farmland of whole cities that had supported the losing side (which throughout most of the struggle could legitimately claim to be the government of Rome!); the descendants of Sulla's victims were deprived of political rights along with their fathers' property; and the political "rules of the game" were re-written to lock in place the domination of Sulla and the aristocrats who had supported him. But this sort of savagery against defeated political opponents had by that point become, if not usual, certainly well-sanctioned by precedent. The senatorial enemies of Tiberius Gracchus, a politician who perhaps unintentionally mounted a challenge in 133 to the senate's supremacy, beat him to death in a public assembly as he was seeking reelection to a public office he currently held and which was supposed to render his person sacred and inviolable (Plutarch, *Tiberius Gracchus* 18.1–19.6; Appian, *Civil Wars* 1.14–17). His younger brother Gaius, who went about his attempt 10 years later to undermine the position of the senate in a much more systematic fashion, also was killed and his supporters butchered after his opponents in the senate and their followers stormed the Aventine hill where the Gracchans had sought to defend themselves against just such an attack. The chief of his enemies offered its weight in gold for his head, which he duly paid (Plutarch, *Gaius Gracchus* 14.1–17.6; Appian, *Civil Wars* 1.25–26). At the close of the second century, an emulator of the Gracchi, Saturninus, and his followers died when their enemies clambered up onto the roof of the senate house, where Saturninus and the others were being kept after surrendering in exchange for promises of safety, tore the roof-tiles off the building, and used them to stone to death those inside (Plutarch, *Marius* 31.1–4; Appian, *Civil Wars* 1.32).

The willingness to find a basis for civil peace that could accommodate at least some of the aspirations and demands on both sides, which had played so crucial a role in gradually ending the struggle between patricians and plebeians in the fifth and fourth centuries, is nowhere in evidence here. The senate in fact signaled its victory over Gaius Gracchus by restoring the great temple of Concord on the Capitoline Hill, the very temple whose establishment had marked an important stage in the settlement of the political differences between patricians and plebeians in 367 (Plutarch, *Gaius Gracchus* 17.6). But now, almost two and a half centuries later, it represented anything but a demonstration of mutual willingness to find a basis for future cooperation. Quite the reverse: civic peace had become very much like military peace, something imposed on the vanquished by the victors that emphasized the powerlessness of the former and the supremacy of the latter, an object lesson in the consequences of forgetting that simple fact of life.

To account for the change, one need only look to the alterations in Rome's military and diplomatic circumstances. In the mid-fourth century, the city had been struggling for its very survival. Cooperation and mutual accommodation within the Republic was imperative, both between rich and poor and among those at the top of the social hierarchy. By the age of the Gracchi, however, those struggles were a thing of the past. Rome had conquered Italy; it had destroyed its age-old rival Carthage in 146; it had beaten the fabled kingdoms of Hellenistic Greece and Asia repeatedly; it had tamed the Gauls and Spain. While the senatorial majority was willing to allow limited economic reforms to satisfy some of the grievances that had fostered the movements the Gracchi and others had led, it refused to tolerate what it perceived as challenges to its rule. And although the scare that the Cimbri and Teutones caused at the end of the second century did bring about a temporary closing of ranks within the aristocracy, it did not last.

In a way, then, one can draw something of a parallel between the rules of empire as the Athenians spelled them out to the Melians and the sway that the senate exercised over affairs in Italy and at Rome. When the two sides were near equals, as in the Social War, then right and justice were on the table and peace had to comprise a measure of equity if reconciliation was to be achieved. But otherwise, the politically strong did what they could and the politically weak suffered what they had to, just as in the military sphere. Much the same attitude characterized the Romans' treatment of their subjects abroad. Gone were the days when security concerns led to efforts at reconciliation with those Rome had conquered and their incorporation in the Republic's military system. By the latter half of the second century, Rome appeared invincible to everyone, including the Romans themselves. Rome had never extended citizenship to those beyond Italy; even formal alliances with foreign states had not been offered quickly. Without a sense of military urgency, the Romans saw little need to keep provincials overseas happy with their lot. So they did little to impede the atrocities, oppression, and increasing financial exploitation that Roman governors, tax collectors, and money lenders perpetrated in the later second and first centuries. The Romans did not have to care. Challenges, when they arose were to be repressed savagely, whether at home or abroad, out of concern that a failure to respond, to demonstrate overwhelming strength, would seem to be weakness and simply invite more of the same.

Consequently, those who, like the Gracchi or Saturninus, entertained hopes of dominating the political landscape at Rome had to accumulate immense resources – particularly glory and wealth and the followers and allies these would attract – to have any chance of success. Such political capital could only be gained from war, and so, not surprisingly, the figures who tower over the events of the Republic's final decades are the great generals – Pompey and Caesar, like Marius and Sulla before them. The political implications of how foreign affairs, and particularly warfare, were conducted by commanders abroad, who had always been factors in decisions about war and peace, now assumed an increasing prominence. Pompey crafted his great settlement of the East following his victory in the Republic's final struggle with Mithradates, the king of Pontus in Asia Minor, as much with an eye towards laying the foundations for his political ascendancy in Rome as towards assuring Rome's in the Near East. Caesar's ruthless triumph-hunting in Gaul and his decisions there on matters of war and peace likewise aimed at strengthening his hand against his opponents in political struggles back home. Ultimately, their rivals, unwilling or unable to find a way to accommodate the great power these men had amassed, sought to destroy them.

The failure of all parties – the senatorial leadership, Pompey, and even, despite his protestations, Caesar – to work seriously for peace doomed the Republic to another round of civil war, although whether any sort of accommodation, any sort of peace, was possible without the establishment of a monarchy is very much open to doubt. But without question, after the 17 years of internecine bloodletting that followed, ending civil war was only possible under the monarchy of Caesar's adopted son Augustus. Following the utter defeat of all his rivals, Augustus, like the statesmen of the early and middle Republic before him, sought to impose a peace that could provide a basis for a lasting reconciliation with those he had humbled. As with the Latin and Italian upper classes defeated in the Republic's earlier conquests, Augustus took surviving aristocrats who came to terms with the new regime into a junior partnership. His collaborators received tangible benefits in exchange, less from the first emperor's clemency than out of his concern to maximize his political strength and preclude challenges to his fragile new order (Syme 1939: 349–86). Likewise, Augustus curtailed the abuses suffered by Rome's subjects abroad in order to prevent them from lending support to a challenger's bid to overthrow him. *Pax* was celebrated as never before in Augustan Rome: the goddess achieved a prominence no earlier age had ever accorded her, embodied most vividly in the *Ara Pacis*, the great altar to Augustan Peace, still standing in Rome today (Weinstock 1960: 44–50). Caution, calculation, and fear led Augustus, like his Republican predecessors, to seek a peace that could reconcile former enemies to their new subordination and secure the cooperation of the vanquished in defending the victor's rule.

The formula worked – because neither side really had any choice but to make it work. Yet the result ushered in an age of unprecedented peace for the Romans and their subjects, the *pax Romana*, the basis for an increasing prosperity now that wars had been removed to distant frontiers where they were fought by professional armies.

Urbanization and the arts flourished, and if there were costs (as there certainly were), they were more than offset by the benefits that a growing cultural integration brought, benefits that, along with the gradual extension of citizenship to the entire population of the Empire, made of Rome's former subjects its staunchest defenders when the great era of military crisis opened in the third century and ended the Roman peace forever.[8]

Notes

1 On what follows, see Rosenstein 1999: 196–205 with further references.
2 Polybius 2.24.1–17; on the interpretation of this passage, see Brunt 1971: 44–60, and, contra, Lo Cascio 1999: 166–70.
3 Livy 22.49.15, 22.58.1–61.15; Lazenby 1978: 84–85; Brunt 1971: 419 however puts the figure at 30,000.
4 Nearly 69,000 were taken in the years 297–293 alone, according to Livy (Oakley 1993: 25). These numbers are unlikely to be very accurate, but they at least suggest the scale on which enslavements were occurring.
5 See the inscription from ca. 172 detailing the list of charges Rome levied against the Macedonian king Perseus in justification of its war against him: SIG^3 II 643, (translated in Lewis and Reinhold 1990: 195–96); the charges are also reflected in Livy 42.13.5–9.
6 Note the senate's angry reaction when the island republic of Rhodes attempted to mediate between Rome and Perseus during the conflict mentioned in the preceding note: Polybius 29.19.1–11. After its victory in 167 Rome severely punished the Rhodians' temerity: Gruen 1984: 569–73.
7 See, most recently, Mouritsen 1998, who challenges the usual view that the allies sought Roman citizenship and only went to war when their demand was rebuffed.
8 I would like to thank Kurt Raaflaub and the other participants in the colloquium for helpful comments, and especially Deborah Boedeker for her extraordinary services and Robin Yates for lending me his shoes.

References

Brunt, Peter. 1971. *Roman Manpower*. Oxford.
Cornell, T. J. 1995. *The Beginnings of Rome. Italy and Rome from the Bronze Age to the Punic Wars (c. 1000–264 BC)*. London.
Eckstein, Arthur. 2006. "Conceptualizing Roman Imperial Expansion under the Republic: An Introduction." In Nathan Rosenstein and Robert Morstein-Marx (eds.), *A Companion to the Roman Republic*, 568–90. Oxford.
Galinski, Karl. 1996. *Augustan Culture*. Princeton.
Gruen, Erich. 1984. *The Hellenistic World and the Coming of Rome*. Berkeley.
Harris, William. 1979. *War and Imperialism in Republican Rome, 327–70 BC*. Oxford.
Hölkeskamp, Karl. 1993. "Conquest, Competition and Consensus: Roman Expansion in Italy and the Rise of the *Nobilitas*." *Historia* 42: 12–39.
Lazenby, J. F. 1978. *Hannibal's War. A Military History of the Second Punic War*. Norman, OK.
Lewis, Naphtali, and Meyer Reinhold (eds.). 1990. *Roman Civilization: Selected Readings, 1: The Republic and the Augustan Age*. New York.

Lo Cascio, Elio. 1999. "The Population of Roman Italy in Town and Country." In John Bintliff and Kostas Sbonias (eds.), *Reconstructing Past Population Trends in Mediterranean Europe (3000 BC–AD 1800)*, 161–71. Oxford.

——. 2001. "Recruitment and the Size of the Roman Population from the Third to the First Century BCE." In Walter Scheidel (ed.), *Debating Roman Demography*, 111–37. Leiden.

Marshall, Anthony. 1984. "Symbols and Showmanship in Roman Public Life: The Fasces." *Phoenix* 38: 120–41.

Mattern, Susan. 1999. *Rome and the Enemy. Imperial Strategy in the Principate*. Berkeley.

Mouritsen, Henrik. 1998. *Italian Unification: A Study in Ancient and Modern Historiography*. London.

Oakley, Stephen. 1993. "The Roman Conquest of Italy." In Rich and Shipley 1993: 9–37.

Raaflaub, Kurt. 1996. "Born to Be Wolves? Origins of Roman Imperialism." In Robert Wallace and Edward Harris (eds.), *Transitions to Empire*, 273–314. Norman.

——. 2005. "From Protection and Defense to Offense and Participation: Stages in the Conflict of the Orders." In Kurt Raaflaub (ed.), *Social Struggles in Archaic Rome. New Perspectives on the Conflict of the Orders*. Expanded and updated edn., 185–222. Oxford.

Rawlings, Louis. 1998. "Condottieri and Clansmen. Early Italian Raiding, Warfare and the State." In Keith Hopwood (ed.), *Organised Crime in Antiquity*, 97–128. London.

Rich, John. 1976. *Declaring War in the Roman Republic in the Period of Transmarine Expansion*. Brussels.

——. 1993. "Fear, Greed, and Glory: The Causes of Roman War-making in the Middle Republic." In Rich and Shipley 1993: 38–68.

——, and Graham Shipley (eds.). 1993. *War and Society in the Roman World*. London.

Rosenstein, Nathan. 1986. "*Imperatores Victi*: The Case of C. Hostilius Mancinus." *Classical Antiquity* 5: 230–52.

——. 1999. "Republican Rome." In Kurt Raaflaub and Nathan Rosenstein (eds.), *War and Society in the Ancient and Medieval Worlds*, 190–216. Washington, DC.

——. 2004. *Rome at War. Farms, Families, and Death in the Middle Republic*. Chapel Hill.

Scullard, H. H. 1981. *Festivals and Ceremonies of the Roman Republic*. Ithaca.

Sherwin White, A. N. 1973. *The Roman Citizenship*. 2nd edn. Oxford.

Syme, Ronald. 1939. *The Roman Revolution*. Oxford.

Weinstock, Stefan. 1960. "Pax and the 'Ara Pacis'." *Journal of Roman Studies* 50: 44–58.

Ziolkowski, Adam. 1993. "*Urbs direpta*, or How the Romans Sacked Cities." In Rich and Shipley 1993: 69–91.

14

The Price of Peace in Ancient Rome

Carlin A. Barton

For Erich S. Gruen

Modern notions of "justice" and "mercy" are two keys to understanding ancient Roman notions of peace.

When might a modern American demand "justice?" Chances are, it is when she is the injured party, when her rights have been violated by others and she feels entitled, according to the provisions of the social contract, to compensation, indemnification. When might a modern American appeal for mercy? Often, it is when she is in the wrong, when she is the one who "owes" and is entreating for the mitigation or suspension of the system of compensations, the remedies provided by the social contract. But there is another situation in which a modern American might plead for mercy rather than justice. If she is mugged in an alley and a knife is at her throat, or she has been defeated in a struggle and there is a gun to the back of her head chances are that – however injured she might feel – she will not clamor for "justice." She is more likely to beg for "mercy." When there is no social contract at all, mercy is as close to one as she can get.

The Latin noun *pax*, like the Latin nouns *fides, pudor, religio, pergamen, piaculum lustrum, flagitium*, and like the Latin verbs *sancire, sacrare, mactare*, had two opposite valences, poised, as it were, on the two opposite poles of a balance beam.[1] *Pax* (peace) for the Romans could be a form of justice or a form of mercy; it might be a type of covenant or it might signal the absence of any contractual relationship.

Modern English suppresses the "darker" meaning of Roman *pax*, or subsumes the "darker" meaning in the "lighter."[2] In our notion of peace, the child of Roman *pax*, the non-contractual aspects have been assimilated into the contractual. "Peace" and "mercy" sound only gentle notes in English. They are the social contract or its benevolent suspension. We are liable to forget or ignore the knife at the throat. The ideas that we associate with "peace" in modern English are serenity and tranquility. We think of "peace" as a stable state, a benevolent state of calm, a state free from turmoil or strife. "Peace" for us is the opposite of lawless chaos, the stormy disorder, suffering and conflict of war or the absence of the social contract. "Peace" is a state associated in our minds with "justice." By the period of the Roman civil wars and early Empire, the opposing senses of Roman *pax* will have undergone the same conflation; increasingly *pax* will display its docile and eirenic aspects – the *animi tranquilla pax* (tranquility of mind) of Lucretius (5.1229, 6.75), the *placidissima* (most quiet) *pax* of Cicero (*Tusculan Disputations* 5.48) – but it might still flash its razor edge. The Romans could still, to use Mattingly's famous translation of the words of Calgacus, the leader of the Britons' last stand, "make a desolation and call it peace" (*solitudinem faciunt, pacem appellant* [Tacitus, *Agricola* 30.6]).[3] The gradual suppression of the darker side of *pax*, in the Roman world – as in ours – was an evolution that revealed, one might say, the price of peace.

To step back, there are reasons that our notions of peace differ from those of the Romans of the Republic. Like all peoples without a powerful centralized state system exercising a monopoly of violence, the Romans relied above all on an acute sense of shame and carefully formalized traditional patterns of behavior to suppress the vendetta within the community. All of these governing forces were based on notions of exchange and interdependence.[4] Reciprocity was the positive balancing force within the culture and, in so far as it operated at all, between cultures. The compensatory system devised by the Romans worked as the stabilizing mechanism within the culture; it *was* their notion of justice. The Romans tended to think of the good conditions for the Republic not as a fixed or stable state free from tensions, but rather as a dramatic, tense, laborious, balancing act – not unlike a handshake.[5]

It is very important to understand that, for the Romans of the Republic, the negative, destabilizing forces, the forces of chaos and civil war, arose from the very same principles of reciprocity as did justice and order. Both the "healthy" equilibrations and the "sick" vendetta (the internecine violence that the balancing system was designed to suppress) operated on the same principles of retribution. The exchanges that held the culture together could produce the great violent alternations and fluctuations that threatened the community with dissolution. The positive and negative forces were not different in nature but in measure; the fluctuations and reciprocities of Roman justice were those that could be modulated, controlled; the furious and centrifugal swings of violence and the vendetta were those that could not be controlled and adjusted. The latter could and finally did disrupt and destroy the commonwealth.

Before the outbreak of the civil wars, the Romans did not conceive of two antithetical states, a serene "peace" and a tumultuous "war" in the way that we do. Nor did they place a high value on calm or rest or leisure. They associated absence of tension and energetic activity as absence of spirit, the absence of vitality. "Peace" in our sense would have been considered enervating – and even dangerous.[6] Peace and leisure slackened the sinews, destroyed the self-discipline that preserved the state, for the debilitated and undisciplined man was also the licentious and greedy man. *Peace and prosperity led directly to civil strife and the destruction of the social contract.* And so, words that we would associate with peace and leisure (*otium, inertia, desidia, ignavia, socordia*), were associated with cowardice and the absence of will, effective energy, *virtus*. Words associated with strenuous activity and tension (*labor, industria, exercitio, disciplina, duritia, studium, vigilantia*), signaled energy, vigor, vitality, heightened being.[7]

Our notions of peace are inseparable from our notions of justice. But if we think of our modern Western icon of justice, the blindfolded goddess holding a set of scales, we will notice two things: firstly, justice for us is the *motionless goddess*, the power at the center determining the stable state, not listing to one side or the other, holding a set of scales on which the plates are forever equally balanced. Secondly, when we imagine peace, we assume it to be a *happy* state, a benevolent one in which there is contentment, equity, freedom. Peace is a state of repose, not of repression. If one wants to understand ancient Roman notions of justice and how they relate to peace and reconciliation, one needs, first of all, to remove the goddess from the picture. The scales have to operate on their own. And they are never in a fixed state; they are always in motion. Social relations within the Republic were imagined as fluid and reciprocal, in an endless process of being negotiated, balanced, adjusted – in order to avoid civil war. Outside of the Republic, the stabilizing systems of exchange hardly existed or were fragile at best. Being citizens of modern states (however "democratic" these states may be in conception), we rely on being regulated, rather passively, from the center. The Romans of the Republic were incessantly and necessarily involved in the balancing, regulating system.

There were times in the Republic, especially in exclusively civic contexts, when *pax* was a synonym for a contract (*pactio, sponsio, foedus, societas, stipulatio*). But the Romans made a sharp distinction between two spheres, *domi* and *militiae*: there was "home" and there was "war." Outside of the Republic *pax* rang of war, defeat, humiliation, compulsion; it often formed part of a matrix of words associated with surrender, supplication, confession (*deditio, supplicatio, confessio*).[8] One sued for peace on one's knees, with one's arms extended in supplication. This peace was the settlement, the order imposed by the gods on man or by the victor on the conquered.

Perhaps the most common notion of *pax* in the Republic (including, and especially, the *pax deorum*, peace with the gods) was of a set of strictures imposed from the top down – whether by a mistress, a victorious general, or a god – in response to the entreaties of the defeated . The phrases one meets focus on "petitions for peace": *pacem precibus exposcere, pacem petere*,[9] *expetere, impetrare, obsecrare*,[10] *quaerere, exquirere*. "Peace and mercy [are] obtained by entreaty from the gods" (*pax veniaque ab dis impetrata* [Livy 1.31.7]). It is this idea of *pax* that is implied in the common expression *pace* (by the leave, by the sufferance, or by the indulgence of someone, especially someone whom you imagine to be hostile). In Plautus' *Mercator* (678) Dorippa supplicates Apollo, begging him to grant her a peace, *pacem dare*, to grant health and safety to her family, and to spare her son (*parcas gnato pace propitius*). Amphitruo, at the end of Plautus' play of the same name, is resigned to having been cuckolded by Jupiter: "I make no complaint," he declares, "at being permitted to have Jupiter as partner in my blessings." Amphitruo then bids his serving girl to prepare the vessels so that he might, with sacrificial offerings, "entreat peace (*pacem expetere*) of the omnipotent god."

This *pax* was, for the Romans, consequent upon, and associated with surrender (*deditio*) and supplication (*supplicatio*) and with the plea for mercy (*deprecatio, postulatio ignoscendi*). And surrender, *deditio*, was associated, in the Roman mind, with the confession of defeat and the broken spirit. Ovid's conquered lover surrenders to Cupid with the following words: "I confess! I am your new prize, your booty. I stretch forth my defeated hands, submissive to your commands. There is no need of war; I entreat for peace and pardon" (*veniam pacemque rogamus* [*Amores* 1.2.19-21]).

The Romans were glad to dictate a peace settlement to their defeated enemy, but were unhappy at the thought of accepting one or even negotiating for one. The Roman tradition was to impose rather to seek peace, *pacem dare* not *pacem petere*.[11] Julius Caesar tells the story of how Quintus Cicero responded to the Gauls who had trapped him and his army in their winter camp. The Gauls offered the Romans a peace on lenient terms. Quintus Cicero responded with these audacious words: "It was not the habit," he replied, "of the Roman people to accept terms from an enemy. *But, if the Gauls would lay down their arms he would intercede with Caesar on their behalf*" (*De bello Gallico* 5.41). Polybius (27.8), Livy (42.62.7), and Plutarch (*Mor.* 197E-F) tell the story of the Roman general Publius Licinius, defeated by Perseus of Macedon in 171 BCE. When the enemy sent envoys to impose a settlement on the Romans, the vanquished Licinius imperiously advised the victor to submit his plea to Rome. In Appian's account of the Spanish Wars, Quintus Pompeius Aulus, even while attempting, out of desperation, to negotiate secretly with the Numantines in 139 BCE, ostentatiously advised them to surrender to the Romans, explaining that the only terms of settlement the Romans considered worthy of themselves were for the enemy to surrender and yield to the Romans' discretion (Appian *Iberica* 13.79). Livy imagined the desperate Romans proudly declaring, after suffering the last and worst of their three great defeats by Hannibal in 216 BCE: "Neither these disasters nor the defections of their allies ever moved the Romans to breathe a word about peace . . . so great was the spirit (*animus*) in the city at that time" (22.61.13–14).[12]

When Hostilius Mancinus and Tiberius Gracchus brought their soldiers home alive from Numantia in 137 BCE the Roman senate treated both them and their negotiated treaty with contempt (Plut. *Ti. Gracchus* 5–7; see Rosenstein, this vol.). In an extended and moving story retrojecting, in part, the situation of Mancinus and Gracchus, Livy's general Spurius Postumius extracted his men alive, if horribly humiliated, from the Caudine Forks, after they had been trapped there by a Samnite army in 321 BCE. He saved his soldiers by a negotiated peace, an act of mercy on the part of the Samnite general Pontius. According to Livy, upon Postumius' return to Rome, the Senate not only rejected the peace, but publicly humiliated its author (9.1–12). One can compare these stories to the stories of the Romans' hostile response to negotiations with Pyrrhus of Epirus in the third century and to Sulla's negotiated peace with Mithridates in the first (Cicero, *Pro Murena* 32).

The desirable end of war for the Romans of the Republic was not, then, a matter of negotiations or reconciliation, but of breaking the enemy's spirit, making the enemy confess defeat, making the enemy "say uncle." To quote Livy: "The spirit of a man was considered broken for all time (*animum in perpetuum vinci*) from whom the confession had been extorted that [and here we have the kind of confession that was put into the mouth of the defeated] 'he had been overcome, not by craft or by accident, but in a just and pious confrontation of arms'" (42.47.8).

Deditio (surrendering, suing for peace) and its companion *deprecatio* (pleading for mercy) were the acts of someone whose spirit had been broken, someone whose *animus* was *fractus*, someone who, as we say in English, had "cracked."[13] When, for instance, in 345/44 BCE the Capuans, with tears and entreaties, surrendered into the *dicio*, the *fides*, the discretion of the Romans, "the senators were," in Livy's words, "greatly disturbed at the fickleness of human fortune: that a people so formidable in their wealth, so illustrious for their luxury and arrogance should be so broken in spirit (*adeo infractos gereret animos*) that they would surrender themselves and all their possessions into the power of another state" (Livy 7.31.6).

Surrender, *deditio*, for the Romans was absolute.[14] In the Romans' mind, all power went to the victor. *Deditio*, to the Romans, did not guarantee to the defeated even the minimum of human rights – not life, not property – nothing. In a famous case of misunderstanding reported by Polybius (20.9–10, 36.4.1–4) and Livy (36.27–28), the Aetolians did not understand the nature of the Roman *fides* into which they were surrendering or how absolutely the Romans considered the *confessi* to be crushed. The Aetolians thought that they still retained some measure of agency, that they could negotiate a treaty, a contract. They did not understand that Roman peace, like the peace of the gods, was what the powerful, out of mercy, left you with.[15] Appian's Publius Lentulus makes the distinction between a *deditio* and a treaty: "Let [the Carthaginians] surrender at [their] discretion, as is the custom of the vanquished, ... and then we will see what we will do. Whatever we grant them they will then take in the light of a favor (*charis*) and not of a compact (*suntheke*). When they surrender into our discretion, we take away their arms, and when their persons are in our possession and they see that there is nothing they can call their own, their spirits will be tamed and they will welcome whatever we allow them to have as a gift bestowed upon them by us" (Appian, *Bellum Punicum* 9.64; trans. White, slightly modified).

The *dediticii* surrendered into the *fides* of the victorious general. (Here it is important to point out that the word *fides* might indicate the restraint of power *or* the unrestrained fullness of power.) Those who confessed, surrendered, and sued for peace hoped for the best but expected the worst. Livy's Capuans addressed the Roman senators: "We have surrendered *everything* into your discretion (*dicio*) and that of the Roman people: the people of Campania, with their city, their lands, the shrines of the gods; everything divine and human. Whatever we shall afterwards suffer, we will suffer as your *dediticii*" (Livy 7.31.4). The Syracusan embassy that came to Marcellus in 212 BCE to seek peace from the Romans, declared, according to Livy, "[We have come] to hand over to you our arms and to surrender ourselves, our city and its walls. We will reject no lot imposed on us by you" (25.29.3). I believe that it was a conflation of the two senses of *pax* (and *fides*) that misled scholars like Rudolf von Jhering (1894), Eugen Täubler (1913), and Emil Seckel (1915) to think that *deditio in fidem* was a form of contract or treaty; they forgot that *fides* as the unlimited power, the will, and discretion of the victorious general was a sort of inverted mirror-image of the *fides*, the self-restraint of the party to a contract, that the *pax* of the battlefield was the inversion of the *pax* of the forum.

The Romans of the late Republic, like the Greeks, believed that the defeated and suppliant *should* be respected, that submissive behavior *should* evoke the force of self-restraint, the mercy of the powerful. "We spare the *dediticii*," says Petronius' Eumolpus (*Satyricon* 107). According to Publilius Syrus, "The greatest praise a man can receive is that 'he could injure – but he chooses not to' " (397, ed. Friedrich).[16] "To crush a suppliant is not an act of valor but of cruelty," he says elsewhere (682). Sallust's general Quintus Marcius Rex responds to the pleas for help of the Catilinarian conspirator and general Gaius Manlius: "Whatever it is that they seek to obtain from the senate, let them put down their weapons and proceed to Rome as suppliants. The senate of the Roman people has always acted with such mildness and pity that no one has ever sought assistance from it in vain" (*Catilina* 34.1). Livy's Titus Quinctius Flamininus declares, "One should meet an armed enemy with a hostile spirit; it is best to show a very gentle spirit toward the defeated" (Livy 33.12.9). According to the emperor Claudius, "It had pleased the ancestors to show as much forbearance to a suppliant as they showed persistence against a foe" (Tacitus, *Annales* 12.20).[17]

Indeed, the Romans of the late Republic and early Empire consistently imagined that there was a time in the past when they had treated the suppliant defeated well. Cicero, in his defense of Roscius, addresses the judges: "All of you are well aware that the Roman people [were] formerly reckoned very lenient even to their enemies" (*Pro Roscio Amerino* 53.154; cf. 52.150). "Truly, our Roman ancestors [...] preferred to pardon rather than to avenge the injuries they endured," says Sallust (*Catilina* 9.5; cf. 12.4).[18]

On the other hand, Cicero reminds us, the Romans were inclined to despise the suppliant and those who begged for their lives.[19] Indeed, Cicero pleads for mercy for Milo on the grounds that the latter is not pleading for it. "As we are wont to have more sympathy for those who do not ask for it than for those who urgently implore it, how much more sympathy, then, ought we to have for our most stalwart citizens" (*Pro Milone* 34.92). Virgil may have conceived the prophetic mission of the Romans to have been "to tame the proud and spare the submissive" (*parcere subiectis et debellare superbos* [*Aeneid* 6.853]), but when he imagined the vanquished Turnus, in the sight of his people, on his knees, extending his right hand and beseeching gaze in supplication to Aeneas, Aeneas famously showed him no mercy (12.930–31, 936–37).[20] Tacitus asserts that "Human beings are wont to hate those whom they have injured" (*Agricola* 42.3). "Cruelty is not broken," Publilius Syrus declares, "but fed by tears" (114 Friedrich ed.).[21]

According to Josephus, when in 37 BCE the Hasmonean Antigonus threw himself at the feet of Antony's general Sosius, the latter, far from pitying the suppliant Antigonus, burst into uncontrollable laughter, called him "Antigona," and put him into irons before executing him (*Bellum Iudaicum* 1.353 and 357). According to Polybius, Scipio Aemilianus treated with similar scorn the suppliant Hasdrubal, son of Gisgo, when he surrendered to the Romans at the end of the Third Punic War (38.20.1–6).[22]

In 173 BCE the Ligurian Statellates, after surrendering unconditionally into the *fides populi Romani*, were deprived of arms, their strongholds destroyed, and they and all their belongings were sold into slavery by the Roman general Popilius Laenas. On that occasion the senate reacted: "The senators thought it atrocious that the Statellates . . . having surrendered into the *fides* of the Roman people – should have been brutalized and destroyed by every example of extreme cruelty. No one ever afterwards would dare to surrender themselves" (Livy 42.8).

André Piganiol believed that prior to the second century BCE Roman *fides* bound the victorious Romans in mutual obligations with their defeated, but that after that date the Romans were as likely to insult and injure the surrendered as not (1950: 339–47).[23] After reviewing the evidence, Franz Hampl came to the conclusion that the Romans of the early Republic, like many Amerindians, determined whether to incorporate or destroy, to adopt or cruelly dispose of their defeated enemies, on a case-to-case basis and that there was neither a moral imperative to be merciful nor a reproach attached to brutality (1957/1973: 116–42, esp. 121–22). Richard Heinze came to a similar conclusion after surveying the portrayals of supplication in Roman literature (1960: 30).[24]

The Roman response to the entreaties of the defeated could not be calculated, any more than the responses of soldiers or muggers or rapists to the pleas of their victims. And it was, I would argue, the very arbitrariness and unpredictability of the response of the conquerors that, for the Romans, demonstrated the fulness of their power, their *fides*. *Powerful men could be merciful – but they were not obligated to be.* Not to be restrained, tied, bound, obligated was to be *sui iuris*, a law unto oneself; to the Roman, this was the height of power. It was, in truth, an impossible and unobtainable ideal of power *within the contractual obligations of civic society*, but it could be realized on the battlefield.

Everything changed with the civil wars and the destruction of the consensus that preserved the social contract within the state. Henceforward, the distinction between "home" and "war" no longer held.

As Jean-Marie André has shown in his exhaustive study of the notion of *otium*, it is with the civil wars, the vendetta unleashed with all its fury, that *otium*, a quiet state of inactivity much like our "peace," becomes a positive value, along with the word *pax*. The ideal of a fixed, permanent, benevolent *status quo*, a state free from the endless equilibrations, the tensions and disturbances of the Republican balancing system, an *otium commune*, a *pax civilis*, appears in Cicero's thought simultaneously with the conviction that the tensions of public life had become insufferable (Barton 2001: 124).

Beginning in the civil war period there appeared in Rome a longing for and appreciation of the fixed and stable state, the type of quiescent harmony advertized by Augustus on the *Ara Pacis*. The notion of peace was still that of a set of conditions dictated from the top down, but such a peace was increasingly felt to be endurable, and finally desirable. In order to suppress the great centrifugal swings of violence that wracked Rome periodically throughout the last century of the Republic, it would be necessary to suppress the balancing system, the system of justice as reciprocity, and to replace it with a merciful peace guaranteed by the prince, the man who emerged victorious from the bloodbath of the civil wars. The emperor became, in the word of Philo Judaeus (2.567), the "guardian of the peace" (*eirenephulax*), the god holding the scales *still*.

In his book, *The Power of Images in the Age of Augustus*, Paul Zanker reproduces a gold coin of C. Lentulus (1988: fig. 74). It shows Augustus extending a hand to the fallen Republic. It is a gesture of mercy similar to that found on the Boscoreale cups, where Augustus extends a hand to the suppliant enemy (Kuttner 1995: Plate I:2). In Augustus' own words "he *preferred* to pardon rather than exterminate" (*Res Gestae* 3.2). But the Republic is, nevertheless, permanently on its knees, permanently the suppliant, permanently pleading for mercy from the divine king. The Republican forces had, as Horace depicted them, "bitten the dust" (*Carmina* 2.7.9–12). The Romans understood this; they understood that the *pax Augusta* (like the *pax deorum* or the *pax Romana* of the Empire) was not simply a state of tranquility.

Exhausted and defeated by a century of intermittent but bloody civil wars, the Romans accepted that the emperor's mercy was as close to a social contract as they would henceforth get. The Romans' celebration of the *pax Augusta* indicated their willingness to accept submission – to go from being citizens to being subjects – and to live at the indulgence, the mercy of the king. The peace of Augustus, like the peace of the gods, seemed worth the price. But many beneficiaries of the *pax Romana*, like Tacitus' British chieftain Calgacus, found that peace somewhat costlier than it sounds to us. So, I might suggest, might many of the beneficiaries of the *pax Americana*.

Notes

1 *Fides* (respect or inhibition before a bond, or power without restrictions); *pudor* (a sense of inhibition, fear of violating one's bonds or the shame of having violated one's bonds); *religio* (inhibition, restraint before a bond or obligation, or the violation of a bond or obligation); *pergamen* (the dirt that is purged, or the purgation); *piaculum* (a sin, a slip or breach or omission in the performance of ritual or the act of undoing or compensating for the breach or omission); *lustrum* (the dirt washed away or the cleansing); *flagitium* (an outrage or the punishment of an outrage); *sacrare* (to set aside positively or negatively, to bless or curse); *sancire* (to sanction positively or negatively, to authorize or to punish); *mactare* (to honor, to increase or to slay or punish).

2 In English, *fides* becomes our positive "faith," *sacer* becomes our positive "sacred," *religio* becomes our positive "religion."

3 Translations are my own unless otherwise noted.

4 Seneca articulates the traditional Roman idea of justice as: "to render to each his due: gratitude for a benefit, retaliation for an injury" (*Epistulae* 81.7). For extended discussions of reciprocal relations within Roman society see Barton 2001.

5 It is possible that the *stipulatio* bond, like the *tessera* bond, was conceptualized as something in two pieces (the *stipula* or the *tessera*) that fit together, and that, as in the case of the handshake, it was the mirroring/fitting function that produced the contract.

6 As has been frequently observed, war served a positive function in the Roman mind; it offered the annealing opposition, the *metus hostilis*, the "counterweight of fear" that galvanized the Roman spirit. Having an enemy encouraged the discipline, labor and solidarity that

kept the Roman people strong. This sentiment survived into the Empire. "The British," according to Tacitus, "showed greater ferocity than the Gauls, as they had not yet been softened by long years of peace. And we are told that the Gauls also once flourished in war; then indolence together with peace made their appearance, and so courage and liberty have been lost together" (*Agricola* 11.4). See Polybius 6.18.1–3; Sallust, *Bellum Iugurthinum* 41, 87.4; *Catilina* 10.1–6; Valerius Maximus 7.2.1, 3; Livy 1.19.4; Velleius Paterculus 2.1.1–2; Plutarch, *Cato Maior* 27.1–3; Florus 1.34.19, 1.47; Augustine, *De civitate dei* 1.30–31; Brink and Walbank 1954: 97–122, esp. 103–04; Walbank 1957: 697; Fuchs 1958: 363–85; Earl 1961: 13, 15, 41–49, 98, 104; Knoche 1962: 111ff.; Strasburger 1965: 41–42; Astin 1967: 276–80; Lind 1979: 8–9, 54.

7 André 1966.

8 *Otium* was the word that would have been used most often for a state of calm peace. It also evolved a more positive aspect.

9 Cicero, *Pro Fonteio* 30: "Other people entreat the *pax* and pardon of the gods; these people (the irreligious Gauls) wage war against the immortal gods themselves."

10 Plautus, *Amphitruo* 388 (the slave Sosia to Mercury): "I beg you *per pacem* to let me speak to you without getting thrashed."

11 See Klingner 1979: 614–44, esp. 616.

12 Plutarch's defiant Cato the Younger addresses those Italians of Utica who were on the point of surrendering to Julius Caesar: "It is for the defeated to beg and for the wrong-doer to appeal for mercy" (*Cato Minor* 64.5). On the reluctance of Cato to be a suppliant, see also Sen., *De prov.* 2.10. Seneca was proud of the fact that even under the tyranny of Messalina and Narcissus he never played the clinging suppliant (*non e manibus ullius supplex pependi* [*Nat. quaest.* 4A *praefatio* 16]). "Even if he falls," Seneca declares, "he fights on his knees" (*De prov.* 2.6. Cf. Cicero, *Pro rege Deiotaro* 13.36). Livy's Roman soldiers trapped at the Caudine Forks in 320 BCE deprived the victorious Samnites of the sweetest part of their victory by refusing to confess defeat. Indeed the Romans had the nerve to send legates to the Samnites to suggest a *pax aequa* (a settlement based on acknowledged equality of rights) or, failing that, to provoke the enemy into giving battle to the death (9.4.1–2).

13 "Overwhelmed, I am compelled to confess" (Ovid, *Met.* 9.545). "[T]hey had wrung a confession from the conquered" (Livy 36.45.6). "Tiberius Caesar forced a clear confession of submission from the Dalmatians such as that which Augustus had wrested from Spain" (Velleius Paterculus 2.39.3). For other examples of extorting confession, see Livy 7.30.9; Seneca, *De clem.* 1.1.7 (with bitter irony); *Epistulae* 82.7; Suetonius, *Galba* 10.5.

14 On *deditio* see Schulten 1901: cols. 2359–2363; Täubler 1913: 14–28; Seckel 1915: 18–19; Heuss 1933: esp. 60–77; Paradisi 1941: 285–324; Piganiol 1950: 339–47; Gruen 1982: 50–68. For the absolute quality of *deditio* see Täubler 1913: 16–20.

15 Here follows an example of the treatment of the defeated. The early Roman king Tarquinius asked the representatives of the Collatini: "Do you give yourselves and the people of Collatia, town, lands, water, boundary markers, shrines, and all provisions and utensils divine and human, into my power and that of the Roman people?" "We do." "And I accept" (Livy 1.38.2). (The surrender is an exchange but not one that establishes a contract.)

16 See Freyburger 1988: 501–28, esp. 521–23.

17 According to the Roman general Flamininus, "Good men (*agathous andras*) ought to be stern and hot-blooded in combat, noble and high-minded if worsted, but moderate, mild and benevolent when they conquer" (Polybius 18.37.7). Cf. Cicero, *De officiis* 1.11.33–35; Livy 7.31.7; 30.42.17; 36.27.6–8; 37.6.6; 37.45.7–8; 42.62.11; Gelzer 1933: 129–66, esp. 137, 164–65; Weinstock 1957: 211–47, esp. 220; Rosenstein 1990: 116. For examples of Romans respecting the suppliant, see Dittenberger 1917: no. 618 = Sherk 1960: no. 35; Terence, *Andria* 282–98; Caesar, *De bello civili* 3.98; Cicero, *Pro Marcello* 4.12; Livy 5.27, 7.30–31, 26.49.7–10; Piganiol 1950: 342–43.

18 "Apart from their very ancient custom of sparing the defeated, the Romans gave exceptional
    proof of their clemency by the peace that they gave to Hannibal and the Carthaginians"
    (Livy 33.12.7; cf. 31.31.1–16; 37.45.7–9). "The greater your power the greater the restraint
    you need to exercise" (Livy 34.7.15). "The greater we are, the more humbly we must
    behave" (Cicero, *De officiis* 1.26.90). "The more power you possess, the more you must
    bear patiently" (Seneca, *Troades* 254).
19 Compare Seneca, *De ira* 2.33.1: "Those whom they injure they also hate."
20 Neither did Aeneas spare good Queen Dido even when she begged.
21 Brutus wrote to Cicero in May 43 that he feared that compliance with the powerful only
    provoked them to do worse: "To refrain from bearing down on the unfortunate I judge
    more honorable than to endlessly concede to the powerful what may inflame their greed
    and arrogance" (Cicero, *Ad Brutum* 10.2 [= 1.4.2]).
22 Compare also Maecenas' poetic plea for mercy (*Fragmenta Poetarum Latinorum*, Morel
    ed., frag. 4, p. 102) with Seneca's sneering commentary on it (*Epistulae* 101.10–12). Brutus
    reacts equally harshly to what he perceives as the shame of Cicero's supplication (Cicero,
    Ad Brutum 17.6 [=1.17.6], 25.8 + 11 [=1.16.8 + 11]). For more humiliations of the
    suppliant see: Plautus, *Asinaria* 682–730; *Cistellaria* 458ff.; *Mercator* 983–997; Sallust,
    Bellum Iugurthinum 91.5–7; Livy 9.1.3–10; Propertius 2.14.11–12; Suetonius, *Augustus*
    13.2. Compare the sentiments expressed in Seneca, *De ira* 1.2.4; *De tranquillitate* 11.5;
    Epistulae 7.5; Lactantius, *Institutiones divinae* 6.20.
23 For Sallust, the cruel treatment of the suppliant began with Sulla (*Catilina* 11–12).
24 For the difficulty of attributing a single range of motivations or behaviors to Roman treat-
    ment of the defeated in war see Gruen 1984. See also Bux 1948: 201–30, esp. 212, 215–16;
    Rich 1993: 38–68; Ziolkowski 1993: 69–91.

References

André, Jean-Marie. 1966. *L'otium dans la vie morale et intellectuelle Romaine*. Paris.

Astin, A. E. 1967. *Scipio Aemilianus*. Oxford.

Barton, Carlin. 2001. *Roman Honor*. Berkeley.

Brink, C. O., and Walbank, F. W. 1954. "The Construction of the Sixth Book of Polybius."
    Classical Quarterly n. s. 4: 97–122.

Bux, Ernst. 1948. "*Clementia Romana*: Ihr Wesen und ihre Bedeutung für die Politik des
    römischen Reiches." *Würzburger Jahrbücher für die Altertumswissenschaft* 3: 201–30.

Earl, Donald. 1961. *The Political Thought of Sallust*. Cambridge.

Freyburger, G. 1988. "Supplication grecque et supplication romaine." *Latomus* 47: 501–28.

Fuchs, Harald. 1958. "Der Friede als Gefahr." *Harvard Studies in Classical Philology* 25:
    363–85.

Gelzer, Matthias. 1933. "Römische Politik bei Fabius Pictor." *Hermes* 68: 129–66.

Gruen, Erich S. 1982. "Greek *pistis* and Roman *fides*." *Athenaeum* 60: 50–68.

——. 1984. *The Hellenistic World and the Coming of Rome*. Berkeley.

Hampl, Franz. 1973. "'Stoische Staatsethik' und frühes Rom" [1957]. In Richard Klein (ed.),
    Das Staatsdenken der Römer, 116–42. Darmstadt.

Heinze, Richard. 1960. "*Supplicium*." In Erick Burck (ed.), *Vom Geist des Römertums:
    Ausgewählte Aufsätze*, 28–41. Darmstadt.

Heuss, Alfred. 1933. *Die völkerrechtlichen Grundlagen der römischen Aussenpolitik in republi-
    kanischer Zeit*. Leipzig.

Jhering, Rudolf von. 1968 (orig. 1894). *Geist des römischen Rechts*. 2 vols. Darmstadt.

Klingner, Friedrich. 1979. "Virgil und die Idee des Friedens." In *Römische Geisteswelt; Essays
    zur lateinischen Literatur*, 614–44. Stuttgart.

Knoche, Ulrich. 1962. "Der Beginn des römischen Sittenverfalls." In Knoche, *Vom Selbstverständnis der Römer. Gesammelte Aufsätze*, 99–123. Heidelberg.

Kuttner, Anne. 1995. *Dynasty and Empire in the Age of Augustus*. Berkeley.

Lind, L. R. 1979. "Tradition of Roman Moral Conservatism." In Carl Deroux (ed.), *Studies in Latin Literature and Roman History*, I: 7–58. Brussels.

Paradisi, Bruno. 1941. "*Deditio in fidem.*" In *Studi di storia e diritto in onore di Arrigo Solmi*, 285–324. Milan.

Piganiol, André. 1950. "*Venire in fidem.*" *Revue internationale des droits de l'antiquité* 5: 339–47.

Rich, John. 1993. "Fear, Greed and Glory: the Causes of Roman War-Making in the Middle Republic." In John Rich and Graham Shipley (eds.), *War and Society in the Roman World*, 38–68. New York.

Rosenstein, Nathan. 1990. *Imperatores Victi*. Berkeley.

Schulten. 1901. "*Dediticii.*" *Paulys Realencyclopädie der classischen Altertumswissenschaft*, vol. 4.2. cols. 2359–63. Stuttgart.

Seckel, Emil. 1915. *Über Krieg und Recht in Rom*. Berlin.

Sherk, Robert. 1960. *Roman Documents from the Greek East*. Baltimore.

Strasburger, Hermann. 1965. "Poseidonios on Problems of the Roman Empire." *Journal of Roman Studies* 55: 40–53.

Täubler, Eugen. 1913. *Imperium Romanum. Studien zur Entwicklungsgeschichte des römischen Reichs*. Leipzig.

Walbank, F. W. 1957. *A Historical Commentary on Polybius*, vol. 1. Oxford.

Weinstock, Stefan. 1957. "*Victor* and *Invictus.*" *Harvard Theological Review* 50: 211–47.

Zanker, Paul. 1988. *The Power of Images in the Age of Augustus*, trans. Alan Shapiro. Ann Arbor.

Ziolkowski, Adam. 1993. "*Urbs direpta*, or How the Romans Sacked Cities." In John Rich and Graham Shipley (eds.), *War and Society in the Roman World*, 69–91. New York.

15

The Gates of War (and Peace): Roman Literary Perspectives

Jeri Blair DeBrohun

> At the present day, civilized opinion is a curious mental mixture. The military instincts and ideals are as strong as ever, but are confronted by reflective criticisms which sorely curb their ancient freedom. Innumerable writers are showing up the bestial side of military service. Pure loot and mastery seem no longer morally avowable motives, and pretexts must be found for attributing them solely to the enemy. England and we, our army and navy authorities repeat without ceasing, arm solely for "peace," Germany and Japan it is who are bent on loot and glory. "Peace" in military mouths today is a synonym for "war expected." The word has become a pure provocative, and no government wishing peace sincerely should allow it ever to be printed in a newspaper. Every up-to-date Dictionary should say that "peace" and "war" mean the same thing, now *in posse*, now *in actu*. It may even reasonably be said that the intensely sharp competitive *preparation* for war by the nations *is the real war*, permanent, unceasing; and that the battles are only a sort of public verification of the mastery gained during the "peace" interval (William James [1910]).

> The word "pax" denotes conquest no less than its desired consummation, and clever Ovid devised the label "perpetuam pacem paciferumque ducem" [perpetual peace and peace-bringing leader] (*Fasti* 4.408)" (Sir Ronald Syme [1989: 116]).

The potential scope of this chapter is immense. To begin, two generalizations are worth making which, though sweeping, are nonetheless true. First, virtually all of extant Roman literature, from its very beginnings through the end of antiquity, reflects, either explicitly or implicitly, a concern with war and peace. The Romans were, at their core, a martial people, who traced their origins back to the god of war, and whose historical development is readily described in terms of a long series of armed conflicts. In their conception of war, as one would expect, they made a clear distinction between campaigns waged against foreign enemies and civil wars between their own citizens. Foreign wars, whether purely imperialistic or fought in response to provocation by enemy peoples, were viewed as necessary and positive exertions of Rome's innate power and civilizing influence. The Romans were proud of their martial heritage and military successes, and this was reflected in their literature. Civil wars, on the other hand, were recognized as a deplorable but unfortunately repeated occurrence throughout the city's history. Romulus' legendary murder of his twin Remus found regular expression in Roman literature as a precursor for the fratricide that characterized civil war. Second, while the Romans often expressed a desire for peace, and for a leader who would establish and ensure a lasting peace, the concept behind the Latin *pax* is often best rendered as "pacification." One need not be as cynical as Syme in the epigraph quoted above to acknowledge that for the Romans peace was essentially the consequence of successfully prosecuted warfare (see Barton, Rosenstein, this vol.).

The focus of this chapter will be narrower, a close consideration of one specific Roman image of war and peace that is itself designedly two-sided and mirror-like: the gated temple of Janus, the two-headed deity whose ability to look forward and back simultaneously is reflected in the month that bears his name.[1] Janus' temple was centrally located in Rome, standing between the Forum Romanum and the Forum Julium, near the point where the Argiletum entered the Forum Romanum (Livy 1.19.2; Ovid *Fasti* 1.258; Richardson 1992: 207–08). Numismatic depictions on coins of Nero suggest that the temple was rectangular in form, consisting of two long walls with double doors at the front and back (Richardson ibid.; Hill 1989: 10; Plutarch, *Numa* 20.1). The god's statue showed him with two identical faces looking in opposite directions (Richardson ibid.). According to tradition, the temple was established early in Rome's history, as a means to symbolize whether the state was at war or at peace: if the gates were opened, Rome was at war; if they were closed, the state had achieved peace. The learned antiquarian, historian, and philologist Varro described the etymological origin of the gates' name, as well as the shrine's primary function, in his *De Lingua Latina* (most likely written 47–45 BCE):

> The Janualis gate ⟨was⟩ named after Janus, and therefore a statue of Janus was set up there and a ritual practice was instituted by Pompilius (as Piso writes in his *Annales*) that the gate should always be open, except when there was war nowhere. The tradition has been passed down that the gate was closed when Pompilius was king and after that when Titus Manlius was consul, after the first Carthaginian war was finished, and then opened in the same year (5.165).

Varro's description emphasizes that the gates' natural state was open: they were to be closed only when Rome was entirely free from war. Only two prior closures are mentioned by Varro: the first was by Numa Pompilius, Rome's traditional second king; and the second, two centuries before Varro, at the close of the First Punic War.

One might expect from Varro's brief description that the symbolism of Janus' temple was universal and timeless, not subject to manipulation or reinterpretation. With the advent of the principate (called thus after Augustus' self-styled designation as *princeps*, "first citizen"), however, the gates took on a renewed significance, reflected in a pronounced literary presence. The Battle of Actium (31 BCE), in which the forces of Augustus defeated those of Antony and Cleopatra, effectively concluded a long and difficult period of civil war. It was, however, immediately defined by Augustus and his supporters (and, eventually, by the Romans generally) as a foreign war, in which Italy, under Julius Caesar's heir, defeated the forces of the "East" under Cleopatra and thus brought peace to the world. In addition to the triple triumph held to celebrate the war's completion, the gates of the temple of Janus were ceremoniously closed in 29 BCE (Reinhold 1981–2; Gurval 1995: esp. 19–36). As Augustus himself tells us in his report about his achievements (*Res Gestae* 13), the gates were also closed on two more occasions during his principate.[2]

Not surprisingly, Augustus' closing of Janus' temple, together with the emphasis he himself placed on his performance of the ritual, elicited literary responses from nearly all the major writers of the period. It is not my primary purpose here to enter the debate on whether individual Augustan writers were adherents to or critics of the *princeps*.[3] These authors rarely express their views in transparent language; moreover, each depiction of Janus' gated shrine we will examine appears in the context of a larger work into whose aims and concerns the picture is fully integrated. While the writers' representations of, and attitudes toward, Augustus himself will inevitably form part of our discussion, it is those larger concerns, particularly with the nature of war and peace at Rome, that have the greatest relevance in the present context. The varied and at times competing perspectives on war and peace represented by the authors to be considered here (Livy, Virgil, Horace, and, though perhaps less influentially, Ovid) are all the more meaningful because their works assumed immediate and enduring importance to the Romans themselves for their role in defining and expressing Rome's national character.

We will see that the basic symbolism of Janus' gates remains constant: open gates signify war, closed ones peace. However, the origin of this symbolism, as well as the manner in which the signification worked, were subject to interpretation and imaginative representation. This potential for manipulation was exploited by the writers, who produced dramatically different, even at times contradictory, depictions of Janus' operation in order to provide their own commentaries, direct or oblique, on how war and peace were to be understood by their fellow Romans.

The *Res Gestae* of Augustus

Although chronologically the latest of the texts to be discussed here, Augustus' *Res Gestae* will be considered first.[4] It was one of three documents left by the *princeps* at his death, and a copy of it was to be inscribed on bronze pillars at the entrance of his mausoleum at Rome (Suetonius, *Augustus* 101.4). Since Mommsen (1883: v–vi), it has been recognized that the text divides itself into three sections: offices and honors (1–14); the *princeps'* expenditures on Rome's behalf (15–24), and finally the *Res Gestae* proper (25–35). These divisions, however, are not rigid (Yavetz 1984: 14–15). In addition to the special emphasis granted to events mentioned in the opening and closing chapters, certain concerns (such as Augustus' faithful adherence to ancestral custom or his personal modesty) are highlighted throughout. Nor is the *Res Gestae* a comprehensive list of Augustus' achievements; rather, it offers a highly selective personal account (Yavetz 1984; Ramage 1987; Ridley 2003).

Chapter 13 serves as the culmination of an initial enumeration of the traditional honors awarded to Augustus himself. The closing of Janus' gates is thus granted particular significance among the achievements for which Augustus wished to be remembered by posterity:

> It was the will of our ancestors that the gateway of Janus Quirinus should be shut when peace had been gained by victories on land and sea throughout the whole empire of the Roman people; from the foundation of the city down to my birth, tradition records that it

was shut only twice, but while I was the leading citizen the senate resolved that it should be shut on three occasions (trans. Brunt and Moore, modified).

This passage is interesting for the manner and language in which Augustus chose to represent his actions and underscore their significance. He places his achievements carefully in a context of ancestral tradition and Republican constitutional procedure: it was Rome's ancestors (*maiores*) whose will established the custom regarding the closing of Janus' temple, and the Senate who decreed its closure in each instance during Augustus' career. He uses the traditional record of only two prior closings to good advantage. In the whole expanse of the period before his birth, he reminds us, the temple was closed only twice altogether (*priusquam nascerer... bis omnino*); but during his principate, three closings were decreed *(ter me principe)*. By thus dividing Rome's history into the years before and after his own birth, then emphasizing his three closures of Janus over the two previously recorded, Augustus claims that his birth and rule ushered in a new era, in which peace was dramatically more prevalent than in Rome's past.[5] For the reader determined to approach the *Res Gestae* in literary terms, the alliterative and etymological connections between **priusquam** *nascerer* and *me* **principe** underline Augustus' peculiar role as the originator of a new era of peace.

The *princeps* also emphasizes that the right to close Janus' gates was reserved exclusively for those who had secured peace throughout the entire empire through military victory (*terra marique esset parta victoriis pax*). Nowhere in extant Roman literature is the close association between peace and military victory made more explicit. What Varro had stated in negative terms – the gates were to remain open "except when there was war nowhere" (*nisi cum bellum sit nusquam*) – is here phrased much more positively.

In addition, Augustus refers to the god by his title *Quirinus*, which associates Janus with a native Italian god of war and was understood in antiquity to suggest that he was, in one of his aspects, a war god.[6] From the third century on, moreover, Quirinus was assimilated to the deified Romulus, and it was as Romulus that he played a central role in Augustus' self-representation. Thus, Janus' epithet Quirinus, and the alignment it suggests in the *Res Gestae*, of Augustus-Romulus-war god, is not surprising, especially if Augustus means to emphasize both his military achievement and his role as founder of a new era for Rome.[7]

As Varro's passage indicates, however, Janus' temple had closer ties to Rome's second king, Numa Pompilius, to whom the first closure is regularly attributed. It has recently been noticed that Augustus took some pains to associate himself with the peaceful, religious Numa in addition to Rome's martial first founder (Galinsky 1996: 34–7, 84, 282, 346). While the clear emphasis placed on his military victories associates him more intimately with Romulus, Augustus' attention to Janus' temple itself, and the pride he takes in recalling its closure under his auspices, may well have been meant to promote an identification of his achievements with those of both Romulus and Numa. Understandably, since only the closing, not opening, of the gates symbolizes Augustus' (repeated) achievement of peace, the *Res Gestae* includes no mention of the ceremonial opening of the gates between closures: "Janus opened is less on show than Janus closed" (Syme 1989:115).

Livy's Janus: Indicator of Peace and War (*index pacis bellique*)

Livy presents Rome's foundation in two phases, through the reigns of its first two kings. Romulus founded Rome and led its citizens to victory in the wars that established their sovereignty over their Italian neighbors. Romulus' successor, Numa, took the following initial action as king (1.19.1–2):

> When he had thus gained the kingship, he prepared to give the new city, founded by force of arms, a wholly new foundation based on law, statutes, and rituals. And perceiving that men could not grow used to these things in the midst of wars, since their natures grew wild and savage through warfare, he thought that his fierce people needed to be softened by the disuse of arms, and he built the temple of Janus at the bottom of the Argiletum, as an indicator of peace and war, that when open it might signify that the nation was in arms, when closed that all the people round about were pacified.[8]

Livy makes peace the theme for Numa's reign, in contrast to the preceding era of war under Romulus. Following Romulus' foundation of the city by means of force (*urbem... conditam vi et armis*), Numa offers Rome a new, second foundation in law and religion (*iure... legibusque ac moribus*). This stark contrast, as well as the necessity of both rulers' contributions for the full establishment of the Roman state, are again made explicit at the end of Livy's treatment of Numa: "Thus two successive kings, each in a different way, the first by war, the second by peace, promoted the state's growth" (1.21.6: *Ita duo deinceps reges, alius alia via, ille bello, hic pace, civitatem auxerunt*).[9]

The first act of Numa's new foundation of Rome is the establishment of Janus' shrine, prompted by a specific motivation: Numa recognized that continued warfare made the Romans' character increasingly savage (*efferari militia animos*) and that, in fact, they were already a "fierce people" (*ferocem populum*). His belief that these bellicose tendencies "must be softened by disuse of arms" (*mitigandum... armorum desuetudine*) led him to build the temple of Janus, "as an indicator of peace and war" (*indicem pacis bellique*). Thus, although Livy presents Numa's Janus in neutral terms, as a simple signifier (*indicem*), Numa's expressed motive suggests an expectation (or at least desire) that the temple itself, as a symbolic witness, might somehow hold the potential to effect (or at least encourage) periods of peace among a people whose initial experiences and primary inclinations were martial. Numa's temple, like the king himself, has closer associations with peace than with war.

Ogilvie (1965: 95) observes that Livy's depiction of war's effects on the minds of the Romans reflects an unusual perspective:

> Whereas other Romans accepted war and military service as fields in which a man's *virtus* could be seen to best advantage, L. rejects that assumption. For him war itself is degrading – *efferari militia animos*. This is a heterodox notion, found only among Romans of his time (e.g. Horace, *Epode* 7; cf. Tacitus, *Hist.* 3.25, 31, 33). His chief care is peace... There-fore the replacement of the *metus hostilis* [fear of the enemy] by the *metus deorum* [fear of

the gods] which was a political *pis aller* to Sallust and others was for L. a consummation devoutly to be wished.

Within Livy's narrative, Numa's concern with war's deleterious effects is a reflection of the king's own almost preternaturally peaceful character. Numa's perception that typical Roman character, in contrast, is essentially bellicose appears to be borne out when, in the next sentence, Livy provides a wider chronological perspective on war and peace at Rome by reporting the history of the gates' operation since Numa's initial closure (1.19.3–4a):

> Twice since Numa's reign has it been closed: once in the consulship of Titus Manlius, after the conclusion of the First Punic War; the second time, which the gods permitted our own generation to witness, was after the battle of Actium, when the emperor Caesar Augustus had brought about peace on land and sea.

Livy's report is consistent with those of Varro and Augustus: as of the time he wrote, the temple gates had been closed only twice in all the centuries since Numa initiated the ritual.[10] From all three accounts, the reader readily infers that at every other period in Rome's history the gates of Janus were open, suggesting a state of nearly continual war since the city's foundation.

We will return to examine Livy's report on the gates' three closures more closely below. Let us now consider Numa's concerns just after the treaties were secured that led to the gate's first closing (1.19.4):

> Numa closed the temple after first securing the good will of all the neighboring tribes by alliances and treaties. And fearing lest relief from anxiety on the score of foreign perils might lead men who had hitherto been held back by fear of their enemies (*metus hostium*) and by military discipline into extravagance and idleness, he thought the very first thing to do, as being the most efficacious with a populace which was ignorant and, in those early days, uncivilized, was to imbue them with the fear of the gods (*deorum metus*).

These lines express the common Greco-Roman view that prolonged periods of peace were prone to lead to luxurious living and, eventually, to moral decline (Ogilvie 1965: 94–95 with references). Not surprisingly, Livy's Numa has a ready response: peace, if it is to be maintained with dignity, requires the discipline offered by law and religion, based on firmly established legal and religious institutions (1.19–21). These include the creation of a priesthood for Jupiter (the *flamen Dialis*):

> But since he thought that in a warlike state there would be more kings like Romulus than like Numa, and that they would themselves go into battles, he was concerned that the sacrificial duties of the kingship should not be abandoned, and so he established a *flamen* for Jupiter to serve as his perpetual priest, and he outfitted him with a conspicuous dress and with the royal curule chair (1.20.2).

Despite his own exclusively peaceful rule, Numa conceives of Rome as a "warlike state," as if this were its essential character, a city whose leaders are more likely to model themselves on their militarily inclined first ruler than on their more peaceable second king, and in which a separate, royal priesthood is required to ensure the continued practice of religious ritual.

Livy opens his final chapter on Numa's reign (1.21.1–2) with an idealized picture of a Roman people whose minds have been thoroughly converted from the concentration on war that characterized Romulus' reign (1.21.1 closely recalls 1.19.1) to a preoccupation with piety. No doubt is left about the source and infectious nature of this altered Roman mindset:

> And while the people themselves were shaping their own character based on the morals of their king, as their unique example, the neighboring peoples also, who previously had considered that a camp, not a city had been set up in their midst, as a disturbance to the general peace, came to feel such reverence that they considered it sacrilege to harm a state so completely turned toward the worship of the gods (1.21.2).

Numa is an *exemplum*; specifically, he is one of the positive models Livy in his preface promises his readers for their emulation (*Praef.* 10). More than that, he is an ideal paradigm of the discipline and piety Livy bemoans as lacking in his own time (*Praef.* 9–11; Feldherr 1998: 70). The historian even characterizes Numa as a "unique example" (*unici exempli*), perhaps recalling the singular role he played among Rome's early kings (and indeed, among all the city's leaders) as a ruler devoted entirely to peace.

Livy's narration of Numa's reign ends with a recapitulation of Rome's twofold foundation (1.21.5):

> Of all Numa's services, the greatest was his guardianship, throughout the time of his rule, no less of peace than of his kingdom. Thus two kings in succession, each in a different way, the first through war, the second through peace, increased the state … The state was strong and well balanced in the arts of both war and peace.

Livy's final words suggest that a well-balanced state can only be achieved when periods of successful war are followed by eras of perfect peace under the leadership of peace-minded rulers. Might we not conclude here that Livy offers a subtle challenge to Augustus, whose own recent closure of Janus' gates, with its accompanying proclamation of universal peace, raised hope that he would now himself follow the example of Numa?[11]

Let us return now to Livy's description of the closures of Janus' gates and consider them more closely in the context of his treatment of Numa's reign (1.19.2–4). When Livy introduces the symbolism of the gates, he follows the tradition associating closure with universal peace (*pacatos circa omnes populos*). In his narrative, the description of the surrounding peoples as "pacified" looks both backward and forward. It recalls Romulus' consolidation of Rome's power through military victory over the city's neighbors and anticipates Numa's own effective pacification, through the power of his example, not only of his fellow Romans but also of their neighbors, who are understandably reluctant to attack such a pious city.

By contrast, Livy explicitly states that subsequent closures by Titus Manlius and Augustus both occurred after the successful completion of wars. Only Numa's closure occurred "after securing the goodwill of all the neighboring peoples through alliances and treaties." While this representation of Numa is consistent with the historian's overall portrayal of this king as unique in all of Rome's history in his exclusive

concern with peace and peaceful relations, it reminds the reader that later closures will necessarily be preceded by a period of war for which the gates have been
opened.

As suggested above, Livy's treatment of Numa might include a challenge to
Augustus to follow this king's genuinely peaceful example. In closing, let us consider an additional link between Numa and Augustus suggested by Livy's language.
As we have seen, Livy explicitly denotes Numa as a paradigm (*exemplum*) to his fellow
Romans both of the principles of peaceful relations and policies and of the ideals of
moral discipline that in his own time have decayed to the point of near extinction. As
far as Augustus is concerned, at the most obvious level, like Titus Manlius, he follows
the example of Numa when he closes the temple of Janus. Although he does this
after a war (*post bellum*), which might appear to associate him more immediately with
the gates' second closure by Manlius, Livy's description establishes a more intimate
connection between Numa's and Augustus' closures by emphasizing that "the gods
granted [the latter] to our generation to witness" (1.19.3). Livy's explicit mention of
a divine gift is surely intended to associate Rome's current leader closely with his pious
forebear. At the same time, the gods' intention in granting this favor to Livy's contemporary audience suggests that Augustus, like Numa, might serve as a model for his
fellow Romans.[12] Here too, perhaps, Livy offers a hint that contemporary Romans,
including the historian himself, will be observing Augustus' reign attentively, hoping
that he will ensure a lasting era of peace.

Virgil's *Aeneid*: The Gates of War

The most powerfully dramatic portrayal of Janus' gates is found in Virgil's *Aeneid*.
While Livy's Janus was closely associated with a unique era of peace, Virgil's depiction
reflects a preoccupation with war, and especially with the uneasy blurring of the definitions of civil versus foreign war in the celebrations following the Battle of Actium.
The gates appear prominently at two critical moments in the epic: their future closure
under Augustus is promised by Jupiter in his prophecy to Venus in Book 1; later, in
Book 7, Juno forces them open, thereby instigating the wars of the poem's "Iliadic"
second half.[13]

Jupiter's prophecy to Venus (*Aen.* 1.257–96) promises a glorious future for Rome,
beginning with Aeneas' successful war in Italy and culminating in a future age of peace
under Augustus (286–96):

> A Trojan Caesar will be born from glorious ancestry, whose power will end at the Ocean,
> whose fame at the stars, a Julius, a name handed down from great Iulus. Him you, without
> worry, will someday receive in the heavens, weighed down with the spoils of the East; this
> man, too, will be invoked in prayers. At that time wars will cease and rough ages soften;
> hoary Faith and Vesta, Quirinus with his brother Remus will give laws. The gates of war,
> grim with iron and close-fitting bars, will be closed; within, impious Rage (*Furor impius*),
> sitting on savage arms, his hands fast bound behind with a hundred brazen knots, shall
> roar in the ghastliness of blood-stained lips.[14]

Jupiter's optimistic speech succeeds in reassuring Venus but contains troubling ambiguities and distortions. Two of the more notorious appear in this section and are important for our consideration of Virgil's description of the gates of war: the ambiguity of *Caesar* (whether Julius or Augustus is meant) in line 286, and the promise of a harmonious reunion of Quirinus/Romulus and Remus in Rome's future era of peace (line 292). In addition, Virgil's depiction of the gates themselves, and of their operation, also involves a distortion both of their traditional function and of the meaning Augustus himself attached to their closure under his auspices.

I assume here that Virgil is referring to Augustus throughout lines 286–96 and that the primary historical moment evoked in the passage is Augustus' first closure of Janus' gates in 29 BCE, as part of the celebration of his victory at Actium.[15] This is not to say, however, that Virgil's words in 286–90 are unambiguous. The combination of *Caesar*, *Iulius*, and the mention of deification would no doubt remind the contemporary Roman reader of Augustus' adoptive father. Yet without special pleading, Julius cannot be imagined to arrive in heaven "weighted down with Eastern spoils."

O'Hara notes that "the riddle of the description of the man forces the reader to think about both the bloody civil wars before and after Julius' death, and the similarities between Julius and Augustus" (1990: 161). To anticipate my argument, this connection of both men not just with war, but specifically with civil war, is one of the primary reasons that Virgil has Jupiter, at the culmination of his prophecy, introduce Augustus in terms that call attention to his relationship with his adoptive father. For it is with civil war that Virgil is particularly concerned in these final lines. Significantly, the reminder of the connection between the two men is immediately followed by an assurance of perhaps the most important difference between them: only Augustus at last brought an end to civil war, as signified by his closure of Janus' temple in 29 BCE (alluded to in 291–96). Yet Virgil's depiction of the gates of war (and especially of *Furor impius*), even more than his use of *Caesar*, undermines the prophecy's assurance of a peaceful future by suggesting that civil war might someday be rekindled.

In these lines, as elsewhere in the *Aeneid* (esp. 6.791–95), Augustus ushers in a new Golden Age for Rome. Virgil's picture initially appears to be more optimistic than Livy's, whose Numa saw his fellow Romans as a people who had grown fierce through war and whose spirits required "softening" (*mitigandum*). Even during his own peaceful reign, Numa continued to prophesy Rome's future as a "warlike state" (*bellicosa civitas*). Virgil's Jupiter, in contrast, promises a future era when wars will cease altogether and generations will "soften" (*mitescent*) as if on their own volition. The following lines, however, modify the prediction of universal peace in 291. The promise that Quirinus/Romulus and his brother Remus will rule together specifically alludes to the end of civil war; and civil war, not war generally, remains the focus through the end of the passage.

An obvious problem is posed by the use of a reconciliation between Romulus and Remus to symbolize the end of (civil) war, a clear contradiction of accepted legend.[16] As was noted earlier, Romulus' legendary murder of his brother, one of Rome's primary foundation myths, was also viewed as a natural analogy for the fratricide of civil war. Virgil's use of Quirinus for Romulus is suggestive here; for Quirinus is, specifically, the deified Romulus, and his identification by that name distinguishes him from his twin. In addition, Quirinus is one of Janus' titles, later used of the god by Augustus himself (*R.G.* 13, quoted above). Virgil's reference to Romulus as Quirinus, followed by the gates' closure, implicitly associates this event with the more successful twin. This allusion, and the *princeps'* own suggestion of a link between himself and Romulus-Quirinus, complete the complex of associations. Before we offer an interpretation of these connections, let us consider Virgil's depiction of the gates of Janus' temple.

Jupiter's optimistic tenor changes when he concludes his vision of Rome's future with a frightening image of the gates of war and, especially, of *Furor impius* bound in chains within them. Livy's neutral "indicator of peace and war" (*index pacis bellique*) is unrecognizable in Virgil's "grim portals of War" (*dirae... Belli portae*). Virgil found the inspiration for this depiction in two models. For *dirae portae*, he drew on Ennius' epic *Annales* (fr. 225–6 Skutsch: "after foul Discord [*Discordia taetra*] broke open the iron gateposts and gates of war"), and his portrait of *Furor impius* was based on a painting by Apelles which Augustus later placed in his own Forum (D. Servius, on *Aen.* 1.294; Pliny, *Natural History* 35.27). Pliny (ibid. 35.23) reports that the painting depicted "an image of War with its hands tied behind its back, while Alexander in his chariot triumphs over it." As a result of Virgil's artistic combination of these models, the temple that in Livy serves as a passive barometer of war and peace becomes a fortress endowed with the superhuman strength necessary to ensure the perpetual forced imprisonment of *Furor*, whose gore-covered lips utter forth an eternal roar.

Two aspects are particularly significant here. First, the portrait of *Furor* as an indestructible creature, restrained but still howling (and bloodied), is by no means a reassuring image of perpetual peace. Even worse, in the world of Virgil's *Aeneid*, nearly without exception, fortified strongholds, even when controlled by divine ordinance, are eventually breached either by stealth or force.[17] As we will see, this proves true for the gates of war in Book 7. That Jupiter's prediction concerns a time far in the future, outside the scope of the epic's narrative, is limited consolation.

Let us look briefly at one example of a breached stronghold whose description, and eventual opening, in several respects parallels the final image in Jupiter's prophecy. The roar (*fremet*, 296) of imprisoned *Furor* echoes the sound of the winds chained within the cave of Aeolus earlier in Book 1 (52–59; *fremunt*, 56). Jupiter himself, fearful of the winds' uncontrollable power, has buried them under massive mountains and placed Aeolus in command over them (60–63). Aeolus is to check or release the winds, when ordered, according to a fixed covenant (*foedere certo*, 62). Juno's initial act in the *Aeneid* is to persuade Aeolus to violate this covenant, force open the cavernous prison, and unleash the winds. This causes the storm that shipwrecks Aeneas' fleet. After Poseidon has calmed the storm, Venus approaches Jupiter with her concerns for Aeneas' future. Jupiter's prophecy promises an end to Aeneas' trials, but its final image, of a powerful disruptive force imprisoned under Jupiter's sanction, uncomfortably recalls the start of the narrative sequence.

A second, especially problematic aspect of *Furor* is its characterization as *impius*. For *Furor impius*, especially appearing right after the mention of Romulus and Remus, must represent civil war.[18] Thus Virgil's Jupiter closes his prophecy with a distorted picture of the gates' traditional function. In their next appearance, in Book 7, an association with civil war accurately describes their use within the action of the poem's narrative. In their present context, however, their apparently exclusive connection with civil war raises problems. Most obviously, if their closure ensures the confinement of *Furor impius*, how could they ever be opened, and how is a just war against foreign enemies to be declared? This problem, too, is addressed in Book 7, but it remains open at the end of Jupiter's prophecy.

First, however, let us consider how we are to interpret Virgil's allusion to Augustus' closure of Janus' gates in Book 1. Virgil's complex imagery does not lend itself to a straightforward reading. Since, as we have seen, lines 292–96 specifically evoke the end of civil war, an allusion to Augustus can only be meaningfully attached to the closure of 29 BCE, after the battle of Actium. In one sense, this is unsurprising, since Augustus' victory in this battle is also the climactic endpoint of the prophetic imagery on Aeneas' shield in Book 8. Yet in Book 1 an allusion to Actium is not unproblematic because Augustus himself defined his victory as the end of a foreign war, fought against Cleopatra and the forces of the East, and because, within the prophecy itself, line 291 introduces the new, gentler age for Rome as an era when all wars will cease (*positis bellis*). This notion of universal peace is more appropriate to the traditional associations of Janus' closures.

Virgil's narrowing of the gates' signification from universal peace to the end of civil war in the context of Augustus' closure may be read in two ways: more positively, it implies that the victory at Actium simultaneously ended all Rome's wars, foreign and domestic, and it provided an end, at last, to a long era of civil war; less positively, it reminds the Romans that the attainment of peace, celebrated by Janus' closure after Actium, came also at the cost associated with the impiety of civil war. In addition, the link between Romulus/Quirinus, Augustus, and Janus suggests, positively, a close association between Rome's deified first founder and the future deification of Augustus as the founder of a new age of peace. Negatively, it implies that, just as the peaceful reunion between Romulus and his brother Remus is impossible, so also there was only one victor in the most recent civil war that led to Rome's new foundation. Finally, the depiction of *Furor impius* as an indestructible creature, in concert with the recollection of Julius Caesar in 286–88, may well be meant to suggest that the fulfillment of Jupiter's prophecy has not yet been fully assured.

The gates' next appearance, in *Aeneid 7*, is preceded by Juno's resolve to put the final touch on her instigation of war between Latins and Trojans (lines 572–73). The Latins, spurred on by the interventions of Juno's agent Allecto, collectively demand that King Latinus declare war: "Immediately they all demand unholy war (*infandum bellum*), against the omens, against the oracles of the gods, with perverse will" (583–84). Latinus, unable to prevail against such pressure, warns his people of the impiety of their plan, abdicates his power, and retreats to his palace. At this point, with the Latins on the cusp of declaring *infandum bellum*, Virgil depicts the traditional ceremony to be carried out whenever the gates of war are opened, then returns to the poem's action (601–22):

> There was a custom in Hesperian Latium, which thenceforth the Alban
> cities held holy, as now does Rome, mistress of the world,
> when they first rouse the war-god to battle,
> be it Getae or Arabs or Hyrcanians against whom their hands
> prepare to carry tearful war, or to march on India's sons
> and pursue the Dawn, and reclaim their standards from the Parthians.
> There are twin gates of war (so men call them),
> hallowed by religious awe and the terrors of fierce Mars:
> a hundred brazen bolts close them, and the eternal strength of iron,
> and Janus their guardian never quits the threshold.
> Here, when the sentence of the Fathers is firmly fixed on war,
> the Consul, arrayed in Quirinal robe and Gabine cincture,
> with his own hand unbars the grating portals,
> with his own lips calls forth war; then the rest of the warriors take up the cry,
> and brazen horns blare out their hoarse accord.
> Then, too, Latinus was bidden to proclaim war on the sons of Aeneas,
> with such custom, and to unclose the grim gates.
> But the father withheld his hand, shrank back from the
> hateful office, and buried himself in blind darkness.
> Then the queen of the gods, gliding from the sky,
> with her own hand dashed in the lingering doors, and on their turning hinges
> Saturn's daughter burst open the iron-bound gates of war.

Virgil's imaginative description of the ceremonial opening of Janus' gates suggests that the tradition was passed down from the remote past of the peoples of Italy to the Romans, who then performed it throughout their own history.[19] Emphasis is placed on the religious piety and moral authority required for the declaration of war.[20] In solemn ceremony, with full support of the senators and citizens, the consul himself unlocks the gates and symbolically calls forth war, expressed not in personified form but with the concrete *pugnas*. Virgil's description of the gates themselves recalls that which ended Jupiter's prophecy, but with certain notable exceptions. Here the gates are holy (*sacrae*, 608) rather than *dirae* (*Aen.* 1.293), and Janus is explicitly named as their *custos* (line 610). The associations with civil war (Quirinus and Remus, *Furor impius*) are absent. The emphasis in these lines is on Mars, Rome's ancestor and god of war. The savagery and pain of war are not ignored (cf. *saevi formidine Martis*, 608; *lacrimabile bellum*, 604), but these are necessary elements of any war. Perhaps most importantly, the gates are opened to initiate foreign wars. It is not difficult to imagine that Virgil's account of the ritual reflects the ceremony as it was performed by Augustus.

In line 616, Virgil returns to his primary narrative; *more* (custom) in line 617 recalls *mos* in line 601 and suggests a seamless transition between modern Rome and ancient Latium. In this instance, however, as Virgil's readers know from the previous events in Book 7, the demand on Latinus to open the gates is not morally sanctioned.[21] Latinus himself recognizes this and, dreading what is to come, refuses to complete the ritual. With terrible swiftness, Juno slips down from the sky and, with her own hand, forces open the gates that hesitate even at her divine touch.[22] When Juno suddenly appears, the reader immediately senses a transformation. Lines 621–22 are modeled closely on those from Ennius' *Annales* quoted earlier, as now Virgil's Juno replaces Ennius' *Discordia taetra* as the divine force releasing war's madness. Yet Virgil excludes any simple allegory. Juno's descent itself reminds us that we have not shifted from the human to the divine realm. Instead, she has brought to earth her capacity to unleash (and conjure?) *Furor impius*. Just as Juno has engineered the events leading up to the violent eruption of war, her divine power is required to complete the process. And it is surely *Furor impius* that is released from the *Belli portae*. Although Virgil includes here no picture of *Furor*, his readers will have forgotten neither the terrifying creature whose character is suited to the *infandum bellum* the Latins have demanded nor its associations with civil war. And, of course, readers know of the future coalescence of the two peoples, which marks their conflict, opened by the ritual Latinus is expected to perform, as a precursor of civil war. This adds meaning to Latinus' refusal to engage in a "hateful office" (*foeda ministeria*), a description more suitable for Juno's actions.

Virgil thus manages to present two conflicting pictures of the gates of war – their traditional, appropriate opening for foreign wars versus their improper employment to instigate civil war – without, however, neatly separating the two. He does not present two different sets of gates, but two different pictures of the same set. The reference to the gates as "twin portals" (*geminae portae*, 607), which evokes Janus' title *Geminus*, is perhaps also meant as a subtle pointer to the poet's own double image. In this instance, Virgil's ambiguity, and the implications it suggests, cannot simply be attributed to Jupiter as perhaps is possible in Book 1. Virgil means for his readers to see that the gates are capable of signifying different, even contradictory ideas simultaneously. Juno's intervention in opening the gates shows that they are not only a mortal construction but part of the divine machinery of the universe. For Juno, the gates are as they were described in Jupiter's prophecy. In the domestic ("civil") conflict between the gods Jupiter and Juno, which fuels the (civil) wars within the poem, Jupiter's gates, exclusively concerned with *Furor impius*, represent well the poem's divine conflict between Juno's *furor* and Jupiter's determination to control it.

Virgil's twofold depiction of the gates has complicated implications in the human sphere as well, both within the epic and for his readers. The Latins' intention to use the gates' traditional ritual to declare what they perceive as a foreign war, but what is also, at least proleptically, a civil war, serves as a reminder that this distinction is not always clear. Here, as in Jupiter's prophecy, the Roman reader might think of Augustus and Actium. Virgil's dual picture also reminds us of the ritual's inherent ambiguity. If Janus closed signifies universal peace, both foreign and domestic, should his ceremonial opening not be employed for both foreign and civil conflicts? For the Romans, of course, as Latinus' refusal indicates, this would be sacrilege.

Virgil's allusion to Augustus' historical opening of the gates occurs in the description of the ritual's tradition (*Aen.* 7.601–15) and serves as an example of how and when the ceremony is properly performed: with full civic participation and to announce the initiation of a foreign campaign. The contrasting pictures of Rome's *Belli portae*, therefore, perhaps simultaneously remind the Romans of the civil wars in their past, recent and ancient, and express hope that in the future (starting with Augustus) the gates would only ever be used to signify unambiguously the initiation and successful completion of foreign wars.

Horace, *Odes* 4.15: Janus, Devoid of Wars

Horace first mentions the shrine of Janus in his final *Ode* (4.15), which most likely dates to 13/12 BCE (Fraenkel 1957: 449). The poem celebrates certain achievements of Augustus and demonstrates lyric poetry's ideal suitability as a medium for such praise.[23] As Putnam has shown (1986: 262–306), one of the primary means Horace employs to convey how much Rome, with the principate now fully established, has changed for the better, is the allusive recollection and revision of certain moments in his own earlier poetry and in the poems of his contemporary, Virgil. This connection between Horace and Virgil is especially significant for our consideration of Horace's depiction of Janus. In his portrayal of the god's shrine, Horace reverses the central features of Virgil's image, shifting the emphasis from war, both domestic and foreign, to universal peace. Horace also employs certain aspects of Virgil's depiction in new contexts, further highlighting his own, more unreservedly positive, depiction of Augustan peace.

As the first stanza ends and the second begins, Horace proclaims that the age (*aetas*) of Caesar Augustus has ushered in a long-desired era of restored peace for Rome. The poem's central stanzas offer a catalogue of the blessings Augustus has restored to Rome (lines 4b–16) followed by an assurance that his protection has secured a peaceful future for the city (17–24):

> Your age, Caesar, has returned plentiful crops to the fields and restored to our Jove the standards snatched from the arrogant doorposts of the Parthians, and it has closed the Janus of Quirinus, devoid of wars (*vacuum duellis/Ianum Quirini clausit*), and has cast reins on license that wandered beyond the right bounds, and it banished faults and recalled the ancient arts, through which the Latin name and Italian might grew strong, and the fame and majesty of our rule was spread to the rising of the sun from its western bed. With Caesar as guardian of our circumstances (*custode rerum*), no civil rage or force will drive away peaceful leisure (*non furor civilis aut vis exiget otium*), nor will wrath, which forges swords and makes enemies of wretched cities. Not those who drink the deep Danube will break Julian laws, nor the Getae, nor the Seres or faithless Parthians, nor those born by the river Tanais (lines 4b–24).

One of the preeminent images used to exemplify Rome's new *aetas* is the closing of Janus' temple. Horace's contemporaries must have been struck by the dramatic contrast between this image and Virgil's *Belli portae*. In Jupiter's prophecy in *Aeneid* Book 1, the eternal roar of (civil) war's *Furor impius*, forcibly imprisoned within the gates' stronghold, serves as a warning that the violence of war, if not guarded carefully, is ever poised to burst forth anew (as it does in Book 7, with Juno's help). For Horace, however, closure means that Janus' shrine, and by extension Rome itself, is entirely devoid of wars. Horace also reverses Virgil's more positive depiction of the traditional ritual of the gates' opening (in *Aeneid* 7.601–15). There, too, the gates were ceremoniously unlocked by the consul so that war could be summoned forth. Horace's image, juxtaposed to that of Virgil, suggests not only that all wars have ended in the new age, but also that there is no potential, within Rome, for their renewal.

Horace further recalls and revises Virgil's image most clearly in lines 17–20. The reference to Caesar as "guardian of affairs" (*custos rerum*), positioned at the beginning of stanza five, looks back to "Janus of Quirinus" (*Ianum Quirini*, see below) at the opening of stanza three. Janus is regularly designated as *custos* of his temple, and he was so described by Virgil (*Aeneid* 6.610: *nec custos abstitit limine Ianus*). In *Ode* 4.15, Horace's Caesar himself takes on the role of guardian of the state (17). In replacing Janus with Augustus here, Horace highlights the idea that the one responsible for the temple's closure is, in fact, the state's protector. What Augustus' guardianship means, and how it is related to his assumption of Janus' role, is seen in the lines that follow, which again take their meaning from Horace's reversal of Virgil's image.

For Horace, under Augustus' protection civil rage, force, and wrath (*furor civilis, vis*, and *ira*) are kept outside the state, while peaceful leisure (*otium*) alone is protected inside. *Furor civilis* vividly recalls Virgil's *Furor impius* and makes explicit Horace's understanding of Virgil's image. Horace recognized the problems inherent in Virgil's picture of Janus' gates. He no doubt realized, as Virgil had, that the madness of civil war, which, by definition, involves only Rome's citizens, might most suitably be imagined as dwelling within the city's boundaries. While Virgil's memorable portrait of an indestructible *Furor*, restrained but still roaring and bloodied, suggests continued fear of the re-emergence of civil war, Horace's desire to present Rome as entirely protected from war, foreign or civil, requires the expulsion of *furor civilis* from the city and, through Augustus' strength as *custos rerum*, the protection of *otium*, which alone remains in the city.

Virgil's *Belli portae* are again relevant when Horace turns to Rome's foreign enemies (21–24). A similar list of potential Roman foes appeared in Virgil's description of the gates' opening to signify the initiation of foreign war in *Aen*. 7. There it was the Romans who actively pursued war against their enemies (7.604–6). Horace avoids any suggestion of Roman aggression. "Breaking" (*rumpent*, line 22), used for the action of Rome's enemies, recalls Juno's forced opening of the gates in Virgil's epic (*Belli ferratos rumpit Saturnia postis*; *Aen*. 7.622), but the threat concerns "Julian laws" (*edicta Iulia*), not the gates of war. In Horace's ode, Augustus' Rome focuses not on war, but on the protection of lawful order.

More subtly, Horace replaces Virgil's imagery with his own language of confinement and exclusion at other moments in his poem's central stanzas. The mention of Janus' closure in line 9 is immediately followed by the imposition of reins not on madness, but on license, which would otherwise wander outside the bounds of correctness. Horace's words suggest that, once he had removed any need for concern with war, the *princeps* rightly turned his attention to moral reform. In lines 11–12, faults (*culpae*) are expelled and Rome's "ancient arts" (*veteres artes*) are recalled.[24] The latter is surely a reference to another Virgilian perspective on war and peace, expressed in Anchises' prophecy of Rome's future and spoken to his son in the Underworld (6.851–853):

> You, Roman, remember to rule nations with your power
> (these will be your arts), to impose the custom of peace,
> to spare the humbled and conquer the proud.

In his ode, Horace manages to allude to Rome's success in war without mentioning it directly. The results of Rome's victories are the subject of lines 13–16.

Like Augustus in the *Res Gestae*, Horace refers to Janus by using his designation as *Quirinus*, a traditional title that also reflects Augustus' own representation of his closures – though here with a slight variation: the god's temple is "the Janus of Quirinus." In light of Horace's later replacement of Janus with Augustus himself as *custos*, and of his desire to emphasize only Janus' peaceful associations, his words ("your age, Caesar, has closed the Janus of Quirinus") may well suggest to his readers that Rome's new founder, Augustus, has now fully replaced its original one, and that the old associations of Janus, with Romulus and the god of war, have now been replaced by only peaceful ones. This reading might also reassure those who recalled the gates' troubling association, in *Aeneid* 1, with both Quirinus–Romulus and his brother Remus.

Horace was concerned to present in his final ode a depiction of the Augustan age that demonstrated, both in its message and in its language and imagery, the peaceful nature of the new era. He chose to express this in part by alluding to, and revising, certain troubling passages in Virgil's poetry, including especially the vividly imagined portrait of the *Belli portae* and their prisoner, *Furor impius*. He signaled his intentions cleverly and indirectly, by opening with a *recusatio*: he had desired to write of "battles and conquered cities" but was stopped by Apollo, who warned that the theme was too much for him (1–3). This immediately leads to the elaborate praise of Caesar's new age. As Fraenkel notes, a more obvious reason for Horace's abandonment of martial subjects is evidenced in the poem's central stanzas: "now that peace and order have been restored, a poet has better things to do than write about battles (*proelia loqui*)."[25] In the new age initiated by Augustus' closure of Janus' temple, war has been banished not only from Rome but also from Horace's poetry.

Revision of Virgil's Janus again appears in Horace's letter to Augustus (*Epistle* 2.1), a poem nearly contemporary with *Odes* 4. After noting Virgil's favor with the *princeps* (247), Horace, also in a *recusatio*, includes among the subjects he would sing for Augustus, if he were able, "the ending of wars throughout the world under your auspices, and the bars holding fast Janus, the guardian of peace" (*tuisque/auspiciis totum confecta duella per orbem,/claustraque custodem pacis cohibentia Ianum;* 254–55). Here, too, peace, not war, is protected inside Janus' gates, although this time Horace retains Virgil's image of a locked stronghold, which was perhaps too forceful for his peaceful intentions in *Ode* 4.15. Under Augustus' auspices, Janus, who protects peace, is himself held fast, a firm reminder that in the new age of peace his temple is never again to be opened.

Ovid's Janus: Nothing to Do with War (*nil mihi cum bello*)

The differences in the depictions of Janus' gates in Livy, Virgil, and Horace exemplify well how individual Roman writers – even those working in the same period – can use the same image to convey different reflections, emphases, and ideas about the nature of war and peace at Rome. When Ovid takes up the same subject in his *Fasti* (a poem left unfinished on the poet's death in 17 CE), he explicitly and mischievously raises questions about the precise function of Janus' temple on which he knows his readers have received competing answers in his predecessors' works.

After a brief formal prologue, Ovid opens his poem on the Roman calendar with a dialogue between the narrator and the god Janus himself. The Janus episode is both the first and the longest in the entire poem (1.63–288). As the first speaker, Janus is a character within the poem and serves a programmatic role as a primary representative of the poem's themes and concerns (Hardie 1991). Two programmatic aspects of Janus' character are especially relevant here. First, as an informant Janus is decidedly given to ambiguity: he often provides ambivalent answers or refuses to choose between competing explanations for a single phenomenon, and in at least one instance explicitly concerned with our topic, he offers what appears to be contradictory information. Ovid exploits this aspect of Janus' character fully when the god answers questions about the operation of his temple's gates in relation to war and peace. Second, and significantly in the present context, Janus associates himself much more closely with peace than with war. Peace is a central theme of the *Fasti*, and in his own statements on war and peace, Janus places himself firmly on the side of the latter.

In *Fasti* 1.117–24, Janus describes his guardianship of the world, including a peculiar version of his control over war and peace:

> Whatever you see anywhere – sky, sea, clouds, earth – all things are closed and opened by my hand. The guardianship of this vast universe depends on me alone, and the right to turn its hinge is entirely mine. When I choose to send forth peace from her tranquil dwelling, she freely walks every path. But the whole world would be filled with deadly slaughter, if unyielding bars should not hold the wars locked inside.

Although Janus here speaks of his powers in cosmological terms, the language evokes the image of the god's temple at Rome. Lines 121–24 combine and revise aspects of both Virgil's and Horace's pictures. Janus asserts that he controls the movements of both peace and war, and indeed it appears that both have abodes, in separate quarters, within the god's temple. Whereas Virgil personifies war's Furor, Ovid presents an agile, anthropomorphic Peace, who can be sent forth by Janus from her own "tranquil dwelling" (*placidis tectis*) to wander the world freely. Peace's personification and freedom of movement also distinguish her from Horace's *otium* in *Ode* 4.15 or *pax* in *Ep.* 2.1, which are both represented as fully protected inside. Wars, meanwhile, as in Virgil's picture, are kept imprisoned behind unyielding locks but retain their destructive power, as well as the potential for future release.

Janus claims absolute control over both war and peace, but his relations with peace are clearly the more amicable. When at home, she imparts her own calm quality to her dwelling. When the god releases her, she readily spreads her influence throughout the world. In Virgil's picture of Janus' gates, peace was not mentioned directly but was represented only through the imprisonment of war. For Horace, even in a Rome "devoid of war" peace was carefully guarded by Caesar as *custos*. In Ovid, however, Janus' Peace is at least as comfortable abroad as at home: when she is released, her influence is felt everywhere (*perpetuas vias*, 122). Because Janus makes no distinction between domestic and foreign war, his words also suggest a more universal notion of war than we have seen thus far: should war be unleashed, it will fill the whole world with battle.

Later in the dialogue, Janus describes his role in an idealized Saturnian Golden Age in Italy, before Justice was banished from the earth (*Fasti* 1.247–55a):

> "I was in power at that time, when earth could endure the presence of gods, and divinities moved freely in the abodes of men. Human wickedness had not yet put Justice to flight (she was the last of the gods to abandon the earth). Instead of fear, honor itself ruled the people, without force. No work was required to dispense justice to just men. I had nothing to do with war: I protected peace and doorways (*nil mihi cum bello: pacem postesque tuebar*)," and, showing the key, he said "these are the arms I bear."

Ovid's Janus insists here that there was a time when he had nothing to do with war. The abrupt break between *bello* and *pacem* in the middle of line 253 emphatically marks Janus' original detachment from warfare. Although there is no direct reference to his shrine in these lines, the linkage of *pacem postesque* reminds us that his original association with gates was exclusively peaceful.

Ovid's narrator presses Janus for further information, asking about the origins and operation of his temple at Rome.[26] Most significantly, Janus is explicitly asked the question to which Virgil and Horace had offered conflicting answers: "But why do you hide in times of peace and open your gates when men take up arms?" (277: *at cur pace lates motusque recluderis armis?*). The god responds immediately (279–82):

> So that when the soldiers have been sent forth to war, their entrance upon return will be open, too, my gate, unbarred, stands fully open. I shut the doors in peace, so that peace cannot depart, and under Caesar's divine protection I will be closed for a long time.

These lines, Janus' final words in the poem, present an interesting problem: the meaning Janus attributes to his temple's opening and closure revises, even contradicts, his earlier explanation in lines 121–24.[27] Let us begin, as Janus does, with the reasons for the temple's opening. Janus does not deny that the opened gates signify the release of war.[28] Avoiding, however, any reference to war's madness, the god offers an altogether different explanation: the gates are unbarred so that those who have left the city to wage war will know that Rome's guardian stands ready to welcome them with easy entrance on their return home. The god's language implies that the army's departure for war, not that of war itself, was the reason his gates were opened; and "to war" (*ad bella*) suggests that war was already outside before Janus' bolts were removed. It appears that the god wishes to deemphasize his responsibility for war itself, though his earlier words in 123–24 made clear that war could only be unleashed under his authority.

As in Horace *Ode* 4.15, Ovid's Janus here keeps peace, not war, inside his gates, and Caesar is responsible for the continuation of this peace. But Ovid's depiction also differs from Horace's in a significant respect. For Horace, Caesar (and Janus' gates) protect peace against the malevolent forces (*furor civilis, vis, ira*) that would attempt to banish it from Rome. Ovid's Janus, however, also operating with the aid of Caesar's divine guidance, does not simply protect peace but confines it behind his gates, as if fearing that it might depart from the state on its own volition if not restrained. Peace's confinement uncomfortably recalls the imprisonment of war in Janus' earlier description, an image that in turn recalls Virgil's barricaded *Furor impius* in *Aeneid* 1.

Here, too, Janus' explanation involves a distortion of his earlier description of his gates' operation. Again, it is not a full contradiction, for we noted earlier that Ovid's personified Peace appears to have her own domestic residence (*placidis tectis*) inside the gates but separate from war's prison (121–22). Although Janus' words in 121–24 clearly suggest that Peace is only able to roam freely when wars are confined, they do not, strictly speaking, exclude the possibility that both war and Peace are in their respective abodes at the same time.

The problem of Janus' emphasis on peace's forced imprisonment in line 281 remains, however, since lines 121–22 suggest that little pressure needs to be exerted by the god to ensure that *Pax* acts according to his desires. Ovid's poetic purpose here is twofold. By having Janus concentrate on war's imprisonment in the earlier passage, then shift his emphasis, in his later speech, to the confinement of peace, Ovid recalls the depictions of Janus in his two poetic predecessors and highlights the contradiction between them. At the same time, within the context of the present dialogue itself, Janus' later distortion of the implications of his earlier speech underlines what is new about Ovid's own picture: not peace's confinement itself, but rather the representation of Peace as a living entity, analogous to Virgil's *Furor*, who will, if allowed, leave the presumably more limited confines of her tranquil dwelling in order to spread her influence freely (*libera*, 122) throughout the world. Ovid's personified *Pax*, although of course more amiable than Virgil's *Furor*, nonetheless chafes at her confinement. If the idea of Peace's release is construed narrowly, as it is by Ovid's Janus in 281, it can be taken to mean that she willingly departs from Rome, leaving only war within the city.

Ovid's deliberately ambiguous depiction of Janus' operation not only points to the limitations of the images of the gods' gates in Virgil and Horace but also illuminates the problems inherent in the idea itself of Janus' shrine as an indicator of the nature of war and peace and the inability of the image ever to represent fully, without contradiction, the notion of universal peace. Ovid presses on his audience the realization that it is not enough for peace to be protected inside the city, with the forces of war outside; nor should there be an idea that if peace were released to roam wherever she wanted, she would exist only outside Rome, while war alone remained inside. In an ideal world, peace, and only peace, should be present everywhere at once.

For the Romans, as was noted at the outset of this chapter, the most prevalent meaning of *pax* was, in fact, "pacification" as a result of successful warfare. Thus it is difficult to imagine an adequate representation of their notion of universal peace.

The lines that follow Janus' last words in the dialogue (277–83), concluding the god's episode in the *Fasti*, present a final image of Janus' double vision that is suggestive of a more essentially Roman conception of world peace:

> (The god) finished speaking, and lifting up his eyes that see in opposite directions, he surveyed all that existed in the whole world. Peace was there, and the reason for your triumph, Germanicus, already the Rhine had handed over its waters as your slaves. O Janus, let peace and the servants of peace endure forever, and may peace's author never abandon his work.

Ovid signals to his readers that Janus is ideally capable of seeing, and thus perhaps also understanding, from two opposite perspectives simultaneously. When Janus surveys the entire world, what he immediately sees is peace (*pax erat*, 283). Juxtaposed to peace is "a reason for triumph" (*causa triumphi*), a vivid reminder of the intimate link between peace and military victory, followed by a vision of a personified Rhine surrendering its waters that would be well suited to the placards carried in triumphal processions. The narrator's prayer in the final couplet reinforces the idea that perpetual peace depends upon continued success in war.

Conclusions

History's most successful imperialists, the Romans of the Republic had for nearly 400 years practiced war and peace alternately with stunning success as they acquired their Mediterranean empire. The last century of the Republic, however, witnessed an alarming change: from the time of Sulla through the end of the Republic, no foreign war was without its repercussions in civil conflict. Foreign and civil war had become much the same thing, culminating in the Battle of Actium. It was among Augustus' greatest achievements at last to disentangle the two. Prominent among the symbolic means Augustus employed to celebrate his accomplishment and to announce the new age of peace it had initiated were the gates of Janus, closed three times during his principate. The impact the resuscitation of this antiquated custom had on his Roman contemporaries is reflected in the gates' prominence in Augustan literature. Livy, Virgil, Horace, and Ovid each provide in their depictions of Janus both a judgement, explicit or implicit, on the *princeps'* achievement itself, and an individual perspective on whether, and to what extent, the nature of war and peace in Rome's future might genuinely and permanently be changed from that in the city's past.

Notes

1 The seminal work on Janus in Roman literature, though with different emphasis, is Syme 1979; also Syme 1989. Cf. also Putnam 1986: 275–77; Herbert-Brown 1994: 185–96; Fowler 1998; Green 2000.

2   On the occasions and dates of the three closings, see esp. Syme 1978; 1979: 25; 1989. For arguments that the third closure was proposed but not carried out, see Gruen 1985: 54 n.13; Ridley 2003: 114–15.

3   Exemplary discussions of this subject include Wallace-Hadrill 1982, 1985; Griffin 1984; White 1993.

4   On the *Res Gestae* as literature, see Brunt and Moore 1967: 2–3, who place it in the tradition of the *elogia* inscribed in memory of a Roman of high achievement after his death. Cf. also Ramage 1987; Ridley 2003: 51–66, 229–31.

5   Suetonius clearly read Augustus' words in this manner. In *Augustus* 22.1, he states the case more explicitly: "The temple of Janus Quirinus, closed only twice before his time since the founding of the city, he closed three times in a much briefer period, having won peace on land and sea." Cf. Herbert-Brown 1994: 188–89 with bibliography. On Augustan peace symbolism, see also Raaflaub, this vol.

6   Macrobius *Saturn.* 1.9.16: *Quirinum, quasi bellorum potentem, ab hasta quam Sabini curin vocant* ("Quirinus, as if powerful over wars, from the spear which the Sabines call curis").

7   Scott 1925; also Hinds 1992 with bibliography. Romulus was, in some versions, associated with the foundation of Janus' temple; for a brief summary, see Richardson 1992: 207.

8   Translations of Livy are taken, with occasional modification, from those of B. O. Foster *et al.* for the Loeb Classical Library.

9   Esp. useful for this treatment of Livy's Numa were: Levene 1993: 134–37, 147; Miles 1995: 120–27, 149–50; Feldherr 1998: 69–71, 156.

10   Livy's knowledge of only one closure provides a *terminus ante quem* of 25 BCE for this passage; cf. Syme 1979.

11   Unfortunately, Numa's prescience about the innate savagery of the Roman character is immediately borne out when his successor is chosen in 1.22.2: "He was not only unlike the king just before him but was fiercer (*ferocior*) even than Romulus." This drastic turn suggests that in Livy's view such interludes of peace, while difficult to achieve, are impossible to maintain in Rome's "warlike state."

12   In Pref. 10, Livy states that the special value of history is that it allows the reader to "look at the lessons provided by example" (*exempli documenta. . . intueri*).

13   For Jupiter's prophecy, see esp. O'Hara 1990: 128–63; for the gates in Book 7, Fowler 1998 with bibliography.

14   Translations of Virgil are taken, with occasional modification, from those of H. R. Fairclough for the Loeb Classical Library.

15   *Pace* O'Hara. For a summary of the most relevant arguments, with bibliography of the debate since O'Hara 1990, see Harrison 1996.

16   O'Hara 1990: 151–54. Wiseman 1995: 144–46 sees here an allusion to Augustus and Agrippa.

17   *E.g.* Troy's walls breached by stealth, *Aen.* 2.13–245; Priam's palace forced open by Pyrrhus, *Aen.* 2.479–85.

18   Cf. Virgil *Georgics* 1.511, where *Mars impius* rages in a world full of civil strife.

19   Syme (1989: 15): "A picture of fantasy."

20   *Certa sententia* in 7.611 recalls the *certo foedere* under which Aeolus was to control the gates of the winds' prison in 1.62.

21   The threefold prelude to war set in motion by the fury Allecto under Juno's direction is summarized in 7.572–84.

22   Juno's forcing of the gates in Book 7 echoes Aeolus' forced opening of the winds' cavern in Book 1; cf. Fowler 1998: 172 n. 24.

23   Fraenkel 1957: 449–53; Putnam 1986: 262–306. For an overview of differing views of the poem, see Griffin 2002, with notes.

24   These lines also reverse the imagery of *Ode* 3.24.25–32; Putnam 1986: 278–79.

25 One more martial reference appears in lines 5–7, when Horace recalls that Rome's stand-ards, "snatched from the arrogant doorposts of the Parthians" (*derepta Parthorum superbis postibus*), have been restored to their rightful place. Parthia also appears in *Ep.* 2.1.256. On the importance of Parthia to Horace's representation of Janus, see Syme 1989.

26 Janus' version of his origins differs from Livy's foundation under Numa; instead, he attrib-utes his shrine's foundation to the Romans' gratitude for the god's help in repelling the assault on Rome by the Sabine King Titus Tatius.

27 The contradiction of lines 123–24 in 281 is noted by Hardie 2001 (64 n.52). For a different understanding of these lines, see Herbert-Brown 1994: 185–96; Green 2000.

28 *Dempta sera* in 280 recalls *rigidae serae* in 124.

References

Brunt, P. A., and M. M. Moore (eds.). 1967. *Res Gestae Divi Augusti*. Oxford.

Feldherr, A. M. 1998. *Spectacle and Society in Livy's History*. Berkeley.

Fowler, Don. 1998. "Opening the Gates of War (*Aen.* 7.601–40)." In Hans-Peter Stahl (ed.), *Vergil's* Aeneid: *Augustan Epic and Political Context*, 155–74. London.

Fraenkel, E. 1957. *Horace*. Oxford.

Galinsky, K. 1996. *Augustan Culture: An Interpretive Introduction*. Princeton.

Green, S. J. 2000. "Multiple Interpretations of the Opening and Closing of the Temple of Janus: A Misunderstanding of Ovid *Fasti* 1.281." *Mnemosyne* 53: 302–09.

Griffin, Jasper. 1984. "Augustus and the Poets: 'Caesar qui cogere posset'." In Millar and Segal 1984: 189–218.

——. 2002. "Look Your Last on Lyric: Horace *Odes* 4.15." In T. P. Wiseman (ed.), *Classics in Progress. Essays on Ancient Greece and Rome*, 311–32. Oxford.

Gruen, E. 1985. "Augustus and the Ideology of War and Peace." In R. Winkes (ed.), *The Age of Augustus*, 51–72. Louvain.

Gurval, R. A. 1995. *Actium and Augustus*. Ann Arbor.

Hardie, P. 1991. "The Janus Episode in Ovid's *Fasti*." *Materiali e discussioni per l'analisi dei testi classici* 26: 47–64.

Harrison, S. J. 1996. "*Aeneid* 1.286: Julius Caesar or Augustus?" *Papers of the Leeds Latin Seminar* 9: 127–33.

Herbert-Brown, G. 1994. *Ovid and the* Fasti. *An Historical Study*. Oxford.

Hill, P. 1989. *The Monuments of Ancient Rome as Coin Types*. London.

Hinds, S. 1992. "*Arma* in Ovid's *Fasti* Part 2: Genre, Romulean Rome and Augustan Ideology." *Arethusa* 25: 113–53.

James, William. 1910. "The Moral Equivalent of War." *Association for International Concili-ation: Leaflet No. 27*: 3–20.

Levene, D. S. 1993. *Religion in Livy*. Leiden.

Miles, G. B. 1995. *Livy. Reconstructing Early Rome*. Ithaca.

Millar, F., and E. Segal (eds.). 1984. *Caesar Augustus: Seven Aspects*. Oxford.

Mommsen, Th. 1883. *Res Gestae Divi Augusti*. Berlin.

Ogilvie, R. M. 1965. *A Commentary on Livy, Books 1–5*. Oxford.

O'Hara, James. 1990. *Death and the Optimistic Prophecy in Vergil's* Aeneid. Princeton.

Putnam, M. C. J. P. 1986. *Artifices of Eternity. Horace's Fourth Book of Odes*. Ithaca and London.

Ramage, E. 1987. *The Nature and Purpose of Augustus'* Res Gestae. *Historia* Einzelschriften 54. Wiesbaden.

Reinhold, Meyer. 1981–82. "The Declaration of War against Cleopatra," *Classical Journal* 77: 97–103.

Richardson, Lawrence, Jr. 1992. *A Topographical Dictionary of Ancient Rome.* Baltimore and London.

Ridley, Ronald. 2003. *The Emperor's Retrospect. Augustus'* Res Gestae *in Epigraphy, Historiography and Commentary.* Studia Hellenistica 39. Leuven and Dudley.

Scott, Kenneth. 1925. "The Identification of Augustus with Romulus-Quirinus." *Transactions of the American Philological Association* 56: 82–105.

Syme, Ronald. 1978. *History in Ovid.* Oxford.

——. 1979. "Problems about Janus." *American Journal of Philology* 100: 188–212 = *Roman Papers*, III, ed. E. Badian, 1179–1197. Oxford, 1979.

——. 1989. "Janus and Parthia in Horace." In J. Diggle, J. B. Hall, and H. D. Jocelyn (eds.), *Studies in Latin Literature and Its Tradition, in Honour of C. O. Brink.* Cambridge Philological Society, Supp. 15, 113–24 = id., *Roman Papers*, VI, ed. Anthony R. Birley, 441–50. Oxford, 1991.

Wallace-Hadrill, Andrew. 1982. "The Golden Age and Sin in Augustan Ideology." *Past and Present* 95: 19–36.

——. 1985. "Propaganda and Dissent? Augustan Moral Legislation and the Love-Poets." *Klio* 67: 180–84.

White, Peter. 1993. *Promised Verse. Poets in the Society of Augustan Rome.* Cambridge, MA.

Wiseman, T. P. 1995. *Remus. A Roman Myth.* Cambridge.

Yavetz, Zvi. 1984. "The *Res Gestae* and Augustus' Public Image." In Millar and Segal 1984: 1–36.

16

Early Christian Views on Violence, War, and Peace

Louis J. Swift

> They shall beat their swords into plowshares and their spears into pruning hooks; nation shall not lift up sword against nation, neither shall they learn war any more (*Isaiah* 2.4).
>
> But I say to you, "Do not resist one who is evil. But if anyone strikes you on the right cheek, turn to him the other also" (*Matthew* 5.39).

Isaiah's prophecy (see Krüger, this vol.) and Jesus' injunction to his followers leave little doubt about the kind of relationship that ought to obtain between private individuals and between communities of all kinds, whether they be families, tribes, or nation states. From its beginning in the early days of the Roman Empire, the Christian message has consistently echoed the theme of peace and forgiveness which is present in the Gospels and the earliest canonical writings. From the angels' greeting at Bethlehem to Jesus' words to Peter about putting away the sword, to Christ's words to the apostles in the upper room, to Paul's message about the "Gospel of Peace," the texts constantly remind the new Christian communities of the spirit which permeated Jesus' life and teachings and which should prevail in their own internal and external relations.[1]

Developments in Christianity over the first five centuries of its history, however, clearly attest to the difficulties which adherents of the new religion encountered in trying to live out the implications of the Scriptural injunctions concerning peace. Differences in how to interpret Scriptural texts from both the Old and the New Testaments, ambiguities about how to apply the principles of peace, changes in the political, social, and cultural milieu in which Christians found themselves, and the variable attitudes which Christians adopted toward the ruling power all played a role in tempering, altering or, as some would argue, compromising the pacific message of the New Testament.

Fundamental to all these variances in Christian beliefs and practices during the early centuries is the fact that Christianity is an incarnational religion. If it proposes a future for humankind which is ultimately outside the world of time, the means of reaching that future are deeply immersed in temporal realities, which are subject to the vagaries and limitations, the blessings and the shortcomings of the human condition. Thus, on the momentous issues of war and peace, which are fraught with complexity and ambiguities, we should not be surprised to find uncertainties, inconsistencies, and changes of outlook among Christians as the centuries progressed. If the quest for peace is one constant in the Christians' scheme of values, the proper way of pursuing it had to be worked out over time and was always developed amid the temporal circumstances which prevailed at a particular moment in history.

It is traditional and helpful to divide early Christian views about peace and war roughly into two periods or stages before and after Constantine's accession in 312 CE.[2] This division is appropriate not simply because of the spiritual and material advantages which flowed to the Christian Church after the emperor embraced Christianity but because of the unexpected and strikingly different environment in which the Christians found themselves *vis-à-vis* their own responsibilities toward society and politics. As we shall see, new circumstances created new issues which were addressed in new ways.

Nonetheless, in discussing the pre- and post-Constantinian ages, it is important to avoid viewing the latter period as representing a complete volte-face in the Christian community on the issue of war and peace. This popular view belies certain historical realities and does little justice to Christian thought and practice on either side of the divide.[3] It is fair to argue, I believe, that in both periods there were Christians who opposed violence and Christians who found no problem with participation in violent activities, whether they involved warfare or police actions. Though we can legitimately argue for a major shift in the *dominant* outlook of Christians toward war and military service after Constantine – a shift which had enormous consequences both for Christianity and the western world – it is, I believe, inaccurate simply to classify the two stages of the Christian approach to violence and war as pacifist versus belligerent or as principled versus expedient. Minority views were present in both periods, and although there were major changes in attitudes after Constantine, there was also some continuity in this period with actions and attitudes of the earlier centuries.

Before Constantine

One of the more important consistencies involved the Church's general stance *vis-à-vis* the empire during the first three centuries of its existence when Christians were subject to periodic persecution. If one notable Christian source describes Rome as a beast waging war on the saints or as a harlot drunk with the blood of the "martyrs of Jesus" (*Revelation* 13, 17), it was much more typical for Christians in this period to acknowledge the wisdom of Paul's injunction, "Let every person be subject to the governing authorities. For there is no authority except from God ..." (*Romans* 13.1). If Christian writers had harsh things to say about the state during sporadic periods of violent repression, their general outlook regarding the exercise of temporal power was consistently positive, and like their pagan contemporaries, they recognized the benefits of the relative peace which prevailed throughout the empire.[4] Indeed, both before and after Constantine some Christian writers saw the hand of God promoting the growth of Christianity through the imperial exercise of power, and we should not assume any general hostility among Christians toward pagan authorities. The moving prayer for the well-being of the realm which concludes the *First Letter of Clement*, written at the beginning of the second century, is a typical expression of the Christians' outlook during these early years. In praying for the emperors he asks God to "guide their decisions . . . according to what is good and acceptable in your eyes so that by dutifully wielding in peace and gentleness the authority you gave them they may gain your favor" (61.1–2).

Early Christian views about Christian participation in the use of force were complicated by the fact that the Scriptures provide no clear-cut and definitive answer to the issue. Christ's own allusions to war and the many warlike images used to describe the Christian life in the New Testament do not, of course, represent an endorsement of violence, but, on the other hand, events such as John the Baptist's response to the soldiers who came to him for advice, Christ's praise for the Centurion at Capernaum, and Peter's acceptance of Cornelius[5] all made it more difficult to conclude absolutely that all aspects of physical force are in principle ruled out for Christians. Indeed, Israelite victories recounted in the Old Testament were a source of pride for Steven and Paul (*Acts* 7.45; 13.19; *Hebr.* 11.32–34), and early Christian apologists such as Justin (*Dialogue with Trypho* 91), Irenaeus (*Against Heresies* 4.24) and Tertullian (*Against Marcian* 3.18.6) saw military events and personages of the Old Testament as prefigurations of events in the New. In such a context early Christian writers were forced to deal with texts which appeared to run counter to their basic beliefs about peace.[6] They did so, as we shall see, in a number of ways.

The relative absence of direct comment on the issue in the Christian scriptures may actually be due to the small numbers of Christians in the army. At least during the first 100 years of Christianity the social status of many believers, as well as the issues of violence and idolatry, would seem to have posed serious barriers to enlistment, and since there was no involuntary conscription during this period, Christians could easily avoid military service if they chose to do so. Indeed, at this juncture in the new religion's history Christians had little role at all to play in public affairs. "They, like most subjects of the Roman Empire, had no active political responsibility; for the time being there was no question of their holding any political or communal office. Along with the obvious moral obligations they only had to comply, as to public life, with the general requirements of peace and obedience" (Von Campenhausen 1968: 155). Thus, it was easy for an early apologist like Justin to claim that Christians were living out the kind of peace foretold by Isaiah. "We who were filled with war and mutual slaughter and every wickedness have each through the whole world changed our warlike weapons – our swords into plowshares and our spears into implements of tillage – and we cultivate piety, righteousness, philanthropy, faith and hope" (*Dialogue with Trypho* 110.3).[7] This assertion and others like it found in Irenaeus (*Against Heresies* 4.34.4), Tertullian (*Against the Jews* 3.10), and Origen (*Against Celsus* 5.33) leave little doubt about the Christians' main concerns when it came to certain aspects of maintaining the empire.

What is striking in the first three centuries is that writers coupled their criticism of Christian participation in war and in any form of violence with strong support for the empire. Despite Justin's words cited above about Christians turning "swords into ploughshares," the apologist insists on their strong loyalty in paying taxes and acknowledging the emperor's authority (*Apol.* 1.17.3). In about 177, the Greek apologist Athenagoras assures Marcus Aurelius that Christians pray for the empire's increase "with all men becoming subject to your sway" (*Supplication for Christians* 37), while at the same time he condemns the slaughter and destruction which often attend the pursuit of that end (*On the Resurrection of the Dead* 19). Christians themselves, he insists, cannot bear to see a man killed even justly (*Supplication* 35), and "when struck, they do not strike again" (ibid. 11). Clearly these writers separated their sense of loyalty to the ruling power from their views about Christian responsibilities regarding its defense. They seem not to have come to grips with the moral issues involved, and perhaps they saw little reason to do so because they knew of few Christians who were in the army or who were intending to join.

In fact, it was on this latter point that a prominent critic took the Christians to task. Around 180, the pagan writer Celsus composed a detailed critique of Christianity entitled *The True Doctrine*,[8] and in this work he faulted the Christians for not doing their part to protect the emperor and the realm: "If everyone were to do the same as you, he says, there would be nothing to prevent him from being abandoned, alone and deserted, while earthly things would come into the power of the most lawless and savage barbarians" (*Against Celsus* 8.68). Clearly the issue of Christians in the army had now become a public one, and from Celsus' perspective at least, the Christians were rejecting military service on a large scale.

However, it appears that Celsus was not fully informed on this matter. In the reign of Marcus Aurelius (161–180) we get references to the miracle of the rain which saved a Roman legion (*Legio XII Fulminata*) from defeat in a battle with the Germans and Sarmatians.[9] Tertullian (*Apology* 5.6) and Eusebius (*Ecclesiastical History* 5.5) attribute this miracle to the prayers of Christians in the legion whereas pagan sources (Dio Cassius 72.14 and *The Lives of the Later Caesars, Marcus Antoninus* 24.4) recount the miracle but make no mention of Christians. The historical facts surrounding the event are subject to interpretation, but what is important is that there were enough Christians in the legion to gain acceptance of the miracle among the Christian community, and neither Tertullian nor Eusebius offers any indication that the Christians' presence was a source of scandal. This silence is particularly ironic for Tertullian who was a strong opponent of Christians' serving in the military.

Tertullian, in fact, was the first Christian writer to confront the issue of military service in a coherent and detailed fashion.[10] In dealing with this complicated and prolific writer, it is important to remember that he was a strong and uncompromising apologist for Christianity, that he regularly used his formidable talent to tailor his argument to the issue at hand, and that according to tradition he grew more rigorous as he grew older, eventually ending up outside the mainstream of Christianity in the Montanist heresy. Thus, it is sometimes difficult to determine how widely his remarks about Christian participation in war reflected the views of contemporary Christian communities at large. Be that as it may, he is, together with Origen, the most articulate and persuasive proponent of Christian pacifism during the entire pre-Constantinian period.

In his *Apology*, which was probably composed at the end of the second century, Tertullian himself acknowledges the presence of Christians in the Roman army, and he even takes pride in the spread of Christianity to all segments of Roman society. "We no less than you sail the sea, serve in the army, farm the land, buy and sell" (42.3; cf. 37.4). Like Justin and Athenagoras he underscores the loyalty of Christians to the empire and their desire for its continued prosperity. "We pray without ceasing for all emperors, for their prolonged life, for a secure empire, for protection of the imperial palaces, for brave armies" (30.4). Christians are not only loyal but are an integral part of the Roman social fabric who have no taste for Armageddon and who enjoy the peace of the empire. Almost in the same breath, however, he asks rhetorically, "What kind of war would we, who willingly submit to the sword, not be ready or eager for . . . if it were not for the fact that according to our doctrine it is more permissible to be killed than to kill" (37.4).

When he faced the issue of military service directly, Tertullian rejected Christian participation of any kind. He articulated his reasons in two treatises commonly dated in the early years of the third century, *On Idolatry* and *On the Crown*. In the first of these he asks whether a Christian could serve in a public office if he remained free of idolatry. His answer is sardonically affirmative if all the required and regular responsibilities of office were avoided such as offering sacrifice, taking oaths and sentencing men to prison. Thus, Christians shall have no part in managing state affairs.

Dealing in the same treatise with the question of whether a Christian may join the army or a soldier in the army could be admitted to baptism, Tertullian replies more directly. After dismissing arguments for serving in the military on the basis of Scriptural models like Moses, Joshua, and the centurion in the Gospels, he argues that "the Lord, by taking away Peter's sword disarmed every soldier thereafter. We are not allowed to wear a uniform that symbolizes a sinful act" (19.3). For Tertullian the military oath (*sacramentum*) is irreconcilable with the promise (*sacramentum*) made at baptism; service to both Caesar and Christ is impossible.[11]

Perhaps just as telling, however, is the apologist's rejection of arguments posed by those who disagree with him. It is clear that some Christians were taking a different stance toward service in the army and were using examples from both the Old and the New Testaments to justify their action. Tertullian will have none of this. As he says elsewhere, in disarming Peter, Christ "cursed the works of the sword ever after" (*On Patience* 3).

In another treatise (*On the Crown*), he praises a Christian legionnaire's refusal to accept a military crown in honor of the emperor Caracalla's accession to power. Here again he distinguishes between Christian converts proposing to enter the service and those converted while in the army. With respect to the former he argues that all military service, involving as it does issues of bloodshed and idolatry, forecloses the possibility of "carrying the title of Christian from the camp of life to the camp of darkness" (11.4). For those converted while already serving in the army he recommends that they abandon their commitment, "as many have done," but he admits the theoretical possibility of their remaining in uniform. To do so, however, they will have to "engage in all kinds of quibbling to avoid offending God in ways that are forbidden to men even outside the service" (11.4–6).

Though Tertullian clearly considers this latter option a practical impossibility, it would appear that he was facing certain realities both in and outside the Christian community. If deserters following his advice did manage to escape capital punishment, they lost all material benefits which would accrue to them when they were mustered out of the army. What is more, during and after Septimius Severus' reign (193–211) civil offices were often filled by military men, who could spend an entire career without ever being involved in war or police duties.[12] Under such circumstances it is not inconceivable that some Christians saw little danger to their faith if they stayed in the lower ranks where they would not be involved in idolatry or bloodshed. This general mindset would at least explain why the legionnaire was singled out by Tertullian for special praise as an exception, and why individual Christians were citing Scripture to justify military service. In any event, it appears that despite his strong objections, a growing number of Christians were, in fact, remaining in the service, and since Tertullian is so vehement about the issue of Christians and violence, it seems likely that their number must have been significant.

Cyprian of Carthage, who was Tertullian's successor as the most prominent African Christian writer, seems to share the ambiguities of earlier authors. He decries homicide (*On the Dress of Virgins* 11), criticizes the vanity of military life (*To Donatus* 11), objects to the distinction which is often made between private and public morality in taking human life (ibid. 6), and advises that one who has received the Eucharist should not stain his hands with the sword (*On the Goodness of Patience* 14). Nonetheless, he seems to feel that wars are inevitable (*On Mortality* 2), and he prays for the success of the Roman armies in warding off enemies (*To Demetrianus* 20). In short, like his predecessors he maintains a strong disposition toward peace and at the same time recognizes the need for a forceful means of maintaining such peace in the contemporary world. He does not endorse Christian service in the army, but it is hard to place him in the pacifist camp with Tertullian. In large measure it appears that the issue never seems to have been a pressing one for him.

Tertullian's Greek contemporary, Clement of Alexandria, whose writings attempt in many ways to demonstrate the compatibility between Christianity and Greco-Roman culture, is in much the same position as Cyprian. Though he speaks of wars as inspired by demons (*Exhortation to the Greeks* 3.42) and says to his fellow Christians, "In peace, not in war are we trained" (*The Teacher* 1.12), he follows the common practice of describing the Christian life in military terms (e.g. *Exhortation to the Greeks* 11.116–17; *Miscellanies* 6.14), compares Christ to a military commander (*The Teacher* 1.7) and, in addressing the issue of every person's calling, advises, "If you were in the army when you were seized by the knowledge of God, obey the Commander who gives just commands" (*Exhortation to the Greeks* 10.100). Once again, although Clement is sensitive to the need for defending the safety of the state, the moral issue of Christian participation in violent action seems not to have been seriously joined in his mind.

Such was not the case, however, with his pupil, Origen, who was the most outstanding theologian of the pre-Constantinian era and the most articulate proponent of Christian pacifism. His views on war and peace appear mostly in his *Against Celsus,* an apologetic work written in the mid-third century in which he attempts to counter Celsus' detailed objections to Christianity (mentioned earlier).[13] In responding to Celsus' urging that Christians "assist the emperor with all [their] strength ..., fight for him and ... serve in his army if he requires it either as a soldier or a general," Origen answers that Christians provide for the emperor's needs "'through prayers, supplications, petitions and thanksgiving for all men, especially for the emperors and all those in authority' (*I Timothy* 2.1–2). To be sure, the more pious a man is the more effectively does he assist the emperors – more so than the troops that go out and kill as many as possible on the battle line" (8.73). However unconvincing this response may have appeared to pagan contemporaries, it underscores the fact that in Origen's mind the issue of state security and peace involved a struggle against the powers of evil, which are as much inside as outside human individuals or groups, and not everyone plays the same role in this struggle.

Origen is here redefining the kind of loyalty which Christians owe to the empire; service must be in the realm of the spirit or not at all. He makes this argument by comparing Christians to pagan priests who were freed from military service even during wartime. "Though they keep their right hands clean, the Christians fight through their prayers to God on behalf of those doing battle in a just cause and on behalf of an emperor who is ruling justly in order that all opposition and hostility toward those who are acting rightly may be eliminated" (8.73). Origen acknowledges the possibility of a justified war, but he insists that "we [Christians] have come in response to Jesus' commands to beat into plowshares the rational swords of conflict and arrogance and to change into pruning hooks those spears that we used to fight with. For we no longer take up the sword against any nation nor do we learn the art of war anymore" (5.33).

At the same time Origen is aware that his position represented a marked departure from what is found in the Old Testament, and he faces this issue by means of history and allegory. He argues that in the Jews' case denying them the right to wage war or inflict physical punishment on wrongdoers was "nothing short of consigning them to complete destruction when an enemy attacked their nation" (*Against Celsus* 7.26). With the end of the Jewish state, however, there was no longer a need for using physical force among God's people, who, in any case, were not to be identified with any particular nation. Whatever forces were needed to keep the barbarians at bay could be entrusted to the armies of Rome, but in that context Christians still remained under a prohibition because the meaning of Christ's words about perishing by the sword is very clear. "We must beware of unsheathing the sword simply because we are in the army or for the sake of avenging private injuries or under any other pretext because Christ's teaching in the Gospels considers all of these uses an abomination" (*Commentariorum Series* 102). It is notable in this remark that service itself in the army seems not to be excluded, but such service does not justify taking human life. This stance seems akin to what we saw above in Tertullian's *On the Crown* and appears to indicate that there is some acknowledgement of the legitimacy of Christians serving in the army if they avoid bloodshed.

Origen shows his faithfulness to the Alexandrian allegorical approach to Scripture by interpreting passages in the Old Testament which seem to endorse acts of violence as actually containing a spiritual message for Christian readers. Thus, for example, when the psalmist says, "Every morning I killed all the sinners on earth" (*Ps.* 101.8), he is really referring to the destruction of all thoughts and desires that are opposed to the truth (*Against Celsus* 7.22). Elsewhere Origen is quite blunt about the absolute need to read the Old Testament passages in this light. "Unless those carnal wars (i.e. of the Old Testament) were a symbol of spiritual wars, I do not think that the Jewish historical books would ever have been passed down by the apostles to be read by Christ's followers in their churches" (*Homilies on Joshua* 15.1). This approach addresses many of the problems connected with wars and violent action depicted in the Old Testament, problems which writers both before and after Origen faced with varying degrees of success.

After Constantine's Accession

Following the accession of Constantine, what Tertullian had considered impossible (*Apology* 21.24) actually came to pass. The emperor, at least in his attitude and actions, had become Christian, and some adherents to the faith saw themselves living in a new dispensation in which the Roman empire and Christianity were joint works of God. This view was most clearly expressed by Eusebius of Caesarea in 336, when he delivered an ebullient address to Constantine.

> By the command, as it were, of the one God two blessings sprouted forth simultaneously, that is, the Roman empire and the doctrine of true piety ... Concomitant with the proclamation of the One God and the one way of knowing him, a single empire held sway among men, and the whole human race was converted to peace and friendship when all men recognized each other as brothers and discovered their natural kinship (*In Praise of Constantine* 16.4–7).

The rhetoric in these words only serves to underline the fact that the task for Christians was no longer to pit their religion against the ruling power but to determine the limits of cooperation between the two. Not surprisingly, the tack they pursued was twofold. Some were so taken with their new state of legitimacy that their sense of loyalty to the empire led them to endorse the exercise of temporal power unreservedly. Thus, Eusebius could speak of Constantine as being "armed ... against his foes with the standards given him by the Savior from above" (ibid. 2.3). The bishop likened the emperor's victory over his enemies to the triumph of Moses over the Pharaoh at the Red Sea (*Ecclesiastical History* 9.9) and claimed that "God made him such a consistently triumphant ruler and glorious victor over his enemies that no one ever heard the like of him in human memory" (*Life of Constantine* 1.6). The most telling aspect of these remarks is the fact that earlier pacifist arguments about force and bloodshed are totally submerged, and in place of adamant opposition to Christian involvement in coercive measures by the state we get a quite simplistic amalgam of Christian and temporal ends.

Eusebius' approach, however, did not stand alone. In both the eastern and western parts of the empire there were signs of a more reflective approach toward violence and of reservations about any easy convergence of spiritual and temporal aims. To be sure, the church father, Basil the Great (ca. 329–379), insists that "even in the military profession one can maintain perfect love for God" (*Letter* 106), and he cites military figures in the New Testament, including the centurion at Capernaum and Cornelius in *Acts*, as models of the Christian life.[14] Nonetheless, although he claims that "our predecessors did not consider killing in war as murder but ... made allowances for those who fought on the side of moderation and piety," he recommends that those involved in bloodshed should "abstain from communion for three years" (*Letter* 188.13). Clearly for him violence and contact with things sacred remained a problem, but he could not exclude the use of physical force altogether. Basil's contemporary Athanasius also sought to deal with the issue of distinguishing war from murder when he argued for the way in which circumstances alter the moral character of an action. "One is not supposed to kill," he says, "but killing in battle is both lawful and praiseworthy" (*Letter to Amun*). The question no longer is whether a Christian may take human life but what conditions are required to justify such action. At this juncture in the Church's history it seems that if Christian ideals of peace, forgiveness, and forbearance were to continue to play a role in the public arena, they would have to be integrated into larger questions. Specifically, what had to be faced was the problem of maintaining the principles of Christian love when the demands of statecraft called for the use of force.

The two writers who sparked the most reflection on this question in the fourth century and who largely determined subsequent discussion of the matter in the west were Ambrose and Augustine. Ambrose (ca. 339–397) was a layman and was actually functioning as the governor of the province of Aemilia-Liguria in northern Italy at the time when he was chosen to be bishop of Milan in 374.[15] With such a background it is not surprising that his views on the use of force were much influenced by Roman sentiments of loyalty, courage, and public responsibility. He says frankly that "the kind of courage which is involved in defending the empire against barbarians or protecting the weak on the home front or allies against plunderers is wholly just" (*On the Duties of the Clergy* 1.27.129). He speaks with admiration about Old Testament figures such as Joshua, Jonathan, and Judas Maccabeus (*Duties* 1.40.195) and makes a clear distinction between using force for one's own advantage and doing so on behalf of one's country. Nothing "goes against nature as much as doing violence to another person for the sake of one's own advantage," but "it is much more commendable to protect one's country from destruction than to protect oneself from danger" (*Duties* 3.3.23).

This distinction between the private and public use of force becomes very explicit in Ambrose's remarks about the proper response when an individual is being physically attacked. In such instances total non-resistance is called for. "It does not seem to me that a Christian who is both wise and just should try to save his own life at the expense of another's. Indeed, even if a man comes up against an armed thief, he cannot return blow for blow lest in the act of protecting himself he weaken the virtue of love" (*Duties* 3.4.27). In defending oneself by taking another's life, an individual inevitably destroys that which unites people to God and which is the foundation of all the virtues (*Discourse on Psalm* 118.18.45; *Discourse on Psalm* 36.37). Harming an assailant to protect one's own life is tantamount to preferring a human good to a divine one and is a reversal of the proper hierarchy of values which should obtain in all human relationships.

That same hierarchy of values, however, calls for a very different approach when a third party is involved. In such cases one is not only permitted but obliged to intervene even with the use of lethal force. "For anyone who does not prevent an injury to a companion, if he can do so, is as much at fault as he who inflicts it. Following this principle holy Moses provided an early proof of his courage. For when he saw a Jew being injured by an Egyptian, he defended his countryman to the point of killing the Egyptian and hiding him in the sand" (*Duties* 1.36.178). It is difficult to overestimate the importance of the distinction which Ambrose makes here between self-defense and defending another. The point is significant because it appears that in the minds of many contemporary Christians the question had to do with their responsibilities now that they were becoming increasingly active in the conduct of government. Whereas earlier they could avoid involvement in statecraft if they found it incompatible with their Christian values, now it was these values themselves, seen in a new context, which not only allowed them to employ physical force in certain circumstances, but, if Ambrose is correct, required them to do so.

Nonetheless, Ambrose is aware that "military courage itself very often militates against peace" and that "the whole purpose of virtue and physical courage is to re-establish peace when war is over" (*Discourse on Ps.* 118.21.17). In the conduct of war Christians are obliged to follow the Gospel injunctions about loving enemies (ibid. 118.15.15–22), for ultimately the struggle for peace is waged not with barbarians, heretics, or other nations but within the individual soul. "The peace which removes the enticement of the passions and calms the perturbations of the spirit is loftier than that which puts down the invasion of barbarians. For it is a greater thing to resist the enemy inside you than the one far off" (*On Jacob* 2.6.29).

Despite these observations, the ambiguities involved in the Christians' use of physical force are not all resolved. The kind of peace Ambrose talks about will come only at the end of time (*Discourse on Psalm* 36.22); in the interim the struggle with internal and external forces that threaten to forestall progress in the pursuit of peace goes on. Such is the problem Augustine had to face in providing the early Christian world with his own nuanced ideas about peace and war and about the ways in which these opposing concepts can coexist in the world of time.

Augustine is frequently credited or blamed for developing what is often called the "theory of the just war."[16] This reputation is ironic inasmuch as he never wrote a treatise on the subject, and his comments on the issue are scattered throughout his works, including sermons, commentaries, letters, and apologetic pieces, all of which address a wide variety of problems or issues. Thus, what he has to say about war and peace ought rightly to be described as a collection of observations or insights, and we do better to think not about his "theory of the just war" but of his attitude and approach to the justified war. It is important also to remember that the world he lived in was both violent and oppressive, and this fact inevitably influenced his thinking on the use of force in a Christian context.[17]

Fundamental to Augustine's views about war and peace is his conviction about the human condition and about the role of the state in human society. In this matter it is hard to overemphasize the importance of Original Sin in his thinking. As a consequence of Adam's rebellion, the human race had become a "mass of sin" (*To Simplicianus on Diverse Questions* 1.2.16), which was fundamentally at odds with God and merited his condemnation (*City of God* 21.12). Despite the salvation effected by Christ, human proclivities toward self-interest and the lower appetites remain almost irresistible, and the lust to dominate (*libido dominandi* in Augustine's famous phrase) prevails. In such a context Augustine follows St. Paul in arguing that God wills the civil order as a means of punishing wrongdoers and restraining evil.

> Surely it is not in vain that we have such institutions as the power of the king, the death penalty of the judge, the hooks of the executioner, the weapons of the soldier, the stringency of the overlord, and even the strictness of a good father. All these things have their own method, reason, motive, and benefit. Where they are feared, evil men are held in check, and the good enjoy greater peace among the wicked (*Letter* 153.6.16).

If Augustine did not endorse Eusebius' notion of the state as God's direct agent in promoting the growth of Christianity, he did see temporal rule as functioning in the fashion of a father exercising "tough love" by restraining wrongdoing and thus assuring a degree of peace in society (i.e. "tranquility of order" [*City of God* 19. 13]).

> To achieve a minimal kind of benefit, it [the earthly city] desires an earthly peace and strives to obtain this through war ... When victory goes to those who have fought in the more upright cause, who would doubt that such a victory should be celebrated? Who would doubt that the resulting peace is desirable? These are blessings and are unquestionably gifts from God (ibid. 15.4).

Although Augustine cautions against taking earthly peace as our ultimate destiny (ibid.), he nevertheless sees it as a foretaste of eternal peace (*Letter* 189.6), and he insists that "everybody desires peace just as everyone wants joy. Even those who opt for war want nothing else but victory; thus their aim is glorious peace through war" (*City of God* 19.12).

This is the thrust of his specific advice to the Roman general, Boniface, who was having qualms of conscience about reconciling his role with the demands of the Christian faith. "Peace should be your aim; war should be a matter of necessity so that God might free you from necessity and preserve you in peace ... Even in the act of war be careful to maintain a peaceful disposition so that by defeating your foes you can bring them the benefits of peace" (*Letter* 189.6).[18] The "necessity" which Augustine talks about here is created by the sinful nature of the world. "It is the other side's wrongdoing that compels the wise man to wage just wars" (*City of God* 19.7). We should have no illusions about the realities of war, but at the same time we should recognize that we cannot entirely escape them because "in the great ebb and flow of human affairs no people has ever been granted such security that it did not have to fear attacks on its life here below" (ibid. 17.13). Ultimately, it is one's attitude in the midst of these inevitabilities that matters. "Waging war and expanding the empire by conquering other peoples strikes evil men as a fortunate thing, but to good men it is simply a necessity. Since, however, it would be worse for good men to be under the thumb of wrongdoers, it is not out of line to describe such a necessity as 'fortunate'" (ibid. 4.15).

Elsewhere Augustine voices this viewpoint in greater detail by drawing out the analogy of a father who uses "benign severity" in correcting his son but in the process does not stop loving his offspring.

> By analogy, if the earthly city observes Christian principles, even its wars will be waged with the benevolent purpose that better provision might be made for the defeated to live harmoniously together in justice and godliness. Anyone whose freedom to do evil is curtailed is subject to a beneficial kind of restraint since nothing is less fortunate than the good fortune of sinners (*Letter* 138.14; cf. 173.2).

However persuasive or unpersuasive Augustine's argument is here, his remarks indicate how far we have come from the position of the pre-Constantinian writers. For them the notion of waging war with a benevolent purpose was simply out of court, and if "benign severity" was not totally foreign to their thinking, the exercise of it on a large scale and with Christian participation certainly was.

Nonetheless, well-known and oft-cited Scriptural texts remained a problem for Augustine to address. Both Old Testament wars and New Testament injunctions about the use of the sword had to be faced. With respect to the Old Testament, Augustine was at pains to counter the Manichaean claim that a violent and vindictive Yahweh who commanded Moses to slay his enemies was at odds with the spirit of Jesus and was foreign to Christian thinking. In defending the identity of the God of the Old Testament and the God of the New he argued that Moses was acting out of obedience rather than savagery and that God was using Moses to punish wrongdoers. In all such actions the real evil lies elsewhere.

> What rightly deserves censure in war is the desire to do harm, cruel vengeance, a disposition that remains unappeased and implacable, a savage spirit of rebellion, a lust for domination and other such things. The reason why good men in the face of violent resistance even undertake wars at God's command or the command of legitimate authority is to inflict just punishment on things like these (*Against Faustus* 22.74).

No longer do we have Origen's allegorical reading of Scripture or his argument that the New Testament supersedes the Old. What we have is the kind of benign severity described above. Like Ambrose before him, Augustine is arguing that violence and the internal spirit of love are not incompatible. "It is not military duty (*militia*)," he says in one of his sermons (302.15), "but malice of heart (*malitia*) that forestalls the doing of good." Thus, it was Moses' "holy zeal and a desire that the people entrusted to him be subject to the one true God" which stood behind the prophet's slaying of idol worshipers among the Israelites (*Against Faustus* 22.79). "When one reads Moses' prayer for the sinful Israelites, who would not conclude that he did what he did out of deep love rather than any cruelty?" (ibid.).

The same focus on internal dispositions rather than outward actions appears in Augustine's handling of New Testament texts. Christ's admonition about turning the other cheek pertains to the heart where "virtue has its dwelling" (*Against Faustus* 22.76) rather than to outward actions. Christ himself did not follow his own injunction literally (*Letter* 138.13; cf. *On the Lord's Sermon* 1.19.57–58), and "this text does not forbid punishment which serves as a corrective" (ibid. 1.20.63). Christ's command about not resisting evil was aimed "to forestall our taking the kind of delight in revenge which feeds on another's misfortune. It was not meant to encourage us to neglect the correction of others" (*Letter* 47.5). As a consequence of this approach Augustine could cite David in the Old Testament as well as the centurion, Cornelius, and the soldiers who questioned John the Baptist about what they should do as evidence against the assumption "that it is impossible for anyone to serve God while on active duty in the army" (*Letter* 189.4). Once again the very instances which Tertullian rejected as justification for the use of force are now being presented in an entirely different light and are used to provide warrant for some form of physical coercion.

"Some" is the proper term here because in Augustine's mind both the right to wage war (*ius ad bellum*) and the conduct of war (*ius in bello*) are circumscribed by conditions. Although Augustine does not go into these conditions at length, they are important because they established certain ground rules for the discussion of the issues in subsequent centuries. With respect to the *ius ad bellum*, an offensive war must be initiated by a legitimate authority, and it must be undertaken either to avenge injuries "if some nation or state ... has neglected to punish a wrong committed by its citizens or to return something that was wrongfully taken" (*Questions on the Heptateuch* 6.10). Although Augustine does not talk much about defensive wars, we can conclude on the basis of the foregoing that he considered such conflicts legitimate. He as much as acknowledges this fact when he notes in the *City of God* (3.10) that some of Rome's wars were legitimate because they were waged not out of a "desire for glory but the need to protect its own liberty and safety."

With respect to the *ius in bello*, Augustine is again not very profuse. His most important point is that once peace has been achieved, mercy must be shown to the vanquished. "Just as we use force on a man as long as he resists and rebels, so, too, we should show him mercy once he has been vanquished or captured, especially when there is no fear of a future disturbance of the peace" (*Letter* 189.6).

Amid his defense of coercive actions by the state, we should note that Augustine had no illusions about the cost of war and the propensity of governing powers to use their vast resources to create in the public mind a favorable climate for war.[19] Rome was little different from modern states in its ability to employ public rhetoric (in Rome's case the poets, philosophers, political figures, and historians as well as the visual arts) to exalt the established political order and to hide the ways in which violence in its many forms is both a corrupt and corrupting dimension in a society which is preoccupied with its "prodigal pleasures" and its security. Augustine was not insensitive to the way in which the Rome of his time ignored the inherent moral shortcomings which its own writers made plain, and he comments on the delusions involved in the pursuit of glory.

> The lust to dominate inflicts great evils on the human race and wears it down . . . Tear away the false and misleading disguise so that we may see the facts as they are. Let no one say to me, 'This man or that one is great because he fought with so and so and beat him' . . . Gladiators, too, are victorious . . . but I think it is better to suffer the consequences of any kind of lethargy than to seek glory in that kind of fighting (*City of God* 3.14).

In response to such realities in human society Augustine pleads for grief and prayer for release from the necessities of a fallen world. In talking about the evils that attend even just wars he claims that "any one who endures these things or thinks about them without sorrow in his heart is all the more unfortunate in considering himself happy because he no longer possesses any human sensitivity" (*City of God* 19.7). Much the same is said about the magistrate who will of necessity make mistakes in condemning the innocent and in shedding blood despite his best intentions. For such a person Augustine advises that it is more consonant with his humanity to "recognize the misery involved in that necessity, [to] loathe it in himself, and if he is reverent and wise, [to] cry to God, 'Deliver me from my necessities'"(*City of God* 19.6, quoting *Ps.* 25.17).

These are the texts to be kept foremost in mind in considering Augustine's views on the justified war. And they are texts, I believe, which stand behind those Christians in post-Constantinian times who both held responsible positions in the public sphere and attempted in varying degrees to retain the spirit of their pre-Constantinian forebears.

The new outlook developed in the fourth century did not mean the demise of all pacifist sentiments in the Christian community.[20] In addition to the prohibition against participation in acts of violence by clergy, there were other indications that the difficulty of reconciling bloodshed with Christian love had not been totally surmounted. Even though much of the evidence on this point is couched in hagiographical and liturgical writings, which must be used with caution, the documents give us a good insight into some popular views of the time.

The most notable example of Christian opposition to war in the fourth century is Martin of Tours who in 356 abandoned his position in the army, proclaiming that since he wished to be a soldier of Christ, "it [was] not right for [him] to fight" (*Life of Martin* 4). Though the historicity of this action has been challenged, what is significant is that Martin's biographer, Sulpicius Severus, writing at the end of the fourth century, did not hesitate to present Martin's anti-militarist stance as a commendable example for Christians to follow. Early in the next century Paulinus, Bishop of Nola (409–431), took a similar stance in urging an acquaintance to give up his military career because "the man who fights with the sword is an agent of death . . . For this reason the Lord says, 'You cannot serve two masters,' that is, both the one God and mammon, both God and Caesar" (*Letter* 25.3, quoting Matt. 6.24). With much rhetorical flourish Paulinus also extolled his colleague Victricius, Bishop of Rouen, who apparently was converted while in military service, for throwing down [his] "weapons of blood in order to put on the weapons of peace" (*Letter* 18.7). Similar praise is found in Rome in Pope Damasus' epigrams commending the military martyrs Achilles and

Nereus who "threw down their shields and military trappings and bloody spears. Confessing Christ, they rejoiced in carrying his triumphal sign" (*Epigram* 8.4–7). In Spain the military martyrs Emeterius and Chelidonius are commemorated in a hymn by Prudentius which was used in liturgical ceremonies. Of them the Christian poet says, "They abandon the banners of Caesar and choose the emblem of the cross" (*Crowns of Martyrdom* 1.34). Though we cannot be sure that bloodshed as such was the sole or even the primary reason for these individuals' change of heart, what is significant is that long after Constantine they are praised for refusing to fight, and their actions were meant to stir the faith and admiration of others.

Such texts hardly indicate that pacifist sentiments had wide appeal or were a strong undercurrent in Roman society in the post-Constantinian age. What they do suggest is that the endorsement of Christian participation in war was never free of difficulties, and in some circles the pacifist arguments of earlier centuries lived on. If there were tensions of one kind on this issue before Constantine, there were tensions of another after his accession. In light of the human capacity for doing evil and the problem of knowing clearly and unequivocally what response is called for, it is difficult to see how it could have been otherwise. The problem of war and violence – however justified these may be by particular moral standards – is a product of the problem of evil and of the human obligation to limit its impact in a world which we neither fully understand nor fully control. These aspects of human experience continue to be with us, and so, too, does the ambiguity of using physical force in a way that genuinely leads to a more peaceful world.

Notes

1 *Luke* 2.14: "Glory to God in the highest, and on earth peace among men with whom he is pleased." *Matthew* 26.52: "Put your sword back into its place, for all who take the sword will perish by the sword." *John* 20.19: "On the evening of that day, the first day of the week, the doors being shut where the disciples were, for fear of the Jews, Jesus came and stood among them and said to them, 'Peace be with you'." *Ephesians* 6.14–16: "Stand, therefore, having girded your loins with truth and having put on the breastplate of righteousness, and having shod your feet with the equipment of the gospel of peace; above all taking the shield of faith with which you can quench all the flaming darts of the evil one." With slight variations, I have followed the Revised Standard Version of the New Testament throughout.

2 All dates are CE. As one can imagine, the bibliography on war and peace in early Christianity is considerable. Two traditional starting places, albeit somewhat dated at this point, are Bainton 1960 and Harnack 1980 (orig. edn. 1905). For studies taking a pacifist position on the issue, see Cadoux 1919 and Hornus 1980.

3 As H. von Campenhausen (1968: 160) noted many years ago, we should avoid posing the question of war and military service in "broad and undiscriminating terms, in a mode in which it never existed for the ancient Church or for the Church in any age." Not only the answer but the form of the question can vary from period to period.

4 Kurt Aland (1968: 124) rightly sums up the prevailing attitude of Christians in this period. "The Roman state is their state; that which damages the State, damages them; that which is beneficial to the state is also beneficial to them."

 5 *Luke* 3.14: "Soldiers also asked him, 'And we, what shall we do?' And he said to them, 'Rob
    no one by violence or by false accusation, and be content with your wages'." *Matt.* 8.10:
    "When Jesus heard him, he marveled and said, 'Truly, I say to you, not even in Israel have
    I found such faith'." *Acts* 10.44–48: "While Peter was saying this, the Holy Spirit fell on all
    who heard the word . . . Then Peter declared, 'Can anyone forbid water for baptizing these
    people who have received the Holy Spirit just as we have?' And he commanded them to be
    baptized in the name of Jesus Christ."
 6 Harnack's remark (1980: 35) in reference to wars enjoined by God in the Old Testament
    makes the point well. "How can one reject wars generally and in every sense if God himself
    brings them about and leads them? Apparently there are necessary and just wars!"
 7 The translation here and for Athenagoras below is that found in Robinson and Donaldson
    1996. Except where noted, the English renderings of the ancient authors are my own.
 8 Celsus' text is not extant, but we have long excerpts in *Against Celsus*, a defense against the
    pagan critic which Origen composed in the mid-third century, some 70 or 80 years after
    Celsus wrote. For Origen's treatise I have followed the translation of Chadwick 1965.
 9 In addition to the literary sources we have an illustration of the event on the column of
    Marcus Aurelius. See Daniel 1965: p. 44.
10 For the dates of Tertullian's works, see Barnes 1985; for recent general studies with good
    bibliographies, Osborn 1997; Rankin 1995; for Tertullian's exegetical principles, Jansen
    1982: 191–207.
11 Some modern critics argue that Tertullian's rejection of military service is based on
    the demands of pagan worship, which was an integral part of Roman military life. This
    is the view of Helgeland 1986 who sees a close connection between idolatrous activities in
    the army and religious aspects of the gladiatorial games. "It is small wonder, then, that so
    many Church Fathers should have criticized involvement with the military and condemned
    the games in the same breath" (47). Nonetheless, I believe that Tertullian's remarks indic-
    ate that for him the issue of bloodshed was also a major obstacle to service in the army. For
    a detailed and quite comprehensive treatment of the whole problem of Christians and the
    military in both the pre- and post-Constantinian eras, see Helgeland 1979.
12 In their role as civil servants "many, for their full 25 years, did nothing but write; many
    attended magistrates as messengers, ushers, confidential agents, and accountants, measuring
    their promotion from chair to chair, from office to office." See MacMullen 1963: 157.
13 For an excellent study of the relationship between Origen's exegetical principles and his
    political views, consult Caspary 1979; more generally for Origen's exegesis, Trigg 1983.
14 *Homily* 18.7. It is notable that the specific New Testament examples rejected by Tertullian
    as a justification for Christian participation in the army are here held up as exemplars of
    virtue. Elsewhere (Swift 1986), I have focused on the scriptural dimensions of the issue of
    war and peace in early Christianity.
15 For a recent comprehensive study of Ambrose, see McLynn 1994; for Ambrose's views on
    war, Swift 1970.
16 The bibliography on Augustine is unending. Fundamental is Brown 2000. See also the very
    recent biography of James O'Donnell (2005). For the bishop's views on war and military
    service, see especially the excellent analysis of Markus 1983; consult also Deane 1963; Swift
    1973, 1983; Russell 1975; Lenihan 1988; Cahill 1994; and Dodaro 1994.
17 It is significant that the Bishop of Hippo followed Ambrose in rejecting violence in matters
    of self-defense. "I do not approve of killing another man in order to avoid being killed
    oneself unless one happens to be a soldier or public official and thus acting not on his
    own behalf but for the sake of others or for the city in which he lives" (*Letter* 47.5). The
    evil in taking another's life in such a situation lies in the fact that it involves an inordinate
    desire (*libido*) for things of this world, including temporal life itself. However, like Ambrose,
    Augustine believes that this danger is no longer present when a third party is involved.

18 Nonetheless, peacekeeping holds a higher place in Augustine's mind as he makes clear to Darius, an ambassador sent to North Africa to negotiate a peace with rebel forces. "Preventing war through persuasion and seeking or attaining peace through peaceful means rather than through war are more glorious things than slaying men with the sword" (*Letter* 229.2). On Augustine's preoccupation with peace, see Lenihan 1988, and for the bishop's influence on subsequent ages, see Lenihan 1996; Russell 1975.

19 See Dodaro 1994, whose study adds a new dimension to our understanding of Augustine's views on war and is in my view essential reading for all subsequent discussion of the issues. See also Hanby 2005: esp. 124–28.

20 For the survival of pacifist sentiments in the fourth century, see Fontaine 1980.

References

Aland, K. 1968. "The Relationship between Church and State in Early Times: A Reinterpretation." *Journal of Theological Studies* 19: 15–27.

Bainton, R. H. 1960. *Christian Attitudes Toward War and Peace: A Historical Survey and Critical Re-Evaluation*. Nashville.

Barnes, T. D. 1985. *Tertullian: A Historical and Literary Study*. Reissue, New York.

Brown, P. 2000. *Augustine of Hippo. A Biography. A New Edition with an Epilogue*. Berkeley.

Cadoux, C. J. 1919. *The Early Christian Attitude to War*. New York.

Cahill, L. S. 1994. *Love Your Enemies: Discipleship, Pacifism, and Just War Theory*. Minneapolis.

Campenhausen, H. von. 1968. "Christians in Military Service in the Early Church." In H. von Campenhausen (ed.), *Tradition and Life in the Church*, 160–70. Trans. A.V. Littledale. Philadelphia.

Caspary, G. E. 1979. *Politics and Exegesis: Origen and the Two Swords*. Berkeley.

Chadwick, H. 1965. *Origen: Contra Celsum*. New York.

Daniel, G. 1965. *The Art of the Romans*. New York.

Deane, H. A. 1963. *The Political and Social Ideas of St. Augustine*. New York.

Dodaro, R. 1994. "Eloquent Lies, Just Wars and the Politics of Persuasion: Reading Augustine's *City of God* in a 'Postmodern' World." *Augustinian Studies* 25: 77–137.

Fontaine, J. 1980. "Le culte des martyrs militaires et son expression poétique au IVe siècle." *Augustinianum* 20: 141–71.

Hanby, M. 2005. "*Democracy and its Demons*." In J. Doody, K. L. Hughes, and K. Paffenroth (eds.), *Augustine and Politics*, 117–144. New York.

Harnack, A. von. 1980. *Militia Christi. The Christian Religion and the Military in the First Three Centuries*. Trans. D. M. Gracie. Philadelphia, German ed. 1905.

Helgeland, J. 1979. "Christians and the Roman Army from Marcus Aurelius to Constantine." *Aufstieg und Niedergang der Römischen Welt* II.23.1: 724–834.

——. 1986. "The Early Church and War: The Sociology of Idolatry." In Reid 1986: 34–47.

Hornus, J.-M. 1980. *It Is Not Lawful for Me to Fight: Early Christian Attitudes to War*. Rev. ed. Trans. A. Kreider and O. Coburn. Scottsdale.

Jansen, J. F. 1982. "Tertullian and the New Testament." *The Second Century* 2: 191–207.

Lenihan, D. A. 1988. "The Just War Theory in the Work of St. Augustine." *Augustinian Studies* 19: 37–70.

——. 1996. "The Influence of Augustine's Just War: The Early Middle Ages." *Augustinian Studies* 27: 55–93.

MacMullen, R. 1963. *Soldier and Civilian in the Later Roman Empire*. Cambridge, MA.

McLynn, N. B. 1994. *Ambrose of Milan: Church and Court in a Christian Capital*. Berkeley.

Markus, R. A. 1983. "St. Augustine's views on the 'Just War'." *Studies in Church History* 20:
     1–13.

O'Donnell, James J. 2005. *Augustine: A New Biography.* New York.

Osborn, E. 1997. *Tertullian: First Theologian of the West.* Cambridge.

Rankin, D. 1995. *Tertullian and the Church.* Cambridge.

Reid, C. R. Jr. (ed.). 1986. *Peace in a Nuclear Age.* Washington, DC.

Robinson A., and Donaldson J. (eds.). 1996. *The Ante-Nicene Fathers.* Grand Rapids. Reprint
     of 1885.

Russell, F. H. 1975. The Just War in the Middle Ages. Cambridge.

Swift, L. J. 1970. "St. Ambrose on Violence and War." *Transactions and Proceedings of the
     American Philological Association* 101: 533–43.

——. 1973. "Augustine on War and Killing: Another View." *Harvard Theological Review* 66:
     369–83.

——. 1983. *The Early Church Fathers on War and Military Service.* Wilmington.

——. 1986. "Search the Scriptures: Patristic Exegesis and the *Ius Belli*." In Reid 1986: 48–68.

Trigg, J. W. 1983. *Origen: the Bible and Philosophy in the Third Century Church.* Atlanta.

Zampaglione, G. 1973. *The Idea of Peace in Antiquity.* Trans. R. Dunn. Notre Dame.

17

Fight for God – But Do So with Kindness: Reflections on War, Peace, and Communal Identity in Early Islam*

Fred M. Donner

Preliminaries

The formulation "War and Peace," to which this volume is devoted, orients us in a very specific direction, by presenting war and peace as the relevant polar opposites – or, more exactly, by implying that war is the main, or even the only, opposite of peace. That they are diametrically opposed is clear, but focusing on them may limit our vision by obscuring some other possibilities that may also be worth considering. For, while war can definitely be viewed as a state of "un-peace" or "peacelessness," it is clear that "peace" cannot so simply be defined merely as the absence of war (except, perhaps, in a narrowly diplomatic sense). That is, "peace" is a concept of greater breadth or range than war, and one that can be negated by a variety of kinds of stress, distress, unrest, disturbance, and so on, most of which would not qualify, for most of us, as "war." When we say, for example, that someone is "at peace with himself," we may indeed mean that he is free of "warring emotions" within himself. But our reference to "warring emotions" is, of course, a metaphor, by which we try to express some of the inner turmoil and distress that attend times of severe emotional upset by drawing a parallel between them and the physical traumas of actual war. So the opposite of being "at peace with oneself" is actually something like being "at odds with oneself" or "subject to unstable or changing emotions." Peace is also sometimes defined as tranquillity or quiet (as, e.g. in the phrase "peace and quiet"), so in this sense, its opposite – or an opposite – would be "noise" or "clamor."

A full understanding of the meaning of "peace," then, requires us to look not only at its opposite in war, but also at such things as harmony (within a person, within a community or society), coherence, spiritual wholeness, and an absence of strife or contention in general. And, since the existence of differences between individuals and groups – differences in outlook or beliefs, differences in interests, goals, and the methods adopted to attain them – are often the crucial element shaping the presence of stresses, tensions, and conflict within a society, the key questions become, "How does a tradition or community deal with differences?" "To what extent does it tolerate differences?" The word "reconciliation" – initially also part of this volume's overall theme – implies recognition of the existence of differences, and some effort to reduce the tension and conflict they may cause. This may be achieved by emphasizing common ground and "agreeing to disagree" on the rest, or by one party changing its mind on a key issue (whether through persuasion or a simple change of heart), or by interpreting the differences in such a manner that they do not appear, after all, to be so essentially different. Reconciliation, at any rate, seems to reject the idea of resolving differences simply by coercing one side to follow the other, by imposing uniformity.

It is especially important to transcend the restricted vision of the "peace vs. war" dichotomy when trying to describe the thought-world of the earliest Islamic community (or, as I prefer to call it, the early community of Believers). This is because warfare (and peace as the absence of warfare) is generally associated with the activities of states or other large political groupings; yet, for the earliest community of Believers (early seventh century), we have little reliable documentation about the state, or for that matter about political activity or political ideals of any kind. For the beginnings of Islam we are almost completely lacking in contemporary sources of a truly documentary character; the single exception – and it is a huge exception – is the Muslim holy book or scripture, the Qur'an, which in my view must be considered something that crystallized and was set down in definitive written form already within a few years of Muhammad's death in 632.[1] For our present purposes, then, the Qur'an can be accepted as a kind of quasi-documentary source for the very first stage in the growth of the community of Believers, and as such it provides us with a unique window into the thought-world of the earliest Believers, of Muhammad and his first followers.

When we look in that window, however, we find no shred of concern for a state, or for political organization of any kind; the Qur'an is almost completely devoid of it. That a state did emerge somehow during Muhammad's lifetime and that it developed rapidly thereafter is well known, but it is known from somewhat later literary sources and documents, so that for the earliest phases of this process we must rely on guesswork (to which we try to lend some measure of plausibility by calling it educated). The Qur'an's lack of any reference to a state or to political organization is one of the main reasons why later Muslim political theorists, over the centuries right up until today, have struggled to reach any consensus on just what constitutes "Islamic government." It is well-nigh impossible to do so when the most fundamental Islamic text, the Qur'an, is silent on what kind of political order Believers should establish, or how power should be exercised, or who should hold it, or how power should be transferred. The vague injunction, "O Believers! Obey God and obey the apostle and those in authority from among you" (Surat al-Nisa' (4): 59), is a slender foundation on which to build a political theory, although of course Muslims through the ages have been forced to try to do so, for want of anything else.

The Qur'an does use the word "war" (*harb*) and related words a few – about a half-dozen – times. "Peace" (*salam*) is much more frequently invoked in the Qur'an – over forty times – but most of these instances are formulaic appeals to it as a greeting, or speak vaguely of someone being at peace with his Lord; very few relate to actual peace or peacemaking in a human society. Yet the Qur'an also contains many other passages that, while not referring explicitly to war or peace, do relate to questions of social tranquility and harmony, social conflict, strife, and how they are to be dealt with, which I take to be the true concern of this volume. To look only at the "peace vs. war" theme, narrowly defined, then, would force us to neglect a rich trove of material in the Qur'an on how to handle such things as tension and contention within the community and within oneself, which should rightly be placed within the broad semantic field of "peace and the absence thereof."

My further comments will be organized into three separate themes: the Qur'an's injunctions on relations with unbelievers (Second section); the Qur'an's injunctions on relations among Believers, and on just how Believers were to be defined in the earliest community (Third section); and what sources of somewhat later date tell us about the early Islamic state and the way it handled considerations of war, peace, and reconciliation during the early Islamic years, ca. 630–700 (Fourth section).

The Qur'an on Relations with Unbelievers

The Qur'an conveys a single very clear religious message, addressed forcefully and uncompromisingly to everyone who hears or reads it. (And, we should note here, the Qur'an seems to be directed mainly at individuals: it speaks to you and me.) It divides humankind unambiguously into two groups, Believers and unbelievers.[2] It tells us that, as individuals, we are all faced with the stark choice of either believing in the one God, or not, and on the basis of that choice and of our behavior in support of it, we will either be rewarded at the Last Judgment with eternal bliss in heaven, or condemned to eternal torment in hell. This basic complex of ideas was, of course, already widely known in the Near East when Muhammad preached in Arabia in the early seventh century – Judaism, Christianity, and Zoroastrianism, among others, said similar things. But the Qur'an's way of presenting these ideas is particularly forceful. It hammers away insistently at this theme, reminding us repeatedly and in various ways that unbelievers will face "grievous punishment" (*'adhab alim*). It makes it painfully clear that if we meet death without having made the right choice, no amount of special pleading will get us off the hook: we will pay. It depicts, on the surface of the discourse, a very black and white moral world, divided between Believers and unbelievers.

This stark vision of the world as divided into two realms, of good and evil, is not unrelated to the question of warfare and strife. The doctrine of a single God is preached to all the world, and everyone is expected to respond to this appeal. The failure of people to respond properly is taken as an affront against God. Numerous passages in the Qur'an authorize Believers to fight unbelievers, if the latter attack the Believers, or speak of resisting unbelievers who "make war on God and His messenger." "The only punishment of those who wage war against God and His messenger, and who try to spread corruption on the earth, is that they should be killed, or crucified, or that their hands and feet should be cut off on opposite sides, or that they should be imprisoned. That is a disgrace for them in this life, and in the afterlife there shall be for them a great punishment" (Surat al-Ma'ida (5): 33). Some passages do not even seem to have the defensive character of the previous verse: "Fight those who do not believe in God, nor in the Last Day, nor forbid that which God and His messenger have forbidden, nor follow the true law (*wa la yadinuna din al-haqq*)" (Surat al-Tawba (9): 29). In short, Qur'anic discourse on unbelievers does not appear, at first, to portray a world where "reconciliation" is an operative concept; for between Believers and unbelievers, who represent the greatest affront to God in their denial of His oneness, there can in principle be no reconciliation.

And yet, when we look a bit more closely at the text of the Qur'an, we find that many of its denunciations of unbelievers, some of them (as we have seen) of hair-raising asperity, are followed by mitigating or "escape" clauses – not in the sense of offering any concession on the matter of belief, which is simply not negotiable, but by suggesting that some concession may be made, either because the unbelievers have shown repentance, or for other reasons less clear. For example: "So when the sacred months have passed, kill the idolaters wherever you find them, and take them captive and besiege them and lie in wait for them in every ambush. But if they repent and perform prayer and offer the sin-tax (*zakat*), let them go their way, for God is forgiving and merciful. And if any of the idolaters asks for your protection, grant it to him so that he may hear the word of God; then deliver him to his place of safety. That is because they are a people who do not know" (ibid. 5–6).[3] These verses suggest that unbelievers can be granted tolerant treatment not only by repenting and showing that they are Believers after all, but apparently simply because they are ignorant and need time to "come around" to being Believers. Another verse accuses the Jews of having broken their covenant with God and distorted their scriptures, "excepting a few of them – so pardon them and forgive; for surely God loves those who treat others with kindness" (Surat al-Ma'ida (5): 13). The opening of the verse, which offers a hard-edged condemnation of Jews as renegades from the true faith, is tempered by the "escape clause" which emphasizes forgiveness and acceptance for those Jews who are not seen as stubborn resisters. Passages such as this one also make clear how thoroughly, in the Qur'an's world-view, the question of belief or unbelief is the result of an *individual* decision, not a matter of collective identity. You are judged not because of what you are or to which group you belong, but because of what you do, of what choices you, as an individual with free will, have made.

Such "escape clauses" have the effect of softening the overall tone of the text, and are so frequent in the Qur'an that they must be considered a characteristic feature of Qur'anic discourse.[4] They represent, in effect, the *yin* and *yang* of the Qur'an's world-view and of its style, complementary opposites that make up the whole. It is the tension between this *yin* and *yang* that enables the Qur'an to tread the ground between, on the one hand, doing its main job, which is to get us to believe in God (perhaps by frightening us into it!), and on the other, providing sufficient flexibility to accommodate the reality of human nature, with its hesitation, vacillation, and tendency to procrastinate and change one's mind. This, I think, is part of the reason why as a religious text the Qur'an has proven so effective over fourteen centuries: through the myriad distractions and confusions and moral fuzziness that we all experience in daily life, the Qur'an – both in its content and its style – focuses our minds again on what is, or what it wants us to believe is, of ultimate importance; yet it keeps a certain balance with its "escape clauses," leaving up to us the decision on whether a particular situation demands enforcement of a stricture, or observance of the injunction to be forgiving. I will note here in passing that this "*yin/yang*" quality of Qur'anic discourse also has a less fortunate consequence: it makes it relatively easy to distort the Qur'an's message by quoting a short passage out of context, for whatever purpose – either by quoting the blood-curdling injunctions against unbelief without the mitigating appeals to mercy, or by quoting the injunctions to forgiveness without mentioning the basic principles they are introduced to temper. Both techniques constitute polemic, differing only in their goals – whether Muslim apologetic, or "Islam-bashing."

To sum up this part of our reflections: the Qur'an conveys a double message on the question of relations with unbelievers. Given the Qur'an's harsh denunciations of unbelief and unbelievers and the sharp line it draws between unbelievers and Believers, it would be entirely misleading to characterize the Qur'an as eirenic; as a whole, the Qur'an is a tough and generally uncompromising condemnation of idolatry and unbelief. The Qur'an's goal, after all, is to persuade us that Belief in the one God and proper worship of Him is God's due, that it is morally essential, and therefore that anything less than Belief in God is intolerable; and a system of beliefs that finds something intolerable is not, under any circumstances, a very promising basis for tolerance. We must assume, then, that the earliest community of Believers, in the time of Muhammad and his followers, adopted a similarly tough stance. Yet, by the same token, the Qur'an cannot be characterized simply as militantly aggressive either, because its most strident injunctions seem to be focused mainly on defensive situations, and because it contains frequent mitigating clauses which enjoin forgiveness in at least some circumstances, even when dealing with unbelievers. And so we must conclude that Muhammad's community probably also made practical allowances of various kinds for unbelievers – idolators – in some cases, when they were viewed as non-hostile, or likely to "come around" to true Belief given a certain amount of leniency and time.

There is one further aspect of this issue that needs to be considered. The assertiveness of the Qur'an in confronting unbelievers is rooted in the Qur'an's desire to see the whole human community living peaceably in accordance with God's revealed will. The ultimate objective of the Qur'an, in other words, is not war, but peace. From the Qur'an's perspective, recognition of God's oneness is non-negotiable, and unbelievers are those who are in rebellion against the patent truth of God's existence and unity. This is why many Qur'anic passages on fighting unbelievers have a defensive tone; the mere fact of unbelief is an act of aggression against God's oneness. We may view Believers as aggressively fomenting war against unbelievers, or we may view unbelievers as being by their nature at war with God. Our judgment on who "starts" this war, in other words, is largely dependent on our point of view.

Relations among Believers, and the Definition of Believer

When we move to the question of how the Qur'an presents the nature of human interactions within the community of Believers, we find a radically different picture. In this context, the individual is of course forcefully enjoined to do good works, but this is defined not only as showing piety and devotion to God, but also as being conciliatory and forgiving in one's behavior towards others – that is, toward other Believers. We find this set of essentially conciliatory ideas reflected in a number of key terms in the Qur'an. One of the most frequently encountered (ca. 100 times) is the word *ihsan*, which can be translated loosely as "charity" or "kindliness," and its correlated adjectives (e.g. *muhsin*, "one who is charitable"). This term is often used as an alternative designation for Believers; for example, typical passages note that "those who submit their faces to God are *muhsin*," or enjoins Believers to treat their parents with *ihsan* (e.g. Surat al-Baqara (2): 112). A few offer a more detailed description of just what *ihsan* entails. For example, one passage promises paradise for those God-fearing or pious persons "who give of their wealth in good times and bad, and who restrain [their] anger, and forgive people; for God loves the *muhsinin*."[5] So *ihsan* comprises, among other things, generosity, self-control, and forgiveness.

Other passages also emphasize the importance of showing forgiveness (*'afw*), seeking reconciliation (*sulh*), and avoiding aggressiveness: "The repayment of evil is evil like it, but whoever forgives and seeks reconciliation, his reward is with God, for [God] does not love those who oppress."[6] A few verses later, the Qur'an enjoins Believers to be patient and forgiving. One passage instructs Believers to "reconcile your differences" (Surat al-Anfal (8): 1; cf Surat al-Baqara (2): 224, ". . . and make peace between men"), and another says, "If two parties of Believers quarrel, make peace among them. The Believers are brethren, so make peace between your brothers" (Surat al-Hujurat (49), 9–10). Yet another verse states, ". . . help one another in righteousness and piety, not in sin and aggression."[7] There are even passages enjoining Believers to seek reconciliation between estranged spouses, to be gentle to one's enemies, and for husbands not to behave graspingly with a woman's dowry if their marriage is anulled before consummation, but rather to give up the half the husband is by custom and the letter of the law entitled to retain, on the grounds that "that is closer to God-fearingness."[8]

The Qur'an, in other words, strongly encourages Believers to treat one another with kindness, charity, forgiveness, and to seek compromise and conciliation. But what, then, are we to make of the Islamic tradition of "enjoining the right and forbidding the wrong" (*al-amr bi l-ma'ruf wa l-nahy 'an al-munkar*), which is mentioned in the Qur'an? Those who are familiar with later Islamic tradition know that this idea was sometimes used as a pretext for what we would consider a "holier-than-thou" meddling in your neighbors' affairs. Famous anecdotes in later Islamic law texts relating to this doctrine, for example, speak of men of known piety being offended by the fact that a neighbor was playing music (considered irreligious by some), and responding by entering the neighbor's house uninvited and smashing the offending musical instruments. Such behavior bespeaks a harshly intolerant attitude even within the community of Believers. But a recent definitive examination of these traditions (Cook 2000) shows quite convincingly that such intolerance is a particular formulation that arose only in certain circles in a particular historical context, and indeed was a minority formulation. It was counterbalanced in the tradition by other attitudes that stood firmly on such principles as the inviolability of the home from such meddlesome invasions of privacy. Most important for our purposes, this study reveals that the Qur'an itself in no way requires, or even encourages, such a meddlesome stance; the Qur'an seems only to be enjoining Believers in a very general, moral sense, to stand as a community unified in being mindful of good and evil and striving to be good (ibid. 13–17). There is no reason, therefore, to assume from the Qur'an that the early community espoused the kind of intolerance that some of the Qur'an's later interpreters did.

Earlier we considered the importance of difference, and of how difference is negotiated, as a crucial factor in how a tradition deals with such questions as peace and war. As we have seen, the Qur'an offers significant evidence of a desire to establish peaceful relations *within* the community of Believers. We might, however, say, "well, it is easy to establish peaceful relations among people who all agree (all are Believers), because that removes a basic difference between them" – although that charge is perhaps a bit unfair given the many practical matters on which even fellow-Believers might disagree. Still, the fact remains that for the Qur'an the basic divide is between Believers and unbelievers, and so for our purposes a great deal rests on exactly how the Qur'an defines Believers and unbelievers. Who is, or could be, in fact, a member of the "in-group" of Believers? This brings us to the question of religious tolerance and the notion of religious community among the earliest Believers, as we find that reflected in the Qur'an.

Later Muslim tradition, which crystallized in the three centuries after the time of the prophet Muhammad (i.e., especially during the eighth and ninth centuries), offers a very clear vision of how Muslims should relate to people of other religions. In the tradition's view, Muslims have constituted a distinct religious confession from the days of Muhammad's first preaching. As adherents of a distinct religion, Muslims (according to this view) are not to tolerate idolatry (polytheism) at all, and are to treat "peoples of the Book" – that is other monotheists, mainly Christians and Jews – with only a grudging tolerance in exchange for the latter's payment of a poll-tax symbolizing their inferior status.[9] Christians and Jews are accorded this tolerance because they are, after all, monotheists, even though they espouse what is, in the view of later Muslim tradition, a defective form of monotheism. This vision of how Muslims related to non-Muslims has generally been accepted by Western scholars, and was considered by everyone – Muslim and non-Muslim alike – to have applied in the earliest community, at the time of the prophet Muhammad, as well as in later times.

Although this view is well-entrenched in scholarship on early Islam, there is reason to think that it is fundamentally mistaken at least as far as its relevance to the foundational period of the community of Believers is concerned. For, when we examine the text of the Qur'an – which, to repeat, is our best and almost our only source of reliable evidence about the intellectual world of the earliest community – we find numerous passages that appear to cast doubt upon the later idea that Believers are to be so categorically distinguished from Christians and Jews. Rather, the intellectual world depicted in the Qur'an seems to be one in which the community was significantly more ecumenical in nature, or we might say, more flexible or tolerant in its self-definition, than the later strict dichotomy between "Muslim" and "Non-Muslim" would imply.

In order to make the case for my revisionist theory, however, we need first to attend to some crucial matters of vocabulary. Later Muslim tradition – and, following it, Western scholarship and popular writing – generally used the terms "Islam" and "Muslim" when speaking of the prophet Muhammad's community and the religious movement inaugurated by him. (Consider even the title of this chapter: War, Peace, and Communal Identity in Early *Islam*.) But, when we examine the text of the Qur'an, we notice a striking fact: the Qur'an uses the terms "Islam" and "Muslim" relatively sparingly, whereas it speaks very frequently of "Believers" (*mu'minun*), and there is no doubt that the audience to which the Qur'an addresses itself is called, and presumably called itself, Believers – not "Muslims." (Consider the common Qur'anic invocations, "O you who Believe…", etc.) This is why, as I noted at the beginning, I prefer to speak of Muhammad's community as "the community of Believers" rather than as "the Muslim community" or just "the Muslims."

Now, to some this may appear to be mere hair-splitting; they may insist that "Believers" and "Muslims" mean the same thing – and, indeed, later Muslim tradition generally makes this claim and treats the two terms as, roughly speaking, synonymous. The problem is that the Qur'an itself, in a few crucial passages, makes clear that "Believer" and "Muslim," while related in some way, are *not* simple synonyms. Full demonstration of this hypothesis, which I have tried to provide elsewhere (Donner 2002–3), is beyond the scope of this chapter, but consider the following passage: "The bedouins have said, '*amanna*' ['we believe']. Say [to them]: 'You do not Believe; rather, say '*aslamna*' ['we have submitted/become Muslims'], for Belief has not entered your hearts" (Surat al-Hujarat (49): 14). This verse makes it clear, I think, that in the Qur'an's usage, *islam* and *iman*, Islam and Belief, Muslim and Believer, are not simple equivalents. One could go much deeper into the significance and implications of this distinction, but that would be a detour from the topic of this chapter, to which we must return.

Since the Qur'an is addressed primarily to "Believers," what exactly is it that these Believers believe in? Again, the Qur'an makes it clear at various points what the essentials are. A Believer is one who believes in the oneness of God, in the Last Judgment (possibly the imminent Last Judgment), in the need to live righteously according to God's revealed law. The important fact here is that this cluster of beliefs – one God, Last Day, righteous behavior according to the law – was something that the "peoples of the book" – Christians and Jews – could, and in many cases did, subscribe to. In other words, there is no reason why the Qur'anic term "Believers" (*mu'minun*) could not have applied to some Christians and Jews; unlike the later usage of "Muslim," the terms "Believer" and "Christian" or "Jew" were not mutually exclusive. Or, to put it yet another way, the early community of Believers could – and, very probably, did – include some Christian and Jewish Believers.

Again, we turn to the Qur'an for further confirmation. "There are some peoples of the book who Believe in God and what was sent down to you and what was sent down to them" (Surat Al 'Imran (3): 199). Some other passages make it clear that such Believing peoples of the Book will attain paradise: "If the peoples of the book Believe and are pious (*ittaqaw*), we shall efface their evil deeds from them (*la-kaffarna 'anhum sayyi'atihim*) and shall admit them to the gardens of delight. If they obey the Torah and the Gospel and that which was sent down to them from their Lord, they shall eat from above, and from beneath their feet. Among them is a provident/moderate community (*ummatun muqtasidatun*), but many of them do evil."[10] This passage states quite directly that those individuals among the peoples of the book who embrace right Belief and right action are to be counted among the Believers and will be rewarded in the afterlife.

Conversely, those peoples of the book who do *not* believe, those among the "many of them [who] do evil," are not only excluded from the ranks of Believers, they are to be actively combatted. Another Qur'anic verse states, "Of those who were brought the Book, fight such as do not believe in God and the last day, and who do not forbid what God and His apostle have forbidden, and who do not obey the true *din*, until, being completely subdued, they pay tribute from their hand" (Surat al-Bara'a (9), 29). Peoples of the book who do not believe are even, at times, equated with unbelievers (*kafirun*): "For the unbelievers among them, we have prepared a painful punishment. But for those of them who are grounded in knowledge, and the Believers who believe in what was sent down to you and what was sent down before you and those who observe prayer and those who bring alms and the Believers in God and the Last Day – to those We shall bring a great reward" (Surat al-Nisa' (4), 161–62). Like many others, this passage makes it clear that the boundary dividing Believers/saved from unbelievers/damned is one that falls across the ranks of the peoples of the book. People are to be saved not because of their confessional identity, but because, whatever their confessional identity, they are Believers, in word and deed.

The central idea contained in the Qur'an, then, seems to be that salvation comes from proper piety, avoidance of sinful behavior, coupled with a basic belief in the one God and the Last Day. It does not matter to which monotheist community one belongs, for Belief – particularly in the sense of right or righteous action – transcends one's identification with a particular community. Those who Believe and are righteous are to be saved, whatever confession they ascribe to; those who are sinful, on the other hand, will be punished, regardless of their confession.

We can summarize this third part of our exploration, dealing with the Qur'an's perspective on relations among Believers, as follows. Here the Qur'an seems to be very positive in its tone: it emphasizes that Believers should treat other Believers with kindness, forgiveness, forbearance, tolerance, and so on. This is perhaps not so surprising. More interesting, I think, is the fact that the Qur'an seems to offer the basis for a kind of openness and inclusiveness with the traditional monotheisms – Judaism and Christianity. This is particularly important because the majority of people with whom the earliest Arabian Believers would make contact in the Near East – Syria, Iraq, Egypt – would be Christians and Jews. The Qur'an decidedly does not draw a sharp dichotomy between Muslims and Christians or Jews, as later Muslim tradition would do, but focuses on the concept of a community of Believers which is confessionally open – that is, that included (i.e. tolerated) Believers who followed Qur'anic law, or Jewish Believers who followed the Torah, or Christian Believers who followed the Gospels. This seems to be reflected in Qur'anic verses such as the following, which speaks of Believers who die fighting "in God's way" and will, therefore, attain paradise: "[This is] a promise which is binding upon Him [i.e. upon God], in the Torah, the Gospels, and the Qur'an; and who is more faithful to his promise than God?" (Surat al-Tawba (9): 111). Exactly how these Christian, Jewish, and Qur'anic Believers related to one another in day-to-day terms in the earliest community of Believers, above all in such matters as ritual practice, is something that still remains to be clarified; perhaps we can envision them as different congregations, each following their traditional practices of worship, within a single larger community of Believers led by Muhammad.

That the Believers were to be sharply differentiated on a religious basis from unbelievers of various kinds, with whom relations must often have been hostile, can hardly be doubted from what the Qur'an tells us. But we see that the Qur'an also makes it clear that the Believers' community embraced not only Muslims – Qur'anic Believers – but also Believing Christians and Jews, and so provided a basis for a fundamental toleration across the confessional barrier separating those groups. The kindliness and tolerance that the Qur'an enjoins among Believers, then, would presumably apply to all Believers, whether Qur'anic/Muslim, Christian, or Jewish. This initial ecumenical character of the community of Believers of Muhammad's time seems, unfortunately, to have been eclipsed within a few generations, by which time the community had come to identify itself more narrowly with Muslims – Qur'anic Believers – and had re-defined the position of Christians and Jews as now being outside its boundaries. This, too, is a process that needs to be further clarified, but it represented, of course, a step away from the early community's original ecumenical qualities, and was linked with a hermeneutical re-reading of both the Qur'an and other early Islamic texts in a manner that was designed to disguise or conceal this very ecumenism towards other monotheists.

War, Peace, and Reconciliation in the Early Islamic State

Finally, we must consider the question of war and peace in the context of the early Islamic state – in its embryonic form during Muhammad's life and as it developed subsequently under the "commanders of the Believers," who succeeded Muhammad as heads of the movement he started. This is a project that necessitates moving to a different set of sources – first because, as noted earlier, the Qur'an does not make reference to a state or to political institutions, and second, because the Qur'an in any case can tell us only about the time of the prophet, not about the subsequent history of the community. The early Islamic state is therefore something we learn about mainly from an extensive Islamic chronicle literature in Arabic, which was compiled between a century and three centuries after Muhammad's death, although many reports in these chronicles may draw on somewhat older oral reports. We can also glean some hints about what the early state may have been like from a few surviving inscriptions, coins, and papyri; these offer very fragmented bits of information, but have the advantage – unlike the later chronicles – of being documentary in character (an effort to use these is found in Donner 1986). It is the chronicle literature, however, that for better or for worse provides the bulk of our evidence.[11]

These chronicles offer us a clear vision of a series of state-sponsored wars of expansion mounted by Muhammad's followers, spreading first throughout Arabia and then into the neighboring lands of the Near East – Syria, Iraq, Iran, Egypt – and beyond.[12] The shock troops for this expansion may have been pastoral nomadic or settled village tribesmen from various parts of Arabia, but the leadership cadres – the commanders, governors, and above all, the "commanders of Believers" or heads of the movement after Muhammad's death – were mainly townsmen of Mecca and Medina, and many were of the prophet's own tribe of Quraysh. According to our chronicles, the "commanders of the Believers" (*amir al-mu'minin*; later commonly called caliphs) dispatched the armies of conquest to various fronts and directed their activities from their capital in Medina. Their goal, our chronicles make clear, was to spread "Islam" – recognition of God's oneness and submission to God's will – to the far corners of the earth, and to force the two "evil empires" of their age – the Byzantine and Sasanian states – to submit. It was the Muslims' religious duty to engage in *jihad*, "striving" (in God's way), clearly equated in this context with undertaking armed military action against unbelievers and for this reason sometimes simply equated with "holy war" (p. 309 below). *Jihad* is mentioned frequently in the Qur'an, as are injunctions for the Believers to engage in fighting (*qital*) against unbelievers, but the chronicles depict the early Islamic state as organizing and leading this activity. This policy led, naturally enough, to major clashes between the armies of the Muslims and those of the empires, clashes that, notwithstanding the much larger size of the Byzantine and Sasanian forces, resulted in resounding victories for the Muslims at places like Yarmuk in Syria, Qadisiyya in Iraq, and Nihavand in Iran in the 630s and 640s. In between such major clashes, the Believers' armies busied themselves with subduing the countryside in these areas and in forcing the towns and cities, most of which were walled and fortified, either to submit to them and pay tribute, or to face conquest by force and the attendant pillage that inevitably would come after it. The overall picture offered by these chronicles is, then, one of religiously-based strife and intolerance launched by the state.

Some parts of this picture drawn by the chronicles may describe fairly accurately key features of the early expansion of the Believers into the Near East. It seems to me, for example, that the movement must have been at least loosely directed from the center, even if we want to view skeptically the chronicles' occasional claim that virtually every detail of the conquests on distant fronts was cleared with Medina (Donner 1995). Nor do I doubt that the Believers had armies, or that those armies confronted the armies of the great empires on the battlefield, and that they sometimes won. A Syriac source from the late seventh century, John Bar Penkaye, describes the *mhaggraye* (as the Syriac texts call the Muslims) as launching regular raiding campaigns every year during which they seized large amounts of booty and many captives, and this seems to provide independent confirmation of the martial activities of the early Believers.[13] And, as we have seen already, many Qur'anic passages fit the idea of the early Believers' movement as one of militant and uncompromising piety.

On the other hand, the picture presented by the chronicles embodies certain conceptual difficulties and probably misrepresents some aspects of the expansion of the Believers' movement. First and foremost, this picture is firmly rooted in the later Islamic view of the world as sharply divided between a community of Muslims and everyone else; for this reason, its descriptions of the conquest campaigns emphasize this "us versus them" quality when discussing the arrival of "Muslims" in a new area. However, our re-interpretation of the character of the earliest community as one of Believers (rather than Muslims), outlined in the third part of this chapter, obviously suggests that we need to reconsider this question. If the community and polity that was expanding from Arabia into the adjacent lands of the Near East saw itself at first as a community of monotheist Believers, as proposed above, even of rigorously monotheist Believers, then from the perspective of many towns and villages in the Near East, these Arabian Believers may have come as religious reformers, urging the people in these towns to do better by their monotheism and to live righteously, rather than as religious zealots brandishing a sword and demanding conversion to a totally new religion, or death. The chronicles' presentation of a series of grand conquests also probably exaggerates their role, because the notion of a divinely-supported victory of "Muslims" over non-Muslims was part of a later program to justify the Believers' rule. Most localities in the Near East were, after all, already occupied by monotheists (Jews or Christians or even Zurvanite Zoroastrians), so in most cases conversion to monotheism was not at issue. This tempers, once again, the image of the conquests and the kind of harsh, coercive confessional intolerance one sometimes associates with it.

On the other hand, we should not overdo here the emphasis on peacefulness among the early Believers; we must remember that our aforementioned Syriac source, John Bar Penkaye, *does* speak of annual raids by the Believers during which they took booty and captives – which does not sound very peace-loving. Furthermore, the likelihood that the early Believers were attempting to overthrow the existing empires (Byzantine and Sasanian), which they saw as sinful, oppressive establishments hopelessly mired in evil and impiety, makes it impossible to argue that Islam came in all circumstances simply as a "religion of peace," as some of its present-day apologists like to claim, even though kindness and forgiveness, as we have seen, constitute a significant theme in Qur'anic discourse. But Bar Penkaye also states that "among them [i.e. among the *mhaggraye* making these raids] there were many Christians...," so whatever the basis of this raiding was, it seems to have been independent of any perceived dichotomy between Believers and Christians.

The annals of the early community of Believers in the decades following Muhammad's death in 632 also inform us of another kind of strife: internal dissension and even open fighting among the Believers themselves, mostly over the question of leadership, particularly during the two "civil wars" (656–661 and 680–692).

The chronicles describe in considerable (and often contradictory) detail the events of these two periods of strife.[14] It is difficult to see in these reports much evidence of the Qur'an's spirit of forgiveness and tolerance among Believers that was discussed in the third section above; some of the events of these civil wars were brutal.[15] There are, however, some indicators that this intra-communal violence greatly troubled many people; for example, some prominent Believers withdrew from public life, went into seclusion, and steadfastly refused to get involved on the part of any of the combatants, suggesting that they felt intense distaste for such activities. The later chronicles, moreover, referred to these events using the Qur'anic word *fitna*, a pejorative with overtones of temptation and seduction – implying that the strife itself, the two *fitnas*, were episodes when Believers succumbed to the temptation to pursue worldly interests, or were seduced by the lust for power.[16]

The question of *jihad*, or "striving in God's way," is perhaps an appropriate one on which to close our reflections.[17] As noted above, the early Islamic – or Believers' – state seems to have been motivated partly by this concept, which (unlike a number of other things we find in the chronicle descriptions of early Islam) has strong roots in the Qur'an itself. The Qur'an often enjoins the Believers to "strive (*jahidu*) in God's way with one's wealth and oneself," that is, to expend both money and personal effort to advance God's cause.[18] There are Qur'anic passages that seem to equate *jihad* with fighting under certain circumstances (often, as we have noted above, in defense of the community of Believers when it is attacked by others). Many passages use the word fighting itself – *qital*. But other Qur'anic verses make it clear that *jihad* means a wide range of activities, from inner struggle against unbelief to quiet proselytization to active physical fighting. The striking thing is that the Qur'anic injunctions to *jihad* are all directed (as is the Qur'an itself) to the individual Believer. The later Islamic state, however, appropriated this injunction and applied it to the state, using it as the basis for legitimizing, in the name of the faith, state-sponsored *jihad* as an institution for realizing the state's goal of military expansion – and the securing of booty, tax revenues, and lands.

As in so many other cases, the Qur'an, in its use of the term *jihad*, tempers its apparently hard-edge attitudes, for there is at least one verse that links *jihad* to *ihsan*, kindliness or charity: "Those who have striven for us (*jahadu fina*) we shall guide in our paths; surely God is with the charitable."[19] This passage, it seems to me, provides a perfect epigram that captures the essence of the Qur'an's – and, I think, the early community of Believers' – complex, and perhaps ambivalent, attitude toward questions of peace, war, and reconciliation. "Fight for God – but do so with kindness." This encapsulates the tension between two counterpoised ideals – militant monotheist piety, and forgiving human kindness – that makes it difficult to reach a simplistic judgment on what the attitude of the earliest community of Believers may have been – or, therefore, on what the "essential" Islamic position on peace and war is. But this same tension has also created for Muslims in all periods a space for fruitful and creative reinterpretation of these issues, as they strive to decide what Islam means for them in their day and under their particular historical circumstances.

Notes

* In romanizing Arabic words, I have eschewed most diacritics, which Arabists generally do not need and non-Arabists cannot use. I quote the Qur'an by specific *suras* (chapters), given by name and number followed by verse number (e.g. Surat al-Baqara (2): 1); translations are usually my own. All dates are CE.

1 For my justification of this claim, see Donner 1998: ch. 1.

2 The "hypocrites" (*munafiqun*) are not viewed by the Qur'an as occupying a moral middle ground between belief and unbelief; rather, they are portrayed as people who merely disguise themselves as Believers, but are fundamentally unbelievers – and, as unbelievers, they receive the Qur'an's unstinting condemnation.

3 On *zakat* as a payment due in expiation of sins committed while one was yet in a state of unbelief, see Bashear 1993.

4 Muhammad Qasim Zaman observed, in responding to this paper, that this form of "escape clause" discourse is also reflected in the later Muslim juristic literature, presumably reflecting the impact of the Qur'an's style.

5 Surat Al 'Imran (3): 132–33. "...*al-ladhina yunfiquna fi l-sarra'i wa l-darra'i wa l-kazimin al-ghayz wa l-'affin 'an al-nas wa llahu yuhibbu al-muhsinin*."

6 Surat al-Shura (42): 40. "...*wa jaza'u sayyi'atin sayyi'atun mithluha fa-man 'afa wa aslaha fa-ujru-hu 'ala llahi innahu la yuhibbu al-zalimin*..."

7 Surat al-Ma'ida (5), v. 3. "...*wa ta'awunu 'ala l-birri wa l-taqwa wa la ta'awanu 'ala l-ithmi wa-l-'udwani*..."

8 Surat al-Nisa' (4): 128 [estrangement]; Surat Al 'Imran (3): 158 [enemies]; Surat al-Baqara (2): 237 [dowry].

9 For a brief introduction to the traditional view, see *Encyclopaedia of Islam*, 2nd ed. (Leiden: E. J. Brill, 1960-), "Dhimma" (Claude Cahen), "Ahl al-kitab" (G. Vajda). A fuller treatment is Fattal 1958.

10 Surat al-Ma'ida (5), 65–66. See also verse 58, which also makes clear to the *ahl al-kitab* the importance of observing the Torah and Gospel.

11 On the chronicle literature, see Khalidi 1994; Noth and Conrad 1994; Donner 1998; Robinson 2003. An extensive collection of reports is found in the voluminous *History* of Muhammad ibn Jarir al-Tabari (d. 923); see Yarshater 1985–99.

12 For an overview, see Donner 2005: 28–51. More detailed studies are Donner 1981 (on Arabia, Syria, Iraq); Butler 1902; Gibb 1923; Zarrinkub 1975; Taha 1989. For some chronicle reports, see *History of al-Tabari* (Yarshater 1985–99), vols. 11–14, or Hitti 1916, a translation of part of the *Kitab futuh al-buldan* ("Conquest of the lands") by Ahmad ibn Jabir al-Baladhuri (d. 892).

13 See Brock 1987; Bar Penkaye's text was published, with a partial French translation, in Mingana 1908; further commentary on the relevant passages is found in Hoyland 1997: 194–200.

14 An overview of the civil wars can be found in Hawting 1987 or Kennedy 1986; for chronicle reports, see *The History of al-Tabari* (Yarshater 1985–99), vols. 15–17 and 19–21.

15 For example, the battle of Karbala' (October, 680) or the battle of the Harra (summer, 683). On the former, which became the focus of Shi'ite martyrology, see the sympathetic overview in Jafri 1979: 174–221; on the latter, see Kister 1977.

16 See *Encyclopaedia of Islam*, "Fitna" (L. Gardet). For a fuller discussion, see As-Sirri 1990.

17 The literature on *jihad* is vast. A recent survey of this broad subject is Cook 2005. For *jihad* in the Qur'an, see Firestone 1999.

18 See also the nice phrase in Surat al-Taghabun (64): 16, which enjoins Believers to observe their duty to God – "hear, obey, and spend!"

19 Surat al-'Ankabut (29): 69. *"…wa al-ladhina jahadu fina la-nahdiyanna-hum subulan wa-inna llaha la-ma'a l-muhsinin…"*

References

As-Sirri, Ahmed. 1990. *Religiös-politische Argumentation im frühen Islam (610–85). Der Begriff Fitna: Bedeutung und Funktion.* Frankfurt a.M.

Bashear, Suliman. 1993. "On the Origins and Development of the Meaning of zakat in Early Islam." *Arabica* 40: 84–113.

Brock, Sebastian. 1987. "North Mesopotamia in the Late Seventh Century: Book XV of John Bar Penkaye's Rîs Melle." *Jerusalem Studies in Arabic and Islam* 9: 51–75.

Butler, Alfred J. 1902. *The Arab Conquest of Egypt and the Last Thirty Years of the Roman Dominion.* Oxford.

Cook, David. 2005. *Understanding Jihad.* Berkeley.

Cook, Michael. 2000. *Commanding Right and Forbidding Wrong in Islamic Thought.* Cambridge.

Donner, Fred M. 1981. *The Early Islamic Conquests.* Princeton.

——. 1986. "The Origins of the Islamic State." *JAOS* 106: 283–96.

——. 1995. "Centralized Authority and Military Autonomy in the Early Islamic Conquests." In Averil Cameron (ed.), *The Byzantine and Early Islamic Near East,* III: *States, Resources, and Armies,* 337–60. Princeton.

——. 1998. *Narratives of Islamic Origins.* Princeton.

——. 2002–3. "From Believers to Muslims: Confessional Self-Identity in the Early Islamic Community." *Al-Abhath* 50–51: 9–53.

——. 2005. "The Islamic Conquests." In Youssef Choueiri (ed.), *A Companion to the History of the Middle East,* 28–51. Malden and Oxford.

Fattal, Antoine. 1958. *Le statut légal des non-musulmans en pays d'Islam.* Beirut.

Firestone, Reuven. 1999. *Jihad: the Origin of Holy War in Islam.* New York.

Gibb, Hamilton A. R. 1923. *The Arab Conquests in Central Asia.* London.

Hawting, G. R. 1987. *The First Dynasty of Islam: The Umayyad Caliphate, 661–750.* Carbondale.

Hitti, Philip K. 1916. *The Origins of the Islamic State.* New York.

Hoyland, Robert. 1997. *Seeing Islam as Others Saw It.* Princeton.

Jafri, S. H. M. 1979. *The Origin and Early Development of Shi'a Islam.* London.

Kennedy, Hugh. 1986. *The Prophet and the Age of the Caliphates.* London.

Khalidi, Tarif. 1994. *Arabic Historical Thought in the Classical Period.* Cambridge.

Kister, M. J. 1977. "The Battle of the Harra: Some Socio-Economic Aspects." In Myriam Rosen-Ayalon (ed.), *Studies in Memory of Gaston Wiet,* 33–49. Jerusalem.

Mingana, Alfons (ed.). 1908. *Sources Syriaques,* I. Leipzig.

Noth, Albrecht, and Lawrence I. Conrad. 1994. *The Early Arabic Historical Tradition: A Source-Critical Study.* Princeton.

Robinson, Chase F. 2003. *Islamic Historiography.* Cambridge.

Taha, 'Abdulwahid Dhanun. 1989. *The Muslim Conquest and Settlement of North Africa and Spain.* London.

Yarshater, Ehsan (ed.). 1985–99. *The History of al-Tabari.* 39 vols. Albany.

Zarrinkub, 'Abd al-Husain. 1975. "The Arab Conquest of Iran and Its Aftermath." In *The Cambridge History of Iran,* IV: 1–56. Cambridge.

18

Peace, Reconciliation, and Alliance in Aztec Mexico

Ross Hassig

Peace and reconciliation played little role in an Aztec society where war dominated. Aztec society as we know it, is as it was when the Spaniards reached it, a young, energetic empire, without the cultural elaboration that would doubtless have come in its maturity. But the Aztecs were not always as the Spaniards recorded them: they began their march to power only in 1428 and thus, when Hernan Cortés reached Mexico, they had been an empire for just over 90 years and were still expanding.[1]

The Image of the Aztecs

The popular image of the Aztecs is of a warlike society engaging in human sacrifice on a massive scale. And this is true, at least in part (Durán 1967: 2.345). The Aztecs' lack of emphasis on peace, however, does not mean that they lived in a state of Hobbesian warfare of all against all. They did have allies, and it is the nature of these non-war relations that is of interest here.

Peace was desirable and attainable personally, at the individual level, but politically, peace did not mean amiable coexistence, but subordination. In essence, for the Aztecs, everyone was either a subordinate or a target. Peace was achieved by hierarchy, the placement of all groups in a loosely ordered relationship to all other groups, and even in this, the Aztecs sought cooption, not mutual cooperation.

Peace and Society

Is peace merely the opposite of war? If so, there were many peaceful periods in Aztec history, but it is difficult to distinguish these intervals of non-war from respite between wars, and there is little evidence to suggest that peace was a goal in itself. If, however, peace is viewed as a philosophical, religious, or political ideology, it was lacking in Aztec society and its absence begs explanation. But rather than seeing peace as a natural state and its absence as demanding explanation, it is perhaps more useful to assess peace in relation to social systems, since some appear to foster peace and others do not. In short, rather than simply existing in peace, societies encourage it or not, and even then, it is not societies as wholes, but groups or institutions in societies that can translate their goals to the societal whole.

As far as can be determined from the extant documentation, the Aztecs lacked a peace god, lacked rites for peace, and lacked any ritual cleansing for the readmission of soldiers into peaceful society.[2] Conquest was a primary political goal, and war, as its necessary handmaiden, was suitably exalted. Death in war was the most honored status one could attain, and warriors slain in battle went to the heaven of the sun from which they returned as precious birds and butterflies after four years (Sahagún 1950–82: 3.49).

The question for the Aztecs was not how to coexist peacefully with other polities, but how to bring all other polities into a hierarchical relationship with themselves on top. There could be peace only with the subordinated, the dead, or with those too distant or yet too powerful to be conquered. This did not prevent the Aztecs from entering into alliances. They did, but these all proved to be temporary.[3] Throughout most of Mesoamerica there were courteously observed manners and conventions regarding wars and foreign relations, such as inquiring about one's intentions before engaging in war, or observing the immunity of foreign ambassadors (Clavigero 1787: 1.355). Long-term peaceful relations, however, seem not to have been a goal.

If there are to be peace movements within a society, regardless of whether peace is a major social goal, the groups or institutions fostering peace must have interests that are better served by non-war than war, whether these groups are religiously or intellectually committed to it or simply see it as more beneficial to other economic, social, or political activities. But where are such groups or interests in ancient Mexico? To inquire effectively, the differences between city-states and empires in Mesoamerica must first be explored.

City-states

Encompassing the areas of high civilization extending from Central Mexico to northern Honduras, Mesoamerican societies during Aztec times were overwhelmingly either city-states or empires. And the nature or warfare, peace, and alliance differed between them.

While city-states are often viewed as the fundamental building blocks of empires, the latter are not simply the former writ large or in aggregate but qualitatively different. Briefly, there were a series of differences between city-states and empires in Mesoamerica. City-states in Mesoamerica were, of course, significantly smaller than empires, each controlling a hinterland within a radius of approximately eight miles

(Hassig 1997). This radius was defined by the diurnal cycle within which the center can exercise effective political and economic control[4] over the 40 percent of the population that was rural (Cook and Borah 1971: 9–10), which rose to over 50 percent in the densely populated Valley of Mexico (Sanders 1976: 150). Thus dominating relatively discrete hinterlands, city-states engaged in a variety of economic and social interactions among themselves. While city-states occupied independent territories, battles were common between them but they did not aim at conquest.[5] They were fought to legitimate the ruler's position, to maintain the boundaries of the city's hinterland against encroachment by neighboring cities, and to insure domination of its tributary towns. Both of these ends, ruler legitimacy and boundary maintenance, could be achieved by raids rather than outright wars. The goal in the case of ruler legitimacy was for the king to achieve enough success to boast of his feats and thus elevate himself. And for boundary maintenance, raids were sufficient to uphold the appearance of strength and thus insure that towns did not shift their loyalties to the seemingly stronger rulers of neighboring cities. Failure to maintain boundaries could mean the weakening and demise of the city-state as an independent kingdom. So while city-states did not generally engage in wars of conquest, there were persistent, albeit intermittent, wars and a certain tension between neighbors. Trade and other forms of social interaction, such as religious rituals, created some regional coherence, but integration at the political level was rare.

As a consequence of their own rather limited military goals, with only rare exceptions, Mesoamerican city-states differed from empires in a series of ways. First, they were generally ethnically homogeneous, if not among the entire population, then certainly among the nobility.[6] Second, they trained and relied on nobles for soldiers, relegating commoners to the role of cannon-fodder, much like the peasant supporters of medieval European knights (Hassig 1992: 101–02). Third, they frequently engaged in the torture and humiliation of captives since their goals were to demonstrate their dominance over enemies and thereby elevate themselves. Consequently, captives in city-states are often depicted as humiliated – nude, bound, and trodden underfoot (e.g. Baudez and Mathews 1978: 32; Flannery et al. 1981: 75–77, 80, 87, 90–92). All these practices are tied directly to city-states engaging in wars to maintain boundaries, secure tributaries, and glorify and legitimate their rulers, but not to conquer and expand.

Empires

Mesoamerican empires differ markedly from city-states. The most obvious characteristic is their control over significantly larger areas than city-states. Empires were themselves controlled from capital cities, so the question is both how and why empires emerged from those cities and not from others.

"Why?" is perhaps not answerable in any general sense, as the instigating cause may be historically particular and rest on a specific constellation of persons and circumstances that cannot be generalized from example to example.[7] But "how?" is more general and its mechanics can, I believe, be explained.

The enormous costs of distance limited the ability of city-states to conquer and exploit their neighbors, but Mexican empires were not as constrained by this limitation as all of them arose in especially favorable and densely populated regions. In the case of the Aztecs, the adjacent cities did not lie outside the sixteen miles distance that would make their control by another center enormously difficult and thus insulated them from conquest. In and around the densely populated Valley of Mexico, they were far closer to each other. As a result, the city-states that became empires already possessed at least the nucleus of the political and military machinery needed to control nearby cities. Being far closer, distance offered them little protection from conquest and control. And this proximity could operate not merely between adjacent cities within the valley, but throughout its expanse, as its vast lakes permitted quick and inexpensive control via canoes that would have been virtually impossible over similar distances by land (Hassig 1985: 28–40, 56–66, 133).

While empires contrast with city-states in many ways, there are a series of differences that can be meaningfully discussed in relation to the characteristics noted above. First, drawing on far larger populations and intermarrying with the rulers of the conquered towns, they are ethnically heterogenous, even at the elite level. Second, empires rely on far larger armies than do city-states and, consequently, tend to rely on both nobles and commoners, training the latter to have nearly to the skill of the former (Hassig 1988: 59–72). Third, they do not generally conquer to humiliate or degrade the enemy, who are accordingly not depicted that way.[8] Empires do sometimes sacrifice captives, but these are not shown nude or degraded and the goal is a political one, to demonstrate power to the tributary rulers, not to denigrate their people. The reason for this contrast lies in the goal of the empire, which is expansionistic, to incorporate the conquered at least economically as tributaries. Once such a system was successfully begun, the influx of tributary wealth allowed the capital city-state to expand its internal political system to a size adequate to the increased areas it now controlled.

Political Integration in the Aztec Empire

The Aztec empire nevertheless remained a center-out empire, with all political control flowing out from the capital and all tributary wealth flowing in. It was able to retain the essentially engorged structures of a city-state by exercising power hegemonically rather than dominating territorially (Hassig 1985: 90–103).

The Aztecs conquered independent city-states to exact tribute,[9] which they did without eliminating or replacing local leaders or imposing their own social, economic, religious, and political practices. Rather, they left the local leadership and social customs in place, thereby virtually eliminating the need to garrison troops locally, impose political cadre, indoctrinate the populace, or impose any of a number of costly control mechanisms frequently needed to control conquered peoples (Hassig 1985: 99–100). Instead, they extracted moderate amounts of tribute which the local leadership paid, and they did so not by force, but by power – by raising and maintaining the perception that they could and would impose their will if thwarted. The Aztecs did not destroy their enemies so much as yoke them into a single economic entity, and they did so in a way that made their empire essentially self-perpetuating.

Without cultural indoctrination or the ready availability of force to compel compliance, the risks of revolt might seem to be constant. The system would appear to be dangerously unstable. Yet this empire generally produced peace, albeit of a subservient sort. Revolts were infrequent (Hassig 1988); indeed, they were extremely rare in relation to the apparent ease with which they might have occurred. In the absence of enculturation, which is generally a multi-generational phenomenon, some other form of "re-education," or the direct application of force, preferably in conjunction with the removal of the tributaries' ability to mount armed resistance – why did this imperial system produce as much internal peace as it did?

Other Mechanisms of Integration

Cultural imperialism was not much in evidence in Mesoamerica. Societies did not tell others how to live or what to believe, though the politically or culturally dominant did influence others informally. The Aztecs conformed to this hands-off pattern, yet they did practice two integration strategies, one a direct imposition and the other a widespread practice they turned to their own advantage.

The first, and the one cultural change they imposed, was calendrical. Having a polytheistic religion, the Aztecs did not possess exclusive religious truth and therefore did not conquer to impose their beliefs. Instead, they left intact the religious beliefs, practices, or godly pantheons of others. But they did alter their calendars.[10]

Very briefly, with few exceptions, the same calendrical structure was common throughout Mesoamerica, though how it was employed differed between the Maya and Mexican areas (Caso 1971). In Mexico, everyone shared the same 365-day solar calendar of eighteen 20-day months plus five "waste" days, coupled with a 260-day sacred calendar fundamentally composed of twenty 13-day cycles. These two cycles ran simultaneously to yield a still larger cycle of 52-years, the "Calendar Round," after which the entire cycle began anew.

The names of the days, months, and years might differ among the various societies, but the structure was shared. However, there was no uniformity among the calendars in starting dates because the calendar had no internal leap-year correction. Since people operate on days, but solar years determining the seasons are 365.2422 days long, some calendrical adjustment is necessary to bring the year and the days into agreement. As a result, while the calendar *system* was shared throughout Mexico, the specific correlation of dates to actual days was not, as each city could make its own leap-year correction. When and how leap-year corrections are inserted into the solar calendar is merely a matter of convention – ours was dictated by Pope Gregory in 1582 and remains in force (Moyer 1982) – and essentially of a political decision.

When its subordinates held festivals for specific gods was of no concern to the Aztecs, but when they made their tribute payments was. The Aztecs wanted to coordinate these payments, forcing everyone to bring in their obligations and pledge fealty at the same time – presumably to make the pageantry more impressive politically – and they fixed those times at the beginning of four of their months, at approximately quarterly intervals.[11] But effecting this in the face of an array of even slightly variant calendars would require individual notification, a costly and probably ineffective means. The only feasible system was the imposition of some means of self-coordination. Thus, when the Aztecs expanded, the only major cultural change they imposed was their calendar, not for supernatural reasons, but to create an empire that was chronologically linked, that could, by its own efforts, respond to temporally precise tribute demands.[12] So while the Aztec empire was not a unified religious, social, political, or economic entity, it established synchronous unity with considerable coordination.

The second change imposed by the Aztecs did not demand a cultural shift, but took advantage of an already widespread practice. Following conquest, the Aztecs inserted themselves into the existing patterns of noble intermarriage. That noble intermarriage was a key element to the creation of peace in Mexico, while it failed abysmally in Europe, was a result of other, broader social patterns common among the Aztecs.

Marriage and Nobility

Polygyny (having multiple wives) was widespread among the nobles of Mesoamerica (Carrasco 1984); rulers in particular were polygynous, and part of the purpose was to produce multiple offspring. The focus of royal marriages tends to be on the production of sons as future rulers, but perhaps more important in Aztec society was the production of daughters to marry to allied kings and cement political ties. Royal family intermarriage was common among both city-states and empires, but in empires the practice was often greatly expanded. Among the Aztecs, this pattern began with the empire and it was tied to another change that occurred at that time, concerning the succession of their kings to the throne.

Polygyny and Power

When the Aztecs were tributaries to other cities early in their history, their kings named one of their sons to succeed to the throne in a patrilineal though not primogenitor pattern.[13] When they became an empire, however, this system was replaced by one in which kings did not choose their successors; rather, after the death of the reigning king the successor was chosen by the upper nobles from among the proven warriors of their class.[14] In addition to being a proven warrior and upper noble, an often overlooked consideration was the need to have women of marriageable or near-marriageable age to cement political alliances, which typically meant already having daughters, and that, in turn, meant being older. Thus, with empire, the age of Aztec rulers at succession jumped nearly a generation from the pre-imperial practice.

Empires also had more allies or tributaries than city-states, and each of these political relationships was best tied by marriage between the respective ruling families. Thus empire increased the demand for kings' daughters which, in turn, expanded normal royal polygyny to a vastly increased scale, hyperpolygyny. Expanding the number of the wives of kings would not greatly alter the structure of Aztec society, since they had a large population and very few kings. But hyperpolygyny was not restricted just to the king and his direct line. Every upper noble who aspired to be king – and that pool had greatly increased – now had to have many wives before election, which meant that polygyny on a greatly expanded scale spread among the upper nobles. In short, empire caused the influx of new wealth which fueled the growth of Aztec nobility in both numbers and importance; as a result of the shift in the succession system that accompanied empire, the number of potential aspirants for the throne multiplied; and the need for royal daughters to tie the growing number of tributary towns to Tenochtitlan meant that not only the king but also all those aspiring to the throne had to have more wives. So, once expansion cemented the new political/social system in place, it, in turn, encouraged additional imperial warfare.

Commoners and Empire

Increasing and expanding wealth and power might explain noble support for imperial expansion. But why would the commoners support it?

The martial needs of city-states in Mexico were generally met by their nobility who were educated and militarily trained in special noble schools (*calmecac*). Empires, however, had vastly greater military needs on many fronts and required far larger armies to maintain and expand their areas of domination. And even though Tenochtitlan was the largest city, with at least 200,000 residents in 1519 (Calnek 1973), the demands of an expanding empire were greater than the resources that could be drawn from its nobility alone. This demand was met by involving commoners as well as nobles. In general, the high logistical costs of expansion without means of transport other than the human back effectively limited, if not outright prohibited, the employment of untrained commoners. "Cannon-fodder" is cheap in the eyes of the military elite around the world, but only if its use is also cheap. And in Mexico, without wheeled vehicles or draft animals, it was not. The Aztecs overcame this limitation by introducing commoner schools (*telpochcalli*) which, though scaled back from noble schools, nevertheless provided years of military training to commoners who could now approach noble levels of expertise.

Providing commoners with advanced military training requires, however, that the society is not so repressive that revolt is the likely result. So how and why did the Aztecs successfully incorporate trained commoners *en masse* into the military?

Social mobility is relatively uncommon in archaic states. As a rule of thumb, in such societies a maximum of 5–10 percent of the population can be sustained as elites,[15] as they depend upon the commoners for their support, and the commoners, in turn, can support only so many nobles. So any upward mobility by commoners tends to increase pressure on existing elites and the possibility of their social decline. Consequently, nobles usually maintain class lines vigorously. Commoner merchants might become prosperous, and commoner priests might gain status, but neither become nobles or benefit directly from the public purse as does the nobility. But in Aztec society, with its need for a large, trained military, commoners who excelled in warfare did enjoy such benefits, and they began doing so following the introduction of commoner schools during the reign of King Moteuczoma Ilhuicamina (1440–68; Durán 1967: 2.211–14). Those who excelled could be elevated to the status of hereditary lower nobles (*cuauhpilli*). So the Aztec class system was not as rigid as it was in many other archaic states, and it offered the possibility of upward social mobility, which doubtlessly played a role in quelling any unrest and the danger it could provoke among trained commoners.

How often such a warrior-commoner was elevated is uncertain. Initially, it must have been too frequent in the eyes of the nobility, as tighter requirements were implemented during the reign of King Tizoc (1481–6; Torquemada 1975–83: 1.252) and then again under King Moteuczoma Xocoyotl (1502–20; Durán 1967: 2.403–4). Indeed, actual examples of upward mobility by meritorious warrior-commoners may have been, or have become, rare, but the possibility alone would have functioned like the pervasive American myth of being able to become President even if you were born in a log cabin. But while commoner men only rarely became nobles through their own exertions, the same was not true of women.

Nobles in Mexico practiced polygyny while commoners were restricted to monogamy by economic realities if not by law. Yet the biological reality of roughly equal male-to-female births meant that Aztec elites necessarily married commoner women as well as noble, and more of the former than the latter. Such marriages did not transform these wives into nobles, but it had this effect on their offspring.

Marriage of commoner women by noble men provided for upward mobility for some commoners, but it had another, no doubt unintended, impact. Since only a small percentage of elites can be sustained by the commoners, any movement upward of new members put greater pressure on those already there. The system could not simply absorb more and more commoners. If some were moving up, then others had to move down. In the case of Tenochtitlan, this affected those nobles who were four degrees of kinship away from the king. That is, if nobles failed to become or to marry higher nobles more closely linked to the king, they were marginalized and dropped out of the nobility and back into the ranks of commoners. So Aztec hyperpolygyny not only fueled upward mobility for commoners, it demanded downward mobility for peripheral nobles who, most likely, continued to claim noble status long after their economic circumstances had ceased to justify it.

Support for the Empire

While it is unquestionable that the nobles benefited from the wealth that flowed in from imperial expansion, in fact, virtually everyone in Aztec society profited. Priests were supported through their temples, which received state support in the form of lands taken as tribute. Merchants benefited by the incorporation of lands that were thereby rendered safer for them, and their transport was speeded by the imposition of tributary obligations to supply human porters (*tlamemes*) and maintain the roads through regions producing exotic materials that flowed into Tenochtitlan to supply the craftsmen there. And commoners benefited as well, by booty from war, by possible social promotions, and by increased wealth flowing to the wards (*calpolli*) into which they were organized. Even the households of those killed in battle were given additional financial support. So virtually everyone benefited, both materially and socially.

War, then, would seem to have had many supporters and few detractors among the Aztecs. But what happened to those they conquered? Empires are always substantially supported by the wealth they extract from those they vanquish. It is axiomatic that tributaries lose some of their wealth, but the losses accrue primarily to the commoner producers and not to their king.

Inevitable Conquest

The Aztecs are touted as an empire with all the conquests that suggests, but many more of their tributaries submitted "voluntarily" than actually fell by force of arms. The Aztecs frequently bypassed towns to reach other targets, and the mere passage of their victorious armies returning home was often sufficient to induce local rulers to submit to the empire, especially since the Aztec armies were usually larger than the towns through which they passed.

As for towns actually vanquished, they could surrender at any point. Sometimes towns would be asked to provide a seemingly innocent commodity or service to the Aztecs, as they did when they asked Chalco for stone to expand the main temple in Tenochtitlan (Durán 1967: 2.135–38; *Crónica mexicana* 1975: 287–89). All such solicitations were *de facto* requests for subservience, and their rejection offered sufficient and justifiable grounds for declaring war. Other times, targeted towns would be visited by Aztec ambassadors requesting submission, the rejection of which was likewise adequate cause for war. Wars that were carried to their ultimate climax were publicly announced in Tenochtitlan, the levies were communicated to the commoner wards, and the needed men were raised, equipped, and retrained for five to eight days before departing. The armies would then march toward the target, often along parallel routes to speed their journey, until they reached the town, where they would build their camp. Once fully assembled, the attack would be signaled at dawn to maximize the daylight hours. The two sides would meet and fight until either the Aztecs were repulsed, in which case they would withdraw and return at a later time, or they prevailed, typically by breaking through the opposing lines or by turning the enemies' flanks and encircling them. If the army withdrew to the city, or if the enemy leaders refused to submit after the defeat of their army, the Aztecs would enter the city and sack it (see Hassig 1988: 85–183 for fuller discussion).

At any point, however, the war could be stopped: after the enemy learned of the impending attack, after the army was raised, once it was on the march, when it reached the target, during the battle, after defeat, or after the sack of the city; and the earlier the submission, the lighter their tributary obligations. So while Aztec conquests did demonstrate their military power, they were not necessarily undertaken expressly for that purpose. Rather, they offered the targeted opponent a range of options; not independence, of course, but a wide gradient of conditions under which they would be subordinated.

While virtually all segments of Aztec society profited from the tributary empire, who benefited by combat and how differed by class. The tribute that flowed into the empire in regular payments went directly to the king and to those to whom he had given tributary lands, such as various lords and temples. The bulk of it, however, remained with the king who decided to whom it should be allocated or in what amounts, including additional meritorious nobles and the commoner wards. As they disproportionately benefited from war, it would seem obvious that the upper nobles would push for it, while the commoners would resist it. But such does not appear to have been the case.

From the perspective of the empire, any form of voluntary submission was preferable to conquest as it was less costly in men and material, and it was much better than sacking a city, as that crippled its ability to pay tribute. But from the perspective of the commoners, who made up the bulk of the army, only combat offered the prospect of rewards for feats of arms, including the possibility of rising into the noble ranks, and only by sacking a city were most of the commoners able to secure some immediate gain, including capturing townspeople, which was significantly easier than taking warriors on the battlefield. To be sure, nobles could participate in the sacking, but being a minority of the military, their shares would likewise be proportionately smaller and would ultimately mean a reduced share in later, diminished, tribute. Moreover, while feats of arms would burnish their reputations and aid in securing political offices, the incentive of upward mobility was significantly smaller for them than for the commoners. As a result, the higher nobles who already had their status, had a far greater interest in the submission of cities before conquest while the commoners had a greater incentive to carry combat through to the bitter end, and so too did the lowest nobles who were in imminent danger of dropping into the commoner class.

Assimilation and Disruption

What, though, was the fate of the conquered? They all paid tribute, though in different amounts according to the extent of their resistance and the products of the region. And while any tribute paid diminished the wealth of that region, the burden as always fell on the commoners. They paid their assessed quotas to their ward heads from which it flowed to the king in the traditional manner, except that the local king was now no longer the top of the tribute system. The king in turn paid a portion of what he received to the Aztec empire.

Of course, the reliability of new tributaries remained in doubt, as they were near their traditional allies who might offer assistance. In most cases, the relatively weak former allies did not present a problem to the Aztecs, but occasionally cities were conquered that had formidable allies, such as Tepeyacac (Tepeaca, Puebla), which had been allied to Tlaxcallan. To ensure that there would be no relapse, Tepeyacac was uniquely required to give as part of its tribute a captive to be sacrificed in Tenochtitlan. As this captive could not come from the other Aztec tributaries around it, the demand effectively forced Tepeyacac to engage in continuous war with its former allies, creating a constant friction between them and minimizing the likelihood that they would break away from the Aztec dominions (*Matricula de Tributos* 1980: 11v; see also Hassig 1988: 350).

Compliance with the Aztecs' tribute demands did not guarantee peace in the system, though, and revolts were not uncommon. The simple exercise of power to compel compliance is not sustainable in the long term. There is little reason to assume that tributaries grew comfortable with the status quo. But the Aztec system achieved peaceful coherence more subtly than simply by economic extraction backed up by the fear of force.

For instance, merely complying with the tribute demands altered the local social system by reducing the noble class in the tributary cities. Because of the limits on how much the commoners could produce and how much of that could be extracted in tribute, the loss of some tribute siphoned off by the empire resulted in the swelling of the Aztec noble classes and the shrinkage of tributary nobles in the provinces. While the data are slim, the "four-degree principle" that seems to have prevailed among the Aztecs was probably sustained by the influx of tribute, without which three degrees of kinship perhaps represented a more typical limit. And if such had been the case in the provinces, their economic loss may have reduced the local nobility closer to two degrees of kinship before the social drop, generating considerable disaffection in lesser nobles though perhaps greater loyalty and coherence among the uppers.

Another change arising from being conquered was the receipt of another wife for the tributary king, a practice that was often reciprocal, with the subordinated king giving one of his daughters to the Aztec ruler. While this might appear to be a symbolic gesture cementing the new relationship, its consequences went much further. The impact of an additional wife from a tributary ruler was minor for the Aztec king's domestic order. But it had enormous consequences for the tributary ruler.

Succession and Alliance

Aztec imperial practice aside, the widespread pattern in central Mexico was for rulers to be succeeded by sons. Since kings were polygynous, they often had many sons. The one chosen, however, was not necessarily the bravest or smartest, as desirable as those attributes were in a king, but the son by the king's politically most important wife. And who that was depended on the hierarchy of political alliances: typically, it would be the king's son by the wife from the most powerful kingdom with which he was allied (Carrasco 1984).

Succession, however, is much like a bequest: there are no heirs until the benefactor dies; until then, there are only heirs apparent and heirs expectant. As for royal succession, the fortunes of kingdoms rose and fell, so that the wife who was the politically most important at marriage might not be at the death of the king, with corresponding consequences for her son. Consequently, there was often a coterie of brothers who might become king.

Once a city had been conquered by the Aztecs, however, this changed. The Aztec wife was not only the most politically important at marriage, the disproportionate power and stability of the Aztec empire virtually guaranteed that her son would succeed to the throne. The impact of this was felt both within the kingdom and without.

Since the Aztecs did not conquer entire allied regions at once, local alliances were not retained intact. Regional alliances were overlapping as they were virtually continuous, with each city the center of its own series of alliances that only partially overlapped with those of any other city. Indeed, only imperial conquest created alliance boundaries, however fluid. And new imperial boundaries severed some of the political ties that the newly subjugated city-state had created through marriage, with the result that the royal wives whose natal homes were within the empire were politically strengthened, whereas those from outside were weakened. But whether their fortunes waxed or waned, all royal wives were eclipsed by the ruler's new Aztec wife, the importance of their home cities diminished as the tie to Tenochtitlan became pivotal, and the prospects of their sons to succeed to the throne dimmed.

But it was not just the sons who lost in this system. The king of the new ally was also threatened because he had already demonstrated weakness in submitting. He was also now cut off from political support from his maternal and spousal kin. Thus, he was threatened in fact or in perception by his sons and by his erstwhile allies. His only options were to rebel against the Aztecs to reassert the traditional order. His recent defeat had already demonstrated that this course was likely to be futile, and attempting it risked incurring far more onerous penalties, including his potential ousting. His other alternative was to cleave strongly to the Aztecs to secure their support from these internal and external threats. The latter was the common result of conquest.

Of course, the severing of traditional alliances and the implantation of a new pivotal alliance had a similarly great impact beyond the empire. Cities that had previously been allied to now-conquered cities yet remained independent themselves, also lost support they had previously enjoyed, as their traditional allies were reoriented toward Tenochtitlan. Their internal succession system was disrupted, new allies had to be sought, and reigning kings looked after their own security. Subjugation thus roiled alliances within and without imperial boundaries, weakening kings on both sides, and rendering further conquests easier.

The internal consequence of tributary conquest, however, was not simply that the king was threatened, weakened, and became a more reliable Aztec ally. It was that, within one generation, a maternal Aztec would be on the throne of the tributary province and he would, in turn, have at least one Aztec wife to further cement the kin ties that bound his kingdom to Tenochtitlan.

Moreover, within that generation, the towns surrounding that tributary would most likely be conquered as well, setting the stage for the establishment of new political ties via marital alliances with their traditional allies who were now Aztec tributaries as well. Their rulers would similarly be seeking political support through Aztec marital alliances and with those of other Aztec tributaries in the region, so that an entirely new regionally stable system of pro-Aztec alliances would emerge.

Hence the peace that Tenochtitlan did not seek in its public and political practices was in fact a consequence of how they dealt with the subordinated cities and provinces. The empire grew by immediate conquest, but it was the creation of elite marital ties and the subsequent ascent of Aztec offspring to the thrones of subject cities that created an extensive area of relative peace.

Proving the Case

It is easy to assert any number of "true" causes of any phenomenon when there is only one example to be explained, which is the case with the Aztec empire. So is there any contrary example that might shed some light on the validity of this explanation? I believe so (or I would not have raised the issue in the first place): the conquest of the Chalca city-states.

Chalca and its allied cities occupied the southeastern corner of the Valley of Mexico and were the Aztecs' most implacable foes until they were conquered in 1464–5.[16] Then, instead of permitting the reigning kings to remain and govern, as was typical, the Aztecs removed them and imposed governors (*cuauhtlatoque;* Chimalpahin 1965: 39–48).

Whatever the reason for imposing these governors in the first place – perhaps the need to act decisively against powerful cities that near to Tenochtitlan, or their vigorous and sustained resistance to Aztec domination – the removal of the local kings probably represents an attempt to supplant the ruling lineages of the Chalca cities. Yet the effort failed. The "governors" were removed again and the local nobility allowed to regain their thrones over a period of eight years, from 1486 through 1493 (ibid. 39–48, 110). Permitting the restoration of the local rulers did not create grateful and loyal tributaries, however, a fact of which Cortés took full advantage during his conquest of Mexico.[17] And this begs the question of why not?

The reason lies in the inverse of the success of the empire elsewhere, the lack of marital ties. Because the Aztecs did not leave the indigenous rulers on the thrones of the Chalca cities, they did not exchange brides with them. And since the attempt to graft new rulers atop the Chalca ruling trees failed, when the local ruling lineages were allowed to regain their thrones, they had no kin ties to the Aztec state, and the successors to these kings were born of Chalca noblewomen, not Aztec. The more gradual supplanting of local rulers by half-local/half-Aztec successors was generally effective; the wholesale imposition of Aztecs on conquered thrones was not. And the Aztec failure to weave their kin webs in the Chalca cities demonstrates most compellingly the effectiveness of this technique when it was employed.

Peace and the Social System

The ultimate question is where peace is located in the Aztec social system. And the answer is, nowhere. Peace as a goal existed at a personal level in Aztec society, but it was not a political, religious, or intellectual aspiration: there was no room for it in the social system. Virtually everyone benefited from warfare, kings, nobles, commoners, priests, merchants, and artisans. It fueled their economy, permitted their social mobility, and fed their gods. And while the kings and upper nobles undoubtedly benefited most from this system of warfare, in a seeming paradox commoners and lower nobles profited more from wars that were carried to their most violent and destructive ends than from those that ended prematurely because of the enemy's submission.

So was there peace, beyond that of the dead? Yes. The peace was not, however, a general condition of human society but one that was internal to the empire. Peaceful relations did not exist between independent polities in the Aztec world: reconciliation was not between equals, but between subordinates and superiors, and alliances were concluded not with partners, but by the conquered with the conqueror. In short, peace in the Aztec world was not a condition of peoples and states, but of hierarchies. Peace for the Aztecs was peace through domination.

Notes

1   García Icazbalceta 1886–92: 3.252; Herrera 1934–57: 6.210; Barlow 1949: 121; Sahagún 1950–82: 8.1; Mengin 1952: 446; Chimalpahin 1965: 90, 93, 192; Durán 1967: 2.80–81; Mendieta 1971: 150; Alvarado Tezozomoc 1975b: 108; *Anales de Cuauhtitlan* 1975: 66; *Códice Ramírez* 1975: 51; *Crónica mexicana* 1975: 249; Ixtlilxóchitl 1975–77: 2.79–80; Torquemada 1975–83: 1.198; Berlin and Barlow 1980: 16; Dibble 1981: 10.

2   There is some possible evidence of such a cleansing ritual in the Tlacaxipehualiztli festival that ended the war season, but such an interpretation is a stretch. The Tlacaxipehualiztli ceremony was a state-level event, whose most important celebration was held in Tenochtitlan's main ceremonial precinct, where conquests were glorified. If there were purification rituals, they would most likely have been held at the local level, in *calpolli* (ward) temples, since most warriors were drawn from the *calpollis*, and such local rituals, if they differ from the main celebration, which seems unlikely, are generally not recorded.

3   The Aztec alliance with Tetzcoco and Tlacopan endured as long as the empire, but the relationships within it shifted. What began either as a relatively equal alliance, or an equal one between Tetzcoco and Tenochtitlan, with Tlacopan occupying a slightly subordinate position, grew into one which Tenochtitlan clearly dominated.

4   Stephens 1971. While the relatively dense packing of cities on the landscape in Mexico was a reflection of how far most could effectively exercise their political control within a day's march, that in turn was severely constrained by the lack of draft animals or wheeled vehicles in Mexico. Travel by foot over existing roads meant an average of sixteen miles per day, or an eight-mile radius for a round trip which was typical for markets, with armies being about a third slower owing to the dynamics of large-scale marches.

5   See Acuña (1982–87: passim) for conflicts between city-states and their traditional enemies, which were ongoing and never resolved, either by victory or defeat.

6   See Acuña (1982–87: passim) for the ethnicity of rulers throughout Mesoamerica.

7 Benjamin Cohen (1973) has grouped explanations of imperialism into three broad types: empires that expand as a result of some inherent dynamic of the expanding center (a phenomenon that Marxists often claim for capitalism); those that expand as a result of some feature of the periphery, such as some polity's weakness that renders it incapable of maintaining order and stable relations, which in turn forces the center to step in; and those that expand from a simple power imbalance in the international system that causes stronger centers to expand in order to control the weakness inherent in anarchic situations. Each or all of these explanations may apply in different circumstances, but they deal more with "how?" than "why?," reflect political stances more than explanations, and offer precious little insight in specific cases; in particular, they do not explain a case where a stable empire is overthrown by a generally weaker opponent with essentially the same structure.

8 The primary examples are the Stone of Tizoc and the recently discovered *cuauhxicalli* attributed to Moteuczoma Ilhuicamina. See Hassig 1992: 414 n. 8.

9 See the tribute lists in the *Matricula de Tributos* (1980) and the *Codex Mendoza* (Berdan and Anawalt 1992).

10 For a fuller discussion of the Aztec calendar, how it functioned, and how the Aztecs changed it, see Hassig 2001.

11 The tribute months were Tlacaxipehualiztli, Etzalcualiztli, Ochpaniztli, and Panquetzaliztli, whose festival days were 80, 100, 80, and 100 days apart in the solar year (Borah and Cook 1963: 45–50; Berdan 1976: 138).

12 The Aztecs made two specific changes that allow us to see the spread of their calendar throughout Mexico: they shifted the year-beginning month from Tlacaxipehualiztli to Atl Cahualo and they shifted the beginning of the 52-year Calendar Round and it's associated New Fire ceremony from the year 1 *Tochtli* (1 Rabbit) to 2 *Calli* (2 House). For a fuller discussion, see Hassig 2001: 121–72.

13 The pattern for the three pre-imperial kings was Acamapichtli (1372–91), followed by his son Huitzilihuitl (1391–1417), who was followed by his son Chimalpopoca (1417–27).

14 The pattern for the six imperial kings was Itzcoatl (1427–40), great uncle of Chmalpopoca, then to Moteuczoma Ilhuicamina (1440–68) who was Itzcoatl's nephew, then to Axayacatl (1468–81), who was the grandson of Moteuczoma Ilhicamina, then to Tizoc (1481–86), his brother, then to Ahuitzotl (1486–1502), his brother, then to Moteuczoma Xocoyotl (1502–20), his nephew. Moteuczoma Xocoyotl was killed during the Conquest, and was then succeeded by his brother, Cuitlahua (1520), who was succeeded by his first cousin (1521–25), though the circumstances of the Conquest may have yielded atypical successions.

15 Sjoberg 1960: 10; Crone 1989: 15–16; Hicks 1999: 409–11, 419. Because of the nature of the data, or lack thereof, these are no more than estimates.

16 García Icazbalceta 1886–92: 3.306; Herrera 1934–57: 6.211; Barlow 1949: 122; Sahagún 1950–82: 8.1; Chimalpahin 1965: 101, 1464; *Anales de Cuauhtitlan* 1975: 53; Ixtlilxóchitl 1975–77: 2.126; Torquemada 1975–83: 1.226–27.

17 Oviedo y Valdés 1959: 4.115; Cortés 1963: 136–38, 150; López de Gómara 1965–66: 2.237–38, 263–64; Durán 1967: 2.563; Ixtlilxóchitl 1975–77: 1.458–59, 462, 2.250, 256; Aguilar 1977: 95; Díaz del Castillo 1977: 1.460–69, 2.9–10.

References

Acuña, René (ed.). 1982–87. *Relaciones Geográficas del Siglo XVI*. 9 vols. Mexico City.

Aguilar, Francisco de. 1977. *Relación breve de la conquista de la Nueva España*. Jorge Gurría Lacroix (ed.). Mexico City.

Alvarado Tezozomoc, Hernándo. 1975a. *Crónica mexicana y Códice Ramírez.* Manuel Orozco y Berra (ed.). Mexico City.

———. 1975b. *Crónica mexicayotl.* Ed. by Adrián León. Mexico City.

Anales de Cuauhtitlan. 1975. In *Códice Chimalpopoca* 1975: 3–68.

Barlow, Robert H. (ed.). 1949. "El Códice Azcatitlán." *Journal de la Société des Américanistes* 38: 101–35.

Baudez, Claude F., and Peter Mathews. 1978. "Capture and Sacrifice at Palenque." In Robertson and Jeffers 1978: 31–40.

Berdan, Frances F. 1976. "A Comparative Analysis of Aztec Tribute Documents." *Actas del XLI Congreso International de Americanistas*, vol. 2: 131–42. Mexico City.

———, and Patricia Rieff Anawalt (eds.). 1992. *The Codex Mendoza.* 4 vols. Berkeley and Los Angeles.

Berlin, Heinrich, and Robert H. Barlow (eds. and trans.). 1980. *Anales de Tlatelolco.* Mexico City.

Borah, Woodrow, and Sherburne F. Cook. 1963. *The Aboriginal Population of Central Mexico on the Eve of the Spanish Conquest.* Ibero-Americana 45. Berkeley.

Calnek, Edward F. 1973. "The Localization of the Sixteenth Century Map Called the Maguey Plan." *American Antiquity* 38: 190–95.

Carrasco, Pedro. 1984. "Royal Marriages in Ancient Mexico." In Harvey and Prem 1984: 41–81.

Caso, Alfonso. 1971. "Calendrical Systems of Central Mexico." In Gordon F. Ekholm and Ignacio Bernal (eds.), *Handbook of Middle American Indians* 10: 333–48. Austin.

Chimalpahin, Francisco de San Anton Muñón. 1965. *Relaciones originales de Chalco Amaquemecan.* Ed. and trans. by S. Rendón. Mexico City.

Clavigero, Francisco. 1787. The History of Mexico. Trans. Charles Cullen. 2 vols. London.

Códice Chimalpopoca. 1975. *Códice Chimalpopoca: Anales de Cuauhtitlan y Leyenda de los Soles.* Feliciano Velázquez (ed. and trans.). Mexico City.

Códice Ramírez. 1975. In Alvarado Tezozomoc 1975a: 17–149.

Cohen, Benjamin J. 1973. *The Question of Imperialism: The Political Economy of Dominance and Dependence.* New York.

Cook, Sherburne F., and Woodrow Borah. 1971. *Essays in Population History.* Vol. 1. Berkeley and Los Angeles.

Cortés, Hernán. 1963. *Cartas y documentos.* Mexico City.

Crone, Patricia. 1989. *Pre-Industrial Societies.* Oxford.

Crónica mexicana. 1975. In Alvarado Tezozomoc 1975a: 151–701.

Denevan, William M. (ed.). 1976. *The Native Population of the Americas in 1492.* Madison.

Díaz del Castillo, Bernal. 1977. *Historia verdadera de la conquista de la Nueva España.* Ed. by Joaquin Ramírez Cabaña. 2 vols. Mexico City.

Dibble, Charles (ed. and trans.). 1981. *Codex en Cruz.* 2 vols. Salt Lake City.

Durán, Diego. 1967. *Historia de las Indias de Nueva España e islas de la tierra firme.* Ángel Ma. Garibay K. (ed.). 2 vols. Mexico City.

Flannery, Kent V., Joyce Marcus, and Stephen Kowalewski. 1981. "The Preceramic and Formative of the Valley of Oaxaca." In Jeremy Sabloff (ed.), *Handbook of Middle American Indians*, Supplement 1: 48–93. Austin.

Galloway, Patricia. 1997. *The Hernando de Soto Expedition: History, Historiography, and "Discovery" in the Southeast.* Lincoln, NE.

García Icazbalceta, Joaquin (ed.). 1886–92. *Nueva colección de documentos para la historia de México.* 5 vols. Mexico City.

Harvey, H. R., and Hanns J. Prem (eds.). 1984. *Explorations in Ethnohistory: Indians of Central Mexico in the Sixteenth Century.* Albuquerque.

Hassig, Ross. 1985. *Trade, Tribute, and Transportation: The Sixteenth-Century Political Economy of the Valley of Mexico*. Norman.

———. 1988. *Aztec Warfare: Imperial Expansion and Political Control*. Norman.

———. 1992. *War and Society in Ancient Mesoamerica*. Berkeley and Los Angeles.

———. 1997. "Leagues in Mexico vs. Leagues in Florida: How Good Were Estimates?" In Galloway 1997: 234–45.

———. 2001. *Time, History, and Belief in Aztec and Colonial Mexico*. Austin.

Herrera, Antonio de. 1934–57. *Historia general de los hechos de los castellanos en las islas y tierra firme del mar oceano*. Antonio Ballesteros y Beretta, Ángel Altolaguirre, et al. (eds.). 17 vols. Madrid.

Hicks, Frederic. 1999. "The Middle Class in Ancient Central Mexico." *Journal of Anthropological Research* 55: 409–27.

Ixtlilxóchitl, Fernándo de Alva. 1975–77. *Obras Históricas*. Edmundo O. Gorman (ed.). 2 vols. Mexico City.

López de Gómara, Francisco. 1965–66. *Historia general de las Indias*. Pilar Guibelalde (ed.). 2 vols. Barcelona.

Matrícula de tributos. 1980. *Matrícula de tributos (Códice de Moctezuma)*. Graz.

Mendieta, Gerónimo de. 1971. *Historia eclesiástica indiana*. Joaquin Garcia Icazbalceta (ed.). Mexico City.

Mengin, Ernest. 1952. "Commentaire du Codex Mexicanus Nos 23–24." *Journal de la Société des Américanistes* 41: 387–498.

Moyer, Gordon. 1982. "The Gregorian Calendar." *Scientific American* 246.5: 144–52.

Oviedo y Valdés, Gonzalo Fernández de. 1959. *Historia general y natural de las Indias*. Juan Perez de Tudela Buesco (ed.). 5 vols. Madrid.

Robertson, Merle Greene, and Donnan Call Jeffers (eds.). 1978. *Tercera Mesa Redonda de Palenque*, Vol. IV. Monterey.

Sahagún, Bernardino de. 1950–82. *General History of the Things of New Spain: Florentine Codex*. Trans. Arthur J. O. Anderson and Charles E. Dibble. 13 vols. Salt Lake City.

Sanders, William T. 1976. "The Population of the Teotihuacan Basin, the Basin of Mexico, and the Central Mexican Symbiotic Region in the Sixteenth Century." In Denevan 1976: 85–150.

Sjoberg, Gideon. 1960. *The Preindustrial City: Past and Present*. New York.

Stephen, G. Edward. 1971. "Variation in County Size: A Theory of Segmental Growth." *American Sociological Review* 36: 451–61.

Torquemada, Juan de. 1975–83. *Monarquía indiana*. 7 vols. Mexico City.

19

War and Peace in the Inca Heartland

Catherine Julien

What has been written about Andean warfare has largely been about the Incas (Bram 1941; Rowe 1946; Murra 1986 [1978]; D'Altroy 2002: 205–30).[1] The Spaniards who wrote about the Inca expansion were the direct heirs to Inca rule and wanted to know something about how their predecessors had unified such a large territory, stretching from north of Quito (in modern Ecuador) to just below Santiago (modern Chile). Some documentary sources drew from oral testimony or from local historical genres and offer a more ethnographic picture of warfare than other kinds of source materials. What I will do in this essay is develop a perspective on how Inca warfare developed in the region near Cuzco, the Inca capital, by isolating indigenous voices about the events of a century or more before Europeans arrived in the Andes. I want to learn about how the practice of war changed as empire became the goal and explore the question of the role peace played in the process.

One reason to isolate the voices of specific individuals or groups is to cast what they say against more general treatments of the Inca expansion. Sometimes Andean voices speak about particular situations, and what they say has an ethnographic feel. There is less of this kind of material for the Andes than for other parts of the ancient world, in part because Andean technologies for writing or recording were not understood or described by Europeans who first entered the Inca empire. Something like warfare can only be understood from an internal perspective; so every effort will be made in this essay to tease out a perspective on it from the small corpus of promising source material.

Preliminaries

The most promising sources for this sort of enterprise concern the region around Cuzco, the Inca capital. I will rely heavily in this chapter on a series of interviews conducted by the Viceroy Francisco de Toledo as he traveled along the main Inca road between Jauja and Cuzco (1570–1), and later, during his stay in Cuzco itself (1571–2).[2] The transcripts of these interviews are known as the "Informaciones de Toledo" (hereafter *Informaciones*). Toledo asked former Inca subjects about how they had governed themselves before the Inca expansion, both in times of peace and war, and about the Inca annexation of their territory. Most of the individuals interviewed had been adults by 1533, the year the Spaniards first arrived in Cuzco. Since the Inca expansion took place a century or more before this time, they were not speaking from personal knowledge but from what their "fathers and grandfathers" had told them. Toledo also interviewed members of the Inca dynastic lineage and others in the Cuzco valley about how the Incas had come to dominate the region of the capital itself. What we can glean from such Andean memories gives us something close to an internal view of the Inca expansion.

Other material for this essay comes from historical narratives about the Inca past written by Spanish authors but incorporating Inca historical genres (Julien 2000a). One of these is the *Historia Indica* of Pedro Sarmiento de Gamboa (1906 [1572]). The Inca conquest of the region between Cuzco and Jauja occurred during the rule of Pachacuti, the 9th Inca of the dynastic list, and his son, Thupa Inca Yupanqui. Sarmiento appears to have drawn from a life history of Pachacuti. Juan de Betanzos uses this same material in his *Suma y narración*, written two decades before (1987 [1551–7]). The Incas used knotted cords called *khipus* to record both accounting data and narrative, and a *khipu* account of the life of Pachacuti was still in the hands of Pachacuti's lineage when Betanzos wrote (Julien 2000a: 128–29). Betanzos was an interpreter who spoke the Inca language well and thus had no need of translators. He was married to a high-born woman of the lineage of the 10th Inca and could have known and conversed with those who kept the *khipus*. There are other *khipu* sources embedded in Spanish narratives of the Inca past. For instance, several Spanish authors appear to have used a list of the conquests of Thupa Inca transcribed from a *khipu* that was presented by the descendants of this Inca with a petition in 1569 (Rowe 1985).

The chronological framework used in this essay derives from these Spanish and Inca sources. Using the sequence of 11 Incas from the *Historia Indica* and estimating the average rule as about 30 years (which may be generous), a correlation with the Christian calendar may be constructed (table 19.1). Using this kind of projection, Inca origins date to the late eleventh century.[3]

The *Informaciones*: Witnesses from the Region Between Jauja and Cuzco

The first interviews in Jauja were conducted with four *caciques* (a Caribbean term used everywhere in the Americas to describe persons in authority) from the subdivision of Huringuancas, one of three in the Jauja province. One of them, Felipe Poma

Table 19.1 Correlation between Inca Genealogy and the European Calendar

1) Spanish arrival in Cuzco	December 1533
2) Death of the 11th Inca	About 1526–8
3) Beginning of the Inca expansion (when the 9th Inca was young)	Beginning of the 14th century
4) Consolidation of Inca control in the Cuzco valley (when the 4th Inca was young)	Mid-12th century
5) The time of origins (when the 1st Inca and his siblings emerged from the cave at Pacaritambo)	Late 11th century

Macao, had been a *curaca* (the local term for a hereditary provincial official in the Inca administration, often used synonymously with *cacique*; Julien 1982: 122–26). Specifically, he had been head of a *pachaca* (an administrative unit of 100 households). He testified that, before the time of the Inca empire, there had been *cincheconas* (captains) in time of war. These had not been hereditary but were chosen on the basis of their abilities, as observed in combat situations (f. 28v). His testimony was seconded by other Huringuanca witnesses. The name *cinchecona* was translated by more than one Huringuanca witness as "now this one is valiant" (*agora es este valiente*, f. 17). Another *curaca*, Hernando Apachin, noted that each town (*pueblo*) governed itself "in the manner of communities" (f. 32), and here the interpreter is supplying a comparison to Spanish forms.[4] Another witness, Alonso Cama, testified that *cincheconas* were chosen when the town had to defend itself. A *cinchecona* was the sort of person who would inspire the people to fight and who would himself fight in the vanguard. These traits had to be demonstrated. None of the Huringuanca witnesses mentioned inheritance of the position by descendants. Only one noted that the *cinchecona* served in peace as well as wartime (f. 28). Hernando Apachin, seconded by Alonso Cama (ff. 33, 36v–37), testified that wars were fought "for women and lands." He also indicated that *cincheconas* actually promoted conflict:

> These *cincheconas* wanted there to be continuous warfare since the people would hold festivals in their honor and respect them more; and when they defeated some towns, the women would come out with jugs of maize beer and other things to offer them so that they would not kill them, and the young girls likewise, and they would offer themselves to these *cincheconas*, to be their women (f. 33).

One of the witnesses, Diego Lucana, was not born in Jauja. He was in charge of the Cañares, Chachapoyas and Llaquas (f. 22), all of them *mitimaes* (colonists) settled in Jauja by the Incas (Rowe 1982). There is no telling to which of these groups he belonged, but at least the first two lived in the northern highlands, a great distance from Jauja, and it is likely that he came from that region. Lucana testified that, before the Incas, *cincheconas* were chosen because they were valiant in war, and that they "were respected" in peacetime. Before the Incas, there had been no large provinces, nor any tribute. He also said that *cincheconas* had been around since the "creation of the world," and that some had emerged from springs, others from rivers, rocks, or narrow holes (f. 23v). Lucana appears to be describing a primordial form of government.

Unlike any of the other witnesses interviewed in the region between Jauja and Cuzco, Lucana indicated that there was an expectation that the offspring of a *cinchecona* would be *cinchecona* as well:

> ... and if, in the lifetime of a *cinchecona* it happened that a *cinchecona* had sons, and he sent some of them to war with some people, and when it happened that one fought valiantly, the people said he would be a good *cinchecona* and they elected him to the office, and he became *cinchecona* after the death of his father and he looked after them and defended them. And if a *cinchecona* had two or three able and valiant sons, they were all elected as *cincheconas*, and when the sons of the *cincheconas* were young, they named others until they were older, but if they were not valiant, they were not elected to be *cincheconas* (f. 24).

Inheritance of the qualities associated with a *cinchecona* was expected, but these had to be demonstrated nonetheless.

Precisely for the Cañar region, there is evidence for hereditary rulers. In the *Historia Indica*, the leader of the Cañares is identified as Cañar Capac, or "the *capac* of the Cañares" (Sarmiento de Gamboa 1906: ch. 44: 87). Since Sarmiento's sources were Incas, we are here dealing with Inca understandings. The Incas themselves were *capac*, that is, they recognized a hereditary status that passed through the descendants of Manco Capac and a sister, who had emerged from the central window at Pacaritambo, eleven generations before the Spaniards arrived. *Capac* status was not something the Incas had known they possessed all along: it was revealed to them in several episodes by a solar deity connected with warfare (Julien 2000a: 23–42). The Incas Sarmiento interviewed described the leaders of a number of powerful prehispanic groups as *capac*. They were obstacles to the Inca expansion, and the Cañar Capac was one of them. Diego Lucana's testimony, despite the use of the term *cinchecona*, accords well with information from Inca sources about the Cañar region. *Cinchecona* status was not inherited, but the qualities associated with it were expected to be transferred to the next generation who still had to demonstrate them.

Only one of the Huringuanca witnesses said anything about the effective size of political units. Alonso Pomaguala testified that "each division had a *cinchecona*, and that in this valley of Jauja, up to the moiety of the Ananguancas, the *cincheconas* took care of them" (f. 17v). This seems to indicate that the political units in the valley were not necessarily small, and that there had been an effective boundary between the territories that later became Huringuanca and Ananguanca. Alonso Camo, also from Huringuancas, confirms this impression: the towns near each other got along well; the conflict was with towns that were "not so close." These more distant people would attack them to take their lands and their women (ff. 37–37v).

So far, the testimonies concerned defense. Yet an armed response to an attack was not the only option: some witnesses gave evidence that a choice could be offered between war and peace – on the agressor's terms. Diego Lucana testified that, when a town did not want to submit peacefully, the *cincheconas* and their followers would make war on them, kill them, and take their lands. If people decided to submit peacefully, they would keep their lands and become "vassals" of the others (f. 24–24v). Just what was expected from these "vassals" is unknown, beyond implicit subordination. Alonso Camo, one of the Jauja witnesses, also talked about negotiated peace:

> ... when one place [*lugar*] or town/people [*pueblo*] defeated another, they [the agressors] took their lands and destroyed them and killed the people, but when they [the agressors] came in peace and the people swore obedience to them, the people were allowed to stay in their towns, and no damage was done to them. And they [the agressors] would say that they wanted to speak with them, and that they [the people] should not be afraid because they came in peace (f. 37v).

Obviously in the case of war the people attacked stood to lose everything, not just their lands. What did the agressor gain if peace was chosen? The people swore their obedience, but what did this mean? Perhaps some kind of tribute was expected afterwards, although many witnesses testified that they had not paid tribute to an overlord before the Incas. Another possibility is that the people who were subordinated became allies: subordinate in status, but free, except when their superiors called on them for support, perhaps to go to war or for defense.

The same choice is mentioned by other witnesses in the towns between Jauja and Cuzco. In the next town, Guamanga (modern Ayacucho), Antonio Guaman Cucho, from Chirua in Tanquigua (Cook 1975: 278), corroborated the testimony of the Jauja witnesses but added to the repertory of choices arising from attack by one group on another:

> This witness had heard from his father and grandfather and other oldtimers that sometimes they [the agressors] would take part of their *chacaras* [cultivated fields] and leave others. When the local people who had fled learned about it, they could get their lands back by trading animals and cloth (f. 41v).

What seems to be described in this statement is that some local people fled, while others stayed. Those who fled lost their lands. Nothing was said about what happened to the others, and they may have simply been left alone.

In this case, aggression does not seem to have been motivated by a desire for land; otherwise, there would have been little reason to return the land. Still, one of the Jauja witnesses, Felipe Poma Macao, gave a classic materialist reason for territorial expansion:

> When one *pueblo* experienced a large expansion in its population, it would provoke wars with others to take their *chacaras* [cultivated fields], foodstuffs and women ... (f. 28v).

We do not know how common it was to go to war over land, but a number of witnesses mentioned it. Taking land was usually accompanied by killing the people on it. As Don Felipe Poma Macao noted, "when some towns defeated others, they killed all the people and took over their lands and their towns and divided them up among themselves and their captains, setting their own boundary markers" (f. 29). Andean people were strongly tied to the local landscape and killing everyone may have been the only means of acquiring a clear title to the land.

By killing everyone, the conquerors may also have intended to prevent retaliation. Only one witness, however, mentioned revenge as part of the cycle of conflict. Baltasar

Guaman Llamoca, from the province of Soras (in the highlands south of Ayacucho) explained what happened after a successful raid:

> When some people defeated others, and the defeated people fled, the winners arrived in their town and took their wives, women, clothing, livestock and everything they could find and left. When the people from that town returned, they made alliances with other groups and went to war again over what had been taken from them (f. 45).

This sounds like the other side of the coin described above – there was no intention of restoring what had been taken. (Yet this conflict was not over land.)

Fighting for the sole purpose of taking spoils – what we could call raiding – can have been an end in itself. It was also the result of a successful campaign that may have been motivated by other reasons. Two witnesses describe the handling of spoils. Juan Chancavilca and Alonso Quia Guanaco, from Parinacochas (in the highlands south of Ayacucho), noted that the *cincheconas* did not keep all the spoils for themselves but divided them among all who had participated (f. 52, cf. 50).

In addition to the reasons given so far, other, seemingly more minor provocations could result in armed conflict. Alonso Quia Guanaco said they went to war over "very small matters, like stealing firewood in the territory of others, or cutting pasture, or because of some offense committed by a particular person" (f. 50). Two Incas, interviewed in towns close to Cuzco, mentioned similar causes for aggression. Cristóbal Cusi Guaman, interviewed in Limatambo, said that wars might result from taking firewood and pasture from the lands of others (f. 56). Joan Sona, interviewed in Mayo, said that wars over water and lands were very ordinary and that arguments, too, brought about armed conflict (f. 67). Such local disputes suggest that neighboring towns did not always get along as well as one of the witnesses indicated.

The *Informaciones*: Witnesses from the Cuzco Valley

Groups questioned in the Cuzco valley were expected to provide information about Inca usurpation of their lands. Of the three groups interviewed, two were related to the Incas – the *ayllo* (here lineage) descended from Sauasiray and the *ayllo* descended from Ayar Ucho (also called Alcabizas); the third, the Guallas, was not. Since they describe events that occurred prior to the Inca expansion, their statements can be compared with what people elsewhere said about pre-Inca warfare.

The Inca genealogical account that underpins the *Historia Indica* begins with a story about Manco Capac and seven siblings crawling out of the central window of three at Pacaritambo, a place about 25 km. south of Cuzco. The siblings – the Ayar brothers and sisters – resided in several places before settling permanently in Cuzco. Just before their move to Cuzco they lived at Matagua. The Inca odyssey is described in terms of looking for good lands (Sarmiento de Gamboa 1906: ch. 12: 35). To test a site as a potential settlement, a rod (*vara*) was thrown; how it penetrated the ground was read as a sign of fertility. When the Inca siblings reached the Cuzco valley, one of the women, Mama Guaco, threw two golden rods. The one that revealed fertile soil landed in Guanaypata, a place "two harquebus shots from Cuzco," inhabited by the Guallas (ibid. ch. 13: 38–39).

Returning first to Matagua, Manco Capac, the progenitor of the dynastic line, sent another brother off to a stone boundary-marker where now the church of Santo Domingo in Cuzco stands. The brother went to the appointed place, sat there, and turned to stone, becoming a marker of Inca possession. Moving to this spot, the Incas also began their campaign to usurp the water and lands of the Guallas (ibid. ch. 13: 39–40).

Fifteen Guallas were interviewed in Cuzco during the Toledo interviews. They testified that their lands were on some terraces on a slope past San Blas, one of the parishes of Cuzco. The Incas had introduced people into their lands on two occasions. Fearing Inca cruelty, the Guallas fled with their *cinchecona*, Apo Caua, looking for new lands; they settled 20 leagues (100 km.) from Cuzco, in a town named after them where they were still living at the time (ff. 139–140v).

The next round of aggression occurred when the Incas reached a place near Cuzco, to the southwest, where a *cinchecona* named Copalimayta came out to meet them. Copalimayta was an outsider, but he had been chosen as *cinchecona* by the people of Sauasiray. Sarmiento considers these people non-Incas, while in the *Informaciones* they are represented as relatives of the Incas, though not direct descendants of Manco Capac. Sauasiray is described as having emerged from Sutictoco, one of the three windows at Pacaritambo. Most likely, the Sauasiray and the Incas were part of the same larger group, even though the Incas never represent themselves as subject to any higher authority (Julien 2000a: 241–43). In the fight with the Incas, Copalimayta was taken prisoner. To free himself, he left the region, giving up his lands and property. Manco Capac and Mama Guaco took what he had left and also gained authority over his people (Sarmiento de Gamboa 1906: ch. 13: 40). There had been a battle, but rather than killing the people the Incas appear to have negotiated a settlement.

Five men from the Sauasiray lineage (*ayllo*) were interviewed in the *Informaciones*. They reiterate Sarmiento's statement that Sauasiray had come from Sutictoco and settled near the Guallas, where no one else lived at the time. Since they say nothing about resisting the Incas, their testimony merely establishes their priority in the region and the defeat of their *cinchecona* (f. 136).

The Alcabizas were the next group that resisted the Incas. They were settled "half a harquebus shot from the Incas, where the convent of Santa Clara [now] is" (Sarmiento de Gamboa 1906: ch. 14: 41). After defeating Copalimayta, Manco Capac decided to take the lands of the Alcabizas. The Alcabizas gave him some land, but Manco Capac wanted it all. The strategy, suggested by Mama Guaco, was to take their water. The plan succeeded and the Incas got what they wanted without armed conflict.

Four people identified as Alcabizas were interviewed. They were from the lineage of Ayar Ucho, one of the brothers who emerged with Manco Capac from the center window at Pacaritambo, that is, they were collateral kin (ff. 136v–139). According to the *Historia Indica*, Ayar Ucho turned to stone and became the marker symbolizing the Inca possession of Cuzco. In the Inca account, he left no descendants (Sarmiento de Gamboa: ch. 12: 36–37). This is patently untrue, since his descendants were among the persons interviewed by both Sarmiento and Toledo. Sarmiento even gives some of their names (ibid. ch. 11: 34), flatly contradicting what he says in the next pages. They said nothing about being forced off their lands by the Incas, testifying only that the Guallas and the *ayllos* of Sauasiray and Quizco were already there (f. 137).

Another story about Inca aggression against the Alcabizas dates to the time of Mayta Capac, the fourth Inca (approximately in the mid-twelfth century). After the initial acts of agression which allowed the Incas to establish themselves in the Cuzco valley, there was peace for three generations. Then the young Mayta Capac began to show signs of aggressive behavior. One day, when he was playing with some young Alcabizas and Culunchimas, Mayta Capac injured many of his playmates, killing some. Soon after, he had an argument with an Alcabiza boy over drinking water from a spring and broke the boy's leg, chasing the other Alcabizas who were with him back to their houses, where they hid. The Alcabiza adults decided that it was time to free themselves from Inca domination. They chose ten strong men and went to the place where the Incas lived, determined to kill Mayta Capac and his father, Lloque Yupangui. Mayta Capac was entertaining himself with other boys in the patio when he saw the armed men arriving. He threw bolas at one of them and killed him, then threw again at another. When the Alcabizas turned to run, Mayta Capac went right after them. This defeat only made the Alcabizas more determined to win their freedom. The Alcabizas and Culunchimas joined forces and went to fight Mayta Capac and his supporters. Mayta Capac won the first encounter, then prevailed in another skirmish. In a third encounter, the Alcabizas were defeated by supernatural intervention: a sudden disastrous hailstorm. Mayta Capac kept their *cinchecona* imprisoned until his death (Sarmiento de Gamboa 1906: ch. 17: 45–48).

The Alcabizas told a different story in their testimony for the *Informaciones:* Mayta Capac deceived them out of their lands. When they protested, he responded that they should all marry each other, since they were close kin. They resisted but Mayta Capac and his people started killing them secretly at night as well as committing other acts of treachery. Every day Mayta Capac would introduce more people into their lands, killing a few more at night. Mayta Capac also openly attacked their *cinches,* Apo Mayta and Cullaychima, imprisoning them at Sangahuaci to be tortured and killed. Mayta Capac and his people then entered their lands and took their water. They also cut open their women and took the dead fetuses from their bodies (ff. 137v–138). Here an effort to exterminate a particular group is apparent. Since descent was determined through the male line, killing their fetuses would put an end to the Alcabizas.

Conflicts in the Cuzco valley, then, reflect competition for lands and power. The Incas initially despoiled the Guallas of their lands and only later took the lands belonging to the Alcabizas, moving them to another location in the Cuzco valley. The difference between the treatment of these two groups may have been due to their different ties to the Incas. The Guallas were neither close nor distant relatives of the Incas. The other groups were related in some way to the Incas and managed to coexist with them for some time. The Incas quickly established authority over the Sauasirays at the time Manco Capac and his siblings first arrived in the area. The Alcabizas were descendants of one of Manco Capac's brothers and were much closer kin. Theoretically, they had as much claim to *capac* status as the Incas did.

Betanzos on Inca Warfare

If we take into account what both the Incas and the other peoples of the Cuzco valley told Sarmiento and Toledo the Inca expansion effectively began in the time of Mayta Capac, the 4th Inca (mid-twelfth century?). Much happened before the Incas expanded beyond the Cuzco region under the 8th and 9th Incas, and there is a story in Betanzos and Sarmiento about the growth of Inca power at the regional level through marriage alliance with other groups (Julien 2000a: 233–53). I want to move forward to the time of Pachacuti, the 9th Inca (early fifteenth century?). A life history exists for this Inca which both Betanzos and Sarmiento appear to have used (ibid. 93–130). It begins with the invasion of Cuzco by the Chancas, a group from the region between Cuzco and Jauja, and ends with Pachacuti's death. Pachacuti was personally involved in the conquest of part of the region, and the annexation of Jauja was accomplished by captains during his lifetime, so his life history spans the period of our interest.

If Pachacuti's life history were our only source, we would think the Chanca attack materialized out of thin air. Fortunately there are other ways to gain an understanding of regional power relationships at the time (ibid. 213–22). Suffice it to say here that a vacuum had been created in the region between the Chancas and the Incas by the demise of a polity known as Quichuas (or Quechuas). Both the Chancas (from the west) and Incas (from the east) had usurped Quichua territory (Julien 2000b:139–40). It was only a matter of time until they confronted each other. If we listen to the Inca voices transmitted by Betanzos and Sarmiento, the Chancas were a worthy enemy. I will take from their narratives what is relevant to our discussion of warfare.

Betanzos represents the Chanca lord (*señor de los Chancas*), named Uscovilca, as being head of a great number of people. He had six valiant captains. At the time, he resided at a place called Paucaray, near Parcos. Because he had heard that Viracocha, the 8th Inca, was the most important lord (*señor*) in the region, he decided to find out what kind of power this Viracocha had. Betanzos also noted that Viracocha had assumed this name which meant "god." Uscovilca traveled to Cuzco, dividing his army into three groups. One was to travel via Condesuyo (which means, on a parallel course to the right of the main forces), the other via Andesuyo (on a parallel course to the left), and he would lead the forces down the middle (Betanzos 1987: pt. 1, ch. 6: 22). This was a ritualized movement that imitated the movement of the sun (Julien 2000a: 291–92). The sun had a tie to warfare that the Incas were soon to use.

Uscovilca armed his people with lances, axes, maces, slings, and shields, and gave them dried maize, fish, and meat for the road. He told them that they would share in whatever livestock, women, clothing, gold and silver, slaves or other servants might be taken. Two of the captains took charge of the forces that were to travel on the right and left. These captains were wildly successful and went on conquering all the way to what is now eastern Bolivia. Uscovilca wanted to take Cuzco himself. Viracocha did not want to fight, given that he had had no time to call some of his principal people together, and when Uscovilca sent two messengers to offer him a choice between peaceful submission or battle, he decided on submission. He sent a message to Uscovilca that "he would swear his obedience and that he wanted to eat and drink with him." As the day approached to meet with Uscovilca, Viracocha changed his mind. He decided – perhaps in consultation with others – to avoid Uscovilca entirely and to leave Cuzco. He took his people with him and installed them at Caquia Xaquixaguana, a towering hill not far from Cuzco (Betanzos 1987: pt. 1, ch. 6: 24–25).

The youngest of his sons, feeling that it was wrong to abandon Cuzco to the Chancas, decided to stay with some of his young friends and their servants, nine people in all. Uscovilca heard the news about this plan to defend Cuzco and was overjoyed. He could fight this small contingent of Incas and celebrate a triumph: his victory would be cheap and easy. One of Uscovilca's captains, named Tomay Guaraca, wanted the assignment but Uscovilca kept it for himself (ibid. chs. 6: 25–26, 7: 27–28). Viracocha, in his refuge, only laughed at his youngest son, saying (here Betanzos gives a first person speech):

> Since I am a man who communicates with god, and since I have heard from him and been advised that I cannot win against Uscovilca, I left Cuzco so that Uscovilca would not bring dishonor on me and bad treatment to my people (ibid. ch. 7: 28).

Viracocha refused to return to Cuzco to fight, but a number of important lords (*caciques y señores*) in the Cuzco area decided to support the young Pachacuti.

While Betanzos narrates the events before the Inca-Chanca engagements in several chapters, he barely mentions the battle itself. Uscovilca descended the hill of Carmenga to the center of Cuzco:

> [The Incas and Chancas] engaged in battle and fought from the morning – which was when it began – until midday. And the events of the battle were such that a great number of Uscovilca's soldiers were killed, and none engaged that were not killed. Uscovilca himself was taken and killed, and when his people saw him captured and dead and saw the slaughter of so many of their own, they decided to retreat (ibid. ch. 8: 33).

They regrouped not far from Cuzco along the main road to the North, and sent for reinforcements. They also summoned the two captains who had been sent on parallel courses, who immediately returned, bringing the spoils of all their other victories. All were dismayed by the news of Uscovilca's death (ibid. ch. 8: 33).

What follows is the story of how Pachacuti tried to get his father to accept the insignia of Uscovilca and the clothing and other spoils taken from the defeated Chancas.

> [Pachacuti] went to where his father was and paid him the respect that he was owed as his lord (*señor*) and father, and also put before him the insignia, weapons and clothing of the Chanca Uscovilca whom he had defeated and killed. He begged his father to tread on the insignia of the defeated enemy, and he also begged him to tread on some of Uscovilca's captains who had been taken prisoners and whom he had brought with him, and he made them lie down (ibid. ch. 9: 35).

Betanzos then notes that this was how the Incas celebrated a triumph: they would bring the insignia of the defeated captains and any captains who had been taken alive and parade them into Cuzco where they would be delivered to the ruling Inca who would step on them. In this way, the Inca in authority would accept what they had done. Viracocha refused, even after numerous attempts by Pachacuti to get him to acquiesce. This story, then, concerns not just the defeat of the Chancas, but also the rupture between father and son (ibid. ch. 9: 35–41).

There were still Chancas to be defeated, and they had entered into an alliance with the people of Jaquijaguana, west of Cuzco, who were part of the larger group identified as Incas. This time, instead of waiting for the Chancas to attack Cuzco, Pachacuti went out to meet them. Again, there is no real information about the battle, except that it began when the sun was already high, about ten, and ended in the late afternoon.

What is important is what happened after the battle. First, Pachacuti dealt with Jaquijaguana. Identifying with the Chanca cause, these people had braided their hair like the Chancas. After the battle, they went to Pachacuti and threw themselves on the ground before him. They said they had been unable to resist the Chancas. Many of the Incas who had fought with Pachacuti wanted them killed, "since they had witnessed the deaths of Inca soldiers," but Pachacuti decided to spare them, "since they were *orejones*." (*Orejones*, or "big ears," was the term the Spaniards used to describe those who wore ear spools and, we can infer, were initiated in rites similar to the Inca rite, and hence were Incas in some sense.) Being *orejones*, however, "they should wear their hair short." By wearing their hair long and braided, they had denied their Inca affiliation. Pachacuti sent them home and ordered his captains not to take anything that belonged to them.

The Chancas were another matter. Pachacuti had their captains who had campaigned successfully brought before him. They told him all about their conquests and how, because of their success, they had dared to attack him. Pachacuti responded that, if they had been victorious, it had been because they were following Uscovilca's orders. Since he, Pachacuti, had defeated Uscovilca, "they should have presumed that their luck had run out." To punish them and set an example for others – and perhaps, most importantly, to prevent them from regrouping to fight him again – he had them taken to the site of the battle and, in his presence, hung from posts erected there. Afterwards, he ordered their heads to be cut off and placed on the posts. Their bodies were burned and the ash thrown to the wind from the highest hills. The Chanca dead were to be left where they were lying, to serve as food for the foxes and vultures. Pachacuti thus created a gruesome memorial to the Chanca defeat. The spoils were taken to Cuzco and distributed among those who had fought, "according to the quality of the person" (Betanzos 1987: pt. 1, ch. 10: 44–46).

Various elements of this story echo what witnesses told Toledo about warfare before the time of the Inca expansion. First, a choice was offered between war or negotiated peace. This seems typical of an aggressor who was not looking for lands: war involved risk and the purpose could be achieved by other means. Although we might think that Uscovilca could have negotiated peace with Viracocha rather than fight Pachacuti, it appears that Viracocha had reneged on the peace and was prepared to face a Chanca attack in a place where he could defend himself better. Uscovilca chose an easy victory over a hard one. Second, the Chancas were a large and powerful group, but they were still structured along the principles described by the Toledo witnesses: they were an assemblage of valiant captains or *cincheconas*. Third, spoils were expected, and these too corresponded to those mentioned by the Toledo witnesses: animals, women, metals, clothing. Moreover, sharing the spoils was the sign of a popular captain. Uscovilca was also astute, since he informed his soldiers of this before the battle. What is new is the description of the ritualized movement of armies, the relationship between success and supernatural favor, the ritual of triumph, and the creation of a battle memorial using the bodies of the fallen enemy.

The next major campaign north of Cuzco was directed against a people called the Soras and took place not long after the Chanca defeat. Pachacuti had decided that there were too many local lords claiming to be *capac*, but that "there should be only one: and that was himself" (Betanzos 1987: pt. 1, ch. 18: 87). The way to prove one's *capac* status – to draw the logical conclusion – was success in battle. "The sun was now with him," he reasoned, and we can assume that this supernatural support had had something to do with his recent success. For the next three months, Pachacuti made a great number of sacrifices and ordered a statue to be made of gold that would go into battle with him. Called Cacha, the statue would be carried into battle by one man while a second man kept pace with him, shading the statue from the sun with a small parasol, in the same manner that the Inca was given shade. Just before leaving, sacrifices were made to the sun and the important *huacas* (sacred beings) to insure the success of the campaign (ibid. ch. 18: 87–88).

A great deal of effort during the campaign went into building roads and bridges. These were major works of engineering, and Betanzos devotes a fair amount of space to describing the construction of bridges of plaited straw – in fact, much more than to the battle that followed. At Curahuasi, a place on the road, a great number of people came and submitted peacefully. Pachacuti incorporated them into his army and went on building the road and bridges. Only after crossing the Abancay river did he meet with any resistance: the Soras had been joined by their neighbors, the Lucanas, and some of the remaining Chancas. Pachacuti was happy to hear the news, since "his trip would not be in vain." So he went on building the road and bridges, this time in the direction of Soras territory. Once there, "he attacked them from all directions in such a manner that in short order they were defeated" (ibid. ch. 18: 88–90). So much for describing Inca military strategy.

Again, what happened after the battle is more important. Pachacuti divided his army into three groups, two headed by captains who were Cuzco lords (*señores*) and one by himself. One of the captains was to take his army along a parallel course through Condesuyo, the other through Andesuyo. They were to conquer as they went. Pachacuti would lead the main body of the army down the middle. But first, the prisoners were brought before him. Pachacuti had ordered a great many red tassels made, a palm's length each, and they were brought for him to step on. He had them sewn on long red shirts made for this purpose which the prisoners had to put on. Then their hair was drenched with *chicha* (maize beer) and dusted with maize flour. The women of the important lords (*señores*), summoned from Cuzco, sang a song: "Inca Yupanqui [Pachacuti], son of the sun, defeated the Soras and put tassels on them," followed by the refrain "hayahuaya," repeated frequently. The lords of Cuzco dressed in the finery they had worn into battle. Everyone, with the prisoners in the center, sang and celebrated for a month. Then it was time to return to Cuzco. The prisoners were paraded ahead, causing them great humiliation. The captains who had been sent along on parallel courses rejoined the main army shortly before it reached Cuzco. A great fire was made before the Inca, and some of the animals, fine clothing and maize taken in the campaign were sacrificed in it. The captains brought the insignia, weapons, and captured enemies before Pachacuti and humbly begged him to tread on them. Then the same kind of tassels the Soras wore were brought and he stepped on them. The prisoners taken by the other captains were dressed in long shirts and their hair was treated as the hair of the other prisoners had been. The captains from the Andes had brought many wild lowland animals that were to be used in the punishment of the prisoners. Pachacuti ordered that no food be given to these animals (Betanzos 1987: pt. 1, chs. 18–19: 90–95).

The next day, the entire army headed back to Cuzco. When they were in sight of the city, Pachacuti ordered the army to enter in a particular order. Each group was to sing of its experiences, beginning with Pachacuti and the Soras prisoners and the song that had already been composed. The prisoners were ordered to enter the city crying and singing of their crimes in loud voices, and of how they were subjects and vassals of the "son of the sun," and that there were no forces strong enough to defeat him. The statue of the sun, important sacred objects, and the bodies of earlier Inca rulers had been assembled in the main plaza. Pachacuti had the wild animals taken to the Sangahuaci. The prisoners were closed in with them for three days, and those who survived were allowed to live but deprived of their estates and their positions and ordered to serve the statues and sacred objects assembled there. The insignia and arms and other things taken in battle were placed in a house known as Llaxahuaci, where other battle trophies were to be kept thereafter. Then the men who had gone with Pachacuti were brought before him. They were richly rewarded and given their share of the spoils. Pachacuti named some of them to be lords (*señores*) of the provinces that had belonged to those enemies devoured by the wild animals (ibid. ch. 19: 95–97).

As in the campaign against the Chancas and their allies in Xaquixaguana, great emphasis is placed on ritual both when Inca armies leave for war and after their victorious return. Practices related to the treatment of prisoners and spoils, including prisons and museums for war trophies, may be new. Proof of *capac* status was richly celebrated, and even the prisoners were made to sing in confirmation of it.

Betanzos does not treat Pachacuti's later campaigns in the same detail as this one. The campaign against the lord (*señor*) of Hatuncolla is important for our purposes. This lord was calling himself *capac çapa apo indi chori*, which Betanzos glosses as "king and only lord, son of the sun." Of course, this is the status that Pachacuti claimed (and Uscovilca appears to have claimed before him). The description of Pachacuti's preparations for the campaign is brief; that of the battle follows the usual pattern, that is, it was fiercely fought by both sides, and lasted from morning till late afternoon, and the lord of Hatuncolla was captured and killed. Pachacuti ordered his head to be preserved, probably as a drinking cup. The enemy dead were not to be interred. Instead, they were to be taken away from the battle site and left out in the open. On the site itself, Pachacuti built a house for the sun and installed an image of the sun, to which he made great sacrifices. This was a different kind of memorial (Betanzos 1987: pt. 1, ch. 20: 100–01).

The bodies of fallen Incas were gathered up and housed near the battle site while Pachacuti continued his campaign. The bodies were to be taken back to Cuzco. The Inca believed that the bodies of the dead would be resuscitate at some point. Betanzos describes this first in the Inca language and then translates the passage: "after this world ends all of the people have to rise up from it alive and in the same flesh, just as we are now" (ibid. ch. 20: 101). How much of this represents assimilation of the Christian idea of resurrection is unknown, but there clearly existed some belief that necessitated the preservation of Inca bodies and the destruction of enemy bodies.

The Colla prisoners were bound and marched back to Cuzco in the way described earlier. The spoils were gathered up, including livestock, clothing, gold and silver ornaments, and service personnel. For the first time, Betanzos supplies a term for what was taken after vanquishing an enemy: *piñas*. In Cuzco the prisoners were imprisoned in the Sangahuaci to be eaten by wild animals. The insignia and arms taken were sent to the Llaxahuaci. The spoils were distributed in shares to the participants. The bodies of the Inca dead were preserved and given to their women and children, who also received shares in the spoils. Later, the Incas who were installed as administrators would see that these widows and children received their share of lands or other distributions, and that they would receive them first, before any of the others. After the defeat of the lord of Hatuncolla, other groups from the Lake Titicaca basin submitted peacefully (ibid. ch. 20: 101–2).

This was the last time Pachacuti campaigned in person, and here Betanzo's detailed treatment of campaigning stops. What he narrates about Pachacuti's campaigns clearly focuses on what this Inca invented, or at least elaborated from some pre-existing form. The creation of a statue to be taken into battle, the engineering projects, the invention of rituals associated with the transport of prisoners to Cuzco and their punishment there, the treatment of both enemy and Inca dead, the treatment of the widows and children of the Inca dead, and the invention of a special place to house the insignia and arms of the enemy – all this appears to have originated with Pachacuti. Rituals were needed to reflect Inca power, and institutions to govern the territory over which the Incas claimed authority, and this Inca turned his attention to developing them.

Sarmiento on Inca Warfare

Betanzos says nothing about the Inca conquest of Jauja, but Sarmiento does. This campaign was led by Pachacuti's brother, Capac Yupanqui (Sarmiento de Gamboa 1906: ch. 35: 74). What Sarmiento has to say about the fortresses conquered north of Soras comes from a *khipu* source (Julien 2000a: 147). The material is inserted into a single paragraph:

> In the province of the Quicchuas [Quichuas] he conquered and took the fortress of Tohara and Cayara and the fortress of Curamba; in the Angarares, the fortress of Urcocolla and Guayllapucara and captured their *cinche* named Chuquis Guaman; in the province of Jauja, Siciquilla [Siquilla] Pucara, and in the province of Guayllas [Guaylas], Chungomarca Pillaguamaraca ... (Sarmiento 1906: ch. 44: 87).

Sarmiento's sequencing of this material poses problems, but what we want to note is that the list includes a fortress in Jauja where the people resisted.

The *khipu* source focuses on resistance. Apparently, there was a major effort to resist the Incas (Cieza de León 1986: ch. XLIX: 143), perhaps at Siquilla Pucara, as noted in the *khipu* list. The information we have from the Huringuanca witnesses is not about this battle, but about peaceful submission (see next section). After all, they were descended from the individuals the Incas chose as *curacas*. It is unlikely that those who fought the Incas were rewarded in this way.

Sarmiento has a great deal more to say about Inca warfare than Betanzos, but I will limit myself here to a single later campaign, against the Collas, right after Pachacuti's death. A Colla rebellion broke out while Thupa Inca was campaigning in the lowlands east of Cuzco. One of the Collas in his company fled to the Lake Titicaca region and spread the rumor that Thupa Inca had been killed. The Colla was named Coaquiri, but he took the name Pachacuti Inca, signifying a cataclysmic overturn of the existing order. The Collas took him as their captain. When Thupa Inca heard the news, he left the lowland campaign in the hands of a captain and headed straight for Lake Titicaca. Thupa Inca enlarged his army, naming a few new captains, and went to where the Collas had fortified themselves at Llallagua, Asillo, Arapa and Pucara. He captured the Colla captains, Chuca Chuca and Pachacuti Coaquiri, and "made drums of them." This campaign lasted "for years," during which Thupa Inca carried out "great cruelties" (Sarmiento 1906: chs. 49–50: 96–97).

The places named are located in the region that had submitted peacefully to his father after the conquest of Hatuncolla (ibid. ch. 50: 97). Other source material indicates that this region was organized into provinces that were part of the estate of Thupa Inca and the sun (Rostworowski de Diez Canseco 1993: 269). Similar links exist between the defeat – and virtual extermination of peoples – in the Urubamba valley by Pachacuti and estates that later belonged to that Inca. Extermination or near-extermination of the people occupying a territory may have paved the way for the development of these types of Inca holdings. Both cases involved people who had been Inca subjects and then rebelled, and one case involved people who had at first submitted peacefully to the Incas (Julien 2000c: 70–71).

The *Informaciones*: Non-Inca Witnesses on Inca Warfare

Some of those questioned about the Inca expansion came from places, like Soras, that had been conquered in the time of Pachacuti. They uniformly testified that Pachacuti had annexed their territory. The witnesses interviewed in Jauja said it had been Thupa Inca, reflecting what is known from narratives like the *Historia Indica*.

All witnesses noted that the Inca offered their opponents a choice between war or peaceful submission. Most said the Inca fought until the people submitted, but Don Alonso Quia Guanaco of Parinacochas presented a more specific idea of the Inca policy:

> When they resisted for a few days, the Incas put all of them, large and small, to the knife, and when this was seen and understood by the rest of the people, they submitted out of fear (f. 51).

Another witness, Don Joan Puyquin, whose father had come from the Quito region, said that his father had been the only person the Inca left alive. His people had all been killed in the conquest "because they had resisted him." His father was spared because "he had been very young" and was taken as a servant by Thupa Inca (ff. 58–58v, 60). One of the Inca witnesses, Don Juan Sona, interviewed at Mayo just north of Cuzco, said that the Inca regularly killed all of the people who resisted and that "the only ones left alive were the very small boys."

The best testimony about submission was given by Don Alonso Pomaguala of Huringuancas, who testified that he had learned about the Inca conquest from his father Guamia Chiguala and his grandfather Xaxaguaman, "who were *caciques* named by the Inca." Both had told him that "they had been with the Inca in the conquest of this land" (f. 17). Elsewhere he notes that his great-grandfather, named Capoguala, had negotiated Huringuanca submission to Thupa Inca. Thupa Inca had installed himself on a local mountain top in Huringuancas with an army of 10,000 men. Capoguala, "one of the *cincheconas*," went with ten of his men to meet with the Inca. His people were told to hide until they learned what befell this embassy. The Inca gave his great-grandfather some "ornately-decorated shirts and cloaks, and the kind of cups they drink from called *aquillas*." (*Aquillas* are drinking cups made of precious metal; González Holguín 1952: 689.) Those who were hiding thought the Inca was coming to kill them when they saw the embassy return, but rejoiced when they recognized their own leaders. Capoguala led his people to where the Inca was and they swore their obedience to him. From this group, Thupa Inca recruited an army to continue with him to Ecuador (ff. 19v–20). Pomaguala noted that others who had not submitted to Inca authority had been defeated in battle. Some had been tied up and their lands taken from them (ff. 19v–20).

Interestingly, the Incas chose a fortified site as a place for negotiations. The choice apparently was between submission or attacking a fortified position. One witness, Don Roldan Matara, a *cacique* from Cotabambas (southwest of Cuzco) gave the usual statement to the effect that those who did not peacefully submit and chose to defend themselves were killed and treated with great cruelty. He added that some peoples submitted because they were afraid of what would happen if they did not, but also because the Inca said "he was son of the sun" (f. 65). Like Don Felipe Poma Macao, he noted that those who submitted "went with the Inca, helping him to conquer and annex these lands" (f. 65).

War, or Peace, at any Price

A close reading of select sources pertaining to the conduct of war in the Inca heartland suggests a number of general observations. Before the Inca expansion, warfare had been a more informal practice. Leaders – *cinchecona* – were chosen as the need arose. Their power depended on performance, and they enjoyed nothing more than respect when the threat of war had passed. There were expectations that the abilities of the *cinchecona* would be transmitted to the next generation, and these may have led toward a hereditary status. There were disputes over minor matters like gathering kindling on someone else's land and raids for movable property and women. More serious attempts to remove people from their lands prompted the residents to flee or face decimation. Campaigns may have simply forced people into alliance with more powerful groups for common defense. There may have been rules of engagement, but Andean voices tell us little about the actual conduct of war.

This holds true as well for the Inca expansion. Almost all that was said about battle was that it began and ended during the daylight hours of a single day. A change occurred in the nature of leadership; whether this development was entirely new or harkened back to earlier Andean practice is an open question.[5] The Incas claimed *capac* status, which involved a genealogical tie to a solar supernatural. They must have shown prowess during engagements with those who decided to fight them: warfare was a test of *capac* status. What Inca sources tell us most about, however, concerns the march to the battle site, the construction of roads and bridges along the way, gruesome displays of the enemy dead at or near battle sites, and rituals involving prisoners and spoils on the road home and at permanent sites in the city of Cuzco. The Incas – like the Chancas before them – used a certain marching formation that represented the march of the sun across the sky, presumably expressing their claim to a genealogical connection with this supernatural. A victory offered them an opportunity to create a performance that would reflect and enhance their *capac* status.

Gruesome displays and rituals following victory prove *capac* status but should not obscure a fundamental reality. Claims to *capac* status, no less than those to *cinchecona* status, had to be demonstrated. A great deal was at stake in an Inca campaign. Not only the person who proved that he was *capac* by emerging victorious on the battlefield, but the whole group of Incas had a vested interest in maintaining and preserving this status. We can only imagine that an Inca, having arrived in a territory to be annexed and finding a defensible site where his army could wait until the opponents decided whether they wanted war or peace, must have felt great relief when they came to sue for peace. According to Andean witnesses, a choice between war and peace had been offered before the Incas began to expand, and this choice became a fundamental part of the Inca expansion. Like other empire builders, the Inca aggressors coerced peaceful submission through threats of extermination – or at least humiliation and dire consequences. Thus the contest for power was rigged in favor of peaceful submission to Inca rule. In effect, both sides wanted and needed peace.

With annexation came the *pax Incaica*. The Incas installed governors and organized productive activities in each province, both to provide support for their campaigns and the dynastic cult and to rationalize local economies (Julien 1982, 1988, 1993, ms.). We hear of some notable rebellions, but no province, once annexed, ever successfully recovered its independence. At the time of the Spanish arrival, however, a civil war divided the Andean populations between two Inca brothers who had different territorial bases. One of them was in the process of consolidating his control over his brother's area, when he was captured by Pizarro. The Spaniards entered Cuzco as liberators of the losing side, only to reveal gradually their ultimate plan to usurp authority over the entire Inca empire. Imperial peace established by the Incas remained fragile.

Notes

1 In this essay, the term "Inca" will be used to refer to a person ("the Inca") and a group ("the Incas"). A longer version of this chapter appears in a volume titled *War and Peace in Aboriginal South America* (Julien 2003). I thank Paul Valentine and the editors of *Antropológica* for permission to republish its substance here.
2 Levillier 1940, vol. 2; AGI Lima 28b; AGI Patronato 294, no. 6. All folio references in the text of my essay are to AGI Lima 28b. All transcriptions from this document are my own.
3 The archaeological sequence for the valley of Cuzco extends to the period before the Common Era; so Inca genealogy does not reflect what we know about human occupation in the region. The point is not to reconcile different understandings about the past but to develop a correlation between them. Inca genealogy gives us a real-time framework on which to base a calendar-year estimate for the stories that drew upon an Inca memory of the past.
4 The word *pueblo* has more than one meaning. It was used to refer to the lowest rung in a hierarchy of three urban forms in the Americas: city (*ciudad*), villa (*villa*) and town (*pueblo*). In Spain, the term *lugar* was used instead of *pueblo*. All of these urban forms had a territory associated with them, though in the case of *villas* and *pueblos* this was not extensive. The word *pueblo* could also refer to "a people." I think the Jauja witnesses are using the term to refer to a small, local jurisdiction. Another term that needs discussing is *comunidad*. At the time, there were competing forms of political organization in Spain: one, the *señorío*, or hereditary lordship, involved both a tribute right over a territory and civil and criminal jurisdiction; another, *behetría* or *comunidad*, was the free community, still subject to royal authority but under a local lord of its choice (Glick 1979: ch. 4). The *señorío* had been gaining ground since the eleventh century, but it was to make a real surge in growth in the sixteenth and seventeenth centuries. The third question in Toledo's first questionnaire asked specifically if towns were governed "in the manner of *behetría* or *comunidades*" (f. 14v), prompting responses in these terms.
5 Warfare is hard to study from archaeological traces; so the best studies focus on the Moche on the North Coast of Peru, where painted ceramics as well as elaborate sites of human sacrifice have been found (Bourget 2001).

Documents and Publications

AGI Lima 28B. Ynformaciones hechas por el Virey del Peru don Françisco de Toledo en averiguacion del origen y gobierno de los Yncas, 1570–72. Archivo General de Indias, Sevilla.

AGI Patronato 294, no. 6. Ynformacion de las idolatrias de los Yncas e indios y de como se enterraban, 1571. Archivo General de Indias, Sevilla.

References

Betanzos, Juan de. 1987. *Suma y narración de los Incas* [1551–57]. Madrid.

Bourget, Steve. 2001. "Rituals of Sacrifice: Its Practice at Huaca de la Luna and Its Representation in Moche Iconography." In J. Pillsbury (ed.), *Moche Art and Archaeology in Ancient Peru*, 89–109. Washington, DC.

Bram, Joseph. 1941. *An Analysis of Inca Militarism*. Seattle.

Cieza de León, Pedro de. 1986. *Crónica del Perú. Segunda parte* [1553]. Lima.

Collier, George A., Renato I. Rosaldo, and John D. Wirth (eds.). 1982. *The Inca and Aztec States, 1400–1800: Anthropology and History*. New York.

Cook, Noble David. 1975. *Tasa de la visita general de Francisco de Toledo* [1583]. Lima.

D'Altroy, Terence. 2002. *The Incas*. Oxford.

Glick, Thomas F. 1979. *Islamic and Christian Spain in the Early Middle Ages*. Princeton.

Gonzalez Holguin, Diego. 1952. *Vocabulario de la lengua general de todo el Peru llamada lengua Quichua o del Inca* [1608]. Lima.

Julien, Catherine J. 1982. "Inca Decimal Administration in the Lake Titicaca Region." In Collier et al. 1982: 119–51.

——. 1988. "How Inca Decimal Administration Worked." *Ethnohistory* 35 (1): 257–79.

——. 1993. "Finding a Fit: Archaeology and Ethnohistory of the Incas." In M. Malpass (ed.), *Provincial Inca: Archaeological and Ethnohistorical Assessment of the Impact of the Inca State*, 177–233. Iowa City.

——. 2000a. *Reading Inca History*. Iowa City.

——. 2000b. "El otro sentido de la palabra aymara durante el incanato." *Anales de la Reunión Annual de Etnología ... 1999*, I: 137–46. La Paz.

——. 2000c. *Los Incas*. Madrid.

——. 2003. "War and a Semblance of Peace in the Inca Heartland." In Paul Valentine and Catherine Julien (eds.), *War and Peace in Aboriginal South America*. Antropológica 99–100: 187–218.

——. Ms. *An Inca Information Network*.

Levillier, Roberto. 1940. *Don Francisco de Toledo, supremo organizador del Perú, su vida, su obra (1512–1582)*. 2 vols. Buenos Aires.

Murra, John V. 1986. "The Expansion of the Inca State: Armies, War, and Rebellions" [1978]. In J. Murra and N. Wachtel (eds.), *Anthropological History of Andean Polities*, 49–58. Cambridge.

Rostworowski de Diez Canseco, María. 1993. "Nuevos datos sobre tenencia de tierras reales en el incario." In *Ensayos de historia andina: elites, etnias, recursos*, 105–46. Lima.

Rowe, John Howland. 1946. "Inca Culture at the Time of the Spanish Conquest." In J. Steward (ed.), *Handbook of South American Indians*, 2: 183–330. Washington, DC.

——. 1982. "Inca Policies and Institutions Relating to the Cultural Unification of the Empire." In Collier et al. 1982: 93–118.

——. 1985. "Probanza de los Incas nietos de conquistadores." *Histórica* 9 (2): 193–245.

Sarmiento de Gamboa, Pedro de. 1906. *Geschichte des Inkareiches, von Pedro Sarmiento de Gamboa* [1572]. Ed. Richard Pietschmann. Abhandlungen der königlichen Gesellschaft der Wissenschaften zu Göttingen, philologisch-historische Klasse, n.s. 6, no. 4. Berlin.

20

The Long Peace Among Iroquois Nations

Neta C. Crawford

For three centuries, five and later six Native American nations who had previously engaged in violent and costly conflict forged a peaceful relationship known as the Iroquois League.[1] From about 1450 to 1777 CE the League, located in what is now upstate New York, functioned to reduce conflict among its members and eliminate war among them. Even upon its dissolution during the United States War of Independence, Iroquois League members agreed to dismantle their organization non-violently. North America in this period was far from peaceful; there were ample opportunities for these Native nations to return to violent conflict. How did these peoples forge and maintain their long peace?

The original five nations of the Iroquois League, whose members spoke distinct but closely related languages, were the Cayuga, Mohawk, Oneida, Onondaga, and Seneca. In 1600 they comprised a total population of perhaps one hundred thousand.[2] The Tuscarora nation joined the Iroquois League in about 1720. Some argue that the Iroquois nations were at the least fierce warriors, and possibly an imperialist alliance; on the other hand, some view the Iroquois as an almost saintly group of peaceful nations. The evidence suggests a much more complicated picture than either of these, and indeed, there are startling contradictions in the practices of Iroquois League members. The members of the Iroquois League and the League itself were genuinely democratic; on the other hand, individual members of the five nations were sometimes torturers and cannibals (they took war captives and sometimes ate those captives). In sum, the Iroquois League was both peaceful and violent, egalitarian and characterized by firm gender roles, oriented to the dream world and simultaneously acutely aware of and pragmatic in its dealings with the Dutch, British, French, and other Native American nations. The members of the Five Nations were as complex in their motives and behavior as any other society.

This brief description raises several questions. First, why did the Iroquois nations fight each other before the League's formation? Second, why did the five nations stop fighting each other? Did the fact that these nations were democracies have anything to do with the end of war among them? Third, how did the formation of the League change the pattern of conflict between the League and other Native American nations who were their neighbors, for instance the Algonquins or Hurons? Was the League a war-making alliance? If not originally conceived as a war-making alliance, did the League's existence allow its members to wage war against other nations because near neighbors were not hostile? Dorothy Jones suggests that the League was an "attempt to suppress in-group hostility and turn it outward" (Jones 1982: 23). Or was the League used to extend a regional peace by treaty? Fourth, how did relations among League members and their neighbors change after they came into contact with Europeans? Fifth, what caused the members of the League to resume antagonism after centuries of peace? Finally, what are the lessons of the League for scholars of war and peace?

I argue that the Iroquois nations stopped fighting each other and kept the peace among themselves by forming a "security regime."[3] Specifically, security regimes are principles, rules, and norms that permit nations to be more restrained in their behavior in the belief that others will reciprocate (Jervis 1983).[4] As a security regime the Iroquois League functioned well in decreasing conflict among its members. Further, because it was the basis for diplomacy and collective security, the League was partially successful in enabling the Iroquois nations to adapt to the shocks posed by the Europeans' arrival, that is, massive epidemics and depopulation, disruption of the local economy, and the wars between the Europeans.[5] And although the five and later six nations were not entirely pacific, the League became the foundation for a series of peaceful treaty relations among both Natives and Europeans in the region.

War Among the Five Nations before the Formation of the League

The Mohawk, Oneida, Onondaga, Cayuga, and Seneca nations were formed between 1000 and 1400 CE from "Owasco" peoples (Dennis 1993: 43–75; Snow 1994: 1–33). The myth about the founding of the League holds that war among the five nations was widespread before the formation of the League and archeological evidence supports this view (Dennis 1993: 50, 54). War as a result of boundary disputes appears to have been uncommon, although the Iroquois and other groups did have clear notions of territory and sovereignty (Tooker 1978a; Richter 1992: 32–38). The dominant form of pre-colonial warfare among those nations that would later form the Iroquois League is called "blood feud" or "mourning war" (Snyderman 1948/1978: 7; Wallace 1970: 44–48). Escalation of initially small feuds could lead to war: "Over a period of time ... a sequence of mutually vengeful killings could occur, involving an increasing number of members of the two groups, until finally there were so many unsettled scores left on both sides that a state of chronic 'war' could be said to exist, justifying an endless exchange of forays" (Wallace 1970: 44).

Iroquois families were obliged by tradition and religious belief to seek revenge, and often a replacement, for the death of a family member by either killing or capturing and adopting one of the enemy. This is one reason why warriors were praised for their ability to take captives. Iroquois League nations were not the only Native American nations to make use of this practice: capture by another group could lead to terrible physical abuse, especially for the males, who were forced to run through two rows of male members of the village who inflicted blows on them (running the gauntlet) and sometimes had one or more fingers cut off to mark them as adoptees and limit, at least for a time, their ability to use weapons against their captors. Some captives were killed, and parts of their bodies eaten if they did not meet with the satisfaction of their captors. Those who were chosen for adoption were apparently then treated with kindness and placed with their new families.[6] Daniel Richter notes: "The connection between war and mourning rested on beliefs about the spiritual power that animated all things" (Richter 1992: 32). Specifically,

> Because an individual's death diminished the collective power of a lineage, clan, and village, Iroquois families conducted "Requickening" ceremonies in which the deceased's name, and with it the social role and duties it represented, was transferred to a successor. Such rites filled vacant positions in lineages and villages both literally and symbolically: they assured survivors that the social function and spiritual potency embodied in the departed's name had not disappeared and that the community would endure. In Requickenings, people of high status were usually replaced from within ... but at some point lower in the social scale an external source of surrogates inevitably became necessary. Here warfare made its contribution, for those adopted to "help strengthen the familye in lew of their deceased Freind (sic)" were often captives taken in battle (Richter 1992: 32–33).

In a condition of constant feuding, and if escalation was not uncommon, there was a strong incentive for an end to the killing. The traditional account by native peoples of the League's formation traces it back to a period of intense warfare among the original five nations. Dekanawidah proposed the idea of a league to stop the inter-tribal warfare, and the League was negotiated over several years by Dekanawidah's spokesperson, Hiawatha (Parker 1916: 61–109).[7] In proposing the League and the rituals for "condolence," the founder of the League, Dekanawidah, and his spokesper-son Hiawatha provided an alternative to this form of war and a way to soothe those who were grieving. Thus, at least among the five nations of the League, it was no longer necessary to take captives to replace the dead because the condolence ritual of the League partly fulfilled this mourning function. At the same time the League itself strengthened the bonds between nations and reassured members of the peaceful intentions of other nations within the League.

The Formation of the League

It is difficult to establish precisely when the League of the five Iroquois nations was founded and this determination is related to the purpose of the confederation. Was it a reaction to European contact or a much older indigenous form of organization?

Some scholars believe that the League could only have been formed after Europeans appeared. For example, Peter Farb argues, "An impetus for Iroquois confederation more likely than any vision of a prophetic Dekanwidah may be traced to the first probings by French ships into the Gulf of St. Lawrence, early in the sixteenth century" (Farb 1978: 90). But most suggest the League was formed sometime in the fifteenth century, well before the arrival of Europeans.

Specifically, most accounts place the founding of the Iroquois League between 1000 and 1450 CE, and the weight of the evidence seems to argue for the later date. Arthur Parker and Francis Jennings suggest that the League was formed in 1390 (Parker 1916: 71; Jennings 1993: 77), while Anthony Wallace thinks it happened around 1450, "in a successful endeavor to revive an even more ancient but less formally constructed ethnic confederacy" (Wallace 1970: 41–42). Some Iroquois accounts place the founding of the League one or two generations before the Iroquois first came in contact with Europeans: the French explorer Cartier first encountered Mohawk along the Saint Lawrence in 1534–5 (Tooker 1978a: 420–21). As William Fenton argues, "It is certain, however, that the League was founded before European settlement, probably about 1500 CE give or take 25 years, although arguments for earlier and later dates abound" (Fenton 1985: 16). This would be consistent with archaeological evidence that suggests the founding of the League was "sometime in the late fifteenth century" (Richter 1992: 31). Further, Iroquois oral traditions recall that the final negotiations for the League occurred during a time of a solar eclipse, which would put the founding around 1451 (Tooker 1978a: 420).

In sum, it seems likely that the League of the Iroquois was formed well before the five original nations came into contact with European explorers and settlers, although as Fenton notes, it was "an evolving institution" (Fenton 1985: 16). The negotiations for the formation of the League were probably concluded around 1450, about 85 years before the Mohawks, in the League members' first direct contact with Europeans, met Cartier on the Saint Lawrence. The Seneca nation was the last of the original five nations to decide to join. It appears that other Native nations were asked to join the League upon its formation, notably the Cherokee, Erie, and Delaware, but they declined (Parker 1916: 79–80 and 96).

The "Great Law"

The institution of the League was codified in the Great Law of Peace (or the Great Binding Law) which, although certainly modified over the centuries, comes to modern scholars of the Iroquois through generations of Native oral historians. "Seen as an historical discourse, it is comprised of three main parts: (1) the myth of Deganawidah … ; (2) the legend of the conversion of local chiefs to the cause of peace; (3) the principles of the League – its internal structure and rituals" (Fenton 1985: 15). The narrative also provides a guide to its members on how to recall the Great Law accurately and commit it to memory. "Should two sons of opposite sides of the council fire agree in a desire to hear the reciting of the laws of the Great Peace and so refresh their memories in the way ordained by the founder of the Confederacy, one *sachem* (spokesperson) would be appointed to publicly recite the laws" (Parker 1916: 48).

The Great Law is a comprehensive document which includes the policies, proced- ures, philosophy, and mechanisms of amendment for the League. The main purposes of the League were to achieve general peace and to keep unity and order among the five nations who frequently fought each other before the League's formation. The image is of nations sitting together under a tree of peace. "I Dekanwidah (sic), and the Union Lords now uproot the tallest pine tree and into the cavity thereby made we cast all weapons of war ... We bury them from sight and we plant again the tree. Thus shall the Great Peace be established and hostilities shall no longer be known between the Five Nations but peace to the United People." Every five years the people should assemble and ask each other if they were still of the same mind, that is, if they were still united in the League: "If any of the Five Nations shall not pledge continuance and steadfastness to the pledge of unity then the Great Binding Law shall dissolve" (Parker 1916: 49).

The original members of the Iroquois League were concerned with peace among the five nations but also with threats from other Native nations. Thus, the League could also facilitate collective security. Dekanawidah, the League's founder, said: "We bind ourselves together by taking hold of each other's hands so firmly and forming a circle so strong that if a tree should fall upon it, it could not shake or break it, so that our people and our grandchildren shall remain in a circle in security, peace, and happiness" (quoted in Wallace 1970: 42). They also put a metaphorical eagle on top of the tree to look for threats to the peace from outside the League (Parker 1916: 30, 45). Relations with Native and later non-Native nations were regulated through a series of peace treaties, known as the Covenant Chain, but could also include war.

The League was not conceived as a union that would eliminate all differences between the original five nations, and the Great Law clearly states that the five nations were to be autonomous. Moreover, the rights of each nation, that is their cultural as well as political autonomy, were not to be changed by their membership in the League. "The rites and the festivals of each nation shall remain undisturbed and shall continue as before because they were given by the people of old times as useful and necessary" (Parker 1916: 56). An early eighteenth century observer, Cadwallader Colden, noted that "each of these Nations is an absolute Republick by itself, and every Castle in each Nation makes an independent Republick, and is governed in all publick Affairs by its own *Sachems* or old Men" (Colden 1747/1904: xvi).[8] Fenton argues that "each community had its local ways which it zealously maintained and defended," and notes, "this diversity ... continues to this day" (1985: 9). Historians agree that "each of these Five Nations retained full sovereignty over its own affairs" (Jennings 1985: 37). Each member of the League was free to make war or peace separately (Jennings 1984: 106).

The Great Law provides that all were welcome under the Tree of Peace if they were willing to abide by the laws of the League (Parker 1916: 30). A proposition to establish the "Great Peace" between the League and another nation would be made in councils between Iroquois and the other nation. But the language of the Great Law is unclear about the circumstances for an invitation to join the League and, in fact, the language seems rather bellicose. According to the Great Law, the other nation should be persuaded by reason to join and the request should be made several times if the other nation does not immediately agree to join the League. "If refusal steadfastly follows, the War Chief shall let the bunch of white lake shells drop from his outstretched hand to the ground and shall bound quickly forward and club the offending chief to death. War shall thereby be declared … War must continue until the contest is won by the Five Nations" (ibid. 54). When the League "has for its object the establishment of the Great Peace among the people of an outside nation and that nation refuses to accept the Great Peace, then by such refusal they bring a declaration of war upon themselves from the Five Nations. Then shall the Five Nations seek to establish the Great Peace by conquest of the rebellious nation" (ibid. 52). Once the war was over, the other nation should be disarmed and that nation would observe all the laws of the Great Peace "for all time to come" (ibid. 53).

The insistent, perhaps even militaristic quality of the Great Law's proposal to extend the peace is not clearly supported or refuted by League history. Was an invitation to join the League's alliances with other Native nations or to join the Covenant Chain made only if the outside nation had attacked an Iroquois nation or was an invitation made to neighboring nations as part of a policy of expansion? According to the law of the five nations, whether a nation joined the League of its own free will or as the result of conquest, it could continue its own system of internal government, and it was to be disarmed. The law also said these new nations "must cease all warfare against other nations" (Parker 1916: 53). Newly admitted nations were not to have a right to participate equally in the League councils. In addition, individuals were free to join and leave the individual nations of the League. The Great Law also provides for expelling those nations which do not follow the law of the five nations.

Both the individual member nations of the League and the League itself operated democratically. The League of the Iroquois included a body, the Great Council, for decision making among member nations. Each of the original five nations sent a number of "sachems" or spokespersons to the Great Council, for a total of fifty *sachems*. The *sachems* were to be above gossip and partisanship in order to keep the best interests of the nations in mind. "All their actions shall be marked by calm deliberation" (Parker 1916: 53). If a *sachem* was not performing well or in the best interest of the people, he was to be admonished three times and then he could be removed and replaced (ibid. 34–40). Cadwallader Colden confirms that these practices were still in place in the early eighteenth century: the *sachems* were "generally poorer than the common People" because they gave their wealth away and "every unworthy Action is unavoidably attended with the Forfeiture of their Commission; for their Authority is only the Esteem of the People, and ceases the Moment that Esteem is lost" (Colden 1747/1904: xvii).

Fenton argues that the *sachems* or chiefs "enjoyed great prestige but little power." He clarifies this by saying, "I use 'power' here in the sense of prestige translated into action. In Iroquois polity no one ordered any one else around. Issues were argued to consensus, and if agreement was not reached, the matter was dropped. Even when the chiefs had attained 'one mind', an appeal was made to the people, hoping they would agree" (Fenton 1985: 12, 33). There also seems to have been a clear separation of military and political authority: League *sachems* were not allowed to take part in warfare as leaders – there were separate military chiefs. In practice, the Iroquois nations conducted war and peace negotiations, as well as made alliances, as the collective League and as individual nations.

The League's Great Council met annually in the fall (or at other times when necessary) at Onondaga where they discussed alliance formation, peacemaking, and decided on major wars. Although the nations were formally equal and autonomous, the Great Law outlined different roles for each in decision making within the League council. The Onondaga were designated the keepers of the "fire" (meeting place) and the wampum bead records of the League. The Mohawk and the Seneca nations were known as the older brothers, and the Cayuga and Oneida were younger brothers. Decisions were reached by a series of caucuses: each "brotherhood" talked separately about an issue and came to consensus before consulting the other side. "First the question shall be passed to the Mohawk and Seneca Lords, then it shall be discussed and passed by the Oneida and Cayuga Lords. Their decisions shall then be referred to the Onondaga Lords (Fire Keepers) for final judgment" (Parker 1916: 32). Elisabeth Tooker reports that if the Onondaga received the opinions of the other four nations and disagreed, "they referred it back for further discussion; but in so doing, they had to show that the opinion of the other tribes was in conflict with established custom or with public policy" (Tooker 1978a: 429).[9] The decisions of the Great Council, even in times of great threat, were then to be confirmed by going back to the people of each nation (Parker 1916: 55). A nineteenth century observer, Asher Wright, noted:

> If any individual desired to bring any proposition before the general council, he must first gain the consent of his family, then his clan, next of the four related clans in his end of the council house, then of his nation, and thus in due course … the business would be brought up before the representatives of the confederacy. In the reverse order, the measures of the general council were sent down to the people for their approval. It was a standing rule that all action should be unanimous. Hence, the discussions were continued until all opposition was reasoned down, or the proposed measure was abandoned (quoted in Fenton 1985: 12–13).

Openness in discussing every matter, including war, may have been a problem at times in terms of gaining the element of surprise against the adversaries of the League. During a seventeenth century war with the French, a British envoy advised the Iroquois to "take one or two of your wisest *Sachems*, and one or two chief Captains of each Nation, to be a Council to manage all the affairs of the War. They are to give Orders to the rest of the Officers what they are to do, that your designs may be kept Private, for after it comes among so many People, it is Blazed abroad and your designs are often frustrated" (Colden 1964: 66–67).

The Council functioned as an information and communication center and as a decision making body. The League's members made decisions in the Great Council by consensus. In local matters of revenge warfare against non-league tribes, the Great Council of the League would sometimes remain silent and nations were allowed to make separate alliances with other nations. Other nations not formally in the League were consulted in accordance to their relationship or status with the League and made their views known through the *sachems* of their sponsor in the League (Wallace 1946: 42). Formal allies were talked with as equals, and hopefully persuaded by League oratory. When allies were not persuaded, the League apparently assented to their right to hold a different position.

When the Tuscarora joined the League they were admitted as a junior member, without a formal seat at the fire of the Great Council: Tuscarora chiefs were not made *sachems* and the total number of *sachems* was kept at fifty. They were treated as *de facto* equals by the other five nations and were able to make their views known through their sponsors, the Oneida (Morgan 1851/1901: 93–94; Wallace 1946: 42; Landy 1978: 519; Fenton 1985: 9). On the other hand, apparently, the Tuscarora did not always follow League Council decisions (Boyce 1987: 158–59).

After the League's formation, the evidence of the continuing existence of the League suggests that war among the five and later six nations significantly declined or was entirely eliminated. There is no mention by historians of war among League members after the formation of the League, although there was some fighting, "a quarrel," among Mohawks, Senecas, and Onondagas over captives taken in a war against the Hurons in the 1650s (Snyderman 1948/1978: 14; Richter 1992: 65). Also, to be clear, the increasingly fluid residence patterns in the villages of Native American nations meant that some members of the League nations resided in the villages of other nations and vice versa (White 1991). So, for example, it is entirely possible that Seneca peoples, who made their residence with the Illinois, would join the Illinois in wars against one of the five/six nations. In addition, during the wars on the frontier between the French and British, members of the League sometimes took different sides.[10] But there was no war among the member nations of the League between its formation and its dissolution about 300 years later. Thus, the League functioned well as a security regime.

> A number of generations – no one knows certainly how many – went by before the Five Nations solved most of the problems of keeping their League united. By the time of the English conquest of New Netherland in 1664, the Five Nations had ceased to fight against each other, and they acted as a unit for defense though internal strains continued throughout the League's existence (Jennings 1984: 8).

But if organized war among the members of the League halted, what was the pattern of warfare between League and non-League nations? The next section surveys the complex history of Iroquois war from about 1535 to 1777 and demonstrates that while the Iroquois League nations were not fighting each other, they were often at war with Native and European neighbors. Iroquois war cannot be understood outside the context of the pattern of economic and political relations among Native and European nations in North America.

Character of Wars and Treaties after Contact with Europeans

The pattern and scale of Iroquois war appear to have changed dramatically soon after the first Europeans began to settle in the northeast and trade with the Iroquois and other nations. There is little doubt that prior to contact with Europeans the Iroquois nations fought with their neighbors: evidence includes the fact that the institution of war chiefs was intact and the larger settlements of the Iroquois nations consisted of 30–150 longhouses surrounded by wooden fortifications that Europeans would later describe as "castles" or palisades. The Iroquois also had a fierce reputation. But, whereas native war before contact with Europeans primarily consisted of blood feuds and territorial skirmishes, several new motives and pressures for war were introduced with the European presence.

First, with the Europeans came the epidemic diseases that led to a dramatic decline in Native American populations; the Iroquois increasingly resorted to war to boost their population by "adopting" war captives. "The thousands of deaths from disease led women to demand continual mourning-wars and inspired young men to seize even more captives to requicken the dead" (Richter 1992: 60; also Colden 1964: 8; Wright 1992: 123–24). For example, Richter notes that some of the Iroquois went to war against Native nations in the Carolinas after a small pox epidemic in 1679, and observers in the mid-1600s believed that as many as two-thirds of the people in some Iroquois villages were adoptees (ibid. 65–66, 145).

Second, the fur trade changed the international relations of Native nations in important ways: those nations with access to the fur trade also had access to European weapons, and often allied with a European power. Added firepower also altered the balance of power among native nations. And third, European settlers increasingly encroached on Iroquois land. So, with European settlement of the northeast, the Iroquois began to fight for access to trade goods, to retain their influence in the region among other Native groups and between themselves and the Europeans, and to protect their land from encroachment by the settlers and traders. Often the several reasons for war (desire for captives, access to the fur trade, and control of territory) were intertwined.

From the 1600s to the late 1700s, the Iroquois League members were frequently at war with the other native nations, the British, French, and later, the young United States. Relations with the Dutch, who occupied New Netherland from 1614 to the mid 1700s, were much less antagonistic, and almost entirely focused on trade (Dennis 1993: 119–79). The wars and treaties involving League nations during these years number in the dozens, and no single source has a comprehensive summary of both treaties and wars. Apart from League treaties, the five and six Iroquois nations also made separate treaties with other Native American nations and the Europeans. While it is impossible to discuss all the wars, treaties and alliances of these centuries here, tables 20.1 and 20.2 illustrate the main wars and treaties of select periods.

The "Beaver Wars"

The fur trade began almost as soon as the Europeans began their exploration of the Northeast. French, Dutch, and English colonials were involved in the trade, which entailed Native Americans bringing beaver pelts and other furs to European traders

Table 20.1 The Iroquois Nations' Involvement in War, 1600–1783[11]

1609–27	French (Champlain) allied with Algonquin, Huron and Montagnais attacked Iroquois in an attempt to drive them from the St. Lawrence River valley
1610	French attacked Mohawk
1610s	Mohawk and other Iroquois raids for fur and prisoners against Algonquin and Huron
1615	French attacked Onondaga
1624–8	Mohawk war against the Mohicans in the Hudson Valley area for access to Dutch Fort Orange
1643	Dutch-Mohawk alliance against Wappingers in the lower Hudson Valley
1642–57	French-Iroquois wars
1648–9	Five nations united to attack the Huron Confederacy, who were allied with the French
1650	Petun (Huron Confederacy) defeated and dispersed by Iroquois
1651	Neutrals (Huron Confederacy) defeated and dispersed by Iroquois
1657	Eries (Huron Confederacy) defeated and dispersed by Iroquois
1660	Mohawk war against Mohicans
1663–4	Mohawk war with Algonquins and Abenakis
1663	War by Onondagas, Cayugas, Senecas and Oneidas with Susquehannocks who were trading with Dutch and English
1664	Dutch-Mohawk alliance against the Esopus along the Hudson – ended Esopus' resistance to the Dutch
1665–7	French-Iroquois wars: Louis the XIV gave the order to exterminate Iroquois. Iroquois allied with English
1675–7	Mohawk allied with English colonials to defeat Algonquin attacks on colonies (King Phillip's/Metacomet's War)
1676	Iroquois wars in the west with Illinois, Miamis, Foxes, Ojibwas, Wyandots, and Ottowas for fur trade and captives
1684–9	French-Iroquois wars. English incited the Iroquois to disrupt the French fur trade on the Great Lakes
1687	French attacked Iroquois; the Iroquois counterattacked in 1689, killing 200 French Canadians
1689–97	King William's War: French attacked British and Natives (Part of European War of the Grand Alliance). Iroquois and English fought French and their Native allies
1711–3	Tuscarora attacked colonial settlements in New Bern (North Carolina), killing 140; settlers and Native allies retaliated 1712–3, killing 1010 Tuscarora. The Tuscarora fled north to New York and joined the League
1754–63	French-British territorial conflict; in 1759, 1,000 Iroquois assisted 2,200 British and colonial troops, to besiege and defeat the French at Niagara
1763–5	Pontiac's War: Ottowas, Hurons, Chippewas, Kickapoos and Seneca allied to push the British back; 1763, 300 Senecas ambushed a British wagon train
1775–83	Revolutionary War: Oneidas and Tuscarora with the US; Mohawk, Cayuga, Seneca, and Onondaga allied with the British

Table 20.2 Selected Iroquois Nations Treaties and Conferences, 1624–1701[12]

1624	Treaty for trade between Iroquois and New France
1633	Treaty for trade between Iroquois and New France
1634	Mohawk truce with native Nations in Canada
1643	Treaty of trade between Mohawks and Dutch
1645	Three Rivers Treaty between Mohawk, French, Algonquins, and Hurons
1645	Treaty between Dutch and Mohawks and Mohicans
1653	Five Nations made separate treaties with French
1657/1658	Treaty relations between Onondaga, Oneida, Cayuga, and Seneca with Dutch
1659	Dutch and Mohawk renewed an earlier, 1644, alliance
1664	Treaty of friendship, trade, and mutual aid between Mohawks, Senecas, and English
1665–7	Iroquois nations signed treaties (Mohawk last) with the French
1675	New York's Governor Andros renewed English protection of Mohawks and Mohicans
1677	Two Covenant Chain Treaties negotiated: April and May between New York, Massachusetts, Connecticut with Iroquois and Hudson River Nations; July and August between New York, Maryland, and Virginia to halt their war with the Five Nations and Susquehannocks
1679	Treaty between Five Nations and New York, Maryland, and Virginia
1682	Treaty for Peace between Five Nations and Maryland
1682	Negotiations between French and the Five Nations at Montreal
1684	Five Nations treaty with New York and Virginia; English claimed they were sovereign over the Iroquois while the Iroquois said they were free
1684	New France joined the Covenant Chain but France rejected the agreement
1685	Piscataway Indians of Maryland joined the Covenant Chain
1686	New York renewed the Covenant Chain
1687	French declared their sovereignty over the Iroquois after destroying some Seneca villages
1688	Onondaga, Cayuga, and Oneida met French at Montreal, proclaimed their sovereignty and said they were neutral between the French and British
1689	Covenant Chain renewed between Connecticut and Mohawks
1689	Abenakis and the Mohawks met: the Iroquois rejected a proposal for an alliance to fight against the English
1689	Seneca peace treaty with Ottowas; in January 1690 the treaty was confirmed by the entire League
1692	Shawnees joined the Covenant Chain after the New York government said they could resettle there
1693	Covenant Chain renewed with Governor of New York. Earlier in the year, New York pursued French who had attacked and destroyed three Mohawk villages
1694	Three meetings between Five Nations and English over the Iroquois discussions with the French, which the English disapproved of
1697	Treaty between England and France, but the war continued between French Indian allies and the Iroquois

Continued

Table 20.2 *Continued*

1698	June–August, Iroquois and French conferences where the Iroquois proposed peace
1699–1700	The New York Government pleaded with the Five Nations, in April 1699 and August 1700 not to negotiate with the French. The Iroquois continued negotiations
1701	After many meetings, the Iroquois and the French confirmed a peace treaty and their neutrality between French and British; neutrality reconfirmed in 1703

in exchange for European goods, including weapons. To the South and East, trade with the Dutch appears to have been mutually profitable and relations with the Dutch were relatively peaceful. But to the North, members of the Iroquois League appear to have been at first locked out of the fur trade with the French because the Algonquins, Huron, and Montagnais, who made the initial contact with the Europeans, were attempting to secure a monopoly (Trigger 1978b: 346). But later it is clear that the Iroquois went to war in the late sixteenth century to plunder and to break the exclusive control over trade held by the other Native nations.

Meanwhile the Algonquin, Montagnais, and Huron nations formed various alliances among themselves, and later with the French, to protect their trade monopoly. In some instances, New France directly joined in the conflict among Native nations over access to trade, for example in 1609 when Champlain and his Native allies defeated a Mohawk party of over 300 warriors and in the following year killed nearly 100 Mohawk warriors (Trigger 1978b: 349; Hurley 1985: 112). Jennings argues that "the long antagonism between the French and the Five Nations was created by the French, not by the Iroquois, as a deliberate implementation of a divide and conquer strategy. Every effort by the Iroquois at reconciliation was rebuffed or evaded until finally they exploded" (Jennings 1984: 87). The entire French population of New France in 1650 was about 2,000 people, dispersed in scattered settlements (ibid. 85). With so few French in the New World, the French policies of alliance with Native nations, and also the practice of miscegenation and adoption of Native peoples, makes strategic sense.

The fur trade also caused increased tension among Iroquois League nations. For example, Bruce Trigger argues (1978b: 350) that after 1650 the Mohawk became more "arrogant in their dealings with the other tribes of the confederacy, who needed their permission to pass through the Mohawk River valley to trade with the Dutch." There were also divisions among the five nations over access to trade with the English through Mohawk territory, and conflicts between the Mohawk and Onondaga, and between the Seneca and Onondaga over relationships with the French in 1656 (ibid. 355; Snyderman 1948/1978: 25–26). Tooker notes (1978b: 430) that the existence of the League "did not mean that each tribe ceased to pursue its own national interests as some have supposed." Rather,

> Each tribe continued to seek a policy that would give it advantage in the fur trade,… establishing new or renewing old trade relationships if that course of action seemed

profitable and, as the Great Peace established by the League extended only to its members, going to war if success there promised some advantage.

Regardless of tensions over the fur trade, the Iroquois certainly faced a more dire threat from the French than from each other. In 1642 the Iroquois approached the French at Three Rivers in order to establish trade and peace. They were rejected in their three attempts (Wallace 1946: 89–90; Jennings 1984: 48–50). In 1664, Louis XIV sent an order to French troops to "totally exterminate" the Iroquois.[13] The French extermination program became unnecessary when four of five nations of the Iroquois submitted to a treaty with the French in December 1665. The Mohawk, who did not sign immediately, made an agreement with the French in June 1666; despite the agreement, the French commander found an excuse to burn Mohawk villages and farms in October (Jennings 1984: 131–32). J. D. Hurley argues (1985: 161) that "The peace ... secured by the treaties of 1665–7 ... was never really more than a truce of convenience. Underlying this 'peace', the basic cause of Franco-Iroquois warfare remained: competition for exclusive control of the Great Lakes fur trade."

The Iroquois nations were a buffer between the British and the French. New York's first secretary of Indian Affairs, Robert Livingston, wrote in May 1701: "Of the Five [Iroquois] Nations, I need not enumerate the advantages arising from their firmness to this government [of New York], they having fought our battles for us and been a constant barrier of defence between Virginia and Maryland and the French, and by their constant vigilence have prevented the French from making any descent that way" (quoted in Jennings 1984: xvi). In 1754 British commissioners for trade clearly noted:

> The preserving and securing the friendship of these Indians is in the present situation of affairs an object of the greatest importance ... It is from the steady adherence of these Indians to the British Interests that not only New York but all the other Northern Colonys have hitherto been secured from the fatal effects of the encroachments of a foreign power, and without their friendship and assistance all efforts to check and disappoint the present view of this power may prove ineffectual (quoted in Jones 1982: 29).

Diplomacy, Alliance, and Collective Security

While individual member nations of the League conducted separate diplomacy with other Native nations and the colonizers, the League itself became the basis for Iroquois diplomacy with both Native and European Nations in the seventeenth century. Mathew Dennis argues that, through their diplomacy, the Iroquois sought to bring the European nations into a peaceful relationship based on the notion of Iroquois kinship with Europeans (Dennis 1993). But, whatever the Iroquois League's grand design, the conduct of diplomacy was complex and expansive in geographic character. The popular notion that the Iroquois managed a vast empire may be due in part to the fact that League *sachems* sometimes spoke for other Native nations in negotiations with Europeans, as for instance when they spoke up for the Tuscarora in 1713 (Boyce 1987: 155). The Iroquois also involved Europeans in their diplomacy: at least twice in the 1600s the League asked the Dutch to mediate for them with the French (Dennis 1993: 170 and 247).

In addition the Iroquois League managed a complex system of alliances, the "Covenant Chain," beginning in 1677 with two treaties negotiated at Albany between the Iroquois, Delaware, and the colonies of New York, Connecticut, Massachusetts, Maryland, and Virginia. Jennings argues (1984: xvii–xviii): "The Chain is the reason there was peace between colonies and tribes in the 'middle colonial' region during the long period from 1677–1755."

> The Chain organized trade between Indians and colonials over a vast region ... It recruited warriors in joint struggles of Indians and English colonials to conquer New France. It organized systematic retreats of Indians from defeats in New England and southern colonies into sanctuaries in New York, Pennsylvania, and Iroquoia. Chain negotiations covered the peaceful retreat of Indians from eastern Pennsylvania to the Ohio region beyond the Appalachians. And Chain arrangements opened the west to English settlement. The Chain's arrangements, rather than incessant ferocious war, explain how the Iroquois achieved leadership and occasionally the power of command over other tribes.

Alliances also existed between the Iroquois nations and many other Native nations. These agreements varied between those among equals, as in the case of the Delaware-Iroquois alliance, and those where Native nations, for example the Susqehannock, were under the "protection" of the Iroquois (Jennings 1985: 41). In some cases, especially later in the eighteenth century, it appears that the Iroquois exaggerated their ability to speak for other Native nations bound to the Chain, perhaps to increase their leverage in negotiations with the British (Jones 1982: 34; Jennings 1984: 8; Druke 1987: 32). Several nations that fled the advancing European colonists were treated as "brothers," "cousins," or "nephews" by the League. Europeans called these nations "tributaries" of the League, although Jennings argues that the relationship of these other Native nations to the Iroquois was more reciprocal. "No general rule can be applied, but duality or reciprocity was the principle operating throughout Iroquois political structures; what Europeans called tributaries were known by the Iroquois as *bretheren, cousins,* or *nephews* – statuses that involved Iroquois responsibilities as well as privileges" (Jennings 1984: 8).

The League also began increasingly to function for collective security. For example, even while they made agreements with the colonists the Iroquois debated among themselves and with other Native American groups about whether to throw the English out of the northeast by force. In 1726 the Iroquois, disturbed by the increasing loss of their territory through sale or seizure, proposed that all Indians fight both the British and the French to prevent them from taking all the Native American lands (Jennings 1985: 42–43). Later, in 1761 and again in 1763, the Seneca tried to organize a war against the Europeans, Pontiac's Conspiracy (Wallace 1970: 114–15). In neither period were the Iroquois able to convince all the nations they invited to join for war against the colonists. On the first occasion, in 1726, they were unsuccessful in getting their neighbors to mount any action against the colonists. On the second occasion, the allied Native nations attacked the English in Detroit, Fort Pitt, Niagara, and elsewhere, but despite short-term gains, were ultimately unsuccessful.

Dissolution During the War of Independence

He [King George] has excited domestic insurrections among us, and has endeavoured to bring on the inhabitants of our frontiers, the merciless Indian Savages, whose known rule of warfare is an undistinguished destruction of all ages, sexes and conditions (United States "Declaration of Independence," July 4, 1776).

The British and the colonists each worked hard to keep the Iroquois on their side during the colonial rebellion that became the War of Independence. In 1775, the Continental Congress sent a delegation to the Iroquois in Albany to ask for their neutrality in the coming war against the British while, on the other side, the British argued that the colonists were essentially naughty children. The Iroquois agreed to be neutral on the condition that their hunters be allowed free passage during the war and that actions be limited to the coast. There was some involvement of small groups of Iroquois warriors on both sides, but for the most part the Iroquois kept a low profile. In late 1775, a Mohawk person was killed by a Continental soldier and the next year other Mohawk warriors joined the British against the rebels. In the next two years the neutrality policy gradually disintegrated as both sides exhorted the Iroquois to take up arms for their respective causes.

In 1777 the Six Nations disagreed about their role in the American Revolution. The Oneida and Tuscarora decided to support the continental rebels while the rest of the League, Onondaga, Cayuga, Mohawk and Seneca supported the British in large numbers on the condition that Iroquois land claims be adjudicated (Wallace 1970: 149–83; Tooker 1978a: 434–5). The disagreement resulted in the League "putting out the fire" in Onondaga and dividing the wampum records of their agreements between the two sides. Iroquois nation met Iroquois nation on August 8, 1777 in battle for the first time in more than 300 years at Oriskany, New York (Jennings 1993: 301).

The Iroquois nations that fought for the British did well, and in some battles the Iroquois fielded more troops and suffered more casualties than the red coats. At the battle in Oriskany, ninety-one Iroquois and 33 British died on the British side; at Wyoming Valley on July 3, 1778 the Iroquois fielded 500 combatants, the British 400; at Cherry Valley on November 11, 1778 the Iroquois provided 500 warriors and the British sent 200 (Clodfelter 1992: 199–200).

General Washington, clearly distressed by their role, urged that the Iroquois allied with the British be "destroyed" (quoted in Wright 1992: 139), and part of the Continental army attempted to do just that. Wright notes, "In 1779, General John Sullivan cut down orchards and crops, burning 500 [Iroquois] houses and nearly a million bushels of corn. Colonel Daniel Brodhead, in an infamous attack that became known as the 'squaw campaign', dodged Indian armies but slaughtered women and children" (ibid.). Despite the Continental Army's efforts, in 1781 the Governor of New York had to admit to the Congress that the Iroquois deprived them of "a great portion of our most valuable and well inhabited territory" (ibid.; see also Mann 2005; Williams 2005).

At the conclusion of the war, the Continental army claimed that it also defeated the Native nations that backed the British, and no provisions for the Iroquois were made in the 1783 Treaty of Paris. The young United States' colonies crowded the individual Iroquois nations in a westward expansion, acquiring Iroquois land by various means including treaties, purchase, swindle, and force (Wallace 1970: 141–48). The Iroquois were gradually confined to reservations in New York, Canada, Wisconsin, and Oklahoma. The League was renewed in the late eighteenth century at both Six Nations Reserve in Canada and on the Buffalo Creek Reservation in upstate New York and continues to operate in both the US and Canada (Tooker 1978b: 449–65).

In sum, what should be clear from this short history of Iroquois war after the arrival of European traders is that the severity and probably the frequency of war and diplomacy changed dramatically because of the desire to replace those lost to epidemics and because of the new mix of motives introduced by the European – Native American fur trade. Despite opportunities for the League of the Iroquois to fall apart as a security regime, it remained intact. Individual members of the League were threatened by the increased strength of their neighbors and those nations' direct alliance with the French, who also worked to dissolve the League. The Iroquois responded to these pressures with both insistent diplomatic efforts and by taking up arms against both the French and their Native trading partners. The Iroquois League members' relationship with the Dutch and later the British was less overtly conflictual and quite advantageous to the British. What is interesting is the fact that the League did not dissolve under these pressures, despite the fact that there were differences between League members over relations with the Europeans.

The Iroquois League as a Security Regime

The League of the Iroquois worked to maintain the peace between its member nations for over three centuries, even in the face of strong outside pressures, and despite the fact that individual League members occasionally disagreed with each other and set policies that were sometimes directly opposite each other. League resilience is in stark contrast to relations among other Native nations, including the Iroquois' adversaries, who, under the pressures of European contact sometimes turned upon each other or even disintegrated internally. How did the members of the League keep the peace?

Further, the Iroquois frequently fought Native and European nations during the period considered here (c. 1450–1777 CE). Was the League thus really less a security regime and more an alliance for war-making? Snyderman argues that the original and most important function of the League, as a security regime among five powerful neighbors, gradually evolved into a war-making alliance: "The League was established to arbitrate quarrels among its members ... It was therefore established to promote peace. However, it freed its members from fear and danger of a rear attack and allowed them to devote their individual attention to a single enemy ... The League itself organized for peace became an instrument of war" (Snyderman 1948/1978: 78; also, Morgan 1851/1901: 8). But this interpretation, though plausible, does not quite fit the evidence and also confuses the League with its individual members. The League did offer its members a sense of security about their relations toward each other and foster peace – that was its explicit and intended function. It was the individual members, in nearly all cases, that went to war, not the entire League membership or large coalitions of League members. The evidence of a continuing debate among League members over whom to support in the conflicts between British and French and later between the British and the American Revolutionaries, as well as the practice of individual nations fighting wars of defense and offense apart from the League indicates that the League was not a war-making instrument. Perhaps if the Iroquois had been a war-making alliance, successful European colonization would have been delayed. It was only with Pontiac's Rebellion in the 1760s, that the Iroquois tried to rid North America of, from their perspective, the lying, cheating, land-grabbing Europeans. Instead, the Iroquois League biased the foreign policy of the five nations toward diplomacy and peace negotiations with the Europeans, despite the Iroquois' numeric advantage during much of this period. Thus they hoped to secure Iroquois lands and the benefits of trade, "for Trade & Peace we take to be one thing."[14] Meanwhile the French and the Americans openly spoke of destroying the League and made attempts to do so.

The evidence suggests that the Iroquois League was a robust security regime among the five and later six independent Native nations. The theory is that security regimes should reduce conflict between sovereign states by decreasing the uncertainty and distrust characteristic of the "security dilemma" where what one state does to enhance its security may be seen as a threat to another state. Security regimes, as rules, norms, and decision-making procedures agreed to by all parties, thus are able to mitigate the effects of international anarchy – the lack of an overarching sovereign to keep peace and enforce international agreements. Security regimes facilitate communication, negotiation, and coordination among participants, and thus function to reduce information and transaction costs. As antagonism decreases and trust grows, the security regime may become a pluralistic security community, where a larger sense of common identity and purpose develops even as members retain their political autonomy. The European Union is an example of such a security community.

There is some debate among scholars of international relations about the origins of security regimes. Realist theories suggest that security regimes, if they are formed at all, are imposed by hegemons (dominant states) or that regimes will only form if the interests of all actors converge. Liberal idealists suggest that regimes form when actors renounce short-term self-interest and seek to promote their long-term interest in peace and security. Specifically, Jervis argues that security regimes form when states believe that war is costly and that expansion is not the route to security. Janice Stein agrees (1985: 615): security regimes are likely to form when "leaders … see war as unattractive, with damaging and undesirable consequences. They are likely to do so in the aftermath of protracted, or costly, or indecisive war which failed to achieve its minimum objectives even as it disrupted the economic and social fabric of domestic society." But, as Joseph Nye argues (1987: 375, 377), "If cooperation can be explained on the basis of short-run self-interests, such as avoiding the disproportionate costs of … war, then regimes become a redundant explanation." Limited "cooperation can be based on risk aversion without requiring agreement on the long-term course of history." The Iroquois League suggests that security regimes may form without hegemons and out of a common history.

Once formed, how do security regimes work to maintain peace? Do security regimes change the power relations among states (the structure of international politics), the perception of interests of participants, or conceptions of "identity" within and among regime members? At least in the case of the Iroquois League, all those factors worked to maintain the peace.

What conditions foster the maintenance of security regimes? Is institutionalization a virtue or a hindrance? Does the inertia of habit and "sunk cost" better explain the duration of security regimes (Stein 1985: 610)? In the case of the long peace among the Iroquois, the fact that the League was both highly institutionalized yet flexible facilitated its long duration and eventual reconstitution. Indeed, compared to other security regimes, such as the Concert of Europe, the Iroquois League was highly institutionalized (Crawford 1994). Further, the belief system of the Native nations that comprised the League – its emphasis on peacemaking and consensus building – helped foster long-term stability and commitment.

This leads to the question of whether security regimes that are composed entirely of democracies are more successful than those that contain non-democracies. It appears that security regimes composed entirely of democracies may be more successful than those that consist of non-democracies or are mixed. For example, the Concert of Europe, a security regime which lasted from roughly 1815 to 1914, was composed of both democratic and non-democratic states, and was a much weaker security regime (Jervis 1983; Crawford 1994). The individual nations of the League, and the League itself were extremely democratic, especially in comparison to their European counterparts of the era. Voting rights were universal, regardless of gender or property holding status. There was a separation of civil and military authority. Broad civil and economic rights were in effect. Decisions within nations and among members of the League were taken after public deliberation and consensus building. Indeed, in many respects the League resembles the Kantian ideal of perpetual peace among democratic states (Kant 1983).

Most theories of international relations are based on a reading of relatively recent European history – the past 500 years or so.[15] They are suspicious of the possibility of a long peace among nations that is not based on a balance of power. Yet, an examination of the long peace among the Iroquois suggests that realist claims to cross-cultural and timeless validity – for instance, Hans Morgenthau's first principle of political realism that "politics, like society, is governed by objective laws that have their roots in human nature … and [that nature] has not changed" in thousands of years (1985: 4) – are at best premature.

Notes

1 Although I use it throughout, the word "Iroquois" is not indigenous. Iroquois people called themselves the People of the Long House or Houdenosaunee (Ho-De'-No-Sau-Nee) in the Seneca language. The League of the Iroquois was also called the Five Nations (or the Six Nations, depending on the period in question) or the Confederacy of the Five

Nations (or Six Nations). Because there were several confederacies (e.g. the Illinois and Delaware confederacies) of Native American peoples during and after the exploration and conquest of North America by Europeans and the United States, I usually refer to the Iroquois nations' organization as the League.

2 Rough estimate based on figures in Trigger 1985: 231–41. On problems in estimating Native populations, see Denevan 1992.

3 For a more theoretically oriented discussion and a comparison of the League to the nineteenth century Concert of Europe, see Crawford 1994.

4 Also see Stein 1985; Nye 1987; and Smith 1989.

5 The Iroquois League exemplifies aspects of Kant's idea of a system for perpetual peace. The fact that the Iroquois League was composed of participatory democracies is not coincidental to its success as a security regime: members were inclined, because they were democracies, to use negotiation and consultation to resolve disputes. While much recent international relations scholarship has examined the "zone of peace" among democracies, few have paid attention to Kant's idea of a *league* of peace, of which the Iroquois League is an excellent example. *Perpetual Peace* was published in 1795, and to this day, many consider it a utopian document. Ironically, several thousand miles from autocratic Prussia, such a system had already arisen, endured for over 300 years, and fallen before Kant's essay was published.

6 For a vivid description of the fate of captives, see White 1991: 3–6.

7 Of the several translations of the Great Law made in the nineteenth and twentieth centuries I use the translation by Parker, *The Constitution of the Five Nations* (1916), which appears to be the most widely used version.

8 Colden was reprinted, incorporating both volumes in one, in 1964. Quotes are from the earlier edition, unless indicated by Cornell in parentheses.

9 Wallace (1946: 33, 37) reports yet another order, but also emphasizes the consensus orientation of the caucusing procedure. Also see Dennis 1993: 95.

10 On residence patterns see White 1991.

11 Sources: Hunt 1940; Trigger 1978b; Aquila 1983; Dupuy and Dupuy 1985; White 1991; Clodfelter 1992; Richter 1992.

12 Sources: primarily relies on the "Descriptive Treaty Calendar" in Jennings, Fenton, and Druke 1985b, covering League treaties, conferences and councils from 1613 to 1919.

13 Louis XIV's instructions to the French commander are quoted in Jennings 1984: 131. Also see Dennis 1993: 215, 217.

14 Iroquois spokesperson in 1735, quoted in Fenton 1985: 13.

15 Exceptions among international relations scholars include: Ember, Ember, and Russett 1992; Ross 1993; Russett 1993.

References

Aquila, R. 1983. *The Iroquois Restoration: Iroquois Diplomacy on the Colonial Frontier, 1701–1754*. Detroit.

Bedford, D., and T. Workman. 1997. "The Great Law of Peace: Alternative Inter-Nation(al) Practices and the Iroquoian Confederacy." *Alternatives* 22: 87–111.

Boyce, D. W. 1987. "As the Wind Scatters the Smoke: The Tuscaroras in the Eighteenth Century." In Richter and Merrell 1987: 151–163.

Clodfelter, M. 1992. *Warfare and Armed Conflicts: A Statistical Reference to Casualties and Other Figures, 1618–1991*. Jefferson.

Colden, C. 1747/1904. *The History of the Five Indian Nations of Canada which are Dependent on the Province of New York, and are a Barrier Between the English and the French in that Part of the World.* Vols. 1 and 2. New York.

——. 1964. *The History of the Five Indian Nations Depending on the Province of New York in America.* Ithaca.

Crawford, N. C. 1994. "A Security Regime Among Democracies: Cooperation Among Iroquois Nations." *International Organization* 48: 345–85.

Denevan, M. W. (ed.). 1992. *The Native Population in the Americas in 1492.* Second edition. Madison.

Dennis, M. 1993. *Cultivating a Landscape of Peace: Iroquois – European Encounters in Seventeenth-Century America.* Ithaca.

Druke, M. A. 1987. "Linking Arms: The Structure of Iroquois Intertribal Diplomacy." In Richter and Merrell 1987: 29–39.

Dupuy, R. E., and T. N. Dupuy. 1985. *The Encyclopedia of Military History.* Revised second edition. New York.

Ember, C. R., M. Ember, and B. Russett. 1992. "Peace Between Participatory Polities: A Cross-Cultural Test of the 'Democracies Rarely Fight Each Other' Hypothesis." *World Politics* 44: 573–99.

Farb, P. 1978. *Man's Rise to Civilization: The Cultural Ascent of the Indians of North America.* Second edition. New York.

Fenton, W. N. 1985. "Structure, Continuity, and Change in the Process of Iroquois Treaty Making." In Jennings, Fenton, and Druke 1985a: 3–36.

Hunt, G. T. 1940. *The Wars of the Iroquois: A Study in Intertribal Trade Relations.* Madison.

Hurley, J. D. 1985. *Children or Brethren: Aboriginal Rights in Colonial Iroquoia.* Saskatoon.

Jennings, F. 1984. *The Ambiguous Iroquois Empire: The Covenant Chain Confederation of Indian Tribes with English Colonies.* New York.

——. 1985. "Iroquois Alliances in American History." In Jennings, Fenton, and Druke 1985a: 37–65.

——. 1993. *The Founders of America: How Indians Discovered The Land, Pioneered In It, And Created Great Classical Civilizations; How They Were Plunged Into A Dark Age By Invasion and Conquest; And How They Are Reviving.* New York.

——, W. N. Fenton, and M. A. Druke (eds.). 1985a. *The History and Culture of Iroquois Diplomacy: An Interdisciplinary Guide to the Treaties of the Six Nations and their League.* Syracuse.

——, W. N. Fenton, and M. A. Druke. 1985b. "Descriptive Treaty Calendar." In Jennings, Fenton, and Druke 1985a: 157–208.

Jervis, R. 1983. "Security Regimes." In S. D. Krasner (ed.), *International Regimes,* 173–194. Ithaca.

Jones, D. V. 1982. *License for Empire: Colonialism by Treaty in Early America.* Chicago.

Kant, I. 1983. "To Perpetual Peace: A Philosophical Sketch." In I. Kant (ed.), *Perpetual Peace and Other Essays on Politics, History, and Morals,* 107–43, Indianapolis.

Landy, D. 1978. "Tuscarora among the Iroquois." In Trigger 1978a: 518–24.

Mann, B. A. 2005. *George Washington's War on Native America.* Westport.

Morgan, L. H. 1851/1901. *League of the Ho-Dé-No-Sau-Nee or Iroquois.* Vols. 1 and 2. New York.

Morgenthau, H. 1985. *Politics among Nations: The Struggle for Power and Peace.* Sixth edition. New York.

Nye, J. S. 1987. "Nuclear Learning and U.S. – Soviet Security Regimes." *International Organization* 41: 371–402.

Parker, A. C. 1916. *The Constitution of the Five Nations or the Iroquois Book of the Great Law.* Albany.

Richter, D. K. 1992. *The Ordeal of the Longhouse: The Peoples of the Iroquois League in the Era of European Colonization.* Chapel Hill.

——, and J. H. Merrell. 1987. *Beyond the Covenant Chain: The Iroquois and Their Neighbors in Indian North America, 1600–1800.* Syracuse.

Ross, M. H. 1993. *The Culture of Conflict: Interpretations and Interests in Comparative Perspective.* New Haven.

Russett, B. 1993. *Grasping the Democratic Peace: Principles for a Post – Cold War World.* Princeton.

Smith, R. K. 1989. "Institutionalization as a Measure of Regime Stability: Insights for International Regime Analysis from the Study of Domestic Politics." *Millennium* 18: 227–44.

Snow, D. R. 1994. *The Iroquois.* Cambridge, MA.

Snyderman, G. S. 1948/1978. *Behind the Tree of Peace: A Sociological Analysis of Iroquois Warfare.* New York.

Stein, J. G. 1985. "Detection and Defection: Security 'Regimes' and the Management of International Conflict." *International Journal* 40: 599–627.

Tooker, E. 1978a. "The League of the Iroquois: Its History, Politics, and Ritual." In Trigger 1978a: 418–41.

——. 1978b. "Iroquois since 1820." In Trigger 1978a: 449–65.

Trigger, B. G. (ed.). 1978a. *Northeast, Volume 15 of Handbook of North American Indians.* Washington, DC.

——. 1978b. "Early Iroquoian Contacts with Europeans." In Trigger 1978a: 344–56.

——. 1985. *Natives and Newcomers: Canada's Heroic Age Reconsidered.* Manchester, NH.

Wallace, A. F. C. 1970. *The Death and Rebirth of the Seneca.* New York.

Wallace, P. A. W. 1946. *The White Roots of Peace.* Philadelphia.

White, R. 1991. *The Middle Ground: Indians, Empires, and Republics in the Great Lakes Region, 1650–1815.* Cambridge.

Williams, G. F. 2005. *Year of the Hangman: George Washington's Campaign against the Iroquois.* Yardley.

Wright, R. 1992. *Stolen Continents: The "New World" Through Indian Eyes.* New York.

Index